PRESENTED TO

_____

BY

_____

_____

DATE

THE PROPHETS

נביאים

NEVI'IM

THE PROPHETS

נביאים

NEVI'IM

A new translation of
THE HOLY SCRIPTURES
according to the Masoretic text
SECOND SECTION

THE JEWISH PUBLICATION SOCIETY OF AMERICA
PHILADELPHIA

ISBN 0–8276–0096–8 (cloth-bound)
ISBN 0–8276–0101–8 (leather-bound)
Library of Congress Catalog Card No. 77–87245
Manufactured in the United States of America

PREFACE

Sixty years have passed since The Jewish Publication Society published its first translation of the Bible. The preface to that edition pointed out that translating the Holy Scriptures is nothing new in the history of the Jewish people; translations have been made whenever a substantial part of the people adopted another language as its vernacular. In earlier centuries, translations were made into Aramaic, Greek, and Arabic; in more recent years, into English, German, Yiddish, and many other languages. Those translations were never intended to displace the Hebrew text. They stemmed from the natural desire to make the Bible intelligible to Jews living in various lands of the widespread Diaspora.

But why another translation into English? The reasons are both linguistic and scholarly. Languages in constant use undergo change. Certainly, in the course of the past two generations of growing literary productivity, such changes have been numerous, and sometimes radical. So, if Bible readers are to understand the text, words must be used in their contemporary sense. Indeed, this is one reason for the several new translations of recent years by the Christian communities of England and the United States.

Moreover, it is not just the English language that has changed. A much more precise understanding of biblical Hebrew and a much better knowledge of the biblical world—its geography, peoples, institutions, and customs—are possible today, for archaeologists have brought to light many new records of ancient civilizations, including some heretofore unknown manuscripts of the Hebrew text. By means of a somewhat different type of archaeological research, modern literary scholars have combed the text of the Talmud and the homilies of the Midrash; they have restudied the works of medieval philologists and commentators and there found insights into the Bible text which succeeding generations apparently neglected or forgot, and which have therefore remained unused. All this new material is highly stimulating. Since, however, complete unanimity of interpretation among scholars has not yet been achieved for much of it, our Committee of translators had no choice but to set aside a great deal of unresolved material. The Committee had to find its own answer to the question that was ever before it: What thought did the person who first recorded these words really intend to express?

Aware of their obligation to the English-speaking public to encourage the widest possible use of the Bible, the trustees of The Jewish Publication Society decided to have the Holy Scriptures translated anew. The original Committee of translators consisted of three professors of Bible: H. L. Ginsberg, of the Jewish Theological Seminary of America; Harry M. Orlinsky, of the Hebrew Union College–Jewish Institute of Religion, in New York; and Ephraim A. Speiser, of the University of Pennsylvania. Added to them were three learned rabbis representing the three organized rabbinic bodies in the United States: Max Arzt, Conservative; Bernard J. Bamberger, Reform; and Harry Freedman, Orthodox. Solomon Grayzel, then editor (now editor-emeritus) of The Jewish Publication Society, was also appointed to the Committee as its secretary. In the course of its work, the Committee unfortunately lost two of its members: Dr. Speiser died in 1965, after the translation of *The Torah* had been published, and Rabbi Arzt died in 1975, when the work on *The Prophets* was almost completed.

For the translation of *The Torah,* Dr. Orlinsky served as editor, in association with Dr. Ginsberg; for the translation of *The Prophets,* Dr. Ginsberg served as editor, in association with Dr. Orlinsky. In the case of *The Torah,* Dr. Orlinsky prepared the basic draft, which was then sent, chapter by chapter, to the other members of the working Committee for their comments and suggestions, later to be discussed at regularly scheduled meetings. The procedure was slightly different in the case of *The Prophets.* Individual members of the Committee undertook to prepare a draft of an entire book or a part of a book, but everyone had an opportunity (as in the case of *The Torah*) to criticize the draft and to offer detailed suggestions at periodic Committee sessions, which were presided over by Dr. Bamberger. Differences of opinion were settled by majority vote. The comments of absent members, offered in writing, were also considered. When a book was completed, it was subjected to review and revision as many times as seemed necessary. The drafts were, of course, based on the original, traditional (masoretic) text of the Bible, but there was constant reference to such ancillary material as the Dead Sea Scrolls and such early translations as the Septuagint, Targum, Peshitta, and Vulgate. Medieval commentaries and modern scholarly commentaries and translations were also consulted.

One specific problem for which solutions were sought in all this material deserves special mention, because it illustrates an important aspect of the Committee's work:

The prophetic books contain many passages from which any clear meaning is difficult to extract. In order to provide an intelligible rendering, modern scholars have resorted to emending the Hebrew text. Some of these emendations are derived from ancient versions, especially from the Septuagint and the Targum. The authors of these ancient translations had before them a Hebrew text that sometimes differed from today's traditional text. Where these ancient versions provided no help, some scholars have made conjectural emendations of their own. Many modern English versions contain translations of emended texts, sometimes without citing any departure from the traditional Hebrew text.

The present translation adheres strictly to the traditional Hebrew text, but where the text remained obscure and an alteration of it provided marked clarification, a footnote is offered with a rendering of the suggested emendation. If the emendation is based on one or two ancient versions, the latter are mentioned by name. If several of these ancient versions agree, they are summed up as "ancient versions." Conjectural emendations are introduced by "Emendation yields." Sometimes, however, it was deemed sufficient to change the vowels with which the consonantal text is pronounced. Such modifications are indicated in the footnote as "Change of vocalization yields." In all cases, the emendation is given in a footnote, which may be readily disregarded by those who reject it either on scholarly or on religious grounds. The only exceptions involve such changes in grammatical form as those, say, from second person to third or singular to plural. In such minor instances, the change is incorporated in the text, and the traditional Hebrew is translated in a footnote. (See, for example, Judges 5.7; Zechariah 13.4.)

In addition to emendations, there were certain instances in *The Prophets*— as in *The Torah*— where footnotes were deemed necessary: 1) where the Committee had to admit that it did not understand a word or a passage; 2) where an alternative rendering was possible; 3) where an old rendering, no longer retained, was so well known that its omission would be noticeable (in such a case the traditional rendering was given in a footnote as "Others," usually as found in The Jewish Publication Society translation of 1917); 4) where the understanding of a passage could be facilitated by reference to a comparable passage elsewhere in the Bible (although the forthcoming translation of the third section of the Bible, *The Writings,* sponsored by The Jewish Publication Society, may not render the word or phrase in question precisely in the same way); 5) where textual variants are to be found in some ancient manuscripts or versions of the Bible.

Certain other basic rules, which were followed in *The Torah,* were continued in *The Prophets*: Obsolete words and phrases were avoided, and Hebrew idioms were translated, insofar as possible, by their normal English equivalents. For the second person singular, the modern "you" was used, even when referring to the Deity ("You"), rather than the archaic "thou" ("Thou"). Another obvious difference between this translation and most of the older ones may be noted in the rendering of the Hebrew particle *waw*, which is usually translated "and." Classical Hebrew demanded its frequent use, but there it had the force not only of "and" but also of "however," "but," "yet," "when," and any number of such words or particles—or of none that can be translated into English at all. To render *waw* always by "and" is to misrepresent the Hebrew rather than to be faithful to it. Consequently, the Committee either translated the particle as the sense required or omitted it in translation.

While the chapter and verse divisions found in the printed Bible are indispensable as a system of precise reference, they do not always coincide with the organic divisions of the text. The chapter divisions, whose origin is neither ancient nor Jewish but medieval Christian, sometimes join or separate the wrong paragraphs, sentences, or even parts of sentences. The verse divisions, though of Jewish origin and considerably older, occasionally separate parts of the same sentence or join together parts of different sentences. It is not surprising that Rav Saadia Gaon, the brilliant scholar who translated the Bible into Arabic, in the tenth century, gave no indication of chapter divisions, since they did not exist in his day. More noteworthy is the readiness with which, when sense required it, he joined separate verses of the Hebrew text—whose authority he did not question—into single sentences. Thus, in joining Genesis 7.24 and 8.1 into one sentence, or combining the last part of I Kings 6.38 with 7.1, the present translation is merely following the example of Rav Saadia's. The attentive reader will discover other sentences, in both *The Torah* and *The Prophets*, in which the translators have not hesitated to follow what they considered the logical units of meaning, even when these do not coincide with conventional divisions of chapters and verses. The conventional markings, however, are indicated throughout.

There was one deviation from sequence of text which the Committee felt constrained to make. Occasionally, though rarely, in *The Torah* and in *The Prophets,* the Hebrew does not offer a sequence of thought acceptable in English. In those instances, rather than confuse the reader, the Committee chose to transfer part of a verse to a more logical sentence. Of course, attention is called to such transpositions in a footnote, and the reader will find examples in *The Torah* at Exodus 35.32–34, and in *The Prophets* at Isaiah 18.2.

The Torah was published in 1962, and a revised edition appeared five years later. Three other volumes appeared thereafter which are the work of the same Committee of translators: *The Five Megilloth and Jonah* (1969), *Isaiah* (1973), and *Jeremiah* (1974). The two latter books and *Jonah* are incorporated, with some corrections and revisions, into the complete translation of the prophetic books presented herewith.

In the beginning of the work, neither the trustees of The Jewish Publication Society nor the Committee of translators suspected that the task would be of such magnitude as soon became apparent. By 1965, it was obvious that the one Committee could not complete the translation of the entire Bible within a reasonable period of time. Accordingly, another Committee was entrusted with the translation of the third part of the Holy Scriptures, *Kethubim (The Writings). The Book of Psalms,* translated by the second Committee, was published in 1972. The present volume, like *The Torah,* is the work of the original Committee. The Jewish Publication Society joins the translators in the fervent prayer that their work will find favor with God and man.

The Jewish Publication Society
of America

כ״ה כסלו ה׳תשל״ח
December 5, 1977

GLOSSARY OF TERMS USED
IN THE NOTES

Akkadian	An ancient Semitic language spoken in Mesopotamia; its chief dialects were Babylonian and Assyrian.
Aquila	A second-century convert to Judaism who made a literal translation of the Bible into Greek.
Berakot	One of the treatises of the Mishnah and the Talmud.
Ibn Ezra	Abraham ibn Ezra, a Spanish Jew of the 12th century, who wrote a commentary on the Bible.
Kethib	The way a word, usually unvocalized, is written in the Bible; see *qere*.
Kimhi	Rabbi David Kimhi (Radak), a Bible commentator and grammarian who lived in Southern France in the late 12th and early 13th centuries.
Masorah	The text of the Bible as transmitted, with vowel signs and accents.
Mishnah	The code of Jewish Law prepared by Rabbi Judah haNasi about 200 of the Common Era. The word is usually followed by the name of the relevant treatise.
Peshitta	A Christian translation of the Bible into Syriac, parts of which are said to have been made in the first century of the Common Era.
Qere	The way the Masorah requires a word to be read, especially when it diverges from the *kethib*.
Qumran	The site of the caves where Bible manuscripts were found in 1949/50. The manuscripts are identified by such symbols as 4QSam^a (for manuscript *a* of Samuel, found in the fourth cave of Qumran); 1QIs^a (for manuscript *a* of Isaiah found in the first cave of Qumran).

Rashbam   Rabbi Shmuel ben Meir, a grandson of Rashi, who commented on a part of the Bible (the Torah).

Rashi   Rabbi Shlomo Yitzhaki, the best-known Jewish commentator on the Bible; he lived in France at the end of the 11th century.

Saadia   A *gaon*, i.e., a head of a Babylonian talmudic academy, in the early part of the 10th century. His works include the famous translation of the Bible into Arabic.

Septuagint   The oldest Jewish translation of the Bible into Greek. The Torah translation dates from the third century Before the Common Era; other books of the Bible were translated somewhat later.

Syriac   See *Peshitta*.

Targum   A Jewish translation of the Bible into Aramaic, a language once widely spoken in Western Asia, of which Syriac was a later development.

Ugaritic   A language current in northern Syria in the second millennium Before the Common Era. Both the language and its literature have shed much light on the Hebrew Bible.

Vulgate   The Latin translation of the Bible made by the Church Father Jerome about the year 400 of the Common Era. It became the official Bible of the Roman Catholic Church.

TABLE OF SCRIPTURAL READINGS

Readings on Weekly Sabbaths

THE TORAH		THE PROPHETS
GENESIS		
בראשית	1.1-6.8	Isaiah 42.5-43.10 (42.5-21)ᵃ
נח	6.9-11.32	Isaiah 54.1-55.5 (54.1-10)
לך לך	12.1-17.27	Isaiah 40.27-41.16
וירא	18.1-22.24	II Kings 4.1-37 (4.1-23)
חיי שרה	23.1-25.18	I Kings 1.1-31
תולדת	25.19-28.9	Malachi 1.1-2.7
ויצא	28.10-32.3	Hosea 12.13-14.10
		(add 12.7-13.5)
וישלח	32.4-36.43	Hosea 11.7-12.12
		(Obadiah 1.1-21)
וישב	37.1-40.23	Amos 2.6-3.8
מקץ	41.1-44.17	I Kings 3.15-4.1
ויגש	44.18-47.27	Ezekiel 37.15-28
ויחי	47.28-50.26	I Kings 2.1-12
EXODUS		
שמות	1.1-6.1	Isaiah 27.6-28.13; 29.22, 23
		(Jeremiah 1.1-2.3)
וארא	6.2-9.35	Ezekiel 28.25-29.21
בא	10.1-13.16	Jeremiah 46.13-28
בשלח	13.17-17.16	Judges 4.4-5.31 (5.1-31)

ᵃ*Parentheses indicate Sephardi ritual.*

THE TORAH   THE PROPHETS

DEUTERONOMY

דברים	1.1-3.22	Isaiah 1.1-27
ואתחנן	3.23-7.11	Isaiah 40.1-26
עקב	7.12-11.25	Isaiah 49.14-51.3
ראה	11.26-16.17	Isaiah 54.11-55.5
שפטים	16.18-21.9	Isaiah 51.12-52.12
כי תצא	21.10-25.19	Isaiah 54.1-10
כי תבוא	26.1-29.8	Isaiah 60.1-22
נצבים	29.9-30.20	Isaiah 61.10-63.9
וילך	31.1-30	Isaiah 55.6-56.8
האזינו	32.1-52	II Samuel 22.1-51
וזאת הברכה	33.1-34.12	Joshua 1.1-18 (1.1-9)

Readings on Special Sabbaths

	THE TORAH	THE PROPHETS
Sabbath coinciding with Rosh Hodesh	Weekly portion and Numbers 28.9-15	Isaiah 66.1-24, 23
Sabbath immediately preceding Rosh Hodesh	Weekly portion	I Samuel 20.18-42
Shekalim	Weekly portion and Exodus 30.11-16	II Kings 12.1-17 (11.17-12.17)
Zakor	Weekly portion and Deuteronomy 25.17-19	I Samuel 15.2-34 (15.1-34)
Parah	Weekly portion and Numbers 19.1-22	Ezekiel 36.16-38 (36.16-36)

	THE TORAH	THE PROPHETS
Ha-Hodesh	Weekly portion and Exodus 12.1-20	Ezekiel 45.16-46.18 (45.18-46.15)
Sabbath ha-Gadol	Weekly portion	Malachi 3.4-24
First Sabbath Hanukkah	Weekly portion and Numbers 7.1-11 plus the verses relating to the prince *(nasi)* of the day corresponding to the day of Hanukkah	Zechariah 2.14-4.7
Second Sabbath Hanukkah	Weekly portion and Hanukkah portions as above	I Kings 7.40-50

Readings for the Days of Awe

	THE TORAH	THE PROPHETS
New Year, 1st Day	Genesis 21.1-34; Numbers 29.1-6	I Samuel 1.1-2.10
2d Day	Genesis 22.1-24; Numbers 29.1-6	Jeremiah 31.1-19
Sabbath Shubah	Weekly portion	Hosea 14.2-10; Micah 7.18-20, or Hosea 14.2-10; Joel 2.15-17 (Hosea 14.2-10; Micah 7.18-20)
Day of Atonement, Morning	Leviticus 16.1-34; Numbers 29.7-11	Isaiah 57.14-58.14
Afternoon	Leviticus 18.1-30	Jonah 1.1-4.11; Micah 7.18-20

Readings on Festivals

	THE TORAH	THE PROPHETS
Shavuoth, 1st Day	Exodus 19.1-20.23; Numbers 28.26-31	Ezekiel 1.1-28; 3.12
2d Day	Deuteronomy 15.19- 16.17ᵃ	
	Numbers 28.26-31	Habakkuk 3.1-19 (2.20-3.19)

Readings on Week-Day Occasions

Purim	Exodus 17.8-16	
Ninth of Ab,		
Morning	Deuteronomy 4.25- 40	Jeremiah 8.13-9.23
Afternoon	Exodus 32.11-14; 34.1-10	Isaiah 55.6-56.8 (Hosea 14.2-10; Micah 7.18-20)
Public Fasts	Exodus 32.11-14; 34.1-10	Isaiah 55.6-56.8 (none)

ᵃ*On Sabbath, 14.22-16.17*

CONTENTS

THE PROPHETS – NEVI'IM

יהושע
JOSHUA

יהושע
JOSHUA

1 After the death of Moses the servant of the LORD, the LORD said to Joshua son of Nun, Moses' attendant:

2 "My servant Moses is dead. Prepare to cross the Jordan, together with all this people, into the land which I am giving to the Israelites. 3 Every spot on which your foot treads I give to you, as I promised Moses. 4 Your territory shall extend from the wilderness and the Lebanon to the Great River, the River Euphrates [on the east]—the whole Hittite country—and up to the Mediterranean*a* Sea on the west. 5 No man shall be able to resist you as long as you live. As I was with Moses, so I will be with you; I will not fail you or forsake you.

6 "Be strong and resolute, for you shall apportion to this people the land that I swore to their fathers to give them. 7 But you must be very strong and resolute to observe faithfully all the Teaching that My servant Moses enjoined upon you. Do not deviate from it to the right or to the left, that you may be successful wherever you go. 8 Let not this Book of the Teaching cease from your lips, but recite it day and night, so that you may observe faithfully all that is written in it. Only then will you prosper in your undertakings and only then will you be successful.

9 "I charge you: Be strong and resolute; do not be terrified or dismayed, for the LORD your God is with you wherever you go."

10 Joshua thereupon gave orders to the officials of the people: 11 "Go through the camp and charge the people thus: Get provisions ready, for in three days' time you are to cross the Jordan,

---

a Heb. "Great."

in order to enter and occupy the land which the LORD your God is giving you as a possession."

¹² Then Joshua said to the Reubenites, the Gadites, and the half-tribe of Manasseh, ¹³ "Remember what Moses the servant of the LORD enjoined upon you, when he said: 'The LORD your God is granting you a haven; He is assigning this territory to you.' ¹⁴ Let your wives, children, and livestock remain in the land which Moses assigned to you *b*-on this side of*-b* the Jordan; but every one of your fighting men shall go across armed*c* in the van of your kinsmen. And you shall assist them ¹⁵ until the LORD has given your kinsmen a haven, such as you have, and they too have gained possession of the land which the LORD your God has assigned to them. Then you may return to the land on the east side of the Jordan, which Moses the servant of the LORD assigned to you as your possession, and you may occupy it."

¹⁶ They answered Joshua, "We will do everything you have commanded us and we will go wherever you send us. ¹⁷ We will obey you just as we obeyed Moses; let but the LORD your God be with you as He was with Moses! ¹⁸ Any man who flouts your commands and does not obey every order you give him shall be put to death. Only be strong and resolute!"

2 Joshua son of Nun secretly sent two spies from Shittim, saying, "Go, reconnoiter the region of Jericho." So they set out, and they came to the house of a harlot named Rahab and lodged there. ² The king of Jericho was told, "Some men have come here tonight, Israelites, to spy out the country." ³ The king of Jericho thereupon sent orders to Rahab: "Produce the men who came to you and entered your house, for they have come to spy out the whole country." ⁴ The woman, however, had taken the two men and hidden them. "It is true," she said, "the men did come to me, but I didn't know where they were from. ⁵ And at dark, when the gate was about to be closed, the men left; and I don't know where the men went. Quick, go after them, for you can overtake

---

b-b Lit. "across."
c Meaning of Heb. uncertain.

them."—⁶ Now she had taken them up to the roof and hidden them under some stalks of flax which she had lying on the roof.—⁷ So the men pursued them in the direction of the Jordan down to the fords; and no sooner had the pursuers gone out than the gate was shut behind them.

⁸ ᵃ⁻The spies⁻ᵃ had not yet gone to sleep when she came up to them on the roof. ⁹ She said to the men, "I know that the LORD has given the country to you, because dread of you has fallen upon us, and all the inhabitants of the land are quaking before you. ¹⁰ For we have heard how the LORD dried up the waters of the Sea of Reeds for you when you left Egypt, and what you did to Sihon and Og, the two Amorite kings across the Jordan, whom you doomed.ᵇ ¹¹ When we heard about it, we lost heart, and no man had any more spirit left because of you; for the LORD your God is the only God in heaven above and on earth below. ¹² Now, since I have shown loyalty to you, swear to me by the LORD that you in turn will show loyalty to my family. Provide me with a reliable sign ¹³ that you will spare the lives of my father and mother, my brothers and sisters, and all who belong to them, and save us from death." ¹⁴ The men answered her, "Our persons are pledged for yours, even to death! If you do not disclose this mission of ours, we will show you true loyalty when the LORD gives us the land."

¹⁵ She let them down by a rope through the window—for her dwelling was at the outer side of the city wall and she lived in the actual wall. ¹⁶ She said to them, "Make for the hills, so that the pursuers may not come upon you. Stay there in hiding three days, until the pursuers return; then go your way."

¹⁷ But the men warned her, "We will be released from this oath which you have made us take ¹⁸ [unless,] when we invade the country, you tie this length of crimson cord to the window through which you let us down. Bring your father, your mother, your brothers, and all your family together in your house; ¹⁹ and if anyone ventures outside the doors of your house, his blood will be on his head, and we shall be clear. But if a hand is laid on

---

ᵃ⁻ᵃ *Heb. "They."*
ᵇ *I. e. placed under* ḥerem, *which meant the annihilation of the inhabitants. Cf. Deut. 2.34ff.*

anyone who remains in the house with you, his blood shall be on our heads. 20 And if you disclose this mission of ours, we shall likewise be released from the oath which you made us take." 21 She replied, "Let it be as you say."

She sent them on their way, and they left; and she tied the crimson cord to the window.

22 They went straight to the hills and stayed there three days, until the pursuers turned back. And so the pursuers, searching all along the road, did not find them.

23 Then the two men came down again from the hills and crossed over. They came to Joshua son of Nun and reported to him all that had happened to them. 24 They said to Joshua, "The LORD has delivered the whole land into our power; in fact, all the inhabitants of the land are quaking before us."

3 Early next morning, Joshua and all the Israelites set out from Shittim and marched to the Jordan. They did not cross immediately, but spent the night there. 2 Three days later, the officials went through the camp 3 and charged the people as follows: "When you see the Ark of the Covenant of the LORD your God being borne by the levitical priests, you shall move forward. Follow it—4 but keep a distance of some two thousand cubits from it, never coming any closer to it—so that you may know by what route to march, since it is a road you have not traveled before." 5 And Joshua said to the people, "Purify yourselves,ᵃ for tomorrow the LORD will perform wonders in your midst."

6 Then Joshua ordered the priests, "Take up the Ark of the Covenant and advance to the head of the people." And they took up the Ark of the Covenant and marched at the head of the people.

7 The LORD said to Joshua, "This day, for the first time, I will exalt you in the sight of all Israel, so that they shall know that I will be with you as I was with Moses. 8 For your part, command the priests who carry the Ark of the Covenant as follows: When

ᵃ *See Exod. 19.10, 15.*

6

you reach the edge of the waters of the Jordan, make a halt in the Jordan."

9 And Joshua said to the Israelites, "Come closer and listen to the words of the LORD your God. 10 By this," Joshua continued, "you shall know that a living God is among you, and that He will dispossess for you the Canaanites, Hittites, Hivites, Perizzites, Girgashites, Amorites, and Jebusites: 11 the Ark of the Covenant of the Sovereign of all the earth is advancing before you into the Jordan. 12 Now select twelve men from the tribes of Israel, one man from each tribe. 13 When the feet of the priests bearing the Ark of the LORD, the Sovereign of all the earth, come to rest in the waters of the Jordan, the waters of the Jordan—the water coming from upstream—will be cut off and will stand in a single heap."

14 When the people set out from their encampment to cross the Jordan, the priests bearing the Ark of the Covenant were at the head of the people. 15 Now the Jordan keeps flowing over its entire bed throughout the harvest season. But as soon as the bearers of the Ark reached the Jordan, and the feet of the priests bearing the Ark dipped into the water at its edge, 16 the waters coming down from upstream piled up in a single heap a great way off, at*b* Adam, the town next to Zarethan; and those flowing away downstream to the Sea of the Arabah (the Dead Sea) ran out completely. So the people crossed near Jericho. 17 The priests who bore the Ark of the LORD's Covenant stood on dry land exactly in the middle of the Jordan, while all Israel crossed over on dry land, until the entire nation had finished crossing the Jordan.

4 When the entire nation had finished crossing the Jordan, the LORD said to Joshua, 2 "Select twelve men from among the people, one from each tribe, 3 and instruct them as follows: Pick up twelve stones from the spot exactly in the middle of the Jordan, where the priests' feet are standing; take them along with you and deposit them in the place where you will spend the night."

b *So* kethib; qere *"from."*

4 Joshua summoned the twelve men whom he had designated among the Israelites, one from each tribe; 5 and Joshua said to them, "Walk up to the Ark of the LORD your God, in the middle of the Jordan, and each of you lift a stone onto his shoulder—corresponding to the number of the tribes of Israel. 6 This shall serve as a symbol among you: in time to come, when your children ask, 'What is the meaning of these stones for you?' 7 you shall tell them, 'The waters of the Jordan were cut off because of the Ark of the LORD's Covenant; when it passed through the Jordan, the waters of the Jordan were cut off.' And so these stones shall serve the people of Israel as a memorial for all time."

8 The Israelites did as Joshua ordered. They picked up twelve stones, corresponding to the number of the tribes of Israel, from the middle of the Jordan—as the LORD had charged Joshua—and they took them along with them to their night encampment and deposited them there.

9 Joshua also set up twelve stones in the middle of the Jordan, at the spot where the feet of the priests bearing the Ark of the Covenant had stood; and they have remained there to this day.

10 The priests who bore the Ark remained standing in the middle of the Jordan until all the instructions that the LORD had ordered Joshua to convey to the people had been carried out. And so the people speedily crossed over, *-just as Moses had assured Joshua in his charge to him.-* 11 And when all the people finished crossing, the Ark of the LORD and the priests advanced to the head of the people.

12 The Reubenites, the Gadites, and the half-tribe of Manasseh went across armed*b* in the van of the Israelites, as Moses had charged them.*c* 13 About forty thousand shock troops went across, at the instance of the LORD, to the steppes of Jericho for battle.

14 On that day the LORD exalted Joshua in the sight of all Israel, so that they revered him all his days as they had revered Moses.

15 The LORD said to Joshua, 16 "Command the priests who bear the Ark of the Pact to come up out of the Jordan." 17 So Joshua commanded the priests, "Come up out of the Jordan." 18 As soon

---

a-a Connection of clause uncertain; cf. Deut. 31.7-8.
b Meaning of Heb. uncertain.
c See Num. 32.20-22.

as the priests who bore the Ark of the LORD's Covenant came up out of the Jordan, and the feet of the priests stepped onto the dry ground, the waters of the Jordan resumed their course, flowing over its entire bed as before.

¹⁹ The people came up from the Jordan on the tenth day of the first month, and encamped at Gilgal on the eastern border of Jericho. ²⁰ And Joshua set up in Gilgal the twelve stones they had taken from the Jordan. ²¹ He charged the Israelites as follows: "In time to come, when your children ask their fathers, 'What is the meaning of those stones?' ²² tell your children: 'Here the Israelites crossed the Jordan on dry land.' ²³ For the LORD your God dried up the waters of the Jordan before you until you crossed, just as the LORD your God did to the Sea of Reeds, which He dried up before us until we crossed. ²⁴ Thus all the peoples of the earth shall know how mighty is the hand of the LORD, and you shall fear the LORD your God always."

5 When all the kings of the Amorites on the western side of the Jordan, and all the kings of the Canaanites near the Sea, heard how the LORD had dried up the waters of the Jordan for the sake of the Israelites until they crossed over, they lost heart, and no spirit was left in them because of the Israelites.

² At that time the LORD said to Joshua, "Make flint knives and proceed with a second circumcision of the Israelites." ³ So Joshua had flint knives made, and the Israelites were circumcised at Gibeath-haaraloth.ᵃ

⁴ This is the reason why Joshua had the circumcision performed: All the people who had come out of Egypt, all the males of military age, had died during the desert wanderings after leaving Egypt. ⁵ Now, whereas all the people who came out of Egypt had been circumcised, none of the people born after the exodus, during the desert wanderings, had been circumcised. ⁶ For the Israelites had traveled in the wilderness forty years, until the

ᵃ *I.e. "the Hill of Foreskins."*

9

entire nation—the men of military age who had left Egypt—had perished; because they had not obeyed the LORD, and the LORD had sworn never to let them see the land which the LORD had sworn to their fathers to give us, a land flowing with milk and honey. 7 But He had raised up their sons in their stead; and it was these that Joshua circumcised, for they were uncircumcised, not having been circumcised on the way. 8 After the circumcising of the whole nation was completed, they remained where they were, in the camp, until they recovered.

9 And the LORD said to Joshua, "Today I have rolled away from you the disgrace of Egypt."*b* So that place was called Gilgal,*c* as it still is.

10 Encamped at Gilgal, in the steppes of Jericho, the Israelites offered the passover sacrifice on the fourteenth day of the month, toward evening.

11 On the day after the passover offering, on that very day, they ate of the produce of the country, unleavened bread and parched grain. 12 On that same day,*d* when they ate of the produce of the land, the manna ceased. The Israelites got no more manna; that year they ate of the yield of the land of Canaan.

13 Once, when Joshua was near Jericho, he looked up and saw a man standing before him, drawn sword in hand. Joshua went up to him and asked him, "Are you one of us or of our enemies?" 14 He replied, "No, I am captain of the LORD's host. Now I have come!" Joshua threw himself face down to the ground and, prostrating himself, said to him, "What does my lord command his servant?" 15 The captain of the LORD's host answered Joshua, "Remove your sandals from your feet, for the place where you stand is holy." And Joshua did so.

6 Now Jericho was shut up tight because of the Israelites; no one could leave or enter.

2 The LORD said to Joshua, "See, I will deliver Jericho and her

b *I.e. of the Egyptian bondage.*
c *Interpreted as "rolling."*
d *Lit. "on the day after."*

king [and her] warriors into your hands. ³ Let all your troops
march around the city and complete one circuit of the city. Do
this six days, ⁴ with seven priests carrying seven ram's horns
preceding the Ark. On the seventh day, march around the city
seven times, with the priests blowing the horns. ⁵ And when a
long blast is sounded on the horn—as soon as you hear that
sound of the horn—all the people shall give a mighty shout.
Thereupon the city wall will collapse, and the people shall advance, every man straight ahead."

⁶ Joshua son of Nun summoned the priests and said to them,
"Take up the Ark of the Covenant, and let seven priests carrying
seven ram's horns precede the Ark of the LORD." ⁷ And he instructed the people, "Go forward, march around the city, with
the vanguard marching in front of the Ark of the LORD." ⁸ When
Joshua had instructed the people, the seven priests carrying
seven ram's horns advanced before the LORD, blowing their
horns; and the Ark of the LORD's Covenant followed them. ⁹ The
vanguard marched in front of the priests who were blowing the
horns, and the rear guard marched behind the Ark, with the
horns sounding all the time. ¹⁰ But Joshua's orders to the rest of
the people were, "Do not shout, do not let your voices be heard,
and do not let a sound issue from your lips until the moment that
I command you, 'Shout!' Then you shall shout."

¹¹ So he had the Ark of the LORD go around the city and complete one circuit; then they returned to camp and spent the night
in camp. ¹² Joshua rose early the next day; and the priests took
up the Ark of the LORD, ¹³ while the seven priests bearing the
seven ram's horns marched in front of the Ark of the LORD,
blowing the horns as they marched. The vanguard marched in
front of them, and the rear guard marched behind the Ark of the
LORD, with the horns sounding all the time. ¹⁴ And so they
marched around the city once on the second day and returned to
the camp. They did this six days.

¹⁵ On the seventh day, they rose at daybreak and marched
around the city, in the same manner, seven times; that was the

only day that they marched around the city seven times. [16] On the seventh round, as the priests blew the horns, Joshua commanded the people, "Shout! For the LORD has given you the city. [17] The city and everything in it are to be proscribed for the LORD; only Rahab the harlot is to be spared, and all who are with her in the house, because she hid the messengers we sent. [18] But you must beware of that which is proscribed, or else you will be proscribed:[a] if you take anything from that which is proscribed, you will cause the camp of Israel to be proscribed; you will bring calamity upon it. [19] All the silver and gold and objects of copper and iron are consecrated to the LORD; they must go into the treasury of the LORD."

[20] So the people shouted when the horns were sounded. When the people heard the sound of the horns, the people raised a mighty shout and the wall collapsed. The people rushed into the city, every man straight in front of him, and they captured the city. [21] They exterminated everything in the city with the sword: man and woman, young and old, ox and sheep and ass. [22] But Joshua bade the two men who had spied out the land, "Go into the harlot's house and bring out the woman and all that belong to her, as you swore to her." [23] So the young spies went in and brought out Rahab, her father and her mother, her brothers and all that belonged to her—they brought out her whole family and left them outside the camp of Israel.

[24] They burned down the city and everything in it. But the silver and gold and the objects of copper and iron were deposited in the treasury of the House of the LORD. [25] Only Rahab the harlot and her father's family were spared by Joshua, along with all that belonged to her, and she dwelt among the Israelites—as is still the case. For she had hidden the messengers that Joshua sent to spy out Jericho.

[26] At that time Joshua pronounced this oath: "Cursed of the LORD be the man who shall undertake to fortify this city of Jericho: he shall lay its foundations at the cost of his firstborn, and set up its gates at the cost of his youngest."

---

[a] *I.e. be put to death; cf. Lev. 27.28-29.*

²⁷ The LORD was with Joshua, and his fame spread throughout the land.

7 The Israelites, however, violated the proscription: Achan son of Carmi son of Zabdi son of Zerah, of the tribe of Judah, took of that which was proscribed, and the LORD was incensed with the Israelites.

² Joshua sent men from Jericho to Ai, which lies close to Beth-aven—east of Bethel—with orders to go up and spy out the country. So the men went up and spied out Ai. ³ They returned to Joshua and reported to him, "Not all the troops need go up. Let two or three thousand men go and attack Ai; do not trouble all the troops to go up there, for [the people] there are few." ⁴ So about three thousand of the troops marched up there; but they were routed by the men of Ai. ⁵ The men of Ai killed about thirty-six of them, pursuing them outside the gate as far as Shebarim, and cutting them down along the descent. And the heart of the troops ^{a-}sank in utter dismay.^{-a}

⁶ Joshua thereupon rent his clothes. He and the elders of Israel lay until evening with their faces to the ground in front of the Ark of the LORD; and they strewed earth on their heads. ⁷ "Ah, Lord GOD!" cried Joshua. "Why did You lead this people across the Jordan only to deliver us into the hands of the Amorites, to be destroyed by them? If only we had been content to remain on the other side of the Jordan! ⁸ O Lord, what can I say after Israel has turned tail before its enemies? ⁹ When the Canaanites and all the inhabitants of the land hear of this, they will turn upon us and wipe out our very name from the earth. And what will You do about Your great name?"

¹⁰ But the LORD answered Joshua: "Arise! Why do you lie prostrate? ¹¹ Israel has sinned! They have broken the covenant by which I bound them. They have taken of the proscribed and put it in their vessels; they have stolen; they have broken faith! ¹² Therefore, the Israelites will not be able to hold their ground

^{a-a} Lit. "melted and turned to water."

13

against their enemies; they will have to turn tail before their enemies, for they have become proscribed. I will not be with you any more unless you root out from among you what is proscribed. [13] Go tell the people to purify themselves. Order them: Purify yourselves for tomorrow. For thus says the LORD, the God of Israel: Something proscribed is in your midst, O Israel, and you will not be able to stand up to your enemies until you have purged the proscribed from among you. [14] Tomorrow morning you shall present yourselves by tribes. Whichever tribe the LORD indicates[b] shall come forward by clans; the clan which the LORD indicates shall come forward by ancestral houses, and the ancestral house that the LORD indicates shall come forward man by man. [15] Then he who is [c]indicated for proscription,[c] and all that is his, shall be put to the fire, because he broke the covenant of the LORD and because he committed an outrage in Israel."

[16] Early next morning, Joshua had Israel come forward by tribes; and the tribe of Judah was indicated. [17] He then had the clans of Judah come forward, and the clan of Zerah was indicated. Then he had the clan of Zerah come forward by [d]ancestral houses,[d] and Zabdi was indicated. [18] Finally he had his ancestral house come forward man by man, and Achan son of Zerah son of Zabdi, of the tribe of Judah, was indicated.

[19] Then Joshua said to Achan, "My son, pay honor to the LORD, the God of Israel, and make confession to Him. Tell me what you have done; do not hold anything back from me." [20] Achan answered Joshua, "It is true, I have sinned against the LORD, the God of Israel. This is what I did: [21] I saw among the spoil a fine Shinar mantle, two hundred shekels of silver, and a wedge of gold weighing fifty shekels, and I coveted them and took them. They are buried in the ground in my tent, with the silver under it."[e]

[22] Joshua sent messengers, who hurried to the tent; and there it[e] was, buried in his tent, with the silver underneath. [23] They took them from the tent and brought them to Joshua and all the Israelites, and displayed[f] them before the LORD. [24] Then Joshua, and all Israel with him, took Achan son of Zerah—and the silver,

---

[b] Lit. "catches."
[c-c] Or "caught in the net."
[d-d] So some Heb. mss. and some ancient versions; most mss. and editions have "men."
[e] I.e. the mantle.
[f] Meaning of Heb. uncertain.

the mantle, and the wedge of gold—his sons and daughters, and his ox, his ass, and his flock, and his tent, and all his belongings, and brought them up to the Valley of Achor. 25 And Joshua said, "What calamity you have brought upon us! The LORD will bring calamity upon you this day." And all Israel pelted him with stones. They put them to the fire and stoned them. 26 They raised a huge mound of stones over him, which is still there. Then the anger of the LORD subsided. That is why that place was named the Valley of Achor[g]—as is still the case.

8 The LORD said to Joshua, "Do not be frightened or dismayed. Take all the fighting troops with you, go and march against Ai. See, I will deliver the king of Ai, his people, his city, and his land into your hands. 2 You shall treat Ai and her king as you treated Jericho and her king; however, you may take the spoil and the cattle as booty for yourselves. Now set an ambush against the city behind it."

3 So Joshua and all the fighting troops prepared for the march on Ai. Joshua chose thirty thousand men, valiant warriors, and sent them ahead by night. 4 He instructed them as follows: "Mind, you are to lie in ambush behind the city; don't stay too far from the city, and all of you be on the alert. 5 I and all the troops with me will approach the city; and when they come out against us, as they did the first time, we will flee from them. 6 They will come rushing after us until we have drawn them away from the city. They will think, 'They are fleeing from us the same as last time'; but while we are fleeing before them, 7 you will dash out from your ambush and seize the city, and the LORD your God will deliver it into your hands. 8 And when you take the city, set it on fire. Do as the LORD has commanded. Mind, I have given you your orders."

9 With that, Joshua sent them off, and they proceeded to the ambush; they took up a position between Ai and Bethel—west of Ai—while Joshua spent the night with the rest of the troops.

---

[g] *Connected with* 'akhar *"to bring calamity upon"; cf. v. 25.*

¹⁰ Early in the morning, Joshua mustered the troops; then he and the elders of Israel marched upon Ai at the head of the troops. ¹¹ All the fighting force that was with him advanced near the city and encamped to the north of Ai, with a hollow between them and Ai.— ¹² He selected about five thousand men and stationed them as an ambush between Bethel and Ai, west of the city. ¹³ Thus the main body of the army was disposed on the north of the city, but the far end of it was on the west. (This was after Joshua had *-spent the night-ᵃ in the valley.ᵇ)—¹⁴ When the king of Ai saw them, he and all his people, the inhabitants of the city, rushed out in the early morning to the ᶜ-meeting place,-ᶜ facing the Arabah, to engage the Israelites in battle; for he was unaware that a force was lying in ambush behind the city. ¹⁵ Joshua and all Israel fled in the direction of the wilderness, as though routed by them. ¹⁶ All the troops in the city gathered to pursue them; pursuing Joshua, they were drawn out of the city. ¹⁷ Not a man was left in Ai or in Bethel who did not go out after Israel; they left the city open while they pursued Israel.

¹⁸ The LORD then said to Joshua, "Hold out the javelin in your hand toward Ai, for I will deliver it into your hands." So Joshua held out the javelin in his hand toward the city. ¹⁹ As soon as he held out his hand, the ambush came rushing out of their station. They entered the city and captured it; and they swiftly set fire to the city. ²⁰ The men of Ai looked back and saw the smoke of the city rising to the sky; they had no room for flight in any direction. The people who had been fleeing to the wilderness now became the pursuers. ²¹ For when Joshua and all Israel saw that the ambush had captured the city, and that smoke was rising from the city, they turned around and attacked the men of Ai. ²² Now the other [Israelites] were coming out of the city against them, so that they were between two bodies of Israelites, one on each side of them. They were slaughtered, so that no one escaped or got away. ²³ The king of Ai was taken alive and brought to Joshua.

²⁴ When Israel had killed all the inhabitants of Ai who had pursued them into the open wilderness, and all of them, to the

---

ᵃ⁻ᵃ *So with some mss. (cf. v. 9); most mss. and editions read "marched."*
ᵇ *Syriac reads "with the troops"; cf. v. 9.*
ᶜ⁻ᶜ *Emendation yields "descent"; cf. 7.5.*

last man, had fallen by the sword, all the Israelites turned back to Ai and put it to the sword.

[25] The total of those who fell that day, men and women, the entire population of Ai, came to twelve thousand.

[26] Joshua did not draw back the hand with which he held out his javelin until all the inhabitants of Ai had been exterminated. [27] However, the Israelites took the cattle and the spoil of the city as their booty, in accordance with the instructions that the LORD had given to Joshua.

[28] Then Joshua burned down Ai, and turned it into a mound of ruins for all time, a desolation to this day. [29] And the king of Ai was impaled on a stake until the evening. At sunset, Joshua had the corpse taken down from the stake and it was left lying at the entrance to the city gate. They raised a great heap of stones over it, which is there to this day.

[30] At that time Joshua built an altar to the LORD, the God of Israel, on Mount Ebal, [31] as Moses, the servant of the LORD, had commanded the Israelites—as is written in the Book of the Teaching of Moses[d]—an altar of unhewn stone upon which no iron had been wielded. They offered on it burnt offerings to the LORD, and brought sacrifices of well-being. [32] And there, on the stones, he inscribed a copy of the Teaching which Moses had written for the Israelites. [33] All Israel—stranger and citizen alike —with their elders, officials, and magistrates, stood on either side of the Ark, facing the levitical priests who carried the Ark of the LORD's Covenant. Half of them faced Mount Gerizim and half of them faced Mount Ebal, as Moses the servant of the LORD had commanded them of old, in order to bless the people of Israel. [34] After that, he read all the words of the Teaching, the blessing and the curse, just as is written in the Book of the Teaching.[e] [35] There was not a word of all that Moses had commanded which Joshua failed to read in the presence of the entire assembly of Israel, including the women and children and the strangers who accompanied them.

[d] See Deut. 27.3-8.
[e] See Deut. 27.11-28.68.

9 When all the kings *a*-west of-*a* the Jordan—in the hill country, in the Shephelah, and along the entire coast of the Mediterranean Sea up to the vicinity of Lebanon, the [land of the] Hittites, Amorites, Canaanites, Perizzites, Hivites, and Jebusites—learned of this, 2 they gathered with one accord to fight against Joshua and Israel.

3 But when the inhabitants of Gibeon learned how Joshua had treated Jericho and Ai, 4 they for their part resorted to cunning. They set out *b*-in disguise:-*b* they took worn-out sacks for their asses, and worn-out waterskins that were cracked and patched; 5 they had worn-out, patched sandals on their feet, and thread-bare clothes on their bodies; and all the bread they took as provision was dry and crumbly. 6 And so they went to Joshua in the camp at Gilgal and said to him and to the men of Israel, "We come from a distant land; we propose that you make a pact with us." 7 The men of Israel replied to the Hivites, "But perhaps you live among us; how then can we make a pact with you?"*c*

8 They said to Joshua, "We will be your subjects." But Joshua asked them, "Who are you and where do you come from?" 9 They replied, "Your servants have come from a very distant country, because of the fame of the LORD your God. For we heard the report of Him: of all that He did in Egypt, 10 and of all that He did to the two Amorite kings on the other side of the Jordan, King Sihon of Heshbon and King Og of Bashan who lived in Ashtaroth. 11 So our elders and all the inhabitants of our country instructed us as follows, 'Take along provisions for a trip, and go to them and say: "We will be your subjects; come make a pact with us." ' 12 This bread of ours, which we took from our houses as provision, was still hot when we set out to come to you; and see how dry and crumbly it has become. 13 These wineskins were new when we filled them, and see how they have cracked. These clothes and sandals of ours are worn out from the very long journey." 14 The men *b*-took [their word]

a-a Lit. "across."
b-b Meaning of Heb. uncertain.
c Cf. Deut. 7.2.

because of[-b] their provisions, and did not inquire of the LORD.
15 Joshua established friendship with them; he made a pact with them to spare their lives, and the chieftains of the community gave them their oath.

16 But when three days had passed after they made this pact with them, they learned that they were neighbors, living among them. 17 So the Israelites set out, and on the third day they came to their towns; these towns were Gibeon, Chephirah, Beeroth, and Kiriath-jearim. 18 But the Israelites did not attack them, since the chieftains of the community had sworn to them by the LORD, the God of Israel. The whole community muttered against the chieftains, 19 but all the chieftains answered the whole community, "We swore to them by the LORD, the God of Israel; therefore we cannot touch them. 20 This is what we will do to them: We will spare their lives, so that there may be no wrath against us because of the oath that we swore to them." 21 And the chieftains declared concerning them, "They shall live!" And they became hewers of wood and drawers of water for the whole community, as the chieftains had decreed concerning them.

22 Joshua summoned them and spoke to them thus: "Why did you deceive us and tell us you lived very far from us, when in fact you live among us? 23 Therefore, be accursed! Never shall your descendants cease to be slaves, hewers of wood and drawers of water for the House of my God." 24 But they replied to Joshua, "You see, your servants had heard that the LORD your God had promised His servant Moses to give you the whole land and to wipe out all the inhabitants of the country on your account; so we were in great fear for our lives on your account. That is why we did this thing. 25 And now we are at your mercy; do with us what you consider right and proper." 26 And he did so; he saved them from being killed by the Israelites. 27 That day Joshua made them hewers of wood and drawers of water—as they still are—for the community and for the altar of the LORD, in the place that He would choose.

10 When King Adoni-zedek of Jerusalem learned that Joshua had captured Ai and proscribed it, treating Ai and its king as he had treated Jericho and its king, and that, moreover, the people of Gibeon had come to terms with Israel and remained among them, ² *ᵃ*he was*ᵃ* very frightened. For Gibeon was a large city, like one of the royal cities—in fact, larger than Ai—and all its men were warriors. ³ So King Adoni-zedek of Jerusalem sent this message to King Hoham of Hebron, King Piram of Jarmuth, King Japhia of Lachish, and King Debir of Eglon: ⁴ "Come up and help me defeat Gibeon; for it has come to terms with Joshua and the Israelites."

⁵ The five Amorite kings—the king of Jerusalem, the king of Hebron, the king of Jarmuth, the king of Lachish, and the king of Eglon, with all their armies—joined forces and marched on Gibeon, and encamped against it and attacked it. ⁶ The people of Gibeon thereupon sent this message to Joshua in the camp at Gilgal: "Do not fail your servants; come up quickly and aid us and deliver us, for all the Amorite kings of the hill country have gathered against us." ⁷ So Joshua marched up from Gilgal with his whole fighting force, all the trained warriors.

⁸ The LORD said to Joshua, "Do not be afraid of them, for I will deliver them into your hands; not one of them shall withstand you." ⁹ Joshua took them by surprise, marching all night from Gilgal. ¹⁰ The LORD threw them into a panic before Israel: [Joshua] inflicted a crushing defeat on them at Gibeon, pursued them in the direction of the Beth-horon ascent, and harried them all the way to Azekah and Makkedah. ¹¹ While they were fleeing before Israel down the descent from Beth-horon, the LORD hurled huge stones on them from the sky, all the way to Azekah, and they perished; more perished from the hailstones than were killed by the Israelite weapons.

¹² On that occasion, when the LORD routed the Amorites before

---

ᵃ⁻ᵃ *Heb. "they were."*

the Israelites, Joshua addressed the LORD; he said in the presence of the Israelites:

"Stand still, O sun, at Gibeon,
O moon, in the Valley of Aijalon!"
[13] And the sun stood still
And the moon halted,
While a nation wreaked judgment on its foes

—as is written in the Book of Jashar.[b] Thus the sun halted in midheaven, and did not press on to set, for a whole day; [14] for the LORD fought for Israel. Neither before nor since has there ever been such a day, when the LORD acted on words spoken by a man. [15] Then Joshua together with all Israel returned to the camp at Gilgal.

[16] Meanwhile, those five kings fled and hid in a cave at Makkedah. [17] When it was reported to Joshua that the five kings had been found hiding in a cave at Makkedah, [18] Joshua ordered, "Roll large stones up against the mouth of the cave, and post men over it to keep guard over them. [19] But as for the rest of you, don't stop, but press on the heels of your enemies and harass them from the rear. Don't let them reach their towns, for the LORD your God has delivered them into your hands." [20] When Joshua and the Israelites had finished dealing them a deadly blow, they were wiped out, except for some fugitives who escaped into the fortified towns. [21] The whole army returned in safety to Joshua in the camp at Makkedah; no one so much as snarled[c] at the Israelites. [22] And now Joshua ordered, "Open the mouth of the cave, and bring those five kings out of the cave to me." [23] This was done. Those five kings—the king of Jerusalem, the king of Hebron, the king of Jarmuth, the king of Lachish, and the king of Eglon— were brought out to him from the cave. [24] And when the kings were brought out to Joshua, Joshua summoned all the men of Israel and ordered the army officers who had accompanied him, "Come forward and place your feet on the necks of these kings." They came forward and placed their feet on their necks. [25] Joshua

[b] *Presumably a collection of war songs.*
[c] *Cf. Exod. 11.7.*

said to them, "Do not be frightened or dismayed; be firm and resolute. For this is what the LORD is going to do to all the enemies with whom you are at war." [26] After that, Joshua had them put to death and impaled on five stakes, and they remained impaled on the stakes until evening. [27] At sunset Joshua ordered them taken down from the poles and thrown into the cave in which they had hidden. Large stones were placed over the mouth of the cave, [and there they are] to this very day.

[28] At that time Joshua captured Makkedah and put it and its king to the sword, proscribing it[d] and every person in it and leaving none that escaped. And he treated the king of Makkedah as he had treated the king of Jericho.

[29] From Makkedah, Joshua proceeded with all Israel to Libnah, and he attacked it. [30] The LORD delivered it and its king into the hands of Israel; they put it and all the people in it to the sword, letting none escape. And he treated its king as he had treated the king of Jericho.

[31] From Libnah, Joshua proceeded with all Israel to Lachish; he encamped against it and attacked it. [32] The LORD delivered Lachish into the hands of Israel. They captured it on the second day and put it and all the people in it to the sword, just as they had done to Libnah.

[33] At that time King Horam of Gezer marched to the help of Lachish; but Joshua defeated him and his army, letting none of them escape.

[34] From Lachish, Joshua proceeded with all Israel to Eglon; they encamped against it and attacked it. [35] They captured it on the same day and put it to the sword, proscribing all the people that were in it, as they had done to Lachish.

[36] From Eglon, Joshua marched with all Israel to Hebron and attacked it. [37] They captured it and put it, its king, and all its towns, and all the people that were in it, to the sword. He let none escape, proscribing it and all the people in it, just as he had done in the case of Eglon.

[38] Joshua and all Israel with him then turned back to Debir and

---

d *So several mss; most mss. and the editions read "them."*

attacked it. [39] He captured it and its king and all its towns. They put them to the sword and proscribed all the people in it. They let none escape; just as they had done to Hebron, and as they had done to Libnah and its king, so they did to Debir and its king.

[40] Thus Joshua conquered the whole country:[c] the hill country, the Negeb, the Shephelah, and the slopes, with all their kings; he let none escape, but proscribed everything that breathed—as the LORD, the God of Israel, had commanded. [41] Joshua conquered them from Kadesh-barnea to Gaza, all the land of Goshen, and up to Gibeon. [42] All those kings and their lands were conquered by Joshua at a single stroke, for the LORD, the God of Israel, fought for Israel. [43] Then Joshua, with all Israel, returned to the camp at Gilgal.

11

When the news reached King Jabin of Hazor, he sent messages to King Jobab of Madon, to the king of Shimron, to the king of Achshaph, [2] and to the other kings in the north—in the hill country, in the Arabah south of Chinnereth, in the lowlands, and in the district[a] of Dor on the west; [3] to the Canaanites in the east and in the west; to the Amorites, Hittites, Perizzites, and Jebusites in the hill country; and to the Hivites at the foot of Hermon, in the land of Mizpah. [4] They took the field with all their armies—an enormous host, as numerous as the sands on the seashore—and a vast multitude of horses and chariots. [5] All these kings joined forces; they came and encamped together at the Waters of Merom to give battle to Israel.

[6] But the LORD said to Joshua, "Do not be afraid of them; tomorrow at this time I will have them all lying slain before Israel. You shall hamstring their horses and burn their chariots." [7] So Joshua, with all his fighting men, came upon them suddenly at the Waters of Merom, and pounced upon them. [8] The LORD delivered them into the hands of Israel, and they defeated them and pursued them all the way to Great Sidon [b-]and Misrephoth-maim,[-b] and all the way to the Valley of Mizpeh[c] on the east; they

---

[c] I.e. the whole southern part of Canaan.

[a] Meaning of Heb. uncertain.

[b-b] Change of vocalization yields "and Misrephoth on the west."

[c] Apparently identical with Mizpah in v. 3.

crushed them, letting none escape. [9] And Joshua dealt with them as the LORD had ordered him; he hamstrung their horses and burned their chariots.

[10] Joshua then turned back and captured Hazor and put her king to the sword.—Hazor was formerly the head of all those kingdoms.—[11] They proscribed and put to the sword every person in it. Not a soul survived, and Hazor itself was burned down. [12] Joshua captured all those royal cities and their kings. He put them to the sword; he proscribed them in accordance with the charge of Moses, the servant of the LORD. [13] However, all those towns that are still standing on their mounds were not burned down by Israel; it was Hazor alone that Joshua burned down. [14] The Israelites kept all the spoil and cattle of the rest of those cities as booty. But they cut down their populations with the sword until they exterminated them; they did not spare a soul. [15] Just as the LORD had commanded His servant Moses, so Moses had charged Joshua, and so Joshua did; he left nothing undone of all that the LORD had commanded Moses.

[16] Joshua conquered the whole of this region: the hill country [of Judah], the Negeb, the whole land of Goshen, the Shephelah, the Arabah, and the hill country and coastal plain of Israel— [17] [everything] from Mount Halak, which ascends to Seir, all the way to Baal-gad in *d*-the Valley of the Lebanon-*d* at the foot of Mount Hermon; and he captured all the kings there and executed them.

[18] Joshua waged war with all those kings over a long period. [19] Apart from the Hivites who dwelt in Gibeon, not a single city made terms with the Israelites; all were taken in battle. [20] For it was the LORD's doing to stiffen their hearts to give battle to Israel, in order that they might be proscribed without quarter and wiped out, as the LORD had commanded Moses.

[21] At that time, Joshua went and wiped out the Anakites from the hill country, from Hebron, Debir, and Anab, from the entire hill country of Judah, and from the entire hill country of Israel; Joshua proscribed them and their towns. [22] No Anakites re-

d-d *I.e. the valley between the Lebanon and Anti-Lebanon ranges.*

mained in the land of the Israelites; but some remained in Gaza, Gath, and Ashdod.

²³ Thus Joshua conquered the whole country, just as the LORD had promised Moses; and Joshua assigned it to Israel to share according to their tribal divisions. And the land had rest from war.

12 The following are the kings of the land whom the Israelites defeated and whose territories they occupied:

East of the Jordan, from the Wadi Arnon to Mount Hermon, including the eastern half of the Arabah: ² ªKing Sihon of the Amorites, who resided in Heshbon and ruled over part of Gilead —from Aroer on the bank of the Wadi Arnon and the wadi proper up to the Wadi Jabbok [and] the border of the Ammonites—³ and over the eastern Arabah up to the Sea of Chinnereth and, southward by way of Beth-jeshimoth at the foot of the slopes of Pisgah on the east, down to the Sea of the Arabah, that is, the Dead Sea. ⁴ Also the territory of King Og of Bashan—one of the last of the Rephaim—who resided in Ashtaroth and in Edrei ⁵ and ruled over Mount Hermon, Salcah, and all of Bashan up to the border of the Geshurites and the Maacathites, as also over part of Gilead [down to] the border of King Sihon of Heshbon. ⁶ These were vanquished by Moses, the servant of the LORD, and the Israelites; and Moses, the servant of the LORD, assigned ᵇthat territory⁻ᵇ as a possession to the Reubenites, the Gadites, and the half-tribe of Manasseh.

⁷ And the following are the kings of the land whom Joshua and the Israelites defeated on the west side of the Jordan—from Baal-gad in the Valley of the Lebanon to Mount Halak which ascends to Seir—which Joshua assigned as a possession to the tribal divisions of Israel: ⁸ in the hill country, in the lowlands, in the Arabah, in the slopes,ᶜ in the wilderness, and in the Negeb —[in the land of] the Hittites, the Amorites, the Canaanites, the Perizzites, the Hivites, and the Jebusites. ⁹ They were:

ª *Meaning of vv. 2 and 3 uncertain.*
ᵇ⁻ᵇ *Lit. "it."*
ᶜ *I.e. the slopes of Pisgah; cf. 13.20.*

the king of Jericho 1
the king of Ai, near Bethel, 1
10 the king of Jerusalem 1
the king of Hebron 1
11 the king of Jarmuth 1
the king of Lachish 1
12 the king of Eglon 1
the king of Gezer 1
13 the king of Debir 1
the king of Geder 1
14 the king of Hormah 1
the king of Arad 1
15 the king of Libnah 1
the king of Adullam 1
16 the king of Makkedah 1
the king of Bethel 1
17 the king of Tappuah 1
the king of Hepher 1
18 the king of Aphek 1
the king of Sharon 1
19 the king of Madon 1
the king of Hazor 1
20 the king of Shimron-meron 1
the king of Achshaph 1
21 the king of Taanach 1
the king of Megiddo 1
22 the king of Kedesh 1
the king of Jokneam in the Carmel 1
23 the king of Dor in the district*d* of Dor 1
the king of Goiim in Gilgal 1
24 the king of Tirzah 1
Total number of kings 31.

---

d *Meaning of Heb. uncertain.*

26

13 Joshua was now old, advanced in years. The LORD said to him, "You have grown old, you are advanced in years; and very much of the land still remains to be occupied. ² This is the territory that remains: all the districts of the Philistines and all [those of] the Geshurites, ³ from the Shihor, which is close to Egypt, to the territory of Ekron on the north, are accounted Canaanite, namely, those of the five lords of the Philistines—the Gazites, the Ashdodites, the Ashkelonites, the Gittites, and the Ekronites— and those of the Avvim ⁴ on the south; further, all the Canaanite country from Mearah of the Sidonians to Aphek at the Amorite border ⁵ and the land of the Gebalites, with the whole [Valley of the] Lebanon, from Baal-gad at the foot of Mount Hermon to Lebo-hamath on the east, ⁶ with all the inhabitants of the hill country from the [Valley of the] Lebanon to ᵃ⁻Misrephoth-maim,⁻ᵃ namely, all the Sidonians. I Myself will dispossess ᵇ⁻those nations⁻ᵇ for the Israelites; you have only to apportion ᶜ⁻their lands ᶜ by lot among Israel, as I have commanded you. ⁷ Therefore, divide this territory into hereditary portions for the nine tribes and the half-tribe of Manasseh."

⁸ Now the Reubenites and the Gadites, along with ᶜ⁻the other half-tribe,⁻ᶜ had already received the shares which Moses assigned to them on the east side of the Jordan—as assigned to them by Moses the servant of the LORD: ⁹ from Aroer on the edge of the Wadi Arnon and the town in the middle of the wadi, the entire Tableland [from] Medeba to Dibon, ¹⁰ embracing all the towns of King Sihon of the Amorites, who had reigned in Heshbon, up to the border of the Ammonites; ¹¹ further, Gilead, the territories of the Geshurites and the Maacathites, and all of Mount Hermon, and the whole of Bashan up to Salcah—¹² the entire kingdom of Og, who had reigned over Bashan at Ashtaroth and at Edrei. (He was the last of the remaining Rephaim.) These were defeated and dispossessed by Moses; ¹³ but the Israelites failed to dispossess the Geshurites and the Maacathites, and Ge-

ᵃ⁻ᵃ *See note on 11.8.*
ᵇ⁻ᵇ *Lit. "them."*
ᶜ⁻ᶜ *Lit. "it."*

shur and Maacath remain among Israel to this day. [14] No hereditary portion, however, was assigned to the tribe of Levi, their portion being the fire offerings of the LORD, the God of Israel, as He spoke concerning them.[d]

[15] And so Moses assigned [the following] to the tribe of the Reubenites, for their various clans, [16] and it became theirs: The territory from Aroer, on the edge of the Wadi Arnon and the town in the middle of the wadi, up to Medeba—the entire Tableland—[17] Heshbon and all its towns in the Tableland: Dibon, Bamoth-baal, Beth-baal-meon, [18] Jahaz, Kedemoth, Mephaath, [19] Kiriathaim, Sibmah, and Zereth-shahar [e]in the hill of the valley,[-e] [20] Beth-peor, the slopes of Pisgah, and Beth-jeshimoth—[21] all the towns of the Tableland and the entire kingdom of Sihon, the king of the Amorites, who had reigned in Heshbon. (For Moses defeated him and the Midianite chiefs Evi, Rekem, Zur, Hur, and Reba, who had dwelt in the land as princes of Sihon. [22] Together with the others that they slew, the Israelites put Balaam son of Beor, the augur, to the sword.) [23] The boundary of the Reubenites was the edge of the Jordan. That was the portion of the Reubenites for their various clans—those towns with their villages.

[24] To the tribe of Gad, for the various Gadite clans, Moses assigned [the following], [25] and it became their territory: Jazer, all the towns of Gilead, part of the country of the Ammonites up to Aroer, which is close to Rabbah, [26] and from Heshbon to Ramath-mizpeh and Betonim, and from Mahanaim to the border of Lidbir;[f] [27] and in the Valley, Beth-haram, Beth-nimrah, Succoth, and Zaphon—the rest of the kingdom of Sihon, the king of Heshbon —down to the edge of the Jordan and up to the tip of the Sea of Chinnereth on the east side of the Jordan. [28] That was the portion of the Gadites, for their various clans—those towns with their villages.

[29] And to the half-tribe of Manasseh Moses assigned [the following], so that it went to the half-tribe of Manasseh, for its various clans, [30] and became their territory: Mahanaim,[g] all of

[d] See Deut. 18.1.
[e-e] Emendation yields "in the hill country; and in the Valley. . . ."
[f] Change of vocalization yields "Lo-debar"; cf. II Sam. 9.4,5; 17.27.
[g] Lit. "from Mahanaim."

28

Bashan, the entire kingdom of Og king of Bashan, and all of Havvoth-jair*h* in Bashan, 60 towns; [31] and part of Gilead, and Ashtaroth and Edrei, the royal cities of Og in Bashan, were assigned to the descendants of Machir son of Manasseh—to a part of the descendants of Machir—for their various clans.

[32] Those, then, were the portions that Moses assigned in the steppes of Moab, on the east side of the Jordan. [33] But no portion was assigned by Moses to the tribe of Levi; the LORD, the God of Israel, is their portion, as He spoke concerning them.*d*

14 And these are the portions that the Israelites acquired in the land of Canaan, that were assigned to them by the priest Eleazar, by Joshua son of Nun, and by the heads of the ancestral houses of the Israelite tribes, [2] the portions that fell to them by lot, as the LORD had commanded through Moses for the nine and a half tribes. [3] For the portion of the other two and a half tribes had been assigned to them by Moses on the other side of the Jordan. He had not assigned any portion among them to the Levites; [4] for whereas the descendants of Joseph constituted two tribes, Manasseh and Ephraim, the Levites were given no share in the land, but only some towns to live in, with the pastures for their livestock and cattle. [5] Just as the LORD had commanded Moses, so the Israelites did when they apportioned the land.

[6] The Judites approached Joshua at Gilgal, and Caleb son of Jephunneh the Kenizzite said to him: "You know what instructions the LORD gave at Kadesh-barnea to Moses, the man of God, concerning you and me. [7] I was forty years old when Moses the servant of the LORD sent me from Kadesh-barnea to spy out the land, and I gave him a forthright report. [8] While my companions who went up with me took the heart out of the people, I was loyal to the LORD my God. [9] On that day, Moses promised on oath, 'The land on which your foot trod shall be a portion for you and your descendants forever, because you were loyal to the LORD my God.' [10] Now the LORD has preserved me, as He promised. It is

---

h *See note on Num. 32.41.*

forty-five years since the LORD made this promise to Moses, when Israel was journeying through the wilderness; and here I am today, eighty-five years old. [11] I am still as strong today as on the day that Moses sent me; my strength is the same now as it was then, for battle and for activity.[a] [12] So assign to me this hill country as the LORD promised on that day. Though you too heard on that day that Anakites are there and great fortified cities, if only the LORD is with me, I will dispossess them, as the LORD promised."

[13] So Joshua blessed Caleb son of Jephunneh and assigned Hebron to him as his portion. [14] Thus Hebron became the portion of Caleb son of Jephunneh the Kenizzite, as it still is, because he was loyal to the LORD, the God of Israel.— [15] The name of Hebron was formerly Kiriath-arba: [Arba] was the great man among the Anakites.

And the land had rest from war.

15 The portion that fell by lot to the various clans of the tribe of Judah lay farthest south, down to the border of Edom, which is the Wilderness of Zin. [2] Their southern boundary began from the tip of the Dead Sea, from the tongue that projects southward. [3] It proceeded to the south of the Ascent of Akrabbim, passed on to Zin, ascended to the south of Kadesh-barnea, passed on to Hezron, ascended to Addar, and made a turn to Karka. [4] From there it passed on to Azmon and proceeded to the Wadi of Egypt; and the boundary ran on to the Sea. That shall be your southern boundary.

[5] The boundary on the east was the Dead Sea up to the mouth of the Jordan. On the northern side, the boundary began at the tongue of the Sea at the mouth of the Jordan. [6] The boundary ascended to Beth-hoglah and passed north of Beth-arabah; then the boundary ascended to the Stone of Bohan son of Reuben. [7] The boundary ascended [a-from the Valley of Achor to Debir and turned north-a] to Gilgal,[b] facing the Ascent of Adummim which

[a] Lit. "and to go out and come in."

[a-a] Meaning of Heb. uncertain.

[b] Apparently identical with Geliloth, 18.17.

is south of the wadi; from there the boundary continued to the waters of En-shemesh and ran on to En-rogel. [8] Then the boundary ascended into the Valley of Ben-hinnom, along the southern flank of the Jebusites—that is, Jerusalem. The boundary then ran up to the top of the hill which flanks the Valley of Hinnom on the west, at the northern end of the Valley of Rephaim. [9] From that hilltop the boundary curved to the fountain of the Waters of Nephtoah and ran on to the towns of Mount Ephron; then the boundary curved to Baalah—that is, Kiriath-jearim. [10] From Baalah the boundary turned westward to Mount Seir,[c] passed north of the slope of Mount Jearim—that is, Chesalon—descended to Beth-shemesh, and passed on to Timnah. [11] The boundary then proceeded to the northern flank of Ekron; the boundary curved to Shikkeron, passed on to Mount Baalah, and proceeded to Jabneel; and the boundary ran on to the Sea. [12] And the western boundary was the edge of the Mediterranean Sea. Those were the boundaries of the various clans of the Judites on all sides.

[13] In accordance with the LORD's command to Joshua, Caleb son of Jephunneh was given a portion among the Judites, namely, Kiriath-arba—that is, Hebron. ([Arba] was the father of Anak.) [14] Caleb dislodged from there the three Anakites: Sheshai, Ahiman, and Talmai, descendants of Anak. [15] From there he marched against the inhabitants of Debir—the name of Debir was formerly Kiriath-sepher—[16] and Caleb announced, "I will give my daughter Achsah in marriage to the man who attacks and captures Kiriath-sepher." [17] His kinsman Othniel the Kenizzite[d] captured it; and Caleb gave him his daughter Achsah in marriage.

[18] [e-]When she came [to him], she induced him[-e] to ask her father for some property. She dismounted from her donkey, and Caleb asked her, "What is the matter?" [19] She replied, "Give me a present; for you have given me away as Negeb-land;[f] so give me springs of water." And he gave her Upper and Lower Gulloth.[g]

[20] This was the portion of the tribe of the Judites by their clans: [21] The towns at the far end of the tribe of Judah, near the border of Edom, in the Negeb, were: Kabzeel, Eder, Jagur,

[c] *Not the Seir of Edom.*
[d] *Cf. 14.6, 14.*
[e-e] *Meaning of Heb. uncertain. Some Greek mss. read "He induced her"; cf. Judg. 1.14.*
[f] *I.e. as a dry land, that is, without a dowry.*
[g] *I.e. "springs."*

²² Kinah, Dimonah, Adadah, ²³ Kedesh, Hazor, Ithnan, ²⁴ Ziph, Telem, Bealoth, ²⁵ Hazor-hadattah, Kerioth-hezron—that is, Hazor—²⁶ Amam, Shema, Moladah, ²⁷ Hazar-gaddah, Heshmon, Beth-pelet, ²⁸ Hazar-shual, Beer-sheba, Biziothiah, ²⁹ Baalah, Iim, Ezem, ³⁰ Eltolad, Chesil, Hormah, ³¹ Ziklag, Madmannah, Sansannah, ³² ʰ-Lebaoth, Shilhim,-ʰ Ain and Rimmon.ⁱ Total: 29ʲ towns, with their villages.

³³ In the Lowland: Eshtaol, Zorah, Ashnah, ³⁴ Zanoah, En-gannim, Tappuah, Enam, ³⁵ Jarmuth, Adullam, Socoh, Azekah, ³⁶ Shaaraim, Adithaim, Gederah, and Gederothaim—14ᵏ towns, with their villages.

³⁷ Zenan, Hadashah, Migdal-gad, ³⁸ Dilan, Mizpeh, Joktheel, ³⁹ Lachish, Bozkath, Eglon, ⁴⁰ Cabbon, Lahmas, Chithlish, ⁴¹ Gederoth, Beth-dagon, Naamah, and Makkedah: 16 towns, with their villages.

⁴² Libnah, Ether, Ashan, ⁴³ Iphtah, Ashnah, Nezib, ⁴⁴ Keilah, Achzib, and Mareshah: 9 towns, with their villages.

⁴⁵ Ekron, with its dependencies and villages. ⁴⁶ From Ekron westward, all the towns in the vicinity of Ashdod, with their villages—⁴⁷ Ashdod, its dependencies and its villages—Gaza, its dependencies and its villages, all the way to the Wadi of Egypt and the edge of the Mediterranean Sea.

⁴⁸ And in the hill country: Shamir, Jattir, Socoh, ⁴⁹ Dannah, Kiriath-sannah—that is, Debir—⁵⁰ Anab, Eshtemoh, Anim, ⁵¹ Goshen, Holon, and Giloh: 11 towns, with their villages.

⁵² Arab, Dumah, Eshan, ⁵³ Janum, Beth-tappuah, Aphekah, ⁵⁴ Humtah, Kiriath-arba—that is, Hebron—and Zior: 9 towns, with their villages.

⁵⁵ Maon, Carmel, Ziph, Juttah, ⁵⁶ Jezreel, Jokdeam, Zanoah, ⁵⁷ Kain, Gibeah, and Timnah: 10 towns, with their villages.

⁵⁸ Halhul, Beth-zur, Gedor, ⁵⁹ Maarath, Beth-anoth, and Eltekon: 6 towns, with their villages.ˡ

ʰ⁻ʰ *Cf. below 19.6.*
ⁱ *Cf. Ain, Rimmon, 19.7 below, and I Chron. 4.32; En-rimmon, Neh. 11.29.*
ʲ *The number is uncertain. Some of the same towns are listed under Simeon, cf. 19.1-9; so Rashi.*
ᵏ *The number is uncertain. Tappuah and Enam may have been one place; so Rashi on basis of 17.7.*
ˡ *Septuagint adds: Tekoa, Ephrathah—that is, Bethlehem—Peor, Etam, Kulon, Tatam, Sores, Karem, Gallim, Bether, and Manach—11 towns, with their villages.*

⁶⁰ Kiriath-baal—that is, Kiriath-jearim—and Rabbah: 2 towns, with their villages.

⁶¹ In the wilderness: Beth-arabah, Middin, Secacah, ⁶² Nibshan, Ir-melah,*ᵐ* and En-gedi: 6 towns, with their villages.

⁶³ But the Judites could not dispossess the Jebusites, the inhabitants of Jerusalem; so the Judites dwell with the Jebusites in Jerusalem to this day.

16 The portion that fell by lot to the Josephites ran from the Jordan at Jericho—from the waters of Jericho east of the wilderness. From Jericho it ascended through the hill country to Bethel. ² From Bethel it ran to Luz and passed on to the territory of the Archites at Ataroth, ³ descended westward to the territory of the Japhletites as far as the border of Lower Beth-horon and Gezer, and ran on to the Sea. ⁴ Thus the Josephites—that is, Manasseh and Ephraim—received their portion.

⁵ The territory of the Ephraimites, by their clans, was as follows: The boundary of their portion ran from Atroth-addar on the east to Upper Beth-horon, ⁶ and the boundary ran on to the Sea. And on the north, the boundary proceeded from Michmethath to the east of Taanath-shiloh and passed beyond it up to the east of Janoah; ⁷ from Janoah it descended to Ataroth and Naarath, touched on Jericho, and ran on to the Jordan. ⁸ Westward, the boundary proceeded from Tappuah to the Wadi Kanah and ran on to the Sea. This was the portion of the tribe of the Ephraimites, by their clans, ⁹ together with the towns marked off*ᵃ* for the Ephraimites within the territory of the Manassites—all those towns with their villages. ¹⁰ However, they failed to dispossess the Canaanites who dwelt in Gezer; so the Canaanites remained in the midst of Ephraim, as is still the case. But they had to perform forced labor.

ᵐ *Or "the City of Salt."*
ᵃ *Meaning of Heb. uncertain.*

17 And this is the portion that fell by lot to the tribe of Manasseh—for he was Joseph's firstborn. Since Machir, the firstborn of Manasseh and the father of Gilead, was a valiant warrior, Gilead and Bashan were assigned to him. ² And now assignments were made to the remaining Manassites, by their clans: the descendants of Abiezer, Helek, Asriel, Shechem, Hepher, and Shemida. Those were the male descendants of Manasseh son of Joseph, by their clans.

³ ᵃNow Zelophehad son of Hepher son of Gilead son of Machir son of Manasseh had no sons, but only daughters. The names of his daughters were Mahlah, Noah, Hoglah, Milcah, and Tirzah. ⁴ They appeared before the priest Eleazer, Joshua son of Nun, and the chieftains, saying: "The LORD commanded Moses to grant us a portion among our male kinsmen." So, in accordance with the LORD's instructions, they were granted a portion among their father's kinsmen. ⁵ Ten districts fell to Manasseh, apart from the lands of Gilead and Bashan, which are across the Jordan. ⁶ Manasseh's daughters inherited a portion in these together with his sons, while the land of Gilead was assigned to the rest of Manasseh's descendants.

⁷ The boundary of Manasseh ran from Asher to Michmethath, which lies near Shechem. The boundary continued to the right, toward the inhabitants of En-tappuah.—⁸ The region of Tappuah belonged to Manasseh; but Tappuah, on the border of Manasseh, belonged to the Ephraimites.—⁹ Then the boundary descended to the Wadi Kanah. Those towns to the south of the wadi belonged to Ephraim as an enclave among the towns of Manasseh. The boundary of Manasseh lay north of the wadi and ran on to the Sea. ¹⁰ What lay to the south belonged to Ephraim, and what lay to the north belonged to Manasseh, with the Sea as its boundary. [This territory] was contiguous with Asher on the north and with Issachar on the east. ¹¹ Within Issachar and Asher, Manasseh possessed Beth-shean and its dependencies, Ibleam

ᵃ *Cf. Num. 27.1-11.*

and its dependencies, the inhabitants of Dor and its dependencies, the inhabitants of En-dor and its dependencies, the inhabitants of Taanach and its dependencies, and the inhabitants of Megiddo and its dependencies: *b*-these comprised three regions.*-b*

¹² The Manassites could not dispossess [the inhabitants of] these towns, and the Canaanites stubbornly remained in this region. ¹³ When the Israelites became stronger, they imposed tribute on the Canaanites; but they did not dispossess them.

¹⁴ The Josephites complained to Joshua, saying, "Why have you assigned as our portion a single allotment and a single district, seeing that we are a numerous people whom the LORD has blessed so greatly?" ¹⁵ "If you are a numerous people," Joshua answered them, "go up to the forest country and clear an area for yourselves there, in the territory of the Perizzites and the Rephaim, seeing that you are cramped in the hill country of Ephraim." ¹⁶ "The hill country is not enough for us," the Josephites replied, "and all the Canaanites who live in the valley area have iron chariots, both those in Beth-shean and its dependencies and those in the Valley of Jezreel." ¹⁷ But Joshua declared to the House of Joseph, to Ephraim and Manasseh, "You are indeed a numerous people, possessed of great strength; you shall not have one allotment only. ¹⁸ The hill country shall be yours as well; true, it is forest land, but you will clear it and possess it to its farthest limits. And you shall also dispossess the Canaanites, even though they have iron chariots and even though they are strong."

18 The whole community of the Israelite people assembled at Shiloh, and set up the Tent of Meeting there. The land was now under their control; ² but there remained seven tribes of the Israelites which had not yet received their portions. ³ So Joshua said to the Israelites, "How long will you be slack about going and taking possession of the land which the LORD, the God of your fathers, has given you? ⁴ Appoint three men of each tribe;

b-b *Meaning of Heb. uncertain.*

I will send them out to go through the country and write down a description of it for purposes of apportionment, and then come back to me. ⁵ They shall divide it into seven parts—Judah shall remain by its territory in the south, and the House of Joseph shall remain by its territory in the north.—⁶ When you have written down the description of the land in seven parts, bring it here to me. Then I will cast lots for you here before the LORD our God. ⁷ For the Levites have no share among you, since the priesthood of the LORD is their portion; and Gad and Reuben and the half-tribe of Manasseh have received the portions which were assigned to them by Moses the servant of the LORD, on the eastern side of the Jordan."

⁸ The men set out on their journeys. Joshua ordered the men who were leaving to write down a description of the land, "Go, traverse the country and write down a description of it. Then return to me, and I will cast lots for you here at Shiloh before the LORD."

⁹ So the men went and traversed the land; they described it in a document, town by town, in seven parts, and they returned to Joshua in the camp at Shiloh. ¹⁰ Joshua cast lots for them at Shiloh before the LORD, and there Joshua apportioned the land among the Israelites according to their divisions.

¹¹ The lot of the tribe of the Benjaminites, by their clans, came out first. The territory which fell to their lot lay between the Judites and the Josephites. ¹² The boundary on their northern rim began at the Jordan; the boundary ascended to the northern flank of Jericho, ascended westward into the hill country and ran on to the Wilderness of Beth-aven. ¹³ From there the boundary passed on southward to Luz, to the flank of Luz—that is, Bethel; then the boundary descended to Atroth-addar [and] to the hill south of Lower Beth-horon. ¹⁴ The boundary now turned and curved onto the western rim; and the boundary ran southward from the hill on the south side of Beth-horon till it ended at Kiriath-baal—that is, Kiriath-jearim—a town of the Judites. That was the western rim. ¹⁵ The southern rim: From the outskirts of Kiriath-jearim,

the boundary passed westward*a* and ran on to the fountain of the Waters of Nephtoah. [16] Then the boundary descended to the foot of the hill by the Valley of Ben-hinnom at the northern end of the Valley of Rephaim; then it ran down the Valley of Hinnom along the southern flank of the Jebusites to En-rogel. [17] Curving northward, it ran on to En-shemesh and ran on to Geliloth, facing the Ascent of Adummim, and descended to the Stone of Bohan son of Reuben. [18] It continued northward to the edge of the Arabah and descended into the Arabah. [19] The boundary passed on to the northern flank of Beth-hoglah, and the boundary ended at the northern tongue of the Dead Sea, at the southern end of the Jordan. That was the southern boundary. [20] On their eastern rim, finally, the Jordan was their boundary. That was the portion of the Benjaminites, by their clans, according to its boundaries on all sides.

[21] And the towns of the tribe of the Benjaminites, by its clans, were: Jericho, Beth-hoglah, Emek-keziz, [22] Beth-arabah, Zemaraim, Bethel, [23] Avvim, Parah, Ophrah, [24] Chephar-ammonah, Ophni, and Geba—12 towns, with their villages. [25] Also Gibeon, Ramah, Beeroth, [26] Mizpeh, Chephirah, Mozah, [27] Rekem, Irpeel, Taralah, [28] Zela, Eleph, and Jebus*b*—that is, Jerusalem—Gibeath [and] Kiriath:*c* 14 towns, with their villages. That was the portion of the Benjaminites, by their clans.

19

The second lot fell to Simeon. The portion of the tribe of the Simeonites, by their clans, lay inside the portion of the Judites. [2] Their portion comprised: Beer-sheba—or Sheba—Moladah, [3] Hazar-shual, Balah, Ezem, [4] Eltolad, Bethul,*a* Hormah, [5] Ziklag, Beth-marcaboth, Hazar-susah, [6] *b*-Beth-lebaoth, and Sharuhen*-b*—13 towns, with their villages. [7] Ain, Rimmon, Ether, and Ashan: 4 towns, with their villages—[8] together with all the villages in the vicinity of those towns, down to Baalath-beer [and] Ramath-negeb. That was the portion of the tribe of the Simeonites, by their clans. [9] The portion of the Simeonites was part of

a *Emendation yields "eastward."*
b *Heb. "the Jebusite."*
c *Emendation yields "and Kiriath-jearim."*

a *15.30 reads "Chesil."*
b-b *15.32 reads "Shilhim."*

the territory of the Judites; since the share of the Judites was larger than they needed, the Simeonites received a portion inside their portion.

¹⁰ The third lot emerged for the Zebulunites, by their clans. The boundary of their portion: Starting at Sarid, ¹¹ their boundary*c* ascended westward to Maralah, touching Dabbesheth and touching the wadi alongside Jokneam. ¹² And it also ran from Sarid along the eastern side, where the sun rises, past the territory of Chisloth-tabor and on to Daberath and ascended to Japhia. ¹³ From there it ran [back] to the east, toward the sunrise, to Gath-hepher, to Eth-kazin, and on to Rimmon, where it curved to Neah. ¹⁴ Then it turned—that is, the boundary on the north— to Hannathon. Its extreme limits*d* were the Valley of Iphtah-el, ¹⁵ Kattath, Nahalal, Shimron, Idalah, and Bethlehem: 12 towns, with their villages. ¹⁶ That was the portion of the Zebulunites by their clans—those towns, with their villages.

¹⁷ The fourth lot fell to Issachar, the Issacharites by their clans. ¹⁸ Their territory comprised: Jezreel, Chesulloth, Shunem, ¹⁹ Hapharaim, Shion, Anaharath, ²⁰ Rabbith, Kishion, Ebez, ²¹ Remeth, En-gannim, En-haddah, and Beth-pazzez. ²² The boundary touched Tabor, Shahazimah, and Beth-shemesh; and their boundary ran to the Jordan: 16 towns, with their villages. ²³ That was the portion of the tribe of the Issacharites, by their clans—the towns with their villages.

²⁴ The fifth lot fell to the tribe of the Asherites, by their clans. ²⁵ Their boundary*c* ran along Helkath, Hali, Beten, Achshaph, ²⁶ Allammelech, Amad, and Mishal; and it touched Carmel on the west, and Shihor-libnath. ²⁷ It also ran*e* along the east side to Beth-dagon, and touched Zebulun and the Valley of Iphtah-el to the north, [as also] Beth-emek and Neiel; *f*-then it ran to Cabul on the north,*f* ²⁸ Ebron,*g* Rehob, Hammon, and Kanah, up to Great Sidon. ²⁹ The boundary turned to Ramah and on to the fortified city of Tyre; then the boundary turned to Hosah *f*-and it ran on westward to Mehebel,*f* Achzib, ³⁰ Ummah, Aphek, and Rehob: 22 towns, with their villages. ³¹ That was the portion of

---

c I.e. the southern one.
d I.e. the northwest corner, opposite the starting point, Sarid.
e I.e. from Helkath, v. 25.
f-f Meaning of Heb. uncertain.
g Some Heb. mss., as well as Josh. 21.30 and I Chron. 6.59, read "Abdon."

the tribe of the Asherites, by their clans—those towns, with their villages.

³² The sixth lot fell to the Naphtalites, the Naphtalites by their clans. ³³ *ʰTheir boundary ran from Heleph, Elon-bezaanannim, Adami-nekeb, and Jabneel to Lakkum, and it ended at the Jordan. ³⁴ The boundary then turned westward to Aznoth-tabor and ran from there to Hukok. It touched Zebulun on the south, and it touched Asher on the west, and Judah at the Jordan on the east. ³⁵ Its fortified towns were Ziddim, Zer, Hammath, Rakkath, Chinnereth, ³⁶ Adamah, Ramah, Hazor, ³⁷ Kedesh, Edrei, En-hazor, ³⁸ Iron, Migdal-el, Horem, Beth-anath, and Beth-shemesh: 19 towns, with their villages. ³⁹ That was the portion of the tribe of the Naphtalites, by their clans—the towns, with their villages.

⁴⁰ The seventh lot fell to the tribe of the Danites, by their clans. ⁴¹ Their allotted territory comprised: Zorah, Eshtaol, Ir-shemesh, ⁴² Shaalabbin, Aijalon, Ithlah, ⁴³ Elon, Timnah, Ekron, ⁴⁴ Eltekeh, Gibbethon, Baalath, ⁴⁵ Jehud, Bene-berak, Gath-rimmon, ⁴⁶ Mejarkon, and Rakkon, at the border near Joppa. ⁴⁷ But the territory of the Danites slipped from their grasp. So the Danites migrated and made war on Leshem.ⁱ They captured it and put it to the sword; they took possession of it and settled in it. And they changed the name of Leshem to Dan, after their ancestor Dan. ⁴⁸ That was the portion of the tribe of the Danites, by their clans —those towns, with their villages.

⁴⁹ When they had finished allotting the land by its boundaries, the Israelites gave a portion in their midst to Joshua son of Nun. ⁵⁰ At the command of the LORD they gave him the town that he asked for, Timnath-serah in the hill country of Ephraim; he fortified the town and settled in it.

⁵¹ These are the portions assigned by lot to the tribes of Israel by the priest Eleazar, Joshua son of Nun, and the heads of the ancestral houses, before the LORD at Shiloh, at the entrance of the Tent of Meeting.

ʰ *The geography of vv. 33-35 is unclear in part.*
ⁱ *Called Laish in Judg. 18.7ff.*

20 When they had finished dividing the land, [1] the LORD said to Joshua: [2] "Speak to the Israelites: Designate the cities of refuge —about which I commanded you through Moses—[3] to which a manslayer who kills a person by mistake, unintentionally, may flee. They shall serve you as a refuge from the blood avenger. [4] He shall flee to one of those cities, present himself at the entrance to the city gate, and plead his case before the elders of that city; and they shall admit him into the city and give him a place in which to live among them. [5] Should the blood avenger pursue him, they shall not hand the manslayer over to him, since he killed the other person without intent and had not been his enemy in the past. [6] He shall live in that city until he can stand trial before the assembly, [and remain there] until the death of the high priest who is in office at that time. Thereafter, the manslayer may go back to his home in his own town, to the town from which he fled."

[7] So they set aside Kedesh in the hill country of Naphtali in Galilee, Shechem in the hill country of Ephraim, and Kiriath-arba —that is, Hebron—in the hill country of Judah. [8] And across the Jordan, east of Jericho, they assigned Bezer in the wilderness, in the Tableland, from the tribe of Reuben; Ramoth in Gilead from the tribe of Gad; and Golan in Bashan from the tribe of Manasseh. [9] Those were the towns designated[a] for all the Israelites and for aliens residing among them, to which anyone who killed a person unintentionally might flee, and not die by the hand of the blood avenger before standing trial by the assembly.

21 The heads of the ancestral houses of the Levites approached the priest Eleazer, Joshua son of Nun, and the heads of the ancestral houses of the Israelite tribes, [2] and spoke to them at Shiloh in the land of Canaan, as follows: "The LORD commanded through Moses that we be given towns to live in, along

___
[a] *Meaning of Heb. uncertain.*

with their pastures for our livestock." [3] So the Israelites, in accordance with the LORD's command, assigned to the Levites, out of their own portions, the following towns with their pastures:

[4] The [first] lot among the Levites fell to the Kohathite clans. To the descendants of the priest Aaron, there fell by lot 13 towns from the tribe of Judah, the tribe of Simeon, and the tribe of Benjamin; [5] and to the remaining Kohathites [there fell] by lot 10 towns from the clans of the tribe of Ephraim, the tribe of Dan, and the half-tribe of Manasseh.

[6] To the Gershonites [there fell] by lot 13 towns from the clans of the tribe of Issachar, the tribe of Asher, the tribe of Naphtali, and the half-tribe of Manasseh in Bashan.

[7] [And] to the Merarites, by their clans—12 towns from the tribe of Reuben, the tribe of Gad, and the tribe of Zebulun. [8] The Israelites assigned those towns with their pastures by lot to the Levites—as the LORD had commanded through Moses.

[9] From the tribe of the Judites and the tribe of the Simeonites were assigned the following towns, which will be listed by name; [10] they went to the descendants of Aaron among the Kohathite clans of the Levites, for the first lot had fallen to them. [11] To them were assigned in the hill country of Judah Kiriath-arba—that is, Hebron—together with the pastures around it. [Arba was] the father of the Anokites.[a] [12] They gave the fields and the villages of the town to Caleb son of Jephunneh as his holding. [13] But to the descendants of Aaron the priest they gave Hebron—the city of refuge for manslayers—together with its pastures, Libnah with its pastures, [14] Jattir with its pastures, Eshtemoa with its pastures, [15] Holon with its pastures, Debir with its pastures, [16] Ain with its pastures, Juttah with its pastures, and Beth-shemesh with its pastures—9 towns from those two tribes. [17] And from the tribe of Benjamin: Gibeon with its pastures, Geba with its pastures, [18] Anathoth with its pastures, and Almon with its pastures—4 towns. [19] All the towns of the descendants of the priest Aaron, 13 towns with their pastures.

[a] *Elsewhere Anakites; cf. Num. 13.22; Deut. 9.2.*

20 [b]As for the other clans of the Kohathites, the remaining Levites descended from Kohath, the towns in their lot were: From the tribe of Ephraim 21 they were given, in the hill country of Ephraim, Shechem—the city of refuge for manslayers—with its pastures, Gezer with its pastures, 22 Kibzaim with its pastures, and Beth-horon with its pastures—4 towns. 23 From the tribe of Dan, Elteke with its pastures, Gibbethon with its pastures, 24 Aijalon with its pastures, and Gath-rimmon with its pastures—4 towns. 25 And from the half-tribe of Manasseh, Taanach with its pastures, and Gath-rimmon with its pastures—2 towns. 26 All the towns for the remaining clans of the Kohathites came to 10, with their pastures.

27 To the Gershonites of the levitical clans: From the half-tribe of Manasseh, Golan in Bashan—the city of refuge for manslayers—with its pastures, and Beeshterah with its pastures—2 towns. 28 From the tribe of Issachar: Kishion with its pastures, Dobrath with its pastures, 29 Jarmuth with its pastures, and En-gannim with its pastures—4 towns. 30 From the tribe of Asher: Mishal with its pastures, Abdon with its pastures, 31 Helkath with its pastures, and Rehob with its pastures—4 towns. 32 From the tribe of Naphtali, Kedesh in Galilee—the city of refuge for manslayers—with its pastures, Hammoth-dor with its pastures, and Kartan with its pastures—3 towns. 33 All the towns of the Gershonites, by their clans, came to 13 towns, with their pastures.

34 To the remaining Levites, the clans of the Merarites: From the tribe of Zebulun, Jokneam with its pastures, Kartah with its pastures, 35 Dimnah with its pastures, and Nahalal with its pastures—4 towns.[c] 36 From the tribe of Gad, Ramoth in Gilead—the city of refuge for manslayers—with its pastures, Mahanaim with its pastures, 37 Heshbon with its pastures, and Jazer with its pastures—4 towns in all. 38 All the towns which went by lot to the Merarites, by their clans—the rest of the levitical clans—came to 12 towns. 39 All the towns of the Levites within the holdings of the Israelites came to 48 towns, with their pastures. 40 [d]Thus

[b] Explicating v. 5.
[c] Some mss. and editions add the following (cf. I Chron. 6.63-64), "And from the tribe of Reuben: Bezer with its pastures, Jahaz with its pastures, Kedemoth with its pastures, and Mephaath with its pastures—4 towns."
[d] Meaning of verse uncertain.

those towns were assigned, every town with its surrounding pasture; and so it was with all those towns.

[41] The LORD gave to Israel the whole country which He had sworn to their fathers that He would give them; they took possession of it and settled in it. [42] The LORD gave them rest on all sides, just as He had promised to their fathers on oath. Not one man of all their enemies withstood them; the LORD delivered all their enemies into their hands. [43] Not one of the good things which the LORD had promised to the House of Israel was lacking. Everything was fulfilled.

22 Then Joshua summoned the Reubenites, the Gadites, and the half-tribe of Manasseh, [2] and said to them, "You have observed all that Moses the servant of the LORD commanded you, and have obeyed me in everything that I commanded you. [3] You have not forsaken your kinsmen through the long years down to this day, but have faithfully observed the Instruction of the LORD your God. [4] Now the LORD your God has given your kinsmen rest, as He promised them. Therefore turn and go to your homes, to the land of your holdings beyond the Jordan which Moses the servant of the LORD assigned to you. [5] But be very careful to fulfill the Instruction and the Teaching that Moses the servant of the LORD enjoined upon you, to love the LORD your God and to walk in all His ways, and to keep His commandments and hold fast to Him, and to serve Him with all your heart and soul." [6] Then Joshua blessed them and dismissed them, and they went to their homes.

[7] To the one half-tribe of Manasseh Moses had assigned territory in Bashan, and to the other Joshua assigned [territory] on the west side of the Jordan, with their kinsmen.[a]

Furthermore, when Joshua sent them[b] off to their homes, he blessed them [8] and said to them, "Return to your homes with great wealth—with very much livestock, with silver and gold, with

---

[a] *I.e. the other nine tribes.*
[b] *I.e. the two and a half tribes.*

copper and iron, and with a great quantity of clothing. Share the spoil of your enemies with your kinsmen." 9 So the Reubenites, the Gadites, and the half-tribe of Manasseh left the Israelites at Shiloh, in the land of Canaan, and made their way back to the land of Gilead, the land of their own holding, which they had acquired by the command of the LORD through Moses. 10 When they came to the region of the Jordan in the land of Canaan, the Reubenites and the Gadites and the half-tribe of Manasseh built an altar there by the Jordan, a great conspicuous altar.

11 A report reached the Israelites: "The Reubenites, the Gadites, and the half-tribe of Manasseh have built an altar opposite the land of Canaan, in the region of the Jordan, across from the Israelites." 12 When the Israelites heard this, the whole community of the Israelites assembled at Shiloh to make war on them. 13 But [first] the Israelites sent the priest Phinehas son of Eleazar to the Reubenites, the Gadites, and the half-tribe of Manasseh in the land of Gilead, 14 accompanied by ten chieftains, one chieftain from each ancestral house of each of the tribes of Israel; they were every one of them heads of ancestral houses of the contingents of Israel. 15 When they came to the Reubenites, the Gadites, and the half-tribe of Manasseh in the land of Gilead, they spoke to them as follows:

16 "Thus said the whole community of the LORD: What is this treachery that you have committed this day against the God of Israel, turning away from the LORD, building yourselves an altar and rebelling this day against the LORD! 17 Is the sin of Peor, which brought a plague upon the community of the LORD, such a small thing to us? We have not cleansed ourselves from it to this very day; 18 and now you would turn away from the LORD! If you rebel against the LORD today, tomorrow He will be angry with the whole community of Israel. 19 If it is because the land of your holding is unclean, cross over into the land of the LORD's own holding, where the Tabernacle of the LORD abides, and acquire holdings among us. But do not rebel against the LORD, and do not rebel against us by building for yourselves an altar other than

the altar of the LORD our God. 20 When Achan son of Zerah violated the proscription, anger struck the whole community of Israel; he was not the only one who perished for that sin."

21 The Reubenites, the Gadites, and the half-tribe of Manasseh replied to the heads of the contingents of Israel: They said, 22 "God, the LORD God! God, the LORD God! He knows, and Israel too shall know! If we acted in rebellion or in treachery against the LORD, do not vindicate us this day! 23 If we built an altar to turn away from the LORD, if it was to offer burnt offerings or meal offerings upon it, or to present sacrifices of well-being upon it, may the LORD Himself demand [a reckoning]. 24 We did this thing only out of our concern that, in time to come, your children might say to our children, 'What have you to do with the LORD, the God of Israel? 25 The LORD has made the Jordan a boundary between you and us, O Reubenites and Gadites; you have no share in the LORD!' Thus your children might prevent our children from worshiping the LORD. 26 So we decided to provide [a witness] for ourselves by building an altar—not for burnt offerings or [other] sacrifices, 27 but as a witness between you and us, and between the generations to come—that we may perform the service of the LORD before Him^c with our burnt offerings, our sacrifices, and our offerings of well-being; and that your children should not say to our children in time to come, 'You have no share in the LORD.' 28 We reasoned: should they speak thus to us and to our children in time to come, we would reply, 'See the replica of the LORD's altar,^c which our fathers made—not for burnt offerings or sacrifices, but as a witness between you and us.' 29 Far be it from us to rebel against the LORD, or to turn away this day from the LORD and build an altar for burnt offerings, meal offerings, and sacrifices other than the altar of the LORD our God which stands before His Tabernacle."

30 When the priest Phinehas and the chieftains of the community—the heads of the contingents of Israel—who were with him heard the explanation given by the Reubenites, the Gadites, and the Manassites, they approved. 31 The priest Phinehas son of

^c I.e. at Shiloh.

Eleazar said to the Reubenites, the Gadites, and the Manassites, "Now we know that the LORD is in our midst, since you have not committed such treachery against the LORD. You have indeed saved the Israelites from punishment by the LORD."

³² Then the priest Phinehas son of Eleazar and the chieftains returned from the Reubenites and the Gadites in the land of Gilead to the Israelites in the land of Canaan, and gave them their report. ³³ The Israelites were pleased, and the Israelites praised God; and they spoke no more of going to war against them, to ravage the land in which the Reubenites and Gadites dwelt.

³⁴ The Reubenites and the Gadites named the altar ["Witness"], meaning, "It is a witness between us and them that the LORD is [our] God."

23 Much later, after the LORD had given Israel rest from all the enemies around them, and when Joshua was old and well advanced in years, ² Joshua summoned all Israel, their elders and commanders, their magistrates and officials, and said to them: "I have grown old and am advanced in years. ³ You have seen all that the LORD your God has done to all those nations on your account, for it was the LORD your God who fought for you. ⁴ See, I have allotted to you, by your tribes, [the territory of] these nations that still remain, and that of all the nations that I have destroyed, from the Jordan to the Mediterranean Sea in the west. ⁵ The LORD your God Himself will thrust them out on your account and drive them out to make way for you, and you shall occupy their land as the LORD your God promised you.

⁶ "But be most resolute to observe faithfully all that is written in the book of the Teaching of Moses, without ever deviating from it to the right or to the left, ⁷ and without intermingling with these nations which are left among you. Do not utter the names of their gods or swear by them; do not serve them or bow down to them. ⁸ But hold fast to the LORD your God as you have done to this day.

⁹ "The LORD has driven out great, powerful nations on your account, and not a man has withstood you to this day. ¹⁰ A single man of you would put a thousand to flight, for the LORD your God Himself has been fighting for you, as He promised you. ¹¹ For your own sakes, therefore, be most mindful to love the LORD your God. ¹² For should you turn away and attach yourselves to the remnant of those nations—to those that are left among you—and intermarry with them, you joining them and they joining you, ¹³ know for certain that the LORD your God will not continue to drive these nations out before you; they shall become a snare and a trap for you, a scourge to your sides and thorns in your eyes, until you perish from this good land which the LORD your God has given you.

¹⁴ "I am now going the way of all the earth. Acknowledge with all your heart and soul that not one of the good things that the LORD your God promised you has failed to happen; they have all come true for you, not a single one has failed. ¹⁵ But just as every good thing that the LORD your God promised you has been fulfilled for you, so the LORD can bring upon you every evil thing until He has wiped you off this good land which the LORD your God has given you. ¹⁶ If you break the covenant which the LORD your God enjoined upon you, and go and serve other gods and bow down to them, then the LORD's anger will burn against you, and you shall quickly perish from the good land which He has given you."

24

Joshua assembled all the tribes of Israel at Schechem. He summoned Israel's elders and commanders, magistrates and officers; and they presented themselves before God. ² Then Joshua said to all the people, "Thus said the LORD, the God of Israel: In olden times, your forefathers—Terah, father of Abraham and father of Nahor—lived beyond the Euphrates and worshiped other gods. ³ But I took your father Abraham from beyond the Euphrates and led him through the whole land of

Canaan and multiplied his offspring. I gave him Isaac, ⁴ and to Isaac I gave Jacob and Esau. I gave Esau the hill country of Seir as his possession, while Jacob and his children went down to Egypt.

⁵ "Then I sent Moses and Aaron, and I plagued Egypt with [the wonders] that I wrought in their midst, after which I freed you —⁶ I freed your fathers—from Egypt, and you came to the Sea. But the Egyptians pursued your fathers to the Sea of Reeds with chariots and horsemen. ⁷ They cried out to the LORD, and He put darkness between you and the Egyptians; then He brought the Sea upon them, and it covered them. Your own eyes saw what I did to the Egyptians.

"After you had lived a long time in the wilderness, ⁸ I brought you to the land of the Amorites who lived beyond the Jordan. They gave battle to you, but I delivered them into your hands; I annihilated them for you, and you took possession of their land. ⁹ Thereupon Balak son of Zippor, the king of Moab, made ready to attack Israel. He sent for Balaam son of Beor to curse you, ¹⁰ but I refused to listen to Balaam; he had to bless you, and thus I saved you from him.

¹¹ "Then you crossed the Jordan and you came to Jericho. The citizens of Jericho and the Amorites, Perizzites, Canaanites, Hittites, Girgashites, Hivites, and Jebusites fought you, but I delivered them into your hands. ¹² I sent a plague*a* ahead of you, and it drove them out before you—[just like] the two Amorite kings —not by your sword or by your bow. ¹³ I have given you a land for which you did not labor and towns which you did not build, and you have settled in them; you are enjoying vineyards and olive groves which you did not plant.

¹⁴ "Now, therefore, revere the LORD and serve Him with undivided loyalty; put away the gods that your forefathers served beyond the Euphrates and in Egypt, and serve the LORD. ¹⁵ Or, if you are loath to serve the LORD, choose this day which ones you are going to serve—the gods that your forefathers served beyond

---

ª *See note at Exod. 23.28.*

the Euphrates, or those of the Amorites in whose land you are settled; but I and my household will serve the LORD."

¹⁶ In reply, the people declared, "Far be it from us to forsake the LORD and serve other gods! ¹⁷ For it was the LORD our God who brought us and our fathers up from the land of Egypt, the house of bondage, and who wrought those wondrous signs before our very eyes, and guarded us all along the way that we traveled and among all the peoples through whose midst we passed. ¹⁸ And then the LORD drove out before us all the peoples —the Amorites—that inhabited the country. We too will serve the LORD, for He is our God."

¹⁹ Joshua, however, said to the people, "You will not be able to serve the LORD, for He is a holy God. He is a jealous God; He will not forgive your transgressions and your sins. ²⁰ If you forsake the LORD and serve alien gods, He will turn and deal harshly with you and make an end of you, after having been gracious to you." ²¹ But the people replied to Joshua, "No, we will serve the LORD!" ²² Thereupon Joshua said to the people, "You are witnesses against yourselves that you have by your own act chosen to serve the LORD." "Yes, we are!" they responded. ²³ "Then put away the alien gods that you have among you and direct your hearts to the LORD, the God of Israel." ²⁴ And the people declared to Joshua, "We will serve none but the LORD our God, and we will obey none but Him."

²⁵ On that day at Shechem, Joshua made a covenant for the people and he made a fixed rule for them. ²⁶ Joshua recorded all this in a book of divine instruction. He took a great stone and set it up at the foot of the oak in the sacred precinct of the LORD; ²⁷ and Joshua said to all the people, "See, this very stone shall be a witness against us, for it heard all the words that the LORD spoke to us; it shall be a witness against you, lest you break faith with your God." ²⁸ Joshua then dismissed the people to their allotted portions.

²⁹ After these events, Joshua son of Nun, the servant of the LORD, died at the age of one hundred and ten years. ³⁰ They buried him on his own property, at Timnath-serah in the hill country of Ephraim, north of Mount Gaash. ³¹ Israel served the LORD during the lifetime of Joshua and the lifetime of the elders who lived on after Joshua, and who had experienced all the deeds that the LORD had wrought for Israel.

³² The bones of Joseph, which the Israelites had brought up from Egypt, were buried at Shechem, in the piece of ground which Jacob had bought for a hundred *kesitahs*[b] from the children of Hamor, Shechem's father, and which had become a heritage of the Josephites.

³³ Eleazar son of Aaron also died, and they buried him on the hill of his son Phinehas, which had been given to him in the hill country of Ephraim.

[b] *See note at Gen. 33.19.*

שופטים

JUDGES

שׁוֹפְטִים
JUDGES*

1 After the death of Joshua, the Israelites inquired of the LORD, "Which of us shall be the first to go up against the Canaanites and attack them?" ² The LORD replied, "Let [the tribe of] Judah go up. I now deliver the land into their hands." ³ Judah then said to their brother-tribe Simeon, "Come up with us to our allotted territory and let us attack the Canaanites, and then we will go with you to your allotted territory." So Simeon joined them.

⁴ When Judah advanced, the LORD delivered the Canaanites and the Perizzites into their hands, and they defeated ten thousand of them at Bezek. ⁵ At Bezek, they encountered Adoni-bezek, engaged him in battle, and defeated the Canaanites and the Perizzites. ⁶ Adoni-bezek fled, but they pursued him and captured him; and they cut off his thumbs and his big toes. ⁷ And Adoni-bezek said, "Seventy kings, with thumbs and big toes cut off, used to pick up scraps under my table; as I have done, so God has requited me." They brought him to Jerusalem and he died there.

⁸ The Judites attacked Jerusalem and captured it; they put it to the sword and set the city on fire. ⁹ After that the Judites went down to attack the Canaanites who inhabited the hill country, the Negeb, and the Shephelah.

¹⁰ The Judites marched against the Canaanites who dwelt in Hebron, and they defeated Sheshai, Ahiman, and Talmai. (The name of Hebron was formerly Kiriath-arba.) ¹¹ From there they marched against the inhabitants of Debir (the name of Debir was formerly Kiriath-sepher). ¹² And Caleb announced, "I will give my daughter Achsah in marriage to the man who attacks and

---

*This is the traditional rendering of *shophetim*, which, however, in the text is rendered "chieftains." The corresponding verb *shaphat* is usually translated not "judged" but "ruled" or "led"

53

captures Kiriath-sepher." [13] His younger kinsman, Othniel the Kenizzite,[a] captured it; and Caleb gave him his daughter Achsah in marriage. [14] [b-]When she came [to him], she induced him to ask her father for some property. She dismounted from her donkey, and Caleb asked her, "What is the matter?" [15] She replied, "Give me a present, for you have given me away as Negeb-land; give me springs of water." And Caleb gave her Upper and Lower Gulloth.[-b]

[16] The descendants of the Kenite, the father-in-law of Moses, went up with the Judites from the City of Palms to the wilderness of Judah; and they went and settled among the people[c] in the Negeb of Arad. [17] And Judah with its brother-tribe Simeon went on and defeated the Canaanites who dwelt in Zephath. They proscribed it, and so the town was named Hormah.[d] [18] And Judah captured[e] Gaza and its territory, Ashkelon and its territory, and Ekron and its territory.

[19] The LORD was with Judah, so that they took possession of the hill country; but they were not able to dispossess the inhabitants of the plain, for they had iron chariots. [20] They gave Hebron to Caleb, as Moses had promised; and he drove the three Anakites out of there. [21] The Benjaminites did not dispossess the Jebusite inhabitants of Jerusalem; so the Jebusites have dwelt with the Benjaminites in Jerusalem to this day.

[22] The House of Joseph, for their part, advanced against Bethel, and the LORD was with them. [23] While the House of Joseph were scouting at Bethel (the name of the town was formerly Luz), [24] their patrols[f] saw a man leaving the town. They said to him, "Just show us how to get into the town, and we will treat you kindly." [25] He showed them how to get into the town; they put the town to the sword, but they let the man and all his relatives go free. [26] The man went to the Hittite country. He founded a city and named it Luz, and that has been its name to this day.

[a] Cf. Josh. 14.6, 14.
[b-b] Cf. Josh. 15.18-19 and notes.
[c] Meaning of Heb. uncertain. Emendation yields "Amalekites"; cf. I Sam. 15.6.
[d] I.e. "Proscribed." Cf. notes at Num. 21.2-3.
[e] Septuagint reads "But Judah did not capture Gaza. . . ." Gaza is in the coastal plain referred to in v. 19.
[f] Lit. "watchmen."

²⁷ Manasseh did not dispossess [the inhabitants of] Beth-shean and its dependencies, or [of] Taanach and its dependencies, or the inhabitants of Dor and its dependencies, or the inhabitants of Ibleam and its dependencies, or the inhabitants of Megiddo and its dependencies. The Canaanites persisted in dwelling in this region. ²⁸ And when Israel gained the upper hand, they subjected the Canaanites to forced labor; but they did not dispossess them. ²⁹ Nor did Ephraim dispossess the Canaanites who inhabited Gezer; so the Canaanites dwelt in their midst at Gezer.

³⁰ Zebulun did not dispossess the inhabitants of Kitron or the inhabitants of Nahalol, so the Canaanites dwelt in their midst, but they were subjected to forced labor. ³¹ Asher did not dispossess the inhabitants of Acco or the inhabitants of Sidon, Ahlab, Achzib, Helbah, Aphik, and Rehob. ³² So the Asherites dwelt in the midst of the Canaanites, the inhabitants of the land, for they did not dispossess them. ³³ Naphtali did not dispossess the inhabitants of Beth-shemesh or the inhabitants of Beth-anath. But they settled in the midst of the Canaanite inhabitants of the land, and the inhabitants of Beth-shemesh and Beth-anath had to perform forced labor for them.

³⁴ The Amorites pressed the Danites into the hill country; they would not let them come down to the plain. ³⁵ The Amorites also persisted in dwelling in Har-heres, in Aijalon, and in Shaalbim. But the hand of the House of Joseph bore heavily on them and they had to perform forced labor. ³⁶ The territory of the Amorites[g] extended from the Ascent of Akrabbim—from Sela—onward.

2

An angel of the LORD came up from Gilgal to Bochim and said, "I brought you up from Egypt and I took you into the land which I had promised on oath to your fathers. And I said, 'I will never break My covenant with you. ² And you, for your part, must make no covenant with the inhabitants of this land; you must tear down their altars.' But you have not obeyed Me—look what you have done! ³ Therefore, I have resolved not to drive them out

---

ᵍ *Some Septuagint mss. read "Edomites."*

before you; they shall become your oppressors,[a] and their gods shall be a snare to you." [4] As the angel of the LORD spoke these words to all the Israelites, the people broke into weeping. [5] So they named that place Bochim,[b] and they offered sacrifices there to the LORD.

[6] When Joshua dismissed the people, the Israelites went to their allotted territories and occupied the land. [7] The people served the LORD during the lifetime of Joshua and the lifetime of the older people who lived on after Joshua and who had witnessed all the marvelous deeds that the LORD had wrought for Israel. [8] Joshua son of Nun, the servant of the LORD, died at the age of one hundred and ten years, [9] and was buried on his own property, at Timnath-heres[c] in the hill country of Ephraim, north of Mount Gaash. [10] And all that generation were likewise gathered to their fathers.

Another generation arose after them, which had not experienced [the deliverance of] the LORD or the deeds that He had wrought for Israel. [11] And the Israelites did what was offensive to the LORD. They worshiped the Baalim [12] and forsook the LORD, the God of their fathers, who had brought them out of the land of Egypt. They followed other gods, from among the gods of the peoples around them, and bowed down to them; they provoked the LORD. [13] They forsook the LORD and worshiped Baal and the Ashtaroth.[d] [14] Then the LORD was incensed at Israel, and He handed them over to foes[e] who plundered them. He surrendered them to their enemies on all sides, and they could no longer hold their own against their enemies. [15] In all their campaigns, the hand of the LORD was against them to their undoing, as the LORD had declared and as the LORD had sworn to them; and they were in great distress. [16] Then the LORD raised up chieftains who delivered them from those who plundered them. [17] But they did not heed their chieftains either; they went astray after other gods and bowed down to them. They were quick to turn aside from the way their fathers had followed in obedience to the commandments of

---

[a] *So Targum and other ancient versions. Meaning of Heb. uncertain.*
[b] *I.e. "weepers."*
[c] *Some mss. read "Timnath-serah"; cf. Josh. 24.30.*
[d] *Canaanite female deities.*
[e] *Lit. "plunderers."*

the LORD; they did not do right. [18] When the LORD raised up chieftains for them, the LORD would be with the chieftain and would save them from their enemies during the chieftain's lifetime; for the LORD would be moved to pity by their moanings because of those who oppressed and crushed them. [19] But when the chieftain died, they would again act basely, even more than *f*-the preceding generation-*f*—following other gods, worshiping them, and bowing down to them; they omitted none of their practices and stubborn ways.

[20] Then the LORD became incensed against Israel, and He said, "Since that nation has transgressed the covenant that I enjoined upon their fathers and has not obeyed Me, [21] I for My part will no longer drive out before them any of the nations that Joshua left when he died." [22] For it was in order to test Israel by them —[to see] whether or not they would faithfully walk in the ways of the LORD, as their fathers had done—[23] that the LORD had left those nations, instead of driving them out at once, and had not delivered them into the hands of Joshua.

3 *a*These are the nations that the LORD left so that He might test by them all the Israelites who had not known any of the wars of Canaan, [2] so that succeeding generations of Israelites might be made to experience war—but only those who had not known the *b*-former wars:-*b* [3] the five principalities*c* of the Philistines and all the Canaanites, Sidonians, and Hivites who inhabited the hill country of the Lebanon from Mount Baal-hermon to Lebo-hamath.*d* [4] These served as a means of testing Israel, to learn whether they would obey the commandments which the LORD had enjoined upon their fathers through Moses.

[5] The Israelites settled among the Canaanites, Hittites, Amorites, Perizzites, Hivites, and Jebusites; [6] they took their daughters to wife and gave their own daughters to their sons, and they worshiped their gods. [7] The Israelites did what was offensive to the LORD; they ignored the LORD their God and wor-

f-f *Lit. "their fathers."*

a *The sentence structure of vv. 1-2 is uncertain.*
b-b *Lit. "them formerly."*
c *Lit. "lords."*
d *See note at Num. 13.21.*

shiped the Baalim and the Asheroth. [8] The LORD became incensed at Israel and surrendered them to King Cushan-rishathaim of Aram-naharaim; and the Israelites were subject to Cushan-rishathaim for eight years. [9] The Israelites cried out to the LORD, and the LORD raised a champion for the Israelites to deliver them: Othniel the Kenizzite, a younger kinsman of Caleb. [10] The spirit of the LORD descended upon him and he became Israel's chieftain. He went out to war, and the LORD delivered King Cushan-rishathaim of Aram into his hands. He prevailed over Cushan-rishathaim, [11] and the land had peace for forty years.

When Othniel the Kenizzite died, [12] the Israelites again did what was offensive to the LORD. And because they did what was offensive to the LORD, the LORD let King Eglon of Moab prevail over Israel. [13] [Eglon] brought the Ammonites and the Amalekites together under his command, and went and defeated Israel and occupied the City of Palms. [14] The Israelites were subject to King Eglon of Moab for eighteen years.

[15] Then the Israelites cried out to the LORD, and the LORD raised up a champion for them: the Benjaminite Ehud son of Gera, a left-handed man. It happened that the Israelites sent tribute to King Eglon of Moab through him. [16] So Ehud made for himself a two-edged dagger, a *gomed* in length, which he girded on his right side under his cloak. [17] He presented the tribute to King Eglon of Moab. Now Eglon was a very stout man. [18] When [Ehud] had finished presenting the tribute, he dismissed the people who had conveyed the tribute. [19] But he himself returned from Pesilim, near Gilgal, and said, "Your Majesty, I have a secret message for you." [Eglon] thereupon commanded, "Silence!" So all those in attendance left his presence; [20] and when Ehud approached him, he was sitting alone in his cool upper chamber. Ehud said, "I have a message for you from God"; whereupon he rose from his seat. [21] Reaching with his left hand, Ehud drew the dagger from his right side and drove it into [Eglon's][e] belly. [22] The fat closed over the blade and the hilt went in after the

[e] *Heb. "his."*

blade—for he did not pull the dagger out of his belly—and the filth*f* came out.

²³ Stepping out into the vestibule,*f* Ehud shut the doors of the upper chamber on him and locked them. ²⁴ After he left, the courtiers returned. When they saw that the doors of the upper chamber were locked, they thought, "He must be relieving himself in the cool chamber." ²⁵ They waited a long time; and when he did not open the doors of the chamber, they took the key and opened them—and there their master was lying dead on the floor! ²⁶ But Ehud had made good his escape while they delayed; he had passed Pesilim and escaped to Seirah. ²⁷ When he got there, he had the ram's horn sounded through the hill country of Ephraim, and all the Israelites descended with him from the hill country; and he took the lead. ²⁸ "Follow me closely," he said, "for the LORD has delivered your enemies, the Moabites, into your hands." They followed him down and seized the fords of the Jordan against the Moabites; they let no one cross. ²⁹ On that occasion they slew about 10,000 Moabites; they were all robust and brave men, yet not one of them escaped. ³⁰ On that day, Moab submitted to Israel; and the land was tranquil for eighty years.

³¹ After him came Shamgar *g*son of Anath,*g* who slew six hundred Philistines with an oxgoad. He too was a champion of Israel.

4 The Israelites again did what was offensive to the LORD—Ehud now being dead. ² And the LORD surrendered them to King Jabin of Canaan, who reigned in Hazor. His army commander was Sisera, whose base was Harosheth-goiim. ³ The Israelites cried out to the LORD; for he had nine hundred iron chariots, and he had oppressed Israel ruthlessly for twenty years.

⁴ Deborah, wife of Lappidoth, was a prophetess; she led Israel at that time. ⁵ She used to sit under the Palm of Deborah, between Ramah and Bethel in the hill country of Ephraim, and the Israelites would come to her for decisions.

f Meaning of Heb. uncertain.
g-g Or "the Beth-anathite."

⁶ She summoned Barak son of Abinoam, of Kedesh in Naphtali, and said to him, "The LORD, the God of Israel, has commanded: Go, march up to Mount Tabor, and take with you ten thousand men of Naphtali and Zebulun. ⁷ And I will draw Sisera, Jabin's army commander, with his chariots and his troops, toward you up to the Wadi Kishon; and I will deliver him into your hands." ⁸ But Barak said to her, "If you will go with me, I will go; if not, I will not go." ⁹ "Very well, I will go with you," she answered. "However, there will be no glory for you in the course you are taking, for then the LORD will deliver Sisera into the hands of a woman." So Deborah went with Barak to Kedesh. ¹⁰ Barak then mustered Zebulun and Naphtali at Kedesh; ten thousand men marched up *-after him;-* and Deborah also went up with him.

¹¹ Now Heber the Kenite had separated *-from the other Kenites,-* descendants of Hobab, father-in-law of Moses, and had pitched his tent at Elon-bezaananim, which is near Kedesh.

¹² Sisera was informed that Barak son of Abinoam had gone up to Mount Tabor. ¹³ So Sisera ordered all his chariots—nine hundred iron chariots—and all the troops he had to move from Harosheth-goiim to the Wadi Kishon. ¹⁴ Then Deborah said to Barak, "Up! This is the day on which the LORD will deliver Sisera into your hands: the LORD is marching before you." Barak charged down Mount Tabor, followed by the ten thousand men, ¹⁵ and the LORD threw Sisera and all his chariots and army into a panic *-before the onslaught of Barak.-* Sisera leaped from his chariot and fled on foot ¹⁶ as Barak pursued the chariots and the soldiers as far as Harosheth-goiim. All of Sisera's soldiers fell by the sword; not a man was left.

¹⁷ Sisera, meanwhile, had fled on foot to the tent of Jael, wife of Heber the Kenite; for there was friendship between King Jabin of Hazor and the family of Heber the Kenite. ¹⁸ Jael came out to greet Sisera and said to him, "Come in, my lord, come in here, do not be afraid." So he entered her tent, and she covered him with a blanket. ¹⁹ He said to her, "Please let me have some water; I am thirsty." She opened a skin of milk and gave

ᵃ⁻ᵃ *Lit. "at his feet."*
ᵇ⁻ᵇ *Lit. "from Cain"; cf. 1.16.*
ᶜ⁻ᶜ *Lit. "at the edge of the sword before Barak."*

him some to drink; and she covered him again. ²⁰ He said to her, "Stand at the entrance of the tent. If anybody comes and asks you if there is anybody here, say 'No.' " ²¹ Then Jael wife of Heber took a tent pin and grasped the mallet. When he was fast asleep from exhaustion, she approached him stealthily and drove the pin through his temple till it went down to the ground. Thus he died.

²² Now Barak appeared in pursuit of Sisera. Jael went out to greet him and said, "Come, I will show you the man you are looking for." He went inside with her, and there Sisera was lying dead, with the pin in his temple.

²³ On that day God subdued King Jabin of Hazor before the Israelites. ²⁴ The hand of the Israelites bore harder and harder on King Jabin of Canaan, until they destroyed King Jabin of Canaan.

5 On that day Deborah and Barak son of Abinoam sang:

> ² ᵃWhen ᵇlocks go untrimmed⁻ᵇ in Israel,
> When people dedicate themselves—
> Bless the LORD!

> ³ Hear, O kings! Give ear, O potentates!
> I will sing, will sing to the LORD,
> Will hymn the LORD, the God of Israel.

> ⁴ O LORD, when You came forth from Seir,
> Advanced from the country of Edom,
> The earth trembled;
> The heavens dripped,
> Yea, the clouds dripped water,
> ⁵ The mountains quakedᶜ—
> Before the LORD, Him of Sinai,
> Before the LORD, God of Israel.

ᵃ *In many parts of this poem the meaning is uncertain.*
ᵇ⁻ᵇ *Apparently an expression of dedication; cf. Num. 6.5.*
ᶜ *Taking* nazelu *as a by-form of* nazollu; *cf. Targum.*

6 In the days of Shamgar *d*-son of Anath,*d*
In the days of Jael, caravans*e* ceased,
And wayfarers went
By roundabout paths.
7 Deliverance ceased,
Ceased in Israel,
Till you*f* arose, O Deborah,
Arose, O mother, in Israel!
8 When they chose new gods,
g-Was there a fighter then in the gates?*g*
No shield or spear was seen
Among forty thousand in Israel!

9 My heart is with Israel's leaders,
With the dedicated of the people—
Bless the LORD!
10 You riders on tawny she-asses,
You who sit on saddle rugs,
And you wayfarers, declare it!
11 Louder than the *h*-sound of archers,*h*
There among the watering places
Let them chant the gracious acts of the LORD,
His gracious deliverance of Israel.
Then did the people of the LORD
March down to the gates!
12 Awake, awake, O Deborah!
Awake, awake, strike up the chant!
Arise, O Barak;
Take your captives, O son of Abinoam!

13 Then was the remnant made victor over the mighty,
The LORD's people*i* won my victory over the warriors.

---

d-d *Or "the Beth-anathite."*
e *Or "roads."*
f *Heb.* qamti, *archaic second person singular feminine.*
g-g *Meaning of Heb. uncertain; others "then was war in the gates."*
h-h *Or "thunder peals"; meaning of Heb. uncertain.*
i *Reading* 'am *(with* pathah) Adonai; *so many Heb. mss.*

¹⁴ From Ephraim came they whose roots are in Amalek;
After you, your kin Benjamin;
From Machir came down leaders,
From Zebulum such as hold the marshal's staff.
¹⁵ And Issachar's chiefs were with Deborah;
As Barak, so was Issachar—
Rushing after him into the valley.

Among the clans of Reuben
Were great decisions of heart.
¹⁶ Why then did you stay among the sheepfolds
And listen as they pipe for the flocks?
Among the clans of Reuben
Were great searchings of heart!
¹⁷ Gilead tarried beyond the Jordan;
And Dan—why did he linger ʲ⁻by the ships?⁻ʲ
Asher remained at the seacoast
And tarried at his landings.
¹⁸ Zebulum is a people ᵏ⁻that mocked at death, ⁻ᵏ
Naphtali—on the open heights.

¹⁹ Then the kings came, they fought:
The kings of Canaan fought
At Taanach, by Megiddo's waters—
They got no spoil of silver.
²⁰ The stars fought from heaven,
From their courses they fought against Sisera.
²¹ The torrent Kishon swept themˡ away,
The raging torrent, the torrent Kishon.

March on, my soul, with courage!

²² Then the horses' hoofs pounded
ᵐ⁻As headlong galloped the steeds.⁻ᵐ

ʲ⁻ʲ Or "at Onioth," a presumed designation of Dan's region.
ᵏ⁻ᵏ Lit. "belittled its life to die."
ˡ I.e. the kings of Canaan (v. 19).
ᵐ⁻ᵐ Lit. "From the gallopings, the gallopings of his steeds."

23 "Curse Meroz!" said the angel of the LORD.
"Bitterly curse its inhabitants,
Because they came not to the aid of the LORD,
To the aid of the LORD among[n] the warriors."

24 Most blessed of women be Jael,
Wife of Heber the Kenite,
Most blessed of women in tents.
25 He asked for water, she offered milk;
In a princely bowl she brought him curds.
26 Her [left] hand reached for the tent pin,
Her right for the workmen's hammer.
She struck Sisera, crushed his head,
Smashed and pierced his temple.
27 At her feet he sank, lay outstretched,
At her feet he sank, lay still;
Where he sank, there he lay—destroyed.

28 Through the window peered Sisera's mother,
Behind the lattice she whined:[o]
"Why is his chariot so long in coming?
Why so late the clatter of his wheels?"
29 The wisest of her ladies give answer;
She, too, replies to herself:
30 "They must be dividing the spoil they have found:
A damsel or two for each man,
Spoil of dyed cloths for Sisera,
Spoil of embroidered cloths,
A couple of embroidered cloths
Round every neck as spoil."

31 So may all Your enemies perish, O LORD!
But may His friends be as the sun rising in might!

And the land was tranquil forty years.

[n] *Or "against."*
[o] *Or "gazed"; meaning of Heb. uncertain.*

6 Then the Israelites did what was offensive to the LORD, and the LORD delivered them into the hands of the Midianites for seven years. ² The hand of the Midianites prevailed over Israel; and because of Midian, the Israelites *ª*provided themselves with refuges in the caves and strongholds of the mountains.*ᵃ* ³ After the Israelites had done their sowing, Midian, Amalek, and the Kedemites would come up and raid them; ⁴ they would attack them, destroy*ᵇ* the produce of the land all the way to Gaza, and leave no means of sustenance in Israel, not a sheep or an ox or an ass. ⁵ For they would come up with their livestock and their tents, swarming as thick as locusts; they and their camels were innumerable. Thus they would invade the land and ravage it. ⁶ Israel was reduced to utter misery by the Midianites, and the Israelites cried out to the LORD.

⁷ When the Israelites cried to the LORD on account of Midian, ⁸ the LORD sent a prophet to the Israelites who said to them, "Thus said the LORD, the God of Israel: I brought you up out of Egypt and freed you from the house of bondage. ⁹ I rescued you from the Egyptians and from all your oppressors; I drove them out before you, and gave you their land. ¹⁰ And I said to you, 'I the LORD am your God. You must not worship the gods of the Amorites in whose land you dwell.' But you did not obey Me."

¹¹ An angel of the LORD came and sat under the terebinth at Ophrah, which belonged to Joash the Abiezrite. His son Gideon was then beating out wheat inside a winepress in order to keep it safe from the Midianites. ¹² The angel of the LORD appeared to him and said to him, "The LORD is with you, valiant warrior!" ¹³ Gideon said to him, "Please, my lord, if the LORD is with us, why has all this befallen us? Where are all His wondrous deeds about which our fathers told us, saying, 'Truly the LORD brought us up from Egypt'? Now the LORD has abandoned us and delivered us into the hands of Midian!" ¹⁴ The LORD turned to him and

---

ᵃ⁻ᵃ *Meaning of Heb. uncertain.*
ᵇ *I.e. by grazing their livestock.*

said, "Go in this strength of yours and deliver Israel from the Midianites. I herewith make you My messenger." [15] He said to Him, "Please, my lord, how can I deliver Israel? Why, my clan is the humblest in Manasseh, and I am the youngest in my father's household." [16] The LORD replied, "I will be with you, and you shall defeat Midian to a man." [17] And he said to Him, "If I have gained Your favor, give me a sign that it is You who are speaking to me: [18] do not leave this place until I come back to You and bring out my offering and place it before You." And He answered, "I will stay until you return."

[19] So Gideon went in and prepared a kid, and [baked] unleavened bread from an ephah of flour. He put the meat in a basket and poured the broth into a pot, and he brought them out to Him under the terebinth. As he presented them, [20] the angel of God said to him, "Take the meat and the unleavened bread, put them on yonder rock, and spill out the broth." He did so. [21] The angel of the LORD held out the staff that he carried, and touched the meat and the unleavened bread with its tip. A fire sprang up from the rock and consumed the meat and the unleavened bread. And the angel of the LORD vanished from his sight. [22] Then Gideon realized that it was an angel of the LORD; and Gideon said, "Alas, O Lord GOD! For I have seen an angel of the LORD face to face."

[23] But the LORD said to him, "All is well; have no fear, you shall not die." [24] So Gideon built there an altar to the LORD and called it ᶜ⁻Adonai-shalom.⁻ᶜ To this day it stands in Ophrah of the Abiezrites.

[25] That night the LORD said to him: "Take the ᵃ⁻young bull⁻ᵃ belonging to your father and another bull seven years old; pull down the altar of Baal which belongs to your father, and cut down the sacred post which is beside it. [26] Then build an altar to the LORD your God, on ᵃ⁻the level ground⁻ᵃ on top of this stronghold. Take the other bull and offer it as a burnt offering, using the wood of the sacred post that you have cut down." [27] So Gideon took ten of his servants and did as the LORD had told him; but as he was afraid to do it by day, on account of his father's house-

ᶜ⁻ᶜ *I.e. "My lord, 'All-is-well.'"*

hold and the townspeople, he did it by night. ²⁸ Early the next morning, the townspeople found that the altar of Baal had been torn down and the sacred post beside it had been cut down, and that the second bull had been offered on the newly built altar. ²⁹ They said to one another, "Who did this thing?" Upon inquiry and investigation, they were told, "Gideon son of Joash did this thing!" ³⁰ The townspeople said to Joash, "Bring out your son, for he must die: he has torn down the altar of Baal and cut down the sacred post beside it!" ³¹ But Joash said to all who had risen against him, "Do you have to contend for Baal? Do you have to vindicate him? Whoever fights his battles shall be dead by morning! If he is a god, let him fight his own battles, since it is his altar that has been torn down!" ³² That day they named him*d* Jerubbaal, meaning "Let Baal contend with him, since he tore down his altar."

³³ All Midian, Amalek, and the Kedemites joined forces; they crossed over and encamped in the Valley of Jezreel. ³⁴ The spirit of the LORD enveloped Gideon; he sounded the horn, and the Abiezrites rallied behind him. ³⁵ And he sent messengers throughout Manasseh, and they too rallied behind him. He then sent messengers through Asher, Zebulun, and Naphtali, and they came up to meet the Manassites.*e*

³⁶ And Gideon said to God, "If You really intend to deliver Israel through me as You have said—³⁷ here I place a fleece of wool on the threshing floor. If dew falls only on the fleece and all the ground remains dry, I shall know that You will deliver Israel through me, as You have said." ³⁸ And that is what happened. Early the next day, he squeezed the fleece and wrung out the dew from the fleece, a bowlful of water. ³⁹ Then Gideon said to God, "Do not be angry with me if I speak just once more. Let me make just one more test with the fleece: let the fleece alone be dry, while there is dew all over the ground." ⁴⁰ God did so that night: only the fleece was dry, while there was dew all over the ground.

d *I.e. Gideon.*
e *Heb. "them."*

7 Early next day, Jerubbaal—that is, Gideon—and all the troops with him encamped above En-harod,*a* while the camp of Midian was in the plain to the north of him, at Gibeath-moreh.*b* 2 The LORD said to Gideon, "You have too many troops with you for Me to deliver Midian into their hands; Israel might claim for themselves the glory due to Me, thinking, 'Our own hand has brought us victory.' 3 Therefore, announce to the men, 'Let anybody who is timid and fearful turn back, *c*as a bird flies from Mount Gilead.' "*-c* Thereupon, 22,000 of the troops turned back and 10,000 remained.

4 "There are still too many troops," the LORD said to Gideon. "Take them down to the water and I will sift*d* them for you there. Anyone of whom I tell you, 'This one is to go with you,' that one shall go with you; and anyone of whom I tell you, 'This one is not to go with you,' that one shall not go." 5 So he took the troops down to the water. Then the LORD said to Gideon, "Set apart all those who *e*lap up the water with their tongues like dogs*-e* from all those who get down on their knees to drink." 6 Now those who "lapped" the water into their mouths by hand numbered three hundred; all the rest of the troops got down on their knees to drink. 7 Then the LORD said to Gideon, "I will deliver you and I will put Midian into your hands through the three hundred 'lappers'; let the rest of the troops go home." 8 *c*So [the lappers] took the provisions and horns that the other men had with them,*-c* and he sent the rest of the men of Israel back to their homes, retaining only the three hundred men.

The Midianite camp was below him, in the plain. 9 That night the LORD said to him, "Come, attack*f* the camp, for I have delivered it into your hands. 10 And if you are afraid to attack, first go down to the camp with your attendant Purah 11 and listen to what they say; after that you will have the courage to attack the camp." So he went down with his attendant Purah to the outposts of the

---

a Or "the Spring of Harod."
b Or "the Hill of Moreh."
c-c Meaning of Heb. uncertain.
d Lit. "smelt."
e-e Actually, using their hands as a dog uses its tongue; see v. 6.
f Lit. "descend upon"; so in vv. 10 and 11.

warriors who were in the camp.—[12] Now Midian, Amalek, and all the Kedemites were spread over the plain, as thick as locusts; and their camels were countless, as numerous as the sands on the seashore.—[13] Gideon came there just as one man was narrating a dream to another. "Listen," he was saying, "I had this dream: There was a commotion[c]—a loaf of barley bread was whirling through the Midianite camp. It came to a tent and struck it, and it fell; it turned it upside down, and the tent collapsed." [14] To this the other responded, "That can only mean the sword of the Israelite Gideon son of Joash. God is delivering Midian and the entire camp into his hands."[g]

[15] When Gideon heard the dream told and interpreted, he bowed low. Returning to the camp of Israel, he shouted, "Come on! The LORD has delivered the Midianite camp into your hands!" [16] He divided the three hundred men into three columns and equipped every man with a ram's horn and an empty jar, with a torch in each jar. [17] "Watch me," he said, "and do the same. When I get to the outposts of the camp, do exactly as I do. [18] When I and all those with me blow our horns, you too, all around the camp, will blow your horns and shout, 'For the LORD and for Gideon!' "

[19] Gideon and the hundred men with him arrived at the outposts of the camp, at the beginning of the middle watch, just after the sentries were posted. [h-]They sounded the horns and smashed the jars that they had with them,[-h] [20] and the three columns blew their horns and broke their jars. Holding the torches in their left hands and the horns for blowing in their right hands, they shouted, "A sword for the LORD and for Gideon!" [21] They remained standing where they were, surrounding the camp; but the entire camp ran about yelling, and took to flight. [22] For when the three hundred horns were sounded, the LORD turned every man's sword against his fellow, throughout the camp, and the entire host fled as far as Beth-shittah and on to Zererah—as far as the outskirts of Abel-meholah near Tabbath.

[23] And now the men of Israel from Naphtali and Asher and

[g] *The loaf of bread symbolizes the agricultural Israelites; the tent, the nomadic Midianites.*
[h-h] *Emendation yields "He sounded the horn and smashed the jar that he had with him."*

from all of Manasseh rallied for the pursuit of the Midianites. ²⁴ Gideon also sent messengers all through the hill country of Ephraim with this order: ⁱ "Go down ahead of the Midianites and seize their access to the water all along the Jordan down to Beth-barah." So all the men of Ephraim rallied and seized the waterside down to Beth-barah by the Jordan. ²⁵ They pursued the Midianites and captured Midian's two generals, Oreb and Zeeb. They killed Oreb at the Rock of Oreb and they killed Zeeb at the Winepress of Zeeb; and they brought the heads of Oreb and Zeeb from the other side of the Jordan to Gideon.

8 And the men of Ephraim said to him, "Why did you do that to us—not calling us when you went to fight the Midianites?" And they rebuked him severely. ² But he answered them, "After all, what have I accomplished compared to you? Why, Ephraim's gleanings are better than Abiezer's vintage! ³ God has delivered the Midianite generals Oreb and Zeeb into your hands, and what was I able to do compared to you?" And when he spoke in this fashion, their anger against him abated.

⁴ Gideon came to the Jordan and crossed it. The three hundred men with him were famished, but still in pursuit. ⁵ He said to the people of Succoth, "Please give some loaves of bread to the men who are following me, for they are famished, and I am pursuing Zebah and Zalmunna, the kings of Midian." ⁶ But the officials of Succoth replied, ^a-"Are Zebah and Zalmunna already in your hands,^{-a} that we should give bread to your troops?" ⁷ "I swear," declared Gideon, "when the LORD delivers Zebah and Zalmunna into my hands, I'll thresh^b your bodies upon desert thorns and briers!" ⁸ From there he went up to Penuel and made the same request of them; but the people of Penuel gave him the same reply as the people of Succoth. ⁹ So he also threatened the people of Penuel: "When I come back safe, I'll tear down this tower!"

¹⁰ Now Zebah and Zalmunna were at Karkor with their army of

ⁱ *Meaning of rest of verse uncertain.*

^{a-a} *Lit. "Is the palm of Zebah and Zalmunna in your hand."*

^b *I.e., throw them naked in a bed of thorns and trample them; but exact meaning uncertain.*

about 15,000; these were all that remained of the entire host of the Kedemites, for the slain numbered 120,000 fighting men.[c] [11] Gideon marched up the road of the tent dwellers, up to east of Nobah and Jogbehah, and routed the camp, which was off guard. [12] Zebah and Zalmunna took to flight, with Gideon[d] in pursuit. He captured Zebah and Zalmunna, the two kings of Midian, and threw the whole army into panic.

[13] On his way back from the battle at the Ascent of Heres, Gideon son of Joash [14] captured a boy from among the people of Succoth and interrogated him. The latter drew up for him a list of the officials and elders of Succoth, seventy-seven in number. [15] Then he came to the people of Succoth and said, "Here are Zebah and Zalmunna, about whom you mocked me, saying, [a-]"Are Zebah and Zalmunna already in your hands,[-a] that we should give your famished men bread?' " [16] And he took the elders of the city and, [bringing] desert thorns and briers, he punished[e] the people of Succoth with them. [17] As for Penuel, he tore down its tower and killed the townspeople.

[18] Then he asked Zebah and Zalmunna, "Those men you killed at Tabor, [f]what were they like?"[-f] "They looked just like you," they replied, "like sons of a king." [19] "They were my brothers," he declared, "the sons of my mother. As the LORD lives, if you had spared them, I would not kill you." [20] And he commanded his oldest son Jether, "Go kill them!" But the boy did not draw his sword, for he was timid, being still a boy. [21] Then Zebah and Zalmunna said, "Come, you slay us; for strength comes with manhood." So Gideon went over and killed Zebah and Zalmunna, and he took the crescents that were on the necks of their camels.

[22] Then the men of Israel said to Gideon, "Rule over us—you, your son, and your grandson as well; for you have saved us from the Midianites." [23] But Gideon replied, "I will not rule over you myself, nor shall my son rule over you; the LORD alone shall rule over you." [24] And Gideon said to them, "I have a request to make

---

[c] Lit. "men who drew the sword."
[d] Heb. "him."
[e] Meaning of Heb. uncertain; emendation yields "threshed"; cf. v. 7.
[f-f] Others, "Where are they?"

of you: Each of you give me the earring he received as booty."
(They[g] had golden earrings, for they were Ishmaelites.) [25] "Certainly!" they replied. And they spread out a cloth, and everyone
threw onto it the earring he had received as booty. [26] The weight
of the golden earrings that he had requested came to 1700 shekels of gold; this was in addition to the crescents and the pendants and the purple robes worn by the kings of Midian and in
addition to the collars on the necks of their camels. [27] Gideon
made an ephod of [h]this gold[-h] and set it up in his own town of
Ophrah. There all Israel went astray after it, and it became a
snare to Gideon and his household.

[28] Thus Midian submitted to the Israelites and did not raise its
head again; and the land was tranquil for forty years in Gideon's
time.

[29] So Jerubbaal son of Joash retired to his own house. [30] Gideon
had seventy sons of his own issue, for he had many wives. [31] A son
was also born to him by his concubine in Shechem, and he named
him Abimelech. [32] Gideon son of Joash died at a ripe old age, and
was buried in the tomb of his father Joash at Ophrah of the
Abiezrites.

[33] After Gideon died, the Israelites again went astray after the
Baalim, and they adopted Baal-berith as a god. [34] The Israelites
gave no thought to the LORD their God, who saved them from all
the enemies around them. [35] Nor did they show loyalty to the
house of Jerubbaal-Gideon in return for all the good that he had
done for Israel.

9

Abimelech son of Jerubbaal went to his mother's brothers in
Shechem and spoke to them and to the whole clan of his mother's
family. He said, [2] "Put this question to all the citizens of Shechem:
Which is better for you, to be ruled by seventy men—by all the
sons of Jerubbaal—or to be ruled by one man? And remember,
I am your own [a]flesh and blood."[-a] [3] His mother's brothers said

[g] *I.e. the Midianites. The author explains that the Midianites wore earrings like the Ishmaelites, who were better known to his contemporaries.*
[h-h] *Heb. "it."*
[a-a] *Lit. "bone and flesh."*

all this in his behalf to all the citizens of Shechem, and they were won over to Abimelech; for they thought, "He is our kinsman." ⁴ They gave him seventy shekels from the temple of Baal-berith; and with this Abimelech hired some worthless and reckless fellows, and they followed him. ⁵ Then he went to his father's house in Ophrah and killed his brothers, the sons of Jerubbaal, seventy men on one stone. Only Jotham, the youngest son of Jerubbaal, survived, because he went into hiding.

⁶ All the citizens of Shechem and all Beth-millo convened, and they proclaimed Abimelech king at the terebinth of the pillar ᵇ at Shechem. ⁷ When Jotham was informed, he went and stood on top of Mount Gerizim and called out to them in a loud voice, "Citizens of Shechem!" he cried, "Listen to me, that God may listen to you.

⁸ "Once the trees went to anoint a king over themselves. They said to the olive tree, 'Reign over us.' ⁹ But the olive tree replied, 'Have I, through whom God and men are honored, stopped yielding my rich oil, that I should go and wave above the trees?' ¹⁰ So the trees said to the fig tree, 'You come and reign over us.' ¹¹ But the fig tree replied, 'Have I stopped yielding my sweetness, my delicious fruit, that I should go and wave above the trees?' ¹² So the trees said to the vine, 'You come and reign over us.' ¹³ But the vine replied, 'Have I stopped yielding my new wine, which gladdens God and men, that I should go and wave above the trees?' ¹⁴ Then all the trees said to the thornbush, 'You come and reign over us.' ¹⁵ And the thornbush said to the trees, 'If you are acting honorably in anointing me king over you, come and take shelter in my shade; but if not, may fire issue from the thornbush and consume the cedars of Lebanon!'

¹⁶ "Now then, if you acted honorably and loyally in making Abimelech king, if you have done right by Jerubbaal and his house and have requited him according to his deserts—¹⁷ considering that my father fought for you and saved you from the Midianites at the risk of his life, ¹⁸ and now you have turned on my father's household, killed his sons, seventy men on one stone,

ᵇ Meaning of Heb. uncertain.

and set up Abimelech, the son of his handmaid, as king over the citizens of Shechem just because he is your kinsman—[19] if, I say, you have this day acted honorably and loyally toward Jerubbaal and his house, have joy in Abimelech and may he likewise have joy in you. [20] But if not, may fire issue from Abimelech and consume the citizens of Shechem and Beth-millo, and may fire issue from the citizens of Shechem and Beth-millo and consume Abimelech!"

[21] With that, Jotham fled. He ran to Beer and stayed there, because of his brother Abimelech.

[22] Abimelech held sway over Israel for three years. [23] Then God sent a spirit of discord between Abimelech and the citizens of Shechem, and the citizens of Shechem broke faith with Abimelech—[24] to the end that the crime committed against the seventy sons of Jerubbaal might be avenged, and their blood recoil upon their brother Abimelech, who had slain them, and upon the citizens of Shechem, who had abetted him in the slaying of his brothers. [25] The citizens of Shechem planted ambuscades against him on the hilltops; and they robbed whoever passed by them on the road. Word of this reached Abimelech.

[26] Then Gaal son of Ebed and his companions came passing through Shechem, and the citizens of Shechem gave him their confidence. [27] They went out into the fields, gathered and trod out the vintage of their vineyards, and made a festival. They entered the temple of their god, and as they ate and drank they reviled Abimelech. [28] Gaal son of Ebed said, "Who is Abimelech and who are [we] Shechemites, that we should serve him? [b-]This same son of Jerubbaal and his lieutenant Zebul once served the men of Hamor, the father of Shechem;[-b] so why should we serve him? [29] Oh, if only this people were under my command, I would get rid of Abimelech! One[c] would challenge Abimelech, 'Fill up your ranks and come out here!' "

[30] When Zebul, the governor of the city, heard the words of Gaal son of Ebed, he was furious. [31] He sent messages to Abimelech at Tormah[d] to say, "Gaal son of Ebed and his companions

<hr>

[c] *Septuagint reads "I."*
[d] *Called "Arumah" in v. 41.*

have come to Shechem and they are inciting[b] the city against you.
[32] Therefore, set out at night with the forces you have with you
and conceal yourself in the fields. [33] Early next morning, as the
sun rises, advance on the city. He and his men will thereupon
come out against you, and you will do to him whatever you find
possible."

[34] Abimelech and all the men with him set out at night and
disposed themselves against Shechem in four hiding places.
[35] When Gaal son of Ebed came out and stood at the entrance to
the city gate, Abimelech and the army with him emerged from
concealment. [36] Gaal saw the army and said to Zebul, "That's an
army marching down from the hilltops!" But Zebul said to him,
"The shadows of the hills look to you like men." [37] Gaal spoke
up again, "Look, an army is marching down from Tabbur-erez,
and another column is coming from the direction of Elon-
meonenim." [38] "Well," replied Zebul, "where is your boast,
'Who is Abimelech that we should serve him'? There is the army
you sneered at; now go out and fight it!"

[39] So Gaal went out at the head of the citizens of Shechem and
gave battle to Abimelech. [40] But he had to flee before him, and
Abimelech pursued him, and many fell slain, all the way to the
entrance of the gate. [41] Then Abimelech stayed in Arumah,[e] while
Zebul expelled Gaal and his companions and kept them out of
Shechem.

[42] The next day, when people went out into the fields, Abimelech was informed. [43] Taking the army, he divided it into three
columns and lay in ambush in the fields; and when he saw the
people coming out of the city, he pounced upon them and struck
them down. [44] While Abimelech and the column[f] that followed
him dashed ahead and took up a position at the entrance of the
city gate, the other two columns rushed upon all that were in the
open and struck them down. [45] Abimelech fought against the city
all that day. He captured the city and massacred the people in it;
he razed the town and sowed it with salt.

[46] When all the citizens of the Tower of Shechem[g] learned of

[e] Cf. "Tormah" in v. 31.
[f] Heb. "columns."
[g] Perhaps identical with Beth-millo of vv. 6 and 20.

this, they went into the tunnel[h] of the temple of El-berith.[i]
[47] When Abimelech was informed that all the citizens of the
Tower of Shechem had gathered [there], [48] Abimelech and all the
troops he had with him went up on Mount Zalmon. Taking an ax[j]
in his hand, Abimelech lopped off a tree limb and lifted it onto
his shoulder. Then he said to the troops that accompanied him,
"What you saw me do—quick, do the same!" [49] So each of the
troops also lopped off a bough; then they marched behind
Abimelech and laid them against the tunnel, and set fire to the
tunnel over their heads. Thus all the people of the Tower of
Shechem also perished, about a thousand men and women.

[50] Abimelech proceeded to Thebez; he encamped at Thebez
and occupied it. [51] Within the town was a fortified tower; and all
the citizens of the town, men and women, took refuge there.
They shut themselves in, and went up on the roof of the tower.
[52] Abimelech pressed forward to the tower and attacked it. He
approached the door of the tower to set it on fire. [53] But a woman
dropped an upper millstone on Abimelech's head and cracked his
skull. [54] He immediately cried out to his attendant, his arms-
bearer, "Draw your dagger and finish me off, that they may not
say of me, 'A woman killed him!' " So his attendant stabbed him,
and he died. [55] When the men of Israel saw that Abimelech was
dead, everyone went home.

[56] Thus God repaid Abimelech for the evil he had done to his
father by slaying his seventy brothers; [57] and God likewise repaid
the men of Shechem for all their wickedness. And so the curse
of Jotham son of Jerubbaal was fulfilled upon them.

10 After Abimelech, Tola son of Puah son of Dodo, a man of
Issachar, arose to deliver Israel. He lived at Shamir in the hill
country of Ephraim. [2] He led Israel for twenty-three years; then
he died and was buried at Shamir.

[3] After him arose Jair the Gileadite, and he led Israel for

---

[h] *Cf. I Sam. 13.6; others "citadel."*
[i] *Called "Baal-berith" in v. 4.*
[j] *Heb. plural.*

twenty-two years. (^{4} He had thirty sons, who rode on thirty burros and owned thirty boroughs^a in the region of Gilead; these are called Havvoth-jair^b to this day.) ^{5} Then Jair died and was buried at Kamon.

^{6} The Israelites again did what was offensive to the LORD. They served the Baalim and the Ashtaroth, and the gods of Aram, the gods of Sidon, the gods of Moab, the gods of the Ammonites, and the gods of the Philistines; they forsook the LORD and did not serve Him. ^{7} And the LORD, incensed with Israel, surrendered them to the Philistines and to the Ammonites. ^{8} That year they battered and shattered the Israelites—for^c eighteen years—all the Israelites beyond the Jordan, in [what had been] the land of the Amorites in Gilead. ^{9} The Ammonites also crossed the Jordan to make war on Judah, Benjamin, and the House of Ephraim. Israel was in great distress.

^{10} Then the Israelites cried out to the LORD, "We stand guilty before You, for we have forsaken our God and served the Baalim." ^{11} But the LORD said to the Israelites, "[I have rescued you] from the Egyptians, from the Amorites, from the Ammonites, and from the Philistines. ^{12} The Sidonians, Amalek, and Maon^d also oppressed you; and when you cried out to Me, I saved you from them. ^{13} Yet you have forsaken Me and have served other gods. No, I will not deliver you again. ^{14} Go cry to the gods you have chosen; let them deliver you in your time of distress!" ^{15} But the Israelites implored the LORD: "We stand guilty. Do to us as You see fit; only save us this day!" ^{16} They removed the alien gods from among them and served the LORD; and He could not bear the miseries of Israel.

^{17} The Ammonites mustered and they encamped in Gilead; and the Israelites massed and they encamped at Mizpah. ^{18} The troops—the officers of Gilead—said to one another, "Let the man who is the first to fight the Ammonites be chieftain over all the inhabitants of Gilead."

---

^{a} *Imitating the pun in the Heb., which employs* ʿayarim *first in the sense of "donkeys" and then in the sense of "towns."*
^{b} *I.e. "the villages of Jair"; cf. Num. 32.41.*
^{c} *Meaning of Heb. uncertain; perhaps "enough for" or "continuing for."*
^{d} *Septuagint reads "Midian."*

11 Jephthah the Gileadite was an able warrior, who was the son of a prostitute. Jephthah's father was Gilead; 2 but Gilead also had sons by his wife, and when the wife's sons grew up, they drove Jephthah out. They said to him, "You shall have no share in our father's property, for you are the son of an outsider."ᵃ 3 So Jephthah fled from his brothers and settled in the Tob country. Men of low character gathered about Jephthah and went out raiding with him.

4 Some time later, the Ammonites went to war against Israel. 5 And when the Ammonites attacked Israel, the elders of Gilead went to bring Jephthah back from the Tob country. 6 They said to Jephthah, "Come be our chief, so that we can fight the Ammonites." 7 Jephthah replied to the elders of Gilead, "You are the very people who rejected me and drove me out of my father's house. How can you come to me now when you are in trouble?" 8 The elders of Gilead said to Jephthah, "Honestly, we have now turned back to you. If you come with us and fight the Ammonites, you shall be our commander over all the inhabitants of Gilead." 9 Jephthah said to the elders of Gilead, "[Very well,] if you bring me back to fight the Ammonites and the LORD delivers them to me, I am to be your commander." 10 And the elders of Gilead answered Jepthah, "The LORD Himself shall be witness between us: we will do just as you have said."

11 Jephthah went with the elders of Gilead, and the people made him their commander and chief. And Jephthah repeated all these terms before the LORD at Mizpah.

12 Jephthah then sent messengers to the king of the Ammonites, saying, "What have you against me that you have come to make war on my country?" 13 The king of the Ammonites replied to Jephthah's messengers, "When Israel came from Egypt, they seized the land which is mine, from the Arnon to the Jabbok as far as the Jordan. Now, then, restore it peaceably."

ᵃ Lit. "another woman."

[14] Jephthah again sent messengers to the king of the Ammonites. [15] He said to him, "Thus said Jephthah: Israel did not seize the land of Moab or the land of the Ammonites. [16] When they left Egypt, Israel traveled through the wilderness to the Sea of Reeds and went on to Kadesh. [17] Israel then sent messengers to the king of Edom, saying, 'Allow us to cross your country.' But the king of Edom would not consent. They also sent a mission to the king of Moab, and he refused. So Israel, after staying at Kadesh, [18] traveled on through the wilderness, skirting the land of Edom and the land of Moab. They kept to the east of the land of Moab until they encamped on the other side of the Arnon; and, since Moab ends at the Arnon, they never entered Moabite territory.

[19] "Then Israel sent messengers to King Sihon of the Amorites, the king of Heshbon. Israel said to him, 'Allow us to cross through your country to our homeland.' [20] But Sihon would not trust Israel to pass through his territory. Sihon mustered all his troops, and they encamped at Jahaz; he engaged Israel in battle. [21] But the LORD, the God of Israel, delivered Sihon and all his troops into Israel's hands, and they defeated them; and Israel took possession of all the land of the Amorites, the inhabitants of that land. [22] Thus they occupied all the territory of the Amorites from the Arnon to the Jabbok and from the wilderness to the Jordan.

[23] "Now, then, the LORD, the God of Israel, dispossessed the Amorites before His people Israel; and should you possess their land? [24] Do you not hold what Chemosh your god gives you to possess? So we will hold on to everything that the LORD our God has given us to possess.

[25] "Besides, are you any better than Balak son of Zippor, king of Moab? Did he start a quarrel with Israel or go to war with them?

[26] "While Israel has been occupying Heshbon and its dependencies, and Aroer and its dependencies, and all the towns along the Arnon for three hundred years, why have you not tried to recover them all this time? [27] I have done you no wrong; yet you

are doing me harm and making war on me. May the LORD, who judges, decide today between the Israelites and the Ammonites!" ²⁸ But the king of the Ammonites paid no heed to the message that Jephthah sent him.

²⁹ Then the spirit of the LORD came upon Jephthah. He marched through Gilead and Manasseh, passing Mizpeh of Gilead; and from Mizpeh of Gilead he crossed over [to] the Ammonites. ³⁰ And Jephthah made the following vow to the LORD: "If you deliver the Ammonites into my hands, ³¹ then whatever comes out of the door of my house to meet me on my safe return from the Ammonites shall be the LORD's and shall be offered by me as a burnt offering."

³² Jephthah crossed over to the Ammonites and attacked them, and the LORD delivered them into his hands. ³³ He utterly routed them—from Aroer as far as Minnith, twenty towns—all the way to Abel-cheramin. So the Ammonites submitted to the Israelites.

³⁴ When Jephthah arrived at his home in Mizpah, there was his daughter coming out to meet him, with timbrel and dance! She was an only child; he had no other son or daughter. ³⁵ On seeing her, he rent his clothes and said, "Alas, daughter! You have brought me low; you have become my troubler! For I have ᵇ⁻uttered a vow⁻ᵇ to the LORD and I cannot retract." ³⁶ "Father," she said, "you have uttered a vow to the LORD; do to me as you have vowed, seeing that the LORD has vindicated you against your enemies, the Ammonites." ³⁷ She further said to her father, "Let this be done for me: let me be for two months, and I will go with my companions and lamentᶜ upon the hills and there bewail my maidenhood." ³⁸ "Go," he replied. He let her go for two months, and she and her companions went and bewailed her maidenhood upon the hills. ³⁹ After two months' time, she returned to her father, and he did to her as he had vowed. She had never known a man. So it became a custom in Israel ⁴⁰ for the maidens of Israel to go every year, for four days in the year, and chant dirges for the daughter of Jephthah the Gileadite.

ᵇ⁻ᵇ Lit. "opened my mouth."
ᶜ Lit. "descend" i.e. with weeping; cf. Isa. 15.3.

12 The men of Ephraim mustered and crossed [the Jordan] to Zaphon. They said to Jephthah, "Why did you march to fight the Ammonites without calling us to go with you? We'll burn your house down over you!" [2] Jephthah answered them, "I and my people were in a bitter conflict with the Ammonites; and I summoned you, but you did not save me from them. [3] When I saw that you were no saviors, I risked my life and advanced against the Ammonites; and the LORD delivered them into my hands. Why have you come here now to fight against me?" [4] And Jephthah gathered all the men of Gilead and fought the Ephraimites. The men of Gilead defeated the Ephraimites; for [a-]they had said, "You Gileadites are nothing but fugitives from Ephraim—being in Manasseh is like being in Ephraim."[-a] [5] The Gileadites held the fords of the Jordan against the Ephraimites. And when any fugitive from Ephraim said, "Let me cross," the men of Gilead would ask him, "Are you an Ephraimite?"; if he said, "No," [6] they would say to him, "Then say *shibboleth*"; but he would say "*sibboleth*," not being able to pronounce it correctly. Thereupon they would seize him and slay him by the fords of the Jordan. Forty-two thousand Ephraimites fell at that time.

[7] Jephthah led Israel six years. Then Jephthah the Gileadite died and he was buried in one of the towns of Gilead.

[8] After him, Ibzan of Bethlehem[b] led Israel. [9] He had thirty sons, and he married off thirty daughters outside the clan and brought in thirty girls from outside the clan for his sons. He led Israel seven years. [10] Then Ibzan died and was buried in Bethlehem.

[11] After him, Elon the Zebulunite led Israel; he led Israel for ten years. [12] Then Elon the Zebulunite died and was buried in Aijalon, in the territory of Zebulun.

[13] After him, Abdon son of Hillel the Pirathonite led Israel. [14] He had forty sons and thirty grandsons, who rode on seventy

[a-a] *Meaning of Heb. uncertain.*
[b] *I.e. Bethlehem in Zebulun; cf. Josh. 19.15.*

jackasses. He led Israel for eight years. ¹⁵ Then Abdon son of Hillel the Pirathonite died. He was buried in Pirathon, in the territory of Ephraim, on the hill of the Amalekites.

13 The Israelites again did what was offensive to the LORD, and the LORD delivered them into the hands of the Philistines for forty years.

² There was a certain man from Zorah, of the stock of Dan, whose name was Manoah. His wife was barren and had borne no children. ³ An angel of the LORD appeared to the woman and said to her, "You are barren and have borne no children; but you shall conceive and bear a son. ⁴ Now be careful not to drink wine or other intoxicant, or to eat anything unclean. ⁵ For you are going to conceive and bear a son; let no razor touch his head, for the boy is to be a nazirite to God from the womb on. He shall be the first to deliver Israel from the Philistines."

⁶ The woman went and told her husband, "A man of God came to me; he looked like an angel of God, very frightening. I did not ask him where he was from, nor did he tell me his name. ⁷ He said to me, 'You are going to conceive and bear a son. Drink no wine or other intoxicant, and eat nothing unclean, for the boy is to be a nazirite to God from the womb to the day of his death!' "

⁸ Manoah pleaded with the LORD. "Oh, my Lord!" he said, "please let the man of God that You sent come to us again, and let him instruct us how to act with the child that is to be born." ⁹ God heeded Manoah's plea, and the angel of God came to the woman again. She was sitting in the field and her husband Manoah was not with her. ¹⁰ The woman ran in haste to tell her husband. She said to him, "The man who came to me before*a* has just appeared to me." ¹¹ Manoah promptly followed his wife. He came to the man and asked him: "Are you the man who spoke to my wife?" "Yes," he answered. ¹² Then Manoah said, "May your words soon come true! What rules shall be observed for the boy?" ¹³ The angel of the LORD said to Manoah, "The woman

---

ᵃ *Lit. "in the day."*

must abstain from all the things against which I warned her. [14] She must not eat anything that comes from the grapevine, or drink wine or other intoxicant, or eat anything unclean. She must observe all that I commanded her."

[15] Manoah said to the angel of the LORD, "Let us detain you and prepare a kid for you." [16] But the angel of the LORD said to Manoah, "If you detain me, I shall not eat your food; and if you present a burnt offering, offer it to LORD."—For Manoah did not know that he was an angel of the LORD. [17] So Manoah said to the angel of the LORD, "What is your name? We should like to honor you when your words come true." [18] The angel said to him, "You must not ask for my name; it is unknowable!"

[19] Manoah took the kid and the meal offering and offered them up on the rock to the LORD; *b*-and a marvelous thing happened-*b* while Manoah and his wife looked on. [20] As the flames leaped up from the altar toward the sky, the angel of the LORD ascended in the flames of the altar, while Manoah and his wife looked on; and they flung themselves on their faces to the ground.—[21] The angel of the LORD never appeared again to Manoah and his wife.— Manoah then realized that it had been an angel of the LORD. [22] And Manoah said to his wife, "We shall surely die, for we have seen a divine being." [23] But his wife said to him, "Had the LORD meant to take our lives, He would not have accepted a burnt offering and meal offering from us, nor let us see all these things; and He would not have made such an announcement to us."

[24] The woman bore a son, and she named him Samson. The boy grew up, and the LORD blessed him. [25] The spirit of the LORD first moved him in the encampment of Dan, between Zorah and Eshtaol.

14 Once Samson went down to Timnah; and while in Timnah, he noticed a girl among the Philistine women. [2] On his return, he told his father and mother, "I noticed one of the Philistine women in Timnah; please get her for me as a wife." [3] His father

---

b-b *Meaning of Heb. uncertain.*

and mother said to him, "Is there no one among the daughters of your own kinsmen and among all our^a people, that you must go and take a wife from the uncircumcised Philistines?" But Samson answered his father, "Get me that one, for she is the one that pleases me." ⁴ His father and mother did not realize that this was the LORD's doing: He was seeking a pretext against the Philistines, for the Philistines were ruling over Israel at that time. ⁵ So Samson and his father and mother went down to Timnah.

When he^b came to the vineyards of Timnah [for the first time], a full-grown lion came roaring at him. ⁶ The spirit of the LORD gripped him, and he tore him asunder with his bare hands as one might tear a kid asunder; but he did not tell his father and mother what he had done. ⁷ Then he went down and spoke to the woman, and she pleased Samson.

⁸ Returning the following year to marry her, he turned aside to look at the remains of the lion; and in the lion's skeleton he found a swarm of bees, and honey. ⁹ He scooped it into his palms and ate it as he went along. When he rejoined his father and mother, he gave them some and they ate it; but he did not tell them that he had scooped the honey out of a lion's skeleton.

¹⁰ So his father came down to the woman, and Samson made a feast there, as young men used to do. ¹¹ When they^c saw him, they designated thirty companions to be with him. ¹² Then Samson said to them, "Let me propound a riddle to you. If you can give me the right answer during the seven days of the feast, I shall give you thirty linen tunics and thirty sets of clothing; ¹³ but if you are not able to tell it to me, you must give me thirty linen tunics and thirty sets of clothing." And they said to him, "Ask your riddle and we will listen." ¹⁴ So he said to them:

"Out of the eater came something to eat,
Out of the strong came something sweet."

For three days they could not answer the riddle.

¹⁵ On the seventh^d day, they said to Samson's wife, "Coax your husband to provide us with the answer to the riddle; else we shall put you and your father's household to the fire; have you invited

---

^a *Heb. "my."*
^b *Heb. "they."*
^c *I.e. the people of Timnah.*
^d *Septuagint and Syriac read "fourth."*

us here*e* in order to impoverish us?" [16] Then Samson's wife harassed him with tears, and she said, "You really hate me, you don't love me. You asked my countrymen a riddle, and you didn't tell me the answer." He replied, "I haven't even told my father and mother; shall I tell you?" [17] During the rest of the seven days of the feast she continued to harass him with her tears, and on the seventh day he told her, because she nagged him so. And she explained the riddle to her countrymen. [18] On the seventh day, before the sunset, the townsmen said to him:

> "What is sweeter than honey,
> And what is stronger than a lion?"

He responded:

> "Had you not plowed with my heifer,
> You would not have guessed my riddle!"

[19] The spirit of the Lord gripped him. He went down to Ashkelon and killed thirty of its men. He stripped them and gave the sets of clothing to those who had answered the riddle. And he left in a rage for his father's house.

[20] Samson's wife then married one of those who had been his wedding companions.

15 Some time later, in the season of the wheat harvest, Samson came to visit his wife, bringing a kid as a gift. He said, "Let me go into the chamber to my wife." But her father would not let him go in. [2] "I was sure," said her father, "that you had taken a dislike to her, so I gave her to your wedding companion. But her younger sister is more beautiful than she; let her become your wife instead." [3] Thereupon Samson declared, "Now the Philistines can have no claim against me for the harm I shall do them."

[4] Samson went and caught three hundred foxes. He took torches and, turning [the foxes] tail to tail, he placed a torch between each pair of tails. [5] He lit the torches and turned [the foxes] loose among the standing grain of the Philistines, setting fire to stacked grain, standing grain, vineyards, [and]*a* olive trees.

e Reading halom, *with some Heb. mss. and Targum.*

a So Targum.

6 The Philistines asked, "Who did this?" And they were told, "It was Samson, the son-in-law of the Timnite, who took Samson's[b] wife and gave her to his wedding companion." Thereupon the Philistines came up and put her and her father[c] to the fire. 7 Samson said to them, "If that is how you act, I will not rest until I have taken revenge on you." 8 [d-]He gave them a sound and thorough thrashing.[-d] Then he went down and stayed in the cave of the rock of Etam.

9 The Philistines came up, pitched camp in Judah and spread out over Lehi. 10 The men of Judah asked, "Why have you come up against us?" They answered, "We have come to take Samson prisoner, and to do to him as he did to us." 11 Thereupon three thousand men of Judah went down to the cave of the rock of Etam, and they said to Samson, "You knew that the Philistines rule over us; why have you done this to us?" He replied, "As they did to me, so I did to them." 12 "We have come down," they told him, "to take you prisoner and to hand you over to the Philistines." "But swear to me," said Samson to them, "that you yourselves will not attack me." 13 "We won't," they replied. "We will only take you prisoner and hand you over to them; we will not slay you." So they bound him with two new ropes and brought him up from the rock.

14 When he reached Lehi, the Philistines came shouting to meet him. Thereupon the spirit of the LORD gripped him, and the ropes on his arms became like flax that catches fire; the bonds melted off his hands. 15 He came upon a fresh jawbone of an ass and he picked it up; and with it he killed a thousand men. 16 Then Samson said:

"With the jaw of an ass,
Mass upon mass!
With the jaw of an ass
I have slain a thousand men."

17 As he finished speaking, he threw the jawbone away; hence that place was called Ramath-lehi.[e]

18 He was very thirsty and he called to the LORD, "You Yourself

b *Heb. "his."*
c *Many mss. read "her father's household"; cf. 14.15.*
d-d *Lit. "He smote them leg as well as thigh, a great smiting."*
e *I.e. "Jawbone Heights."*

have granted this great victory through Your servant; and must I now die of thirst and fall into the hands of the uncircumcised?" ¹⁹ So God split open the hollow which is at Lehi, and the water gushed out of it; he drank, regained his strength, and revived. That is why it is called to this day "En-hakkore*f* of Lehi."

²⁰ He led Israel in the days of the Philistines for twenty years.

16 Once Samson went to Gaza; there he met a whore and slept with her. ² *ª*The Gazites [learned]*b* that Samson had come there, so they gathered and lay in ambush for him in the town gate the whole night; and all night long they kept whispering to each other, "When daylight comes, we'll kill him." ³ But Samson lay in bed only till midnight. At midnight he got up, grasped the doors of the town gate together with the two gateposts, and pulled them out along with the bar. He placed them on his shoulders and carried them off to the top of the hill that is near Hebron.

⁴ After that, he fell in love with a woman in the Wadi Sorek, named Delilah. ⁵ The lords of the Philistines went up to her and said, "Coax him and find out what makes him so strong, and how we can overpower him, tie him up, and make him helpless; and we'll each give you eleven hundred shekels of silver."

⁶ So Delilah said to Samson, "Tell me, what makes you so strong? And how could you be tied up and made helpless?" ⁷ Samson replied, "If I were to be tied with seven fresh tendons, that had not been dried,*c* I should become as weak as an ordinary man." ⁸ So the lords of the Philistines brought up to her seven fresh tendons, that had not been dried. She bound him with them, ⁹ while an ambush was waiting in her room. Then she called out to him, "Samson, the Philistines are upon you!" Whereat he pulled the tendons apart, as a strand of tow comes apart at the touch of fire. So the secret of his strength remained unknown.

f Understood as "The Spring of the Caller."
ª Meaning of parts of verse uncertain.
b Septuagint reads "were told."
c For use as bowstrings.

¹⁰ Then Delilah said to Samson, "Oh, you deceived me; you lied to me! Do tell me now how you could be tied up." ¹¹ He said, "If I were to be bound with new ropes that had never been used, I would become as weak as an ordinary man." ¹² So Delilah took new ropes and bound him with them, while an ambush was waiting in a room. And she cried, "Samson, the Philistines are upon you!" But he tore them off his arms like a thread. ¹³ Then Delilah said to Samson, "You have been deceiving me all along; you have been lying to me! Tell me, how could you be tied up?" He answered her, "If you weave seven locks of my head into the web."ᵈ ¹⁴ And she pinned it with a pegᵉ and cried to him, "Samson, the Philistines are upon you!" Awaking from his sleep, he pulled out the peg, the loom,ᶠ and the web.

¹⁵ Then she said to him, "How can you say you love me, when you don't confide in me? This makes three times that you've deceived me and haven't told me what makes you so strong." ¹⁶ Finally, after she had nagged him and pressed him constantly, he was wearied to death ¹⁷ and he confided everything to her. He said to her, "No razor has ever touched my head, for I have been a nazirite to God since I was in my mother's womb. If my hair were cut, my strength would leave me and I should become as weak as an ordinary man."

¹⁸ Sensing that he had confided everything to her, Delilah sent for the lords of the Philistines, with this message: "Come up once more, for he has confided everything to me." And the lords of the Philistines came up and brought the money with them. ¹⁹ She lulled him to sleep on her lap. Then she called in a man, and she had him cut off the seven locks of his head; thus she weakened himᵍ and made him helpless: his strength slipped away from him. ²⁰ She cried, "Samson, the Philistines are upon you!" And he awoke from his sleep, thinking he would break looseᶠ and shake himself free as he had the other times. For he did not know that the LORD had departed from him. ²¹ The Philistines seized him and gouged out his eyes. They brought him down to Gaza and

---

ᵈ *Septuagint adds "and pin it with a peg to the wall, I shall become as weak as an ordinary man. So Delilah put him to sleep and wove the seven locks of his head into the web."*
ᵉ *Septuagint adds "to the wall."*
ᶠ *Meaning of Heb. uncertain.*
ᵍ *Taking* wattaḥel *as equivalent to* wattaḥal; *cf. vv. 7, 11, and 17.*

shackled him in bronze fetters, and he became a mill slave in the prison. ²² After his hair was cut off, it began to grow back.

²³ Now the lords of the Philistines gathered to offer a great sacrifice to their god Dagon and to make merry. They chanted,

"Our god has delivered into our hands
Our enemy Samson."

²⁴ ʰWhen the people saw him, they sang praises to their god, chanting,

"Our god has delivered into our hands
The enemy who devastated our land,
And who slew so many of us."

²⁵ As their spirits rose, they said, "Call Samson here and let him dance for us." Samson was fetched from the prison, and he danced for them. Then they put him between the pillars. ²⁶ And Samson said to the boy who was leading him by the hand, "Let go of me and let me feel the pillars that the temple rests upon, that I may lean on them." ²⁷ Now the temple was full of men and women; all the lords of the Philistines were there, and there were some three thousand men and women on the roof watching Samson dance. ²⁸ Then Samson called to the LORD, "O Lord GOD! Please remember me, and give me strength just this once, O God, to take revenge of the Philistines, if only for one of my two eyes." ²⁹ He embraced the two middle pillars that the temple rested upon, one with his right arm and one with his left, and leaned against them; ³⁰ Samson cried, "Let me die with the Philistines!" and he pulled with all his might. The temple came crashing down on the lords and on all the people in it. Those who were slain by him as he died outnumbered those who had been slain by him when he lived.

³¹ His brothers and all his father's household came down and carried him up and buried him in the tomb of his father Manoah, between Zorah and Eshtaol. He had led Israel for twenty years.

ʰ *This verse would read well after v. 25.*

17 There was a man in the hill country of Ephraim whose name was Micah.*ᵃ* ² He said to his mother, "The eleven hundred shekels of silver that were taken from you, so that you uttered an imprecation*ᵇ* which you repeated in my hearing—I have that silver; I took it." "Blessed of the LORD be my son," said his mother.*ᶜ* ³ He returned the eleven hundred shekels of silver to his mother; but his mother said, "I herewith consecrate the silver to the LORD, transferring it to my son to make a sculptured image and a molten image. I now return it to you." ⁴ So when he gave the silver back to his mother, his mother took two hundred shekels of silver and gave it to a smith. He made of it a sculptured image and a molten image, which were kept in the house of Micah.

⁵ Now the man Micah had a house of God; he had made an ephod and teraphim and he had inducted one of his sons to be his priest. ⁶ In those days there was no king in Israel; every man did as he pleased.

⁷ There was a young man from Bethlehem of Judah, from the clan seat of Judah; he was a Levite and had resided there as a sojourner. ⁸ This man had left the town of Bethlehem of Judah to take up residence wherever he could find a place. On his way, he came to the house of Micah in the hill country of Ephraim. ⁹ "Where do you come from?" Micah asked him. He replied, "I am a Levite from Bethlehem of Judah, and I am traveling to take up residence wherever I can find a place." ¹⁰ "Stay with me," Micah said to him, "and be a father and a priest to me, and I will pay you ten shekels of silver a year, an allowance of clothing, and your food." *ᵈ⁻*The Levite went.*⁻ᵈ* ¹¹ The Levite agreed to stay with the man, and the youth became like one of his own sons. ¹² Micah inducted the Levite, and the young man became his priest and remained in Micah's shrine. ¹³ "Now I know," Micah told himself, "that the LORD will prosper me, since the Levite has become my priest."

ᵃ *"Micaihu" here and in v. 4.*
ᵇ *Cursing anyone who knew the whereabouts of the silver and did not disclose it; cf. Lev. 5.1; I Kings 8.31.*
ᶜ *In order to nullify the imprecation.*
ᵈ⁻ᵈ *Force of Heb. uncertain.*

18 In those days there was no king in Israel, and in those days the tribe of Dan was seeking a territory in which to settle; for to that day no territory had fallen to their lot among the tribes of Israel. ² The Danites sent out five of their number, from their clan seat at Zorah and Eshtaol—valiant men—to spy out the land and explore it. "Go," they told them, "and explore the land." When they had advanced into the hill country of Ephraim as far as the house of Micah, they stopped there for the night. ³ While in the vicinity of Micah's house, they recognized the speech*ᵃ* of the young Levite, so they went over and asked him, "Who brought you to these parts? What are you doing in this place? What is your business here?" ⁴ He replied, "Thus and thus Micah did for me —he hired me and I became his priest." ⁵ They said to him, "Please, inquire of God; we would like to know if the mission on which we are going will be successful." ⁶ "Go in peace," the priest said to them, "the LORD views with favor the mission you are going on." ⁷ The five men went on and came to Laish. They observed the people in it dwelling carefree, after the manner of the Sidonians, a tranquil and unsuspecting people, with no one in the land to molest them and *ᵇ*with no hereditary ruler.*ᵇ* Moreover, they were distant from the Sidonians and had no dealings with anybody.

⁸ When [the men] came back to their kinsmen at Zorah and Eshtaol, their kinsmen asked them, "How did you fare?" ⁹ They replied, "Let us go at once and attack them! For we found that the land was very good, and you are sitting idle! Don't delay; go and invade the land and take possession of it, ¹⁰ for God has delivered it into your hand. When you come, you will come to an unsuspecting people; and the land is spacious and nothing on earth is lacking there."

¹¹ They departed from there, from the clan seat of the Danites, from Zorah and Eshtaol, six hundred strong, girt with weapons of war. ¹² They went up and encamped at Kiriath-jearim in Judah.

ᵃ Lit. "voice." The men could tell by his dialect that he came from Judah and was therefore a former neighbor of the Danites; cf. vv. 11-12.
ᵇ⁻ᵇ Meaning of Heb. uncertain.

That is why that place is called "the Camp of Dan" to this day; it lies west of Kiriath-jearim. [13] From there they passed on to the hill country of Ephraim and arrived at the house of Micah. [14] Here the five men who had gone to spy out the Laish region remarked to their kinsmen, "Do you know, there is an ephod in these houses, and teraphim, and a sculptured image and a molten image? Now you know what you have to do." [15] So they turned off there and entered the home of the young Levite at Micah's house and greeted him. [16] The six hundred Danite men, girt with their weapons of war, stood at the entrance of the gate, [17] while the five men who had gone to spy out the land went inside and took the sculptured image, the ephod, the teraphim, and the molten image. The priest was standing at the entrance of the gate, and the six hundred men girt with their weapons of war, [18] while those men entered Micah's house and took ⌐the sculptured image, the molten image, the ephod, and the household gods.⌐ The priest said to them, "What are you doing?" [19] But they said to him, "Be quiet; put your hand on your mouth! Come with us and be our father and priest. Would you rather be priest to one man's household or be priest to a tribe and clan in Israel?" [20] The priest was delighted. He took the ephod, the household gods, and the sculptured image, and he joined the people.

[21] They set out again, placing the children, the cattle, and their household goods in front. [22] They had already gone some distance from Micah's house, when the men in the houses near Micah's mustered and caught up with the Danites. [23] They called out to the Danites, who turned around and said to Micah, "What's the matter? Why have you mustered?" [24] He said, "You have taken my priest and the gods that I made, and walked off! What do I have left? How can you ask, 'What's the matter'?" [25] But the Danites replied, "Don't do any shouting at us, or some desperate men might attack you, and you and your family would lose your lives." [26] So Micah, realizing that they were stronger than he, turned back and went home; and the Danites went on their way, [27] taking the things Micah had made and the priest he

---

ᶜ⁻ᶜ *Lit. "the sculptured image of the ephod, and the household gods, and the molten image."*

had acquired. They proceeded to Laish, a people tranquil and unsuspecting, and they put them to the sword and burned down the town. [28] There was none to come to the rescue, for it was distant from Sidon and they had no dealings with anyone; it lay in the valley of Beth-rehob.

They rebuilt the town and settled there, [29] and they named the town Dan, after their ancestor Dan who was Israel's son. Originally, however, the name of the town was Laish. [30] The Danites set up the sculptured image for themselves; and Jonathan son of Gershom son of Manasseh,[d] and his descendants, served the priests to the Danite tribe until the land went into exile. [31] They maintained[b] the sculptured image that Micah had made throughout the time that the House of God stood at Shiloh.

19 In those days, when there was no king in Israel, a Levite residing at the other end of the hill country of Ephraim took to himself a concubine from Bethlehem in Judah. [2] Once his concubine deserted[a] him, leaving him for her father's house in Bethlehem in Judah; and she stayed there a full four months. [3] Then her husband set out, with an attendant and a pair of donkeys, and went after her to woo her and to win her back. She admitted him into her father's house; and when the girl's father saw him, he received him warmly. [4] His father-in-law, the girl's father, pressed him, and he stayed with him three days; they ate and drank and lodged there. [5] Early in the morning of the fourth day, he started to leave; but the girl's father said to his son-in-law, "Eat something to give you strength, then you can leave." [6] So the two of them sat down and they feasted together. Then the girl's father said to the man, "Won't you stay overnight and enjoy yourself?" [7] The man started to leave, but his father-in-law kept urging him until he turned back and spent the night there. [8] Early in the morning of the fifth day, he was about to leave, when the girl's father said, "Come, have a bite." The two of them ate, dawdling until past noon. [9] Then the man, his concubine, and his attendant

---

[d] *Heb.* משה *with* נ *suspended, indicating an earlier reading,* Moses; *cf. Exod. 2.22.*

[a] *Lit. "played the harlot."*

started to leave. His father-in-law, the girl's father, said to him, "Look, the day is waning toward evening; do stop for the night. See, the day is declining; spend the night here and enjoy yourself. You can start early tomorrow on your journey and head for home."

10 But the man refused to stay for the night. He set out and traveled as far as the vicinity of Jebus—that is, Jerusalem; he had with him a pair of laden donkeys, and his concubine *b*-was with him.*-b* 11 Since they were close to Jebus, and the day was very far spent, the attendant said to his master, "Let us turn aside to this town of the Jebusites and spend the night in it." 12 But his master said to him, "We will not turn aside to a town of aliens who are not of Israel, but will continue to Gibeah. 13 Come," he said to his attendant, "let us approach one of those places and spend the night either in Gibeah or in Ramah." 14 So they traveled on, and the sun set when they were near Gibeah of Benjamin.

15 They turned off there and went in to spend the night in Gibeah. He went and sat down in the town square, but nobody took them indoors to spend the night. 16 In the evening, an old man came along from his property *c*-outside the town.*-c* (This man hailed from the hill country of Ephraim and resided at Gibeah, where the townspeople were Benjaminites.) 17 He happened to see the wayfarer in the town square. "Where," the old man inquired, "are you going to, and where do you come from?" 18 He replied, "We are traveling from Bethlehem in Judah to the other end of the hill country of Ephraim. That is where I live. I made a journey to Bethlehem of Judah, and now I am on my way *d*-to the House of the Lord,*-d* and nobody has taken me indoors. 19 We have both bruised straw and feed for our donkeys, and bread and wine for me and your handmaid,*e* and for the attendant *f*-with your servants.*f* We lack nothing." 20 "Rest easy," said the old man. "Let me take care of all your needs. Do not on any account spend the night in the square." 21 And he took him into his house. He mixed fodder for the donkeys; then they bathed their feet and ate and drank.

b-b *Emendation yields "and his attendant."*
c-c *Lit. "in the field."*
d-d *Meaning of Heb. uncertain; emendation yields "to my home"; cf. v. 29.*
e *I.e. the concubine.*
f-f *I.e. "with us."*

²² While they were enjoying themselves, the men of the town, a depraved lot, had gathered about the house and were pounding on the door. They called to the aged owner of the house, "Bring out the man who has come into your house, so that we can be intimate with him." ²³ The owner of the house went out and said to them, "Please, my friends, do not commit such a wrong. Since this man has entered my house, do not perpetrate this outrage. ²⁴ Look, here is my virgin daughter, and his concubine. Let me bring them out to you. Have your pleasure of them, do what you like with them; but don't do that outrageous thing to this man." ²⁵ But the men would not listen to him, so the man seized his concubine and pushed her out to them. They raped her and abused her all night long until morning; and they let her go when dawn broke.

²⁶ Toward morning the woman came back; and as it was growing light, she collapsed at the entrance of the man's house where her husband was. ²⁷ When her husband arose in the morning, he opened the doors of the house and went out to continue his journey; and there was the woman, his concubine, lying at the entrance of the house, with her hands on the threshold. ²⁸ "Get up," he said to her, "let us go." But there was no reply. So the man placed her on the donkey and set out for home. ²⁹ When he came home, he picked up a knife, and took hold of his concubine and cut her up limb by limb into twelve parts. He sent them throughout the territory of Israel. ³⁰ And everyone who saw it cried out, "Never has such a thing happened or been seen from the day the Israelites came out of the land of Egypt to this day! Put your mind to this; take counsel and decide."

20 Thereupon all the Israelites—from Dan to Beer-sheba and [from] the land of Gilead—marched forth, and the community assembled to a man before the LORD at Mizpah. ² All the leaders of the people [and] all the tribes of Israel presented themselves in the assembly of God's people, 400,000 fighting men on foot.—³ The Benjaminites heard that the Israelites had come up to Mizpah.ᵃ—The Israelites said, "Tell us, how did this evil thing happen?" ⁴ And the Levite, the husband of the murdered woman, replied, "My concubine and I came to Gibeah of Benjamin to spend the night. ⁵ The citizens of Gibeah set out to harm me. They gathered against me around the house in the night; they meant to kill me, and they ravished my concubine until she died. ⁶ So I took hold of my concubine and I cut her in pieces and sent them through every part of Israel's territory. For an outrageous act of depravity had been committed in Israel. ⁷ Now you are all Israelites; produce a plan of action here and now!"

⁸ Then all the people rose, as one man, and declared, "We will not go back to our homes, we will not enter our houses! ⁹ But this is what we will do to Gibeah: [we will wage war] against it according to lot. ¹⁰ We will take from all the tribes of Israel ten men to the hundred, a hundred to the thousand, and a thousand to the ten thousand to supply provisions for the troops—ᵇto prepare for their going to Geba in Benjaminᵇ for all the outrage it has committed in Israel." ¹¹ So all the men of Israel, united as one man, massed against the town. ¹² And the tribes of Israel sent men through the whole tribeᶜ of Benjamin, saying, "What is this evil thing that has happened among you? ¹³ Come, hand over those scoundrels in Gibeah so that we may put them to death and stamp out the evil from Israel." But the Benjaminites would not yield to the demand of their fellow Israelites.

¹⁴ So the Benjaminites gathered from their towns to Gibeah in order to take the field against the Israelites. ¹⁵ ᵈOn that day the Benjaminites mustered from the towns 26,000 fighting men, mustered apart from the inhabitants of Gibeah; 700 picked men ¹⁶ of all this force—700 picked men—were left-handed. Every one of them could sling a stone at a hair and not miss. ¹⁷ The men of Israel other than Benjamin mustered 400,000 fighting men, warriors to a man. ¹⁸ They proceeded to Bethel and inquired of God; the Israelites asked, "Who of us shall advance first to fight the Benjaminites?" And the LORD replied, "Judah first." ¹⁹ So the

ᵃ *This sentence is continued at v. 14 below.*
ᵇ⁻ᵇ *Emendation yields "for those who go to requite Gibeah."*
ᶜ *Heb. plural.*
ᵈ *Meaning of parts of vv. 15 and 16 uncertain.*

Israelites arose in the morning and encamped against Gibeah.
²⁰ The men of Israel took the field against the Benjaminites; the
men of Israel drew up in battle order against them at Gibeah.
²¹ But the Benjaminites issued from Gibeah, and that day they
struck down 22,000 men of Israel.

²² Now the army—the men of Israel—rallied and again drew up
in battle order at the same place as they had on the first day.
²³ For the Israelites had gone up and wept before the LORD un-
til evening. They had inquired of the LORD, "Shall we again
join battle with our kinsmen the Benjaminites?" And the LORD
had replied, "March against them." ²⁴ The Israelites advanced
against the Benjaminites on the second day. ²⁵ But the Benjaminites came out from Gibeah against them on the second day and
struck down 18,000 more of the Israelites, all of them fighting
men.

²⁶ Then all the Israelites, all the army, went up and came to
Bethel and they sat there, weeping before the LORD. They fasted
that day until evening, and presented burnt offerings and offerings of well-being to the LORD. ²⁷ The Israelites inquired of the
LORD (for the Ark of God's Covenant was there in those days,
²⁸ and Phineas son of Eleazar son of Aaron the priest ministered
before Him in those days), "Shall we again take the field against
our kinsmen the Benjaminites, or shall we not?" The LORD answered, "Go up, for tomorrow I will deliver them into your
hands."

²⁹ Israel put men in ambush against Gibeah on all sides. ³⁰ And
on the third day, the Israelites went up against the Benjaminites,
as before, and engaged them in battle at Gibeah. ³¹ The Benjaminites dashed out to meet the army and were drawn away from the
town onto the roads, of which one runs to Bethel and the other
to Gibeah. As before, they started out by striking some of the men
dead in the open field, about 30 men of Israel.

³² The Benjaminites thought, "They are being routed before us
as previously." But the Israelites had planned: "We will take to
flight and draw them away from the town to the roads." ³³ And

while the main body of the Israelites had moved away from their positions and had drawn up in battle order at Baal-tamar, the Israelite ambush was rushing out from its position at Maareh-geba.[e] [34] Thus 10,000 picked men of all Israel came to a point south of[f] Gibeah, and the battle was furious. Before they realized that disaster was approaching, [35] the LORD routed the Benjaminites before Israel. That day the Israelites slew 25,100 men of Benjamin, all of them fighting men. [36] Then the Benjaminites realized that they were routed.[g] Now the Israelites had yielded ground to the Benjaminites, for they relied on the ambush which they had laid against Gibeah. [37] One ambush quickly deployed against Gibeah, and the other ambush advanced and put the whole town to the sword.

[38] A time had been agreed upon by the Israelite men with those in ambush: When a huge column of smoke was sent up from the town, [39] the Israelite men were to turn about in battle. Benjamin had begun by striking dead about 30 Israelite men, and they thought, "They are being routed before us as in the previous fighting." [40] But when the column, the pillar of smoke, began to rise from the city, the Benjaminites looked behind them, and there was the whole town going up in smoke to the sky! [41] And now the Israelites turned about, and the men of Benjamin were thrown into panic, for they realized that disaster had overtaken them. [42] They retreated before the men of Israel along the road to the wilderness, where the fighting caught up with them; meanwhile those [h]from the towns[-h] were massacring them in it. [43] [i]They encircled the Benjaminites, pursued them, and trod them down [from] Menuhah to a point opposite Gibeah on the east. [44] 19,000 men of Benjamin fell that day, all of them brave men. [45] They turned and fled to the wilderness, to the Rock of Rimmon; but [the Israelites] picked off another 5,000 on the roads and, continuing in hot pursuit of them up to Gidom, they slew 2,000 more. [46] Thus the total number of Benjaminites that fell that day came to 25,000 fighting men, all of them brave.

[e] *Emendation yields "west of Gibeah."*
[f] *So many Heb. mss. and Targum; most mss. and the editions read "opposite."*
[g] *This sentence is continued by v. 45.*
[h-h] *Meaning of Heb. uncertain; emendation yields "in the town" (i.e. Gibeah).*
[i] *Meaning of verse uncertain.*

⁴⁷ But 600 men turned and fled to the wilderness, to the Rock of Rimmon; they remained at the Rock of Rimmon four months. ⁴⁸ The men of Israel, meanwhile, turned back to the rest of the Benjaminites and put them to the sword—towns, people, cattle —everything that remained. Finally, they set fire to all the towns that were left.

21 Now the men of Israel had taken an oath at Mizpah: "None of us will give his daughter in marriage to a Benjaminite."

² The people came to Bethel and sat there before God until evening. They wailed and wept bitterly, ³ and they said, "O Lord God of Israel, why has this happened in Israel, that one tribe must now be missing from Israel?" ⁴ Early the next day, the people built an altar there, and they brought burnt offerings and offerings of well-being.

⁵ The Israelites asked, "Is there anyone from all the tribes of Israel who failed to come up to the assembly before the Lord?" For a solemn oath had been taken concerning anyone who did not go up to the Lord at Mizpah: "He shall be put to death." ⁶ The Israelites now relented toward their kinsmen the Benjaminites, and they said, "This day one tribe has been cut off from Israel! ⁷ What can we do to provide wives for those who are left, seeing that we have sworn by the Lord not to give any of our daughters to them in marriage?"

⁸ They inquired, "Is there anyone from the tribes of Israel who did not go up to the Lord at Mizpah?" Now no one from Jabesh-gilead had come to the camp, to the assembly. ⁹ For, when the roll of the troops was taken, not one of the inhabitants of Jabesh-gilead was present. ¹⁰ So the assemblage dispatched 12,000 of the warriors, instructing them as follows: "Go and put the inhabitants of Jabesh-gilead to the sword, women and children included. ¹¹ This is what you are to do: Proscribe every man, and every woman who has known a man carnally." ¹² They found among the inhabitants of Jabesh-gilead 400 maidens who had not

known a man carnally; and they brought them to the camp at Shiloh, which is in the land of Canaan.[a]

¹³ Then the whole community sent word to the Benjaminites who were at the Rock of Rimmon, and offered them terms of peace. ¹⁴ Thereupon the Benjaminites returned, and they gave them the girls who had been spared from the women of Jabesh-gilead. [b-]But there were not enough of them.[-b]

¹⁵ Now the people had relented toward Benjamin, for the LORD had made a breach in the tribes of Israel. ¹⁶ So the elders of the community asked, "What can we do about wives for those who are left, since the women of Benjamin have been killed off?" ¹⁷ For they said, "There must be a saving remnant for Benjamin, that a tribe may not be blotted out of Israel; ¹⁸ yet we cannot give them any of our daughters as wives," since the Israelites had taken an oath: "Cursed be anyone who gives a wife to Benjamin!"

¹⁹ They said, "The annual feast of the LORD is now being held at Shiloh." (It lies north of Bethel, east of the highway that runs from Bethel to Shechem, and south of Lebonah.)

²⁰ So they instructed the Benjaminites as follows: "Go and lie in wait in the vineyards. ²¹ As soon as you see the girls of Shiloh coming out to join in the dances, come out from the vineyards; let each of you seize a wife from among the girls of Shiloh, and be off for the land of Benjamin. ²² And if their fathers or brothers come to us to complain, we shall say to them, [b-]'Be generous to them for our sake! We could not provide any of them with a wife on account of the war, and you would have incurred guilt if you yourselves had given them [wives].' "[-b]

²³ The Benjaminites did so. They took to wife, from the dancers whom they carried off, as many as they themselves numbered. Then they went back to their own territory, and rebuilt their towns and settled in them. ²⁴ Thereupon the Israelites dispersed, each to his own tribe and clan; everyone departed for his own territory.

²⁵ In those days there was no king in Israel; everyone did as he pleased.

ᵃ *I.e. west of the Jordan, while Jabesh-gilead is east of the Jordan.*
ᵇ⁻ᵇ *Meaning of Heb. uncertain.*

שמואל א

I SAMUEL

שְׁמוּאֵל א
I SAMUEL

1 There was a man from *a*-Ramathaim of the Zuphites,-*a* in the hill country of Ephraim, whose name was Elkanah son of Jeroham son of Elihu son of Tohu son of Zuph, an Ephraimite. ² He had two wives, one named Hannah and the other Peninnah; Peninnah had children, but Hannah was childless. ³ This man used to go up from his town every year to worship and to offer sacrifice to the LORD of Hosts at Shiloh.—Hophni and Phinehas, the two sons of Eli, were priests of the LORD there.

⁴ One such day, Elkanah offered a sacrifice. He used to give portions to his wife Peninnah and to all her sons and daughters; ⁵ but to Hannah he would give one portion *b*-only—though-*b* Hannah was his favorite—for the LORD had closed her womb. ⁶ Moreover, her rival, to make her miserable, would taunt her that the LORD had closed her womb. ⁷ *c*-This happened-*c* year after year: Every time she went up to the House of the LORD, the other would taunt her, so that she wept and would not eat. ⁸ Her husband Elkanah said to her, "Hannah, why are you crying and why aren't you eating? Why are you so sad? Am I not more devoted to you than ten sons?"

⁹ After they had eaten and drunk at Shiloh, Hannah rose.*d* —The priest Eli was sitting on the seat near the doorpost of the temple of the LORD.—¹⁰ In her wretchedness, she prayed to the LORD, weeping all the while. ¹¹ And she made this vow: "O LORD of Hosts, if You will look upon the suffering of Your maidservant and will remember me and not forget Your maidservant, and if You will grant Your maidservant a male child, I will dedicate him

---

a-a Heb. "Ramathaim-zophim." In 1.19; 2.11; 7.17; 15.34; 19.18, etc. the town is called Ramah; and 9.5 ff. shows that it was in the district of Zuph.
b-b Meaning of Heb. uncertain.
c-c Lit. "Thus he did."
d Septuagint adds "and stood before the LORD."

to the LORD for all the days of his life; and no razor shall ever touch his head."

¹² As she kept on praying before the LORD, Eli watched her mouth. ¹³ Now Hannah was praying in her heart; only her lips moved, but her voice could not be heard. So Eli thought she was drunk. ¹⁴ Eli said to her, "How long will you make a drunken spectacle of yourself? ᵉ⁻Sober up!"⁻ᵉ ¹⁵ And Hannah replied, "Oh no, my lord! I am a very unhappy woman. I have drunk no wine or other strong drink, but I have been pouring out my heart to the LORD. ¹⁶ Do not take your maidservant for a worthless woman; I have only been speaking all this time out of my great anguish and distress." ¹⁷ "Then go in peace," said Eli, "and may the God of Israel grant you what you have asked of Him." ¹⁸ She answered, "You are most kind to your handmaid." So the woman left, and she ate, and was no longer downcast. ¹⁹ Early next morning they bowed low before the LORD, and they went back home to Ramah.

Elkanah knewᶠ his wife Hannah and the LORD remembered her. ²⁰ Hannah conceived, and at the turn of the year bore a son. She named him Samuel,ᵍ meaning, "I asked the LORD for him." ²¹ And when the man Elkanah and all his household were going up to offer to the LORD the annual sacrifice and his votive sacrifice, ²² Hannah did not go up. She said to her husband, "When the child is weaned, I will bring him. For when he has appeared before the LORD, he must remain there for good." ²³ Her husband Elkanah said to her, "Do as you think best. Stay home until you have weaned him. May the LORD fulfill ʰ⁻His word."⁻ʰ So the woman stayed home and nursed her son until she weaned him.

²⁴ When she had weaned him, she took him up with her, along with ⁱ⁻three bulls,⁻ⁱ one ephah of flour, and a jar of wine. And ᵇ⁻though the boy was still very young,⁻ᵇ she brought him to the House of the LORD at Shiloh. ²⁵ After slaughtering the bull, they brought the boy to Eli. ²⁶ She said, "Please, my lord! As you live,

ᵉ⁻ᵉ Lit. "Remove your wine from you."
ᶠ Cf. note at Gen. 4.1.
ᵍ Connected with sha'ul me'el; "asked of God"; cf. vv. 17, 27-28.
ʰ⁻ʰ Septuagint and 4QSamᵃ (a Samuel fragment from Qumran) read "the utterance of your mouth." The translators herewith express their thanks to Professor Frank M. Cross, Jr., for graciouly making available to them copies of his unpublished Samuel fragments.
ⁱ⁻ⁱ Septuagint and 4QSamᵃ read "a three-year-old (cf. Gen. 15.9) bull and bread"; cf. v. 25.

my lord, I am the woman who stood here beside you and prayed to the LORD. ²⁷ It was this boy I prayed for; and the LORD has granted me what I asked of Him. ²⁸ I, in turn, hereby lend^j him to the LORD. For as long as he lives he is lent to the LORD." And they^k bowed low there before the LORD.

2 And Hannah prayed:

> My heart exults in the LORD;
> ^aI have triumphed^{-a} through the LORD.
> ^bI gloat^{-b} over my enemies;
> I rejoice in Your deliverance.

> ² There is no holy one like the LORD,
> Truly, there is none beside You;
> There is no rock like our God.

> ³ Talk no more with lofty pride,
> Let no arrogance cross your lips!
> For the LORD is an all-knowing God;
> By Him actions are measured.

> ⁴ The bows of the mighty are broken,
> And the faltering are girded with strength.
> ⁵ Men once sated must hire out for bread;
> Men once hungry hunger no more.
> While the barren woman bears seven,
> The mother of many is forlorn.
> ⁶ The LORD deals death and gives life,
> Casts down into Sheol and raises up.
> ⁷ The LORD makes poor and makes rich;
> He casts down, He also lifts high.
> ⁸ He raises the poor from the dust,
> Lifts up the needy from the dunghill,

---

^j *From the same root as that of the verb rendered "asked for" in v. 20.*
^k *Heb. "he"; cf. 2.11. A reading in the Talmud (Berakot 61a) implies that Elkanah was there.*

^{a-a} *Lit. "My horn is high."*
^{b-b} *Lit. "My mouth is wide."*

Setting them with nobles,
Granting them seats of honor.
For the pillars of the earth are the LORD's;
He has set the world upon them.
⁹ He guards the steps of His faithful,
But the wicked perish in darkness—
For not by strength shall man prevail.

¹⁰ The foes of the LORD shall be shattered;
He will thunder against them in the heavens.
The LORD will judge the ends of the earth.
He will give power to His king,
ᶜ⁻And triumph to⁻ᶜ His anointed one.

¹¹ Then Elkanah*d* [and Hannah] went home to Ramah; and the boy entered the service of the LORD under the priest Eli.

¹² Now Eli's sons were scoundrels; they paid no heed to the LORD. ¹³ This is how the priests used to deal with the people: When anyone brought a sacrifice, the priest's boy would come along with a three-pronged fork while the meat was boiling, ¹⁴ and he would thrust it into ᵉ⁻the cauldron, or the kettle, or the great pot, or the small cooking-pot;⁻ᵉ and whatever the fork brought up, the priest would take away ᶠ⁻on it.⁻ᶠ This was the practice at Shiloh with all the Israelites who came there. ¹⁵ [But now] even before the suet was turned into smoke, the priest's boy would come and say to the man who was sacrificing, "Hand over some meat to roast for the priest; for he won't accept boiled meat from you, only raw." ¹⁶ And if the man said to him, "Let them first turn the suet into smoke, and then take as much as you want," he would reply, "No, hand it over at once or I'll take it by force." ¹⁷ The sin of the young men against the LORD was very great, for the men treated the LORD's offerings impiously.

¹⁸ Samuel was engaged in the service of the LORD as an attendant, girded with a linen ephod. ¹⁹ His mother would also make a little robe for him and bring it up to him every year, when she

---

ᶜ⁻ᶜ *Lit. "And will raise the horn of."*
d *See note k at 1.28.*
ᵉ⁻ᵉ *These vessels have not been distinguished precisely.*
ᶠ⁻ᶠ *Targum and Septuagint add "for himself."*

made the pilgrimage with her husband to offer the annual sacrifice. [20] Eli would bless Elkanah and his wife, and say, "May the LORD grant[g] you offspring by this woman in place of the loan she made to the LORD." Then they would return home. [21] For[h] the LORD took note of Hannah; she conceived and bore three sons and two daughters. Young Samuel meanwhile grew up in the service of the LORD.

[22] Now Eli was very old. When he heard all that his sons were doing to all Israel, and how they lay with the women who [i-]performed tasks[-i] at the entrance of the Tent of Meeting, [23] he said to them, "Why do you do such things? I get evil reports about you from the people on all hands. [24] Don't, my sons! It is no favorable report I hear the people of the LORD spreading about. [25] If a man sins against a man, the LORD may pardon[i] him; but if a man offends against God, who can [i-]obtain pardon[-i] for him?" But they ignored their father's plea; for the LORD was resolved that they should die. [26] Young Samuel, meanwhile, grew in esteem and favor both with God and with men.

[27] A man of God came to Eli and said to him, "Thus said the LORD: Lo, I revealed Myself to your father's house in Egypt when they were subject to the House of Pharaoh, [28] and I chose them from among all the tribes of Israel to be My priests—to ascend My altar, to burn incense, [and] to carry an ephod[j] before Me— and I assigned to your father's house all offerings by fire of the Israelites. [29] Why, then, do you [k-]maliciously trample upon the sacrifices and offerings which I have commanded?[-k] You have honored your sons more than Me, feeding on the first portions of every offering of My people Israel.[l] [30] Assuredly—declares the LORD, the God of Israel—I intended for you and your father's house to remain in My service forever. But now—declares the LORD—far be it from Me! For I honor those who honor Me, but those who spurn Me shall be dishonored. [31] A time is coming

g *4QSam^a and Septuagint read "repay."*
h *4QSam^a reads "And."*
i-i *Meaning of Heb. uncertain.*
j *Here a device for obtaining oracles (cf. 14.3; 23.6, 9-12), not a garment as in v. 18 above.*
k-k *Meaning of Heb. uncertain. Emendation yields "gaze (cf. Septuagint) grudgingly upon the sacrifices and offerings which I have commanded" (connecting* ma' on *with* 'oyen, *"keeping a jealous eye"; see I Sam. 18.9); cf. v. 32 and note m below.*
l *See vv. 15-16.*

when I will break your power and that of your father's house, and there shall be no elder in your house. [32] You will gaze grudgingly*[m]* at all the bounty that will be bestowed on Israel, but there shall never be an elder in your house. [33] *[i]*-I shall not cut off all your offspring from My altar; [but,] to make your eyes pine and your spirit languish, all the increase in your house shall die as [ordinary] men.-*[i]* [34] And this shall be a sign for you: The fate of your two sons Hophni and Phinehas—they shall both die on the same day. [35] And I will raise up for Myself a faithful priest, who will act in accordance with My wishes and My purposes. I will build for him an enduring house, and he shall walk before My anointed evermore. [36] And all the survivors of your house shall come and bow low to him for the sake of a money fee and a loaf of bread, and shall say, 'Please, assign me to one of the priestly duties, that I may have a morsel of bread to eat.' "

3 Young Samuel was in the service of the LORD under Eli. In those days the word of the LORD was rare; prophecy was not widespread. [2] One day, Eli was asleep in his usual place; his eyes had begun to fail and he could barely see. [3] The lamp of God had not yet gone out, and Samuel was sleeping in the temple of the LORD where the Ark of God was. [4] The LORD called out to Samuel, and he answered, "I'm coming." [5] He ran to Eli and said, "Here I am; you called me." But he replied, "I didn't call you; go back to sleep." So he went back and lay down. [6] Again the LORD called, "Samuel!" Samuel rose and went to Eli and said, "Here I am; you called me." But he replied, "I didn't call, my son; go back to sleep."—[7] Now Samuel had not yet experienced the LORD; the word of the LORD had not yet been revealed to him.—[8] The LORD called Samuel again, a third time, and he rose and went to Eli and said, "Here I am; you called me." Then Eli understood that the LORD was calling the boy. [9] And Eli said to Samuel, "Go lie down. If you are called again, say, 'Speak, LORD,

[m] Cf. note k-k above.

108

for Your servant is listening.' " And Samuel went to his place and lay down. [10] The LORD came, and stood there, and He called as before: "Samuel! Samuel!" And Samuel answered, "Speak, for Your servant is listening." [11] The LORD said to Samuel: "I am going to do in Israel such a thing that both ears of anyone who hears about it will tingle. [12] In that day I will fulfill against Eli all that I spoke concerning his house, from beginning to end. [13] And I declare to him that I sentence his house to endless punishment for the iniquity he knew about—how his sons committed sacrilege *a-at will-a*—and he did not rebuke them. [14] Assuredly, I swear concerning the house of Eli that the iniquity of the house of Eli will never be expiated by sacrifice or offering."

[15] Samuel lay there until morning; and then he opened the doors of the House of the LORD. Samuel was afraid to report the vision to Eli, [16] but Eli summoned Samuel and said, "Samuel, my son"; and he answered, "Here." [17] And [Eli] asked, "What did He say to you? Keep nothing from me. *b-Thus and more may God do to you-b* if you keep from me a single word of all that He said to you!" [18] Samuel then told him everything, withholding nothing from him. And [Eli] said, "He is the LORD; He will do what He deems right."

[19] Samuel grew up and the LORD was with him: He did not leave any of Samuel's *c* predictions unfulfilled. [20] All Israel, from Dan to Beersheba, knew that Samuel was trustworthy as a prophet of the LORD. [21] And the LORD continued to appear at Shiloh: the LORD

4 revealed Himself to Samuel at Shiloh with the word of the LORD; [1] and Samuel's word went forth to all Israel.

*a*Israel marched out to engage the Philistines in battle; they encamped near Eben-ezer, while the Philistines encamped at Aphek. [2] The Philistines arrayed themselves against Israel; and when the battle was fought,*b* Israel was routed by the Philistines,

---

a-a *Meaning of Heb. uncertain. Septuagint reads "against God."*
b-b *A formula of adjuration.*
c *Heb. "his."*

a *Preceding this, Septuagint has "In those days, the Philistines gathered for war against Israel."*
b *Meaning of Heb. uncertain.*

who slew about four thousand men on the field of battle. [3] When the [Israelite] troops returned to the camp, the elders of Israel asked, "Why did the LORD put us to rout today before the Philistines? Let us fetch the Ark of the Covenant of the LORD from Shiloh; thus He will be present among us and will deliver us from the hands of our enemies." [4] So the troops sent men to Shiloh; there Eli's two sons, Hophni and Phinehas, were in charge of the Ark of the Covenant of God, and they brought down from there the Ark of the Covenant of the LORD of Hosts Enthroned on the Cherubim.

[5] When the Ark of the Covenant of the LORD entered the camp, all Israel burst into a great shout, so that the earth resounded. [6] The Philistines heard the noise of the shouting and they wondered, "Why is there such a loud shouting in the camp of the Hebrews?" And when they learned that the Ark of the LORD had come to the camp, [7] the Philistines were frightened; for they said, "God has come to the camp." And they cried, "Woe to us! Nothing like this has ever happened before. [8] Woe to us! Who will save us from the power of this mighty God? He is the same God who struck the Egyptians with every kind of plague in the wilderness! [9] Brace yourselves and be men, O Philistines! Or you will become slaves to the Hebrews as they were slaves to you. Be men and fight!" [10] The Philistines fought; Israel was routed, and they all fled to their homes. The defeat was very great, thirty thousand foot soldiers of Israel fell there. [11] The Ark of God was captured, and Eli's two sons, Hophni and Phinehas, were slain.

[12] A Benjaminite ran from the battlefield and reached Shiloh the same day; his clothes were rent and there was earth on his head.[c] [13] When he arrived, he found Eli sitting on a seat, waiting beside the road—his heart trembling for the Ark of God. The man entered the city to spread the news, and the whole city broke out in a cry. [14] And when Eli heard the sound of the outcry and asked, "What is the meaning of this uproar?" the man rushed over to tell Eli. [15] Now Eli was ninety-eight years old; his eyes were fixed in a blind stare. [16] The man said to Eli, "I am the one

---

[c] *I.e. as a sign of mourning.*

who came from the battlefield; I have just fled from the battlefield." [Eli] asked, "What happened, my son?" 17 The bearer of the news replied, "Israel fled before the Philistines and the troops also suffered a great slaughter. Your two sons, Hophni and Phinehas, are dead, and the Ark of God has been captured." 18 When he mentioned the Ark of God, [Eli] fell backward off the seat beside*b* the gate, broke his neck and died; for he was an old man and heavy. He had been a chieftain of Israel for forty years.

19 His daughter-in-law, the wife of Phinehas, was with child, about to give birth. When she heard the report that the Ark of God was captured and that her father-in-law and her husband were dead, she was seized with labor pains, and she crouched down and gave birth. 20 As she lay dying, the women attending her said, "Do not be afraid, for you have borne a son." But she did not respond or pay heed. 21 She named the boy Ichabod, meaning, "The glory has departed from Israel"—referring to the capture of the Ark of God and to [the death of] her father-in-law and her husband. 22 "The glory is gone from Israel," she said, "for the Ark of God has been captured."

5 When the Philistines captured the Ark of God, they brought it from Eben-ezer to Ashdod. 2 The Philistines took the Ark of God and brought it into the temple of Dagon and they set it up beside Dagon. 3 Early the next day, the Ashdodites found Dagon lying face down on the ground in front of the Ark of the LORD. They picked Dagon up and put him back in his place; 4 but early the next morning, Dagon was again lying prone on the ground in front of the Ark of the LORD. The head and both hands of Dagon were cut off, lying on the threshold; only *a*-Dagon's trunk was left intact.-*a* 5 That is why, to this day, the priests of Dagon and all who enter the temple of Dagon do not tread on the threshold of Dagon in Ashdod.

6 The hand of the LORD lay heavy upon the Ashdodites, and He wrought havoc among them: He struck *b*-Ashdod and its territory-*b*

a-a *Meaning of Heb. uncertain.*

b-b *Meaning of Heb. uncertain. Septuagint reads differently from our Heb. text; it also mentions mice swarming in the Philistine ships and invading their fields. Cf. the mention of "mice" in 6.4, 18; and the note at 6.1.*

with hemorrhoids. [7] When the men of Ashdod saw how matters stood, they said, "The Ark of the God of Israel must not remain with us, for His hand has dealt harshly with us and with our god Dagon." [8] They sent messengers and assembled all the lords of the Philistines and asked, "What shall we do with the Ark of the God of Israel?" They answered, "Let the Ark of the God of Israel be removed to Gath." So they moved the Ark of the God of Israel [to Gath]. [9] And after they had moved it, the hand of the LORD came against the city, causing great panic; He struck the people of the city, young and old, so that hemorrhoids [a]-broke out-[a] among them. [10] Then they sent the Ark of God to Ekron. But when the Ark of God came to Ekron, the Ekronites cried out, "They have moved the Ark of the God of Israel to us to slay us and our kindred." [11] They too sent messengers and assembled all the lords of the Philistines and said, "Send the Ark of the God of Israel away, and let it return to its own place, that it may not slay us and our kindred." For the panic of death pervaded the whole city, so heavily had the hand of God fallen there; [12] and the men who did not die were stricken with hemorrhoids. The outcry of the city went up to heaven.

6 The Ark of the LORD remained in the territory of the Philistines seven months.[a] [2] Then the Philistines summoned the priests and the diviners and asked, "What shall we do about the Ark of the Lord? Tell us with what we shall send it off to its own place." [3] They answered, "If you are going to send the Ark of the God of Israel away, do not send it away without anything; you must also pay an indemnity to Him. Then you will be healed, and [b]-He will make Himself known to you; otherwise His hand will not turn away from you."-[b] [4] They asked, "What is the indemnity that we should pay to Him?" They answered, "Five golden hemorrhoids and five golden mice, corresponding to the number of lords of the Philistines; for the same plague struck all of you[c] and your lords. [5] You shall make figures of your hemorrhoids and of the

---

[a] *Septuagint continues "and mice invaded their fields"; cf. vv. 4, 5, 18, and note at 5. 6.*
[b-b] *Or "and you will know why His hand would not turn away from you." Meaning of Heb. uncertain.*
[c] *Heb. "them."*

mice that are ravaging your land; thus you shall honor the God of Israel, and perhaps He will lighten the weight of His hand upon you and your gods and your land. ⁶ Don't harden your hearts as the Egyptians and Pharaoh hardened their hearts. As you know, when He made a mockery of them, they had to let Israel*c* go, and they departed. ⁷ Therefore, get a new cart ready and two milch cows that have not borne a yoke; harness the cows to the cart, but take back indoors the calves that follow them. ⁸ Take the Ark of the LORD and place it on the cart; and put next to it in a chest the gold objects you are paying Him as indemnity. Send it off, and let it go its own way. ⁹ Then watch: If it goes up the road to Beth-shemesh, to His own territory, it was He who has inflicted this great harm on us. But if not, we shall know that it was not His hand that struck us; it just happened to us by chance."

¹⁰ The men did so. They took two milch cows and harnessed them to the cart, and shut up their calves indoors. ¹¹ They placed the Ark of the LORD on the cart together with the chest, the golden mice, and the figures of their hemorrhoids. ¹² The cows went straight ahead along the road to Beth-shemesh. They went along a single highroad, lowing as they went, and turning off neither to the right nor to the left; and the lords of the Philistines walked behind them as far as the border of Beth-shemesh.

¹³ The people of Beth-shemesh were reaping their wheat harvest in the valley. They looked up and saw the Ark, and they rejoiced *d*-when they saw [it].-*d* ¹⁴ The cart came into the field of Joshua of Beth-shemesh and it stopped there. They split up the wood of the cart and presented the cows as a burnt offering to the LORD. A large stone was there; ¹⁵ and the Levites took down the Ark of the LORD and the chest beside it containing the gold objects and placed them on the large stone. Then the men of Beth-shemesh presented burnt offerings and other sacrifices to the LORD that day. ¹⁶ The five lords of the Philistines saw this and returned the same day to Ekron.

¹⁷ The following were the golden hemorrhoids that the Philis-

d-d Septuagint reads "as they met it."

tines paid as an indemnity to the LORD: For Ashdod, one; for Gaza, one; for Ashkelon, one; for Gath, one; for Ekron, one. [18] [e]As for the golden mice, their number accorded with all the Philistine towns that belonged to the five lords—both fortified towns and unwalled [f]villages, as far as [-f] the great stone[g] on which the Ark of the LORD was set down, to this day, in the field of Joshua of Beth-shemesh.

[19] [The LORD] struck at the men of Beth-shemesh because [h]they looked into the Ark of the LORD; He struck down seventy men among the people [and] fifty thousand men.[-h] The people mourned, for He had inflicted a great slaughter upon the population. [20] And the men of Beth-shemesh asked, "Who can stand in attendance on the LORD, this holy God? And to whom shall He go up from us?" [21] They sent messengers to the inhabitants of Kiriath-jearim to say, "The Philistines have sent back the Ark of the LORD. Come down and take it into your keeping." [1] The 7 men of Kiraith-jearim came and took up the Ark of the LORD and brought it into the house of Abinadab on the hill; and they consecrated his son Eleazar to have charge of the Ark of the LORD.

[2] A long time elapsed from the day that the Ark was housed in Kiraith-jearim, twenty years in all; and all the House of Israel [a-] yearned after[-a] the LORD. [3] And Samuel said to all the House of Israel, "If you mean to return to the LORD with all your heart, you must remove the alien gods and the Ashtaroth from your midst and direct your heart to the LORD and serve Him alone. Then He will deliver you from the hands of the Philistines." [4] And the Israelites removed the Baalim and Ashtaroth and they served the LORD alone.

[5] Samuel said, "Assemble all Israel at Mizpah, and I will pray to the LORD for you." [6] They assembled at Mizpah, and they drew water and poured it out before the LORD; they fasted that day, and there they confessed that they had sinned against the LORD. And Samuel acted as chieftain of the Israelites at Mizpah.

[e] *Meaning of vv. 18 and 19 uncertain in part.*
[f-f] *Emendation yields "villages, as witness there is."*
[g] *Reading 'eben with some Heb. mss., Septuagint, and Targum; most mss. and editions 'abel, "meadow (?)."*
[h-h] *Force of Heb. uncertain.*

[a-a] *Meaning of Heb. uncertain.*

⁷ When the Philistines heard that the Isrealites had assembled at Mizpah, the lords of the Philistines marched out against Israel. Hearing of this, the Israelites were terrified of the Philistines ⁸ and they implored Samuel, "Do not neglect us and do not refrain from crying out to the LORD our God to save us from the hands of the Philistines." ⁹ Thereupon Samuel took a suckling lamb and sacrificed it as a whole burnt offering to the LORD; and Samuel cried out to the LORD in behalf of Israel, and the LORD responded to him. ¹⁰ For as Samuel was presenting the burnt offering and the Philistines advanced to attack Israel, the LORD thundered mightily against the Philistines that day. He threw them into confusion, and they were routed by Israel. ¹¹ The men of Israel sallied out of Mizpah and pursued the Philistines, striking them down to a point below Beth-car.

¹² Samuel took a stone and set it up between Mizpah and Shen,ᵇ and named it Eben-ezer:ᶜ "For up to now," he said, "the LORD has helped us." ¹³ The Philistines were humbled and did not invade the territory of Israel again; and the hand of the LORD was set against the Philistines as long as Samuel lived. ¹⁴ The towns which the Philistines had taken from Israel, from Ekron to Gath, were restored to Israel; Israel recovered all her territory from the Philistines. There was also peace between Israel and the Amorites.

¹⁵ Samuel judged Israel as long as he lived. ¹⁶ Each year he made the rounds of Bethel, Gilgal, and Mizpah, and acted as judge over Israel at all those places. ¹⁷ Then he would return to Ramah, for his home was there, and there too he would judge Israel. He built an altar there to the LORD.

8 When Samuel grew old, he appointed his sons judges over Israel. ² The name of his firstborn son was Joel, and his second son's name was Abijah; they sat as judges in Beer-sheba. ³ But his sons did not follow in his ways; they were bent on gain, they accepted bribes, and they subverted justice.

ᵇ Otherwise unknown; perhaps identical with "Jeshanah"; cf. Septuagint, also II Chron. 13.19.
ᶜ I.e. "Stone of Help."

⁴ All the elders of Israel assembled and came to Samuel at Ramah, ⁵ and they said to him, "You have grown old, and your sons have not followed your ways. Therefore appoint a king for us, to govern us like all other nations." ⁶ Samuel was displeased that they said "Give us a king to govern us." Samuel prayed to the LORD, ⁷ and the LORD replied to Samuel, "Heed the demand of the people in everything they say to you. For it is not you that they have rejected; it is Me they have rejected as their king. ⁸ Like everything else they have done ever since I brought them out of Egypt to this day—forsaking Me and worshiping other gods—so they are doing to you. ⁹ Heed their demand; but warn them solemnly, and tell them about the practices of any king who will rule over them."

¹⁰ Samuel reported all the words of the LORD to the people, who were asking him for a king. ¹¹ He said, "This will be the practice of the king who will rule over you: He will take your sons and appoint them as his charioteers and horsemen, and they will serve as outrunners for his chariots. ¹² He will appoint them as his chiefs of thousands and of fifties; or they will have to plow his fields, reap his harvest, and make his weapons and the equipment for his chariots. ¹³ He will take your daughters as perfumers, cooks, and bakers. ¹⁴ He will seize your choice fields, vineyards, and olive groves, and give them to his courtiers. ¹⁵ He will take a tenth part of your grain and vintage and give it to his eunuchs and courtiers. ¹⁶ He will take your male and female slaves, your choice ᵃ⁻young men,⁻ᵃ and your asses, and put them to work for him. ¹⁷ He will take a tenth part of your flocks, and you shall become his slaves. ¹⁸ The day will come when you cry out because of the king whom you yourselves have chosen; and the LORD will not answer you on that day."

¹⁹ But the people would not listen to Samuel's warning. "No," they said. "We must have a king over us, ²⁰ that we may be like all the other nations: Let our king rule over us and go out at our head and fight our battles." ²¹ When Samuel heard all that the people said, he reported it to the LORD. ²² And the LORD said to

ᵃ⁻ᵃ *Septuagint reads "cattle."*

Samuel, "Heed their demands and appoint a king for them."
Samuel then said to the men of Israel, "All of you go home."

9 There was a man of Benjamin whose name was Kish son of
Abiel son of Zeror son of Becorath son of Aphiah, a Benjaminite,
a man of substance. ² He had a son whose name was Saul, an
excellent young man; no one among the Israelites was hand-
somer than he; *a*he was a head taller*-a* than any of the people.

³ Once the asses of Saul's father Kish went astray, and Kish said
to his son Saul, "Take along one of the servants and go out and
look for the asses." ⁴ He passed into the hill country of Ephraim.
He crossed the district of Shalishah, but they did not find them.
They passed through the district of Shaalim, but they were not
there. They traversed the [entire] territory of Benjamin, and still
they did not find them. ⁵ When they reached the district of Zuph,
Saul said to the servant who was with him, "Let us turn back, or
my father will stop worrying about the asses and begin to worry
about us." ⁶ But he replied, "There is a man of God in that town,
and the man is highly esteemed; everything that he says comes
true. Let us go there; perhaps he will tell us about the errand on
which we set out." ⁷ "But if we go," Saul said to his servant, "what
can we bring the man? For the food in our bags is all gone, and
there is nothing we can bring to the man of God as a present.
What have we got?" ⁸ The servant answered Saul again, "I happen to have a quarter-shekel of silver. I can give that to the man
and he will tell us about our errand."—⁹ *b*Formerly in Israel,
when a man went to inquire of God, he would say, "Come, let us
go to the seer," for the prophet of today was formerly called a
seer.—¹⁰ Saul said to his servant, "A good idea; let us go." And
they went to the town where the man of God lived.

¹¹ As they were climbing the ascent to the town, they met some
girls coming out to draw water, and they asked them, "Is the seer
in town?" ¹² "Yes," they replied. "He is up there ahead of you.
*c*Hurry, for he has just come to town*-c* because the people have

---

ᵃ⁻ᵃ Lit. *"taller from his shoulders up."*
ᵇ *This verse explains the term "seer" in v. 11.*
ᶜ⁻ᶜ *Septuagint reads* 'atta kayyom ba *"He has just come." Emendation yields "Hurry, for
he has just now reached* (attah Kayom ba, *so Septuagint) the gate; cf. v. 18.*

a sacrifice at the shrine today. [13] As soon as you enter the town, you will find him before he goes up to the shrine to eat; the people will not eat until he comes; for he must first bless the sacrifice and only then will the guests eat. Go up at once, for you will find him right away." [14] So they went up to the town; and as they were entering the town,[d] Samuel came out toward them, on his way up to the shrine.

[15] Now the day before Saul came, the LORD had revealed the following to Samuel: [16] "At this time tomorrow, I will send a man to you from the territory of Benjamin, and you shall anoint him ruler of My people Israel. He will deliver My people from the hands of the Philistines; for I have taken note of [e]My people,[e] their outcry has come to Me."

[17] As soon as Samuel saw Saul, the LORD declared to him, "This is the man that I told you would govern My people." [18] Saul approached Samuel inside the gate and said to him, "Tell me, please, where is the house of the seer?" [19] And Samuel answered Saul, "I am the seer. Go up ahead of me to the shrine, for you shall eat with me today; and in the morning I will let you go, after telling you whatever may be on your mind. [20] As for your asses that strayed three days ago, do not concern yourself about them, for they have been found. And for whom is all Israel yearning, if not for you and all your ancestral house?" [21] Saul replied, "But I am only a Benjaminite, from the smallest of the tribes of Israel, and my clan is the least of all the clans of the tribe[f] of Benjamin! Why do you say such things to me?"

[22] Samuel took Saul and his servant and brought them into the hall, and gave them a place at the head of the guests, who numbered about thirty. [23] And Samuel said to the cook, "Bring the portion which I gave you and told you to set aside." [24] The cook lifted up the thigh and [g]what was on it,[g] and set it before Saul. And [Samuel] said, [h]"What has been reserved is set before you. Eat; it has been kept for you for this occasion, when I said I was inviting the people."[h] So Saul ate with Samuel that day. [25] They

---

[d] *Emendation yields "gate"; cf. v. 18.*
[e-e] *Septuagint and Targum read "the plight of My people"; cf. Exod. 3.7.*
[f] *Heb. plural.*
[g-g] *Meaning of Heb. uncertain. Emendation yields "the broad tail."*
[h-h] *Meaning of Heb. uncertain.*

then descended from the shrine to the town, and [i][Samuel] talked with Saul on the roof.

26 Early, at[i] the break of day, Samuel called to Saul on the roof. He said, "Get up, and I will send you off." Saul arose, and the two of them, Samuel and he, went outside. 27 As they were walking toward the end of the town, Samuel said to Saul, "Tell the servant to walk ahead of us"—and he walked ahead—"but you stop here a moment and I will make known to you the word of God."

10 Samuel took a flask of oil and poured some on Saul's[a] head and kissed him, and said, "The LORD herewith [b]anoints you ruler[b] over His own people. 2 When you leave me today, you will meet two men near the tomb of Rachel in the territory of Benjamin, [c]at Zelzah,[c] and they will tell you that the asses you set out to look for have been found, and that your father has stopped being concerned about the asses and is worrying about you, saying: 'What shall I do about my son?' 3 You shall pass on from there until you come to the terebinth of Tabor. There you will be met by three men making a pilgrimage to God at Bethel. One will be carrying three kids, another will be carrying three loaves of bread, and the third will be carrying a jar of wine. 4 They will greet you and offer you two loaves of bread, which you shall accept. 5 After that, you are to go on to [d]the Hill[d] of God, where the Philistine prefects reside. There, as you enter the town, you will encounter a band of prophets coming down from the shrine, preceded by lyres, timbrels, flutes, and harps, and they will be [e]speaking in ecstasy.[e] 6 The spirit of the LORD will grip you, and you will speak in ecstasy along with them; you will become another man. 7 And once these signs have happened

---

[i-i] *Meaning of Heb. uncertain. Septuagint reads "They spread a bed for Saul on the roof, and he lay down. At. . . ."*

[a] *Heb. "his."*

[b-b] *Septuagint and Vulgate read "anoints you ruler over His people Israel, and you will govern the people of the LORD and deliver them from the hands of their foes round about. And this is the sign for you that the LORD anoints you."*

[c-c] *Meaning of Heb. uncertain.*

[d-d] *Or "Gibeah."*

[e-e] *Others "prophesying"; cf. Num. 11.25 and note.*

to you, *f*-act when the occasion arises,*-f* for God is with you. [8] After that, you are to go down to Gilgal ahead of me, and I will come down to you to present burnt offerings and offer sacrifices of well-being.*f* Wait seven days until I come to you and instruct you what you are to do next."

[9] As [Saul] turned around to leave Samuel, God gave him another heart; and all those signs were fulfilled that same day. [10] And when they came there, to *d*-the Hill,*-d* he saw a band of prophets coming toward him. Thereupon the spirit of God gripped him, and he spoke in ecstasy among them. [11] When all who knew him previously saw him speaking in ecstasy together with the prophets, the people said to one another, "What's happened to *g*-the son of Kish?*-g* Is Saul too among the prophets?" [12] But another person there spoke up and said, "And who are their fathers?" Thus the proverb arose: "Is Saul too among the prophets?" [13] And when he stopped speaking in ecstasy, he entered the shrine.

[14] Saul's uncle asked him and his servant, "Where did you go?" "To look for the asses," he replied. "And when we saw that they were not to be found, we went to Samuel." [15] "Tell me," said Saul's uncle, "what did Samuel say to you?" [16] Saul answered his uncle, "He just told us that the asses had been found."But he did not tell him anything of what Samuel had said about the kingship.

[17] Samuel summoned the people to the LORD at Mizpah [18] and said to them, "Thus said the LORD, the God of Israel: 'I brought Israel out of Egypt, and I delivered you from the hands of the Egyptians and of all the kingdoms that oppressed you.' [19] But today you have rejected your God who delivered you from all your troubles and calamities. For you said, 'No,*h* set up a king over us!' Now station yourselves before the LORD, by your tribes and clans."

[20] Samuel brought forward each of the tribes of Israel, and the lot indicated the tribe of Benjamin. [21] Then Samuel brought forward the tribe of Benjamin by its clans, and the clan of the

---

f-f See *11. 5-15.*

g-g To refer to a person merely as "the son (ben) of . . ." is slighting; cf. *20. 27, 30, 31;* Isa. *7.4.*

h So many Heb. mss. and ancient versions. Other mss. and editions read "to Him."

Matrites was indicated; and then[i] Saul son of Kish was indicated. But when they looked for him, he was not to be found. [22] They inquired of the LORD again, [j-]"Has anyone else come here?"[-j] And the LORD replied, "Yes; he is hiding among the baggage." [23] So they ran over and brought him from there; and when he took his place among the people, he stood a head taller than all the people. [24] And Samuel said to the people, "Do you see the one whom the LORD has chosen? There is none like him among all the people." And all the people acclaimed him, shouting, "Long live the king!"

[25] Samuel expounded to the people the rules of the monarchy, and recorded them in a document which he deposited before the LORD. Samuel then sent the people back to their homes. [26] Saul also went home to Gibeah, accompanied by [k-]upstanding men[-k] whose hearts God had touched. [27] But some scoundrels said, "How can this fellow save us?" So they scorned him and brought him no gift. [l-]But he pretended not to mind.[-l]

11 Nahash the Ammonite marched up and besieged Jabesh-gilead. All the men of Jabesh-gilead said to Nahash, "Make a pact with us, and we will serve you." [2] But Nahash the Ammonite answered them, "I will make a pact with you on this condition, that everyone's right eye be gouged out; I will make this a humiliation for all Israel." [3] The elders of Jabesh said to him, "Give us seven days' respite, so that we may send messengers throughout the territory of Israel; if no one comes to our aid, we will surrender to you." [4] When the messengers came to Gibeah of Saul and gave this report in the hearing of the people, all the people broke into weeping.

[5] Saul was just coming from the field driving the cattle; and Saul asked, "Why are the people crying?" And they told him about the situation of the men of Jabesh. [6] When he heard these things, the spirit of God gripped Saul and his anger blazed up.

[i] *Septuagint reads "then he brought up the family of the Matrites by their men and. . . ."*
[j-j] *Septuagint reads "Has the man come here?"*
[k-k] *In contrast to "scoundrels" (v. 27); understanding Heb.* ḥayil *as the equivalent of* bene ḥayil, *as read by Septuagint and 4QSam^a.*
[l-l] *Lit. "But he was as one who holds his peace." Septuagint and 4QSam^a read "About a month later," connecting with what follows.*

⁷ He took a yoke of oxen and cut them into pieces, which he sent by messengers throughout the territory of Israel, with the warning, "Thus shall be done to the cattle of anyone who does not follow Saul and Samuel into battle!" Terror from the LORD fell upon the people, and they came out as one man. ⁸ [Saul] mustered them in Bezek, and the Israelites numbered 300,000, the men of Judah 30,000. ⁹ The messengers who had come were told, "Thus shall you speak to the men of Jabesh-gilead: Tomorrow, when the sun grows hot, you shall be saved." When the messengers came and told this to the men of Jabesh-gilead, they rejoiced. ¹⁰ The men of Jabesh then told [the Ammonites], "Tomorrow we will surrender to you, and you can do to us whatever you please."

¹¹ The next day, Saul divided the troops into three columns; at the morning watch they entered the camp and struck down the Ammonites until the day grew hot. The survivors scattered; no two were left together.

¹² The people then said to Samuel, "Who was it said, 'Shall Saul be king over us?' Hand the men over and we will put them to death!" ¹³ But Saul replied, "No man shall be put to death this day! For this day the LORD has brought victory to Israel."

¹⁴ Samuel said to the people, "Come, let us go to Gilgal and there inaugurate the monarchy." ¹⁵ So all the people went to Gilgal, and there at Gilgal they declared Saul king before the LORD. They offered sacrifices of well-being there before the LORD; and Saul and all the men of Israel held a great celebration there.

12 Then Samuel said to all Israel, "I have yielded to you in all you have asked of me and have set a king over you. ² Henceforth the king will be your leader.

"As for me, I have grown old and gray—but my sons are still with you—and I have been your leader from my youth to this day.

³ Here I am! Testify against me, in the presence of the LORD and in the presence of His anointed one: Whose ox have I taken, or whose ass have I taken? Whom have I defrauded or whom have I robbed? From whom have I taken a bribe ᵃ⁻to look the other way?⁻ᵃ I will return it to you." ⁴ They responded, "You have not defrauded us, and you have not robbed us, and you have taken nothing from anyone." ⁵ He said to them, "The LORD then is witness, and His anointed is witness, ᵇ⁻to your admission⁻ᵇ this day that you have found nothing in my possession." Theyᶜ responded, "He is!"

⁶ Samuel said to the people, ᵈ⁻"The LORD [is witness], He who appointed⁻ᵈ Moses and Aaron and who brought your fathers out of the land of Egypt. ⁷ Come, stand before the LORD while I cite against you all the kindnesses that the LORD has done to you and your fathers.

⁸ "When Jacob came to Egypt,ᵉ . . . your fathers cried out to the LORD, and the LORD sent Moses and Aaron, who brought your fathers out of Egypt and settled them in this place. ⁹ But they forgot the LORD their God; so He delivered them into the hands of Sisera the military commander of Hazor, into the hands of the Philistines, and into the hands of the king of Moab; and these made war upon them. ¹⁰ They cried to the LORD, 'We are guilty, for we have forsaken the LORD and worshiped the Baalim and the Ashtaroth. Oh, deliver us from our enemies and we will serve You.' ¹¹ And the Lord sent Jerubbaal and Bedanᶠ and Jephthah and Samuel, and delivered you from the enemies around you; and you dwelt in security. ¹² But when you saw that Nahash king of the Ammonites was advancing against you, you said to me, 'No, we must have a king reigning over us'—though the LORD your God is your King.

¹³ "Well, the LORD has set a king over you! Here is the king that you have chosen, that you have asked for.

¹⁴ "If you will revere the LORD, worship Him, and obey Him, and will not flout the LORD's command, if both you and the king

ᵃ⁻ᵃ *Septuagint reads "or a pair of sandals? (Cf. Amos 2.6) Testify against me."*
ᵇ⁻ᵇ *Lit. "against you."*
ᶜ *Heb. "he."*
ᵈ⁻ᵈ *Meaning of Heb. uncertain.*
ᵉ *Septuagint adds "the Egyptians oppressed them."*
ᶠ *Septuagint "Barak."*

who reigns over you will follow the LORD your God, [well and good]. [15] But if you do not obey the LORD and you flout the LORD's command, the hand of the LORD will strike you $^{d-}$as it did your fathers.$^{-d}$

[16] "Now stand by and see the marvelous thing that the LORD will do before your eyes. [17] It is the season of the wheat harvest.^{g} I will pray to the LORD and He will send thunder and rain; then you will take thought and realize what a wicked thing you did in the sight of the LORD when you asked for a king."

[18] Samuel prayed to the LORD, and the LORD sent thunder and rain that day, and the people stood in awe of the LORD and of Samuel. [19] The people all said to Samuel, "Intercede for your servants with the LORD your God that we may not die, for we have added to all our sins the wickedness of asking for a king." [20] But Samuel said to the people, "Have no fear. You have, indeed, done all those wicked things. Do not, however, turn away from the LORD your God, but serve the LORD with all your heart. [21] Do not turn away to follow worthless things, which can neither profit nor save but are worthless. [22] For the sake of His great name, the LORD will never abandon His people, seeing that the LORD undertook to make you His people.

[23] "As for me, far be it from me to sin against the LORD and refrain from praying for you; and I will continue to instruct you in the practice of what is good and right. [24] Above all, you must revere the LORD and serve Him faithfully with all your heart; and consider how grandly He has dealt with you. [25] For if you persist in your wrongdoing, both you and your king shall be swept away."

13 Saul was . . .^{a} years old when he became king, and he reigned over Israel two years. [2] Saul picked 3,000 Israelites, of whom 2,000 were with Saul in Michmas^b and in the hill country of Bethel, and 1,000 with Jonathan in Gibeah of Benjamin; the rest of the troops he sent back to their homes. [3] Jonathan struck

---

^{g} *When thunderstorms do not occur in the land of Israel.*

^{a} *The number is lacking in the Heb. text; also, the precise context of the "two years" is uncertain. The verse is lacking in the Septuagint.*

^{b} *So in oldest mss.; other mss. and editions read "Michmash" throughout the chapter.*

down the Philistine prefect in Geba;[c] and the Philistines heard about it. [d-]Saul had the ram's horn sounded throughout the land, saying, "Let the Hebrews hear."[-d]

⁴ When all Israel heard that Saul had struck down the Philistine prefect, and that Israel had [e-]incurred the wrath of[-e] the Philistines, all the people rallied to Saul at Gilgal. ⁵ The Philistines, in turn, gathered to attack Israel: 30,000[f] chariots and 6,000 horsemen, and troops as numerous as the sands of the seashore. They marched up and encamped at Michmas, east of Beth-aven.

⁶ [d-]When the men of Israel saw that they were in trouble—for the troops were hard pressed—the people hid in caves, among thorns, among rocks, in tunnels, and in cisterns. ⁷ Some Hebrews crossed the Jordan, [to] the territory of Gad and Gilead. Saul was still at Gilgal, and the rest of the people rallied to him in alarm.[-d]

⁸ He waited seven days, the time that Samuel [had set].[g] But when Samuel failed to come to Gilgal, and the people began to scatter, ⁹ Saul said, "Bring me the burnt offering and the sacrifice of well-being"; and he presented the burnt offering. ¹⁰ He had just finished presenting the burnt offering when Samuel arrived; and Saul went out to meet him and welcome him. ¹¹ But Samuel said, "What have you done?" Saul replied, "I saw the people leaving me and scattering; you had not come at the appointed time, and the Philistines had gathered at Michmas. ¹² I thought the Philistines would march down against me at Gilgal before I had entreated the LORD, so I [d-]forced myself[-d] to present the burnt offering." ¹³ Samuel answered Saul, [h-]"You acted foolishly in not keeping the commandments that the LORD your God laid upon you! Otherwise[-h] the LORD would have established your dynasty over Israel forever. ¹⁴ But now your dynasty will not endure. The LORD will seek out a man after His own heart, and the LORD will appoint him ruler over His people, because you did not abide by what the LORD had commanded you."

---

[c] *Apparently identical with Gibeah in v. 2.*
[d-d] *Meaning of Heb. uncertain.*
[e-e] *Lit. "became malodorous to."*
[f] *Septuagint and other versions read "three thousand."*
[g] *So some Heb. mss.; other mss., Septuagint, and Targum read "said." Cf. 10.8.*
[h-h] *Change of vocalization yields, "You acted foolishly. If you had kept the commandment the* LORD *your God laid upon you. . . ."*

¹⁵ ⁱ⁻Samuel arose and went up from Gilgal⁻ⁱ to Gibeahʲ of Benjamin. Saul numbered the troops who remained with him—about 600 strong. ¹⁶ Saul and his son Jonathan, and the troops who remained with them, stayed in Geba of Benjamin, while the Philistines were encamped at Michmas. ¹⁷ The raiders came out of the Philistine camp in three columns: One column headed for the Ophrah road that leads to the district of Shual, ¹⁸ another column headed for the Beth-horon road, and the third column headed for the borderᵏ road that overlooks the valley of Zeboim toward the desert.

¹⁹ No smith was to be found in all the land of Israel, for the Philistines were afraid that the Hebrews would make swords or spears. ²⁰ So all the Israelites had to go down to the Philistines to have their plowshares, their mattocks, axes, and coltersˡ sharpened. ²¹ ᵐ The charge for sharpening was a *pim*ⁿ for plowshares, mattocks, three-pronged forks, and axes, and for setting the goads. ²² Thus on the day of the battle, no sword or spear was to be found in the possession of any of the troops with Saul and Jonathan; only Saul and Jonathan had them.

²³ Now the Philistine garrison had marched out to the pass of Michmas.

14 One day, Jonathan son of Saul said to the attendant who carried his arms, "Come, let us cross over to the Philistine garrison on the other side"; but he did not tell his father.— ² Now Saul was staying on the outskirts of Gibeah,ᵃ under the pomegranate tree at Migron, and the troops with him numbered about 600. ³ Ahijah son of Ahitub brother of Ichabod son of Phinehas son of Eli, the priest of the LORD at Shiloh, was there bearing an ephod.—The troops did not know that Jonathan had gone. ⁴ ᵇ⁻At the crossing⁻ᵇ by which Jonathan sought to reach the Philistine

ⁱ⁻ⁱ *Septuagint reads here, "Samuel arose and left Gilgal and went his way. The rest of the people followed Saul to meet the soldiers, and they went from Gilgal."*
ʲ *Sometimes called Geba; cf. vv. 3, 16; 14.5.*
ᵏ *Septuagint reads "Geba."*
ˡ *Meaning of Heb. uncertain. Septuagint reads "sickle."*
ᵐ *Meaning of several terms in this verse uncertain.*
ⁿ *I.e. two-thirds of a shekel.*

ᵃ *See note j at 13.15.*
ᵇ⁻ᵇ *Meaning of Heb. uncertain.*

garrison, there was a rocky crag on one side, and another rocky crag on the other, the one called Bozez and the other Seneh. ⁵ One crag was located on the north, near Michmas, and the other on the south, near Geba.

⁶ Jonathan said to the attendant who carried his arms, "Come, let us cross over to the outpost of those uncircumcised fellows. Perhaps the LORD will act in our behalf, for nothing prevents the LORD from winning a victory by many or by few." ⁷ His arms-bearer answered him, "Do whatever ᶜ⁻you like. You go first,⁻ᶜ I am ᵈ⁻with you, whatever you decide."⁻ᵈ ⁸ Jonathan said, "We'll cross over to those men and let them see us. ⁹ If they say to us, 'Wait until we get to you,' then we'll stay where we are, and not go up to them. ¹⁰ But if they say, 'Come up to us,' then we will go up, for the LORD is delivering them into our hands. That shall be our sign." ¹¹ They both showed themselves to the Philistine outpost and the Philistines said, "Look, some Hebrews are coming out of the holes where they have been hiding." ¹² The men of the outpost shouted to Jonathan and his arms-bearer, "Come up to us, and we'll teach you a lesson." Then Jonathan said to his arms-bearer, "Follow me, for the LORD will deliver them into the hands of Israel." ¹³ And Jonathan clambered up on his hands and feet, his arms-bearer behind him; [the Philistines] fell before Jonathan, and his arms-bearer finished them off behind him. ¹⁴ The initial attack that Jonathan and his arms-bearer made accounted for some twenty men, ᵇ⁻within a space about half a furrow long [in] an acre of land.⁻ᵇ ¹⁵ Terror broke out among all the troops both in the camp [and] in the field; the outposts and the raiders were also terrified. The very earth quaked, and a terror from God ensued.

¹⁶ Saul's scouts in Gibeah of Benjamin saw that the multitude was ᵉ⁻scattering in all directions.⁻ᵉ ¹⁷ And Saul said to the troops with him, "Take a count and see who has left us." They took a count and found that Jonathan and his arms-bearer were missing. ¹⁸ Thereupon Saul said to Ahijah, "Bring the Ark ᶠ of God here";

ᶜ⁻ᶜ Lit. "is in your heart. Incline yourself." Septuagint reads "your heart inclines to."
ᵈ⁻ᵈ Lit. "with you, according to your heart." Septuagint reads "with you; my heart is like your heart."
ᵉ⁻ᵉ Lit. "shaken and going thither." Meaning of Heb. uncertain.
ᶠ Septuagint reads "ephod," and cf. vv. 3; 23.9; 30.7.

for the Ark^f of God was at the time among^g the Israelites. ¹⁹ But while Saul was speaking to the priest, the confusion in the Philistine camp kept increasing; and Saul said to the priest, "Withdraw your hand." ²⁰ Saul and the troops with him assembled and rushed into battle; they found [the Philistines] in very great confusion, every man's sword turned against his fellow. ²¹ ^{b-}And the Hebrews who had previously sided with the Philistines, who had come up with them in the army [from] round about—they too joined the Israelites^{-b} who were with Saul and Jonathan. ²² When all the men of Israel who were hiding in the hill country of Ephraim heard that the Philistines were fleeing, they too pursued them in battle. ²³ Thus the LORD brought victory to Israel that day.

The fighting passed beyond Beth-aven. ²⁴ ^{h-}The men of Israel were distressed^{-h} that day. For Saul had laid an oath upon the troops: "Cursed be the man who eats any food before night falls and I take revenge on my enemies." So none of the troops ate anything. ²⁵ Everybody came to a ⁱ⁻stack of beehives⁻ⁱ where some honey had spilled on the ground. ²⁶ When the troops came to the beehivesⁱ and found the flow of honey there, no one put^b his hand to his mouth, for the troops feared the oath. ²⁷ Jonathan, however, had not heard his father adjure the troops. So he put out the stick he had with him, dipped it into the beehive of honey, and brought his hand back to his mouth; and his eyes lit up. ²⁸ At this one of the soldiers spoke up, "Your father adjured the troops: 'Cursed be the man who eats anything this day.' And so the troops are faint." ²⁹ Jonathan answered, "My father has brought trouble on the people. See for yourselves how my eyes lit up when I tasted that bit of honey. ³⁰ If only the troops had eaten today of spoil captured from the enemy, the defeat of the Philistines would have been greater still!"

³¹ They struck down the Philistines that day from Michmas to Aijalon, and the troops were famished. ³² The troops pounced on the spoil; they took the sheep and cows and calves and

---

^g *Heb. "and."*

^{h-h} *Meaning of Heb. uncertain. Septuagint reads "And all the troops, about 10,000 men, were with Saul; and the battle spread into the hill country of Ephraim. Now Saul committed a rash act."*

ⁱ⁻ⁱ *Meaning of Heb. uncertain; cf. Song of Songs 5.1.*

slaughtered them on the ground, and the troops ate with the blood.[j] [33] When it was reported to Saul that the troops were sinning against the Lord, eating with the blood, he said, "You have acted faithlessly. Roll a large stone over to me today."[k] [34] And Saul ordered, "Spread out among the troops and tell them that everyone must bring me his ox or his sheep and slaughter it here, and then eat. You must not sin against the Lord and eat with the blood." Everyone of the troops brought [l]his own ox with him[-l] that night and slaughtered it there. [35] Thus Saul set up an altar to the Lord; it was the first altar he erected to the Lord.

[36] Saul said, "Let us go down after the Philistines by night and plunder among them until the light of morning; and let us not leave a single survivor among them." "Do whatever you please," they replied. But the priest said, "Let us approach God here." [37] So Saul inquired of God, "Shall I go down after the Philistines? Will You deliver them into the hands of Israel?" But this time He did not respond to him. [38] Then Saul said, "Come forward, all chief officers of the troops, and find out how this guilt was incurred today. [39] For as the Lord lives who brings victory to Israel, even if it was through my son Jonathan, he shall be put to death!" Not one soldier answered him. [40] And he said to all the Israelites, "You stand on one side, and my son Jonathan and I shall stand on the other." The troops said to Saul, "Do as you please." [41] Saul then said to the Lord, the God of Israel, [m-]"Show Thammim."[-m] Jonathan and Saul were indicated by lot, and the troops were cleared. [42] And Saul said, "Cast the lots between my son and me"; and Jonathan was indicated.

[43] Saul said to Jonathan, "Tell me, what have you done?" And Jonathan told him, "I only tasted a bit of honey with the tip of the stick in my hand. I am ready to die." [44] Saul said, "Thus and more may God do:[n] You shall be put to death, Jonathan!" [45] But

[j] *I.e. without the proper rites.*
[k] *Septuagint reads "here."*
[l-l] *Septuagint reads "whatever he had in his possession."*
[m-m] *Meaning of Heb. uncertain. Septuagint reads "Why have You not responded to Your servant today? If this iniquity was due to my son Jonathan or to me, O Lord, God of Israel, show Urim; and if You say it was due to Your people Israel, show Thummim."*
[n] *Many mss. and Septuagint add "to me."*

the troops said to Saul, "Shall Jonathan die, after bringing this great victory to Israel? Never! As the LORD lives, not a hair of his head shall fall to the ground! For he brought this day to pass with the help of God." Thus the troops saved Jonathan and he did not die. ⁴⁶ Saul broke off his pursuit of the Philistines, and the Philistines returned to their homes.

⁴⁷ After Saul had secured his kingship over Israel, he waged war on every side against all his enemies: against the Moabites, Ammonites, Edomites, the Philistines, and the kings⁰ of Zobah; and wherever he turned he worsted [them]. ⁴⁸ He was triumphant, defeating the Amalekites and saving Israel from those who plundered it.

⁴⁹ Saul's sons were: Jonathan, Ishvi,ᵖ and Malchishua; and the names of his two daughters were Merab, the older, and Michal, the younger. ⁵⁰ The name of Saul's wife was Ahinoam daughter of Ahimaaz; and the name of his army commander was Abinerᑫ son of Saul's uncle Ner. ⁵¹ Kish, Saul's father, and Ner, Abner's father, were sons of Abiel.

⁵² There was bitter war against the Philistines all the days of Saul; and whenever Saul noticed any stalwart man or warrior, he would take him into his service.

15 Samuel said to Saul, "I am the one the LORD sent to anoint you king over His people Israel. Therefore, listen to the LORD's command!

² "Thus said the LORD of Hosts: I am exacting the penalty for what Amalek did to Israel, for the assault he made upon them on the road, on their way up from Egypt. ³ Now go, attack Amalek, and proscribeᵃ all that belongs to him. Spare no one, but kill alike men and women, infants and sucklings, oxen and sheep, camels and asses!"

⁴ Saul mustered the troops and enrolled them at Telaim: 200,000 men on foot, and 10,000 men of Judah. ⁵ Then Saul advanced as far as the city of Amalek and ᵇlay in waitᵇ in the wadi.

⁰ *Septuagint and 4QSamᵃ read "king."*
ᵖ *The same as Ishbosheth (II Sam. 2.8) and Eshbaal (I Chron. 8.33).*
ᑫ *Usually "Abner."*

ᵃ *See note at Josh. 6.18.*
ᵇ⁻ᵇ *Meaning of Heb. uncertain.*

130

6 Saul said to the Kenites, "Come, withdraw at once from among the Amalekites, that I may not destroy you along with them; for you showed kindness to all the Israelites when they left Egypt." So the Kenites withdrew from among the Amalekites.

7 Saul destroyed Amalek from Havilah all the way to Shur, which is close to Egypt, 8 and he captured King Agag of Amalek alive. He proscribed all the people, putting them to the sword; 9 but Saul and the troops spared Agag and the best of the sheep, the oxen, the second born,*c* the lambs, and all else that was of value. They would not proscribe them; they proscribed only *b-*what was cheap and worthless.*-b*

10 The word of the LORD then came to Samuel: 11 "I regret that I made Saul king, for he has turned away from Me and has not carried out My commands." Samuel was distressed and he entreated the LORD all night long. 12 Early in the morning Samuel went to meet Saul. Samuel was told, "Saul went to Carmel, where he erected a monument for himself; then he left and went on down to Gilgal."

13 When Samuel came to Saul, Saul said to him, "Blessed are you of the LORD! I have fulfilled the LORD's command." 14 "Then what," demanded Samuel, "is this bleating of sheep in my ears, and the lowing of oxen that I hear?" 15 Saul answered, "They were brought from the Amalekites, for the troops spared the choicest of the sheep and oxen for sacrificing to the LORD your God. And we proscribed the rest." 16 Samuel said to Saul, "Stop! Let me tell you what the LORD said to me last night!" "Speak," he replied. 17 And Samuel said, "You may look small to yourself, but you are the head of the tribes of Israel. The LORD anointed you king over Israel, 18 and the LORD sent you on a mission, saying, 'Go and proscribe the sinful Amalekites; make war on them until you have exterminated them.' 19 Why did you disobey the LORD and swoop down on the spoil *d-*in defiance of the LORD's will?"*-d* 20 Saul said to Samuel, "But I did obey the LORD! I performed the mission on which the LORD sent me: I captured King Agag of Amalek, and I proscribed Amalek, 21 and the troops took

c Targum and Syriac read "fatlings."
d-d Lit. "and do what was evil in the sight of the LORD."

from the spoil some sheep and oxen—the best of what had been
proscribed—to sacrifice to the LORD your God at Gilgal." [22] But
Samuel said:

> "Does the LORD delight in burnt offerings and sacrifices
> As much as in obedience to the LORD's command?
> Surely, obedience is better than sacrifice,
> Compliance than the fat of rams.
> [23] For rebellion is like the sin of divination,
> Defiance, like the iniquity of teraphim.[e]
> Because you rejected the LORD's command,
> He has rejected you as king."

[24] Saul said to Samuel, "I did wrong to transgress the LORD's
command and your instructions; but I was afraid of the troops
and I yielded to them. [25] Please, forgive my offense and come
back with me, and I will bow low to the LORD." [26] But Samuel said
to Saul, "I will not go back with you; for you have rejected the
LORD's command, and the LORD has rejected you as king over
Israel."

[27] As Samuel turned to leave, Saul seized the corner of his robe,
and it tore. [28] And Samuel said to him, "The LORD has this day
torn the kingship over Israel away from you and has given it to
another who is worthier than you. [29] Moreover, the Glory[b] of
Israel does not deceive or change His mind, for He is not human
that He should change His mind." [30] But [Saul] pleaded, "I did
wrong. Please, honor me in the presence of the elders of my
people and in the presence of Israel, and come back with me until
I have bowed low to the LORD your God." [31] So Samuel followed
Saul back, and Saul bowed low to the LORD.

[32] Samuel said, "Bring forward to me King Agag of Amalek."
Agag approached him [f]with faltering steps;[f] and Agag said, "Ah,
bitter death is at hand!"[b]

[33] Samuel said:

> "As your sword has bereaved women,
> So shall your mother be bereaved among women."

And Samuel [b]cut Agag down[b] before the LORD at Gilgal.

---

[e] *Idols consulted for oracles; see Ezek. 21.26; Zech. 10.2.*
[f-f] *From root* ma'ad, *"to falter"; cf. Septuagint.*

³⁴ Samuel then departed for Ramah, and Saul went up to his home at Gibeah of Saul.

³⁵ Samuel never saw Saul again to the day of his death. But Samuel grieved over Saul, because the LORD regretted that He had made Saul king over Israel. ¹ And the LORD said to

16 Samuel, "How long will you grieve over Saul, since I have rejected him as king over Israel? Fill your horn with oil and set out; I am sending you to Jesse the Bethlehemite, for I have decided on one of his sons to be king." ² Samuel replied, "How can I go? If Saul hears of it, he will kill me." The LORD answered, "Take a heifer with you, and say, 'I have come to sacrifice to the LORD.' ³ Invite Jesse to the sacrificial feast, and then I will make known to you what you shall do; you shall anoint for Me the one I point out to you." ⁴ Samuel did what the LORD commanded. When he came to Bethlehem, the elders of the city went out in alarm to meet him and said, "Do you come on a peaceful errand?" ⁵ "Yes," he replied, "I have come to sacrifice to the LORD. Purify yourselves and join me in the sacrificial feast." He also instructed Jesse and his sons to purify themselves and invited them to the sacrificial feast.

⁶ When they arrived and he saw Eliab, he thought: "Surely the LORD's anointed stands before Him." ⁷ But the LORD said to Samuel, "Pay no attention to his appearance or his stature, for I have rejected him. For not as man sees [does the LORD see];ᵃ man sees only what is visible, but the LORD sees into the heart." ⁸ Then Jesse called Abinadab and had him pass before Samuel; but he said, "The LORD has not chosen this one either." ⁹ Next Jesse presented Shammah; and again he said, "The LORD has not chosen this one either." ¹⁰ Thus Jesse presented seven of his sons before Samuel, and Samuel said to Jesse, "The LORD has not chosen any of these."

¹¹ Then Samuel asked Jesse, "Are these all the boys you have?" He replied, "There is still the youngest; he is tending the flock." And Samuel said to Jesse, "Send someone to bring him, for we will not ᵇ⁻sit down to eat⁻ᵇ until he gets here." ¹² So they sent and

---

ᵃ *These words are preserved in the Septuagint.*
ᵇ⁻ᵇ *Meaning of Heb. uncertain.*

brought him. He was [b]ruddy cheeked, bright-eyed,[-b] and hand-some. And the LORD said, "Rise and anoint him, for this is the one." [13] Samuel took the horn of oil and anointed him in the presence of his brothers; and the spirit of the LORD gripped David from that day on. Samuel then set out for Ramah.

[14] Now the spirit of the LORD had departed from Saul, and an evil spirit from the LORD began to terrify him. [15] Saul's courtiers said to him, "An evil spirit of God is terrifying you. [16] Let our lord give the order [and] the courtiers in attendance on you will look for someone who is skilled at playing the lyre; whenever the evil spirit of God comes over you, he will play it[b] and you will feel better." [17] So Saul said to his courtiers, "Find me someone who can play well and bring him to me." [18] One of the attendants spoke up, "I have observed a son of Jesse the Bethlehemite who is skilled in music; he is a stalwart fellow and a warrior, sensible in speech, and handsome in appearance, and the LORD is with him." [19] Whereupon Saul sent messengers to Jesse to say, "Send me your son David, who is with the flock." [20] Jesse took [b]an ass [laden with][-b] bread, a skin of wine, and a kid, and sent them to Saul by his son David. [21] So David came to Saul and entered his service; [Saul] took a strong liking to him and made him one of his arms-bearers. [22] Saul sent word to Jesse, "Let David remain in my service, for I am pleased with him." [23] Whenever the [evil] spirit of God came upon Saul, David would take the lyre and play it;[b] Saul would find relief and feel better, and the evil spirit would leave him.

17 The Philistines assembled their forces for battle; they massed at Socoh of Judah, and encamped at Ephes-dammim, between Socoh and Azekah. [2] Saul and the men of Israel massed and encamped in the valley of Elah. They drew up their line of battle against the Philistines, [3] with the Philistines stationed on one hill and Israel stationed on the opposite hill, the ravine was between them. [4] A champion[a] of the Philistine forces stepped

---

[a] Lit. "the man of the space between," i.e. between the armies.

forward; his name was Goliath of Gath, and he was six cubits and a span tall. [5] He had a bronze helmet on his head, and wore a breastplate of scale armor, a bronze breastplate weighing five thousand shekels. [6] He had bronze greaves on his legs, and a bronze javelin [slung] from his shoulders. [7] The shaft of his spear was like a weaver's bar, and the iron head of his spear weighed six hundred shekels; and the shield-bearer marched in front of him.

[8] He stopped and called out to the ranks of Israel and he said to them, "Why should you come out to engage in battle? I am the Philistine [champion], and you are Saul's servants. Choose[b] one of your men and let him come down against me. [9] If he bests me in combat and kills me, we will become your slaves; but if I best him and kill him, you shall be our slaves and serve us." [10] And the Philistine ended, "I herewith defy the ranks of Israel. Get me a man and let's fight it out!" [11] When Saul and all Israel heard these words of the Philistine, they were dismayed and terror stricken.

[12] David was the son of a certain Ephrathite of Bethlehem in Judah whose name was Jesse. He had eight sons, and in the days of Saul the man was already old, advanced in years.[b] [13] The three oldest sons of Jesse had left and gone with Saul to the war. The names of his three sons who had gone to the war were Eliab the firstborn, the next Abinadab, and the third Shammah; [14] and David was the youngest. The three oldest had followed Saul, [15] and David would go back and forth from attending on Saul to shepherd his father's flock at Bethlehem.

[16] The Philistine stepped forward morning and evening and took his stand for forty days.

[17] Jesse said to his son David, "Take an ephah of this parched corn and these ten loaves of bread for your brothers, and carry them quickly to your brothers in camp. [18] Take these ten cheeses[b] to the captain of their thousand. Find out how your brothers are and bring some token[b] from them." [19] Saul and [c]the brothers[c] and all the men of Israel were in the valley of Elah, in the war against the Philistines.

[b] *Meaning of Heb. uncertain.*
[c-c] *Heb. "they."*

²⁰ Early next morning, David left someone in charge of the flock, took [the provisions], and set out, as his father Jesse had instructed him. He reached the barricade[b] as the army was going out to the battle lines shouting the war cry. ²¹ Israel and the Philistines drew up their battle lines opposite each other. ²² David left his baggage with the man in charge of the baggage and ran toward the battle line and went to greet his brothers. ²³ While he was talking to them, the champion, whose name was Goliath, the Philistine of Gath, stepped forward from the Philistine ranks and spoke the same words as before; and David heard him.

²⁴ When the men of Israel saw the man, they fled in terror. ²⁵ And the men of Israel were saying [among themselves], "Do you see that man coming out? He comes out to defy Israel! The man who kills him will be rewarded by the king with great riches; he will also give him his daughter in marriage and grant exemption[d] to his father's house in Israel." ²⁶ David asked the men standing near him, "What will be done for the man who kills that Philistine and removes the disgrace from Israel? Who is that uncircumcised Philistine that he dares defy the ranks of the living God?" ²⁷ The troops told him in the same words what would be done for the man who killed him.

²⁸ When Eliab, his oldest brother, heard him speaking to the men, Eliab became angry with David and said, "Why did you come down here, and with whom did you leave those few sheep in the wilderness? I know your impudence and your impertinence:[e] you came down to watch the fighting!" ²⁹ But David replied, "What have I done now? I was only asking!" ³⁰ And he turned away from him toward someone else; he asked the same question, and the troops gave him the same answer as before.

³¹ The things David said were overheard and were reported to Saul, who had him brought over. ³² David said to Saul, "Let ʲno man'sʲ courage fail him. Your servant will go and fight that Philistine!" ³³ But Saul said to David, "You cannot go to that Philistine and fight him; you are only a boy, and he has been a

---

[d] *I.e. freedom from royal levies.*
[e] *Lit. "badness of heart."*
[f-f] *Septuagint reads "not my lord's."*

warrior from his youth!" [34] David replied to Saul, "Your servant
has been tending his father's sheep, and if a lion or[b] a bear came
and carried off an animal from the flock, [35] I would go after it and
fight it and rescue it from its mouth. And if it attacked me, I would
seize it by the beard and strike it down and kill it. [36] Your servant
has killed both lion and bear; and that uncircumcised Philistine
shall end up like one of them, for he has defied the ranks of the
living God. [37] The LORD," David went on, "who saved me from
lion and bear will also save me from that Philistine." "Then go,"
Saul said to David, "and may the LORD be with you!"

[38] Saul clothed David in his own garment; he placed a bronze
helmet on his head and fastened [g-]a breastplate on him.[-g] [39] David
girded his sword over his garment. Then he [h-]tried to walk; but[-h]
he was not used to it. And David said to Saul, "I cannot walk in
these, for I am not used to them." So David took them off.
[40] He took his stick, picked a few[i] smooth stones from the wadi,
put them in the pocket[b] of his shepherd's bag and, sling in hand,
he went toward the Philistine.

[41] The Philistine, meanwhile, was coming closer to David,
preceded by his shield-bearer. [42] When the Philistine caught sight
of David, he scorned him, for he was but a boy, ruddy and handsome. [43] And the Philistine called out to David, "Am I a dog that
you come against me with sticks?" The Philistine cursed David by
his gods; [44] and the Philistine said to David, "Come here, and I
will give your flesh to the birds of the sky and the beasts of the
field."

[45] David replied to the Philistine, "You come against me with
sword and spear and javelin; but I come against you in the name
of the LORD of Hosts, the God of the ranks of Israel, whom you
have defied. [46] This very day the LORD will deliver you into my
hands. I will kill you and cut off your head; and I will give [j-]the
carcasses[-j] of the Philistine camp to the birds of the sky and the
beasts of the earth. All the earth shall know that there is a God
in[k] Israel. [47] And this whole assembly shall know that the LORD

g-g *Heb. "clothed him in a breastplate" (cf. v.5), because a breastplate was combined with
a leather jerkin.*
h-h *Septuagint reads "was unable to walk, for. . . ."*
i *Lit. "five."*
j-j *Septuagint reads "your carcass and the carcasses."*
k *So many Heb. mss. and ancient versions; other mss. and the editions read "to."*

can give victory without sword or spear. For the battle is the LORD's, and He will deliver you into our hands."

⁴⁸ When the Philistine began to advance toward him again, David quickly ran up to the battle line to face the Philistine. ⁴⁹ David put his hand into the bag; he took out a stone and slung it. It struck the Philistine in the forehead; the stone sank into his forehead, and he fell face down on the ground. ⁵⁰ Thus David bested the Philistine with sling and stone; he struck him down and killed him. David had no sword; ⁵¹ so David ran up and stood over the Philistine, grasped his sword and pulled it from its sheath; and with it he dispatched him and cut off his head.

When the Philistines saw that their warrior was dead, they ran. ⁵² The men of Israel and Judah rose up with a war cry and they pursued the Philistines all the way to Gai*ˡ* and up to the gates of Ekron; the Philistines fell mortally wounded along the road to Shaarim up to Gath and Ekron. ⁵³ Then the Israelites returned from chasing the Philistines and looted their camp.

⁵⁴ David took the head of the Philistine and brought it to Jerusalem;ᵐ and he put his weapons in his own tent.

⁵⁵ When Saul saw David going out to assault the Philistine, he asked his army commander Abner, "Whose son is that boy, Abner?" And Abner replied, "By your life, Your Majesty, I do not know." ⁵⁶ "Then find out whose son that young fellow is," the king ordered. ⁵⁷ So when David returned after killing the Philistine, Abner took him and brought him to Saul, with the head of the Philistine still in his hand. ⁵⁸ Saul said to him, "Whose son are you, my boy?" And David answered, "The son of your servant Jesse the Bethlehemite."

18 When [David] finished speaking with Saul, Jonathan's soul became bound up with the soul of David; Jonathan loved David as himself. ² Saul took him [into his service] that day and would not let him return to his father's house.—³ Jonathan and David made a pact, because [Jonathan] loved him as himself. ⁴ Jonathan

---

ˡ *Septuagint reads "Gath"; cf. end of verse.*
ᵐ *I.e. after David's capture of Jerusalem (II Sam. 5).*

took off the cloak and tunic he was wearing and gave them to David, together with his sword, bow, and belt. [5] David went out [with the troops], and he was successful in every mission on which Saul sent him, and Saul put him in command of all the soldiers; this pleased all the troops and Saul's courtiers as well. [6] When the [troops] came home [and] David returned from killing the Philistine, *a*-the women of all the towns of Israel came out singing and dancing to greet King Saul*-a* with timbrels, shouting, and sistrums.*b* [7] The women sang as they danced, and they chanted:

Saul has slain his thousands;

David, his tens of thousands!

[8] Saul was much distressed and greatly vexed about the matter. For he said, "To David they have given tens of thousands, and to me they have given thousands. All that he lacks is the kingship!" [9] From that day on Saul kept a jealous eye on David. [10] The next day an evil spirit of God gripped Saul and he began to rave in the house, while David was playing [the lyre], as he did daily. Saul had a spear in his hand, [11] and Saul threw*c* the spear, thinking to pin David to the wall. But David eluded him twice. [12] Saul was afraid of David, for the LORD was with him and had turned away from Saul. [13] So Saul removed him from his presence and appointed him chief of a thousand, *d*-to march at the head of the troops.*-d* [14] David was successful in all his undertakings, for the LORD was with him; [15] and when Saul saw that he was successful, he dreaded him. [16] All Israel and Judah loved David, for he marched at their head.

[17] Saul said to David, "Here is my older daughter Merab, I will give her to you in marriage; in return, you be my warrior and fight the battles of the LORD." Saul thought: "Let not my hand strike him; let the hand of the Philistines strike him." [18] David replied to Saul, "Who am I and *e*-what is my life*-e*—my father's family in Israel—that I should become Your Majesty's son-in-law?" [19] But at the time that Merab, daughter of Saul, should have been given to David, she was given in marriage to Adriel the Meholathite.

---

a-a *Meaning of Heb. uncertain; Septuagint reads "the dancing women came out to meet David from all the towns of Israel."*
b *Meaning of Heb. uncertain.*
c *Change of vocalization yields "raised."*
d-d *Lit. "and he went out and came in before the troops."*
e-e *Meaning of Heb. uncertain. Change of vocalization yields "who are my kin."*

²⁰ Now Michal daughter of Saul had fallen in love with David; and when this was reported to Saul, he was pleased. ²¹ Saul thought: "I will give her to him, and she can serve as a snare for him, so that the Philistines may kill him." So Saul said to David, *ᵇ*"You can become my son-in-law even now through the second one."*⁻ᵇ* ²² And Saul instructed his courtiers to say to David privately, "The king is fond of you and all his courtiers like you. So why not become the king's son-in-law?" ²³ When the king's courtiers repeated these words to David, David replied, "Do you think that becoming the son-in-law of a king is a small matter, when I am but a poor man of no consequence?" ²⁴ Saul's courtiers reported to him, "This is what David answered." ²⁵ And Saul said, "Say this to David: 'The king desires no other bride price than the foreskins of a hundred Philistines, as vengeance on the king's enemies.' "—Saul intended to bring about David's death at the hands of the Philistines.—²⁶ When his courtiers told this to David, David was pleased with the idea of becoming the king's son-in-law. *ᵇ*Before the time had expired,*⁻ᵇ* ²⁷ David went out with his men and killed two hundred*ᶠ* Philistines; David brought their foreskins and *ᵇ*they were counted out*⁻ᵇ* for the king, that he might become the king's son-in-law. Saul then gave him his daughter Michal in marriage. ²⁸ When Saul realized that the LORD was with David *ᵍ⁻*and that Michal daughter of Saul loved him,*⁻ᵍ* ²⁹ Saul grew still more afraid of David; and Saul was David's enemy ever after.

³⁰ The Philistine chiefs marched out [to battle]; and every time they marched out, David was more successful than all the other officers of Saul. His reputation soared.

19 Saul urged his son Jonathan and all his courtiers to kill David. But Saul's son Jonathan was very fond of David, ² and Jonathan told David, "My father Saul is bent on killing you. Be on your guard tomorrow morning; get to a secret place and remain in hiding. ³ I will go out and stand next to my father in the field where you will be, and I will speak to my father about

---

ᶠ Septuagint reads "one hundred," and cf. II Sam. 3.14.
ᵍ⁻ᵍ Septuagint reads "and that all Israel loved him."

you. If I learn anything, I will tell you." ⁴ So Jonathan spoke well of David to his father Saul. He said to him, "Let not Your Majesty wrong his servant David, for he has not wronged you; indeed, all his actions have been very much to your advantage. ⁵ He took his life in his hands and killed the Philistine, and the LORD wrought a great victory for all Israel. You saw it and rejoiced. Why then should you incur the guilt of shedding the blood of an innocent man, killing David without cause?" ⁶ Saul heeded Jonathan's plea, and Saul swore, "As the LORD lives, he shall not be put to death!" ⁷ Jonathan called David, and Jonathan told him all this. Then Jonathan brought David to Saul, and he served him as before.

⁸ Fighting broke out again. David went out and fought the Philistines. He inflicted a great defeat upon them and they fled before him. ⁹ Then an evil spirit of the LORD came upon Saul while he was sitting in his house with his spear in his hand, and David was playing [the lyre]. ¹⁰ Saul tried to pin David to the wall with the spear, but he eluded Saul, so that he drove the spear into the wall. David fled and got away.

That night ¹¹ Saul sent messengers to David's home to keep watch on him and to kill him in the morning. But David's wife Michal told him, "Unless you run for your life tonight, you will be killed tomorrow." ¹² Michal let David down from the window and he escaped and fled. ¹³ Michal then took the household idol, laid it on the bed, and covered it with a cloth; and at its head she put a net of goat's hair. ¹⁴ Saul sent messengers to seize David; but she said, "He is sick." ¹⁵ Saul, however, sent back the messengers to see David for themselves. "Bring him up to me in the bed," he ordered, "that he may be put to death." ¹⁶ When the messengers came, they found the household idol in the bed, with the net of goat's hair at its head. ¹⁷ Saul said to Michal, "Why did you play that trick on me and let my enemy get away safely?" "Because," Michal answered Saul, "he said to me: 'Help me get away or I'll kill you.' "

¹⁸ David made good his escape, and he came to Samuel at

Ramah and told him all that Saul had done to him. He and Samuel went and stayed at Naioth. [19] Saul was told that David was at Naioth in Ramah, [20] and Saul sent messengers to seize David. They[a] saw a band of prophets [b]speaking in ecstasy,[b] with Samuel standing by [c]as their leader;[c] and the spirit of God came upon Saul's messengers and they too began to speak in ecstasy. [21] When Saul was told about this, he sent other messengers; but they too spoke in ecstasy. Saul sent a third group of messengers; and they also spoke in ecstasy. [22] So he himself went to Ramah. When he came to [d]the great cistern at Secu,[d] he asked, "Where are Samuel and David?" and was told that they were at Naioth in Ramah. [23] He was on his way there, to Naioth in Ramah, when the spirit of God came upon him too; and he walked on, speaking in ecstasy, until he reached Naioth in Ramah. [24] Then he too stripped off his clothes and he too spoke in ecstasy before Samuel; and he lay naked all that day and all night. That is why people say, "Is Saul too among the prophets?"

20 David fled from Naioth in Ramah; he came to Jonathan and said, "What have I done, what is my crime and my guilt against your father, that he seeks my life?" [2] He replied, "Heaven forbid! You shall not die. My father does not do anything, great or small, without disclosing it to me; why should my father conceal this matter from me? It cannot be!" [3] David [a]swore further,[a] "Your father knows well that you are fond of me and has decided: Jonathan must not learn of this or he will be grieved. But, as the LORD lives and as you live, there is only a step between me and death." [4] Jonathan said to David, "Whatever you want, I will do it for you."

[5] David said to Jonathan, "Tomorrow is the new moon, and I [b]am to sit with the king at the meal. Instead, let[b] me go and I will hide in the countryside until the third[c] evening. [6] If your father

---

[a] *Heb. "He."*
[b-b] *Cf. note at 10.5.*
[c-c] *Meaning of Heb. uncertain.*
[d-d] *Septuagint reads "the cistern of the threshing floor on the bare height."*

[a-a] *Septuagint reads "replied to him."*
[b-b] *Septuagint reads "will not sit . . . meal. Let. . . . "*
[c] *Septuagint lacks "third."*

142

notes my absence, you say, 'David asked my permission to run down to his home town, Bethlehem, for the whole family has its annual sacrifice there.' 7 If he says 'Good,' your servant is safe; but if his anger flares up, know that he is resolved to do [me] harm. 8 Deal faithfully with your servant, since you have taken your servant into a covenant of the LORD with you. And if I am guilty, kill me yourself, but don't make me go back to your father." 9 Jonathan replied, "Don't talk like that! If I learn that my father has resolved to kill you, I will surely tell you about it." 10 David said to Jonathan, "Who will tell me if*d* your father answers you harshly?" 11 Jonathan said to David, "Let us go into the open"; and they both went out into the open.

12 *e*Then Jonathan said to David, "By the LORD, the God of Israel! I will sound out my father at this time tomorrow, [or] on the third day; and if [his response] is favorable for David, I will send a message to you at once and disclose it to you. 13 But if my father intends to do you harm, may the LORD do thus to Jonathan and more if I do [not] disclose it to you and send you off to escape unharmed. May the LORD be with you, as He used to be with my father. 14 Nor shall you fail to show me the *f*-LORD's faithfulness,*f* while I am alive; nor, when I am dead, 15 shall you ever discontinue your faithfulness to my house—not even after the LORD has wiped out every one of David's enemies from the face of the earth. 16 Thus has Jonathan covenanted with the house of David; and may the LORD requite the enemies of David!"

17 Jonathan, out of his love for David, adjured*g* him again, for he loved him as himself. 18 Jonathan said to him, "Tomorrow will be the new moon; and you will be missed when your seat remains vacant.*h* 19 So the day after tomorrow, go down *i*-all the way*i* to the place where you hid *j*-the other time,*j* and stay close to the Ezel stone. 20 Now I will shoot three arrows to one side of it, as though I were shooting at a mark, 21 and I will order the boy to go and find the arrows. If I call to the boy, 'Hey! the arrows are

---

d *Meaning of Heb. uncertain.*
e *The meaning of several parts of vv. 12-16 is uncertain.*
f-f *I.e. the faithfulness pledged in the covenant before the LORD.*
g *Septuagint reads "swore to."*
h *At the festal meal.*
i-i *Lit. "very much."*
j-j *Lit. "on the day of the incident"; see 19.2 ff.*

on this side of you,' be reassured[k] and come, for you are safe and there is no danger—as the LORD lives! [22] But if, instead, I call to the lad, 'Hey! the arrows are beyond you,' then leave, for the LORD has sent you away. [23] As for the promise we made to each other,[l] may the LORD be [witness] between you and me forever."

[24] David hid in the field. The new moon came, and the king sat down to partake of the meal. [25] When the king took his usual place on the seat by the wall, Jonathan rose[m] and Abner sat down at Saul's side; but David's place remained vacant. [26] That day, however, Saul said nothing. "It's accidental," he thought. [n]"He must be unclean and not yet cleansed."[-n] [27] But on the day after the new moon, the second day, David's place was vacant again. So Saul said to his son Jonathan, "Why didn't the son of Jesse[o] come to the meal yesterday or today?" [28] Jonathan answered Saul, "David begged leave of me to go to Bethlehem. [29] He said, 'Please let me go, for we are going to have a family feast in our town and my brother has summoned me to it. Do me a favor, let me slip away to see my kinsmen.' That is why he has not come to the king's table."

[30] Saul flew into a rage against Jonathan. "You son of a perverse, rebellious woman!" he shouted. "I know that you side with the son of Jesse—to your shame, and to the shame of your mother's nakedness! [31] For as long as the son of Jesse lives on earth, neither you nor your kingship will be secure. Now then, have him brought to me, for he is marked for death." [32] But Jonathan spoke up and said to his father, "Why should he be put to death? What has he done?" [33] At that, Saul threw[p] his spear at him to strike him down; and Jonathan realized that his father was determined to do away with David. [34] Jonathan rose from the table in a rage. He ate no food on the second day of the new moon, because he was grieved about David, and because his father had humiliated him.

[35] In the morning, Jonathan went out into the open for the meeting with David, accompanied by a young boy. [36] He said to

---

[k] Lit. "accept it."
[l] See above, vv. 12-17.
[m] Force of Heb. uncertain; Septuagint "faced him."
[n-n] Heb. construction unclear.
[o] See note at 10.11.
[p] See 18.11 and note.

the boy, "Run ahead and find the arrows that I shoot." And as the boy ran, he shot the arrows past him. [37] When the boy came to the place where the arrows shot by Jonathan had fallen, Jonathan called out to the boy, "Hey, the arrows are beyond you!" [38] And Jonathan called after the boy, "Quick, hurry up. Don't stop!" So Jonathan's boy gathered the arrows and came back to his master.—[39] The boy suspected nothing; only Jonathan and David knew the arrangement.—[40] Jonathan handed the gear to his boy and told him, "Take these back to the town." [41] When the boy got there, David *q*-emerged from his concealment at*-q* the Negeb.*r* He flung himself face down on the ground and bowed low three times. They kissed each other and wept together; David wept the longer.

[42] Jonathan said to David, "Go in peace! For we two have sworn to each other in the name of the LORD: 'May the LORD be [witness] between you and me, and between your offspring and mine, forever!' " [1] David then went his way, and Jonathan returned to the town.

21

[2] David went to the priest Ahimelech at Nob. Ahimelech came out in alarm to meet David, and he said to him, "Why are you alone, and no one with you?" [3] David answered the priest Ahimelech, "The king has ordered me on a mission, and he said to me, 'No one must know anything about the mission on which I am sending you and for which I have given you orders.' So I have *a*-directed [my] young men to*-a* such and such a place. [4] Now then, what have you got on hand? Any*b* loaves of bread? Let me have them—or whatever is available." [5] The priest answered David, "I have no ordinary bread on hand; there is only consecrated bread —provided the young men have kept away from women." [6] In reply to the priest, David said, "I assure you that women have been kept from us, as always. Whenever I went on a mission, even if the journey was a common one, the vessels of the young men were consecrated; all the more then *c*-may consecrated food be

---

q-q Lit. "rose up from beside."
r Identical with the "Ezel Stone," v.19.

a-a Meaning of Heb. uncertain. 4QSam*b* (cf. Septuagint) reads "made an appointment with [my] young men at. . . . "
b Lit. "five."
c-c Meaning of Heb. uncertain in part.

put into their vessels today."*-c* 7 So the priest gave him consecrated bread, because there was none there except the bread of display, which had been removed from the presence of the Lord, to be replaced by warm bread as soon as it was taken away.— 8 Now one of Saul's officials was there that day, *d-*detained before the Lord;*-d* his name was Doeg the Edomite, Saul's *e-*chief herdsman.*-e*

9 David said to Ahimelech, "Haven't you got a spear or sword on hand? I didn't take my sword or any of my weapons with me, because the king's mission was urgent." 10 The priest said, "There is the sword of Goliath the Philistine whom you slew in the valley of Elah; it is over there, wrapped in a cloth, behind the ephod. If you want to take that one, take it, for there is none here but that one." David replied, "There is none like it; give it to me."

11 That day David continued on his flight from Saul and he came to King Achish of Gath. 12 The courtiers of Achish said to him, "Why, that's David, king of the land! That's the one of whom they sing as they dance:

Saul has slain his thousands;
David, his tens of thousands."

13 These words worried David and he became very much afraid of King Achish of Gath. 14 So he concealed his good sense from them; he feigned madness *f-*for their benefit.*-f* He scratched marks on the doors of the gate and let his saliva run down his beard. 15 And Achish said to his courtiers, "You see the man is raving; why bring him to me? 16 Do I lack madmen that you have brought this fellow to rave for me? Should this fellow enter my house?"

22 David departed from there and escaped to the cave*a* of Adullam; and when his brothers and all his father's house heard, they joined him down there. 2 Everyone who was in straits and everyone who was in debt and everyone who was desperate

---

d-d *I.e. excluded from the shrine, perhaps because of ritual impurity.*
e-e *Meaning of Heb. uncertain.*
f-f *Lit. "in their hand"; meaning of Heb. uncertain.*

a *The "cave" in v. 1 is referred to as "stronghold" in vv. 4-5; cf. the same variation in II Sam. 23.13-14; I Chron. 11.15-16.*

joined him, and he became their leader; there were about four hundred men with him. ³ David went from there to Mizpeh of Moab, and. he said to the king of Moab, "Let my father and mother come [and stay] with you, until I know what God will do for me." ⁴ So he ᵇled them to⁻ᵇ the king of Moab, and they stayed with him as long as David remained in the stronghold.ᵃ ⁵ But the prophet Gad said to David, "Do not stay in the stronghold; go at once to the territory of Judah." So David left and went to the forest of Hereth.

⁶ When Saul heard that David and the men with him had been located—Saul was then in Gibeah, sitting under the tamarisk tree on the height, spear in hand, with all his courtiers in attendance upon him—⁷ Saul said to the courtiers standing about him, "Listen, men of Benjamin! Will the son of Jesseᶜ give fields and vineyards to every one of you? And will he make all of you captains of thousands or captains of hundreds? ⁸ Is that why all of you have conspired against me? For no one informs me when my own son makes a pact with the son of Jesse, no one is concernedᵈ for me and no one informs me when my own son has set my servant ᵉ⁻in ambush⁻ᵉ against me, as is now the case."

⁹ Doeg the Edomite, who was standing among the courtiers of Saul, spoke up: "I saw the son of Jesse come to Ahimelech son of Ahitub at Nob. ¹⁰ He inquired of the LORD on his behalf and gave him provisions; he also gave him the sword of Goliath the Philistine." ¹¹ Thereupon the king sent for the priest Ahimelech son of Ahitub and for all the priests belonging to his father's house at Nob. They all came to the king, ¹² and Saul said, "Listen to me, sonᶜ of Ahitub." "Yes, my lord," he replied. ¹³ And Saul said to him, "Why have you and the son of Jesse conspired against me? You gave him food and a sword, and inquired of God for him—that he may rise ᵉ⁻in ambush⁻ᵉ against me, as is now the case."

¹⁴ Ahimelech replied to the king, "But who is there among all your courtiers as trusted as David, son-in-law of Your Majesty and ᶠ⁻obedient to your bidding,ᶠ and esteemed in your house-

ᵇ⁻ᵇ *Targum and Syriac read "left them with."*
ᶜ *See note at 10.11.*
ᵈ *For this meaning of* holeh; *cf. Amos 6.6.*
ᵉ⁻ᵉ *Septuagint reads "as an enemy."*
ᶠ⁻ᶠ *Cf. Isa. 11.14; but meaning of Heb. uncertain.*

hold? ¹⁵ This is the first time that I inquired of God for him; ᵍ-I have done no wrong.ᵍ Let not Your Majesty find fault with his servant [or] with any of my father's house; for your servant knew nothing whatever about all this." ¹⁶ But the king said, "You shall die, Ahimelech, you and all your father's house." ¹⁷ And the king commanded the guards standing by, "Turn about and kill the priests of the LORD, for they are in league with David; they knew he was running away and they did not inform me." But the king's servants would not raise a hand to strike down the priests of the LORD. ¹⁸ Thereupon the king said to Doeg, "You, Doeg, go and strike down the priests." And Doeg the Edomite went and struck down the priests himself; that day, he killed eighty-five men ʰ-who wore the linen ephod.-ʰ ¹⁹ He put Nob, the town of the priests, to the sword: men and women, children and infants, oxen, asses, and sheep—[all] to the sword.

²⁰ But one son of Ahimelech son of Ahitub escaped—his name was Abiathar—and he fled to David. ²¹ When Abiathar told David that Saul had killed the priests of the LORD, ²² David said to Abiathar, "I knew that day, when Doeg the Edomite was there, that he would tell Saul. I ⁱ-am to blame for all the deaths-ⁱ in your father's house. ²³ Stay with me; do not be afraid; for ⁱ-whoever seeks your life must seek my life also.-ⁱ It will be my care to guard you."

23 David was told: "The Philistines are raiding Keilah and plundering the threshing floors." ² David consulted the LORD, "Shall I go and attack those Philistines?" And the LORD said to David, "Go; attack the Philistines and you will save Keilah." ³ But David's men said to him, "Look, we are afraid here in Judah, how much more if we go to Keilah against the forces of the Philistines!" ⁴ So David consulted the LORD again, and the LORD answered him, "March down at once to Keilah, for I am going to deliver the Philistines into your hands." ⁵ David and his men went to Keilah and fought against the Philistines; he drove off their

---

ᵍ⁻ᵍ Lit. "Far be it from me!"
ʰ⁻ʰ Septuagint reads "bearers of the ephod"; cf. note at 2.28.
ⁱ⁻ⁱ Meaning of Heb. uncertain.

cattle and inflicted a severe defeat on them. Thus David saved the inhabitants of Keilah.

⁶ When Abiathar son of Ahimelech fled to David at Keilah, ᵃhe brought down an ephod with him.⁻ᵃ

⁷ Saul was told that David had come to Keilah, and Saul thought, "God has deliveredᵃ him into my hands, for he has shut himself in by entering a town with gates and bars." ⁸ Saul summoned all the troops for war, to go down to Keilah and besiege David and his men. ⁹ When David learned that Saul was planningᵃ to harm him, he told the priest Abiathar to bring the ephod forward. ¹⁰ And David said, "O Lord, God of Israel. Your servant has heard that Saul intends to come to Keilah and destroy the town because of me. ¹¹ Will the citizens of Keilah deliver me into his hands? Will Saul come down, as Your servant has heard? O Lord, God of Israel, tell Your servant!" And the Lord said, "He will." ¹² David continued, "Will the citizens of Keilah deliver me and my men into Saul's hands?" And the Lord answered, "They will." ¹³ So David and his men, about six hundred in number, left Keilah at once and moved about wherever they could. And when Saul was told that David had got away from Keilah, he did not set out.

¹⁴ David was staying ᵃ⁻in the strongholds of the wilderness [of Judah];⁻ᵃ he stayed in the hill country, in the wilderness of Ziph. Saul searched for him constantly, but God did not deliver him into his hands. ¹⁵ David was once at Horesh in the wilderness of Ziph, when David learned that Saul had come out to seek his life. ¹⁶ And Saul's son Jonathan came to David at Horesh and encouraged him in [the name of] God. ¹⁷ He said to him, "Do not be afraid: the hand of my father Saul will never touch you. You are going to be king over Israel and I shall be second to you; and even my father Saul knows this is so." ¹⁸ And the two of them entered into a pact before the Lord. David remained in Horesh, and Jonathan went home.

¹⁹ ᵇSome Ziphites went up to Saul in Gibeah and said, "David is hiding among us in the strongholds of Horesh, at the hill of

ᵃ⁻ᵃ *Meaning of Heb. uncertain.*
ᵇ *The meaning of many parts of 23.19 ff. is uncertain. The events described in 23.19-24.22 are partly parallel in chapter 26, with variations.*

Hachilah south of Jeshimon. ²⁰ So if Your Majesty has the desire to come down, come down, and it will be our task to deliver him into Your Majesty's hands." ²¹ And Saul replied, "May you be blessed of the LORD for the compassion you have shown me! ²² Go now and prepare further. Look around and learn what places he sets foot on [and] who has seen him there, for I have been told he is a very cunning fellow. ²³ Look around and learn in which of all his hiding places he has been hiding, and return to me when you are certain. I will then go with you, and if he is in the region, I will search him out among all the clans of Judah."

²⁴ They left at once for Ziph, ahead of Saul; David and his men were then in the wilderness of Maon, in the Arabah, to the south of Jeshimon. ²⁵ When Saul and his men came to search, David was told about it; and he went down to ᵃ⁻the rocky region⁻ᵃ and stayed in the wilderness of Maon. On hearing this, Saul pursued David in the wilderness of Maon. ²⁶ Saul was making his way along one side of a hill, and David and his men were on the other side of the hill. ᵃ⁻David was trying hard to elude Saul, and Saul and his men were trying to encircle David and his men and capture them,⁻ᵃ ²⁷ when a messenger came and told Saul, "Come quickly, for the Philistines have invaded the land." ²⁸ Saul gave up his pursuit of David and went to meet the Philistines. That is why that place came to be called the Rock of Separation.ᵃ

24 David went from there and stayed in the wildernesses of En-gedi.

² When Saul returned from pursuing the Philistines, he was told that David was in the wilderness of En-gedi. ³ So Saul took three thousand picked men from all Israel and went in search of David and his men ᵃ⁻in the direction of the rocks of the wild goats;⁻ᵃ ⁴ and he came to the sheepfolds along the way. There was a cave there, and Saul went in ᵇ⁻to relieve himself.⁻ᵇ Now David and his men were sitting in the back of the cave.

⁵ David's men said to him, "This is the day of which the LORD

ᵃ⁻ᵃ *Meaning of Heb. uncertain.*
ᵇ⁻ᵇ *Lit. "to cover his feet."*

said to you, 'I will deliver your enemy into your hands; you can do with him as you please.' " ᶜDavid went and stealthily cut off the corner of Saul's cloak. ⁶ But afterward ᵈ⁻David reproached himself⁻ᵈ for cutting off ᵉ⁻the corner of Saul's cloak.⁻ᵉ ⁷ He said to his men, "The LORD forbid that I should do such a thing to my lord—the LORD's anointed—that I should raise my hand against him; for he is the LORD's anointed." ⁸ David rebukedᵃ his men and did not permit them to attack Saul.

Saul left the cave and started on his way. ⁹ Then David also went out of the cave and called after Saul, "My lord king!" Saul looked around and David bowed low in homage, with his face to the ground. ¹⁰ And David said to Saul, "Why do you listen to the people who say, 'David is out to do you harm?' ¹¹ You can see for yourself now that the LORD delivered you into my hands in the cave today. And though ᵃ⁻I was urged⁻ᵃ to kill you, I showed you pity;ᶠ for I said, 'I will not raise a hand against my lord, since he is the LORD's anointed.' ¹² Please, sir,ᵍ take a close look at the corner of your cloak in my hand, for when I cut off the corner of your cloak, I did not kill you. You must see plainly that I have done nothing evil or rebellious, and I have never wronged you. Yet you are bent on taking my life. ¹³ May the LORD judge between you and me! And may He take vengeance upon you for me, but my hand will never touch you. ¹⁴ As the ancient proverb has it: 'Wicked deeds come from wicked men!' My hand will never touch you. ¹⁵ Against whom has the king of Israel come out? Whom are you pursuing? A dead dog? A single flea? ¹⁶ May the LORD be arbiter and may He judge between you and me! May He take note and uphold my cause, and vindicate me against you."

¹⁷ When David finished saying these things to Saul, Saul said, "Is that your voice, my son David?" And Saul broke down and wept. ¹⁸ He said to David, "You are right, not I; for you have treated me generously, but I have treated you badly. ¹⁹ Yes, you have just revealed how generously you treated me, for the LORD delivered me into your hands and you did not kill me. ²⁰ If a man meets his enemy, does he let him go his way unharmed? Surely,

---

ᶜ *Vv. 5b-6 read well after 8a.*
ᵈ⁻ᵈ *Lit. "David's heart struck him."*
ᵉ⁻ᵉ *So several mss. and ancient versions; cf. v. 5. Most mss. and editions read "Saul's corner."*
ᶠ *Understanding the Heb. as an ellipsis of* waṭṭaḥos ʿeni *(cf., e.g., Deut. 7.16).*
ᵍ *Lit. "(my) father," cf. II Kings 5.13.*

the LORD will reward you generously for *h*-what you have done for me this day.*-h* 21 I know now that you will become king, and that the kingship over Israel will remain in your hands. 22 So swear to me by the LORD that you will not destroy my descendants or wipe out my name from my father's house." 23 David swore to Saul, Saul went home, and David and his men went up to the strongholds.

25 Samuel died, and all Israel gathered and made lament for him; and they buried him in Ramah, his home.

David went down to the wilderness of Paran.*a*

2 There was a man in Maon whose possessions were in Carmel. The man was very wealthy; he owned three thousand sheep and a thousand goats. At the time, he was shearing his sheep in Carmel. 3 The man's name was Nabal, and his wife's name was Abigail. The woman was intelligent and beautiful, but the man, a Calebite, was a hard man and an evildoer. 4 David was in the wilderness when he heard that Nabal was shearing his sheep. 5 David dispatched ten young men, and David instructed the young men, "Go up to Carmel. When you come to Nabal, greet him in my name. 6 Say *b*-as follows: 'To life!-*b* Greetings to you and to your household and to all that is yours! 7 I hear that you are now doing your shearing. As you know, your shepherds have been with us; we did not harm them, and nothing of theirs was missing all the time they were in Carmel. 8 Ask your young men and they will tell you. So receive these young men graciously, for we have come on a festive occasion. Please give your servants and your son David whatever you can.'"

9 David's young men went and delivered this message to Nabal in the name of David. When they stopped speaking, 10 Nabal answered David's servants, "Who is David? Who is the son of Jesse? There are many slaves nowadays who run away from their masters. 11 Should I then take my bread and my water,*c* and the meat that I slaughtered for my own shearers, and give them to

---

h-h *Meaning of Heb. uncertain. Emendation yields "the generosity you have shown me."*
a *Septuagint reads "Maon," cf. v. 2 and 23.24, 25.*
b-b *Meaning of Heb. uncertain.*
c *Septuagint reads "wine," and cf. v. 18.*

men who come from I don't know where?" [12] Thereupon David's young men retraced their steps; and when they got back, they told him all this. [13] And David said to his men, "Gird on your swords." Each girded on his sword; David too girded on his sword. About four hundred men went up after David, while two hundred remained with the baggage.

[14] One of [Nabal's] young men told Abigail, Nabal's wife, that David had sent messengers from the wilderness to greet their master, and that he had spurned[b] them. [15] "But the men had been very friendly to us; we were not harmed, nor did we miss anything all the time that we went about with them while we were in the open. [16] They were a wall about us both by night and by day all the time that we were with them tending the flocks. [17] So consider carefully what you should do, for harm threatens our master and all his household; he is such a nasty fellow that no one can speak to him."

[18] Abigail quickly got together two hundred loaves of bread, two jars of wine, five dressed sheep, five *seahs* of parched corn, one hundred cakes of raisin, and two hundred cakes of pressed figs. She loaded them on asses, [19] and she told her young men, "Go on ahead of me, and I'll follow you"; but she did not tell her husband Nabal. [20] She was riding on the ass and going down a trail[b] on the hill, when David and his men appeared, coming down toward her; and she met them.—[21] Now David had been saying, "It was all for nothing that I protected that fellow's possessions in the wilderness, and that nothing he owned is missing. He has paid me back evil for good. [22] May God do thus and more to [d]the enemies of[d] David if, by the light of morning, I leave [e]a single male[e] of his."—[23] When Abigail saw David, she quickly dismounted from the ass and threw herself face down before[b] David, bowing to the ground. [24] Prostrate at his feet, she pleaded, "Let the blame be mine, my lord, but let your handmaid speak to you; hear your maid's plea. [25] Please, my lord, pay no attention to that wretched fellow Nabal. For he is just what his name says: His name means 'boor' and he is a boor.

[d-d] *The phrase is intended to avoid the imprecation of David against himself; it is lacking in the Septuagint.*
[e-e] *Lit. "one who pees against a wall."*

"Your handmaid did not see the young men whom my lord sent. [26] I swear, my lord, as the LORD lives and as you live—the LORD who has kept you from seeking redress by blood with your own hands—let your enemies and all who would harm my lord fare like Nabal! [27] Here is the present which your maidservant has brought to my lord; let it be given to the young men who are the followers of my lord. [28] Please pardon your maid's boldness. For the LORD will grant my lord an enduring house, because my lord is fighting the battles of the LORD, and no wrong is ever to be found in you. [29] And if anyone sets out to pursue you and seek your life, the life of my lord will be bound up in the bundle of life in the care of the LORD; but He will fling away the lives of your enemies as from the hollow of a sling. [30] And when the LORD has accomplished for my lord all the good He has promised you, and has appointed you ruler of Israel, [31] do not let this be a cause of stumbling and of faltering courage to my lord that you have shed blood needlessly and that my lord sought redress with his own hands. And when the LORD has prospered my lord, remember your maid."

[32] David said to Abigail, "Praised be the LORD, the God of Israel, who sent you this day to meet me! [33] And blessed be your prudence, and blessed be you yourself for restraining me from seeking redress in blood by my own hands. [34] For as sure as the LORD, the God of Israel, lives—who has kept me from harming you—had you not come quickly to meet me, not ⁶a single male⁻ᵉ of Nabal's line would have been left by daybreak." [35] David then accepted from her what she had brought him, and he said to her, "Go up to your home safely. See, I have heeded your plea and respected your wish."

[36] When Abigail came home to Nabal, he was having a feast in his house, a feast fit for a king; Nabal was in a merry mood and very drunk, so she did not tell him anything at all until daybreak. [37] The next morning, when Nabal had slept off the wine, his wife told him everything that had happened; and his courage died within him, and he became like a stone. [38] About ten days later

the LORD struck Nabal and he died. ³⁹ When David heard that Nabal was dead, he said, "Praised be the LORD who championed my cause against the insults of Nabal and held back His servant from wrongdoing; the LORD has brought Nabal's wrongdoing down on his own head."

David sent messengers ^fto propose marriage to^f Abigail, to take her as his wife. ⁴⁰ When David's servants came to Abigail at Carmel and told her that David had sent them to her to make her his wife, ⁴¹ she immediately bowed low with her face to the ground and said, "Your handmaid is ready to be your maidservant, to wash the feet of my lord's servants." ⁴² Then Abigail rose quickly and mounted an ass, and with five of her maids in attendance she followed David's messengers; and she became his wife.

⁴³ Now David had taken Ahinoam of Jezreel; so both of them became his wives. ⁴⁴ Saul had given his daughter Michal, David's wife, to Palti son of Laish from Gallim.

26 ^aThe Ziphites came to Saul at Gibeah and said, "David is hiding in the hill of Hachilah facing Jeshimon." ² Saul went down at once to the wilderness of Ziph, together with three thousand picked men of Israel, to search for David in the wilderness of Ziph, ³ and Saul encamped on the hill of Hachilah which faces Jeshimon, by the road. When David, who was then living in the wilderness, learned that Saul had come after him into the wilderness, ⁴ David sent out scouts and made sure that Saul had come. ⁵ David went at once to the place where Saul had encamped, and David saw the spot where Saul and his army commander, Abner son of Ner, lay asleep. Saul lay asleep inside the barricade^b and the troops were posted around him.

⁶ David spoke up and asked Ahimelech the Hittite and Abishai son of Zeruiah, Joab's brother, "Who will go down with me into the camp to Saul?" And Abishai answered, "I will go down with you." ⁷ So David and Abishai approached the troops by night, and found Saul fast asleep inside the barricade,^b his spear stuck

^{f-f} Lit. "and spoke for"; cf. Song of Songs 8.8.
^a Cf. 23.19 and note.
^b Meaning of Heb. uncertain; cf. 17.20.

in the ground at his head, and Abner and the troops sleeping around him. [8] And Abishai said to David, "God has delivered your enemy into your hands today. Let me pin him to the ground with a single thrust of the spear. I will not have to strike him twice." [9] But David said to Abishai, "Don't do him violence! No one can lay hands on the LORD's anointed with impunity." [10] And David went on, "As the LORD lives, the LORD Himself will strike him down, or his time will come and he will die, or he will go down to battle and perish. [11] But the LORD forbid that I should lay a hand on the LORD's anointed! Just take the spear and the water jar at his head and let's be off." [12] So David took away the spear and the water jar at Saul's head, and they left. No one saw or knew or woke up; all remained asleep; a deep sleep from the LORD had fallen upon them.

[13] David crossed over to the other side and stood afar on top of a hill; there was considerable distance between them. [14] And David shouted to the troops and to Abner son of Ner, "Abner, aren't you going to answer?" And Abner shouted back, "Who are you to shout at the king?" [15] And David answered Abner, "You are a man, aren't you? And there is no one like you in Israel! So why didn't you keep watch over your lord the king? For one of [our] troops came to do violence to your lord the king. [16] You have not given a good account of yourself! As the LORD lives, [all of] you deserve to die, because you did not keep watch over your lord, the LORD's anointed. Look around, where are the king's spear and the water jar that were at his head?"

[17] Saul recognized David's voice, and he asked, "Is that your voice, my son David?" And David replied, "It is, my lord king." [18] And he went on, "But why does my lord continue to pursue his servant? What have I done, and what wrong am I guilty of? [19] Now let my lord the king hear his servant out. If the LORD has incited you against me, let Him be appeased[c] by an offering; but if it is men, may they be accursed of the LORD! For they have driven me out today, so that I cannot have a share in the LORD's possession, but am told, 'Go and worship other gods.' [20] Oh, let my blood not

[c] Cf. Amos 5.21.

fall to the ground, away from the presence of the LORD! For the king of Israel has come out to seek a single flea—as if he were hunting a partridge in the hills."

²¹ And Saul answered, "I am in the wrong. Come back, my son David, for I will never harm you again, seeing how you have held my life precious this day. Yes, I have been a fool, and I have erred so very much." ²² David replied, "Here is Your Majesty's spear. Let one of the young men come over and get it. ²³ And the LORD will requite every man for his right conduct and loyalty—for this day the LORD delivered you into my*d* hands and I would not raise a hand against the LORD's anointed. ²⁴ And just as I valued your life highly this day, so may the LORD value my life and may He rescue me from all trouble." ²⁵ Saul answered David, "May you be blessed, my son David. You shall achieve, and you shall prevail."

David then went his way, and Saul returned home.

27 David said to himself, "Some day I shall certainly perish at the hands of Saul. The best thing for me is to flee to the land of the Philistines; Saul will then give up hunting me throughout the territory of Israel, and I will escape him." ² So David and the six hundred men with him went and crossed over to King Achish son of Maoch of Gath. ³ David and his men stayed with Achish in Gath, each man with his family, and David with his two wives, Ahinoam the Jezreelite and Abigail wife of Nabal the Carmelite. ⁴ And when Saul was told that David had fled to Gath, he did not pursue him any more.

⁵ David said to Achish, "If you please, let a place be granted me in one of the country towns where I can live; why should your servant remain with you in the royal city?" ⁶ At that time Achish granted him Ziklag; that is how Ziklag came to belong to the kings of Judah, as is still the case. ⁷ The length of time that David lived in Philistine territory was a year and four months.

⁸ David and his men went up and raided the Geshurites, the

---

d So many mss.; other mss. and editions omit.

Gizrites, and the Amalekites—who were the inhabitants of the region of Olam,ᵃ all the way to Shur and to the land of Egypt.— ⁹ When David attacked a region, he would leave no man or woman alive; he would take flocks, herds, asses, camels, and clothing. When he returned and cameᵇ to Achish, ¹⁰ Achish would ask, "Whereᶜ did you raid today?" and David would reply, "The Negebᵈ of Judah," or "the Negeb of the Jerahmeelites," or "the Negeb of the Kenites." ¹¹ David would leave no man or woman alive to be brought to Gath; for he thought, "They might tell about us: David did this." Such was his practice as long as he stayed in the territory of the Philistines. ¹² Achish trusted David. He thought: ᵉ⁻"He has aroused the wrath of⁻ᵉ his own people Israel, and so he will be my vassal forever."

28 At that time the Philistines mustered their forces for war, to take the field against Israel. Achish said to David, "You know, of course, that you and your men must march out with my forces." ² David answered Achish, "You surely know what your servant will do." "In that case," Achish replied to David, "I will appoint you my bodyguard for life."

³ ᵃNow Samuel had died and all Israel made lament for him; and he was buried in his own town of Ramah. And Saul had forbidden [recourse to] ghosts and familiar spirits in the land.

⁴ The Philistines mustered and they marched to Shunem and encamped; and Saul gathered all Israel, and they encamped at Gilboa. ⁵ When Saul saw the Philistine force, his heart trembled with fear. ⁶ And Saul inquired of the LORD, but the LORD did not answer him, either by dreams or by Urimᵇ or by prophets. ⁷ Then Saul said to his courtiers, "Find me a woman who consults ghosts, so that I can go to her and inquire through her." And his courtiers told him that there was a woman in En-dor who consulted ghosts.

ᵃ *Septuagint reads "Telam" (cf. "Telaim" in 15.4; and "Telem" in Josh. 15.24).*
ᵇ *Change of vocalization yields "brought it"; cf. v. 11.*
ᶜ *So some mss. and Targum; Septuagint and 40Samᵃ read "Whom."*
ᵈ *I.e. the part of the Negeb occupied by these clans.*
ᵉ⁻ᵉ *Cf. note at 13.4.*

ᵃ *The rest of this chapter would read well after chapters 29 and 30.*
ᵇ *A kind of oracle; see note at Exod. 28.30 and I Sam. 14.41.*

[8] Saul disguised himself; he put on different clothes and set out with two men. They came to the woman by night, and he said, "Please divine for me by a ghost. Bring up for me the one I shall name to you." [9] But the woman answered him, "You know what Saul has done, how he has banned [the use of] ghosts and familiar spirits in the land. So why are you laying a trap for me, to get me killed?" [10] Saul swore to her by the LORD: "As the LORD lives, you won't get into trouble over this." [11] At that, the woman asked, "Whom shall I bring up for you?" He answered, "Bring up Samuel for me." [12] Then the woman recognized Samuel,[c] and she shrieked loudly, and said to Saul, "Why have you deceived me? You are Saul!" [13] The king answered her, "Don't be afraid. What do you see?" And the woman said to Saul, "I see a divine being coming up from the earth." [14] "What does he look like?" he asked her. "It is an old man coming up," she said, "and he is wrapped in a robe." Then Saul knew that it was Samuel; and he bowed low in homage with his face to the ground.

[15] Samuel said to Saul, "Why have you disturbed me and brought me up?" And Saul answered, "I am in great trouble. The Philistines are attacking me and God has turned away from me; He no longer answers me, either by prophets or in dreams. So I have called you to tell me what I am to do." [16] Samuel said, "Why do you ask me, seeing that the LORD has turned away from you and has become your adversary?[d] [17] The LORD has done [e]for Himself[e] as He foretold through me: The LORD has torn the kingship out of your hands and has given it to your fellow, to David, [18] because you did not obey the LORD and did not execute His wrath upon the Amalekites. That is why the LORD has done this to you today. [19] Further, the LORD will deliver the Israelites who are with you into the hands of the Philistines. Tomorrow your sons and you will be with me; and the LORD will also deliver the Israelite forces into the hands of the Philistines."

[20] At once Saul flung himself prone on the ground, terrified by Samuel's words. Besides, there was no strength in him, for he had

[c] *Some Septuagint mss. read "Saul."*
[d] *Meaning of Heb. uncertain.*
[e-e] *Some mss. and Septuagint read "to you."*

159

not eaten anything all day and all night. ²¹ The woman went up to Saul and, seeing how greatly disturbed he was, she said to him, "Your handmaid listened to you; I took my life in my hands and heeded the request you made of me. ²² So now you listen to me: Let me set before you a bit of food. Eat, and then you will have the strength to go on your way." ²³ He refused, saying, "I will not eat." But when his courtiers as well as the woman urged him, he listened to them; he got up from the ground and sat on the bed. ²⁴ The woman had a stall-fed calf in the house; she hastily slaughtered it, and took flour and kneaded it, and baked some unleavened cakes. ²⁵ She set this before Saul and his courtiers, and they ate. Then they rose and left the same night.

29

The Philistines mustered all their forces at Aphek, while Israel was encamping at the spring in Jezreel. ² The Philistine lords came marching, each with his units of hundreds and of thousands; and David and his men came marching last, with Achish. ³ The Philistine officers asked, "Who are those Hebrews?" "Why, that's David, the servant of King Saul of Israel," Achish answered the Philistine officers. "He has been with me ᵃ⁻for a year or more,⁻ᵃ and I have found no fault in him from the day he defected until now." ⁴ But the Philistine officers were angry with him; and the Philistine officers said to him, "Send the man back; let him go back to the place you assigned him. He shall not march down with us to the battle, or else he may become our adversary in battle. For with what could that fellow appease his master if not with ᵇ⁻the heads of these men?⁻ᵇ ⁵ Remember, he is the David of whom they sang as they danced:

Saul has slain his thousands;
David, his tens of thousands."

⁶ Achish summoned David and said to him, "As the LORD lives, you are an honest man, and I would like to have you serveᶜ in my forces; for I have found no fault with you from the day you joined me until now. But you are not acceptable to the other lords. ⁷ So

ᵃ⁻ᵃ *Meaning of phrase uncertain.*
ᵇ⁻ᵇ *A euphemism for "our heads."*
ᶜ *Lit. "go out and come in."*

go back in peace, and do nothing to displease the Philistine lords."

⁸ David, however, said to Achish, "But what have I done, what fault have you found in your servant from the day I appeared before you to this day, that I should not go and fight against the enemies of my lord the king." ⁹ Achish replied to David, "I know; you are as acceptable to me as an angel of God. But the Philistine officers have decided that you must not march out with us to the battle. ¹⁰ So rise early in the morning, you and your lord's servants who came with you—ᵈ⁻rise early in the morning,⁻ᵈ and leave as soon as it is light." ¹¹ Accordingly, David and his men rose early in the morning to leave, to return to the land of the Philistines, while the Philistines marched up to Jezreel.

30 By the time David and his men arrived in Ziklag, on the third day, the Amalekites had made a raid into the Negeb and against Ziklag; they had stormed Ziklag and burned it down. ² They had taken the women in it captive, lowborn and highborn alike; they did not kill any, but carried them off and went their way. ³ When David and his men came to the town and found it burned down, and their wives and sons and daughters taken captive, ⁴ David and the troops with him broke into tears, until they had no strength left for weeping. ⁵ David's two wives had been taken captive, Ahinoam of Jezreel and Abigail wife of Nabal from Carmel. ⁶ David was in great danger, for the troops threatened to stone him; for all the troops were embittered on account of their sons and daughters.

But David sought strength in the LORD his God. ⁷ David said to the priest Abiathar son of Ahimelech, "Bring the ephod up to me." When Abiathar brought up the ephodᵃ to David, ⁸ David inquired of the LORD, "Shall I pursue those raiders? Will I overtake them?" And He answered him, "Pursue, for you shall overtake and you shall rescue."

⁹ So David and the six hundred men with him set out, and they

ᵈ⁻ᵈ *Meaning of parts of verse uncertain. Septuagint reads "and go to the place that I have assigned you; and harbor no evil thought in your heart, for you are acceptable to me."*

ᵃ *See note at 2.28.*

came to the Wadi Besor, where a halt was made by those who were to be left behind. [10] David continued the pursuit with four hundred men; two hundred men had halted, too faint to cross the Wadi Besor. [11] They came upon an Egyptian in the open country and brought him to David. They gave him food to eat and water to drink; [12] he was also given a piece of pressed fig cake and two cakes of raisins. He ate and regained his strength, for he had eaten no food and drunk no water for three days and three nights. [13] Then David asked him, "To whom do you belong and where are you from?" "I am an Egyptian boy," he answered, "the slave of an Amalekite. My master abandoned me when I fell ill three days ago. [14] We had raided the Negeb of the Cherethites, and [the Negeb] of Judah, and the Negeb of Caleb; we also burned down Ziklag." [15] And David said to him, "Can you lead me down to that band?" He replied, "Swear to me by God that you will not kill me or deliver me into my master's hands, and I will lead you down to that band." [16] So he led him down, and there they were, scattered all over the ground, eating and drinking and making merry because of all the vast spoil they had taken from the land of the Philistines and from the land of Judah. [17] David attacked them from [b]before dawn until the evening of the next day;[b] none of them escaped, except four hundred young men who mounted camels and got away. [18] David rescued everything the Amalekites had taken; David also rescued his two wives. [19] Nothing of theirs was missing—young or old, sons or daughters, spoil or anything else that had been carried off—David recovered everything. [20] David took all the flocks and herds, [b]which [the troops] drove ahead of the other livestock;[-b] and they declared, "This is David's spoil."

[21] When David reached the two hundred men who were too faint to follow David and who had been left at the Wadi Besor, they came out to welcome David and the troops with him; David came forward with the troops and greeted them. [22] But all the mean and churlish fellows among the men who had accompanied David spoke up, "Since they did not accompany us,[c] we will not

b-b *Meaning of Heb. uncertain.*
c *So some mss. and versions; most mss. and editions read "me."*

give them any of the spoil that we seized—except that each may take his wife and children and go." [23] David, however, spoke up, "You must not do that, [d-]my brothers, in view of[-d] what the LORD has granted us, guarding us and delivering into our hands the band that attacked us. [24] How could anyone agree with you in this matter? The share of those who remain with the baggage shall be the same as the share of those who go down to battle; they shall share alike." [25] So from that day on it was made a fixed rule for Israel, continuing to the present day.

[26] When David reached Ziklag, he sent some of the spoil to the elders of Judah [b-][and] to his friends,[-b] saying, "This is a present for you from our spoil of the enemies of the LORD." [27] [He sent the spoil to the elders] in Bethel,[e] Ramoth-negeb, and Jattir; [28] in Aroer, Siphmoth, and Eshtemoa; [29] in Racal, in the towns of the Jerahmeelites, and in the towns of the Kenites; [30] in Hormah, Bor-ashan, and Athach; [31] and to those in Hebron—all the places where David and his men had roamed.

31 [a]The Philistines attacked Israel, and the men of Israel fled before the Philistines and [many] fell on Mount Gilboa. [2] The Philistines pursued Saul and his sons, and the Philistines struck down Jonathan, Abinadab, and Malchi-shua, sons of Saul. [3] The battle raged around Saul, and [b-]some of the archers[-b] hit him, and he [c-]was severely wounded[-c] by the archers. [4] Saul said to his arms-bearer, "Draw your sword and run me through, so that the uncircumcised may not run me through and make sport of me." But his arms-bearer, in his great awe, refused; whereupon Saul grasped the sword and fell upon it. [5] When his arms-bearer saw that Saul was dead, he too fell on his sword and died with him. [6] Thus Saul and his three sons and his arms-bearer, [d-]as well as all his men,[-d] died together on that day. [7] And when the men of Israel [e-]on the other side of the Valley and on the other side of

---

[d-d] *Meaning of Heb. uncertain. Septuagint reads "after."*
[e] *Called Bethul in Josh. 19.4.*

[a] *I Chron. 10 reproduces this chapter, with minor variations.*
[b-b] *Meaning of Heb. uncertain. Lit. "the archers, men with the bow."*
[c-c] *Construed as* hophal *form; cf. I Kings 2.34.*
[d-d] *Lacking in the Septuagint; I Chron. 10.6 reads "all his house."*
[e-e] *Meaning of Heb. uncertain. I Chron. 10.7 reads "in the Valley."*

the Jordan·^e saw that the men of Israel had fled and that Saul and his sons were dead, they abandoned the towns and fled; the Philistines then came and occupied them.

8 The next day the Philistines came to strip the slain, and they found Saul and his three sons lying on Mount Gilboa. 9 They cut off his head and stripped him of his armor, and they sent them throughout the land of the Philistines, to spread the news ^{f-}in the temples of their idols^{-f} and among the people. 10 They placed his armor in the temple of Ashtaroth, and they impaled his body on the wall of Beth-shan. 11 When ^{g-}the inhabitants of Jabesh-gilead heard about it—what^{-g} the Philistines had done to Saul—12 all their stalwart men set out and marched all night; they removed the bodies of Saul and his sons from the wall of Beth-shan and came^h to Jabesh and burned them there. 13 Then they took the bones and buried them under the tamarisk tree in Jabesh, and they fasted for seven days.

---

^{f-f} *Septuagint and I Chron. 10.9 read "among their idols."*
^{g-g} *I Chron. 10.11 reads "all [the inhabitants of] Jabesh-gilead heard all that."*
^h *I Chron. 10.12 reads "brought them."*

שמואל ב

II SAMUEL

שמואל ב

II SAMUEL

1 After the death of Saul—David had already returned from defeating the Amalekites—David stayed two days in Ziklag. 2 On the third day, a man came from Saul's camp, with his clothes rent and earth on his head; and as he approached David, he flung himself to the ground and bowed low. 3 David said to him, "Where are you coming from?" He answered, "I have just escaped from the camp of Israel." 4 "What happened?" asked David. "Tell me!" And he told him how the troops had fled the battlefield, and that, moreover, many of the troops had fallen and died; also that Saul and his son Jonathan were dead. 5 "How do you know," David asked the young man who brought him the news, "that Saul and his son Jonathan are dead?" 6 The young man who brought him the news answered, "I happened to be at Mount Gilboa, and I saw Saul leaning on his spear, and the chariots and horsemen closing in on him. 7 He looked around and saw me, and he called to me. When I responded, 'At your service,' 8 he asked me, 'Who are you?' And I told him that I was an Amalekite. 9 Then he said to me, 'Stand over me, and finish me off, *-a*for I am in agony and am barely alive.'*-a* 10 So I stood over him and finished him off, for I knew that *-a*he would never rise from where he was lying.*-a* Then I took the crown from his head and the armlet from his arm, and I have brought them here to my lord."

11 David took hold of his clothes and rent them, and so did all the men with him. 12 They lamented and wept, and they fasted until evening for Saul and his son Jonathan, and for the soldiers

a-a *Meaning of Heb. uncertain.*

of the Lord[b] and the House of Israel who had fallen by the sword.
[13] David said to the young man who had brought him the news,
"Where are you from?" He replied, "I am the son of a resident
alien, an Amalekite." [14] "How did you dare," David said to him,
"to lift your hand and kill the Lord's anointed?" [15] Thereupon
David called one of the attendants and said to him, "Come over
and strike him!" He struck him down and he died. [16] And David
said to him, "Your blood be on your own head! Your own mouth
testified against you when you said, 'I put the Lord's anointed to
death.' "

[17] And David intoned this dirge over Saul and his son Jonathan—[18] [a-]He ordered the Judites to be taught [The Song of the]
Bow.[-a] It is recorded in the Book of Jashar.[c]

[19] Your glory, O Israel,
Lies slain on your heights;
How have the mighty fallen!
[20] Tell it not in Gath,
Do not proclaim it in the streets of Ashkelon,
Lest the daughters of the Philistine rejoice,
Lest the daughters of the uncircumcised exult.

[21] O hills of Gilboa—
Let there be no dew or rain on you,
[d-]Or bountiful fields,[-d]
For there the shield of warriors lay rejected,
The shield of Saul,
Polished with oil no more.

[22] From the blood of slain,
From the fat of warriors—
The bow of Jonathan
Never turned back;

[b] *Septuagint reads "Judah."*
[c] *See note at Josh. 10.13.*
[d-d] *Meaning of Heb. uncertain. Emendation yields "springs from the deep"; cf. Ugaritic
shr'thmtm, and see Gen. 7.11; 8.2.*

The sword of Saul
Never withdrew empty.

²³ Saul and Jonathan,
Beloved and cherished,
Never parted
In life or in death!
They were swifter than eagles,
They were stronger than lions!

²⁴ Daughters of Israel,
Weep over Saul,
Who clothed you in crimson and finery,
Who decked your robes with jewels of gold.

²⁵ How have the mighty fallen
In the thick of battle—
Jonathan, slain on your heights!
²⁶ I grieve for you,
My brother Jonathan,
You were most dear to me.
Your love was wonderful to me
More than the love of women.

²⁷ How have the mighty fallen,
The ᵉweapons of warᵉ perished!

2 Some time afterward, David inquired of the Lᴏʀᴅ, "Shall I go up to one of the towns of Judah?" The Lᴏʀᴅ answered, "Yes." David further asked, "Which one shall I go up to?" And the Lᴏʀᴅ replied, "To Hebron." ² So David went up there, along with his two wives, Ahinoam of Jezreel and Abigail wife of Nabal the Carmelite. ³ David also took the men who were with him, each

ᵉ⁻ᵉ *I.e. Saul and Jonathan.*

with his family, and they settled in the towns about Hebron. ⁴ The men of Judah came and there they anointed David king over the House of Judah.

David was told about the men of Jabesh-gilead who buried Saul. ⁵ So David sent messengers to the men of Jabesh-gilead and said to them, "May you be blessed of the LORD because you performed this act of faithfulness to your lord Saul and buried him. ⁶ May the LORD in turn show you true faithfulness; and I too will reward you generously because you performed this act. ⁷ Now take courage and be brave men; for your lord Saul is dead and the House of Judah have already anointed me king over them."

⁸ But Abner son of Ner, Saul's army commander, had taken Ish-bosheth*ᵃ* son of Saul and brought him across to Mahanaim ⁹ and made him king over Gilead, the Ashurites,*ᵇ* Jezreel, Ephraim, and Benjamin—over all Israel. ¹⁰ Ish-bosheth*ᵃ* son of Saul was forty years old when he became king of Israel, and he reigned two years. But the House of Judah supported David. ¹¹ The length of time that David reigned in Hebron over the House of Judah was seven years and six months.

¹² Once Abner son of Ner and the soldiers of Ish-bosheth son of Saul marched out from Mahanaim to Gibeon, ¹³ and Joab son of Zeruiah and the soldiers of David [also] came out.*ᶜ* They confronted one another at the pool of Gibeon: one group sat on one side of the pool, and the other group on the other side of the pool. ¹⁴ Abner said to Joab, "Let the young men come forward and sport*ᵈ* before us." "Yes, let them," Joab answered. ¹⁵ They came forward and were counted off, twelve for Benjamin and Ish-bosheth son of Saul, and twelve of David's soldiers. ¹⁶ Each one grasped his opponent's head*ᵉ* [and thrust] his dagger into his opponent's side; thus they fell together. That place, which is in Gibeon, was called Helkath-hazzurim.*ᶠ*

¹⁷ A fierce battle ensued that day, and Abner and the men of

Israel were routed by David's soldiers. [18] The three sons of Zeruiah[g] were there—Joab, Abishai, and Asahel. Asahel was swift of foot, like a gazelle in the open field. [19] And Asahel ran after Abner, swerving neither right nor left in his pursuit of Abner. [20] Abner looked back and shouted, "Is that you, Asahel?" "Yes, it is," he called back. [21] Abner said to him, "Turn to the right or to the left, and seize one of our boys and strip off his tunic." But Asahel would not leave off. [22] Abner again begged Asahel, "Stop pursuing me, or I'll have to strike you down. How will I look your brother Joab in the face?" [23] When he refused to desist, Abner struck him in the belly with [b-]a backward thrust[-b] of his spear and the spear protruded from his back. He fell there and died on the spot. And all who came to the place where Asahel fell and died halted; [24] but Joab and Abishai continued to pursue Abner. And the sun was setting as they reached the hill of Ammah, [b-]which faces Giah on the road to the wilderness of Gibeon.[-b]

[25] The Benjaminites rallied behind Abner, forming a single company; and they took up a position on the top of a hill. [26] Abner then called out to Joab, "Must the sword devour forever? You know how bitterly it's going to end! How long will you delay ordering your troops to stop the pursuit of their kinsmen?" [27] And Joab replied, "As God lives, [h-]if you hadn't spoken up, the troops would have given up the pursuit of their kinsmen only the next morning."[-h] [28] Joab then sounded the horn, and all the troops halted; they ceased their pursuit of Israel and stopped the fighting. [29] Abner and his men marched through the Arabah all that night and, after crossing the Jordan, they marched [b-]through all of Bithron[-b] until they came to Mahanaim. [30] After Joab gave up the pursuit of Abner, he assembled all the troops and found nineteen of David's soldiers missing, besides Asahel. [31] David's soldiers, on the other hand, [b-]defeated the Benjaminites and the men under Abner and killed three hundred and sixty men.[-b] [32] They bore Asahel away and buried him in his father's tomb in Bethlehem. Then Joab and his men marched all night; day broke upon them in Hebron.

---

[g] *A sister of David, I Chron. 2.16.*
[h-h] *Emendation yields "If you had only spoken up, the troops would already have given up the pursuit of their kinsmen this morning."*

3 The war between the House of Saul and the House of David was long-drawn-out; but David kept growing stronger, while the House of Saul grew weaker.

2 *a*Sons were born to David in Hebron: His firstborn was Amnon, by Ahinoam of Jezreel; 3 his second was Chileab, by Abigail wife of Nabal the Carmelite; the third was Absalom son of Maacah, daughter of King Talmai of Geshur; 4 the fourth was Adonijah son of Haggith; the fifth was Shephatiah son of Abital; 5 and the sixth was Ithream, by David's wife Eglah. These were born to David in Hebron.

6 During the war between the House of Saul and the House of David, Abner supported the House of Saul. 7 Now Saul had a concubine named Rizpah, daughter of Aiah; and [Ish-bosheth] said to Abner, "Why have you lain with my father's concubine?" 8 Abner was very upset by what Ish-bosheth said, and he replied, "Am I a dog's head *b*-from Judah?*-b* Here I have been loyally serving the House of your father Saul and his kinsfolk and friends, and I have not betrayed you into the hands of David; yet this day you reproach me over a woman! 9 May God do thus and more to Abner if I do not do for David as the LORD swore to him—10 to transfer the kingship from the House of Saul, and to establish the throne of David over Israel and Judah from Dan to Beer-sheba." 11 [Ish-bosheth] could say nothing more in reply to Abner, because he was afraid of him.

12 Abner immediately*b* sent messengers to David, saying, *b*-"To whom shall the land belong?" and to say [further],*-b* "Make a pact with me, and I will help you and bring all Israel over to your side." 13 He replied, "Good; I will make a pact with you. But I make one demand upon you: Do not appear before me unless you bring Michal daughter of Saul when you come before me." 14 David also sent messengers to Ish-bosheth son of Saul, to say, "Give me my wife Michal, for whom I paid the bride price*c* of one hundred Philistine foreskins."*d* 15 So Ish-bosheth sent and had

---

a *The list of David's wives and sons in vv. 2-5 differs somewhat from the parallel list in I Chron. 3.1-3. The narrative in v. 1 is resumed in v. 6.*

b-b *Meaning of Heb. uncertain.*

c *Cf. Exod. 22.15; Deut. 20.7; 22.23-29.*

d *Cf. I Sam. 18.27 (where the number is given as "two hundred").*

her taken away from [her] husband, Paltiel son of Laish. [16] Her husband walked with her as far as Bahurim, weeping as he followed her; then Abner ordered him to turn back, and he went back.

[17] Abner had conferred with the elders of Israel, saying, "You have wanted David to be king over you all along. [18] Now act! For the LORD has said concerning David: *'I will deliver-* My people Israel from the hands of the Philistines and all its other enemies through My servant David." [19] Abner also talked with the Benjaminites; then Abner went and informed David in Hebron of all the wishes of Israel and of the whole House of Benjamin.

[20] When Abner came to David in Hebron, accompanied by twenty men, David made a feast for Abner and the men with him. [21] Abner said to David, "Now I will go and rally all Israel to Your Majesty. They will make a pact with you, and you can reign over all that your heart desires." And David dismissed Abner, who went away unharmed.

[22] Just then David's soldiers and Joab returned from a raid, bringing much plunder with them; Abner was no longer with David in Hebron, for he had been dismissed and had gone away unharmed. [23] When Joab and the whole force with him arrived, Joab was told that Abner son of Ner had come to the king, had been dismissed by him, and had gone away unharmed. [24] Joab went to the king and said, "What have you done? Here Abner came to you; why did you let him go? Now he has gotten away! [25] Don't you know that Abner son of Ner came only to deceive you, to learn your comings and goings and to find out all that you are planning?" [26] Joab left David and sent messengers after Abner, and they brought him back from the cistern of Sirah; but David knew nothing about it. [27] When Abner returned to Hebron, Joab took him aside within the gate to talk to him privately;*b* there he struck him in the belly. Thus [Abner] died for shedding the blood of Asahel, Joab's*f* brother.

[28] Afterward, when David heard of it, he said, "Both I and my kingdom are forever innocent before the LORD of shedding the

e So many mss. and versions; most mss. and editions have "He has delivered."
f Heb. "his."

blood of Abner son of Ner. ²⁹ May [the guilt] fall upon the head
of Joab and all his father's house. May the house of Joab never
be without someone suffering from a discharge or an eruption,
or ^{g-}a male who handles the spindle,^{-g} or one slain by the sword,
or one lacking bread."—³⁰ Now Joab and his brother Abishai had
killed Abner because he had killed their brother Asahel during
the battle at Gibeon.—³¹ David then ordered Joab and all the
troops with him to rend their clothes, gird on sackcloth, and make
lament before^h Abner; and King David himself walked behind the
bier. ³² And so they buried Abner at Hebron; the king wept aloud
by Abner's grave, and all the troops wept. ³³ And the king intoned
this dirge over Abner,

"Should Abner have died the death of a churl?
³⁴ Your hands were not bound,
Your feet were not put in fetters;
But you fell as one falls
Before treacherous men!"
And all the troops continued to weep over him.

³⁵ All the troops came to urge David to eat something while it
was still day; but David swore, "May God do thus to me and more
if I eat bread or anything else before sundown." ³⁶ All the troops
^{b-}took note of it^{-b} and approved, ^{b-}just as all the troops approved
everything else the king did.^{-b} ³⁷ That day all the troops and all
Israel knew that it was not by the king's will that Abner son of Ner
was killed. ³⁸ And the king said to his soldiers, "You well know
that a prince, a great man in Israel, has fallen this day. ³⁹ And
today I am weak, even though anointed king; those men, the sons
of Zeruiah, are too savage for me. May the LORD requite the
wicked for their wickedness!"

4 When [Ish-bosheth] son of Saul heard that Abner had died
in Hebron, ^{a-}he lost heart^{-a} and all Israel was alarmed. ² The son
of Saul [had] two company commanders, one named Baanah

^{g-g} I.e. a man fit only for woman's work.
^h I.e. in the procession.
^{a-a} Lit. "his hands weakened"; and so frequently.

and the other Rechab, sons of Rimmon the Beerothite—Benjaminites, since Beeroth too was considered part of Benjamin. [3] The Beerothites had fled to Gittaim, [b]where they have sojourned to this day. ([4]Jonathan son of Saul had a son whose feet were crippled. He was five years old when the news about Saul and Jonathan came from Jezreel, and his nurse picked him up and fled; but as she was fleeing in haste, he fell and was lamed. His name was Mephibosheth.[c]) [5] Rechab and Baanah, sons of Rimmon the Beerothite, started out, and they reached the home of Ish-bosheth at the heat of the day, when he was taking his midday rest. [6] [d-]So they went inside the house, as though fetching wheat, and struck him in the belly.[-d] Rechab and his brother Baanah slipped by, [7] and entered the house while he was asleep on his bed in his bedchamber; and they stabbed him to death. They cut off his head and took his head and made their way all night through the Arabah. [8] They brought the head of Ish-bosheth to David in Hebron. "Here," they said to the king, "is the head of your enemy, Ish-bosheth son of Saul, who sought your life. This day the LORD has avenged my lord the king upon Saul and his offspring."

[9] But David answered Rechab and his brother Baanah, the sons of Rimmon the Beerothite, and said to them, "As the LORD lives, who has rescued me from every trouble: [10] The man who told me in Ziklag that Saul was dead thought he was bringing good news. But instead of rewarding him for the news, I seized and killed him. [11] How much more, then, when wicked men have killed a blameless man in bed in his own house! I will certainly avenge his blood on you, and I will rid the earth of you." [12] David gave orders to the young men, who killed them; they cut off their hands and feet and hung them up by the pool in Hebron. And they took the head of Ish-bosheth and buried it in the grave of Abner at Hebron.

---

[b] *Gittaim was likewise in Benjamin; cf. Neh. 11.31 ff.*
[c] *The original form of the name, Merib-baal, is preserved in I Chron. 8.34; 9.40. Cf. Ish-bosheth (Eshbaal) in II Sam. 2.8, note a. This subject is resumed in chapter 9.*
[d-d] *Meaning of Heb. uncertain. Septuagint reads, "And behold, the woman who kept the door of the house was cleaning wheat. She became drowsy and fell asleep."*

5 *All the tribes of Israel came to David at Hebron and said, "We are your own flesh and blood. ² Long before now, when Saul was king over us, it was you who *led Israel in war;* and the LORD said to you: You shall shepherd My people Israel; you shall be ruler of Israel." ³ All the elders of Israel came to the king at Hebron, and King David made a pact with them in Hebron before the LORD. And they anointed David king over Israel.

⁴ David was thirty years old when he became king, and he reigned forty years. ⁵ In Hebron he reigned over Judah seven years and six months, and in Jerusalem he reigned over all Israel and Judah thirty-three years.

⁶ The king and his men set out for Jerusalem against the Jebusites who inhabited the region. David was told, "You will never get in here! *Even the blind and the lame will turn you back." (They meant: David will never enter here.)*-* ⁷ But David captured the stronghold of Zion; it is now the City of David. ⁸ On that occasion David said, "Those who attack the Jebusites *shall reach the water channel and [strike down] the lame and the blind, who are hateful to David." That is why they say: "No one who is blind or lame may enter the House."*-*

⁹ David occupied the stronghold and renamed it the City of David; David also fortified the surrounding area, from the Millo* inward. ¹⁰ David kept growing stronger, for the LORD, the God of Hosts, was with him.

¹¹ *King Hiram of Tyre sent envoys to David with cedar logs, carpenters, and stonemasons; and they built a palace for David. ¹² Thus David knew that the LORD had established him as king over Israel and had exalted his kingship for the sake of His people Israel.

¹³ After he left Hebron, David took more concubines and wives in Jerusalem, and more sons and daughters were born to David. ¹⁴ These are the names of the children born to him in Jerusalem:

ª *The account in vv. 1-3 and 6-10 is to be found also, with variations, in I Chron. 11.1-9.*
ᵇ⁻ᵇ *Lit. "led Israel out and in."*
ᶜ⁻ᶜ *Meaning of Heb. uncertain.*
ᵈ *A citadel.*
ᵉ *The account in vv. 11-25 is to be found also, with variations, in I Chron. 14.1-16.*

176

*f*Shammua, Shobab, Nathan, and Solomon; [15] Ibhar, Elishua, Nepheg, and Japhia; [16] Elishama, Eliada, and Eliphelet.

[17] *g*When the Philistines heard that David had been anointed king over Israel, the Philistines marched up in search of David; but David heard of it, and he went down to the fastness.*h* [18] The Philistines came and spread out over the Valley of Rephaim. [19] David inquired of the LORD, "Shall I go up against the Philistines? Will You deliver them into my hands?" And the LORD answered David, "Go up, and I will deliver the Philistines into your hands." [20] Thereupon David marched to Baal-perazim, and David defeated them there. And he said, "The LORD has broken through my enemies before me as waters break through [a dam]." That is why that place was named Baal-perazim.*i* [21] The Philistines abandoned their idols there, and David and his men carried them off.

[22] Once again the Philistines marched up and spread out over the Valley of Rephaim. [23] David inquired of the LORD, and He answered, "Do not go up, but circle around behind them and confront them at the baca*c* trees. [24] And when you hear the sound of marching in the tops of the baca trees, then go into action, for the LORD will be going in front of you to attack the Philistine forces." [25] David did as the LORD had commanded him; and he routed the Philistines from Geba all the way to Gezer.

6 David again assembled all the picked men of Israel, thirty thousand strong. [2] *a*Then David and all the troops that were with him set out from Baalim*b* of Judah to bring up from there the Ark of God to which the Name was attached, the name LORD of Hosts Enthroned on the Cherubim.

[3] They loaded the Ark of God onto a new cart and conveyed

---

f *The list in vv. 14-16 is found, in addition to I Chron. 14.4-7, in I Chron. 3.5-8, with variations.*

g *Vv. 17-25 continue the narrative of v. 3.*

h *Probably the stronghold of Adullam (cf. I Sam. 22.4-5).*

i *Interpreted as "Baal of Breaches." Cf. 6.8 below, and the name Perez in Gen. 38.29 and note.*

a *Vv. 2-12 are found also in I Chron. 13.5-14, with variations.*

b *Identical with Baalah, another name for Kiriath-jearim, where the Ark had been kept (cf. I Sam. 6.21; I Chron. 13.6; Josh. 15.9).*

it from the house of Abinadab which was on the hill; and Abinadab's sons, Uzza and Ahio, guided the ᶜ⁻new cart. ⁴ They conveyed it from Abinadab's house on the hill, [Uzzah walking]ᵈ
alongside⁻ᶜ the Ark of God and Ahio walking in front of the Ark.
⁵ Meanwhile, David and all the House of Israel danced before the
LORD to ᵉ⁻[the sound of] all kinds of cypress wood [instruments],⁻ᵉ
with lyres, harps, timbrels, sistrums, and cymbals.

⁶ But when they came to the threshing floor of Nacon, Uzzah
reached out for the Ark of God and grasped it, for the oxen had
stumbled.ᶠ ⁷ The LORD was incensed at Uzzah. And God struck
him down on the spot ᵍ⁻for his indiscretion,⁻ᵍ and he died there
beside the Ark of God. ⁸ David was distressed because the LORD
had inflicted a breach upon Uzzah; and that place was named
Perez-uzzah,ʰ as it is still called.

⁹ David was afraid of the LORD that day; he said, "How can
I let the Ark of the LORD come to me?" ¹⁰ So David would not
bring the Ark to his place in the City of David; instead, he diverted it to the house of Obed-edom the Gittite. ¹¹ The Ark of
the LORD remained in the house of Obed-edom the Gittite
three months, and the LORD blessed Obed-edom and his
whole household.

¹² It was reported to King David: "The LORD has blessed Obed-
edom's house and all that belongs to him because of the Ark of
God." ⁱThereupon David went and brought up the Ark of God
from the house of Obed-edom to the City of David, amid rejoicing. ¹³ When the bearers of the Ark of the LORD had moved
forward six paces, he sacrificed ʲ⁻an ox and a fatling.⁻ʲ ¹⁴ David
whirled with all his might before the LORD; David was girt with
a linen ephod. ¹⁵ Thus David and all the House of Israel brought
up the Ark of the LORD with shouts and with blasts of the horn.

¹⁶ As the Ark of the LORD entered the City of David, Michal
daughter of Saul looked out of the window and saw King David

ᶜ⁻ᶜ *Septuagint and 4QSamᵃ read "cart alongside."*
ᵈ *Cf. vv. 6-7.*
ᵉ⁻ᵉ *Cf. Kimhi; the parallel passage I Chron. 13.8 reads "with all their might and with songs."*
ᶠ *Meaning of Heb. uncertain.*
ᵍ⁻ᵍ *So Targum; I Chron. 13.10 reads "because he had laid a hand on the Ark."*
ʰ *I.e. "the Breach of Uzzah"; cf. 5.20 and note.*
ⁱ *Vv. 12b-14 are found, with variations, in I Chron. 15.25-27; vv. 15-19a, with variations,
in I Chron. 15.28-16.3; vv. 19b-20a, with variations, in I Chron. 16.43.*
ʲ⁻ʲ *4QSamᵃ reads "seven oxen and seven (rams)"; cf. I Chron. 15.26.*

leaping and whirling before the LORD; and she despised him for it.

¹⁷ They brought in the Ark of the LORD and set it up in its place inside the tent which David had pitched for it, and David sacrificed burnt offerings and offerings of well-being before the LORD. ¹⁸ When David finished sacrificing the burnt offerings and the offerings of well-being, he blessed the people in the name of the LORD of Hosts. ¹⁹ And he distributed among all the people— the entire multitude of Israel, man and woman alike—to each a loaf of bread, ^f-a cake made in a pan, and a raisin cake.^{-f} Then all the people left for their homes.

²⁰ David went home to greet his household. And Michal daughter of Saul came out to meet David and said, "Didn't the king of Israel do himself honor today—exposing himself today in the sight of the slavegirls of his subjects, as one of the riffraff might expose himself!" ²¹ David answered Michal, "It was before the LORD who chose me instead of your father and all his family and appointed me ruler over the LORD's people Israel! I will dance before the LORD ²² and dishonor myself even more, and be low in ^k-my own^{-k} esteem; but among the slavegirls that you speak of I will be honored." ²³ So to her dying day Michal daughter of Saul had no children.

7 ^aWhen the king was settled in his palace and the LORD had granted him safety from all the enemies around him, ² the king said to the prophet Nathan: "Here I am dwelling in a house of cedar, while the Ark of the LORD abides in a tent!" ³ Nathan said to the king, "Go and do whatever you have in mind, for the LORD is with you."

⁴ But that same night the word of the LORD came to Nathan: ⁵ "Go and say to My servant David: Thus said the LORD: Are you the one to build a house for Me to dwell in? ⁶ From the day that I brought the people of Israel out of Egypt to this day I

^{k-k} *Septuagint reads "your."*

^a *This chapter is found, with variations, also in I Chron. 17.*

have not dwelt in a house, but have moved about in Tent and Tabernacle. ⁷ As I moved about wherever the Israelites went, did I ever reproach any of the tribal leaders*ᵇ* whom I appointed to care for My people Israel: Why have you not built Me a house of cedar?

⁸ "Further, say thus to My servant David: Thus said the LORD of Hosts: I took you from the pasture, from following the flock, to be ruler of My people Israel, ⁹ and I have been with you wherever you went, and have cut down all your enemies before you. Moreover, I will give you great renown like that of the greatest men on earth. ¹⁰ I will establish a home for My people Israel and will plant them firm, so that they shall dwell secure and shall tremble no more. Evil men shall not oppress them any more as in the past,¹¹ ever since I appointed chieftains over My people Israel. I will give you safety from all your enemies.

"The LORD declares to you that He, the LORD, will establish a house*ᶜ* for you. ¹² When your days are done and you lie with your fathers, I will raise up your offspring after you, one of your own issue, and I will establish his kingship. ¹³ He shall build a house for My name, and I will establish his royal throne forever. ¹⁴ I will be a father to him, and he shall be a son to Me. When he does wrong, I will chastise him *ᵈ⁻*with the rod of men and the affliction of mortals;*⁻ᵈ* ¹⁵ but I will never withdraw My favor from him as I withdrew it from Saul, whom I removed *ᵉ⁻*to make room for you.*⁻ᵉ* ¹⁶ Your house and your kingship shall ever be secure before you;*ᶠ* your throne shall be established forever."

¹⁷ Nathan spoke to David in accordance with all these words and all this prophecy. ¹⁸ Then King David came and sat before the LORD, and he said, "What am I, O Lord GOD, and what is my family, that You have brought me thus far? ¹⁹ Yet even this, O Lord GOD, has seemed too little to You; for You have spoken of Your servant's house also for the future. *ᵍ⁻*May that be the law for the people,*⁻ᵍ* O Lord GOD. ²⁰ What more can David say to You?

You know Your servant, O Lord GOD. [21] [g]For Your word's sake and of Your own accord[g] You have wrought this great thing, and made it known to Your servant. [22] You are great indeed, O LORD God! There is none like You and there is no other God but You, as we have always heard. [23] And who is like Your people Israel, a unique nation on earth, whom God went and redeemed as His people, winning renown for Himself and doing great and marvelous deeds for them[h] [and] for Your land—[driving out][i] nations and their gods before Your people, whom You redeemed for Yourself from Egypt. [24] You have established Your people Israel as Your very own people forever; and You, O LORD, have become their God.

[25] "And now, O LORD God, fulfill Your promise to Your servant and his house forever; and do as You have promised. [26] And may Your name be glorified forever, in that men will say, 'The LORD of Hosts is God over Israel'; and may the house of Your servant David be established before You. [27] Because You, O LORD of Hosts, the God of Israel, have revealed to Your servant that You will build a house for him, Your servant has ventured to offer this prayer to You. [28] And now, O Lord GOD, You are God and Your words will surely come true, and You have made this gracious promise to Your servant. [29] Be pleased, therefore, to bless Your servant's house, that it abide before You forever; for You, O Lord GOD, have spoken. May Your servant's house be blessed forever by Your blessing."

8 [a]Some time afterward, David attacked the Philistines and subdued them; and David took Metheg-ammah[b] from the Philistines. [2] He also defeated the Moabites. He made them lie down on the ground and he measured them off with a cord; he measured out two lengths of cord for those who were to be put to death, and one length for those to be spared.[c] And the Moabites became tributary vassals of David.

[3] David defeated Hadadezer son of Rehob, king of Zobah, who

[h] *Heb. "you," apparently denoting Israel.*
[i] *So I Chron. 17.21.*

[a] *This chapter is reproduced, with some variations, in I Chron. 18.*
[b] *If not a place name, meaning of Heb. uncertain.*
[c] *I.e. he repeatedly doomed twice the number he spared.*

was then on his way to restore his monument[d] at the Euphrates River. [4] David captured 1,700 horsemen and 20,000 foot soldiers of his force; and David hamstrung all the chariot horses, except for 100 which he retained. [5] And when the Arameans of Damascus came to the aid of King Hadadezer of Zobah, David struck down 22,000 of the Arameans. [6] David stationed garrisons in Aram of Damascus, and the Arameans became tributary vassals of David. The LORD gave David victory wherever he went. [7] David took the gold shields[e] carried by Hadadezer's retinue and brought them to Jerusalem; [8] and from Betah and Berothai, towns of Hadadezer, King David took a vast amount of copper.

[9] When King Toi of Hamath heard that David had defeated the entire army of Hadadezer,[10] Toi sent his son Joram to King David to greet him and to congratulate him on his military victory over Hadadezer—for Hadadezer had been at war with Toi. [Joram] brought with him objects of silver, gold, and copper. [11] King David dedicated these to the LORD, along with the other silver and gold that he dedicated, [taken] from all the nations he had conquered:[12] from Edom,[f] Moab, and Ammon; from the Philistines and the Amalekites, and from the plunder of Hadadezer son of Rehob, king of Zobah.

[13] David gained fame [g-]when he returned from defeating[-g] Edom[f] in the Valley of Salt, 18,000 in all. [14] He stationed garrisons in Edom—[h-]he stationed garrisons in all of Edom,[-h] and all the Edomites became vassals of David. The LORD gave David victory wherever he went.

[15] David reigned over all Israel, and David executed true justice among all his people. [16] Joab son of Zeruiah was commander of the army; Jehoshaphat son of Ahilud was recorder; [17] Zadok son of Ahitub and [i-]Ahimelech son of Abiathar[-i] were priests; Seraiah[j] was scribe; [18] Benaiah son of Jehoiada was [k-]commander of[-k] the Cherethites and the Pelethites; and David's sons were priests.

[d] On yad in this sense, cf. 18.18; I Chron. 18.3; I Sam. 15.12. Others "dominion."
[e] Or "quivers."
[f] So several mss., Septuagint, and I Chron. 18.11-13; and cf.v. 14 below. Printed editions and most mss. read "Aram."
[g-g] I Chron. 18.12 and Ps. 60.2 read differently.
[h-h] This phrase is lacking in I Chron. 18.13.
[i-i] Emendation yields "Abiathar son of Ahimelech," cf.,e.g., 20.25; I Sam. 22.20.
[j] "Sheva" in 20.25; "Shavsha" in I Chron. 18.16.
[k-k] So Targum (cf. 20.23; I Chron. 18.17); Heb. "and."

9 David inquired, "Is there anyone still left of the House of Saul with whom I can keep faith for the sake of Jonathan?" [2] There was a servant of the House of Saul named Ziba, and they summoned him to David. "Are you Ziba?" the king asked him. *[a]*"Yes, sir,"*[a]* he replied. [3] The king continued, "Is there anyone at all left of the House of Saul with whom I can keep faith as pledged before God?"*[b]* Ziba answered the king, "Yes, there is still a son of Jonathan whose feet are crippled." [4] "Where is he?" the king asked, and Ziba said to the king, "He is in the house of Machir son of Ammiel, in Lo-debar." [5] King David had him brought from the house of Machir son of Ammiel, at Lo-debar; [6] and when Mephibosheth son of Jonathan son of Saul came to David, he flung himself on his face and prostrated himself. David said, "Mephibosheth!" and he replied, "At your service, sir." [7] David said to him, "Don't be afraid, for I will keep faith with you for the sake of your father Jonathan. I will give you back all the land of your grandfather Saul; moreover, you shall always eat at my table." [8] [Mephibosheth] prostrated himself again, and said, "What is your servant, that you should show regard for a dead dog like me?"

[9] The king summoned Ziba, Saul's steward, and said to him, "I give to your master's grandson everything that belonged to Saul and to his entire family. [10] You and your sons and your slaves shall farm the land for him and shall bring in [its yield] to provide food for your master's grandson*[c]* to live on; but Mephibosheth, your master's grandson, shall always eat at my table."—Ziba had fifteen sons and twenty slaves.—[11] Ziba said to the king, "Your servant will do just as my lord the king has commanded him." *[d]*"Mephibosheth shall eat at my table*[d]* like one of the king's sons."

[12] Mephibosheth had a young son named Mica; and all the members of Ziba's household worked for Mephibosheth. [13] Mephibosheth lived in Jerusalem, for he ate regularly at the king's table. He was lame in both feet.

[a-a] Lit. "Your servant is."
[b] See I Sam. 20.14 and note.
[c] Septuagint reads "household."
[d-d] Septuagint reads "And Mephibosheth ate at David's table."

10 *a*Some time afterward, the king of Ammon died, and his son Hanun succeeded him as king. ² David said, "I will keep faith with Hanun son of Nahash, just as his father kept faith with me." He sent his courtiers with a message of condolence to him over his father. But when David's courtiers came to the land of Ammon, ³ the Ammonite officials said to their lord Hanun, "Do you think David is really honoring your father just because he sent you men with condolences? Why, David has sent his courtiers to you to explore and spy out the city, and to overthrow*b* it." ⁴ So Hanun seized David's courtiers, clipped off one side of their beards and cut away half of their garments at the buttocks, and sent them off. ⁵ When David was told of it, he dispatched men to meet them, for the men were greatly embarrassed. And the king gave orders: "Stop in Jericho until your beards grow back; then you can return."

⁶ The Ammonites realized that they had *c-*incurred the wrath of*-c* David; so the Ammonites sent agents and hired Arameans of Beth-rehob and Arameans of Zobah—20,000 foot soldiers—the king of Maacah [with] 1,000 men, and 12,000 men from Tob. ⁷ On learning this, David sent out Joab and the whole army—[including] the professional fighters. ⁸ The Ammonites marched out and took up their battle position at the entrance of the gate, while the Arameans of Zobah and Rehob and the men of Tob and Maacah took their stand separately in the open. ⁹ Joab saw that there was a battle line against him both front and rear. So he made a selection from all the picked men of Israel and arrayed them against the Arameans,¹⁰ and the rest of the troops he put under the command of his brother Abishai*d* and arrayed them against the Ammonites. ¹¹ [Joab] said, "If the Arameans prove too strong for me, you come to my aid; and if the Ammonites prove too strong for you, I will come to your aid. ¹² Let us be strong and resolute for the sake of our people and the land*e* of our God; and the LORD will do what He deems right."

---

a *This chapter is found also in I Chron. 19.*
b *Emendation yields "reconnoiter"; cf. Deut. 1.22; Josh. 2.2-3.*
c-c *See note at I Sam. 13.4.*
d *Heb. "Abshai."*
e *Lit. "towns."*

¹³ Joab and the troops with him marched into battle against the Arameans, who fled before him. ¹⁴ And when the Ammonites saw that the Arameans had fled, they fled before Abishai and withdrew into the city. So Joab broke off the attack against the Ammonites, and went to Jerusalem.

¹⁵ When the Arameans saw that they had been routed by Israel, they regrouped their forces. ¹⁶ Hadadezer*ᶠ* sent for and brought out the Arameans from across the Euphrates; they came to Helam, led by Shobach, Hadadezer's*ᶠ* army commander. ¹⁷ David was informed of it; he assembled all Israel, crossed the Jordan, and came to Helam. The Arameans drew up their forces against David and attacked him;¹⁸ but the Arameans were put to flight by Israel. David killed 700 Aramean charioteers and 40,000 horsemen;*ᵍ* he also struck down Shobach, Hadadezer's*ʰ* army commander, who died there. ¹⁹ And when all the vassal kings of Hadadezer*ᶠ* saw that they had been routed by Israel, they submitted to Israel and became their vassals. And the Arameans were afraid to help the Ammonites any more.

11 At the turn of the year, the season when kings go out [to battle], David sent Joab with his officers and all Israel with him, and they devastated Ammon and besieged Rabbah; David remained in Jerusalem. ² Late one afternoon, David rose from his couch and strolled on the roof of the royal palace; and from the roof he saw a woman bathing. The woman was very beautiful, ³ and the king sent someone to make inquiries about the woman. He reported, "She is Bathsheba daughter of Eliam [and] wife of Uriah the Hittite." ⁴ David sent messengers to fetch her; she came to him and he lay with her—she had just purified herself after her period—and she went back home. ⁵ The woman conceived, and she sent word to David, "I am pregnant." ⁶ Thereupon David sent a message to Joab, "Send Uriah the Hittite to me"; and Joab sent Uriah to David.

⁷ When Uriah came to him, David asked him how Joab and the

ᶠ *Many editions read "Hadarezer . . . Hadarezer's."*
ᵍ *I Chron. 19.18 reads "foot soldiers."*
ʰ *Heb. "his."*

troops were faring and how the war was going. [8] Then David said to Uriah, "Go down to your house and bathe your feet." When Uriah left the royal palace, a present from the king followed him. [9] But Uriah slept at the entrance of the royal palace, along with the other officers of his lord, and did not go down to his house. [10] When David was told that Uriah had not gone down to his house, he said to Uriah, "You just came from a journey, why didn't you go down to your house?" [11] Uriah answered David, "The Ark and Israel and Judah are located at Succoth, and my master Joab and Your Majesty's men are camped in the open; how can I go home and eat and drink and sleep with my wife? [a-]As you live, by your very life,[-a] I will not do this!" [12] David said to Uriah, "Stay here today also, and tomorrow I will send you off." So Uriah remained in Jerusalem that day. [13] The next day, David summoned him, and he ate and drank with him until he got him drunk; but in the evening, [Uriah] went out to sleep in the same place, with his lord's officers; he did not go down to his home.

[14] In the morning, David wrote a letter to Joab, which he sent with Uriah. [15] He wrote in the letter as follows: "Place Uriah in the front line where the fighting is fiercest; then fall back so that he may be killed." [16] So when Joab was besieging the city, he stationed Uriah at the point where he knew that there were able warriors. [17] The men of the city sallied out and attacked Joab, and some of David's officers among the troops fell; Uriah the Hittite was among those who died.

[18] Joab sent a full report of the battle to David. [19] He instructed the messenger as follows: "When you finish reporting to the king all about the battle, [20] the king may get angry and say to you, 'Why did you come so close to the city to attack it? Didn't you know that they would shoot from the wall? [21] Who struck down Abimelech son of Jerubbesheth?[b] Was it not a woman who dropped an upper millstone on him from the wall at Thebez, from which he died? Why did you come so close to the wall?' Then say: 'Your servant Uriah the Hittite was among those killed.' "

[a-a] *Meaning of Heb. uncertain. Emendation yields "As the* LORD *lives and as you live" (cf. I Sam. 20.3; 25.26; etc.). Lit. "as you live and as your being lives."*

[b] *The earlier form is Jerubbaal (another name for Gideon), Judg. 7.1; on* -bosheth/besheth *for* -baal, *see note at II Sam. 4.4. For the event at Thebez described here, see Judg. 9.35ff.*

²² The messenger set out; he came and told David all that Joab had sent him to say.ᶜ ²³ The messenger said to David, "First the men prevailed against us and sallied out against us into the open; then we drove them back up to the entrance to the gate. ²⁴ But the archers shot at your men from the wall and some of Your Majesty's men fell; your servant Uriah the Hittite also fell." ²⁵ Whereupon David said to the messenger, "Give Joab this message: 'Do not be distressed about the matter. The sword ᵈ⁻always takes its toll.⁻ᵈ Press your attack on the city and destroy it!' Encourage him!"

²⁶ When Uriah's wife heard that her husband Uriah was dead, she lamented over her husband. ²⁷ After the period of mourning was over, David sent and had her brought into his palace; she became his wife and she bore him a son.

12 But the LORD was displeased with what David had done, ¹ and the LORD sent Nathan to David. He came to him and said, "There were two men in the same city, one rich and one poor. ² The rich man had very large flocks and herds, ³ but the poor man had only one little ewe lamb that he had bought. He tended it and it grew up together with him and his children: it used to share his morsel of bread, drink from his cup, and nestle in his bosom; it was like a daughter to him. ⁴ One day, a traveler came to the rich man, but he was loath to take anything from his own flocks or herds to prepare a meal for the guest who had come to him; so he took the poor man's lamb and prepared it for the man who had come to him."

⁵ David flew into a rage against the man, and said to Nathan, "As the LORD lives, the man who did this deserves to die! ⁶ He shall pay for the lamb four times over, because he did such a thing and showed no pity." ⁷ And Nathan said to David, "That man is you! Thus said the LORD, the God of Israel: 'It was I who anointed you king over Israel and it was I who rescued you from the hand of Saul. ⁸ I gave you your master's house and possession of your master's wives; and I gave you the House of Israel and Judah; and if that were not enough, I would give you twice as much more.

ᶜ *Septuagint continues with a recapitulation of vv. 19-21.*
ᵈ⁻ᵈ *Lit. "consumes the like and the like."*

9 Why then have you flouted the command of the LORD and done what displeases Him? You have put Uriah the Hittite to the sword; you took his wife and made her your wife and had him killed by the sword of the Ammonites. 10 Therefore the sword shall never depart from your House—because you spurned Me by taking the wife of Uriah the Hittite and making her your wife.' 11 Thus said the LORD: 'I will make a calamity rise against you from within your own house; I will take your wives and give them to another man before your very eyes and he shall sleep with your wives under this very sun. 12 You acted in secret, but I will make this happen in the sight of all Israel and in broad daylight.' "

13 David said to Nathan, "I stand guilty before the LORD!" And Nathan replied to David, "The LORD has remitted your sin; you shall not die. 14 However, since you have spurned *the enemies of*-*a* the LORD by this deed, the child about to be born to you shall die."

15 Nathan went home, and the LORD afflicted the child that Uriah's wife had borne to David, and it became critically ill. 16 David entreated God for the boy; David fasted, and he went in and spent the night lying*b* on the ground. 17 The senior servants of his household tried to induce him to get up from the ground; but he refused, nor would he partake of food with them. 18 On the seventh day the child died. David's servants were afraid to tell David that the child was dead; for they said, "We spoke to him when the child was alive and he wouldn't listen to us; how can we tell him that the child is dead? He might do something terrible." 19 When David saw his servants talking in whispers, David understood that the child was dead; David asked his servants, "Is the child dead?" "Yes," they replied.

20 Thereupon David rose from the ground; he bathed and anointed himself, and he changed his clothes. He went into the House of the LORD and prostrated himself. Then he went home and asked for food, which they set before him and he ate. 21 His courtiers asked him, "Why have you acted in this manner? While the child was alive, you fasted and wept; but now that the child

a-a *The phrase is intended to avoid saying "spurned the LORD"; cf. Note "d-d" at I Sam. 25.22.*
b *Some Septuagint mss. and 4QSam*ᵃ *add "in sackcloth": cf. I Kings 21.27.*

is dead, you rise and take food!'' ²² He replied, "While the child was still alive, I fasted and wept because I thought: 'Who knows? The LORD may have pity on me, and the child may live.' ²³ But now that he is dead, why should I fast? Can I bring him back again? I shall go to him, but he will never come back to me.''

²⁴ David consoled his wife Bathsheba; he went to her and lay with her. She bore a son and she named him Solomon. The LORD favored him, ²⁵ and He sent a message through the prophet Nathan; and he was named Jedidiah^c at the instance of the LORD.

²⁶ ^dJoab attacked Rabbah of Ammon and captured the royal city. ²⁷ Joab sent messengers to David and said, "I have attacked Rabbah and I have already captured ^e'the water city.^-e ²⁸ Now muster the rest of the troops and besiege the city and capture it; otherwise I will capture the city myself, and my name will be connected with it.'' ²⁹ David mustered all the troops and marched on Rabbah, and he attacked it and captured it. ³⁰ ^fThe crown was taken from the head of their king^g and it was placed on David's head—it weighed a talent of gold, and [on it]^h were precious stones. He also carried off a vast amoung of booty from the city. ³¹ He led out the people who lived there and set them to work with saws, iron threshing boards, and iron axes, or assigned them to brickmaking; David did this to all the towns of Ammon. Then David and all the troops returned to Jerusalem.

13 This happened some time afterward: Absalom son of David had a beautiful sister named Tamar, and Amnon son of David became infatuated with her. ² Amnon was so distraught because of his [half-] sister Tamar that he became sick; for she was a virgin, and it seemed impossible to Amnon to do anything to her. ³ Amnon had a friend named Jonadab, the son of David's brother Shimah; Jonadab was a very clever man. ⁴ He asked him, "Why are you so dejected, O prince, morning after morning? Tell me!''

^c *I.e. "Beloved of the LORD."*
^d *Vv. 26-29 are abridged in I Chron. 20.1b.*
^e-e *Meaning of Heb. uncertain; perhaps the source of the water supply.*
^f *Vv. 30-31 are found also in I Chron. 20.2-3.*
^g *Heb. "malkam," perhaps equivalent to "Milcom," the Ammonite deity; cf. I Kings 11.5.*
^h *So Targum and I Chron. 20.2.*

Amnon replied, "I am in love with Tamar, the sister of my brother Absalom!" [5] Jonadab said to him, "Lie down in your bed and pretend you are sick. When your father comes to to see you, say to him, 'Let my sister Tamar come and give me something to eat. Let her prepare the food in front of me, so that I may look on, and let her serve it to me.' "

[6] Amnon lay down and pretended to be sick. The king came to see him, and Amnon said to the king, "Let my sister Tamar come and prepare a couple of cakes in front of me, and let her bring them to me." [7] David sent a message to Tamar in the palace, "Please go to the house of your brother Amnon and prepare some food for him." [8] Tamar went to the house of her brother Amnon, who was in bed. She took dough and kneaded it into cakes in front of him, and cooked the cakes. [9] She took the *a-*pan and set out [the cakes],-*a* but Amnon refused to eat and ordered everyone to withdraw. After everyone had withdrawn, [10] Amnon said to Tamar, "Bring the food inside and feed me." Tamar took the cakes she had made and brought them to her brother inside. [11] But when she served them to him, he caught hold of her and said to her, "Come lie with me, sister." [12] But she said to him, "Don't, brother. Don't force me. Such things are not done in Israel! Don't do such a vile thing! [13] Where will I carry my shame? And you, you will be like any of the scoundrels in Israel! Please, speak to the king; he will not refuse me to you." [14] But he would not listen to her; he overpowered her and lay with her by force.

[15] Then Amnon felt a very great loathing for her; indeed, his loathing for her was greater than the passion he had felt for her. And Amnon said to her, "Get out!" [16] She pleaded with him, "Please don't *a-*commit this wrong; to send me away would be even worse-*a* than the first wrong you committed against me." But he would not listen to her. [17] He summoned his young attendant and said, "Get that woman out of my presence, and bar the door behind her."—[18] She was wearing an ornamented tunic,*b* for maiden princesses were customarily dressed *c-*in such garments.-*c*

a-a *Meaning of Heb. uncertain.*
b *See Gen. 37.3 and note.*
c-c *Meaning of Heb. uncertain. Emendation yields "(thus) in olden times,"* me'olam.

—His attendant took her outside and barred the door after her. [19] Tamar put dust on her head and rent the ornamented tunic she was wearing; she put her hands on her head,[d] and walked away, screaming loudly as she went. [20] Her brother Absalom said to her, "Was it your brother Amnon[e] who did this to you? For the present, sister, keep quiet about it; he is your brother. Don't brood over the matter." And Tamar remained in her brother Absalom's house, forlorn. [21] When King David heard about all this, he was greatly upset.[f] [22] Absalom didn't utter a word to Amnon, good or bad; but Absalom hated Amnon because he had violated his sister Tamar.

[23] Two years later, when Absalom was having his flocks sheared at Baal-hazor near Ephraim, Absalom invited all the king's sons. [24] And Absalom came to the king and said, "Your servant is having his flocks sheared. Would Your Majesty and your retinue accompany your servant?" [25] But the king answered Absalom, "No, my son. We must not all come, or we'll be a burden to you." He urged him, but he would not go, and he said goodbye to him. [26] Thereupon Absalom said, "In that case, let my brother Amnon come with us," to which the king replied, "He shall not go with you." [27] But Absalom urged him, and he sent with him Amnon and all the other princes.[g]

[28] Now Absalom gave his attendants these orders: "Watch, and when Amnon is merry with wine and I tell you to strike down Amnon, kill him! Don't be afraid, for it is I who give you the order. Act with determination, like brave men!" [29] Absalom's attendants did to Amnon as Absalom had ordered; whereupon all the other princes mounted their mules and fled. [30] They were still on the road when a rumor reached David that Absalom had killed all the princes, and that not one of them had survived. [31] At this, David rent his garment and lay down on the ground, [h]and all his courtiers stood by with their clothes rent.[-h] [32] But Jonadab, the son of David's brother Shimah, said, "My lord must not think that all the young princes have been killed. Only Amnon is dead; for

---

[d] *A gesture of wild grief; cf. Jer. 2.37.*
[e] *Heb. "Aminon."*
[f] *Septuagint adds "but he did not rebuke his son Amnon, for he favored him, since he was his firstborn"; cf. I Kings 1.6.*
[g] *Septuagint adds "and Absalom made a feast fit for a king."*
[h-h] *Septuagint reads "and all his courtiers who were standing by him rent their clothes."*

this has been [i]decided by[i] Absalom ever since his sister Tamar was violated. [33] So my lord the king must not think for a moment that all the princes are dead; Amnon alone is dead."

[34] Meanwhile Absalom had fled.

The watchman on duty looked up and saw a large crowd coming [j]from the road to his rear,[j] from the side of the hill. [35] Jonadab said to the king, "See, the princes have come! It is just as your servant said." [36] As he finished speaking, the princes came in and broke into weeping; and David and all his courtiers wept bitterly, too.

[37] Absalom had fled, and he came to Talmai son of Ammihud, king of Geshur. And [King David] mourned over his son a long time. [38] Absalom, who had fled to Geshur, remained there three years. [39] And [k]King David[k] was pining away for Absalom, for [the king] had gotten over Amnon's death.

14 Joab son of Zeruiah could see that the king's mind was on Absalom; [2] so Joab sent to Tekoa and brought a clever woman from there. He said to her, "Pretend you are in mourning; put on mourning clothes and don't anoint yourself with oil; and act like a woman who has grieved a long time over a departed one. [3] Go to the king and say to him thus and thus." And Joab told her what to say.[a]

[4] The woman of Tekoa came[b] to the king, flung herself face down to the ground, and prostrated herself. She cried out, "Help, O king!" [5] The king asked her, "What troubles you?" And she answered, "Alas, I am a widow, my husband is dead. [6] Your maidservant had two sons. The two of them came to blows out in the fields where there was no one to stop them, and one of them struck the other and killed him. [7] Then the whole clan confronted your maidservant and said, 'Hand over the one who killed his brother, that we may put him to death for the slaying

[i-i] Lit. "determined by the command of."
[j-j] Emendation yields "down the slope of the Horonaim road. The watchman came and told the king 'I see men coming from the Horonaim road.' " Cf. Septuagint.
[k-k] Some Septuagint mss. and 4QSam^a read "the spirit (ruah) of the king."

[a] Lit. "and he put words into her mouth."
[b] So many mss. and printed editions. Most mss. and printed editions read "said."

of his brother, *even though we wipe out the heir.'-c* Thus they would quench the last ember remaining to me, and leave my husband without name or remnant upon the earth." ⁸ The king said to the woman, "Go home. I will issue an order in your behalf." ⁹ And the woman of Tekoa said to the king, "My lord king, may the guilt be on me and on my ancestral house; Your Majesty and his throne are guiltless." ¹⁰ The king said, "If anyone says anything more to you, have him brought to me, and he will never trouble you again." ¹¹ She replied, "Let Your Majesty be mindful of the LORD your God and restrain the blood avenger bent on destruction, so that my son may not be killed." And he said, "As the LORD lives, not a hair of your son shall fall to the ground."

¹² Then the woman said, "Please let your maidservant say another word to my lord the king." "Speak on," said the king. ¹³ And the woman said, "Why then have you planned the like against God's people? In making this pronouncement, Your Majesty condemns himself in that Your Majesty does not bring back his own banished one. ¹⁴ We must all die; we are like water that is poured out on the ground and cannot be gathered up. *ᵈGod will not take away the life of one who makes plans so that no one may be kept banished.ᵈ* ¹⁵ And the reason I have come to say these things to the king, my lord, is that the people have frightened me. Your maidservant thought I would speak to Your Majesty; perhaps Your Majesty would act on his handmaid's plea. ¹⁶ For Your Majesty would surely agree to deliver his handmaid from the hands of anyone [who would seek to] cut off both me and my son from the heritage*ᵉ* of God. ¹⁷ Your maidservant thought, 'Let the word of my lord the king provide comfort; for my lord the king is like an angel of God, understanding everything, good and bad.' May the LORD your God be with you."

¹⁸ In reply, the king said to the woman, "Do not withhold from me anything I ask you!" The woman answered, "Let my lord the king speak." ¹⁹ The king asked, "Is Joab in league with you in all this?" The woman replied, "As you live, my lord the king, *ᶠit is

---

c-c Emendation yields "Thus they would destroy the [last] heir and. . . ."
d-d Meaning of Heb. uncertain. The apparent sense is: God will not punish you for bringing back the banished Absalom.
e I.e. people.
f-f Lit. "there is no turning to the right or to the left of what my lord the king says."

just as my lord the king says.ᶠ Yes, your servant Joab was the one who instructed me, and it was he who ᵍ⁻told your maidservant everything she was to say.⁻ᵍ ²⁰ It was to conceal the real purpose of the matter that your servant Joab did this thing. My lord is as wise as an angel of God, and he knows all that goes on in the land."

²¹ Then the king said to Joab, "I will do this thing. Go and bring back my boy Absalom." ²² Joab flung himself face down on the ground and prostrated himself. Joab blessed the king and said, "Today your servant knows that he has found favor with you, my lord king, for Your Majesty has granted his servant's request." ²³ And Joab went at once to Geshur and brought Absalom to Jerusalem. ²⁴ But the king said, "Let him go directly to his house and not present himself to me." So Absalom went directly to his house and did not present himself to the king.

²⁵ No one in all Israel was so admired for his beauty as Absalom; from the sole of his foot to the crown of his head he was without blemish. ²⁶ When he cut his hair—he had to have it cut every year, for it grew too heavy for him—the hair of his head weighed two hundred shekels by the royal weight. ²⁷ Absalom had three sons and a daughter whose name was Tamar; she was a beautiful woman.

²⁸ Absalom lived in Jerusalem two years without appearing before the king. ²⁹ Then Absalom sent for Joab, in order to send him to the king; but Joab would not come to him. He sent for him a second time, but he would not come. ³⁰ So [Absalom] said to his servants, "Look, Joab's field is next to mine, and he has barley there. Go and set it on fire." And Absalom's servants set the field on fire. ³¹ Joab came at once to Absalom's house and said to him, "Why did your servants set fire to my field?" ³² Absalom replied to Joab, "I sent for you to come here; I wanted to send you to the king to say [on my behalf]: 'Why did I leave Geshur? I would be better off if I were still there. Now let me appear before the king; and if I am guilty of anything, let him put me to death!' " ³³ Joab went to the king and reported to him; whereupon he

ᵍ⁻ᵍ *See note a above.*

194

summoned Absalom. He came to the king and flung himself face down to the ground before the king. And the king kissed Absalom.

15 Some time afterward, Absalom provided himself with a chariot, horses, and fifty outrunners. ² Absalom used to rise early and stand by the road to the city gates; and whenever a man had a case that was to come before the king for judgment, Absalom would call out to him, "What town are you from?" And when he answered, "Your servant is from ᵃ⁻such and such a tribe⁻ᵃ in Israel," ³ Absalom would say to him, "It is clear that your claim is right and just, but there is no one assigned to you by the king to hear it." ⁴ And Absalom went on, "If only I were appointed judge in the land and everyone with a legal dispute came before me, I would see that he got his rights." ⁵ And if a man approached to bow to him, [Absalom] would extend his hand and take hold of him and kiss him. ⁶ Absalom did this to every Israelite who came to the king for judgment. Thus Absalom won away the hearts of the men of Israel.

⁷ After a period of forty^b years had gone by, Absalom said to the king, "Let me go to Hebron and fulfill a vow that I made to the LORD. ⁸ For your servant made a vow when I lived in Geshur of Aram: If the LORD ever brings me back to Jerusalem, I will worship the LORD."^c ⁹ The king said to him, "Go in peace"; and so he set out for Hebron.

¹⁰ But Absalom sent agents to all the tribes of Israel to say, "When you hear the blast of the horn, announce that Absalom has become king in Hebron." ¹¹ Two hundred men of Jerusalem accompanied Absalom; they were invited and went in good faith, suspecting nothing. ¹² Absalom also ^d⁻sent [to fetch]⁻^d Ahithophel the Gilonite, David's counselor, from his town, Giloh, when the sacrifices were to be offered. The conspiracy gained strength, and the people supported Absalom in increasing numbers.

¹³ Someone came and told David, "The loyalty of the men of

ᵃ⁻ᵃ Lit. "one of the tribes."
ᵇ Some Septuagint mss. and Syriac read "four."
ᶜ Some Septuagint mss. add "in Hebron."
ᵈ⁻ᵈ Some Septuagint mss. and 4QSamᵃ read "sent and summoned."

Israel has veered toward Absalom." [14] Whereupon David said to all the courtiers who were with him in Jerusalem, "Let us flee at once, or none of us will escape from Absalom. We must get away quickly, or he will soon overtake us and bring down disaster upon us and put the city to the sword." [15] The king's courtiers said to the king, "Whatever our lord the king decides, your servants are ready." [16] So the king left, followed by his entire household, except for ten concubines whom the king left to mind the palace.

[17] The king left, followed by *e*-all the people,-*e* and they stopped at *f*-the last house.-*f* [18] All *g*-his followers-*g* marched past him, including all the Cherethites and all the Pelethites; and*h* all the Gittites, six hundred men who had accompanied him from Gath, also marched by the king. [19] And the king said to Ittai the Gittite, "Why should you too go with us? Go back and stay with the [new] king, for you are a foreigner and you are also an exile from*i* your country. [20] You came only yesterday; should I make you wander about with us today, when I myself must go wherever I can? Go back, and take your kinsmen with you, [in]*j* true faithfulness." [21] Ittai replied to the king, "As the LORD lives and as my lord the king lives, wherever my lord the king may be, there your servant will be, whether for death or for life!" [22] And David said to Ittai, "Then march by." And Ittai the Gittite and all his men and all the children who were with him marched by.

[23] The whole countryside wept aloud as the troops marched by. The king *k*-crossed the Kidron Valley, and all the troops crossed by the road to-*k* the wilderness. [24] Then Zadok appeared, with all the Levites carrying the Ark of the Covenant of God; and they set down the Ark of God until all the people had finished marching out of the city. *f*-Abiathar also came up.-*f* [25] But the king said to Zadok, "Take the Ark of God back to the city. If I find favor with the LORD, He will bring me back and let me see it and its abode. [26] And if He should say, 'I do not want you,' I am ready; let Him do with me as He pleases." [27] And the king said to the priest

e-e *Septuagint reads "his courtiers."*
f-f *Meaning of Heb. uncertain.*
g-g *Septuagint reads "the people."*
h *Emendation yields "and Ittai and."*
i *So one Heb. ms. and several ancient versions; most mss. and editions read "to."*
j *Meaning of Heb. uncertain. Septuagint reads "and may the LORD show you" (cf., e.g., 2.6).*
k-k *Meaning of Heb. uncertain. Emendation yields "stopped in the Kidron Valley, while all the people marched on before him by way of the Mount of Olives to. . . ."*

Zadok, [-"Do you understand? You return-[to the safety of the city with your two sons, your own son Ahimaaz and Abiathar's son Jonathan. [28] Look, I shall linger in the steppes of the wilderness until word comes from you to inform me." [29] Zadok and Abiathar brought the Ark of God back to Jerusalem, and they stayed there.

[30] David meanwhile went up the slope of the [Mount of] Olives, weeping as he went; his head was covered and he walked barefoot. And all the people who were with him covered their heads and wept as they went up. [31] David [was] told that Ahithophel was among the conspirators with Absalom, and he prayed, "Please, O LORD, frustrate Ahithophel's counsel!"

[32] When David reached the top, where people would prostrate themselves to God, Hushai the Archite was there to meet him, with his robe torn and with earth on his head. [33] David said to him, "If you march on with me, you will be a burden to me. [34] But if you go back to the city and say to Absalom, 'I will be your servant, O king; I was your father's servant formerly, and now I will be yours,' then you can nullify Ahithophel's counsel for me. [35] You will have the priests Zadok and Abiathar there, and you can report everything that you hear in the king's palace to the priests Zadok and Abiathar. [36] Also, their two sons are there with them, Zadok's son Ahimaaz and Abiathar's son Jonathan; and through them you can report to me everything you hear." [37] And so Hushai, the friend of David, reached the city as Absalom was entering Jerusalem.

16

David had passed a little beyond the summit, when Ziba the servant of Mephibosheth came toward him with a pair of saddled asses carrying two hundred loaves of bread, one hundred cakes of raisin, one hundred cakes of figs,[a] and a jar of wine. [2] The king asked Ziba, "What are you doing with these?" Ziba answered, "The asses are for Your Majesty's family to ride on, the bread and figs are for the attendants to eat, and the wine is to be drunk by

---

[-[Meaning of Heb. uncertain. Emendation yields "Look, you and Abiathar return."
[a] Lit. "summer fruit."

any who are exhausted in the wilderness." ³ "And where is your master's son?" the king asked. "He is staying in Jerusalem," Ziba replied to the king, "for he thinks that the House of Israel will now give him back the throne of his grandfather." ⁴ The king said to Ziba, "Then all that belongs to Mephibosheth is now yours!" And Ziba replied, "I bow low. Your Majesty is most gracious to me."

⁵ As King David was approaching Bahurim, a member of Saul's clan—a man named Shimei son of Gera—came out from there, hurling insults as he came. ⁶ He threw stones at David and all King David's courtiers, while all the troops and all the warriors were at his right and his left. ⁷ And these are the insults that he hurled: "Get out, get out, you criminal, you villain! ⁸ The LORD is paying you back for all your crimes against the family of Saul, whose throne you seized. The LORD is handing over the throne to your son Absalom; you are in trouble because you are a criminal!"

⁹ Abishai son of Zeruiah said to the king, "Why let that dead dog abuse my lord the king? Let me go over and cut off his head!" ¹⁰ But the king said, ᵇ-"What has this to do with you,-ᵇ you sons of Zeruiah? He is abusing [me] only because the LORD told him to abuse David; and who is to say, 'Why did You do that?' " ¹¹ David said further to Abishai and all the courtiers, "If my son, my own issue, seeks to kill me, how much more the Benjaminite! Let him go on hurling abuse, for the LORD has told him to. ¹² Perhaps the LORD will look upon my punishmentᶜ and recompense me for the abuse [Shimei] has uttered today." ¹³ David and his men continued on their way, while Shimei walked alongside on the slope of the hill, insulting him as he walked, and throwing stones at him and flinging dirt. ¹⁴ The king and all who accompanied him arrivedᵈ exhausted, and he rested there.

¹⁵ Meanwhile Absalom and all the people, the men of Israel, arrived in Jerusalem, together with Ahithophel. ¹⁶ When Hushai the Archite, David's friend, came before Absalom, Hushai said to

ᵇ⁻ᵇ *Lit. "What have I and you."*
ᶜ *So* kethib; qere *"eye." Ancient versions read "suffering."*
ᵈ *Some Septuagint mss. add "at the Jordan."*

Absalom, "Long live the king! Long live the king!" ¹⁷ But Absalom said to Hushai, "Is this your loyalty to your friend? Why didn't you go with your friend?" ¹⁸ "Not at all!" Hushai replied. "I am for the one whom the LORD and this people and all the men of Israel have chosen, and I will stay with him. ¹⁹ Furthermore, whom should I serve, if not David's*ᵉ* son? As I was in your father's service, so I will be in yours."

²⁰ Absalom then said to Ahithophel, "What do you advise us to do?" ²¹ And Ahithophel said to Absalom, "Have intercourse with your father's concubines, whom he left to mind the palace; and when all Israel hears that you have dared the wrath of your father, all who support you will be encouraged." ²² So they pitched a tent for Absalom on the roof, and Absalom lay with his father's concubines *ᶠ*with the full knowledge*ᶠ* of all Israel.—²³ In those days, the advice which Ahithophel gave was accepted like an oracle sought from God; that is how all the advice of Ahithophel was esteemed both by David and by Absalom.

17

And Ahithophel said to Absalom, "Let me pick twelve thousand men and set out tonight in pursuit of David. ² I will come upon him when he is weary and disheartened, and I will throw him into a panic; and when all the troops with him flee, I will kill the king alone. ³ And I will bring back all the people *ᵃ*to you; when all have come back [except] the man you are after,*ᵃ* all the people will be at peace." ⁴ The advice pleased Absalom and all the elders of Israel. ⁵ But Absalom said, "Summon Hushai the Archite as well, so we can hear what he too has to say." ⁶ Hushai came to Absalom, and Absalom said to him, "This is what Ahithophel has advised. Shall we follow his advice? If not, what do you say?"

⁷ Hushai said to Absalom, "This time the advice that Ahithophel has given is not good. ⁸ You know," Hushai continued, "that your father and his men are courageous fighters, and they are as desperate as a bear in the wild robbed of her whelps. Your

ᵉ *Heb. "his."*
ᶠ⁻ᶠ *Lit. "before the eyes."*

ᵃ⁻ᵃ *Meaning of Heb. uncertain. Septuagint reads "to you as a bride comes back to her husband; you seek the life of but one man, and . . . ."*

father is an experienced soldier, and he will not spend the night with the troops; 9 even now he must be hiding in one of the pits or in some other place. And if any of them[b] fall at the first attack, whoever hears of it will say, 'A disaster has struck the troops that follow Absalom'; 10 and even if he is a brave man with the heart of a lion, he will be shaken—for all Israel knows that your father and the soldiers with him are courageous fighters. 11 So I advise that all Israel from Dan to Beersheba—as numerous as the sands of the sea—be called up to join you, and that you yourself march [c-]into battle.[-c] 12 When we come upon him in whatever place he may be, we'll descend on him [as thick] as dew falling on the ground; and no one will survive, neither he nor any of the men with him. 13 And if he withdraws into a city, all Israel will bring ropes to that city and drag [d-]its stones[-d] as far as the riverbed, until not even a pebble of it is left." 14 Absalom and all Israel agreed that the advice of Hushai the Archite was better than that of Ahithophel.—The LORD had decreed that Ahithophel's sound advice be nullified, in order that the LORD might bring ruin upon Absalom.

15 Then Hushai told the priests Zadok and Abiathar, "This is what Ahithophel advised Absalom and the elders of Israel; this is what I advised. 16 Now send at once and tell David, 'Do not spend the night at the fords of the wilderness, but cross over at once; otherwise the king and all the troops with him will be annihilated.' " 17 Jonathan and Ahimaaz were staying at En-rogel, and a slave girl would go and bring them word and they in turn would go and inform King David. For they themselves dared not be seen entering the city. 18 But a boy saw them and informed Absalom. They left at once and came to the house of a man in Bahurim who had a well in his courtyard. They got down into it, 19 and the wife took a cloth, spread it over the mouth of the well, and scattered groats on top of it, so that nothing would be noticed. 20 When Absalom's servants came to the woman at the house and asked where Ahimaaz and Jonathan were, the woman told them that they had crossed [e-]a bit beyond the water.[-e] They

[b] *Some Septuagint mss. read "the troops" (i.e. Absalom's).*
[c-c] *Ancient versions read "among them."*
[d-d] *Heb. "it."*
[e-e] *Meaning of Heb. uncertain. Targum reads "the Jordan."*

200

searched, but found nothing; and they returned to Jerusalem. ²¹ After they were gone, [Ahimaaz and Jonathan] came up from the well and went and informed King David. They said to David, "Go and cross the water quickly, for Ahithophel has advised thus and thus concerning you." ²² David and all the troops with him promptly crossed the Jordan, and by daybreak not one was left who had not crossed the Jordan.

²³ When Ahithophel saw that his advice had not been followed, he saddled his ass and went home to his native town. He set his affairs in order, and then he hanged himself. He was buried in his ancestral tomb.

²⁴ David had reached Mahanaim when Absalom and all the men of Israel with him crossed the Jordan. ²⁵ Absalom had appointed Amasa army commander in place of Joab; Amasa was the son of a man named Ithra and the ᶠ⁻Israelite, who had married Abigal, daughter of Nahash and sister of Joab's mother Zeruiah.ᶠ ²⁶ The Israelites and Absalom encamped in the district of Gilead. ²⁷ When David reached Mahanaim, Shobi son of Nahash from Rabbath-ammon, Machir son of Ammiel from Lo-debar, and Barzillai the Gileadite from Rogelim, ²⁸ presentedᵍ couches, basins, and earthenware; also wheat, barley, flour, parched grain, beans, lentils, ʰ⁻parched grain,⁻ʰ ²⁹ honey, ⁱ⁻curds, a flock,⁻ⁱ and cheeseʲ from the herd for David and the troops with him to eat. For they knew that the troops must have grown hungry, faint, and thirsty in the wilderness.

18

David mustered the troops who were with him and set over them captains of thousands and captains of hundreds. ² David ᵃ⁻sent out the troops,⁻ᵃ one third under the command of Joab, one third under the command of Joab's brother Abishai son of Zeruiah, and one third under the command of Ittai the Gittite. And David said to the troops, "I myself will march out with you."

ᶠ⁻ᶠ *Some Septuagint mss. and I Chron. 2.12-17 read "Ishmaelite" and give a somewhat different genealogy.*
ᵍ *Brought up from v. 29 for clarity.*
ʰ⁻ʰ *Lacking in the Septuagint and Syriac.*
ⁱ⁻ⁱ *Emendation yields "curds from the flock."*
ʲ *Meaning of Heb. uncertain.*

ᵃ⁻ᵃ *Some Septuagint mss. read "divided the troops into three."*

³ But the troops replied, "No! For if some of us flee, the rest will not be concerned about us; even if half of us should die, the others will not be concerned about us. But ᵇ⁻you are worth ten thousand of us.⁻ᵇ Therefore, it is better for you to support us from the town." ⁴ And the king said to them, "I will do whatever you think best."

So the king stood beside the gate as all the troops marched out by their hundreds and thousands. ⁵ The king gave orders to Joab, Abishai, and Ittai: "Deal gently with my boy Absalom, for my sake." All the troops heard the king give the order about Absalom to all the officers.

⁶ The troops marched out into the open to confront the Israelites,ᶜ and the battle was fought in the forest of Ephraim.ᵈ ⁷ The Israelite troops were routed by David's followers, and a great slaughter took place there that day—twenty thousand men. ⁸ The battle spread out over that whole region, and the forest devoured more troops that day than the sword.

⁹ Absalom encountered some of David's followers. Absalom was riding on a mule, and as the mule passed under the tangled branches of a great terebinth, his hair got caught in the terebinth; he ᵉ⁻was held⁻ᵉ between heaven and earth as the mule under him kept going. ¹⁰ One of the men saw it and told Joab, "I have just seen Absalom hanging from a terebinth!" ¹¹ Joab said to the man who told him, "You saw it! Why didn't you kill him ᶠthen and there?⁻ᶠ I would have owed you tenᵍ shekels of silver and a belt." ¹² But the man answered Joab, "Even if I had a thousand shekels of silver in my hands, I would not raise a hand against the king's son. For the king charged you and Abishai and Ittai in our hearing. 'Watch over my boy Absalom, ʰ⁻for my sake.'⁻ʰ ¹³ If I betrayed myselfⁱ—and nothing is hidden from the king—you would have stood aloof." ¹⁴ Joab replied, ʲ⁻"Then I will not wait for

---

ᵇ⁻ᵇ *So two Heb. mss., Septuagint, and Vulgate; cf. I Kings 1.18 and note. Most mss. and the editions read "Now there are ten thousand like us."*
ᶜ *The usual term in this narrative for the supporters of Absalom.*
ᵈ *Some Septuagint mss. read "Mahanaim"; cf. 17.24.*
ᵉ⁻ᵉ *Meaning of Heb. uncertain. Ancient versions and 4QSamᵃ read "was left hanging"; cf. v.10.*
ᶠ⁻ᶠ *Lit. "to the ground."*
ᵍ *Some Septuagint mss. and 4QSamᵃ read "fifty."*
ʰ⁻ʰ *So some Heb. mss. and ancient versions. Most mss. and editions read "who"—perhaps meaning "whoever you are."*
ⁱ *I.e. by killing Absalom.*
ʲ⁻ʲ *Some Septuagint mss. and Targum read "Therefore, I will begin before you."*

you."·*j* He took three darts in his hand and drove them into Absalom's chest. [Absalom] was still alive in the thick growth of the terebinth, ¹⁵ when ten of Joab's young arms-bearers closed in and struck at Absalom until he died. ¹⁶ Then Joab sounded the horn, and the troops gave up their pursuit of the Israelites; for Joab held the troops in check. ¹⁷ They took Absalom and flung him into a large pit in the forest, and they piled up a very great heap of stones over it. Then all the Israelites fled to their homes.—¹⁸ Now Absalom, in his lifetime, had taken the pillar which is in the Valley of the King and set it up for himself; for he said, "I have no son to keep my name alive." He had named the pillar after himself, and it has been called Absalom's Monument to this day.

¹⁹ Ahimaaz son of Zadok said, "Let me run and report to the king that the LORD has vindicated him against his enemies." ²⁰ But Joab said to him, "You shall not be the one to bring tidings today. You may bring tidings some other day, but you'll not bring any today; for the king's son is dead!" ²¹ And Joab said to a Cushite, "Go tell the king what you have seen." The Cushite bowed to Joab and ran off. ²² But Ahimaaz son of Zadok again said to Joab, "No matter what, let me run, too, behind the Cushite." Joab asked, "Why should you run, my boy, when you have no news *k*·worth telling?"·*-k* ²³ "I am going to run anyway." "Then run," he said. So Ahimaaz ran by way of the Plain, and he passed the Cushite.

²⁴ David was sitting between the two gates.*l* The watchman on the roof of the gate walked over to the city wall. He looked up and saw a man running alone. ²⁵ The watchman called down and told the king; and the king said, "If he is alone, he has news to report." As he was coming nearer, ²⁶ the watchman saw another man running; and he called out to the gatekeeper, "There is another man running alone." And the king said, "That one, too, brings news." ²⁷ The watchman said, "I can see that the first one runs like Ahimaaz son of Zadok"; to which the king replied, "He is a good man, and he comes with good news." ²⁸ Ahimaaz called out and said to the king, "All is well!" He bowed low with his face

k-k Meaning of Heb. uncertain.
l I.e. the inner and outer gateways.

to the ground and said, "Praised be the LORD your God, who has delivered up the men who raised their hand against my lord the king." 29 The king asked, "Is my boy Absalom safe?" And Ahimaaz answered, "I saw *a large crowd when Your Majesty's servant Joab was sending your servant off,-* but I don't know what it was about." 30 The king said, "Step aside and stand over there"; he stepped aside and waited.

31 Just then the Cushite came up; and the Cushite said, "Let my lord the king be informed that the LORD has vindicated you today against all who rebelled against you!" 32 The king asked the Cushite, "Is my boy Absalom safe?" And the Cushite replied, "May the enemies of my lord the king and all who rose against you to do you harm fare like that young man!" 1 *The king **19** was shaken. He went up to the upper chamber of the gateway and wept, moaning these words as he went,* "My son Absalom! O my son, my son Absalom! If only I had died instead of you! O Absalom, my son, my son!"

2 Joab was told that the king was weeping and mourning over Absalom. 3 And the victory that day was turned into mourning for all the troops, for that day the troops heard that the king was grieving over his son. 4 The troops stole into town that day like troops ashamed after running away in battle. 5 The king covered his face and the king kept crying aloud, "O my son Absalom! O Absalom, my son, my son!"

6 Joab came to the king in his quarters and said, "Today you have humiliated all your followers, who this day saved your life, and the lives of your sons and daughters, and the lives of your wives and concubines, 7 by showing love for those who hate you and hate for those who love you. For you have made clear today that the officers and men mean nothing to you. I am sure that if Absalom were alive today and the rest of us dead, you would have preferred it. 8 Now arise, come out and placate your followers! For I swear by the LORD that if* you do not come out, not a single man will remain with you overnight; and that would be a greater

---

ª Counted as 18.33 in some versions.
ᵇ Some Septuagint mss. read "wept."
ᶜ So Septuagint, 4QSamª, and some other Heb. mss., and an ancient masoretic tradition; ordinary texts omit "if."

disaster for you than any disaster that has befallen you from your youth until now." ⁹ So the king arose and sat down in the gateway; and when all the troops were told that the king was sitting in the gateway, all the troops presented themselves to the king.

Now the Israelites had fled to their homes. ¹⁰ All the people throughout the tribes of Israel were arguing: Some said, "The king saved us from the hands of our enemies, and he delivered us from the hands of the Philistines; and just now he had to flee the country because of Absalom. ¹¹ But Absalom, whom we anointed over us, has died in battle; why then do you sit idle instead of escorting the king back?" ¹² The talk of all Israel reached the king in his quarters. So King David sent this message to the priests Zadok and Abiathar, "Speak to the elders of Judah and say, 'Why should you be the last to bring the king back to his palace? ¹³ You are my kinsmen, my own flesh and blood! Why should you be the last to escort the king back?' ¹⁴ And to Amasa say this, 'You are my own flesh and blood. May God do thus and more to me if you do not become my army commander permanently in place of Joab!' " ¹⁵ So [Amasa] swayed the hearts of all the Judites as one man; and they sent a message to the king: "Come back with all your followers."

¹⁶ The king started back and arrived at the Jordan; and the Judites went to Gilgal to meet the king and to conduct the king across the Jordan. ¹⁷ Shimei son of Gera, the Benjaminite from Bahurim, hurried down with the Judites to meet King David, ¹⁸ accompanied by a thousand Benjaminites. ᵈAnd Ziba, the servant of the House of Saul, together with his fifteen sons and twenty slaves, rushed down to the Jordan ahead of the king ¹⁹ while the crossing was being made, to escort the king's family over, and to do whatever he wished. Shimei son of Gera flung himself before the king as he was about to cross the Jordan. ²⁰ He said to the king, "Let not my lord hold me guilty, and do not remember the wrong your servant committed on the day my lord the king left Jerusalem; let Your Majesty give it no thought.

ᵈ *Meaning of parts of the rest of vv. 18 and 19 uncertain.*

21 For your servant knows that he has sinned; so here I have come down today, the first of all the House of Joseph, to meet my lord the king." 22 Thereupon Abishai son of Zeruiah spoke up, "Shouldn't Shimei be put to death for that—insulting the LORD's anointed?" 23 But David said, *"What has this to do with you,*-*e* you sons of Zeruiah, that you should cross me today? Should a single Israelite be put to death today? Don't I*f* know that today I am again king over Israel?" 24 Then the king said to Shimei, "You shall not die;" and the king gave him his oath.

25 Mephibosheth, the grandson of Saul, also came down to meet the king. He had not pared his toenails, or trimmed his mustache, or washed his clothes from the day that the king left until the day he returned safe. 26 When he *g*-came [from]-*g* Jerusalem to meet the king, the king asked him, "Why didn't you come with me, Mephibosheth?" 27 He replied, "My lord the king, my own servant*h* deceived me. *i*-Your servant planned to saddle his ass and ride*-i* on it and go with Your Majesty—for your servant is lame. 28 [Ziba] has slandered your servant to my lord the king. But my lord the king is like an angel of the LORD; do as you see fit. 29 For all the members of my father's family deserved only death from my lord the king; yet you set your servant among those who ate at your table. What right have I to appeal further to Your Majesty?" 30 The king said to him, "You need not speak further. I decree that you and Ziba shall divide the property." 31 And Mephibosheth said to the king, "Let him take it all, as long as my lord the king has come home safe."

32 Barzillai the Gileadite had come down from Rogelin and *j*-passed on to the Jordan with the king, to see his off at*-j* the Jordan. 33 Barzillai was very old, eighty years of age; and he had provided the king with food during his stay at Mahanaim, for he was a very wealthy man. 34 The king said to Barzillai, "Cross over with me, and I will provide for you in Jerusalem at my side." 35 But Barzillai said to the king, "How many years are left to me that I should go up with Your Majesty to Jerusalem? 36 I am now

---

e See note at 16.10.
f Some Septuagint mss. read "you."
g-g So Septuagint. Heb. "entered."
h I.e. Ziba (cf. v. 30 and 9.2 ff.).
i Ancient versions read "Your servant said to him, 'Saddle my ass, that I may ride. . . . ' "
j-j Meaning of Heb. uncertain.

eighty years old. Can I tell the difference between good and bad? Can your servant taste what he eats and drinks? Can I still listen to the singing of men and women? Why then should your servant continue to be a burden to my lord the king? ³⁷ *ʲ*Your servant could barely cross the Jordan*ʲ* with your Majesty! Why should Your Majesty reward me so generously? ³⁸ Let your servant go back, and let me die in my own town, near the graves of my father and mother. But here is your servant Chimham;*ᵏ* let him cross with my lord the king, and do for him as you see fit." ³⁹ And the king said, "Chimham shall cross with me, and I will do for him as you see fit; and anything you want me to do, I will do for you."

⁴⁰ *ˡ*All the troops crossed the Jordan; and when the king was ready to cross, the king kissed Barzillai and bade him farewell; and [Barzillai] returned to his home. ⁴¹ The king passed on to Gilgal, with Chimham accompanying him; and all the Judite soldiers and part of the Israelite army escorted the king across.

⁴² Then all the men of Israel came to the king and said to the king, "Why did our kinsmen, the men of Judah, steal you away and escort the king and his family across the Jordan, along with all David's men?" ⁴³ All the men of Judah replied to the men of Israel, "Because the king is our relative! Why should this upset you? Have we consumed anything that belongs to the king? Has he given us any gifts?" ⁴⁴ But the men of Israel answered the men of Judah, "We have ten shares in the king, and *ᵐ*in David, too, we have more than you.*ᵐ* Why then have you slighted us? Were we not the first to propose that our king be brought back?" However, the men of Judah prevailed over the men of Israel.

20

A scoundrel named Sheba son of Bichri, a Benjaminite, happened to be there. He sounded the horn and proclaimed:

"We have no portion in David,
No share in Jesse's son!
Every man to his tent, O Israel!"

² All the men of Israel left David and followed Sheba son of

ᵏ Heb. Chimhan.
ˡ Meaning of parts of vv. 40-44 uncertain.
ᵐ⁻ᵐ Septuagint reads "we are the firstborn, rather than you."

Bichri; but the men of Judah accompanied their king from the Jordan to Jerusalem. [3] David went to his palace in Jerusalem, and the king took the ten concubines he had left to mind the palace and put them in a guarded place; he provided for them, but he did not cohabit with them. They remained in seclusion until the day they died, in living widowhood.

[4] The king said to Amasa, "Call up the men of Judah to my standard, and report here three days from now." [5] Amasa went to call up Judah, but he took longer than the time set for him. [6] And David said to Abishai, "Now Sheba son of Bichri will cause us more trouble than Absalom. So take your lord's servants and pursue him, before he finds fortified towns and *a*-eludes us."*-a* [7] *b*-Joab's men, the Cherethites and Pelethites, and all the warriors, marched out behind him.*-b* They left Jerusalem in pursuit of Sheba son of Bichri. [8] They were near the great stone in Gibeon when Amasa appeared before them. *a*-Joab was wearing his military dress, with his sword girded over it and fastened around his waist in its sheath; and, as he stepped forward, it fell out.*-a* [9] Joab said to Amasa, "How are you, brother?" and with his right hand Joab took hold of Amasa's beard as if to kiss him. [10] Amasa was not on his guard against the sword in Joab's [left] hand, and [Joab] drove it into his belly so that his entrails poured out on the ground and he died; he did not need to strike him a second time.

Joab and his brother Abishai then set off in pursuit of Sheba son of Bichri, [11] while one of Joab's henchmen stood by *c*-the corpse*-c* and called out, "Whoever favors Joab, and whoever is on David's side, follow Joab!" [12] Amasa lay in the middle of the road, drenched in his blood; and the man saw that everyone stopped. And when he saw that all the people were stopping, he dragged Amasa from the road into the field and covered him with a garment. [13] Once he was removed from the road, everybody continued to follow Joab in pursuit of Sheba son of Bichri. [14] [Sheba] had passed through all the tribes of Israel up to Abel of*d* Beth-maacah; and all the Beerites*e* assembled and followed him inside.

---

a-a *Meaning of Heb. uncertain.*
b-b *Emendation yields "Joab, the Cherethites and Pelethites, and all the warriors marched out behind Abishai."*
c-c *Heb. "him."*
d *Heb. "and." Cf. v. 15 (and "Abel-beth-maacah" in I Kings 15.20 and II Kings 15.29).*
e *Emendation yields "Bichrites"; cf. Septuagint.*

¹⁵ [Joab's men] came and besieged him in Abel of Beth-maacah; they threw up a siege mound against the city ⨍⁻and it stood against the rampart.⨍

All the troops with Joab were ᵍ⁻engaged in battering the wall,⁻ᵍ ¹⁶ when a clever woman shouted from the city, "Listen! Listen! Tell Joab to come over here so I can talk to him." ¹⁷ He approached her, and the woman asked, "Are you Joab?" "Yes," he answered; and she said to him, "Listen to what your handmaid has to say." "I'm listening," he replied. ¹⁸ And she continued, "In olden times people used to say, ᵃ⁻"Let them inquire of Abel,'⁻ᵃ and that was the end of the matter. ¹⁹ I am one of those who seek the welfare of the faithful in Israel. But you seek to bring death upon a mother city in Israel! Why should you destroy the LORD's possession?" ²⁰ Joab replied, "Far be it, far be it from me to destroy or to ruin! ²¹ Not at all! But a certain man from the hill country of Ephraim, named Sheba son of Bichri, has rebelled against King David. Just hand him alone over to us, and I will withdraw from the city." The woman assured Joab, "His head shall be thrown over the wall to you." ²² The woman came to all the people with her clever plan; and they cut off the head of Sheba son of Bichri and threw it down to Joab. He then sounded the horn; all the men dispersed to their homes, and Joab returned to the king in Jerusalem.

²³ Joab was commander of the whole army [of] Israel; Benaiah son of Jehoiada was commander of the Cherethites and the Pelethites; ²⁴ Adoramʰ was in charge of forced labor; Jehoshaphat son of Ahilud was recorder; ²⁵ Shevaⁱ was scribe; and Zadok and Abiathar were priests. ²⁶ Ira the Jairite also served David as priest.

21

There was a famine during the reign of David, year after year for three years. David inquired of the LORD, and the LORD replied, "It is because of the bloodguilt of Saul and [his] house,

---

⨍⁻⨍ Meaning of Heb. uncertain. The phrase would read well in the next verse (". . . a clever woman stood on the rampart and shouted . . .").
ᵍ⁻ᵍ Lit. "destroying, to topple the wall." Septuagint and Targum read "were planning to topple the wall."
ʰ So in I Kings 12.18 and II Chron. 10.18 ("Hadoram"); elsewhere "Adoniram."
ⁱ See note j at 8.17.

for he put some Gibeonites to death." ² The king summoned the Gibeonites and spoke to them.—Now the Gibeonites were not of Israelite stock, but a remnant of the Amorites, to whom the Israelites had given an oath; and Saul had tried to wipe them out in his zeal for the people of Israel and Judah.—³ David asked the Gibeonites, "What shall I do for you? How shall I make expiation, so that you may bless the LORD's own people?" ⁴ The Gibeonites answered him, "We have no claim for silver or gold against Saul and his household; and we have no claim on the life of any other man in Israel." And [David] responded, "Whatever you say I will do for you." ⁵ Thereupon they said to the king, "The man who massacred us and planned to ᵃ⁻exterminate us, so that we⁻ᵃ should not survive in all the territory of Israel—⁶ let seven of his male issue be handed over to us, and we will impale them before the LORD in ᵇ⁻Gibeah of Saul, the chosen of the LORD."⁻ᵇ And the king replied, "I will do so."

⁷ The king spared Mephibosheth son of Jonathan son of Saul, because of the oath before the LORD between the two, between David and Jonathan son of Saul. ⁸ Instead, the king took Armoni and Mephibosheth, the two sons that Rizpah daughter of Aiah bore to Saul, and the five sons that Merabᶜ daughter of Saul bore to Adriel son of Barzillai the Meholathite, ⁹ and he handed them over to the Gibeonites. They impaled them on the mountain before the LORD; all seven of them perished at the same time. They were put to death in the first days of the harvest, the beginning of the barley harvest.

¹⁰ Then Rizpah daughter of Aiah took sackcloth and spread it on a rock for herself, and she stayed there from the beginning of the harvest until rain from the sky fell on ᵈ⁻the bodies;⁻ᵈ she did not let the birds of the sky settle on them by day or the wild beasts [approach] by night. ¹¹ David was told what Saul's concubine Rizpah daughter of Aiah had done. ¹² And David went and took the bones of Saul and of his son Jonathan from the citizens of Jabesh-gilead, who had made off with them from the public

ᵃ⁻ᵃ *Meaning of Heb. uncertain.*
ᵇ⁻ᵇ *Emendation yields, "at Gibeon, on the mountain of the LORD (cf. Septuagint and v. 9).*
ᶜ *So two Heb. mss., many Septuagint mss., and Peshitta; and cf. Targum, Sanhedrin 19b,*
  and I Sam. 18.19. Most mss. o· ᴧ the printed editions read "Michal."
ᵈ⁻ᵈ *Heb. "them."*

square of Beth-shan, where the Philistines had hung them up on the day the Philistines killed Saul at Gilboa. ¹³ He brought up the bones of Saul and of his son Jonathan from there; and he gathered the bones of those who had been impaled. ¹⁴ And they buried the bones of Saul and of his son Jonathan*ᵉ* in Zela, in the territory of Benjamin, in the tomb of his father Kish. And when all that the king had commanded was done, God responded to the plea of the land thereafter.

¹⁵ Again war broke out between the Philistines and Israel, and David and the men with him went down and fought the Philistines; David grew weary, ¹⁶ and *ᵃ*Ishbi-benob*⁻ᵃ* tried to kill David. —He was a descendant of the Raphah;*ᶠ* his bronze spear weighed three hundred shekels and he wore new armor.—¹⁷ But Abishai son of Zeruiah came to his aid; he attacked the Philistine and killed him. It was then that David's men declared to him on oath, "You shall not go with us into battle any more, lest you extinguish the lamp of Israel!"

¹⁸ *ᵍ*After this, fighting broke out again with the Philistines, at Gob; that was when Sibbecai the Hushathite killed Saph, a descendant of the Raphah.*ᶠ* ¹⁹ Again there was fighting with the Philistines at Gob; and Elhanan son of Jaare-oregim*ʰ* the Bethlehemite killed Goliath the Gittite, whose spear had a shaft like a weaver's bar. ²⁰ Once again there was fighting, at Gath. There was a *ᵃ*giant of a man,*⁻ᵃ* who had six fingers on each hand and six toes on each foot, twenty-four in all; he too was descended from the Raphah. ²¹ When he taunted Israel, Jonathan, the son of David's brother Shimei, killed him. ²² Those four were descended from the Raphah in Gath, and they fell by the hands of David and his men.

ᵉ *Septuagint adds "and the bones of those impaled."*
ᶠ *Apparently a race of giants.*
ᵍ *This paragraph is found also in I Chron. 20.4-8; in part, also in IQSamᵃ, with some variations.*
ʰ *Perhaps a duplicate of 'oregim ("weavers") at the end of verse; meaning of Heb. uncertain. I Chron. 20.5 reads "And Elhanan son of Jair killed Lahmi, the brother of Goliath the Gittite."*

22 *a* David addressed the words of this song to the LORD, after the LORD had saved him from the hands of all his enemies and from the hands of Saul. ² He said:

> O LORD, my crag, my fastness, my deliverer!
> ³ O *b-*God, the rock*-b* wherein I take shelter:
> My shield, my *c-*mighty champion,*-c* my fortress and refuge!
> My savior, You who rescue me from violence!

> ⁴ *d-*All praise! I called on the LORD,*-d*
> And I was delivered from my enemies.

> ⁵ For the breakers of Death encompassed me,
> The torrents of Belial*e* terrified me;
> ⁶ The snares of Sheol encircled me,
> The toils of Death engulfed me.

> ⁷ In my anguish I called on the LORD,
> Cried out to my God;
> In His Abode*f* He heard my voice,
> My cry entered His ears.

> ⁸ Then the earth rocked and quaked,
> The foundations of heaven*g* shook—
> Rocked by His indignation.
> ⁹ Smoke went up from His nostrils,
> From His mouth came devouring fire;
> Live coals blazed forth from Him.
> ¹⁰ He bent the sky and came down,
> Thick cloud beneath His feet.

---

a This poem occurs again as Ps. 18, with a number of variations, some of which are cited in the following notes.
b-b Lit. "the God of my rock"; Ps. 18.3 "my God, my rock."
c-c Lit. "horn of rescue."
d-d Construction of Heb. uncertain.
e I.e., the nether world, like "Death" and "Sheol."
f Lit. "Temple."
g Ps. 18.8 "mountains."

¹¹ He mounted a cherub and flew;
*ʰ*He was seen*⁻ʰ* on the wings of the wind.
¹² He made pavilions of darkness about Him,
Dripping clouds, huge thunderheads;
¹³ In the brilliance before Him
Blazed fiery coals.
¹⁴ The LORD thundered forth from heaven,
The Most High sent forth His voice;
¹⁵ He let loose bolts, and scattered them;*ⁱ*
Lightning, and put them to rout.
¹⁶ The bed of the sea was exposed,
The foundations of the world were laid bare
By the mighty roaring of the LORD,
At the blast of the breath of His nostrils.
¹⁷ He reached down from on high, He took me,
Drew me out of the mighty waters;*ʲ*
¹⁸ He rescued me from my enemy so strong,
From foes too mighty for me.
¹⁹ They attacked me on my day of calamity,
But the LORD was my stay.
²⁰ He brought me out to freedom,
He rescued me because He was pleased with me.
²¹ The LORD rewarded me according to my merit,
He requited the cleanness of my hands.

²² For I have kept the ways of the LORD
And have not been guilty before my God;
²³ I am mindful of all His rules
And have not departed from His laws.
²⁴ I have been blameless before Him,
And have guarded myself against sinning—
²⁵ And the LORD has requited my merit,
According to my purity in His sight.

ʰ⁻ʰ *Ps. 18.11 "Gliding."*
ⁱ *I.e., the enemies in v.4.*
ʲ *Cf. v.5.*

²⁶ With the loyal You deal loyally;
With the blameless hero,^k blamelessly.
²⁷ With the pure You act in purity,
And with the perverse You are wily.
²⁸ To humble folk You give victory,
^{l-}And You look with scorn on the haughty.^{-l}

²⁹ You, O LORD, are my lamp;
The LORD lights up my darkness.
³⁰ With You, I can rush a barrier,^m
With my God, I can scale a wall.
³¹ The way of God is perfect,
The word of the LORD is pure.
He is a shield to all who take refuge in Him.
³² Yea, who is a god except the LORD,
Who is a rock except God—
³³ The God, ⁿ⁻my mighty stronghold,⁻ⁿ
Who kept^o my path secure;
³⁴ Who made my legs like a deer's,
And set me firm on the^p heights;
³⁵ Who trained my hands for battle,
So that my arms can bend a bow of bronze!
³⁶ You have granted me the shield of Your protection
^{q-}And Your providence has made me great.^{-q}
³⁷ You have let me stride on freely,
And my feet have not slipped.
³⁸ I pursued my enemies and wiped them out,
I did not turn back till I destroyed them.
³⁹ I destroyed them, I struck them down;
They rose no more, they lay at my feet.
⁴⁰ You have girt me with strength for battle,
Brought low my foes before me,

---

^k *Ps. 18.26 "man."*
^{l-l} *Lit. "And lower Your eyes on the haughty"; Ps. 18.28 "But haughty eyes You humble."*
^m *Cf.* post-biblical gedudiyyoth *"walls," Aramaic* gudda, *"wall."*
ⁿ⁻ⁿ *Ps. 18.33 "who girded me with might."*
^o *Meaning of Heb. uncertain; Ps. 18.33 "maketh."*
^p *Taking* bamothai *as a poetic form of* bamoth; *cf. Hab. 3.19; others "my."*
^{q-q} *Meaning of Heb. uncertain.*

41 Made my enemies turn tail before me,
My foes—and I wiped them out.
42 They looked,[r] but there was none to deliver;
To the LORD, but He answered them not.
43 I pounded them like dust of the earth,
Stamped, crushed them like dirt of the streets.
44 You have rescued me from the strife of peoples,[s]
[t-]Kept me to be[-t] a ruler of nations;
Peoples I knew not must serve me.
45 Aliens have cringed before me,
Paid me homage at the mere report of me.
46 Aliens have lost courage
[q-]And come trembling out of their fastnesses.[-q]

47 The LORD lives! Blessed is my rock!
Exalted be God, the rock
Who gives me victory;
48 The God who has vindicated me
And made peoples subject to me,
49 Rescued me from my enemies,
Raised me clear of my foes,
Saved me from lawless men!
50 For this I sing Your praise among the nations
And hymn Your name:
51 [u-] Tower of victory[-u] to His king,
Who deals graciously with His anointed,
With David and his offspring evermore.

23 These are the last words of David:

[a]The utterance of David son of Jesse,
The utterance of the man [b-]set on high,[-b]
The anointed of the God of Jacob,

[r] *Ps. 18.42 "cried."*
[s] *So some mss. and the Septuagint; most mss. and the printed editions "my people."*
[t-t] *Ps. 18.44 "made me."*
[u-u] Kethib *Ps. 18.51 reads "Who accords wondrous victories."*

[a] *Meaning of much of this poem (vv. 1-7) uncertain.*
[b-b] *4QSam[a] reads "God raised up."*

*c-*The favorite of the songs of Israel:*-c*
2 The spirit of the LORD has spoken through me,
His message is on my tongue;
3 The God of Israel has spoken,
The Rock of Israel said concerning me:
"He who rules men justly,
He who rules in*d* awe of God
4 Is like the light of morning at sunrise,
A morning without clouds—
*e-*Through sunshine and rain
[Bringing]*-e* vegetation out of the earth."
5 Is not my House established before God?
For He has granted me an eternal pact,
Drawn up in full and secured.
Will He not cause all my success
And [my] every desire to blossom?
6 But the wicked shall all
Be raked aside like thorns;
For no one will take them in his hand.
7 Whoever touches them
Must arm himself with iron
And the shaft of a spear;
And they must be burned up on the spot.

8 These are the names*f* of David's warriors: Josheb-basshebeth, a Tahchemonite, the chief officer—he is Adino the Eznite; *g-*[he wielded his spear]*-g* against eight hundred *h-*and slew them*-h* on one occasion.

9 Next to him was Eleazar son of Dodo son of Ahohi. He was one of the three warriors with David when they defied the Philistines gathered there for battle. The Israelite soldiers retreated, 10 but he held his ground. He struck down Philistines until his arm grew tired and his hand stuck to his sword; and the LORD wrought

c-c Or "The favorite of the Mighty One of Israel"; cf. Exod. 15.2. Others "The sweet singer of Israel."
d So many Heb. mss. Most mss. and the printed editions lack "in."
e-e Meaning of Heb. uncertain.
f A number of these names, with variations, are found in I Chron. 11 and 27.
g-g Preserved in I Chron. 11.11; similarly some Septuagint mss. of II Sam.
h-h Lit. "slain."

a great victory that day. Then the troops came back to him—but only to strip [the slain].

[11] Next to him was Shammah son of Age the Ararite. The Philistines had gathered *in force* where there was a plot of ground full of lentils; and the troops fled from the Philistines. [12] But [Shammah] took his stand in the middle of the plot and defended it, and he routed the Philistines. Thus the LORD wrought a great victory.

[13] *Once, during the harvest,* three of the thirty chiefs went down to David at the cave[i] of Adullam, while a force of Philistines was encamped in the Valley of Rephaim. [14] David was then in the stronghold,[i] and a Philistine garrison was then at Bethlehem. [15] David felt a craving and said, "If only I could get a drink of water from the cistern which is by the gate of Bethlehem!" [16] So the three warriors got through the Philistine camp and drew water from the cistern which is by the gate of Bethlehem, and they carried it back. But when they brought it to David he would not drink it, and he poured it out as a libation to the LORD. [17] For he said, "The LORD forbid that I should do this! Can [I drink][j] the blood of the men who went at the risk of their lives?" So he would not drink it. Such were the exploits of the three warriors.

[18] Abishai, the brother of Joab son of Zeruiah, was head of *another three.*[k] He once wielded his spear against three hundred *and slew them.*[h] [19] He won a name among the three;[l] since he was the most highly regarded among the three,[l] he became their leader. However, he did not attain to the three.

[20] Benaiah son of Jehoiada, from Kabzeel, was *a brave soldier*[m] who performed great deeds. He killed the two *[sons] of Ariel of Moab.*[e] Once, on a snowy day, he went down into a pit and killed a lion. [21] He also killed an Egyptian, a huge[n] man. The Egyptian had a spear in his hand, yet [Benaiah] went down against him with a club, wrenched the spear out of the Egyptian's hand, and killed him with his own spear. [22] Such were the exploits of Benaiah son of Jehoiada; and he won a name among the three[l]

---

[i] *See note at I Sam. 22.1.*
[j] *So Septuagint and I Chron. 11.19.*
[k-k] *Two Heb. mss. and Syriac read "the thirty"; cf. vv. 23-24.*
[l] *Emendation yields "thirty."*
[m] *Heb. "the son of a brave soldier."*
[n] *Meaning of Heb. uncertain. I Chron. 11.23 reads "a giant of a man."*

warriors. [23] He was highly regarded among the thirty, but he did not attain to the three. David put him in charge of his bodyguard.[e]

[24] Among the thirty were Asahel, the brother of Joab; Elhanan son of Dodo [from] Bethlehem, [25] Shammah the Harodite, Elika the Harodite, [26] Helez the Paltite, Ira son of Ikkesh from Tekoa, [27] Abiezer of Anathoth, Mebunnai the Hushathite, [28] Zalmon the Ahohite, Maharai the Netophathite, [29] Heleb son of Baanah the Netophathite, Ittai son of Ribai from Gibeah of the Benjaminites, [30] Benaiah of Pirathon, Hiddai of Nahale-gaash, [31] Abi-albon the Arbathite, Azmaveth the Barhumite, [32] Eliahba of Shaalbon, sons of [e]Jashen, Jonathan,[-e] [33] Shammah the Ararite, Ahiam son of Sharar the Ararite, [34] Eliphelet son of Ahasbai son of the Maacathite, Eliam son of Ahithophel the Gilonite, [35] Hezrai the Carmelite, Paarai the Arbite, [36] Igal son of Nathan from Zobah, Bani the Gadite, [37] Zelek the Ammonite, Naharai the Beerothite —the arms-bearer of Joab son of Zeruiah—[38] Ira the Ithrite, Gareb the Ithrite, [39] Uriah the Hittite: thirty-seven in all.[o]

24

[a]The anger of the LORD again[b] flared up against Israel; and He incited David against them, saying, "Go and number Israel and Judah." [2] The king said to Joab, [c]his army commander,[-c] "Make the rounds of all the tribes of Israel, from Dan to Beersheba, and take a census of the people, so that I may know the size of the population." [3] Joab answered the king, "May the LORD your God increase the number of the people a hundredfold, while your own eyes see it! But why should my lord king want this?" [4] However, the king's command to Joab and to the officers of the army remained firm; and Joab and the officers of the army set out, at the instance of the king, to take a census of the people of Israel.

[5] They crossed the Jordan and [d]encamped at Aroer, on the right side of the town, which is in the middle of the wadi of Gad,

---

[o] *Septuagint and I Chron. 11 differ from the foregoing lists in vv. 8-38, and from each other in the number and forms of the names.*

[a] *This chapter is also found, with some variations, in I Chron. 21.1-7.*

[b] *Cf. above 21.1-14.*

[c-c] *I Chron. 21.2 reads "and to the officers of the army"; cf. below v. 4.*

[d-d] *Some Septuagint mss. read "began at Aroer, and from the town, which is . . . Gad, they."*

and*-d* [went on] to Jazer. [6] They continued to Gilead and to the region of *e-*Tahtim-hodshi, and they came to Dan-jaan and around to*-e* Sidon. [7] They went on to the fortress of Tyre and all the towns of the Hivites and Canaanites, and finished at Beersheba in southern Judah. [8] They traversed the whole country, and then they came back to Jerusalem at the end of nine months and twenty days. [9] Joab reported to the king the number of the people that had been recorded: in Israel there were 800,000 soldiers ready to draw the sword, and the men of Judah numbered 500,000.

[10] But afterward David *f-*reproached himself*-f* for having numbered the people. And David said to the LORD, "I have sinned grievously in what I have done. Please, O LORD, remit the guilt of Your servant, for I have acted foolishly." [11] When David rose in the morning, the word of the LORD had come to the prophet Gad, David's seer: [12] "Go and tell David, 'Thus said the LORD: I hold three things over you; choose one of them, and I will bring it upon you.' " [13] Gad came to David and told him; he asked, "Shall a seven-year famine come upon you in the land, or shall you be in flight from your adversaries for three months while they pursue you, or shall there be three days of pestilence in your land? Now consider carefully what reply I shall take back to Him who sent me." [14] David said to Gad, "I am in great distress. Let us fall into the hands of the LORD, for His compassion is great; and let me not fall into the hands of men."*g*

[15] The LORD sent a pestilence upon Israel from morning *e-*until the set time;*-e* and 70,000 of the people died, from Dan to Beersheba. [16] But when the angel extended his hand against Jerusalem to destroy it, the LORD renounced further punishment and said to the angel who was destroying the people, "Enough! Stay your hand!" The angel of the LORD was then by the threshing floor of Araunah the Jebusite. [17] When David saw the angel who was striking down the people, he said to the LORD, "I alone am guilty, I alone have done wrong; but these poor sheep, what have they done? Let Your hand fall upon me and my father's house!"

e-e *Meaning of Heb. uncertain.*
f-f *See note at I Sam. 24.6.*
g *Septuagint adds "So David chose the pestilence. It was the time of the wheat harvest."*

¹⁸ Gad came to David the same day and said to him, "Go and set up an altar to the LORD on the threshing floor of Araunah the Jebusite." ¹⁹ David went up, following Gad's instructions, as the LORD had commanded. ²⁰ Araunah looked out and saw the king and his courtiers approaching him.ʰ So Araunah went out and bowed low to the king, with his face to the ground. ²¹ And Araunah asked, "Why has my lord the king come to his servant?" David replied, "To buy the threshing floor from you, that I may build an altar to the LORD and that the plague against the people may be checked." ²² And Araunah said to David, "Let my lord the king take it and offer up whatever he sees fit. Here are oxen for a burnt offering, and the threshing boards and the gear of the oxen for wood. ²³ All this, ᵉ‑O king,‑ᵉ Araunah gives to Your Majesty. And may the LORD your God," Araunah added, "respond to you with favor!"

²⁴ But the king replied to Araunah, "No, I will buy them from you at a price. I cannot sacrifice to the LORD my God burnt offerings that have cost me nothing." So David bought the threshing floor and the oxen for fifty shekels of silver. ²⁵ And David built there an altar to the LORD and sacrificed burnt offerings and offerings of well-being. The LORD responded to the plea for the land, and the plague against Israel was checked.

ʰ 4QSamᵃ and I Chron. 21.20 add "Araunah (Ornan) was threshing wheat."

מלכים א

I KINGS

מלכים א

I KINGS

1 King David was now old, advanced in years; and though they covered him with bedclothes, he never felt warm. [2] His courtiers said to him, "Let a young virgin be sought for my lord the king, to wait upon Your Majesty and be his attendant;[a] and let her lie in your bosom, and my lord the king will be warm." [3] So they looked for a beautiful girl throughout the territory of Israel. They found Abishag the Shunammite and brought her to the king. [4] The girl was exceedingly beautiful. She became the king's attendant[a] and waited upon him; but the king was not intimate with her.

[5] Now Adonijah son of Haggith [b]went about boasting,[-b] "I will be king!" He provided himself with chariots and horses,[c] and an escort of fifty outrunners. [6] His father had never scolded him: "Why did you do that?" He was the one born after Absalom[d] and, like him, was very handsome.

[7] He conferred with Joab son of Zeruiah and with the priest Abiathar, and they supported Adonijah; [8] but the priest Zadok, Benaiah son of Jehoiada, the prophet Nathan, Shimei and Rei, and David's own fighting men did not side with Adonijah. [9] Adonijah made a sacrificial feast of sheep, oxen, and fatlings at the Zoheleth stone which is near En-rogel; he invited all his brother princes[e] and all the king's courtiers of the tribe of Judah; [10] but he did not invite the prophet Nathan, or Benaiah, or the fighting men, or his brother Solomon. [11] Then Nathan said to Bathsheba, Solomon's mother, "You must have heard that Adonijah son of Haggith has assumed the

[a] *Meaning of Heb. uncertain.*
[b-b] *Or "presumed to think."*
[c] *Others "horsemen"; meaning of Heb.* parash(im) *not always certain.*
[d] *Thus, Absalom having died, Adonijah was David's oldest living son.*
[e] *Lit. "all his brothers, sons of the king."*

kingship without the knowledge of our lord David. [12] Now take my advice, so that you may save your life and the life of your son Solomon. [13] Go immediately to King David and say to him, 'Did not you, O lord king, swear to your maidservant: "Your son Solomon shall succeed me as king, and he shall sit upon my throne"? Then why has Adonijah become king?' [14] While you are still there talking with the king, I will come in after you and confirm your words."

[15] So Bathsheba went to the king in his chamber.—The king was very old, and Abishag the Shunammite was waiting on the king.—[16] Bathsheba bowed low in homage to the king; and the king asked, "What troubles you?" [17] She answered him, "My lord, you yourself swore to your maidservant by the LORD your God: 'Your son Solomon shall succeed me as king, and he shall sit upon my throne.' [18] Yet now Adonijah has become king, and you,[f] my lord the king, know nothing about it. [19] He has prepared a sacrificial feast of a great many oxen, fatlings, and sheep, and he has invited all the king's sons and Abiathar the priest and Joab commander of the army; but he has not invited your servant Solomon. [20] And so the eyes of all Israel are upon you, O lord king, to tell them who shall succeed my lord the king on the throne. [21] Otherwise, when my lord the king lies down with his fathers, my son Solomon and I will be regarded as traitors."

[22] She was still talking to the king when the prophet Nathan arrived. [23] They announced to the king, "The prophet Nathan is here," and he entered the king's presence. Bowing low to the king with his face to the ground, [24] Nathan said, "O lord king, [g]you must have said,[g] 'Adonijah shall succeed me as king and he shall sit upon my throne.' [25] For he has gone down today and prepared a sacrificial feast of a great many oxen, fatlings, and sheep. He invited all the king's sons and the army officers and Abiathar the priest. At this very moment they are eating and drinking with him, and they are shouting, 'Long live King Adonijah!' [26] But he did not invite me your servant, or the priest Zadok, or Benaiah son of Jehoiada, or your servant Solomon. [27] Can this

---

[f] *So many mss. and ancient versions; usual editions "now."*
[g-g] *Or (cf. Rashi, Ralbag, Radak) "have you said . . . ?"*

decision have come from my lord the king, without your telling your servant who is to succeed to the throne of my lord the
king?"

²⁸ King David's response was: "Summon Bathsheba!" She entered the king's presence and stood before the king. ²⁹ And the
king took an oath, saying, "As the LORD lives, who has rescued
me from every trouble: ³⁰ The oath I swore to you by the LORD,
the God of Israel, that your son Solomon should succeed me as
king and that he should sit upon my throne in my stead, I will
fulfill this very day!" ³¹ Bathsheba bowed low in homage to the
king with her face to the ground, and she said, "May my lord King
David live forever!"

³² Then King David said, "Summon to me the priest Zadok, the
prophet Nathan, and Benaiah son of Jehoiada." When they came
before the king, ³³ the king said to them, "Take ʰ⁻my loyal soldiers,⁻ʰ
and have my son Solomon ride on my mule and bring him down
to Gihon. ³⁴ Let the priest Zadok and the prophet Nathan anoint
him there king over Israel, whereupon you shall sound the horn
and shout, 'Long live King Solomon!' ³⁵ Then march up after
him, and let him come in and sit on my throne. For he shall
succeed me as king; him I designate to be ruler of Israel and
Judah." ³⁶ Benaiah son of Jehoiada spoke up and said to the king,
"Amen! And may the LORD, the God of my lord the king, so
ordain. ³⁷ As the LORD was with my lord the king, so may He be
with Solomon; and may He exalt his throne even higher than the
throne of my lord King David."

³⁸ Then the priest Zadok, and the prophet Nathan, and Benaiah
son of Jehoiada went down with the Cherethites and the Pelethites. They had Solomon ride on King David's mule and they led
him to Gihon. ³⁹ The priest Zadok took the horn of oil from the
Tent and anointed Solomon. They sounded the horn and all the
people shouted, "Long live King Solomon!" ⁴⁰ All the people
then marched up behind him, playing on flutes and making merry
till the earth was split open by the uproar.

ʰ⁻ʰ Lit. "your lord's men."

⁴¹ Adonijah and all the guests who were with him, who had just finished eating, heard it. When Joab heard the sound of the horn, he said, "Why is the city in such an uproar?" ⁴² He was still speaking when the priest Jonathan son of Abiathar arrived. "Come in," said Adonijah. "You are a worthy man, and you surely bring good news." ⁴³ But Jonathan replied to Adonijah, "Alas, our lord King David has made Solomon king! ⁴⁴ The king sent with him the priest Zadok and the prophet Nathan and Benaiah son of Jehoiada, and the Cherethites and Pelethites. They had him ride on the king's mule, ⁴⁵ and the priest Zadok and the prophet Nathan anointed him king at Gihon. Then they came up from there making merry, and the city went into an uproar. That's the noise you heard. ⁴⁶ Further, Solomon seated himself on the royal throne; ⁴⁷ further, the king's courtiers came to congratulate our lord King David, saying, 'May God make the renown of Solomon even greater than yours, and may He exalt his throne even higher than yours!' And the king bowed low on his couch. ⁴⁸ And further, this is what the king said, 'Praised be the LORD, the God of Israel who has this day provided a successor to my throne, while my own eyes can see it.' " ⁴⁹ Thereupon, all of Adonijah's guests rose in alarm and each went his own way.

⁵⁰ Adonijah, in fear of Solomon, went at once [to the Tent] and grasped the horns of the altar. ⁵¹ It was reported to Solomon: "Adonijah is in fear of King Solomon and has grasped the horns of the altar, saying, 'Let King Solomon first swear to me that he will not put his servant to the sword.' " ⁵² Solomon said, "If he behaves worthily, not a hair of his head shall fall to the ground; but if he is caught in any offense, he shall die." ⁵³ So King Solomon sent and had him taken down from the altar. He came and bowed before King Solomon, and Solomon said to him, "Go home."

2 When David's life was drawing to a close, he instructed his son Solomon as follows: ² "I am going the way of all the earth; be strong and show yourself a man. ³ Keep the charge of the LORD your God, walking in His ways and following His laws, His commandments, His rules, and His admonitions as recorded in the Teaching of Moses, in order that you may succeed in whatever you undertake and wherever you turn. ⁴ Then the LORD will fulfill the promise that He made concerning me: 'If your descendants are scrupulous in their conduct, and walk before Me faithfully, with all their heart and soul, *ᵃ*your line on the throne of Israel shall never end!'*⁻ᵃ*

⁵ "Further, you know what Joab son of Zeruiah did to me, what he did to the two commanders of Israel's forces, Abner son of Ner and Amasa son of Jether: he killed them, shedding*ᵇ* blood of war in peacetime, staining the girdle of his loins and the sandals on his feet with blood of war.*ᶜ* ⁶ So act in accordance with your wisdom, and see that his white hair does not go down to Sheol in peace.

⁷ "But deal graciously with the sons of Barzillai the Gileadite, for they befriended me when I fled from your brother Absalom; let them be among those that eat at your table.*ᵈ*

⁸ "You must also deal with Shimei son of Gera, the Benjaminite from Bahurim. He insulted me outrageously when I was on my way to Mahanaim; but he came down to meet me at the Jordan,*ᵉ* and I swore to him by the LORD: 'I will not put you to the sword.' ⁹ So do not let him go unpunished; for you are a wise man and you will know how to deal with him and send his gray hair down to Sheol in blood."

¹⁰ So David slept with his fathers, and he was buried in the City of David. ¹¹ The length of David's reign over Israel was forty years: he reigned seven years in Hebron, and he reigned thirty-three years in Jerusalem. ¹² And Solomon sat upon the throne of his father David, and his rule was firmly established.

¹³ Adonijah son of Haggith came to see Bathsheba, Solomon's mother. She said, "Do you come with friendly intent?" "Yes," he replied; ¹⁴ and he continued, "I would like to have a word with

---

ᵃ⁻ᵃ Lit. "there shall never cease to be a man of yours on the throne of Israel." Cf. II Sam. 7.12-16.
ᵇ Meaning of Heb. uncertain.
ᶜ I.e. Joab had thus brought bloodguilt on David's House; see II Sam 3.27 and 20.10.
ᵈ I.e. for whose maintenance you provide; see II Sam. 19.32 ff.
ᵉ See II Sam. 16.5 ff.; 19.17 ff.

you." "Speak up," she said. ¹⁵ Then he said, "You know that the kingship was rightly mine and that all Israel wanted me to reign. But the kingship passed on to my brother; it came to him by the will of the LORD. ¹⁶ And now I have one request to make of you; do not refuse me." She said, "Speak up." ¹⁷ He replied, "Please ask King Solomon—for he won't refuse you—to give me Abishag the Shunammite as wife." ¹⁸ "Very well," said Bathsheba, "I will speak to the king in your behalf."

¹⁹ So Bathsheba went to King Solomon to speak to him about Adonijah. The king rose to greet her and bowed down to her. He sat on his throne; and he had a throne placed for the queen mother, and she sat on his right. ²⁰ She said, "I have one small request to make of you, do not refuse me." He responded, "Ask, mother; I shall not refuse you." ²¹ Then she said, "Let Abishag the Shunammite be given to your brother Adonijah as wife." ²² The king replied to his mother, "Why request Abishag the Shunammite for Adonijah? Request the kingship for him! For he is my older brother, *f*-and the priest Abiathar and Joab son of Zeruiah are on his side."*-f*

²³ Thereupon, King Solomon swore by the LORD, saying, "So may God do to me and even more, if broaching this matter does not cost Adonijah his life! ²⁴ Now, as the LORD lives, who has established me and set me on the throne of my father David and who has provided him*g* with a house, as he promised, Adonijah shall be put to death this very day!" ²⁵ And Solomon instructed Benaiah son of Jehoiada, who struck Adonijah*h* down; and so he died.

²⁶ To the priest Abiathar, the king said, "Go to your estate at Anathoth! You deserve to die, but I shall not put you to death at this time, because you carried the Ark of my Lord GOD before my father David and because you shared all the hardships that my father endured." ²⁷ So Solomon dismissed Abiathar from his office of priest of the LORD—thus fulfilling what the LORD had spoken at Shiloh*i* regarding the house of Eli.

²⁸ When the news reached Joab, he fled to the Tent of the LORD

---

f-f Lit. "and for him and for Abiathar and for Joab son of Zeruiah." Meaning of Heb. uncertain.
g Heb. "me."
h Heb. "him."
i Cf. I Sam. 3.14.

and grasped the horns of the altar—for Joab had sided with Adonijah, though he had not sided with Absalom. ²⁹ King Solomon was told that Joab had fled to the Tent of the Lord and that he was there by the altar; so Solomon sent Benaiah, saying, "Go and strike him down." ³⁰ Benaiah went to the Tent of the Lord and said to him, "Thus said the king: Come out!" "No!" he replied; "I will die here." Benaiah reported back to the king that Joab had answered thus and thus, ³¹ and the king said, "Do just as he said; strike him down and bury him, and remove guilt from me and my father's house for the blood of the innocent that Joab has shed. ³² Thus the Lord will bring his bloodguilt down upon his own head, because, unbeknown to my father, he struck down with the sword two men more righteous and honorable than he —Abner son of Ner, the army commander of Israel, and Amasa son of Jether, the army commander of Judah. ³³ May the guilt for their blood come down upon the head of Joab and his descendants forever, and may good fortune from the Lord be granted forever to David and his descendants, his house and his throne." ³⁴ So Benaiah son of Jehoiada went up and struck him down. And he was buried at his home in the wilderness. ³⁵ In his place, the king appointed Benaiah son of Jehoiada over the army, and in place of Abiathar, the king appointed the priest Zadok.

³⁶ Then the king summoned Shimei and said to him, "Build yourself a house in Jerusalem and stay there—do not ever go out from there anywhere else. ³⁷ On the very day that you go out and cross the Wadi Kidron, you can be sure that you will die; your blood shall be on your own head." ³⁸ "That is fair," said Shimei to the king, "your servant will do just as my lord the king has spoken." And for a long time, Shimei remained in Jerusalem.

³⁹ Three years later, two slaves of Shimei ran away to King Achish son of Maacah of Gath. Shimei was told, "Your slaves are in Gath." ⁴⁰ Shimei thereupon saddled his ass and went to Achish in Gath to claim his slaves; and Shimei returned from Gath with his slaves. ⁴¹ Solomon was told that Shimei had gone from Jerusalem to Gath and back, ⁴² and the king summoned Shimei and said

to him, "Did I not adjure you by the LORD and warn you, 'On the very day that you leave and go anywhere else, you can be sure that you will die,' and did you not say to me, 'It is fair; I accept'? 43 Why did you not abide by the oath before the LORD and by the orders which I gave you?" 44 The king said further to Shimei, "You know all the wrong, which you remember very well, that you did to my father David. Now the LORD brings down your wrongdoing upon your own head. 45 But King Solomon shall be blessed, and the throne of David shall be established before the LORD forever."

46 The king gave orders to Benaiah son of Jehoiada and he went out and struck Shimei[h] down; and so he died.

Thus the kingdom was secured in Solomon's hands.

3 Solomon allied himself by marriage with Pharaoh king of Egypt. He married Pharaoh's daughter and brought her to the City of David [to live there] until he had finished building his palace, and the House of the LORD, and the walls around Jerusalem.

2 The people, however, continued to offer sacrifices at the open shrines, because up to that time no house had been built for the name of the LORD. 3 And Solomon, though he loved the LORD and followed the practices of his father David, also sacrificed and offered at the shrines.

4 The king went to Gibeon to sacrifice there, for that was the largest shrine; on that altar Solomon presented a thousand burnt offerings. 5 At Gibeon the LORD appeared to Solomon in a dream by night; and God said, "Ask, what shall I grant you?" 6 Solomon said, "You dealt most graciously with Your servant my father David, because he walked before You in faithfulness and righteousness and in integrity of heart. You have continued this great kindness to him by giving him a son to occupy his throne, as is now the case. 7 And now, O LORD my God, You have made Your servant king in place of my father David; but I am a young lad,

a-with no experience in leadership.*-a* ⁸ Your servant finds himself in the midst of the people You have chosen, a people too numerous to be numbered or counted. ⁹ Grant, then, Your servant an understanding mind to judge Your people, to distinguish between good and bad; for who can judge this vast people of Yours?"

¹⁰ The LORD was pleased that Solomon had asked for this. ¹¹ And God said to him, "Because you asked for this—you did not ask for long life, you did not ask for riches, you did not ask for the life of your enemies, but you asked for discernment in dispensing justice—¹² I now do as you have spoken. I grant you a wise and discerning mind; there has never been anyone like you before, nor will anyone like you arise again. ¹³ And I also grant you what you did not ask for—both riches and glory all your life —the like of which no king has ever had. ¹⁴ And I will further grant you long life, if you will walk in My ways and observe My laws and commandments, as did your father David."

¹⁵ Then Solomon awoke: it was a dream! He went to Jerusalem, stood before the Ark of the Covenant of the LORD, and sacrificed burnt offerings and presented offerings of well-being; and he made a banquet for all his courtiers.

¹⁶ Later two prostitutes came to the king and stood before him. ¹⁷ The first woman said, "Please, my lord! This woman and I live in the same house; and I gave birth to a child while she was in the house. ¹⁸ On the third day after I was delivered, this woman also gave birth to a child. We were alone; there was no one else with us in the house, just the two of us in the house. ¹⁹ During the night this woman's child died, because she lay on it. ²⁰ She arose in the night and took my son from my side while your maidservant was asleep, and laid him in her bosom; and she laid her dead son in my bosom. ²¹ When I arose in the morning to nurse my son, there he was, dead; but when I looked at him closely in the morning, it was not the son I had borne." ²² The other woman spoke up, "No, the live one is my son, and

---

a-a Lit. *"I do not know to go out and come in"; cf. Nu. 27.17.*

the dead one is yours!" But the first insisted, "No, the dead boy is yours; mine is the live one!" And they went on arguing before the king.

23 The king said, "One says, 'This is my son, the live one, and the dead one is yours'; and the other says, 'No, the dead boy is yours, mine is the live one.' 24 So the king gave the order, "Fetch me a sword." A sword was brought before the king, 25 and the king said, "Cut the live child in two, and give half to one and half to the other."

26 But the woman whose son was the live one pleaded with the king, for she was overcome with compassion for her son. "Please, my lord," she cried, "give her the live child; only don't kill it!" The other insisted, "It shall be neither yours nor mine; cut it in two!" 27 Then the king spoke up. "Give the live child to her," he said, "and do not put it to death; she is its mother."

28 When all Israel heard the decision that the king had rendered, they stood in awe of the king; for they saw that he possessed divine wisdom to execute justice.

4 King Solomon was now king over all Israel. 2 These were his officials:

Azariah son of Zadok—the priest;
3 Elihoreph and Ahijah sons of Shisha—scribes;
Jehoshaphat son of Ahilud—recorder;
4 Benaiah son of Jehoiada—over the army;
Zadok and Abiathar—priests;
5 Azariah son of Nathan—in charge of the prefects;
Zabud son of Nathan the priest—companion of the king;
6 Ahishar—in charge of the palace; and
Adoniram son of Abda—in charge of the forced labor.

7 Solomon had twelve prefects governing all Israel, who provided food for the king and his household; each had to provide food for one month in the year. 8 And these were their names: Ben-hur, in the hill country of Ephraim; 9 Ben-deker, in Makaz,

Shaalbim, Beth-shemesh, and Elon-beth-hanan; [10] Ben-hesed in Arubboth—he governed Socho and all the Hepher area; [11] Ben-abinadab, [in] all of Naphath-dor (Solomon's daughter Taphath was his wife); [12] Baana son of Ahilud [in] Taanach and Megiddo and all Beth-shean, which is beside Zarethan, below Jezreel— from Beth-shean to Abel-meholah as far as the other side of Jokmeam; [13] Ben-geber, in Ramoth-gilead—he governed the villages of Jair son of Manasseh which are in Gilead, and he also governed the district of Argob which is in Bashan, sixty large towns with walls and bronze bars; [14] Ahinadab son of Iddo, in Mahanaim; [15] Ahimaaz, in Naphtali (he too took a daughter of Solomon—Basemath—to wife); [16] Baanah son of Hushi, in Asher and Bealoth;[a] [17] Jehoshaphat son of Paruah, in Issachar; [18] Shimei son of Ela, in Benjamin; [19] Geber son of Uri, in the region of Gilead, the country of Sihon king of the Amorites and Og king of Bashan; [b-]and one prefect who was in the land.[-b]

[20] Judah and Israel were as numerous as the sands of the sea; they ate and drank and were content.

5 Solomon's rule extended over all the kingdoms from the Euphrates to the land of the Philistines and the boundary of Egypt. They brought Solomon tribute and were subject to him all his life. [2] Solomon's daily provisions consisted of 30 *kors* of semolina, and 60 *kors* of [ordinary] flour, [3] 10 fattened oxen, 20 pasture-fed oxen, and 100 sheep and goats, besides deer and gazelles, roebucks and [a-]fatted geese.[-a] [4] For he controlled the whole region west of the Euphrates—all the kings west of the Euphrates, from Tiphsah to Gaza—and he had peace on all his borders round about. [5] All the days of Solomon, Judah and Israel from Dan to Beer-sheba dwelt in safety, everyone under his own vine and under his own fig tree. [6] Solomon had 40,000 stalls of horses for his chariotry and 12,000 horsemen.

[7] [b]All those prefects, each during his month, would furnish provisions for King Solomon and for all who were admitted to

---

[a] *Or "in Aloth."*
[b-b] *Meaning of Heb. uncertain.*

[a-a] *Exact meaning of Heb. uncertain.*
[b] *Resuming the account begun in 4.2.*

King Solomon's table; they did not fall short in anything. [8] They would also, each in his turn, deliver barley and straw for the horses and the swift steeds to the places where they were stationed.

[9] The LORD endowed Solomon with wisdom and discernment in great measure, with understanding as vast as the sands on the seashore. [10] Solomon's wisdom was greater than the wisdom of all the Kedemites and than all the wisdom of the Egyptians. [11] He was the wisest of all men: [wiser] than Ethan the Ezrahite, and Heman, Chalkol, and Darda the sons of Mahol. His fame spread among all the surrounding nations. [12] He composed three thousand proverbs, and his songs numbered one thousand and five. [13] He discoursed about trees, from the cedar in Lebanon to the hyssop that grows out of the wall; and he discoursed about beasts, birds, creeping things, and fishes. [14] Men of all peoples came to hear Solomon's wisdom, [sent] by all the kings of the earth who had heard of his wisdom.

[15] King Hiram of Tyre sent his officials to Solomon when he heard that he had been anointed king in place of his father; for Hiram had always been a friend of David. [16] Solomon sent this message to Hiram: [17] "You know that my father David could not build a house for the name of the LORD his God because of the enemies[c] that encompassed him, until the LORD had placed them under the soles of his feet. [18] But now the LORD my God has given me respite all around; there is no adversary and no mischance. [19] And so I propose to build a house for the name of the LORD my God, as the LORD promised my father David, saying, 'Your son, whom I will set on your throne in your place, shall build the house for My name.' [20] Please, then, give orders for cedars to be cut for me in the Lebanon. My servants will work with yours, and I will pay you any wages you may ask for your servants; for as you know, there is none among us who knows how to cut timber like the Sidonians."

[21] When Hiram heard Solomon's message, he was overjoyed.

[c] *Heb. "war"; cf. Targum.*

"Praised be the LORD this day," he said, "for granting David a wise son to govern this great people." 22 So Hiram sent word to Solomon: "I have your message; I will supply all the cedar and cypress logs you require. 23 My servants will bring them down to the sea from the Lebanon; and at the sea I will make them into floats and [deliver them] to any place that you designate to me. There I shall break them up for you to carry away. You, in turn, will supply the food I require for my household." 24 So Hiram kept Solomon provided with all the cedar and cypress wood he required, 25 and Solomon delivered to Hiram 20,000 *kors* of wheat as provisions for his household and *d*-20 *kors*-*d* of beaten oil. Such was Solomon's annual payment to Hiram.

26 The LORD had given Solomon wisdom, as He had promised him. There was friendship between Hiram and Solomon, and the two of them made a treaty.

27 King Solomon imposed forced labor on all Israel; the levy came to 30,000 men. 28 He sent them to the Lebanon in shifts of 10,000 a month: they would spend one month in the Lebanon and two months at home. Adoniram was in charge of the forced labor. 29 Solomon also had 70,000 porters and 80,000 quarriers in the hills, 30 apart from Solomon's 3,300 officials who were in charge of the work and supervised the gangs doing the work.
31 The king ordered huge blocks of choice stone to be quarried, so that the foundations of the house might be laid with hewn stones. 32 Solomon's masons, Hiram's masons, and the men of Gebal shaped them. Thus the timber and the stones for building the house were made ready.

6 In the four hundred and eightieth year after the Israelites left the land of Egypt, in the month of Ziv—that is, the second month —in the fourth year of his reign over Israel, Solomon began to build the House of the LORD. 2 The House which King Solomon

d-d *Septuagint reads, "20,000 baths."*

built for the LORD was 60 cubits long, 20 cubits wide, and 30 cubits high. [3] The portico in front of the Great Hall of the House was 20 cubits long—along the width of the House—and 10 cubits deep to the front of the House. [4] [a]He made windows for the House, recessed and latticed. [5] Against the outside wall of the House—the outside walls of the House enclosing the Great Hall and the Shrine[b]—he built a storied structure; and he made side chambers all around. [6] The lowest story was five cubits wide, the middle one six cubits wide, and the third seven cubits wide; for he had provided recesses around the outside of the House so as not to penetrate the walls of the House.

[7] When the House was built, only finished stones cut at the quarry were used, so that no hammer or ax or any iron tool was heard in the House while it was being built.

[8] The entrance to the middle[c] [story of] the side chambers was on the right side of the House; and winding stairs led up to the middle chambers, and from the middle chambers to the third story. [9] When he finished building the House, [d]he paneled the House with beams and planks of cedar.[-d] [10] He built the storied structure against the entire House—each story five cubits high, so that it encased the House with timbers of cedar.

[11] Then the word of the LORD came to Solomon, [12] "With regard to this House you are building—if you follow My laws and observe My rules and faithfully keep My commandments, I will fulfill for you the promise that I gave to your father David: [13] I will abide among the children of Israel, and I will never forsake My people Israel."

[14] When Solomon had completed the construction of the House, [15] he paneled the walls of the House on the inside with planks of cedar. He also overlaid the walls on the inside with wood, from the floor of the House to the ceiling. And he overlaid the floor of the House with planks of cypress. [16] Twenty cubits from the rear of the House, he built [a partition] of cedar planks from the floor to the walls;[e] he furnished its interior to serve as

---

[a] *Meaning of parts of vv. 4-6 uncertain.*
[b] *I.e. the inner sanctuary, designated in v. 16 and elsewhere as the "Holy of Holies."*
[c] *Septuagint and Targum read "lowest."*
[d-d] *Meaning of Heb. uncertain.*
[e] *Septuagint reads "rafters."*

a shrine, as the Holy of Holies. [17] *f* The front part of the House, that is, the Great Hall, measured 40 cubits. [18] The cedar of the interior of the House had carvings of gourds and calyxes; it was all cedar, no stone was exposed. [19] In the innermost part of the House, he fixed a Shrine in which to place the Ark of the LORD's Covenant. [20] *b-*The interior of the*-b* Shrine was 20 cubits long, 20 cubits wide, and 20 cubits high. He overlaid it with solid gold; he similarly overlaid [its] cedar altar. [21] Solomon overlaid the interior of the House with solid gold; and he inserted golden chains *g-*into the door of*-g* the Shrine. He overlaid [the Shrine] with gold, [22] so that the entire House was overlaid with gold; he even overlaid with gold the entire altar of the Shrine. And so the entire House was completed.

[23] In the Shrine he made two cherubim of olive wood, each 10 cubits high. [24] [One] had a wing measuring 5 cubits and another wing measuring 5 cubits, so that the spread from wing tip to wing tip was 10 cubits; [25] and the wingspread of the other cherub was also 10 cubits. The two cherubim had the same measurements and proportions: [26] the height of the one cherub was 10 cubits, and so was that of the other cherub.

[27] He placed the cherubim inside the *h-*inner chamber.*-h* Since the wings of the cherubim were extended, a wing of the one touched one wall and a wing of the other touched the other wall, while their wings in the center of the chamber touched each other. [28] He overlaid the cherubim with gold. [29] All over the walls of the House, of both the inner area and the outer area, he carved reliefs of cherubim, palms, and calyxes, [30] and he overlaid the floor of the House with gold, both the inner and the outer areas.

[31] For the entrance of the Shrine he made doors of olive wood, *d-*the pilasters and the doorposts having five sides.*-d* [32] The double doors were of olive wood, and on them he carved reliefs of cherubim, palms, and calyxes. He overlaid them with gold, hammering the gold onto the cherubim and the palms. [33] For the

f *Meaning of vv. 17-22 is unclear in part.*
g-g *Heb. "in front of."*
h-h *I.e. the Shrine.*

entrance of the Great Hall, too, he made doorposts of oleaster wood, *d*-having four sides,*-d* 34 and the double doors of cypress wood, each door consisting of two rounded planks. 35 On them he carved cherubim, palms, and calyxes, overlaying them with gold applied evenly over the carvings. 36 He built the inner enclosure of three courses of hewn stones and one course of cedar beams.

37 In the fourth year, in the month of Ziv, the foundations of the House were laid; 38 and in the eleventh year, in the month of Bul—that is, the eighth month—the House was completed according to all its details and all its specifications.

7 It took him seven years to build it.[1] And it took Solomon thirteen years to build his palace, until his whole palace was completed.

2 He built the *a*-Lebanon Forest House with four rows*-a* of cedar columns, and with hewn cedar beams above the columns. Its length was 100 cubits, its breadth 50 cubits, and its height 30 cubits. 3 It was paneled above with cedar, with the planks[b] that were above on the 45 columns—15 in each row. 4 And there were three rows of window frames, with three tiers of windows facing each other. 5 All the doorways and doorposts[c] had square frames —with three tiers of windows facing each other.

6 He made the portico of columns 50 cubits long and 30 cubits wide; *d*-the portico was in front of [the columns], and there were columns with a canopy in front of them.*-d* 7 He made the throne portico, where he was to pronounce judgment— the Hall of Judgment. It was paneled with cedar from floor to floor.[e]

8 The house that he used as a residence, in the rear courtyard, back of the portico, was of the same construction. Solomon also constructed a palace like that portico for the daughter of Pharaoh, whom he had married.

---

[a] *So called because of the rows of cedar columns. Septuagint reads "three rows" instead of "four rows"; cf. v. 3.*

[b] *Apparently the "planks" connected the columns longitudinally, and the "beams" (v.2) connected the planks transversely.*

[c] *Septuagint reads "windows."*

[d-d] *Meaning of Heb. uncertain.*

[e] *Syriac reads "rafters."*

⁹ All these buildings, from foundation to coping and all the way out to the great courtyard, were of choice stones, hewn according to measure, smooth on all sides.ᶠ ¹⁰ The foundations were huge blocks of choice stone, stones of ten cubits and stones of eight cubits; ¹¹ and above were choice stones, hewn according to measure, and cedar wood. ¹² The large surrounding courtyard had three tiers of hewn stone and a row of cedar beams, the same as for the inner court of the House of the Lᴏʀᴅ, and for the portico of the House.

¹³ King Solomon sent for Hiram and brought him down from Tyre. ¹⁴ He was the son of a widow of the tribe of Naphtali, and his father had been a Tyrian, a coppersmith. He was endowed with skill, ability, and talent for executing all work in bronze.ᵍ He came to King Solomon and executed all his work. ¹⁵ He cast two columns of bronze; one column was 18 cubits high and measured 12 cubits in circumference, [and similarly] the other column. ¹⁶ He made two capitals, cast in bronze, to be set upon the two columns, the height of each of the two capitals being five cubits; ¹⁷ also nets of meshwork with festoons of chainwork for the capitals which were on the top of the columns, seven for each of the two capitals. ¹⁸ He made the columnsʰ so that there were two rows [of pomegranates] encircling the top of the one network, to cover the capitals that were on the top of the pomegranates;ⁱ and he did the same for [the network on] the second capital. ¹⁹ The capitals upon the columns of the portico were of lily design, four cubits high; ²⁰ so also the capitals upon the two columns extended above and next to the bulgeʲ that was beside the network. There were 200 pomegranates in rows around the top of the second capital.ᵏ

²¹ He set up the columns at the portico of the Great Hall; he set up one column on the right and named it Jachin, and he set up the other column on the left and named it Boaz. ²² Upon the

---

ᶠ Lit. "sawed with a saw in the inside and outside."
ᵍ Heb nehosheth means both copper and bronze. In the translation, "copper" is ordinarily used to denote the natural product and "bronze" for the artifacts.
ʰ Two Heb. mss. read "pomegranates."
ⁱ About 50 Heb. mss. read "columns."
ʲ Lit. "belly"; exact force of Heb. uncertain.
ᵏ I.e. each of the two capitals.

top of the columns there was a lily design. Thus the work of the columns was completed.

²³ Then he made the tank^l of cast metal, 10 cubits across from brim to brim, completely round; it was 5 cubits high, and it measured 30 cubits in circumference. ²⁴ There were gourds below the brim completely encircling it—ten to a cubit, encircling the tank; the gourds were in two rows, cast in one piece with it. ²⁵ It stood upon 12 oxen: three facing north, three facing west, three facing south, and three facing east, with the tank resting upon them; their haunches were all turned inward. ²⁶ It was a handbreadth thick, and its brim was made like that of a cup, like the petals of a lily. Its capacity was 2,000 baths.

²⁷ He made the ten laver stands of bronze. The length of each laver stand was four cubits and the width four cubits, and the height was three cubits. ²⁸ The structure of the laver stands was as follows: They had insets,^{m} and there were insets within the frames; ²⁹ and on the insets within the frames were lions, oxen, and cherubim. Above the frames was a stand; and both above and below the lions and the oxen were spirals of hammered metal. ³⁰ Each laver stand had four bronze wheels and [two] bronze axletrees. Its four legs had brackets; the brackets were under the laver, cast ^{d}-with spirals beyond each.$^{-d}$ ³¹ Its funnel, within the crown, rose a cubit above it; this funnel was round, in the fashion of a stand, a cubit and a half in diameter. On the funnel too there were carvings.

But the insets were square, not round. ³² And below the insets were the four wheels. The axletrees of the wheels were [fixed] in the laver stand, and the height of each wheel was a cubit and a half. ³³ The structure of the wheels was like the structure of chariot wheels; and their axletrees, their rims, their spokes, and their hubs were all of cast metal. ³⁴ Four brackets ran to the four corners of each laver stand; the brackets were of a piece with the laver stand. ³⁵ At the top of the laver stand was a round band half a cubit high, and together with the top of the laver stand; its sides and its insets were of one piece with it. ³⁶ ^{d}-On its surface—on its

---

^{l} *Lit. "sea."*
^{m} *Emendation yields "frames."*

sides—and on its insets [Hiram] engraved cherubim, lions, and palms, as the clear space on each allowed,-*d* with spirals round about. [37] It was after this manner that he made the ten laver stands, all of them cast alike, of the same measure and the same form. [38] Then he made ten bronze lavers, one laver on each of the ten laver stands, each laver measuring four cubits and each laver containing forty baths.

[39] He disposed the laver stands, five at the right side of the House and five at its left side; and the tank he placed on the right side of the House, at the southeast [corner].

[40] Hiram also made the lavers, the scrapers, and the sprinkling bowls.

So Hiram finished all the work that he had been doing for King Solomon on the House of the LORD: [41] the two columns, the two globes of the capitals upon the columns; and the two pieces of network to cover the two globes of the capitals upon the columns; [42] the 400 pomegranates for the two pieces of network, two rows of pomegranates for each network, to cover the two globes of the capitals upon the columns; [43] the ten stands and the ten lavers upon the stands; [44] the one tank with the twelve oxen underneath the tank; [45] the pails, the scrapers, and the sprinkling bowls. All those vessels in the House of the LORD which Hiram made for King Solomon were of burnished bronze. [46] The king had them cast *n*-in earthen molds,-*n* in the plain of the Jordan between Succoth and Zarethan. [47] Solomon left all the vessels [unweighed] because of their very great quantity; the weight of the bronze was not reckoned.

[48] And Solomon made all the furnishings that were in the House of the LORD: the altar, of gold; the table for the bread of display, of gold; [49] the lampstands—five on the right side and five on the left—in front of the Shrine, of solid gold; and the petals, lamps, and tongs, of gold; [50] the basins, snuffers, sprinkling bowls, ladles, and fire pans, of solid gold; and the hinge sockets

n-n *Lit. "in the thick of the earth."*

for the doors of the innermost part of the House, the Holy of Holies, and for the doors of the Great Hall of the House, of gold.

51 When all the work that King Solomon had done in the House of the LORD was completed, Solomon brought in the sacred donations of his father David—the silver, the gold, and the vessels —and deposited them in the treasury of the House of the LORD.

8 Then Solomon convoked the elders of Israel—all the heads of the tribes and the ancestral chieftains of the Israelites—before King Solomon in Jerusalem, to bring up the Ark of the Covenant of the LORD from the City of David, that is, Zion. 2 All the men of Israel gathered before King Solomon at the Feast,*a* in the month of Ethanim—that is, the seventh month. 3 When all the elders of Israel had come, the priests lifted the Ark 4 and carried up the Ark of the LORD. Then the priests and the Levites brought the Tent of Meeting and all the holy vessels that were in the Tent. 5 Meanwhile, King Solomon and the whole community of Israel, who were assembled with him before the Ark, were sacrificing sheep and oxen in such abundance that they could not be numbered or counted.

6 The priests brought the Ark of the LORD's Covenant to its place underneath the wings of the cherubim, in the Shrine of the House, in the Holy of Holies; 7 for the cherubim had their wings spread out over the place of the Ark, so that the cherubim shielded the Ark and its poles from above. 8 The poles projected so that the ends of the poles were visible in the Sanctuary in front of the Shrine, but they could not be seen outside; and there they remain to this day. 9 There was nothing inside the Ark but the two tablets of stone which Moses placed there at Horeb, when the LORD made [a covenant] with the Israelites after their departure from the land of Egypt.

10 When the priests came out of the sanctuary—for the cloud had filled the House of the LORD 11 and the priests were not able

---

a I.e. of Booths. Cf Lev. 23.34.

to remain and perform the service because of the cloud, for the Presence of the LORD filled the House of the LORD—[12] then Solomon declared:

"The LORD has chosen
To abide in a thick cloud:
[13] I have now built for You
A stately House,
A place where You
May dwell forever."

[14] Then, with the whole congregation of Israel standing, the king faced about and blessed the whole congregation of Israel. [15] He said:

"Praised be the LORD, the God of Israel, [b]who has fulfilled with deeds the promise He made[-b] to my father David. For He said, [16] 'Ever since I brought My people Israel out of Egypt, I have not chosen a city among all the tribes of Israel for building a House where My name might abide; but I have chosen David to rule My people Israel.'

[17] "Now my father David had intended to build a House for the name of the LORD, the God of Israel. [18] But the LORD said to my father David, 'As regards your intention to build a House for My name, you did right to have that intention. [19] However, you shall not build the House yourself; instead, your son, the issue of your loins, shall build the House for My name.'

[20] "And the LORD has fulfilled the promise that He made: I have succeeded[c] my father David and have ascended the throne of Israel, as the LORD promised. I have built the House for the name of the LORD, the God of Israel; [21] and I have set a place there for the Ark, containing the covenant which the LORD made with our fathers when He brought them out from the land of Egypt."

[22] Then Solomon stood before the altar of the LORD in the presence of the whole community of Israel; he spread the palms of his hands toward heaven [23] and said, "O LORD God of Israel, in the heavens above and on the earth below there is no god like You, who keep Your gracious covenant with Your servants when

b-b *Lit. "who spoke with His own mouth . . . and has fulfilled with His own hand."*
c *Lit. "risen in place of."*

they walk before You in wholehearted devotion; 24 You who have kept the promises You made to Your servant, my father David, fulfilling with deeds the promise You made—as is now the case. 25 And now, O LORD God of Israel, keep the further promise that You made to Your servant, my father David: 'Your line on the throne of Israel shall never end, if only your descendants will look to their way and walk before Me as you have walked before Me.' 26 Now, therefore, O God of Israel, let the promise that You made to Your servant my father David be fulfilled.

27 "But will God really dwell*d* on earth? Even the heavens to their uttermost reaches cannot contain You, how much less this House that I have built! 28 Yet turn, O LORD my God, to the prayer and supplication of Your servant, and hear the cry and prayer which Your servant offers before You this day. 29 May Your eyes be open day and night toward this House, toward the place of which You have said, 'My name shall abide there'; may You heed the prayers which Your servant will offer toward this place. 30 And when You hear the supplications which Your servant and Your people Israel offer toward this place, give heed in Your heavenly abode—give heed and pardon.

31 "Whenever one man commits an offense against another, and the latter utters an imprecation to bring a curse upon him, and comes with his imprecation before Your altar in this House, 32 oh, hear in heaven and take action to judge Your servants, condemning him who is in the wrong and bringing down the punishment of his conduct on his head, vindicating him who is in the right by rewarding him according to his righteousness.

33 "Should Your people Israel be routed by an enemy because they have sinned against You, and then turn back to You and acknowledge Your name, and they offer prayer and supplication to You in this House, 34 oh, hear in heaven and pardon the sin of Your people Israel, and restore them to the land that You gave to their fathers.

35 "Should the heavens be shut up and there be no rain, because they have sinned against You, and then they pray toward

d *II Chron. 6.18 adds "with man."*

this place and acknowledge Your name and repent of their sins, when You answer[e] them, [36] oh, hear in heaven and pardon the sin of Your servants, Your people Israel, after You have shown them the proper way in which they are to walk; and send down rain upon the land which You gave to Your people as their heritage. [37] So, too, if there is a famine in the land, if there is pestilence, blight, mildew, locusts or caterpillars, or if an enemy oppresses them in any of the settlements of the land.

"In any plague and in any disease, [38] in any prayer or supplication offered by any person among all Your people Israel—each of whom knows his own affliction—when he spreads his palms toward this House, [39] oh, hear in Your heavenly abode, and pardon and take action! Render to each man according to his ways as You know his heart to be—for You alone know the hearts of all men—[40] so that they may revere You all the days that they live on the land that You gave to our fathers.

[41] "Or if a foreigner who is not of Your people Israel comes from a distant land for the sake of Your name—[42] for they shall hear about Your great name and Your mighty hand and Your outstretched arm—when he comes to pray toward this House, [43] oh, hear in Your heavenly abode and grant all that the foreigner asks You for. Thus all the peoples of the earth will know Your name and revere You, as does Your people Israel; and they will recognize that Your name is attached to this House that I have built.

[44] "When Your people take the field against their enemy by whatever way You send them, and they pray to the LORD in the direction of the city which You have chosen, and of the House which I have built to Your name, [45] oh, hear in heaven their prayer and supplication and uphold their cause.

[46] "When they sin against You—for there is no man who does not sin—and You are angry with them and deliver them to the enemy, and their captors carry them off to an enemy land, near or far; [47] and then they take it to heart in the land to which they have been carried off, and they repent and make supplication to

[e] *The Septuagint, with a different vocalization, reads "chastise."*

You in the land of their captors, saying: 'We have sinned, we have acted perversely, we have acted wickedly,' [48] and they turn back to You with all their heart and soul, in the land of the enemies who have carried them off, and they pray to You in the direction of their land which You gave to their fathers, of the city which You have chosen, and of the House which I have built to Your name—[49] oh, give heed in Your heavenly abode to their prayer and supplication, uphold their cause, [50] and pardon Your people who have sinned against You for all the transgressions that they have committed against You. Grant them mercy in the sight of their captors that they may be merciful to them. [51] For they are Your very own people that You freed from Egypt, from the midst of the iron furnace. [52] May Your eyes be open to the supplication of Your servant and the supplication of Your people Israel, and may You heed them whenever they call upon You. [53] For You, O Lord God, have set them apart for Yourself from all the peoples of the earth as Your very own, as You promised through Moses Your servant when You freed our fathers from Egypt."

[54] When Solomon finished offering to the LORD all this prayer and supplication, he rose from where he had been kneeling, in front of the altar of the LORD, his hands spread out toward heaven. [55] He stood, and in a loud voice blessed the whole congregation of Israel:

[56] "Praised be the LORD who has granted a haven to His people Israel, just as He promised; not a single word has failed of all the gracious promises that He made through His servant Moses. [57] May the LORD our God be with us, as He was with our fathers. May He never abandon or forsake us. [58] May He incline our hearts to Him, that we may walk in all His ways and keep the commandments, the laws, and the rules, which He enjoined upon our fathers. [59] And may these words of mine, which I have offered in supplication before the LORD, be close to the LORD our God day and night, that He may provide for His servant and for His people Israel, according to each day's needs—[60] to the end that

all the peoples of the earth may know that the LORD alone is God, there is no other. [61] And may you be wholehearted with the LORD our God, to walk in His ways and keep His commandments, even as now."

[62] The king and all Israel with him offered sacrifices before the LORD. [63] Solomon offered 22,000 oxen and 120,000 sheep as sacrifices of well-being to the LORD. Thus the king and all the Israelites dedicated the House of the LORD. [64] That day the king consecrated the center of the court that was in front of the House of the LORD. For it was there that he presented the burnt offerings, the meal offerings, and the fat parts of the offerings of well-being, because the bronze altar that was before the LORD was too small to hold the burnt offerings, the meal offerings, and the fat parts of the offerings of well-being.

[65] So Solomon and all Israel with him—a great assemblage, [coming] from Lebo-hamath to the Wadi of Egypt[f]—observed the Feast[a] at that time before the LORD our God, seven days and again seven days, fourteen days in all. [66] On the eight day[g] he let the people go. They bade the king good-bye and went to their homes, joyful and glad of heart over all the goodness that the LORD had shown to His servant David and His people Israel.

9 When Solomon had finished building the House of the LORD and the royal palace and everything that Solomon had set his heart on constructing, [2] the LORD appeared to Solomon a second time, as He had appeared to him at Gibeon. [3] The LORD said to him, "I have heard the prayer and the supplication which you have offered to Me. I consecrate this House which you have built and I set My name there forever. My eyes and My heart shall ever be there. [4] As for you, if you walk before Me as your father David walked before Me, wholeheartedly and with uprightness, doing all that I have commanded you [and] keeping My laws and My rules, [5] then I will establish your throne of kingship over Israel

---

[f] *I.e. coming from one end of the country to the other.*
[g] *I.e. of the second seven-day feast; cf. II Chron. 7.8-10.*

forever, as I promised your father David, saying, 'Your line on the throne of Israel shall never end.' 6 [But] if you and your descendants turn away from Me and do not keep the commandments [and] the laws which I have set before you, and go and serve other gods and worship them, 7 then I will sweep[a] Israel off the land which I gave them; I will reject[b] the House which I have consecrated to My name; and Israel shall become a proverb and a byword among all peoples. 8 And [c]as for this House, once so exalted,[-c] everyone passing by it shall be appalled and shall hiss.[d] And when they ask, 'Why did the LORD do thus to the land and to this House?,' 9 they shall be told, 'It is because they forsook the LORD their God who freed them from the land of Egypt, and they embraced other gods and worshiped them and served them; therefore the LORD has brought all this calamity upon them.' "

10 At the end of the twenty years[e] during which Solomon constructed the two buildings, the LORD's House and the royal palace—11 since King Hiram of Tyre had supplied Solomon with all the cedar and cypress timber and gold that he required—King Solomon in turn gave Hiram twenty towns in the region of Galilee. 12 But when Hiram came from Tyre to inspect the towns which Solomon had given him, he was not pleased with them. 13 "My brother," he said, "what sort of towns are these you have given me?" So they were named the land of Cabul,[f] as is still the case. 14 However, Hiram sent the king one hundred and twenty talents of gold.

15 This was the purpose of the forced labor which Solomon imposed: It was to build the House of the LORD, his own palace, the Millo,[g] and the wall of Jerusalem, and [to fortify] Hazor, Megiddo, and Gezer. (16 Pharaoh king of Egypt had come up and captured Gezer; he destroyed it by fire, killed the Canaanites who dwelt in the town, and gave it as dowry to his daughter, Solomon's wife.) 17 So Solomon fortified Gezer, lower Beth-horon,

---

[a] Lit. "cut."
[b] Lit. "dismiss from My presence."
[c-c] Targum and some other ancient versions read "and this House shall become a ruin."
[d] An action performed at the sight of ruin to ward off a like fate from the observer; cf. note at Jer. 18.16.
[e] See 6.38-7.1.
[f] Perhaps taken to mean "as nothing."
[g] A citadel.

¹⁸ Baalith, and Tamar*ʰ* in the wilderness, in the land [of Judah], ¹⁹ and all of Solomon's garrison towns, chariot towns, and cavalry towns—everything that Solomon set his heart on building in Jerusalem and in the Lebanon, and throughout the territory that he ruled. ²⁰ All the people that were left of the Amorites, Hittites, and Perizzites, who were not of the Israelite stock—²¹ those of their descendants who remained in the land and whom the Israelites were not able to annihilate—of these Solomon made a slave force, as is still the case. ²² But he did not reduce any Israelites to slavery; they served, rather, as warriors and as his attendants, officials, and officers, and as commanders of his chariotry and cavalry.

²³ These were the prefects that were in charge of Solomon's works and were foremen over the people engaged in the work, who numbered 550.*ⁱ*

²⁴ As soon as Pharaoh's daughter went up from the City of David to the palace which he had built for her, he built the Millo *ᵍ*

²⁵ Solomon used to offer burnt offerings and sacrifices of well-being three times a year on the altar which he had built for the LORD, and *ʲ*he used to offer incense on the one that was before the LORD. And he kept the House in repair.*ʲ*

²⁶ King Solomon also built a fleet of ships at Ezion-geber, which is near Eloth*ᵏ* on the shore of the Sea of Reeds in the land of Edom. ²⁷ Hiram sent servants of his with the fleet, mariners who were experienced on the sea, to serve with Solomon's men. ²⁸ They came to Ophir; there they obtained gold in the amount of four hundred and twenty talents, which they delivered to King Solomon.

10

The queen of Sheba heard of Solomon's fame, *ᵃ*through the name of the LORD,*⁻ᵃ* and she came to test him with hard questions. ² She arrived in Jerusalem with a very large retinue, with camels bearing spices, a great quantity of gold, and precious stones. When she came to Solomon, she asked him all that she

---

ʰ *So kethib, cf. Ezek. 47.19; 48.28; qere Tadmor.*
ⁱ *Their names are not listed in the text.*
ʲ⁻ʲ *Meaning of Heb. uncertain.*
ᵏ *Elsewhere called Elath.*

ᵃ⁻ᵃ *The force of the phrase is uncertain.*

had in mind. ³ Solomon had answers for all her questions; there was nothing that the king did not know, [nothing] to which he could not give her an answer. ⁴ When the queen of Sheba observed all of Solomon's wisdom, and the palace he had built, ⁵ the fare of his table, the seating of his courtiers, the service and attire of his attendants, and his wine service, *ᵇ-and the burnt offerings which he offered at*⁻ᵇ the House of the LORD, she was left breathless.

⁶ She said to the king, "The report I heard in my own land about you and your wisdom was true. ⁷ But I did not believe the reports until I came and saw with my own eyes that not even the half had been told me; your wisdom and wealth surpass the reports that I heard. ⁸ How fortunate are your men and how fortunate are these your courtiers, who are always in attendance on you and can hear your wisdom! ⁹ Praised be the LORD your God, who delighted in you and set you on the throne of Israel. It is because of the LORD's everlasting love for Israel that He made you king to administer justice and righteousness."

¹⁰ She presented the king with one hundred and twenty talents of gold, and a large quantity of spices, and precious stones. Never again did such a vast quantity of spices arrive as that which the queen of Sheba gave to King Solomon.—¹¹ Moreover, Hiram's fleet, which carried gold from Ophir, brought in from Ophir a huge quantity of *almug* wood*ᶜ* and precious stones. ¹² The king used the *almug* wood for decorations in the House of the LORD and in the royal palace, and for harps and lyres for the musicians. Such a quantity of *almug* wood has never arrived or been seen to this day.—¹³ King Solomon, in turn, gave the queen of Sheba everything she wanted and asked for, in addition to what King Solomon gave her out of his royal bounty. Then she and her attendants left and returned to her own land.

¹⁴ The weight of the gold which Solomon received every year was 666 talents of gold, ¹⁵ besides what came from tradesmen, from the traffic of the merchants, and from all the kings of Arabia and the governors of the regions. ¹⁶ King Solomon made 200

ᵇ⁻ᵇ *II Chron. 9.4 reads "... and the procession with which he went up to. ..."*
ᶜ *Others "sandalwood."*

shields of beaten gold—600 shekels of gold to each shield—
[17] and 300 bucklers of beaten gold—three *minas* of gold to each
buckler. The king placed them in the Lebanon Forest House.
[18] The king also made a large throne of ivory, and he overlaid
it with refined gold. [19] Six steps led up to the throne, and the
throne had a back with a rounded top, and arms on either side
of the seat. Two lions stood beside the arms, [20] and twelve lions
stood on the six steps, six on either side. No such throne was ever
made for any other kingdom.[d]

[21] All King Solomon's drinking cups were of gold, and all the
utensils of the Lebanon Forest House were of pure gold: silver
did not count for anything in Solomon's days. [22] For the king had
a Tarshish[e] fleet on the sea, along with Hiram's fleet. Once every
three years, the Tarshish fleet came in, bearing gold and silver,
ivory, apes, and peacocks.

[23] King Solomon excelled all the kings on earth in wealth and
in wisdom. [24] All the world came to pay homage to Solomon and
to listen to the wisdom with which God had endowed him; [25] and
each one would bring his tribute—silver and gold objects, robes,
weapons and spices, horses and mules—in the amount due each
year.

[26] Solomon assembled chariots and horses. He had 1,400 chariots and 12,000 horses, which he stationed[f] in the chariot towns
and with the king in Jerusalem. [27] The king made silver as plentiful in Jerusalem as stones, and cedars as plentiful as sycamores
in the Shephelah. [28] Solomon's horses were procured from Mizraim[g] and Kue. The king's dealers would buy them from Kue at
a fixed price. [29] A chariot imported from Mizraim[g] cost 600 shekels of silver, and a horse 150; these in turn were exported by them[h]
to all the kings of the Hittites and the kings of the Arameans.

11 King Solomon loved many foreign women in addition to
Pharaoh's daughter—Moabite, Ammonite, Edomite, Phoenician,
and Hittite women, [2] from the nations of which the LORD had said

[d] Or "prince"; like Phoenician *mamlakt*.
[e] Probably a fleet of large ships.
[f] So II Chron. *1.14; 9.25;* Heb. here "led."
[g] Usually Egypt, here perhaps Musru, a neighbor of Kue (Cilicia).
[h] I.e. Solomon's dealers.

to the Israelites, "None of you shall join them and none of them shall join you,[a] lest they turn your heart away to follow their gods." Such Solomon clung to and loved. [3] He had seven hundred royal wives and three hundred concubines; and his wives turned his heart away. [4] In his old age, his wives turned away Solomon's heart after other gods, and he was not as wholeheartedly devoted to the LORD his God as his father David had been. [5] Solomon followed Ashtoreth the goddess of the Phoenicians, and Milcom the abomination of the Ammonites.

[6] Solomon did what was displeasing to the LORD and did not remain loyal to the LORD like his father David. [7] At that time, Solomon built a shrine for Chemosh the abomination of Moab on the hill near Jerusalem, and one for Molech the abomination of the Ammonites. [8] And he did the same for all his foreign wives who offered and sacrificed to their gods.

[9] The LORD was angry with Solomon, because his heart turned away from the LORD, the God of Israel, who had appeared to him twice [10] and had commanded him about this matter, not to follow other gods; he did not obey what the LORD had commanded. [11] And the LORD said to Solomon, [b]"Because you are guilty of this[-b]—you have not kept My covenant and the laws which I enjoined upon you—I will tear the kingdom away from you and give it to one of your servants. [12] But, for the sake of your father David, I will not do it in your lifetime; I will tear it away from your son. [13] However, I will not tear away the whole kingdom; I will give your son one tribe, for the sake of My servant David and for the sake of Jerusalem which I have chosen."

[14] So the LORD raised up an adversary against Solomon, the Edomite Hadad, who was of the royal family of Edom. [15] When David [c]was in[-c] Edom, Joab the army commander went up to bury the slain, and he killed every male in Edom; [16] for Joab and all Israel stayed there for six months until he had killed off every male in Edom. [17] But Hadad,[d] together with some Edomite men, servants of his father, escaped and headed for Egypt; Hadad was then a young boy. [18] Setting out from Midian, they came to Paran

---

[a] *I.e. in marriage; cf. Deut. 7.3-4; 23.4, 8-9.*
[b-b] *Lit. "This is with you."*
[c-c] *Emendation yields "defeated"; cf. II Sam. 8.13.*
[d] *Heb. Adad.*

and took along with them men from Paran. Thus they came to
Egypt, to Pharaoh king of Egypt, who gave him a house, assigned
a food allowance to him, and granted him an estate. [19] Pharaoh
took a great liking to Hadad and gave him his sister-in-law, the
sister of Queen Tahpenes, as wife. [20] The sister of Tahpenes bore
him a son, Genubath. Tahpenes weaned[e] him in Pharaoh's palace, and Genubath remained in Pharaoh's palace among the sons
of Pharaoh. [21] When Hadad heard in Egypt that David had been
laid to rest with his fathers and that Joab the army commander
was dead, Hadad said to Pharaoh, "Give me leave to go to my
own country." [22] Pharaoh replied, "What do you lack with me,
that you want to go to your own country?" But he said, "Nevertheless, give me leave to go."

[23] Another adversary that God raised up against Solomon,[f] was
Rezon son of Eliada, who had fled from his lord, King Hadadezer
of Zobah, [24] when David was slaughtering them. He gathered
men about him and became captain over a troop; they went to
Damascus and settled there, and they established a kingdom in
Damascus. [25] He was an adversary of Israel all the days of Solomon, adding to the trouble [caused by] Hadad; he repudiated
[the authority of] Israel and reigned over Aram.

[26] Jeroboam son of Nebat, an Ephraimite of Zeredah, the
son of a widow whose name was Zeruah, was in Solomon's
service; he raised his hand against the king. [27] The circum-
stances under which he raised his hand against the king were
as follows: Solomon built the Millo and repaired the breach of
the city of his father David. [28] This Jeroboam was an able
man, and when Solomon saw that the young man was a capable worker, he appointed him over all the forced labor of the
House of Joseph.

[29] During that time Jeroboam went out of Jerusalem and the
prophet Ahijah of Shiloh met him on the way. He had put on a
new robe; and when the two were alone in the open country,
[30] Ahijah took hold of the new robe he was wearing and tore it
into twelve pieces. [31] "Take ten pieces," he said to Jeroboam.

---

e *Septuagint reads "reared."*
f *Heb. "him."*

"For thus said the LORD, the God of Israel: I am about to tear the kingdom out of Solomon's hands, and I will give you ten tribes. [32] But one tribe shall remain his—for the sake of My servant David and for the sake of Jerusalem, the city which I have chosen out of all the tribes of Israel. [33] For they have forsaken Me; they have worshiped Ashtoreth the goddess of the Phoenicians, Chemosh the god of Moab, and Milcom the god of the Ammonites; they have not walked in My ways, or done what is pleasing to Me, or [kept] My laws and rules, as his father David did. [34] However, I will not take the entire kingdom away from him, but will keep him as ruler as long as he lives for the sake of My servant David whom I chose, and who kept My commandments and My laws. [35] But I will take the kingship out of the hands of his son and give it to you—the ten tribes. [36] To his son I will give one tribe, so that there may be a lamp for My servant David before Me in Jerusalem—the city where I have chosen to establish My name. [37] But you have been chosen by Me; reign[g] wherever you wish, and you shall be king over Israel. [38] If you heed all that I command you, and walk in My ways, and do what is right in My sight, keeping My laws and commandments as My servant David did, then I will be with you and I will build for you a lasting dynasty as I did for David. I hereby give Israel to you; [39] and I will chastise David's descendants for that [sin], though not forever."

[40] Solomon sought to put Jeroboam to death, but Jeroboam promptly fled to King Shishak of Egypt; and he remained in Egypt till the death of Solomon.

[41] The other events of Solomon's reign, and all his actions and his wisdom, are recorded in the book of the Annals of Solomon. [42] The length of Solomon's reign in Jerusalem, over all Israel, was forty years. [43] Solomon slept with his fathers and was buried in the city of his father David; and his son Rehoboam succeeded him as king.

---

[g] *I.e. establish your residence.*

12 Rehoboam went to Shechem, for all Israel had come to Shechem to acclaim him as king. ² Jeroboam son of Nebat learned of it while he was still in Egypt; for Jeroboam had fled from King Solomon, ᵃ⁻and had settled in Egypt.⁻ᵃ ³ They sent for him; and Jeroboam and all the assembly of Israel came and spoke to Rehoboam as follows: ⁴ "Your father made our yoke heavy. Now lighten the harsh labor and the heavy yoke which your father laid on us, and we will serve you." ⁵ He answered them, "Go away for three days and then come back to me." So the people went away.

⁶ King Rehoboam took counsel with the elders who had served his father Solomon during his lifetime. He said, "What answer do you advise [me] to give to this people?" ⁷ They answered him, "If you will be a servant to those people today and serve them, and if you respond to them with kind words, they will be your servants always." ⁸ But he ignored the advice that the elders gave him, and took counsel with the young men who had grown up with him and were serving him. ⁹ "What," he asked, "do you advise that we reply to the people who said to me, 'Lighten the yoke that your father placed upon us'?" ¹⁰ And the young men who had grown up with him answered, "Speak thus to the people who said to you, 'Your father made our yoke heavy, now you make it lighter for us.' Say to them, 'My little finger is thicker than my father's loins. ¹¹ My father imposed a heavy yoke on you, and I will add to your yoke; my father flogged you with whips, but I will flog you with scorpions.' "

¹² Jeroboam and all the people came to Rehoboam on the third day, since the king had told them: "Come back on the third day." ¹³ The king answered the people harshly, ignoring the advice that the elders had given him. ¹⁴ He spoke to them in accordance with the advice of the young men, and said, "My father made your yoke heavy, but I will add to your yoke; my father flogged you with whips, but I will flog you with scorpions." ¹⁵ (The king did not listen to the people; for the LORD had brought it about in

ᵃ⁻ᵃ *II Chron. 10.2 reads "so Jeroboam returned from Egypt."*

order to fulfill the promise which the Lord had made through Ahijah the Shilonite to Jeroboam son of Nebat.) [16] When all Israel saw that the king had not listened to them, the people answered the king:

"We have no portion in David,
No share in Jesse's son!
To your tents, O Israel!
Now look to your own House, O David."

So the Israelites returned to their homes.[b] [17] But Rehoboam continued to reign over the Israelites who lived in the towns of Judah.

[18] King Rehoboam sent Adoram,[c] who was in charge of the forced labor, but all Israel pelted him to death with stones. Thereupon King Rehoboam hurriedly mounted his chariot and fled to Jerusalem. [19] Thus Israel revolted against the House of David, as is still the case.

[20] When all Israel heard that Jeroboam had returned, they sent messengers and summoned him to the assembly and made him king over all Israel. Only the tribe of Judah remained loyal to the House of David.

[21] On his return to Jerusalem, Rehoboam mustered all the House of Judah and the tribe of Benjamin, 180,000 picked warriors, to fight against the House of Israel, in order to restore the kingship to Rehoboam son of Solomon. [22] But the word of God came to Shemaiah, the man of God: [23] "Say to King Rehoboam son of Solomon of Judah, and to all the House of Judah and Benjamin and the rest of the people: [24] Thus said the Lord: You shall not set out to make war on your kinsmen the Israelites. Let every man return to his home, for this thing has been brought about by Me." They heeded the word of the Lord and turned back, in accordance with the word of the Lord.

[25] Jeroboam fortified Shechem in the hill country of Ephraim and resided there; he moved out from there and fortified Penuel. [26] Jeroboam said to himself, "Now the kingdom may well return

[b] Lit. "tents."
[c] Elsewhere called Adoniram; cf. II Sam. 20.24 and note.

to the House of David. ²⁷ If these people still go up to offer sacrifices at the House of the LORD in Jerusalem, the heart of these people will turn back to their master, King Rehoboam of Judah; they will kill me and go back to King Rehoboam of Judah." ²⁸ So the king took counsel and made two golden calves. He said to ᵈ⁻the people,⁻ᵈ "You have been going up to Jerusalem long enough. This is your god, O Israel, who brought you up from the land of Egypt!" ²⁹ He set up one in Bethel and placed the other in Dan. ³⁰ That proved to be a cause of guilt, for the people went to worship [the calf at Bethel and] the one at Dan. ³¹ He also made cult places and appointed priests from the ranks of the people who were not of Levite descent.

³² He stationed at Bethel the priests of the shrines that he had appointed to sacrifice to the calves which he had made. And Jeroboam established a festival on the fifteenth day of the eight month; in imitation of the festival in Judah, he established one at Bethel, and he ascended the altar [there]. ³³ On the fifteenth day of the eighth month—the month in which he had contrived of his own mind to establish a festival for the Israelites—Jeroboam ascended the altar which he had made in Bethel.

13 As he ascended the altar to present an offering, ¹ a man of God arrived at Bethel from Judah at the command of the LORD. While Jeroboam was standing on the altarᵃ to present the offering, the man of God, at the command of the LORD, cried out against the altar: ² "O altar, altar! Thus said the LORD: A son shall be born to the House of David, Josiah by name; and he shall slaughter upon you the priests of the shrines who bring offerings upon you. And human bones shall be burned upon you." ³ He gave a portent on that day, saying, "Here is the portent which the LORD has decreed: This altar shall break apart, and the ashes on it shall be spilled." ⁴ When the king heard what the man of God had proclaimed against the altar in Bethel, Jeroboam stretched out his arm above the altar and cried, "Seize him!" But the arm which he stretched out against him became rigid, and he could not draw it back. ⁵ The altar broke apart and its ashes were spilled

ᵈ⁻ᵈ *Heb. "them."*

ᵃ *I.e. at the top of the steps or ramp.*

—the very portent which the man of God had announced at the LORD's command. ⁶ Then the king spoke up and said to the man of God, "Please entreat the LORD your God and pray for me that I may be able to draw back my arm." The man of God entreated the LORD and the king was able to draw his arm back; it became as it was before.

⁷ The king said to the man of God, "Come with me to my house and have some refreshment; and I shall give you a gift." ⁸ But the man of God replied to the king, "Even if you give me half your wealth, I will not go in with you, nor will I eat bread or drink water in this place; ⁹ for so I was commanded by the word of the LORD: You shall eat no bread and drink no water, nor shall you go back by the road by which you came." ¹⁰ So he left by another road and did not go back by the road on which he had come to Bethel.

¹¹ There was an old prophet living in Bethel; and his sons[b] came and told him all the things that the man of God had done that day in Bethel [and] the words which he had spoken to the king. When they told it to their father, ¹² their father said to them, "Which road did he leave by?" [c]His sons had seen[c] the road taken by the man of God who had come from Judah. ¹³ "Saddle the ass for me," he said to his sons. They saddled the ass for him, and he mounted it ¹⁴ and rode after the man of God. He came upon him sitting under a terebinth and said to him, "Are you the man of God who came from Judah?" "Yes, I am," he answered. ¹⁵ "Come home with me," he said, "and have something to eat." ¹⁶ He replied, "I may not go back with you and enter your home; and I may not eat bread or drink water in this place; ¹⁷ the order I received by the word of the LORD was: You shall not eat bread or drink water there; nor shall you return by the road on which you came." ¹⁸ "I am a prophet, too," said the other, "and an angel said to me by command of the LORD: Bring him back with you to your house, that he may eat bread and drink water." He was lying to him. ¹⁹ So he went back with him, and he ate bread and drank water in his house.

b *Heb. "son."*
c-c *Septuagint reads "And his sons showed."*

²⁰ While they were sitting at the table, the word of the LORD came to the prophet who had brought him back. ²¹ He cried out to the man of God who had come from Judah: "Thus said the LORD: Because you have flouted the word of the LORD and have not observed what the LORD your God commanded you, ²² but have gone back and eaten bread and drunk water in the place of which He said to you, 'Do not eat bread or drink water [there],' your corpse shall not come to the grave of your fathers." ²³ After he had eaten bread and had drunk, he saddled the ass for him— for the prophet whom he had brought back. ²⁴ He set out, and a lion came upon him on the road and killed him. His corpse lay on the road, with the ass standing beside it, and the lion also standing beside the corpse. ²⁵ Some men who passed by saw the corpse lying on the road and the lion standing beside the corpse; they went and told it in the town where the old prophet lived. ²⁶ And when the prophet who had brought him back from the road heard it, he said, "That is the man of God who flouted the LORD's command; the LORD gave him over to the lion which mauled him and killed him in accordance with the word which the LORD had spoken to him." ²⁷ He said to his sons, "Saddle the ass for me," and they did so. ²⁸ He set out and found the corpse lying on the road, with the ass and the lion standing beside the corpse; the lion had not eaten the corpse nor had it mauled the ass. ²⁹ The prophet lifted up the corpse of the man of God, laid it on the ass, and brought it back; ᵈ⁻it was broughtᵈ to the town of the old prophet for lamentation and burial. ³⁰ He laid the corpse in his own burial place; and they lamented over it, "Alas, my brother!" ³¹ After burying him, he said to his sons, "When I die, bury me in the grave where the man of God lies buried; lay my bones beside his. ³² For what he announced by the word of the LORD against the altar in Bethel, and against all the cult places in the towns of Samaria, shall surely come true."

³³ Even after this incident, Jeroboam did not turn back from his evil way, but kept on appointing priests for the shrines from the

---

ᵈ⁻ᵈ *Lit. "it came."*

ranks of the people. He ordained as priests of the shrines any who so desired. ³⁴ Thereby the House of Jeroboam incurred guilt—to their utter annihilation from the face of the earth.

14 At that time, Abijah, a son of Jeroboam, fell sick. ² Jeroboam said to his wife, "Go and disguise yourself, so that you will not be recognized as Jeroboam's wife, and go to Shiloh. The prophet Ahijah lives there, the one who predicted that I would be king over this people. ³ Take with you ten loaves, some wafers, and a jug of honey, and go to him; he will tell you what will happen to the boy." ⁴ Jeroboam's wife did so; she left and went to Shiloh and came to the house of Ahijah. Now Ahijah could not see, for his eyes had become sightless with age; ⁵ but the Lord had said to Ahijah, "Jeroboam's wife is coming to inquire of you concerning her son, who is sick. Speak to her thus and thus. When she arrives, she will be in disguise."

⁶ Ahijah heard the sound of her feet as she came through the door, and he said, "Come in, wife of Jeroboam. Why are you disguised? I have a harsh message for you. ⁷ Go tell Jeroboam: Thus said the Lord, the God of Israel: I raised you up from among the people and made you a ruler over My people Israel; ⁸ I tore away the kingdom from the House of David and gave it to you. But you have not been like My servant David, who kept My commandments and followed Me with all his heart, doing only what was right in My sight. ⁹ You have acted worse than all those who preceded you; you have gone and made for yourself other gods and molten images to vex Me; and Me you have cast behind your back. ¹⁰ Therefore I will bring disaster upon the House of Jeroboam and will cut off from Jeroboam every male, *ᵃ*-bond and free,*ᵃ* in Israel. I will sweep away the House of Jeroboam utterly, as dung is swept away. ¹¹ Anyone belonging to Jeroboam who dies in the town shall be devoured by dogs; and anyone who dies in the open country shall be eaten by the birds of the air; for the Lord has spoken. ¹² As for you, go back home;

ᵃ⁻ᵃ *Meaning of Heb. uncertain; possibly "kinsman and friend," cf. 16.11.*

as soon as you set foot in the town, the child will die. [13] And all Israel shall lament over him and bury him; he alone of Jeroboam's family shall be brought to burial, for in him alone of the House of Jeroboam has some devotion been found to the LORD, the God of Israel. [14] Moreover, the LORD will raise up a king over Israel who will destroy the House of Jeroboam, *b*-this day and even now.*-b*

[15] "The LORD will strike Israel until it sways like a reed in water. He will uproot Israel from this good land which He gave to their fathers, and will scatter them beyond the Euphrates, because they have provoked the LORD by the sacred posts which they have made for themselves. [16] He will forsake Israel because of the sins that Jeroboam committed and led Israel to commit."

[17] Jeroboam's wife got up and left, and she went to Tirzah. As soon as she stepped over the threshold of her house, the child died. [18] They buried him and all Israel lamented over him, in accordance with the word that the LORD had spoken through His servant the prophet Ahijah.

[19] The other events of Jeroboam's reign, how he fought and how he ruled, are recorded in the Annals of the Kings of Israel. [20] Jeroboam reigned twenty-two years; then he slept with his fathers, and his son Nadab succeeded him as king.

[21] Meanwhile, Rehoboam son of Solomon had become king in Judah. Rehoboam was forty-one years old when he became king, and he reigned seventeen years in Jerusalem—the city the LORD had chosen out of all the tribes of Israel to establish His name there. His mother's name was Naamah the Ammonitess. [22] Judah did what was displeasing to the LORD, and angered Him more than their fathers had done by the sins that they committed. [23] They too built for themselves shrines, pillars, and sacred posts on every high hill and under every leafy tree; [24] there were also male prostitutes in the land. [Judah] imitated all the abhorrent practices of the nations which the LORD had dispossessed before the Israelites.

b-b *Meaning of Heb. uncertain.*

²⁵ In the fifth year of King Rehoboam, King Shishak of Egypt marched against Jerusalem ²⁶ and carried off the treasures of the House of the LORD and the treasures of the royal palace. He carried off everything; he even carried off all the golden shields that Solomon had made. ²⁷ King Rehoboam had bronze shields made instead, and he entrusted them to the officers of the guard^c who guarded the entrance to the royal palace. ²⁸ Whenever the king went into the House of the LORD, the guards would carry them and then bring them back to the armory of the guards.

²⁹ The other events of Rehoboam's reign, and all his actions, are recorded in the Annals of the Kings of Judah. ³⁰ There was continual war between Rehoboam and Jeroboam. ³¹ Rehoboam slept with his fathers and was buried with his fathers in the City of David; his mother's name was Naamah the Ammonitess. His son Abijam succeeded him as king.

15 In the eighteenth year of King Jeroboam son of Nebat, Abijam became king over Judah. ² He reigned three years in Jerusalem; his mother's name was ^aMaacah daughter of Abishalom.^{-a} ³ He continued in all the sins that his father before him had committed; he was not wholehearted with the LORD his God, like his father David. ⁴ Yet, for the sake of David, the LORD his God gave him a lamp in Jerusalem, by raising up his descendant after him and by preserving Jerusalem. ⁵ For David had done what was pleasing to the LORD and never turned throughout his life from all that He had commanded him, except in the matter of Uriah the Hittite. ⁶ There was war between Abijam^b and Jeroboam all the days of his life. ⁷ The other events of Abijam's reign and all his actions are recorded in the Annals of the Kings of Judah. ⁸ Abijam slept with his fathers; he was buried in the City of David, and his son Asa succeeded him as king.

⁹ In the twentieth year of King Jeroboam of Israel, Asa became king over Judah. ¹⁰ He reigned forty-one years in Jerusalem; his mother's name was Maacah daughter of Abishalom. ¹¹ Asa did

---

^c *Lit. "runners."*

^{a-a} *II Chron. 13.2 reads "Micaiah daughter of Uriel of Gibeah"; cf. v. 10 below, where Maacah appears as mother of Asa.*
^b *So several mss.; most mss. and the editions read "Rehoboam."*

what was pleasing to the LORD, as his father David had done. [12] He expelled the male prostitutes from the land, and he removed all the idols that his ancestors had made. [13] He also deposed his mother Maacah from the rank of queen mother, because she had made ⸢an abominable thing⸣ for [the goddess] Asherah. Asa cut down her abominable thing and burnt it in the Wadi Kidron. [14] The shrines, indeed, were not abolished; however, Asa was wholehearted with the LORD his God all his life. [15] He brought ⸢into the House of the LORD all the consecrated things of his father and his own consecrated things⸣—silver, gold, and utensils.

[16] There was war between Asa and King Baasha of Israel all their days. [17] King Baasha of Israel advanced against Judah, and he fortified Ramah to prevent anyone belonging to King Asa from going out or coming in. [18] So Asa took all the silver and gold that remained in the treasuries of the House of the LORD as well as the treasuries of the royal palace, and he entrusted them to his officials. King Asa sent them to King Ben-hadad son of Tabrimmon son of Hezion of Aram, who resided in Damascus, with this message: [19] "There is a pact between you and me, and between your father and my father. I herewith send you a gift of silver and gold: Go and break your pact with King Baasha of Israel, so that he may withdraw from me." [20] Ben-hadad responded to King Asa's request; he sent his army commanders against the towns of Israel and captured Ijon, Dan, Abel-beth-maacah, and all Chinneroth, as well as all the land of Naphtali. [21] When Baasha heard about it, he stopped fortifying Ramah and remained in Tirzah.

[22] Then King Asa mustered all Judah, with no exemptions; and they carried away the stones and timber with which Baasha had fortified Ramah. With these King Asa fortified Geba of Benjamin, and Mizpah.

[23] All the other events of Asa's reign, and all his exploits, and all his actions, and the towns that he fortified, are recorded in the Annals of the Kings of Judah. However, in his old age he suffered

---

c-c *Exact meaning of Heb. uncertain.*
d-d *So kethib and II Chron. 15.18.*

from a foot ailment. ²⁴ Asa slept with his fathers and was buried with his fathers in the city of his father David. His son Jehoshaphat succeeded him as king.

²⁵ Nadab son of Jeroboam had become king over Israel in the second year of King Asa of Judah, and he reigned over Israel for two years. ²⁶ He did what was displeasing to the LORD; he continued in the ways of his father, in the sins which he caused Israel to commit. ²⁷ Then Baasha son of Ahijah, of the House of Issachar, conspired against him; and Baasha struck him down at Gibbethon of the Philistines, while Nadab and all Israel were laying siege to Gibbethon. ²⁸ Baasha killed him in the third year of King Asa of Judah and became king in his stead. ²⁹ As soon as he became king, he struck down all the House of Jeroboam; he did not spare a single soul belonging to Jeroboam until he destroyed it—in accordance with the word that the LORD had spoken through His servant, the prophet Ahijah the Shilonite— ³⁰ because of the sins which Jeroboam committed and which he caused Israel to commit, thereby vexing the LORD, the God of Israel.

³¹ The other events of Nadab's reign and all his actions are recorded in the Annals of the Kings of Israel.

³² There was war between Asa and King Baasha of Israel all their days. ³³ In the third year of King Asa of Judah, Baasha son of Ahijah became king in Tirzah over all Israel—for twenty-four years. ³⁴ He did what was displeasing to the LORD; he followed the ways of Jeroboam and the sins which he caused Israel to commit.

16 The word of the LORD came to Jehu son of Hanani against Baasha: ² "Because I lifted you up from the dust and made you a ruler over My people Israel, but you followed the way of Jeroboam and caused My people Israel to sin, vexing Me with their sins—³ I am going to sweep away Baasha and his house. I will make your house like the House of Jeroboam son of Nebat.

⁴ Anyone belonging to Baasha who dies in the town shall be devoured by dogs, and anyone belonging to him who dies in the open country shall be devoured by the birds of the sky."

⁵ The other events of Baasha's reign and his actions and his exploits are recorded in the Annals of the Kings of Israel. ⁶ Baasha slept with his fathers and was buried in Tirzah. His son Elah succeeded him as king.

⁷ But the word of the LORD had come through the prophet Jehu son of Hanani against Baasha and against his house, that it would fare like the House of Jeroboam, ^{a-}which he himself had struck down,^{-a} because of all the evil he did which was displeasing to the LORD, vexing him with his deeds.

⁸ In the twenty-sixth year of King Asa of Judah, Elah son of Baasha became king over Israel, at Tirzah—for two years. ⁹ His officer Zimri, commander of half the chariotry, committed treason against him while he was at Tirzah drinking himself drunk in the house of Arza, who was in charge of the palace at Tirzah. ¹⁰ Zimri entered, struck him down, and killed him; he succeeded him as king in the twenty-sixth year of King Asa of Judah. ¹¹ No sooner had he become king and ascended the throne than he struck down all the House of Baasha; he did not leave a single male of his, nor any kinsman or friend. ¹² Thus Zimri destroyed all the House of Baasha, in accordance with the word that the LORD had spoken through the prophet Jehu—¹³ because of the sinful acts which Baasha and his son Elah committed, and which they caused Israel to commit, vexing the LORD, the God of Israel, with their false gods. ¹⁴ The other events of Elah's reign and all his actions are recorded in the Annals of the Kings of Israel.

¹⁵ During the twenty-seventh year of King Asa of Judah, Zimri reigned in Tirzah for seven days. At the time, the troops were encamped at Gibbethon of the Philistines. ¹⁶ When the troops who were encamped there learned that Zimri had committed treason and had struck down the king, that very day, in the camp, all Israel acclaimed the army commander Omri king over Israel. ¹⁷ Omri and all Israel then withdrew from Gibbethon and laid

^{a-a} *Syntax of Heb. unclear.*

siege to Tirzah. [18] When Zimri saw that the town was taken, he went into the citadel of the royal palace and burned down the royal palace over himself. And so he died—[19] because of the sins which he committed and caused Israel to commit, doing what was displeasing to the LORD and following the ways of Jeroboam. [20] The other events of Zimri's reign, and the treason which he committed, are recorded in the Annals of the Kings of Israel.

[21] Then the people of Israel split into two factions: a part of the people followed Tibni son of Ginath to make him king, and the other part followed Omri. [22] Those who followed Omri proved stronger than those who followed Tibni son of Ginath; Tibni died and Omri became king.

[23] In the thirty-first year of King Asa of Judah, Omri became king over Israel—for twelve years. He reigned in Tirzah six years. [24] Then he bought the hill of Samaria from Shemer for two talents of silver; he built [a town] on the hill and named the town which he built Samaria, after Shemer, the owner of the hill. [25] Omri did what was displeasing to the LORD; he was worse than all who preceded him. [26] He followed all the ways of Jeroboam son of Nebat and the sins which he committed and caused Israel to commit, vexing the LORD, the God of Israel. [27] The other events of Omri's reign, [and] his actions, and the exploits he performed, are recorded in the Annals of the Kings of Israel. [28] Omri slept with his fathers and was buried in Samaria; and his son Ahab succeeded him as king.

[29] Ahab son of Omri became king over Israel in the thirty-eighth year of King Asa of Judah, and Ahab son of Omri reigned over Israel in Samaria for twenty-two years. [30] Ahab son of Omri did what was displeasing to the LORD, more than all who preceded him. [31] Not content to follow the sins of Jeroboam son of Nebat, he took as wife Jezebel daughter of King Ethbaal of the Phoenicians, and he went and served Baal and worshipped him. [32] He erected an altar to Baal in the temple of Baal which he built

in Samaria. ³³ Ahab also made a sacred post. Ahab did more to vex the LORD, the God of Israel, than all the kings of Israel who preceded him.

³⁴ During his reign, Hiel the Bethelite fortified Jericho. He laid its foundations at the cost of Abiram his firstborn, and set its gates in place at the cost of Segub his youngest, in accordance with the words that the LORD had spoken through Joshua son of Nun.^b

17 Elijah the Tishbite, an inhabitant of Gilead, said to Ahab, "As the LORD lives, the God of Israel whom I serve, there will be no dew or rain except at my bidding."

² The word of the LORD came to him: ³ "Leave this place; turn eastward and go into hiding by the Wadi Cherith, which is east of the Jordan. ⁴ You will drink from the wadi, and I have commanded the ravens to feed you there." ⁵ He proceeded to do as the LORD had bidden: he went, and he stayed by the Wadi Cherith which is east of the Jordan. ⁶ The ravens brought him bread and meat every morning and every evening, and he drank from the wadi.

⁷ After some time the wadi dried up, because there was no rain in the land. ⁸ And the word of the LORD came to him: ⁹ "Go at once to Zarephath of Sidon, and stay there; I have designated a widow there to feed you." ¹⁰ So he went at once to Zarephath. When he came to the entrance of the town, a widow was there gathering wood. He called out to her, "Please bring me a little water in your pitcher, and let me drink." ¹¹ As she went to fetch it, he called out to her, "Please bring along a piece of bread for me." ¹² "As the LORD your God lives," she replied, "I have nothing baked, nothing but a handful of flour in a jar and a little oil in a jug. I am just gathering a couple of sticks, so that I can go home and prepare it for me and my son; we shall eat it and then we shall die." ¹³ "Don't be afraid," said Elijah to her. "Go and do as you have said; but first make me a small cake from what you

^b *Cf. Josh. 6.26.*

have there, and bring it out to me; then make some for yourself and your son. [14] For thus said the LORD, the God of Israel: The jar of flour shall not give out and the jug of oil shall not fail until the day that the LORD sends rain upon the ground." [15] She went and did as Elijah had spoken, and she and he and her household had food for a long time. [16] The jar of flour did not give out, nor did the jug of oil fail, just as the LORD had spoken through Elijah.

[17] After a while, the son of the mistress of the house fell sick, and his illness grew worse, until he had no breath left in him. [18] She said to Elijah, "What harm have I done you, O man of God, that you should come here to recall my sin and cause the death of my son?" [19] "Give me the boy," he said to her; and taking him from her arms, he carried him to the upper chamber where he was staying, and laid him down on his own bed. [20] He cried out to the LORD and said, "O LORD my God, will You bring calamity upon this widow whose guest I am, and let her son die?" [21] Then he stretched out over the child three times, and cried out to the LORD, saying, "O LORD my God, let this child's life return to his body!" [22] The LORD heard Elijah's plea; the child's life returned to his body, and he revived. [23] Elijah picked up the child and brought him down from the upper room into the main room, and gave him to his mother. "See," said Elijah, "your son is alive." [24] And the woman answered Elijah, "Now I know that you are a man of God and that the word of the LORD is truly in your mouth."

18 Much later, in the third year,[a] the word of the LORD came to Elijah: "Go, appear before Ahab; then I will send rain upon the earth." [2] Thereupon Elijah set out to appear before Ahab.

The famine was severe in Samaria. [3] Ahab had summoned Obadiah, the steward of the palace. (Obadiah revered the LORD greatly. [4] When Jezebel was killing off the prophets of the LORD, Obadiah had taken a hundred prophets and hidden them, fifty to a cave, and provided them with food and drink.) [5] And Ahab had

---

[a] *I.e. of the drought; see 17.1.*

said to Obadiah, "Go through the land, to all the springs of water and to all the wadis. Perhaps we shall find some grass to keep horses and mules alive, so that we are not left without beasts." 6 They divided the country between them to explore it, Ahab going alone in one direction and Obadiah going alone in another direction. 7 Obadiah was on the road, when Elijah suddenly confronted him. [Obadiah] recognized him and flung himself on his face, saying, "Is that you, my lord Elijah?" 8 "Yes, it is I," he answered. "Go tell your lord: Elijah is here!" 9 But he said, "What wrong have I done, that you should hand your servant over to Ahab to be killed? 10 As the LORD your God lives, there is no nation or kingdom to which my lord has not sent to look for you; and when they said, 'He is not here,' he made that kingdom or nation swear that you could not be found. 11 And now you say, 'Go tell your lord: Elijah is here!' 12 When I leave you, the spirit of the LORD will carry you off I don't know where; and when I come and tell Ahab and he does not find you, he will kill me. Yet your servant has revered the LORD from my youth. 13 My lord has surely been told what I did when Jezebel was killing the prophets of the LORD, how I hid a hundred of the prophets of the LORD, fifty men to a cave, and provided them with food and drink. 14 And now you say, 'Go tell your lord: Elijah is here.' Why, he will kill me!"

15 Elijah replied, "As the LORD of Hosts lives, whom I serve, I will appear before him this very day."

16 Obadiah went to find Ahab, and informed him; and Ahab went to meet Elijah. 17 When Ahab caught sight of Elijah, Ahab said to him, "Is that you, you troubler of Israel?" 18 He retorted, "It is not I who have brought trouble on Israel, but you and your father's House, by forsaking the commandments of the LORD and going after the Baalim. 19 Now summon all Israel to join me at Mount Carmel, together with the four hundred and fifty prophets of Baal and the four hundred prophets of Asherah, b-who eat at Jezebel's table."-b

b-b *I.e. who are maintained by Jezebel.*

²⁰ Ahab sent orders to all the Israelites and gathered the prophets at Mount Carmel. ²¹ Elijah approached all the people and said, "How long will you keep hopping ^cbetween two opinions?^{-c} If the LORD is God, follow Him; and if Baal, follow him!" But the people answered him not a word. ²² Then Elijah said to the people, "I am the only prophet of the LORD left, while the prophets of Baal are four hundred and fifty men. ²³ Let two young bulls be given to us. Let them choose one bull, cut it up, and lay it on the wood, but let them not apply fire; I will prepare the other bull, and lay it on the wood, and will not apply fire. ²⁴ You will then invoke your god by name, and I will invoke the LORD by name; and ^{d-}and let us agree:^{-d} the god who responds with fire, that one is God." And all the people answered, "Very good!"

²⁵ Elijah said to the prophets of Baal, "Choose one bull and prepare it first, for you are the majority; invoke your god by name, but apply no fire." ²⁶ They took the bull that was given them; they prepared it, and invoked Baal by name from morning until noon, shouting, "O Baal, answer us!" But there was no sound, and none who responded; so they performed a hopping dance about the altar that had been set up. ²⁷ When noon came, Elijah mocked them, saying, "Shout louder! After all he is a god. ^{e-}But he may be in conversation, he may be detained, or he may be on a journey,^{-e} or perhaps he is asleep and will wake up." ²⁸ So they shouted louder, and gashed themselves with knives and spears, according to their practice, until the blood streamed over them. ²⁹ When noon passed, they ^{f-}kept raving^{-f} until the hour of presenting the meal offering. Still there was no sound, and none who responded or heeded.

³⁰ Then Elijah said to all the people, "Come closer to me"; and all the people came closer to him. Elijah^g repaired the damaged altar of the LORD. ³¹ He took twelve stones, corresponding to the number of the tribes of the sons of Jacob—to whom the word of the LORD came, saying, "Israel shall be your name"^h—³² and with the stones he built an altar in the name of the LORD. Around the

---

^{c-c} Lit. "on the two boughs."
^{d-d} Lit. "and it shall be."
^{e-e} Meaning of Heb. uncertain.
^{f-f} Others "prophesied"; see Num. 11.25-26.
^g The name is moved up from v. 31 for clarity.
^h See Gen. 35.10.

altar he made a trench large enough for two seahs of seed.[i] 33 He laid out the wood, and he cut up the bull and laid it on the wood. 34 And he said, "Fill four jars with water and pour it over the burnt offering and the wood." Then he said, "Do it a second time"; and they did it a second time. "Do it a third time," he said; and they did it a third time. 35 The water ran down around the altar, and even the trench was filled with water.

36 When it was time to present the meal offering, the prophet Elijah came forward and said, "O Lord, God of Abraham, Isaac, and Israel! Let it be known today that You are God in Israel and that I am Your servant, and that I have done all these things at Your bidding. 37 Answer me, O Lord, answer me, that this people may know that You, O Lord, are God; *for You have turned their hearts backward."-*

38 Then fire from the Lord descended and consumed the burnt offering, the wood, the stones, and the earth; and it licked up the water that was in the trench. 39 When they saw this, all the people flung, themselves on their faces and cried out, "The Lord alone is God: The Lord alone is God!"

40 Then Elijah said to them, "Seize the prophets of Baal, let not a single one of them get away." They seized them, and Elijah took them down to the Wadi Kishon and slaughtered them there.

41 Elijah said to Ahab, "Go up, eat and drink, for there is a rumbling of [approaching] rain," 42 and Ahab went up to eat and drink. Elijah meanwhile climbed to the top of Mount Carmel, crouched on the ground and put his face between his knees. 43 And he said to his servant, "Go up and look toward the Sea." He went up and looked and reported, "There is nothing." Seven times [Elijah] said, "Go back," 44 and the seventh time, [the servant] reported, "A cloud as small as a man's hand is rising in the west." Then [Elijah] said, "Go say to Ahab, 'Hitch up [your chariot] and go down before the rain stops you.'" 45 Meanwhile the sky grew black with clouds; there was wind, and a heavy downpour fell; Ahab mounted his chariot and drove off to Jez-

---

i *I.e. of an area which would require two seahs of seed if sown. Cf. Lev. 27.16; Isa. 5.10.*

reel. [46] The hand of the LORD had come upon Elijah. [j]He tied up
his skirts[j] and ran in front of Ahab all the way to Jezreel.

19 When Ahab told Jezebel all that Elijah had done and how
he had put all the prophets[a] to the sword, [2] Jezebel sent a messenger to Elijah, saying, [b]"Thus and more may the gods do [-b] if by
this time tomorrow I have not made you like one of them."

[3] Frightened,[c] he fled at once for his life. He came to Beersheba, which is in Judah, and left his servant there; [4] he himself
went a day's journey into the wilderness. He came to a broom
bush and sat down under it, and prayed that he might die.
"Enough!" he cried. "Now, O LORD, take my life, for I am no
better than my fathers."

[5] He lay down and fell asleep under a broom bush. Suddenly
an angel touched him and said to him, "Arise and eat." [6] He
looked about; and there, beside his head, was a cake baked on hot
stones and a jar of water! He ate and drank, and lay down again.
[7] The angel of the LORD came a second time and touched him and
said, "Arise and eat, or the journey will be too much for you."
[8] He arose and ate and drank; and with the strength from that
meal he walked forty days and forty nights as far as the mountain
of God at Horeb. [9] There he went into a cave, and there he spent
the night.

Then the word of the LORD came to him. He said to him, "Why
are you here, Elijah?" [10] He replied, "I am moved by zeal for the
LORD, the God of Hosts, for the Israelites have forsaken Your
covenant, torn down Your altars, and put Your prophets to the
sword. I alone am left, and they are out to take my life." [11] "Come
out," He called, "and stand on the mountain before the LORD."

And lo, the LORD passed by. There was a great and mighty
wind, splitting mountains and shattering rocks by the power of
the LORD; but the LORD was not in the wind. After the wind—an
earthquake; but the LORD was not in the earthquake. [12] After the
earthquake—fire; but the LORD was not in the fire. And after the

j-j *Lit. "He bound up his loins."*

[a] *Of Baal; see 18.40.*
b-b *A formula of imprecation. Many Heb. mss. and Septuagint add "to me."*
[c] *So many Heb. mss. and Septuagint; most mss, and the editions read "And he saw, and."*

fire—a soft murmuring sound.*d* 13 When Elijah heard it, he wrapped his mantle about his face and went out and stood at the entrance of the cave. Then a voice addressed him: "Why are you here, Elijah?"14 He answered, "I am moved by zeal for the LORD, the God of Hosts; for the Israelites have forsaken Your covenant, torn down Your altars, and have put Your prophets to the sword. I alone am left, ann they are out to take my life."

15 The LORD said to him, "Go back by the way you came, [and] on to the wilderness of Damascus. When you get there, anoint Hazael as king of Aram. 16 Also anoint Jehu son of Nimshi as king of Israel, and anoint Elisha son of Shaphat of Abel-meholah to succeed you as prophet. 17 Whoever escapes the sword of Hazael shall be slain by Jehu, and whoever escapes the sword of Jehu shall be slain by Elisha. 18 I will leave in Israel only seven thousand—every knee that has not knelt to Baal and every mouth that has not kissed him."

19 He set out from there and came upon Elisha son of Shaphat as he was plowing. There were twelve yoke of oxen ahead of him, and he was with the twelfth. Elijah came over to him and threw his mantle over him. 20 He left the oxen and ran after Elijah, saying: "Let me kiss my father and mother good-bye, and I will follow you." And he answered him, "Go back. What have I done to you?"*e* 21 He turned back from him and took the yoke of oxen and slaughtered them; he boiled *f-*their meat*-f* with the gear*g* of the oxen and gave it to the people, and they ate. Then he arose and followed Elijah and became his attendant.

20

King Ben-hadad of Aram gathered his whole army; thirty-two kings accompanied him with horses and chariots. He advanced against Samaria, laid siege to it, and attacked it. 2 And he sent messengers to Ahab inside the city 3 to say to him, "Thus said Ben-hadad: Your silver and gold are mine, and your beautiful wives and children are mine." 4 The king of Israel replied, "As you say, my lord king: I and all I have are yours." 5 Then the mes-

---

d Others "a still, small voice."
e I.e. I am not stopping you.
f-f Lit. "them, the flesh."
g I.e. using it as firewood; cf. II Sam. 24.22.

sengers came again and said, "Thus said Ben-hadad: When I sent you the order to give me your silver and gold, and your wives and children, 6 I meant that tomorrow at this time I will send my servants to you and they will search your house and the houses of your courtiers and seize everything you*a* prize and take it away."

7 Then the king of Israel summoned all the elders of the land, and he said, "See for yourselves how that man is bent on evil! For when he demanded my wives and my children, my silver and my gold, I did not refuse him." 8 All the elders and all the people said, "Do not obey and do not submit!" 9 So he said to Ben-hadad's messengers, "Tell my lord the king: All that you first demanded of your servant I shall do, but this thing I cannot do." The messenger went and reported this to him. 10 Thereupon Ben-hadad sent him this message: *b-*"May the gods do thus to me and even more,*-b* if the dust of Samaria will provide even a handful for each of the men who follow me!"

11 The king of Israel replied, "Tell him: Let not him who girds on his sword boast like him who ungirds it!"

12 On hearing this reply—while he and the other kings were drinking together at Succoth—he*c* commanded his followers, "Advance!" And they advanced against the city. 13 Then a certain prophet went up to King Ahab of Israel and said, "Thus said the LORD: Do you see that great host? I will deliver it into your hands today, and you shall know that I am the LORD." 14 "Through whom?" asked Ahab. He answered, "Thus said the LORD: Through the aides of the provincial governors." He asked, "Who shall begin the battle?" And he answered, "You."

15 So he mustered the aides of the provincial governors, 232 strong, and then he mustered all the troops—all the Israelites—7,000 strong. 16 They marched out at noon, while Ben-hadad was drinking himself drunk at Succoth together with the thirty-two kings allied with him. 17 The aides of the provincial governors rushed out first. Ben-hadad sent [scouts], who told him, "Some men have come out from Samaria." 18 He said, "If they have come out to surrender, take them alive; and if they have come out for

---

a Several ancient versions read "they."
b-b See note at 19.2.
c I.e. Ben-hadad.

battle, take them alive anyhow." [19] But the others—the aides of the provincial governors, with the army behind them—had already rushed out of the city, [20] and each of them struck down his opponent. The Arameans fled, and Israel pursued them; but King Ben-hadad of Aram escaped on a horse with other horsemen. [21] The king of Israel came out and attacked the horses and chariots, and inflicted a great defeat on the Arameans. [22] Then the prophet approached the king of Israel and said to him, "Go, keep up your efforts, and consider well what you must do; for the king of Aram will attack you at the turn of the year."

[23] Now the ministers of the king of Aram said to him, "Their God is a God of mountains; that is why they got the better of us. But if we fight them in the plain, we will surely get the better of them. [24] Do this: Remove all the kings from their posts and appoint governors in their place. [25] Then muster for yourself an army equal to the army you lost, horse for horse and chariot for chariot. And let us fight them in the plain, and we will surely get the better of them." He took their advice and acted accordingly.

[26] At the turn of the year, Ben-hadad mustered the Arameans and advanced on Aphek to fight Israel. [27] Now the Israelites had been mustered and provisioned, and they went out against them; but when the Israelites encamped against them, they looked like two flocks[d] of goats, while the Arameans covered the land. [28] Then the man of God approached and spoke to the king of Israel, "Thus said the LORD: Because the Arameans have said, 'The LORD is a God of mountains, but He is not a God of lowlands,' I will deliver that great host into your hands; and you shall know that I am the LORD."

[29] For seven days they were encamped opposite each other. On the seventh day, the battle was joined and the Israelites struck down 100,000 Aramean foot soldiers in one day. [30] The survivors fled to Aphek, inside the town, and the wall fell on the 27,000 survivors.

Ben-hadad also fled and took refuge inside the town, in an inner chamber. [31] His ministers said to him, "We have heard that

---

[d] *Meaning of Heb. uncertain.*

the kings of the House of Israel are magnanimous kings. Let us put sackcloth on our loins and ropes on our heads, and surrender to the king of Israel; perhaps he will spare your life." ³² So they girded sackcloth on their loins and wound ropes around their heads, and came to the king of Israel and said, "Your servant Ben-hadad says, 'I beg you, spare my life.' " He replied, "Is he still alive? He is my brother." ³³ The men divined his meaning and quickly *d-*caught the word from him,*-d* saying, "Yes, Ben-hadad is your brother." "Go, bring him," he said. Ben-hadad came out to him, and he invited him into his chariot. ³⁴ Ben-hadad said to him, "I will give back the towns which my father took from your father, and you may set up bazaars for yourself in Damascus as my father did in Samaria." "And I, for my part," [said Ahab,] "will let you go home under these terms." So he made a treaty with him and dismissed him.

³⁵ A certain man, a disciple of the prophets, said to another, at the word of the LORD, "Strike me"; but the man refused to strike him. ³⁶ He said to him, "Because you have not obeyed the LORD, a lion will strike you dead as soon as you leave me." And when he left, a lion came upon him and killed him. ³⁷ Then he met another man and said, "Come, strike me." So the man struck him and wounded him. ³⁸ Then the prophet, disguised by a cloth over his eyes, went and waited for the king by the road. ³⁹ As the king passed by, he cried out to the king and said, "Your servant went out into the thick of the battle. Suddenly a man came over and brought a man to me, saying, 'Guard this man! If he is missing, it will be your life for his, or you will have to pay a talent of silver.' ⁴⁰ While your servant was busy here and there, [the man] got away." The king of Israel responded, "You have your verdict; you pronounced it yourself." ⁴¹ Quickly he removed the cloth from his eyes, and the king recognized him as one of the prophets. ⁴² He said to him, "Thus said the LORD: Because you have set free the man whom I doomed, your life shall be forfeit for his life and your people for his people." ⁴³ Dispirited and sullen, the king left for home and came to Samaria.

21 [The following events] occurred some time afterward: Naboth the Jezreelite owned a vineyard in Jezreel, adjoining the palace of King Ahab of Samaria. ² Ahab said to Naboth, "Give me your vineyard, so that I may have it as a vegetable garden, since it is right next to my palace. I will give you a better vineyard in exchange; or, if you prefer, I will pay you the price in money." ³ But Naboth replied, "The LORD forbid that I should give up to you what I have inherited from my fathers!" ⁴ Ahab went home dispirited and sullen because of the answer that Naboth the Jezreelite had given him: "I will not give up to you what I have inherited from my fathers!" He lay down on his bed and turned away his face, and he would not eat. ⁵ His wife Jezebel came to him and asked him, "Why are you so dispirited that you won't eat?" ⁶ So he told her, "I spoke to Naboth the Jezreelite and proposed to him, 'Sell me your vineyard for money, or if you prefer, I'll give you another vineyard in exchange'; but he answered, 'I will not give my vineyard to you.' " ⁷ His wife Jezebel said to him, "Now is the time to show yourself king over Israel. Rise and eat something, and be cheerful; I will get the vineyard of Naboth the Jezreelite for you."

⁸ So she wrote letters in Ahab's name and sealed them with his seal, and sent the letters to the elders and the nobles who lived in the same town with Naboth. ⁹ In the letters she wrote as follows: "Proclaim a fast and seat Naboth at the front of the assembly. ¹⁰ And seat two scoundrels opposite him, and let them testify against him: 'You have reviled God and king!' Then take him out and stone him to death."

¹¹ His townsmen—the elders and nobles who lived in his town —did as Jezebel had instructed them, just as was written in the letters she had sent them: ¹² They proclaimed a fast and seated Naboth at the front of the assembly. ¹³ Then the two scoundrels came and sat down opposite him; and the scoundrels testified against Naboth publicly as follows: "Naboth has reviled God and

king." Then they took him outside the town and stoned him to death. [14] Word was sent to Jezebel: "Naboth has been stoned to death." [15] As soon as Jezebel heard that Naboth had been stoned to death, she said to Ahab, "Go and take possession of the vineyard which Naboth the Jezreelite refused to sell you for money; for Naboth is no longer alive, he is dead." [16] When Ahab heard that Naboth was dead, Ahab set out for the vineyard of Naboth the Jezreelite to take possession of it.

[17] Then the word of the LORD came to Elijah the Tishbite: [18] "Go down and confront King Ahab of Israel who [resides] in Samaria. He is now in Naboth's vineyard; he has gone down there to take possession of it. [19] Say to him, 'Thus said the LORD: Would you murder and take possession? Thus said the LORD: In the very place where the dogs lapped up Naboth's blood, the dogs will lap up your blood too.' "

[20] Ahab said to Elijah, "So you have found me, my enemy?" "Yes, I have found you," he replied. "Because you have committed yourself to doing what is evil in the sight of the LORD, [21] I will bring disaster upon you. I will make a clean sweep of you, I will cut off from Israel every male belonging to Ahab, [a-]bond and free.[-a] [22] And I will make your house like the House of Jeroboam son of Nebat and like the House of Baasha son of Ahijah, because of the provocation you have caused by leading Israel to sin. [23] And the LORD has also spoken concerning Jezebel: 'The dogs shall devour Jezebel in the field[b] of Jezreel. [24] All of Ahab's line who die in the town shall be devoured by dogs, and all who die in the open country shall be devoured by the birds of the sky.' "

([25] Indeed, there never was anyone like Ahab, who committed himself to doing what was displeasing to the LORD, at the instigation of his wife Jezebel. [26] He acted most abominably, straying after the fetishes just like the Amorites, whom the LORD had dispossessed before the Israelites.)

[27] When Ahab heard these words, he rent his clothes and put sackcloth on his body. He fasted and lay in sackcloth and walked about subdued. [28] Then the word of the LORD came to Elijah the

[a-a] *See note at 14.10.*
[b] *So nine Heb. mss. and the parallel II Kings 9.36, as well as Targum and other ancient versions. Most texts read here "rampart."*

Tishbite: [29] "Have you seen how Ahab has humbled himself before Me? Because he has humbled himself before Me, I will not bring the disaster in his lifetime; I will bring the disaster upon his house in his son's time."

22 [a-]There was a lull of[-a] three years, with no war between Aram and Israel. [2] In the third year, King Jehoshaphat of Judah came to visit the king of Israel. [3] The king of Israel said to his courtiers, "You know that Ramoth-gilead belongs to us, and yet we do nothing to recover it from the hands of the king of Aram." [4] And he said to Jehoshaphat, "Will you come with me to battle at Ramoth-gilead?" Jehoshaphat answered the king of Israel, "I will do what you do; my troops shall be your troops, my horses shall be your horses." [5] But Jehoshaphat said further to the king of Israel, "Please, first inquire of the LORD."

[6] So the king of Israel gathered the prophets, about four hundred men, and asked them, "Shall I march upon Ramoth-gilead for battle, or shall I not?" "March," they said, "and the LORD will deliver [it] into Your Majesty's hands." [7] Then Jehoshaphat asked, "Isn't there another prophet of the LORD here through whom we can inquire?" [8] And the king of Israel answered Jehoshaphat, "There is one more man through whom we can inquire of the LORD; but I hate him, because he never prophesies anything good for me, but only misfortune—Micaiah son of Imlah." But King Jehoshaphat said, "Don't say that, Your Majesty." [9] So the king of Israel summoned an officer and said, "Bring Micaiah son of Imlah at once."

[10] The king of Israel and King Jehoshaphat of Judah were seated on their thrones, arrayed in their robes, on the threshing floor at the entrance of the gate of Samaria; and all the prophets were prophesying before them. [11] Zedekiah son of Chenaanah had provided himself with iron horns; and he said, "Thus said the LORD: With these you shall gore the Arameans till you make an

[a-a] Lit. "They remained."

end of them." [12] And all the other prophets were prophesying similarly, "March upon Ramoth-gilead and triumph! The LORD will deliver it into Your Majesty's hands."

[13] The messenger who had gone to summon Micaiah said to him: "Look, the words of the prophets are with one accord favorable to the king. Let your word be like that of the rest of them; speak a favorable word." [14] "As the LORD lives," Micaiah answered, "I will speak only what the LORD tells me." [15] When he came before the king, the king said to him, "Micaiah, shall we march upon Ramoth-gilead for battle, or shall we not?" He answered him, "March and triumph! The LORD will deliver [it] into Your Majesty's hands." [16] The king said to him, "How many times must I adjure you to tell me nothing but the truth in the name of the LORD?" [17] Then he said, "I saw all Israel scattered over the hills like sheep without a shepherd; and the LORD said, 'These have no master; let everyone return to his home in safety.'" [18] "Didn't I tell you," said the king of Israel to Jehoshaphat, "that he would not prophesy good fortune for me, but only misfortune?" [19] But [Micaiah] said, "I call upon you to hear the word of the LORD! I saw the LORD seated upon His throne, with all the host of heaven standing in attendance to the right and to the left of Him. [20] The LORD asked, 'Who will entice Ahab so that he will march and fall at Ramoth-gilead?' Then one said thus and another said thus, [21] until a certain spirit came forward and stood before the LORD and said, 'I will entice him.' 'How?' the LORD asked him. [22] And he replied, 'I will go out and be a lying spirit in the mouth of all his prophets.' Then He said, 'You will entice and you will prevail. Go out and do it.' [23] So the LORD has put a lying spirit in the mouth of all these prophets of yours; for the LORD has decreed disaster upon you."

[24] Thereupon Zedekiah son of Chenaanah stepped up and struck Micaiah on the cheek, and demanded, "Which way did the spirit of the LORD pass from me to speak with you?" [25] And Micaiah replied, "You'll find out on the day when you try to hide in the innermost room." [26] Then the king of Israel said, "Take

Micaiah and turn him over to Amon, the city's governor, and to Prince Joash, [27] and say, 'The king's orders are: Put this fellow in prison, and let his fare be scant bread and scant water until I come home safe.' " [28] To which Micaiah retorted, "If you ever come home safe, the LORD has not spoken through me." [b]He said further, "Listen, all you peoples!"[-b]

[29] So the king of Israel and King Jehoshaphat of Judah marched upon Ramoth-gilead. [30] The king of Israel said to Jehoshaphat, [c]"Disguise yourself and go[-c] into the battle; but you, wear your robes." So the king of Israel went into the battle disguised. [31] Now the king of Aram had instructed his thirty-two chariot officers: "Don't attack anyone, small or great, except the king of Israel." [32] So when the chariot officers saw Jehoshaphat, whom they took for the king of Israel, they turned upon him to attack him, and Jehoshaphat cried out. [33] And when the chariot officers became aware that he was not the king of Israel, they turned back from pursuing him. [34] Then a man drew his bow at random and he hit the king of Israel between [d]the plates of[-d] the armor; and he said to his charioteer, "Turn [e]the horses[-e] around and get me [f]behind the lines;[-f] I'm wounded." [35] The battle [d]raged all day long,[-d] and the king remained propped up in the chariot facing Aram; the blood from the wound ran down into the hollow of the chariot, and at dusk he died. [36] As the sun was going down, a shout went through the army: "Every man to his own town! Every man to his own district."

[37] So the king died [g]and was brought[-g] to Samaria. They buried the king in Samaria, [38] and they flushed out the chariot at the pool of Samaria. Thus the dogs lapped up his blood and the whores bathed [in it], in accordance with the word that the LORD had spoken.[h]

[39] The other events of Ahab's reign, and all his actions—the ivory palace that he built and all the towns that he fortified—are

[b-b] *Perhaps a notation suggesting that Micaiah was identical with Micah, whose prophecies begin, "Listen, all you peoples," Mic. 1.2.*
[c-c] *Targum and Septuagint read, "I will disguise myself and go."*
[d-d] *Meaning of Heb. uncertain.*
[e-e] *Lit. "your hand," because horses are guided by a pull on the appropriate rein; cf. II Kings 9.23.*
[f-f] *Lit. "outside the camp."*
[g-g] *Lit. "he came."*
[h] *Cf. 21.19.*

all recorded in the Annals of the Kings of Israel. [40] Ahab slept with his fathers, and his son Ahaziah succeeded him as king.

[41] Jehoshaphat son of Asa had become king of Judah in the fourth year of King Ahab of Israel. [42] Jehoshaphat was thirty-five years old when he became king, and he reigned in Jerusalem for twenty-five years. His mother's name was Azubah daughter of Shilhi. [43] He followed closely the course of his father Asa and did not deviate from it, doing what was pleasing to the LORD. [44] However, the shrines did not cease to function, the people still sacrificed and offered at the shrines. [45] And further, Jehoshaphat submitted to the king of Israel. [46] As for the other events of Jehoshaphat's reign and the valor he displayed in battle, they are recorded in the Annals of the Kings of Judah. ([47] He also stamped out the remaining male prostitutes who had survived in the land from the time of his father Asa.)
[48] There was no king in Edom; [i-]a viceroy acted as king. [49] Jehoshaphat[-i] constructed Tarshish[j] ships to sail to Ophir for gold. But he did not sail because the ships were wrecked at Ezion-geber. [50] Then Ahaziah son of Ahab proposed to Jehoshaphat, "Let my servants sail on the ships with your servants"; but Jehoshaphat would not agree. [51] Jehoshaphat slept with his fathers and was buried with his fathers in the city of his father David, and his son Jehoram succeeded him as king.

[52] [Meanwhile,] Ahaziah son of Ahab had become king of Israel, in Samaria, in the seventeenth year of King Jehoshaphat of Judah; he reigned over Israel two years. [53] He did what was displeasing to the LORD, following in the footsteps of his father and his mother, and in those of Jeroboam son of Nebat who had caused Israel to sin. [54] He worshiped Baal and bowed down to him; he vexed the LORD, the God of Israel, just as his father had done.

[i-i] *Emendation yields "the viceroy of King Jehoshaphat."*
[j] *See note at 10.22.*

מלכים ב

II KINGS

מלכים ב

II KINGS

1 After Ahab's death, Moab rebelled against Israel.
² Ahaziah fell through the lattice in his upper chamber at Samaria and was injured. So he sent messengers, whom he instructed: "Go inquire of Baal-zebub, the god of Ekron, whether I shall recover from this injury." ³ But an angel of the LORD said to Elijah the Tishbite, "Go and confront the messengers of the king of Samaria and say to them, 'Is there no God in Israel that you go to inquire of Baal-zebub, the god of Ekron? ⁴ Assuredly, thus said the LORD: You shall not *-rise from the bed you are lying on,-* but you shall die.' " And Elijah went.

⁵ The messengers returned to Ahaziah;*b* and he asked, "Why have you come back?" ⁶ They answered him, "A man came toward us and said to us, 'Go back to the king who sent you, and say to him: Thus said the LORD: Is there no God in Israel that you must send to inquire of Baal-zebub, the god of Ekron? Assuredly, you shall not rise from the bed you are lying on, but shall die.' "
⁷ "What sort of man was it," he asked them, "who came toward you and said these things to you?" ⁸ "A hairy man," they replied, "with a leather belt tied around his waist." "That's Elijah the Tishbite!" he said.

⁹ Then he sent to him a captain of fifty with his fifty men. He climbed up to him, and found him sitting at the top of a hill. "Man of God," he said to him, "by order of the king, come down!"
¹⁰ Elijah replied to the captain of the fifty, "If I am a man of God, let fire come down from heaven and consume you with your fifty men!" And fire came down from heaven and consumed him and his fifty men. ¹¹ The king then sent to him another captain with

---

ᵃ⁻ᵃ Lit. "descend from the bed you have mounted."
ᵇ Heb. "him."

his fifty men; and he *c*-addressed him*-c* as follows: "Man of God, by order of the king, come down at once!" 12 But Elijah answered him, "If I am a man of God, let fire come down from heaven and consume you with your fifty men!" And fire of God came down from heaven and consumed him and his fifty men. 13 Then he sent a third captain of fifty with his fifty men. The third captain of fifty climbed to the top, knelt before Elijah, and implored him, saying, "Oh, man of God, please have regard for my life and the lives of these fifty servants of yours! 14 Already fire has come from heaven and consumed the first two captains of fifty and their men;*d* I beg you, have regard for my life!"

15 Then the angel of the LORD said to Elijah, "Go down with him, do not be afraid of him." So he rose and went down with him to the king. 16 He said to him, "Because you sent messengers to inquire of Baal-zebub the god of Ekron—as if there were no God in Israel whose word you could seek—assuredly, you shall not rise from the bed which you are lying on; but you shall die."

17 And [Ahaziah] died, according to the word of the LORD that Elijah had spoken. Jehoram*e* succeeded him as king, in the second year of King Jehoram son of Jehoshaphat of Judah, for he had no son. 18 The other events of Ahaziah's reign [and] his actions are recorded in the Annals of the Kings of Israel.

2 When the LORD was about to take Elijah up to heaven in a whirlwind, Elijah and Elisha had set out from Gilgal. 2 Elijah said to Elisha, "Stay here, for the LORD has sent me on to Bethel." "As the LORD lives and as you live," said Elisha, "I will not leave you." So they went down to Bethel. 3 Disciples of the prophets at Bethel came out to Elisha and said to him, "Do you know that the LORD will take your master *a*-away from you*-a* today?" He replied, "I know it, too; be silent."

4 Then Elijah said to him, "Elisha, stay here, for the LORD has sent me on to Jericho." "As the LORD lives and as you live," said Elisha, "I will not leave you." So they went on to Jericho. 5 The

---

c-c *Emendation yields "went up and said to him," cf. v. 9.*
d *Lit. "fifties."*
e *Brother of Ahaziah.*

a-a *Lit. "from your head."*

disciples of the prophets who were at Jericho came over to Elisha and said to him, "Do you know that the LORD will take your master *ᵃ⁻*away from you*⁻ᵃ* today?" He replied, "I know it, too; be silent."

⁶ Elijah said to him, "Stay here, for the LORD has sent me on to the Jordan." "As the LORD lives and as you live, I will not leave you," he said, and the two of them went on. ⁷ Fifty men of the disciples of the prophets followed and stood by at a distance from them as the two of them stopped at the Jordan. ⁸ Thereupon Elijah took his mantle and, rolling it up, he struck the water; it divided to the right and left, so that the two of them crossed over on dry land. ⁹ As they were crossing, Elijah said to Elisha, "Tell me, what can I do for you before I am taken from you?" Elisha answered, "Let a *ᵇ⁻*double portion*⁻ᵇ* of your spirit pass on to me." ¹⁰ "You have asked a difficult thing," he said. "If you see me as I am being taken from you, this will be granted to you; if not, it will not." ¹¹ As they kept on walking and talking, a fiery chariot with fiery horses suddenly appeared and separated one from the other; and Elijah went up to heaven in a whirlwind. ¹² Elisha saw it, and he cried out, "Oh, father, father! Israel's chariots and horsemen!" When he could no longer see him, he grasped his garments and rent them in two.

¹³ He picked up Elijah's mantle, which had dropped from him; and he went back and stood on the bank of the Jordan. ¹⁴ Taking the mantle which had dropped from Elijah, he struck the water and said, "Where is the LORD, the God of Elijah?" As he too struck the water, it parted to the right and to the left, and Elisha crossed over. ¹⁵ When the disciples of the prophets at Jericho saw him from a distance, they exclaimed, "The spirit of Elijah has settled on Elisha!" And they went to meet him and bowed low before him to the ground.

¹⁶ They said to him, "Your servants have fifty able men with them. Let them go and look for your master; perhaps the spirit of the LORD has carried him off and cast him upon some mountain or into some valley." "Do not send them," he replied. ¹⁷ But

ᵇ⁻ᵇ *Lit. "two-thirds"; cf. Zech. 13.8.*

they kept pressing him for a long time, until he said, "Send them." So they sent out fifty men, who searched for three days, but did not find him. ¹⁸ They came back to him while he was still in Jericho; and he said to them, "I told you not to go."

¹⁹ The men of the town said to Elisha, "Look, the town is a pleasant place to live in, as my lord can see; but the water is bad and the land causes bereavement." ²⁰ He responded, "Bring me a new dish and put salt in it." They brought it to him; ²¹ he went to the spring and threw salt into it. And he said, "Thus said the LORD: I heal this water; no longer shall death and bereavement come from it!" ²² The water has remained wholesome to this day, in accordance with the word spoken by Elisha.

²³ From there he went up to Bethel. As he was going up the road, some little boys came out of the town and jeered at him, saying, "Go away, baldhead! Go away, baldhead!" ²⁴ He turned around and looked at them and cursed them in the name of the LORD. Thereupon, two she-bears came out of the woods and mangled forty-two of the children. ²⁵ He went on from there to Mount Carmel, and from there he returned to Samaria.

3 Jehoram son of Ahab became king of Israel in Samaria in the eighteenth year of King Jehoshaphat of Judah; and he reigned twelve years. ² He did what was displeasing to the LORD, yet not like his father and mother, for he removed the pillars of Baal that his father had made. ³ However, he clung to the sins which Jeroboam son of Nebat caused Israel to commit; he did not depart from them.

⁴ Now King Mesha of Moab was a sheep breeder; and he used to pay as tribute to the king of Israel ^{a-}a hundred thousand lambs and the wool of a hundred thousand rams.^{-a} ⁵ But when Ahab died, the king of Moab rebelled against the king of Israel. ⁶ So King Jehoram promptly set out from Samaria and mustered all

---

^{a-a} *Or "the wool of 100,000 lambs and of 100,000 rams."*

Israel. ⁷ At the same time, he sent this message to King Jehoshaphat of Judah: "The king of Moab has rebelled against me; will you come with me to make war on Moab?" He replied, "I will go. I will do what you do: my troops shall be your troops, my horses shall be your horses." ⁸ And he asked, "Which route shall we take?" [Jehoram] replied, "The road through the wilderness of Edom."

⁹ So the king of Israel, the king of Judah, and the king of Edom set out, and they marched for seven days until they rounded [the tip of the Dead Sea]; and there was no water left for the army or for the animals that were with them. ¹⁰ "Alas!" cried the king of Israel. "The LORD has brought these three kings together only to deliver them into the hands of Moab." ¹¹ But Jehoshaphat said, "Isn't there a prophet of the LORD here, through whom we may inquire of the LORD?" One of the courtiers of the king of Israel spoke up and said, "Elisha son of Shaphat, who ᵇ-poured water on the hands of-ᵇ Elijah, is here." ¹² "The word of the LORD is with him," said Jehoshaphat. So the king of Israel and Jehoshaphat and the king of Edom went down to him. ¹³ Elisha said to the king of Israel, "What have you to do with me? Go to your father's prophets or your mother's prophets." But the king of Israel said, "Don't [say that], for the LORD has brought these three kings together only to deliver them into the hands of Moab." ¹⁴ "As the LORD of Hosts lives, whom I serve," Elisha answered, "were it not that I respect King Jehoshaphat of Judah, I wouldn't look at you or notice you. ¹⁵ Now then, get me a musician."

As the musician played, the hand of the LORD came upon him, ¹⁶ and he said, "Thus said the LORD: This wadi shall be full of pools. ¹⁷ For thus said the LORD: You shall see no wind, you shall see no rain, and yet the wadi shall be filled with water; and you and your cattle and your pack animals shall drink. ¹⁸ And this is but a slight thing in the sight of the LORD, for He will also deliver Moab into your hands. ¹⁹ You shall conquer every fortified town and every splendid city; you shall fell every good tree and stop up all wells of water; and every fertile field you shall ruin with

ᵇ⁻ᵇ *I.e. personally attended.*

stones." ²⁰ And in the morning, when it was time to present the meal offering, water suddenly came from the direction of Edom and the land was covered by the water.

²¹ Meanwhile, all the Moabites had heard that the kings were advancing to make war on them; ᶜ⁻every man old enough to bear arms⁻ᶜ rallied, and they stationed themselves at the border. ²² Next morning, when they rose, the sun was shining over the water, and from the distance the water appeared to the Moabites as red as blood. ²³ "That's blood!" they said. "The kings must have fought among themselves and killed each other. Now to the spoil, Moab!"

²⁴ They entered the Israelite camp, and the Israelites arose and attacked the Moabites, who fled before them. ᵈ⁻They advanced, constantly attacking⁻ᵈ the Moabites, ²⁵ and they destroyed the towns. Every man threw a stone into each fertile field, so that it was covered over; and they stopped up every spring and felled every fruit tree. ᵉ⁻Only the walls ofᵉ Kir-haresheth were left, and then the slingers surrounded it and attacked it. ²⁶ Seeing that the battle was going against him, the king of Moab led an attempt of seven hundred swordsmen to break a way through to the king of Edom;ᶠ but they failed. ²⁷ So he took his firstborn son, who was to succeed him as king, and offered him up on the wall as a burnt offering. A great wrath came upon Israel, so they withdrew from him and went back to [their own] land.

4 A certain woman, the wife of one of the disciples of the prophets, cried out to Elisha: "Your servant my husband is dead, and you know how your servant revered the LORD. And now a creditor is coming to seize my two children as slaves." ² Elisha said to her, "What can I do for you? Tell me, what have you in the house?" She replied, "Your maidservant has nothing at all in the house, except a jug of oil." ³ "Go," he said, "and borrow vessels outside, from all your neighbors, empty vessels, as many as you can. ⁴ Then go in and shut the door behind you and your

---

ᶜ⁻ᶜ *Lit. "from those old enough to gird on a sword."*
ᵈ⁻ᵈ *Meaning of Heb. uncertain.*
ᵉ⁻ᵉ *Lit. "Until the stones in"; meaning of Heb. uncertain.*
ᶠ *Emendation yields "Aram."*

children, and pour [oil] into all those vessels, removing each one
as it is filled."

⁵ She went away and shut the door behind her and her children.
They kept bringing [vessels] to her and she kept pouring. ⁶ When
the vessels were full, she said to her son, "Bring me another
vessel." He answered her, "There are no more vessels"; and the
oil stopped. ⁷ She came and told the man of God, and he said,
"Go sell the oil and pay your debt, and you and your children can
live on the rest."

⁸ One day Elisha visited Shunem. A wealthy woman lived there,
and she urged him to have a meal; and whenever he passed by,
he would stop there for a meal. ⁹ Once she said to her husband,
"I am sure it is a holy man of God who comes this way regularly.
¹⁰ Let us make a small ᵃ⁻enclosed upper chamber⁻ᵃ and place a
bed, a table, a chair, and a lampstand there for him, so that he
can stop there whenever he comes to us." ¹¹ One day he came
there; he retired to the upper chamber and lay down there. ¹² He
said to his servant Gehazi, "Call that Shunammite woman." He
called her, and she stood before him. ¹³ He said to him, "Tell her,
'You have gone to all this trouble for us. What can we do for you?
Can we speak in your behalf to the king or to the army commander?'" She replied, "I live among my own people." ¹⁴ "What
then can be done for her?" he asked. "The fact is," said Gehazi,
"she has no son, and her husband is old." ¹⁵ "Call her," he said.
He called her, and she stood in the doorway. ¹⁶ And Elisha said,
"At this season next year, you will be embracing a son." She
replied, "Please, my lord, man of God, do not delude your maidservant."

¹⁷ The woman conceived and bore a son at the same season the
following year, as Elisha had assured her. ¹⁸ The child grew up.
One day, he went out to his father among the reapers. ¹⁹ [Sud-
denly] he cried to his father, "Oh, my head, my head!" He said
to a servant, "Carry him to his mother." ²⁰ He picked him up and
brought him to his mother. And the child sat on her lap until

---

ᵃ⁻ᵃ Or "upper wall-chamber"; lit. "an upper chamber of wall(s)."

noon; and he died. [21] She took him up and laid him on the bed of the man of God, and left him and closed the door. [22] Then she called to her husband: "Please, send me one of the servants and one of the she-asses, so I can hurry to the man of God and back." [23] But he said, "Why are you going to him today? It is neither new moon nor sabbath." She answered, [b]"It's all right."[-b]

[24] She had the ass saddled, and said to her servant, "Urge [the beast] on;[c] see that I don't slow down unless I tell you." [25] She went on until she came to the man of God on Mount Carmel. When the man of God saw her from afar, he said to his servant Gehazi, "There is that Shunammite woman. [26] Go, hurry toward her and ask her, 'How are you? How is your husband? How is the child?' " "We are well," she replied. [27] But when she came up to the man of God on the mountain, she clasped his feet. Gehazi stepped forward to push her away; but the man of God said, "Let her alone, for she is in bitter distress; and the LORD has hidden it from me and has not told me." [28] Then she said, "Did I ask my lord for a son? Didn't I say: 'Don't mislead me'?"

[29] He said to Gehazi, [d]"Tie up your skirts,[-d] take my staff in your hand, and go. If you meet anyone, do not greet him; and if anyone greets you, do not answer him. And place my staff on the face of the boy." [30] But the boy's mother said, "As the LORD lives and as you live, I will not leave you!" So he arose and followed her.

[31] Gehazi had gone on before them and had placed the staff on the boy's face; but there was no sound or response. He turned back to meet him and told him, "The boy has not awakened." [32] Elisha came into the house, and there was the boy, laid out dead on his couch. [33] He went in, shut the door behind the two of them, and prayed to the LORD. [34] Then he mounted [the bed] and placed himself over the child. He put his mouth on its mouth, his eyes on its eyes, and his hands on its hands, as he bent over it. And the body of the child became warm. [35] He stepped down, walked once up and down the room, then mounted and bent over him. Thereupon, the boy sneezed seven times, and the boy

---

[b-b] *Heb. "Shalom."*
[c] *The servant runs behind the donkey and urges it on with a stick.*
[d-d] *Lit. "Gird your loins."*

opened his eyes. [36] [Elisha] called Gehazi and said, "Call the Shunammite woman," and he called her. When she came to him, he said, "Pick up your son." [37] She came and fell at his feet and bowed low to the ground; then she picked up her son and left.

[38] Elisha returned to Gilgal. There was a famine in the land, and the disciples of the prophets were sitting before him. He said to his servant, "Set the large pot [on the fire] and cook a stew for the disciples of the prophets." [39] So one of them went out into the fields to gather sprouts. He came across a wild vine and picked from it wild gourds, as many as his garment would hold. Then he came back and sliced them into the pot of stew, for they did not know [what they were]; [40] and they served it for the men to eat. While they were still eating of the stew, they began to cry out: "O man of God, there is death in the pot!"[e] And they could not eat it. [41] "Fetch some flour," [Elisha] said. He threw it into the pot and said, "Serve it to the people and let them eat." And there was no longer anything harmful in the pot.

[42] A man came from Baal-shalishah and he brought the man of God some bread of the first reaping—twenty loaves of barley bread, and some fresh grain [f-]in his sack.[-f] And [Elisha] said, "Give it to the people and let them eat." [43] His attendant replied, "How can I set this before a hundred men?" But he said, "Give it to the people and let them eat. For thus said the LORD: They shall eat and have some left over." [44] So he set it before them; and when they had eaten, they had some left over, as the LORD had said.

5 Naaman, commander of the army of the king of Aram, was important to his lord and high in his favor, for through him the LORD had granted victory to Aram. But the man, though a great warrior, was a leper.[a] [2] Once, when the Arameans were out raiding, they carried off a young girl from the land of Israel, and she

---

[e] *The wild gourds cause severe cramps.*
[f-f] *Or "on the stalk"; perhaps connected with Ugaritic* bṣql.

[a] *Cf. note on Lev. 13.3.*

became an attendant to Naaman's wife. [3] She said to her mistress, "I wish Master could come before the prophet in Samaria; he would cure him of his leprosy." [4] [Naaman] went and told his lord just what the girl from the land of Israel had said. [5] And the king of Aram said, "Go to the king of Israel, and I will send along a letter."

He set out, taking with him ten talents of silver, six thousand shekels of gold, and ten changes of clothing. [6] He brought the letter to the king of Israel. It read: "Now, when this letter reaches you, know that I have sent my courtier Naaman to you, that you may cure him of his leprosy." [7] When the king of Israel read the letter, he rent his clothes and cried, "Am I God, to deal death or give life, that this fellow writes to me to cure a man of leprosy? Just see for yourselves that he is seeking a pretext against me!"

[8] When Elisha, the man of God, heard that the king of Israel had rent his clothes, he sent a message to the king: "Why have you rent your clothes? Let him come to me, and he will learn that there is a prophet in Israel."

[9] So Naaman came with his horses and chariots and halted at the door of Elisha's house. [10] Elisha sent a messenger to say to him, "Go and bathe seven times in the Jordan, and your flesh shall be restored and you shall be clean." [11] But Naaman was angered and walked away. "I thought," he said, "he would surely come out to me, and would stand and invoke the LORD his God by name, and would wave his hand toward the spot, and cure the affected part. [12] Are not the Amanah and the Pharpar, the rivers of Damascus, better than all the waters of Israel? I could bathe in them and be clean!" And he stalked off in a rage.

[13] But his servants came forward and spoke to him. "Sir,"[b] they said, "if the prophet told you to do something difficult, would you not do it? How much more when he has only said to you, 'Bathe and be clean.' " [14] So he went down and immersed himself in the Jordan seven times, as the man of God had bidden; and his flesh became like a little boy's, and he was clean. [15] Returning with his entire retinue to the man of God, he stood before him and ex-

---

[b] Lit. "(My) father."

claimed, "Now I know that there is no God in the whole world except in Israel! So please accept a gift from your servant." [16] But he replied, "As the LORD lives, whom I serve, I will not accept anything." He pressed him to accept, but he refused. [17] And Naaman said, "Then at least let your servant be given two mule-loads of earth; for your servant will never again offer up burnt offering or sacrifice to any god, except the LORD. [18] But may the LORD pardon your servant for this: When my master enters the temple of Rimmon to bow low in worship there, and he is leaning on my arm so that I must bow low in the temple of Rimmon— when I bow low in the temple of Rimmon, may the LORD pardon your servant in this." [19] And he said to him, "Go in peace."

When he had gone some distance from him, [20] Gehazi, the attendant of Elisha the man of God, thought: "My master [c]has let that Aramean Naaman off without accepting what he brought![c] As the LORD lives, I will run after him and get something from him." [21] So Gehazi hurried after Naaman. When Naaman saw someone running after him, he alighted from his chariot to meet him and said, "Is all well?" [22] "All is well," he replied. "My master has sent me to say: Two youths, disciples of the prophets, have just come to me from the hill country of Ephraim. Please give them a talent of silver and two changes of clothing." [23] Naaman said, "Please take two talents." He urged him, and he wrapped the two talents of silver in two bags and gave them, along with two changes of clothes, to two of his servants, who carried them ahead of him. [24] When [Gehazi] arrived at the citadel, he took [the things] from them and deposited them in the house. Then he dismissed the men and they went their way.

[25] He entered and stood before his master; and Elisha said to him, "Where have you been, Gehazi?" He replied, "Your servant has not gone anywhere." [26] Then [Elisha] said to him, "Did not my spirit[d] go along when a man got down from his chariot to meet you? Is this a time to take money in order to buy clothing and olive groves and vineyards, sheep and oxen, and male and female slaves? [27] Surely, the leprosy of Naaman shall cling to you and to

c-c *Lit. "has prevented that Aramean Naaman from having what he brought accepted."*
d *Lit. "heart."*

your descendants forever." And as [Gehazi] left his presence, he was snow-white with leprosy.

6 The disciples of the prophets said to Elisha, "See, the place where we live under your direction is too cramped for us. ² Let us go to the Jordan, and let us each get a log there and build quarters there for ourselves to live in." "Do so," he replied. ³ Then one of them said, "Will you please come along with your servants?" "Yes, I will come," he said; ⁴ and he accompanied them. So they went to the Jordan and cut timber. ⁵ As one of them was felling a trunk, the iron ax head fell into the water. And he cried aloud, "Alas, master, it was a borrowed one!" ⁶ "Where did it fall?" asked the man of God. He showed him the spot; and he cut off a stick and threw it in, and he made the ax head float. ⁷ "Pick it up," he said; so he reached out and took it.

⁸ While the king of Aram was waging war against Israel, he took counsel with his officers and said, ᵃ⁻"I will encamp⁻ᵃ in such and such a place." ⁹ But the man of God sent word to the king of Israel, "Take care not to pass through that place, for the Arameans are encamped there." ¹⁰ So the king of Israel sent word to the place of which the man of God had told him. ᵇ⁻Time and again⁻ᵇ he alerted ᶜ⁻such a place⁻ᶜ and took precautions there. ¹¹ Greatly agitated about this matter, the king of Aram summoned his officers and said to them, "Tell me! Who of us is on the side of the king of Israel?" ¹² "No one, my lord king," said one of the officers. "Elisha, that prophet in Israel, tells the king of Israel the very words you speak in your bedroom." ¹³ "Go find out where he is," he said, "so that I can have him seized." It was reported to him that [Elisha] was in Dothan; ¹⁴ so he sent horses and chariots there and a strong force. They arrived at night and encircled the town.
¹⁵ When the attendant of the man of God rose early and went outside, he saw a force, with horses and chariots, surrounding the

ᵃ⁻ᵃ *Meaning of Heb. uncertain.*
ᵇ⁻ᵇ *Lit. "not once or twice."*
ᶜ⁻ᶜ *Heb. "it."*

town. "Alas, master, what shall we do?" his servant asked him.
¹⁶ "Have no fear," he replied. "There are more on our side than
on theirs." ¹⁷ Then Elisha prayed: "LORD, open his eyes and let
him see." And the LORD opened the servant's eyes and he saw the
hills all around Elisha covered with horses and chariots of fire.
¹⁸ [The Arameans] came down against him, and Elisha prayed to
the LORD: "Please strike this people with a blinding light." And
He struck them with a blinding light, as Elisha had asked.

¹⁹ Elisha said to them, "This is not the road, and that is not the
town; follow me, and I will lead you to the man you want." And
he led them to Samaria. ²⁰ When they entered Samaria, Elisha
said, "O LORD, open the eyes of these men so that they may see."
The LORD opened their eyes and they saw that they were inside
Samaria. ²¹ When the king of Israel saw them, he said to Elisha,
"Father, shall I strike them down?" ²² "No, do not," he replied.
"Did you take them captive with your sword and bow that you
would strike them down? Rather, set food and drink before them,
and let them eat and drink and return to their master." ²³ So he
prepared a lavish feast for them and, after they had eaten and
drunk, he let them go, and they returned to their master. And the
Aramean bands stopped invading the land of Israel.

²⁴ Some time later, King Ben-hadad of Aram mustered his entire army and marched upon Samaria and besieged it. ²⁵ There
was a great famine in Samaria, and the siege continued until a
donkey's head sold for eighty [shekels] of silver and a quarter of
a *kab* of ⁻ᵈdoves' dung⁻ᵈ for five shekels. ²⁶ Once, when the king
of Israel was walking on the city wall, a woman cried out to him:
"Help me, Your Majesty!" ²⁷ "Don't [ask me]," he replied. "Let
the LORD help you! Where could I get help for you, from the
threshing floor or from the winepress? ²⁸ But what troubles you?"
the king asked her. The woman answered, "That woman said to
me, 'Give up your son and we will eat him today; and tomorrow
we'll eat my son.' ²⁹ So we cooked my son and we ate him. The
next day I said to her, 'Give up your son and let's eat him'; but

ᵈ⁻ᵈ *Apparently a popular term for "carob pods," as in Akkadian.*

she hid her son." [30] When the king heard what the woman said, he rent his clothes; and as he walked along the wall, the people could see that he was wearing sackcloth underneath.

[31] He said, "Thus and more may God do to me if the head of Elisha son of Shaphat remains on [e]his shoulders[-e] today." [32] Now Elisha was sitting at home and the elders were sitting with him. The king had sent ahead one of his men; but before the messenger arrived, [Elisha] said to the elders, "Do you see—that son of a murderer has sent someone to cut off my head! Watch when the messenger comes, and shut the door and hold the door fast against him. No doubt the sound of his master's footsteps will follow."

[33] While he was still talking to them, the messenger[f] came to him and said, "This calamity is from the LORD. What more can 7 I hope for from the LORD?" [1] And Elisha replied, "Hear the word of the LORD. Thus said the LORD: This time tomorrow, a *seah* of choice flour shall sell for a shekel at the gate of Samaria, and two *seahs* of barley for a shekel." [2] The aide on whose arm the king was leaning spoke up and said to the man of God, "Even if the LORD were to make windows in the sky, could this come to pass?" And he retorted, "You shall see it with your own eyes, but you shall not eat of it."

[3] There were four men, lepers, outside the gate. They said to one another, "Why should we sit here waiting for death? [4] If we decide to go into the town, what with the famine in the town, we shall die there; and if we just sit here, still we die. Come, let us desert to the Aramean camp. If they let us live, we shall live; and if they put us to death, we shall but die."

[5] They set out at twilight for the Aramean camp; but when they came to the edge of the Aramean camp, there was no one there. [6] For the LORD had caused the Aramean camp to hear a sound of chariots, a sound of horses—the din of a huge army. They said to one another, "The king of Israel must have hired the kings of the Hittites and the kings of Mizraim[a] to attack us!" [7] And they

[e-e] *Lit. "him."*
[f] *Emendation yields "king."*
[a] *Cf. I Kings 10.28 and note g there.*

fled headlong in the twilight, abandoning their tents and horses and asses—the [entire] camp just as it was—as they fled for their lives.

8 When those lepers came to the edge of the camp, they went into one of the tents and ate and drank; then they carried off silver and gold and clothing from there and buried it. They came back and went into another tent, and they carried off what was there and buried it. 9 Then they said to one another, "We are not doing right. This is a day of good news, and we are keeping silent! If we wait until the light of morning, we shall incur guilt. Come, let us go and inform the king's palace." 10 They went and called out to the gatekeepers of the city and told them, "We have been to the Aramean camp. There is not a soul there, nor any human sound; but the horses are tethered and the asses are tethered and the tents are undisturbed."

11 The gatekeepers called out, and the news was passed on into the king's palace. 12 The king rose in the night and said to his courtiers, "I will tell you what the Arameans have done to us. They know that we are starving, so they have gone out of camp and hidden in the fields, thinking: When they come out of the town, we will take them alive and get into the town." 13 But one of the courtiers spoke up, "Let a few[b] of the remaining horses that are still here be taken—'they are like those that are left here of the whole multitude of Israel, out of the whole multitude of Israel that have perished'—and let us send and find out."

14 They took two teams[c] of horses and the king sent them after the Aramean army, saying, "Go and find out." 15 They followed them as far as the Jordan, and found the entire road full of clothing and gear which the Arameans had thrown away in their haste; and the messengers returned and told the king. 16 The people then went out and plundered the Aramean camp. So a *seah* of choice flour sold for a shekel, and two *seahs* of barley for a shekel—as the LORD had spoken.

17 Now the king had put the aide on whose arm he leaned in charge of the gate; and he was trampled to death in the gate by

b *Lit. "five."*
c-c *Meaning of Heb. uncertain.*

the people—just as the man of God had spoken, as he had spoken when the king came down to him. [18] For when the man of God said to the king, "This time tomorrow two *seahs* of barley shall sell at the gate of Samaria for a shekel, and a *seah* of choice flour for a shekel," [19] the aide answered the man of God and said, "Even if the LORD made windows in the sky, could this come to pass?" And he retorted, "You shall see it with your own eyes, but you shall not eat of it." [20] That is exactly what happened to him: The people trampled him to death in the gate.

8 Elisha had said to the woman whose son he revived, "Leave immediately with your family and go sojourn *a-*somewhere else;*-a* for the LORD has decreed a seven-year famine upon the land, and it has already begun." [2] The woman had done as the man of God had spoken; she left with her family and sojourned in the land of the Philistines for seven years. [3] At the end of the seven years, the woman returned from the land of the Philistines and went to the king to complain about her house and farm. [4] Now the king was talking to Gehazi, the servant of the man of God, and he said, "Tell me all the wonderful things that Elisha has done." [5] While he was telling the king how [Elisha] had revived a dead person, in came the woman whose son he had revived, complaining to the king about her house and farm. "My lord king," said Gehazi, "this is the woman and this is her son whom Elisha revived." [6] The king questioned the woman, and she told him [the story]; so the king assigned a eunuch to her and instructed him: "Restore all her property, and all the revenue from her farm from the time she left the country until now."

[7] Elisha arrived in Damascus at a time when King Ben-hadad of Aram was ill. *b-*The king*-b* was told, "The man of God is on his way here," [8] and he said to Hazael, "Take a gift with you and go meet the man of God, and through him inquire of the LORD: Will I recover from this illness?" [9] Hazael went to meet him, taking

a-a *Lit. "wherever you may sojourn."*
b-b *Brought up from v. 8 for clarity.*

with him as a gift forty camel-loads of all the bounty of Damascus. He came and stood before him and said, "Your son, King Benhadad of Aram, has sent me to you to ask: Will I recover from this illness?" [10] Elisha said to him, "Go and say to him, 'You will recover.' However, the LORD has revealed to me that he will die." [11] The man of God *kept his face expressionless-* for a long time; and then he wept. [12] "Why does my lord weep?" asked Hazael. "Because I know," he replied, "what harm you will do to the Israelite people: you will set their fortresses on fire, put their young men to the sword, dash their little ones in pieces, and rip open their pregnant women." [13] "But how," asked Hazael, "can your servant, who is a mere dog, perform such a mighty deed?" Elisha replied, "The LORD has shown me a vision of you as king of Aram." [14] He left Elisha and returned to his master, who asked him, "What did Elisha say to you?" He replied, "He told me that you would recover." [15] The next day, [Hazael] took *a piece of netting,-* dipped it in water, and spread it over his face. So [Benhadad] died, and Hazael succeeded him as king.

[16] In the fifth year of King Joram[d] son of Ahab of Israel—Jehoshaphat had been king of Judah—Joram son of King Jehoshaphat of Judah became king. [17] He was thirty-two years old when he became king, and he reigned in Jerusalem eight years. [18] He followed the practices of the kings of Israel—whatever the House of Ahab did, for he had married a daughter[e] of Ahab—and he did what was displeasing to the LORD. [19] However, the LORD refrained from destroying Judah, for the sake of His servant David, in accordance with His promise to maintain a lamp for his descendants for all time. [20] During his reign, the Edomites rebelled against Judah's rule and set up a king of their own. [21] Joram crossed over to Zair with all his chariotry. *He arose by night and attacked the Edomites, who were surrounding him and the chariot commanders; but-* his troops fled to their homes. [22] Thus Edom fell away from Judah, as is still the case. Libnah likewise fell away at that time.

---

c-c *Meaning of Heb. uncertain.*
d *Throughout this chapter, the name Joram is sometimes written Jehoram.*
e *Emendation yields "sister"; cf. v. 26.*

²³ The other events of Joram's reign, and all his actions, are recorded in the Annals of the Kings of Judah. ²⁴ Joram slept with his fathers and was buried with his fathers in the City of David; his son Ahaziah succeeded him as king.

²⁵ In the twelfth year of King Joram son of Ahab of Israel, Ahaziah son of Joram became king of Judah. ²⁶ Ahaziah was twenty-two years old when he became king, and he reigned in Jerusalem one year; his mother's name was Athaliah daughter of King Omri of Israel. ²⁷ He walked in the ways of the House of Ahab and did what was displeasing to the LORD, like the House of Ahab, for he was related by marriage to the House of Ahab. ²⁸ He marched with Joram son of Ahab to battle against King Hazael of Aram at Ramoth-gilead, but the Arameans wounded Joram. ²⁹ King Joram retired to Jezreel to recover from the wounds which the Arameans had inflicted upon him at Ramah, when he fought against King Hazael of Aram. And King Ahaziah son of Joram of Judah went down to Jezreel to visit Joram son of Ahab while he was ill.

9 Then the prophet Elisha summoned one of the disciples of the prophets and said to him, "Tie up your skirts,^a and take along this flask of oil, and go to Ramoth-gilead. ² When you arrive there, go and see Jehu son of Jehoshaphat son of Nimshi; get him to leave his comrades, and take him into an inner room. ³ Then take the flask of oil and pour some on his head, and say, 'Thus said the LORD: I anoint you king over Israel.' Then open the door and flee without delay."

⁴ The young man, the servant of the prophet, went to Ramoth-gilead. ⁵ When he arrived, the army commanders were sitting together. He said, "Commander, I have a message for you." "For which one of us?" Jehu asked. He answered, "For you, commander." ⁶ So [Jehu] arose and went inside; and [the disciple] poured the oil on his head, and said to him, "Thus said the LORD, the

^a *See note at 4.29.*

God of Israel: I anoint you king over the people of the LORD, over Israel. ⁷ You shall strike down the House of Ahab your master; thus will I avenge on Jezebel the blood of my servants the prophets, and the blood of the other servants of the LORD. ⁸ The whole House of Ahab shall perish, and I will cut off every male belonging to Ahab, ᵇ·bond and free⁻ᵇ in Israel. ⁹ I will make the House of Ahab like the House of Jeroboam son of Nebat, and like the House of Baasha son of Ahijah. ¹⁰ The dogs shall devour Jezebel in the field of Jezreel, with none to bury her." Then he opened the door and fled.

¹¹ Jehu went out to the other officers of his master, and they asked him, "Is all well? What did that madman come to you for?" He said to them, "You know the man and his ranting!" ¹² "You're lying," they said. "Tell us [the truth]." Then he replied, "Thus and thus he said: Thus said the LORD: I anoint you king over Israel!" ¹³ Quickly each man took his cloak and placed it under him,ᶜ on ᵈ·the top step ⁻ᵈ They sounded the horn and proclaimed, "Jehu is king!" ¹⁴ Thus Jehu son of Jehoshaphat son of Nimshi conspired against Joram.

Joram and all Israel had been defending Ramoth-gilead against King Hazael of Aram, ¹⁵ but King Joram had gone back to Jezreel to recover from the wounds which the Arameans had inflicted on him in his battle with King Hazael of Aram.

Jehu said, "If such is your wish, allow no one to slip out of the town to go and report this in Jezreel." ¹⁶ Then Jehu mounted his chariot and drove to Jezreel; for Joram was lying ill there, and King Ahaziah of Judah had gone down to visit Joram. ¹⁷ The lookout was stationed on the tower in Jezreel, and he saw the troop of Jehu as he approached. He called out, "I see a troop!" Joram said, "Dispatch a horseman to meet them and let him ask: Is all well?" ¹⁸ The horseman went to meet him, and he said, "The king inquires: Is all well?" Jehu replied, "What concern of yours is it whether all is well? Fall in behind me." The lookout

ᵇ·ᵇ *See note at I Kings 14.10.*
ᶜ *I.e. Jehu.*
ᵈ·ᵈ *Meaning of Heb. uncertain.*

reported: "The messenger has reached them, but has not turned back." 19 So he sent out a second horseman. He came to them and said, "Thus says the king: Is all well?" Jehu answered, "What concern of yours is it whether all is well? Fall in behind me." 20 And the lookout reported, "The messenger has reached them, but has not turned back. And it looks like the driving of Jehu son of Nimshi, who drives wildly."

21 Joram ordered, "Hitch up [the chariot]!" They hitched up his chariot; and King Joram of Israel and King Ahaziah of Judah went out, each in his own chariot, to meet Jehu. They met him at the field of Naboth the Jezreelite. 22 When Joram saw Jehu, he asked, "Is all well, Jehu?" But Jehu replied, "How can all be well as long as your mother Jezebel carries on her countless harlotries and sorceries?" 23 Thereupon Joram turned his horses^e around and fled, crying out to Ahaziah, "Treason, Ahaziah!" 24 But Jehu drew his bow and hit Joram between the shoulders,^f so that the arrow issued from his chest; and he collapsed in his chariot.

25 Jehu thereupon ordered his officer Bidkar, "Pick him up and throw him into the field of Naboth the Jezreelite. Remember how you and I were riding side by side behind his father Ahab, when the LORD made this pronouncement about him: 26 'I swear, I have taken note of the blood of Naboth and the blood of his sons yesterday—declares the LORD. And I will requite you in this plot —declares the LORD.' So pick him up and throw him unto the plot in accordance with the word of the LORD."

27 On seeing this, King Ahaziah of Judah fled along the road to Beth-haggan. Jehu pursued him and said, "Shoot him down too!" [And they shot him] in his chariot at the ascent of Gur, which is near Ibleam. He fled to Megiddo and died there. 28 His servants conveyed him in a chariot to Jerusalem, and they buried him in his grave with his fathers, in the City of David. (29 Ahaziah had become king over Judah in the eleventh year of Joram son of Ahab.)

^e Lit. "hands"; see note at I Kings 22.34.
^f Lit. "arms."

[30] Jehu went on to Jezreel. When Jezebel heard of it, she painted her eyes with kohl and dressed her hair, and she looked out of the window. [31] As Jehu entered the gate, she called out, "Is all well, Zimri, murderer of your master?"[g] [32] He looked up toward the window and said, "Who is on my side, who?" And two or three eunuchs leaned out toward him. [33] "Throw her down," he said. They threw her down; and her blood spattered on the wall and on the horses, and they trampled her.

[34] Then he went inside and ate and drank. And he said, "Attend to that cursed woman and bury her, for she was a king's daughter." [35] So they went to bury her; but all they found of her were the skull, the feet, and the hands. [36] They came back and reported to him; and he said, "It is just as the LORD spoke through His servant Elijah the Tishbite: The dogs shall devour the flesh of Jezebel in the field of Jezreel; [37] and the carcass of Jezebel shall be like dung on the ground, in the field of Jezreel, so that none will be able to say: 'This was Jezebel.' "

10 Ahab had seventy descendants in Samaria. Jehu wrote letters and sent them to Samaria, to the elders and officials of Jezreel[a] and to the guardians of [the children] of Ahab, as follows: [2] "Now, when this letter reaches you—since your master's sons are with you and you also have chariots and horses, and a fortified city and weapons—[3] select the best and the most suitable of your master's sons and set him on his father's throne, and fight for your master's house." [4] But they were overcome by fear, for they thought, "If the two kings could not stand up to him, how can we?" [5] The steward of the palace and the governor of the city and the elders and the guardians sent this message to Jehu: "We are your subjects, and we shall do whatever you tell us to. We shall not proclaim anyone king; do whatever you like."

[6] He wrote them a second time: "If you are on my side and are ready to obey me, take the heads of the attendants of your master's sons and come[b] to me in Jezreel tomorrow at this time."

[g] *See I Kings 16.8-10.*

[a] *Emendation yields "of the city."*
[b] *Targum and Septuagint read "and bring them."*

Now the princes, seventy in number, were with the notables of the town, who were rearing them. 7 But when the letter reached them, they took the princes and slaughtered all seventy of them; they put their heads in baskets and sent them to him in Jezreel. 8 A messenger came and reported to him: "They have brought the heads of the princes." He said, "Pile them up in two heaps at the entrance of the gate before morning." 9 In the morning he went out and stood there; and he said to all the people, "Are you blameless?ᶜ True, I conspired against my master and killed him; but who struck down all of these? 10 Know, then, that nothing that the LORD has spoken concerning the House of Ahab shall remain unfulfilled, for the LORD has done what he announced through His servant Elijah." 11 And Jehu struck down all that were left of the House of Ahab in Jezreel—and all his notables, intimates, and priests—till he left him no survivor.

12 He then set out for Samaria. On the way, when he was at Beth-eked of the shepherds, 13 Jehu came upon the kinsmen of King Ahaziah of Judah. "Who are you?" he asked. They replied, "We are the kinsmen of Ahaziah, and we have come to pay our respects to the sons of the king and the sons of the queen mother." 14 "Take them alive!" he said. They took them alive and then slaughtered them at the pit of Beth-eked, forty-two of them; he did not spare a single one.

15 He went on from there, and he met Jehonadab son of Rechab coming toward him. He greeted him and said to him, "Are you as wholehearted with me as I am with you?" "I am," Jehonadab replied. "If so," [said Jehu,] "give me your hand." He gave him his hand and [Jehu] helped him into the chariot. 16 "Come with me," he said, "and see my zeal for the LORD." And he was taken along in the chariot. 17 Arriving in Samaria, [Jehu] struck down all the survivors of [the House of] Ahab in Samaria, until he wiped it out, fulfilling the word that the LORD had spoken to Elijah.

18 Jehu assembled all the people and said to them, "Ahab served Baal little; Jehu shall serve him much! 19 Therefore, sum-

ᶜ Or "You are blameless."

mon to me all the prophets of Baal, all his worshipers, and all his priests: let no one fail to come, for I am going to hold a great sacrifice for Baal. Whoever fails to come shall forfeit his life." Jehu was acting with guile in order to exterminate the worshipers of Baal. 20 Jehu gave orders to convoke a solemn assembly for Baal, and one was proclaimed. 21 Jehu sent word throughout Israel, and all the worshipers of Baal came, not a single one remained behind. They came into the temple of Baal, and the temple of Baal was filled from end to end. 22 He said to the man in charge of the wardrobe,*d* "Bring out the vestments for all the worshipers of Baal"; and he brought vestments out for them. 23 Then Jehu and Jehonadab son of Rechab came into the temple of Baal, and they said to the worshipers of Baal, "Search and make sure that there are no worshipers of the LORD among you, but only worshipers of Baal." 24 So they went in to offer sacrifices and burnt offerings. But Jehu had stationed eighty of his men outside and had said, "Whoever permits the escape of a single one of the men I commit to your charge shall forfeit life for life."

25 When Jehu had finished presenting the burnt offering, he said to the guards and to the officers, "Come in and strike them down; let no man get away!" The guards and the officers struck them down with the sword and left them lying where they were; then they proceeded to the interior*e* of the temple of Baal. 26 They brought out the pillars*f* of the temple of Baal and burned them. 27 They destroyed the pillar*g* of Baal, and they tore down the temple of Baal and turned it into latrines, as is still the case. 28 Thus Jehu eradicated the Baal from Israel. 29 However, Jehu did not turn away from the sinful objects by which Jeroboam son of Nebat had caused Israel to sin, namely, the golden calves at Bethel and at Dan.

30 The LORD said to Jehu, "Because you have acted well and done what was pleasing to Me, having carried out all that I desired upon the House of Ahab, four generations of your descendants shall occupy the throne of Israel." 31 But Jehu was not careful to follow the Teaching of the LORD, the God of Israel,

---

d Meaning of Heb. uncertain.
e Lit. "city."
f Emendation yields "sacred posts"; cf. Deut. 12.3.
g Emendation yields "altar."

with all his heart; he did not turn away from the sins that Jeroboam had caused Israel to commit.

32 In those days the LORD began to reduce Israel; and Hazael harassed them throughout the territory of Israel 33 east of the Jordan, all the land of Gilead—the Gadites, the Reubenites, and the Manassites—from Aroer, by the Wadi Arnon, up to Gilead and Bashan.
34 The other events of Jehu's reign, and all his actions, and all his exploits, are recorded in the Annals of the Kings of Israel.
35 Jehu slept with his fathers and he was buried in Samaria; he was succeeded as king by his son Jehoahaz. 36 Jehu reigned over Israel for twenty-two years in Samaria.

11 When Athaliah, the mother of Ahaziah, learned that her son was dead, she promptly killed off all who were of royal stock. 2 But Jehosheba, daughter of King Joram and sister of Ahaziah, secretly took Ahaziah's son Joash away from among the princes who were being slain, and [put]*a* him and his nurse in a bedroom. And they*b* kept him hidden from Athaliah so that he was not put to death. 3 He stayed with her for six years, hidden in the House of the LORD,*c* while Athaliah reigned over the land.

4 In the seventh year, Jehoiada sent for the chiefs of the hundreds of the Carites*d* and of the guards, and had them come to him in the House of the LORD. He made a pact with them, exacting an oath from them in the House of the LORD, and he showed them the king's son. 5 He instructed them: "This is what you must do: One third of those who are on duty for the week *e*shall maintain guard*e* over the royal palace; 6 another third shall be [stationed] at the *f*Sur Gate;*f* and the other third shall be at the gate behind *g*the guards; you shall keep guard over the House on every side.*g* 7 The two divisions of yours who are off duty this

---

a *Cf. II Chron. 22.11.*
b *II Chron. 22.11 reads "she."*
c *Jehosheba was the wife of the high priest Jehoiada; cf. II Chron. 22.11.*
d *Perhaps the Cherethites (cf. II Sam. 20.23) or the Carians. They were members of the king's bodyguard.*
e-e *Heb. "and who keep guard."*
f-f *II Chron. 23.5 reads "Foundation Gate."*
g-g *Meaning of Heb. uncertain.*

week shall keep guard over the House of the LORD for the protection of the king. [8] You shall surround the king on every side, every man with his weapons at the ready; and whoever breaks through the ranks shall be killed. Stay close to the king in his comings and goings."

[9] The chiefs of hundreds did just as Jehoiada ordered: Each took his men—those who were on duty that week and those who were off duty that week—and they presented themselves to Jehoiada the priest. [10] The priest gave the chiefs of hundreds King David's spears[h] and quivers that were kept in the House of the LORD. [11] The guards, each with his weapons at the ready, stationed themselves—from the south end of the House to the north end of the House, at the altar and the House—to guard the king on every side. [12] [Jehoiada] then brought out the king's son, and placed upon him the crown and the insignia.[g] They anointed him and proclaimed him king; they clapped their hands and shouted, "Long live the king!"

[13] When Athaliah heard the shouting of the guards [and] the people, she came out to the people in the House of the LORD. [14] She looked about and saw the king standing by the pillar, as was the custom, the chiefs with their trumpets beside the king, and all the people of the land rejoicing and blowing trumpets. Athaliah rent her garments and cried out, "Treason, treason!" [15] Then the priest Jehoiada gave the command to the army officers, the chiefs of hundreds, and said to them, "Take her out [g-]between the ranks[-g] and, if anyone follows her, put him to the sword." For the priest thought: "Let her not be put to death in the House of the LORD." [16] They cleared a passageway for her and she entered the royal palace through the horses' entrance: there she was put to death.

[17] And Jehoiada solemnized the covenant between the LORD, on the one hand, and the king and the people, on the other—as well as between the king and the people—that they should be the people of the LORD. [18] Thereupon all the people of the land went

[h] *II Chron. 23.9 adds "and shields."*

to the temple of Baal. They tore it down and smashed its altars and images to bits, and they slew Mattan, the priest of Baal, in front of the altars. [Jehoiada] the priest then placed guards over the House of the LORD. 19 He took the chiefs of hundreds, the Carites,*d* the guards, and all the people of the land, and they escorted the king from the House of the LORD into the royal palace by the gate of the guards. And he ascended the royal throne. 20 All the people of the land rejoiced, and the city was quiet. As for Athaliah, she had been put to the sword in the royal palace.

12 Jehoash was seven years old when he became king. 2 Jehoash began his reign in the seventh year of Jehu, and he reigned in Jerusalem forty years. His mother's name was Zibiah of Beer-sheba. 3 All his days Jehoash did what was pleasing to the LORD, as the priest Jehoiada instructed him. 4 The shrines, however, were not removed; the people continued to sacrifice and offer at the shrines.

5 Jehoash said to the priests, "All the money, current money, brought into the House of the LORD as sacred donations—*a-*any money a man may pay as the money equivalent of persons,*-a* or any other money that a man may be minded to bring to the House of the LORD—6 let the priests receive it, each from his benefactor; they, in turn, shall make repairs on the House, wherever damage may be found."

7 But in the twenty-third year of King Jehoash, [it was found that] the priests had not made the repairs on the House. 8 So King Jehoash summoned the priest Jehoiada and the other priests and said to them, "Why have you not kept the House in repair? Now do not accept money from your benefactors any more, but have it donated for the repair of the House." 9 The priests agreed that they would neither accept money from the people nor make repairs on the House.

a-a See Lev. 27.2-8.

¹⁰ And the priest Jehoiada took a chest and bored a hole in its lid. He placed it at the right side of the altar as one entered the House of the LORD, and the priestly guards of the threshold deposited there all the money that was brought into the House of the LORD. ¹¹ Whenever they saw that there was much money in the chest, the royal scribe and the high priest would come up and put the money accumulated in the House of the LORD into bags, and they would count it. ¹² Then they would deliver the money ᵇ⁻that was weighed out⁻ᵇ to the overseers of the work, who were in charge of the House of the LORD. These, in turn, used to pay the carpenters and the laborers who worked on the House of the LORD, ¹³ and the masons and the stonecutters. They also paid for wood and for quarried stone with which to make the repairs on the House of the LORD, and for every other expenditure that had to be made in repairing the House. ¹⁴ However, no silver bowls and no snuffers, basins, or trumpets—no vessels of gold or silver—were made at the House of the LORD from the money brought into the House of the LORD; ¹⁵ this was given only to the overseers of the work for the repair of the House of the LORD. ¹⁶ No check was kept on the men to whom the money was delivered to pay the workers; for they dealt honestly.

¹⁷ Money brought ᶜ⁻as a guilt offering or as a sin offering⁻ᶜ was not deposited in the House of the LORD; it went to the priests.

¹⁸ At that time, King Hazael of Aram came up and attacked Gath and captured it; and Hazael proceeded to march on Jerusalem. ¹⁹ Thereupon King Joash of Judah took all the objects that had been consecrated by his fathers, Kings Jehoshaphat, Jehoram, and Ahaziah of Judah, and by himself, and all the gold that there was in the treasuries of the Temple of the LORD and in the royal palace, and he sent them to King Hazael of Aram, who then turned back from his march on Jerusalem.

²⁰ The other events of Joash's reign, and all his actions, are recorded in the Annals of the Kings of Judah. ²¹ His courtiers formed a conspiracy against Joash and assassinated him at Beth-

ᵇ⁻ᵇ *Meaning of Heb. uncertain.*
ᶜ⁻ᶜ *See Lev. 5.15.*

millo *b*that leads down to Silla.*-b* 22 The courtiers who assassinated him were Jozacar son of Shimeath and Jehozabad son of Shomer. He died and was buried with his fathers in the City of David; and his son Amaziah succeeded him as king.

13 In the twenty-third year of King Joash son of Ahaziah of Judah, Jehoahaz son of Jehu became king over Israel in Samaria —for seventeen years. 2 He did what was displeasing to the LORD. He persisted in the sins which Jeroboam son of Nebat had caused Israel to commit; he did not depart from them. 3 The LORD was angry with Israel and He repeatedly delivered them into the hands of King Hazael of Aram and into the hands of Ben-hadad son of Hazael. 4 But Jehoahaz pleaded with the LORD; and the LORD listened to him, for He saw the suffering that the king of Aram inflicted upon Israel. 5 So the LORD granted Israel a deliverer, and they gained their freedom from Aram; and Israel dwelt in its homes as before. 6 However, they did not depart from the sins which the House of Jeroboam had caused Israel to commit; they persisted in them. Even the sacred post stood in Samaria. 7 *a*In fact, Jehoahaz was left with a force of only fifty horsemen, ten chariots, and ten thousand foot soldiers; for the king of Aram had decimated them and trampled them like the dust under his feet.

8 The other events of Jehoahaz's reign, and all his actions and his exploits, are recorded in the Annals of the Kings of Israel. 9 Jehoahaz slept with his fathers and he was buried in Samaria; his son Joash succeeded him as king.

10 In the thirty-seventh year of King Joash of Judah, Jehoash son of Jehoahaz became king of Israel in Samaria—for sixteen years. 11 He did what was displeasing to the LORD; he did not depart from any of the sins which Jeroboam son of Nebat had caused Israel to commit; he persisted in them.

12 The other events of Joash's reign, and all his actions, and his

---

a This verse would read well after v. 3.

exploits in his war with King Amaziah of Judah, are recorded in the Annals of the Kings of Israel. [13] Joash slept with his fathers and Jeroboam occupied his throne; Joash was buried in Samaria with the kings of Israel.

[14] Elisha had been stricken with the illness of which he was to die, and King Joash of Israel went down to see him. He wept over him and cried, "Father, father! *b*-Israel's chariots and horsemen!"*-b* [15] Elisha said to him, "Get a bow and arrows"; and he brought him a bow and arrows. [16] Then he said to the king of Israel, "Grasp the bow!" And when he had grasped it, Elisha put his hands over the king's hands. [17] "Open the window toward the east," he said; and he opened it. Elisha said, "Shoot!" and he shot. Then he said, "An arrow of victory for the LORD! An arrow of victory over Aram! You shall rout Aram completely at Aphek." [18] He said, "Now pick up the arrows." And he picked them up. "Strike the ground!" he said to the king of Israel; and he struck three times and stopped. [19] The man of God was angry with him and said to him, *c*-"If only you had struck*-c* five or six times! Then you would have annihilated Aram; as it is, you shall defeat Aram only three times."

[20] Elisha died and he was buried. Now bands of Moabites used to invade the land *d*-at the coming of every year.*-d* [21] Once a man was being buried, when the people caught sight of such a band; so they threw the corpse*e* into Elisha's grave and *f*-made off.*-f* When the [dead] man came in contact with Elisha's bones, he came to life and stood up.

[22] King Hazael of Aram had oppressed the Israelites throughout the reign of Jehoahaz. [23] But the LORD was gracious and merciful to them, and He turned back to them for the sake of His covenant with Abraham, Isaac, and Jacob. He refrained from destroying them, and He still did not cast them out from His presence. [24] When King Hazael of Aram died, his son Ben-hadad succeeded him as king; [25] and then Jehoash son of Jehoahaz

b-b On Elisha as defender of Israel, see 6.8-14, 19-23.
c-c Lit. "to strike."
d-d Meaning of Heb. uncertain; emendation yields "year by year."
e Heb. "the man."
f-f Heb. "he made off."

recovered from Ben-hadad son of Hazael the towns which had been taken from his father Jehoahaz in war. Three times Joash defeated him, and he recovered the towns of Israel.

14 In the second year of King Joash son of Joahaz of Israel, Amaziah son of King Joash of Judah became king. ² He was twenty-five years old when he became king, and he reigned twenty-nine years in Jerusalem; his mother's name was Jehoad-dan of Jerusalem. ³ He did what was pleasing to the LORD, but not like his ancestor David; he did just as his father Joash had done. ⁴ However, the shrines were not removed; the people continued to sacrifice and make offerings at the shrines. ⁵ Once he had the kingdom firmly in his grasp, he put to death the courtiers who had assassinated his father the king. ⁶ But he did not put to death the children of the assassins, in accordance with what is written in the Book of the Teaching of Moses, where the LORD commanded, "Parents shall not be put to death for children, nor children be put to death for parents; a person shall be put to death only for his own crime."ᵃ

⁷ He defeated ten thousand Edomites in the Valley of Salt, and he captured Sela in battle and renamed it Joktheel, as is still the case. ⁸ Then Amaziah sent envoys to King Jehoash son of Jehoahaz son of Jehu of Israel, with this message: "Come, let us confrontᵇ each other." ⁹ King Jehoash of Israel sent back this message to King Amaziah of Judah: "The thistle in Lebanon sent this message to the cedar in Lebanon, 'Give your daughter to my son in marriage.' But a wild beast in Lebanon went by and trampled down the thistle. ¹⁰ Because you have defeated Edom, you have become arrogant. Stay home and enjoy your glory, rather than provoke disaster and fall, dragging Judah down with you."

¹¹ But Amaziah paid no heed; so King Jehoash of Israel advanced, and he and King Amaziah of Judah confronted each other at Beth-shemesh in Judah. ¹² The Judites were routed by Israel, and they all fled to their homes. ¹³ King Jehoash son of

ᵃ *Deut. 24.16.*
ᵇ *I.e. in battle.*

Ahaziah of Israel captured King Amaziah son of Jehoash son of Ahaziah of Judah at Beth-shemesh. He marched on Jerusalem, and he made a breach of four hundred cubits in the wall of Jerusalem, from[c] the Ephraim Gate to the Corner Gate. [14] He carried off all the gold and silver and all the vessels that there were in the House of the LORD and in the treasuries of the royal palace, as well as hostages; and he returned to Samaria.

[15] The other events of Jehoash's reign, and all his actions and exploits, and his war with King Amaziah of Judah, are recorded in the Annals of the Kings of Israel. [16] Jehoash slept with his fathers, and was buried in Samaria with the kings of Israel; his son Jeroboam succeeded him as king.

[17] King Amaziah son of Joash of Judah lived fifteen years after the death of King Jehoash son of Jehoahaz of Israel. [18] The other events of Amaziah's reign are recorded in the Annals of the Kings of Judah. [19] A conspiracy was formed against him in Jerusalem and he fled to Lachish; but they sent men after him to Lachish, and they killed him there. [20] They brought back his body on horses, and he was buried with his fathers in Jerusalem, in the City of David.

[21] Then all the people of Judah took Azariah, who was sixteen years old, and proclaimed him king to succeed his father Amaziah. [22] It was he who rebuilt Elath and restored it to Judah, after King [Amaziah] slept with his fathers.

[23] In the fifteenth year of King Amaziah son of Joash of Judah, King Jeroboam son of Joash of Israel became king in Samaria—for forty-one years. [24] He did what was displeasing to the LORD; he did not depart from all the sins that Jeroboam son of Nebat had caused Israel to commit. [25] It was he who restored the territory of Israel from Lebo-hamath to the sea of the Arabah, in accordance with the promise that the LORD, the God of Israel, had made through His servant, the prophet Jonah son of Amittai from Gath-hepher. [26] For the LORD saw the very bitter plight of Israel, with neither bond nor free left, and with none to help

[c] Heb. "at."

Israel. [27] And the LORD resolved not to blot out the name of Israel from under heaven; and he delivered them through Jeroboam son of Joash.

[28] The other events of Jeroboam's reign, and all his actions and exploits, how he fought and recovered Damascus and Hamath *for Judah in Israel,* are recorded in the Annals of the Kings of Israel. [29] Jeroboam slept with his fathers, the kings of Israel, and his son Zechariah succeeded him as king.

15 In the twenty-seventh year of King Jeroboam of Israel, Azariah son of King Amaziah of Judah became king. [2] He was sixteen years old when he became king, and he reigned fifty-two years in Jerusalem; his mother's name was Jecoliah of Jerusalem. [3] He did what was pleasing to the LORD, just as his father Amaziah had done. [4] However, the shrines were not removed; the people continued to sacrifice and make offerings at the shrines. [5] The LORD struck the king with a plague, and he was a leper until the day of his death; he lived *in isolated quarters,* while Jotham, the king's son, was in charge of the palace and governed the people of the land.

[6] The other events of Azariah's reign, and all his actions, are recorded in the Annals of the Kings of Judah. [7] Azariah slept with his fathers, and he was buried with his fathers in the City of David; his son Jotham succeeded him as king.

[8] In the thirty-eighth year of King Azariah of Judah, Zechariah son of Jeroboam became king over Israel in Samaria—for six months. [9] He did what was displeasing to the LORD, as his fathers had done; he did not depart from the sins which Jeroboam son of Nebat had caused Israel to commit. [10] Shallum son of Jabesh conspired against him and struck him down *before the people* and killed him, and succeeded him as king. [11] The other events of Zechariah's reign are recorded in the Annals of the Kings of Israel. [12] This was in accord with the word that the LORD had

c-c *Emendation yields "for Israel."*

a-a *Meaning of Heb. uncertain.*

b-b *Some Septuagint mss. read "at Ibleam."*

spoken to Jehu: "Four generations of your descendants shall occupy the throne of Israel." And so it came about.[c]

[13] Shallum son of Jabesh became king in the thirty-ninth year of King Uzziah of Judah, and he reigned in Samaria one month. [14] Then Menahem son of Gadi set out from Tirzah and came to Samaria; he attacked Shallum son of Jabesh in Samaria and killed him, and he succeeded him as king. [15] The other events of Shallum's reign, and the conspiracy that he formed, are recorded in the Annals of the Kings of Israel.

[16] At that time, [a-][marching] from Tirzah,[-a] Menahem subdued Tiphsah and all who were in it, and its territory; and because it did not surrender, he massacred [its people] and ripped open all its pregnant women.

[17] In the thirty-ninth year of King Azariah of Judah, Menahem son of Gadi became king over Israel in Samaria for ten years. [18] He did what was displeasing to the LORD; throughout his days he did not depart from the sins which Jeroboam son of Nebat had caused Israel to commit. [19] King Pul of Assyria invaded the land, and Menahem gave Pul a thousand talents of silver that he might support him and strengthen his hold on the kingdom. [20] Menahem exacted the money from Israel: every man of means had to pay fifty shekels of silver for the king of Assyria. The king of Assyria withdrew and did not remain in the land. [21] The other events of Menahem's reign, and all his actions, are recorded in the Annals of the Kings of Israel. [22] Menahem slept with his fathers, and his son Pekahiah succeeded him as king.

[23] In the fiftieth year of King Azariah of Judah, Pekahiah son of Menahem became king over Israel in Samaria—for two years. [24] He did what was displeasing to the LORD; he did not depart from the sins which Jeroboam son of Nebat had caused Israel to commit. [25] His aide, Pekah son of Remaliah, conspired against him and struck him down in the royal palace in Samaria; with him

[c] Cf. 10.30.

were fifty Gileadites, *a*-with men from Argob and Arieh;*-a* and he killed him and succeeded him as king.

²⁶ The other events of Pekahiah's reign, and all his actions, are recorded in the Annals of the Kings of Israel.

²⁷ In the fifty-second year of King Azariah of Judah, Pekah son of Remaliah became king over Israel and Samaria—for twenty years. ²⁸ He did what was displeasing to the LORD; he did not depart from the sins which Jeroboam son of Nebat had caused Israel to commit. ²⁹ In the days of King Pekah of Israel, King Tiglath-pileser of Assyria came and captured Ijon, Abel-beth-maacah, Janoah, Kedesh, Hazor—Gilead, Galilee, the entire region of Naphtali; and he deported *d*-the inhabitants*-d* to Assyria.

³⁰ Hoshea son of Elah conspired against Pekah son of Remaliah, attacked him, and killed him. He succeeded him as king in the twentieth year of Jotham son of Uzziah. ³¹ The other events of Pekah's reign, and all his actions, are recorded in the Annals of the Kings of Israel.

³² In the second year of King Pekah son of Remaliah of Israel, Jotham son of King Uzziah of Judah became king. ³³ He was twenty-five years old when he became king, and he reigned sixteen years in Jerusalem; his mother's name was Jerusha daughter of Zadok. ³⁴ He did what was pleasing to the LORD, just as his father Uzziah had done. ³⁵ However, the shrines were not removed; the people continued to sacrifice and make offerings at the shrines. It was he who built the Upper Gate of the House of the LORD. ³⁶ The other events of Jotham's reign, and all his actions, are recorded in the Annals of the Kings of Judah. ³⁷ In those days, the LORD began to incite King Rezin of Aram and Pekah son of Remaliah against Judah. ³⁸ Jotham slept with his fathers, and he was buried with his fathers in the City of his ancestor David; his son Ahaz succeeded him as king.

d-d *Heb. "them."*

16 In the seventeenth year of Pekah son of Remaliah, Ahaz son of King Jotham of Judah became king. [2] Ahaz was twenty years old when he became king, and he reigned sixteen years in Jerusalem. He did not do what was pleasing to the LORD his God, as his ancestor David had done, [3] but followed the ways of the kings of Israel. He even consigned his son to the fire, in the abhorrent fashion of the nations which the LORD had dispossessed before the Israelites. [4] He sacrificed and made offerings at the shrines, on the hills, and under every leafy tree.

[5] Then King Rezin of Aram and King Pekah son of Remaliah of Israel advanced on Jerusalem for battle. They besieged Ahaz, but could not overcome [him]. [6] At that time King Rezin of Aram recovered Elath for Aram;[a] he drove out the Judites from Elath, and Edomites came to Elath and settled there, as is still the case.

[7] Ahaz sent messengers to King Tiglath-pileser of Assyria to say, "I am your servant and your son; come and deliver me from the hands of the king of Aram and from the hands of the king of Israel, who are attacking me." [8] Ahaz took the gold and silver that were on hand in the House of the LORD and in the treasuries of the royal palace and sent them as a gift to the king of Assyria. [9] The king of Assyria responded to his request; the king of Assyria marched against Damascus and captured it. He deported [b]its inhabitants[-b] to Kir and put Rezin to death.

[10] When King Ahaz went to Damascus to greet King Tilgath-pileser of Assyria, he saw the altar in Damascus. King Ahaz sent the priest Uriah a sketch of the altar and a detailed plan of its construction. [11] The priest Uriah did just as King Ahaz had instructed him from Damascus; the priest Uriah built the altar before King Ahaz returned from Damascus. [12] When the king returned from Damascus, and when the king saw the altar, the king drew near the altar, ascended it, [13] and offered his burnt offering and meal offering; he poured his libation, and he dashed the blood of his offering of well-being against the altar. [14] As for

[a] *Emendation yields "Edom."*
[b-b] *Heb. "it."*

the bronze altar which had been before the LORD, he moved it from its place in front of the Temple, ^{c-}between the [new] altar and the House of the LORD,^{-c} and placed it on the north side of the [new] altar. ¹⁵ And King Ahaz commanded the priest Uriah: "On the great^d altar you shall offer the morning burnt offering and the evening meal offering and the king's burnt offering and his meal offering, with the burnt offerings of all the people of the land, their meal offerings and their libations. And against it you shall dash the blood of all the burnt offerings and all the blood of the sacrifices. And I will decide^e about the bronze altar."^e ¹⁶ Uriah did just as King Ahaz commanded.

¹⁷ King Ahaz cut off the insets—the laver-stands—and removed the lavers from them. He also removed the tank from the bronze oxen that supported it and set it on a stone pavement—¹⁸ on account of the king of Assyria.^f He also extended to the House of the LORD ^{c-}the sabbath passage which had been built in the palace and the king's outer entrance.^{-c}

¹⁹ The other events of Ahaz's reign, and his actions, are recorded in the Annals of the Kings of Judah. ²⁰ Ahaz slept with his fathers and was buried with his fathers in the City of David; his son Hezekiah succeeded him as king.

17 In the twelfth year of King Ahaz of Judah, Hoshea son of Elah became king over Israel in Samaria—for nine years. ² He did what was displeasing to the LORD, though not as much as the kings of Israel who preceded him. ³ King Shalmaneser marched against him, and Hoshea became his vassal and paid him tribute. ⁴ But the king of Assyria caught Hoshea in an act of treachery: he had sent envoys to King So of Egypt, and he had not paid the tribute to the king of Assyria, as in previous years. And the king of Assyria arrested him and put him in prison. ⁵ Then the king of Assyria marched against the whole land; he came to Samaria and besieged it for three years. ⁶ In the ninth year of Hoshea, the king of Assyria captured Samaria. He deported the Israelites to As-

^{c-c} *Meaning of Heb. uncertain.*
^d *I.e. the new one.*
^e *I.e. the old one, cf. v.14.*
^f *I.e. because of the metal given him in tribute.*

syria and settled them in Halah, at the [River] Habor, at the River Gozan, and in the towns of Media.

[7] This happened because the Israelites sinned against the LORD their God, who had freed them from the land of Egypt, from the hand of Pharaoh king of Egypt. They worshiped other gods [8] and followed the customs of the nations which the LORD had dispossessed before the Israelites and the customs which the kings of Israel had practiced. [9] The Israelites committed[a] against the LORD their God acts which were not right: They built for themselves shrines in all their settlements, from watchtowers to fortified cities; [10] they set up pillars and sacred posts for themselves on every lofty hill and under every leafy tree; [11] and they offered sacrifices there, at all the shrines, like the nations whom the LORD had driven into exile before them. They committed wicked acts to vex the LORD, [12] and they worshiped fetishes concerning which the LORD had said to them, "You must not do this thing."

[13] The LORD warned Israel and Judah by every prophet [and] every seer, saying: "Turn back from your wicked ways, and observe My commandments and My laws, according to all the Teaching that I commanded your fathers and that I transmitted to you through My servants the prophets." [14] But they did not obey; they stiffened their necks, like their fathers who did not have faith in the LORD their God; [15] they spurned His laws and the covenant which He had made with their fathers, and the warnings He had given them. They went after delusion and were deluded; [they imitated] the nations that were about them, which the LORD had forbidden them to emulate. [16] They rejected all the commandments of the LORD their God; they made molten idols for themselves—two calves—and they made a sacred post and they bowed down to all the host of heaven, and they worshiped Baal. [17] They consigned their sons and daughters to the fire; they practiced augury and divination, and gave themselves over to what was displeasing to the LORD and vexed Him. [18] The LORD was incensed at Israel and He banished them from His presence; none was left but the tribe of Judah alone.

[a] *Meaning of Heb. uncertain.*

¹⁹ Nor did Judah keep the commandments of the LORD their God; they followed the customs that Israel had practiced. ²⁰ So the LORD spurned all the offspring of Israel, and He afflicted them and delivered them into the hands of plunderers, and finally He cast them out from His presence.

²¹ For Israel broke away from the House of David, and they made Jeroboam son of Nebat king. Jeroboam caused Israel to stray from the LORD and to commit great sin, ²² and the Israelites persisted in all the sins which Jeroboam had committed; they did not depart from them. ²³ In the end, the LORD removed Israel from His presence, as He had warned them through all His servants the prophets. So the Israelites were deported from their land to Assyria, as is still the case.

²⁴ The king of Assyria brought [people] from Babylon, Cuthah, Avva, Hamath and Sepharvaim, and he settled them in the towns of Samaria in place of the Israelites; they took possession of Samaria and dwelt in its towns. ²⁵ When they first settled there, they did not worship the LORD; so the LORD sent lions against them which killed some of them. ²⁶ They said to the king of Assyria: "The nations which you deported and resettled in the towns of Samaria do not know the rules of the God of the land; therefore He has let lions loose against them which are killing them—for they do not know the rules of the God of the land." ²⁷ The king of Assyria gave an order: "Send there one of the priests whom you have deported; let him^b go and dwell there, and let him teach them the practices of the God of the land." ²⁸ So one of the priests whom they had exiled from Samaria came and settled in Bethel; he taught them how to worship the LORD. ²⁹ However, each nation continued to make its own gods and to set them up in the cult places which had been made by the people of Samaria; each nation [set them up] in the towns in which it lived. ³⁰ The Babylonians made Succoth-benoth, and the men of Kuth made Nergal, and the men of Hamath made Ashima, ³¹ and the Avvites made Nibhaz and Tartak; and the Sepharvites burned

^b *Heb. "them."*

their children [as offerings] to Adrammelech and Anamelech, the gods of Sepharvaim. [32] They worshiped the LORD, but they also appointed from their own ranks priests of the shrines, who officiated for them in the cult places. [33] They worshiped the LORD, while serving their own gods according to the practices of the nations from which they had been deported. [34] To this day, they follow their former practices. They do not worship the LORD [properly]. They do not follow the laws and practices, the Teaching and Instruction which the LORD enjoined upon the descendants of Jacob—who was given the name Israel—[35] with whom He made a covenant and whom He commanded: "You shall worship no other gods; you shall not bow down to them nor serve them nor sacrifice to them. [36] You must worship only the LORD your God, who brought you out of the land of Egypt with great might and with an outstretched arm: to Him alone shall you bow down and to Him alone shall you sacrifice. [37] You shall observe faithfully, all your days, the laws and the practices, the Teaching and Instruction which I[c] wrote down for you; do not worship other gods. [38] Do not forget the covenant that I made with you; do not worship other gods. [39] Worship only the LORD your God, and He will save you from the hands of all your enemies." [40] But they did not obey; they continued their former practices. [41] Those nations worshiped the LORD, but they also served their idols. To this day their children and their children's children do as their ancestors did.

18

In the third year of King Hoshea son of Elah of Israel, Hezekiah son of King Ahaz of Judah became king. [2] He was twenty-five years old when he became king, and he reigned in Jerusalem twenty-nine years; his mother's name was Abi[a] daughter of Zechariah. [3] He did what was pleasing to the LORD, just as his father David had done. [4] He abolished the shrines and smashed the pillars and cut down the sacred post. He also broke into pieces the bronze serpent which Moses had made, for until

[c] *Heb. "He."*

[a] *II Chron. 29.1 reads "Abijah."*

that time the Israelites had been offering sacrifices to it; it was called Nehushtan. [5] He trusted only in the LORD the God of Israel; there was none like him among all the kings of Judah after him, nor among those before him. [6] He clung to the LORD; he did not turn away from following Him, but kept the commandments which the LORD had given to Moses. [7] And the LORD was always with him; he was successful wherever he turned. He rebelled against the king of Assyria and would not serve him. [8] He overran Philistia as far as Gaza and its border areas, from watchtower to fortified town.

[9] In the fourth year of King Hezekiah, which was the seventh year of King Hoshea son of Elah of Israel, King Shalmaneser of Assyria marched against Samaria and besieged it, [10] and he[b] captured it at the end of three years. In the sixth year of Hezekiah, which was the ninth year of King Hoshea of Israel, Samaria was captured; [11] and the king of Assyria deported the Israelites to Assyria. He [c]settled them in[c] Halah, along the Habor [and] the River Gozan, and in the towns of Media.[12] [This happened] because they did not obey the LORD their God; they transgressed His covenant—all that Moses the servant of the LORD had commanded. They did not obey and they did not fulfill it.

[13] In the fourteenth year of King Hezekiah, King Sennacherib of Assyria marched against all the fortified towns of Judah and seized them. [14] King Hezekiah sent this message to the king of Assyria at Lachish: "I have done wrong; withdraw from me; and I shall bear whatever you impose on me." So the king of Assyria imposed upon King Hezekiah of Judah a payment of three hundred talents of silver and thirty talents of gold. [15] Hezekiah gave him all the silver that was on hand in the House of the LORD and in the treasuries of the palace. [16] At that time Hezekiah cut down the doors and the doorposts[d] of the Temple of the LORD, which King Hezekiah had overlaid [with gold], and gave them to the king of Assyria.

[17] But the king of Assyria sent [e]the Tartan, the Rabsaris, and

---

[b] So some mss. and ancient versions; most mss. and editions read "they."
[c-c] Lit. "led them to."
[d] Meaning of Heb. uncertain.
[e-e] Assyrian titles.

the Rabshakeh⁻ᵉ from Lachish with a large force to King Hezekiah in Jerusalem. They marched up to Jerusalem; and when they arrived, they took up a position near the conduit of the Upper Pool, by the road of the Fuller's Field. ¹⁸ They summoned the king; and Eliakim son of Hilkiah, who was in charge of the palace, Shebna the scribe, and Joah son of Asaph the recorder went out to them.

¹⁹ The Rabshakeh said to them, "You tell Hezekiah: Thus said the Great King, the King of Assyria: What makes you so confident? ²⁰ You must think that mere talk is counsel and valor for war! Look, on whom are you relying, that you have rebelled against me? ²¹ You rely, of all things, on Egypt, that splintered reed of a staff, which enters and punctures the palm of anyone who leans on it! That's what Pharaoh king of Egypt is like to all who rely on him. ²² And if you tell me that you are relying on the LORD your God, He is the very one whose shrines and altars Hezekiah did away with, telling Judah and Jerusalem, 'You must worship only at this altar in Jerusalem.' ²³ Come now, make this wager with my master, the king of Assyria: I'll give you two thousand horses if you can produce riders to mount them. ²⁴ So how could you refuse anything even to the deputy of one of my master's lesser servants, relying on Egypt for chariots and horsemen? ²⁵ And do you think I have marched against this land to destroy it without the LORD? The LORD Himself told me: Go up against that land and destroy it."

²⁶ Eliakim son of Hilkiah, Shebna, and Joah replied to the Rabshakeh, "Please, speak to your servants in Aramaic, for we understand it; do not speak to us in Judean in the hearing of the people on the wall." ²⁷ But the Rabshakeh answered them, "Was it to your master and to you that my master sent me to speak those words? It was precisely to the men who are sitting on the wall— who will have to eat their dung and drink their urine with you." ²⁸ And the Rabshakeh stood and called out in a loud voice in Judean: "Hear the words of the Great King, the King of Assyria. ²⁹ Thus said the king: Don't let Hezekiah deceive you, for he will

not be able to deliver you from my*f* hands. [30] Don't let Hezekiah make you rely on the LORD, saying: The LORD will surely save us: this city will not fall into the hands of the king of Assyria. [31] Don't listen to Hezekiah. For thus said the king of Assyria: Make your peace with me and come out to me,*g* so that you may all eat from your vines and your fig trees and drink water from your cisterns, [32] until I come and take you away to a land like your own, a land of grain [fields] and vineyards, of bread and wine, of olive oil and honey, so that you may live and not die. Don't listen to Hezekiah, who misleads you by saying, 'The LORD will save us.' [33] Did any of the gods of other nations save his land from the king of Assyria? [34] Where were the gods of Hamath and Arpad? Where were the gods of Sepharvaim, Hena, and Ivvah? [And] did they*h* save Samaria from me? [35] Which among all the gods of [those] countries saved their countries from me, that the LORD should save Jerusalem from me?" [36] But the people were silent and did not say a word in reply; for the king's order was: "Do not answer him." [37] And so Eliakim son of Hilkiah, who was in charge of the palace, Shebna the scribe, and Joah son of Asaph the recorder, came to Hezekiah with their clothes rent, and they reported to him what the Rabshakeh had said.

19

When King Hezekiah heard this, he rent his clothes, and covered himself with sackcloth, and went into the House of the LORD. [2] He also sent Eliakim, who was in charge of the palace, Shebna the scribe, and the senior priests, covered with sackcloth, to the prophet Isaiah son of Amoz. [3] They said to him, "Thus said Hezekiah: This day is a day of distress, of chastisement, and of disgrace. *a-*The babes have reached the birthstool, but the strength to give birth is lacking.*-a* [4] Perhaps the LORD your God will take note of all the words of the Rabshakeh, whom his master the king of Assyria has sent to blaspheme the living God, and will mete out judgment for the words that the LORD your God has heard—if you will offer up prayer for the surviving remnant."

f So several mss. and ancient versions; most mss. and editions read "his."
g I.e. to my representative the Rabshakeh.
h I.e. the gods of Samaria.

a-a I.e. the situation is desperate and we are at a loss.

⁵ When King Hezekiah's ministers came to Isaiah, ⁶ Isaiah said to them, "Tell your master as follows: Thus said the LORD: Do not be frightened by the words of blasphemy against Me that you have heard from the minions of the king of Assyria. ⁷ I will delude*ᵇ* him; he will hear a rumor and return to his land, and I will make him fall by the sword in his land."

⁸ The Rabshakeh, meanwhile, heard that [the king] had left Lachish; he turned back and found the king of Assyria attacking Libnah. ⁹ But [the king of Assyria] learned that King Tirhakah of Nubia had come out to fight him; so he again sent messengers to Hezekiah, saying, ¹⁰ "Tell this to King Hezekiah of Judah: Do not let your God, on whom you are relying, mislead you into thinking that Jerusalem will not be delivered into the hands of the king of Assyria. ¹¹ You yourself have heard what the kings of Assyria have done to all the lands, how they have annihilated them; and can you escape? ¹² Were the nations that my predecessors*ᶜ* destroyed —Gozan, Haran, Rezeph, and the Beth-edenites in Telassar— saved by their gods? ¹³ Where is the king of Hamath? And the king of Arpad? And the kings of Lair, Sepharvaim, Hena, and Ivvah?"

¹⁴ Hezekiah took the letter from the messengers and read it. Hezekiah then went up to the House of the LORD and spread it out before the LORD. ¹⁵ And Hezekiah prayed to the LORD and said, "O LORD of Hosts, Enthroned on the Cherubim! You alone are God of all the kingdoms of the earth. You made the heavens and the earth. ¹⁶ O LORD, incline Your ear and hear; open Your eyes and see. Hear the words that Sennacherib has sent to blaspheme the living God! ¹⁷ True, O LORD, the kings of Assyria have annihilated the nations and their lands, ¹⁸ and have committed their gods to the flames and have destroyed them; for they are not gods, but man's handiwork of wood and stone. ¹⁹ But now, O LORD our God, deliver us from his hands, and let all the kingdoms of the earth know that You alone, O LORD, are God."

²⁰ Then Isaiah son of Amoz sent this message to Hezekiah: "Thus said the LORD, the God of Israel: I have heard the prayer

ᵇ Lit. "put a spirit in."
ᶜ Lit. "fathers."

you have offered to Me concerning King Sennacherib of Assyria.
²¹ This is the word that the LORD has spoken concerning him:

"Fair Maiden Zion despises you,
She mocks at you;
Fair Jerusalem shakes
Her head at you.
²² Whom have you blasphemed and reviled?
Against whom made loud your voice
And haughtily raised your eyes?
Against the Holy One of Israel!
²³ Through your envoys you have blasphemed my Lord.
Because you thought,
'Thanks to my vast chariotry,
It is I who have climbed the highest mountains,
To the remotest parts of the Lebanon,
And have cut down its loftiest cedars,
Its choicest cypresses,
And have reached its ᵈ⁻remotest lodge,⁻ᵈ
ᵉ⁻Its densest forest.⁻ᵉ
²⁴ It is I who have drawnᶠ and drunk the waters
of strangers;
I have dried up with the soles of my feet
All the streams of Egypt.'
²⁵ Have you not heard? Of old
I planned that very thing,
I designed it long ago,
And now have fulfilled it.
And it has come to pass,
Laying waste fortified towns
In desolate heaps.
²⁶ Their inhabitants are helpless,
Dismayed and shamed.
They were but grass of the field

ᵈ⁻ᵈ *Isa. 37.24 reads "highest peak."*
ᵉ⁻ᵉ *Lit. "Its farmland forest;" exact meaning of Heb. uncertain.*
ᶠ *Or "dug"; meaning of Heb. uncertain.*

And green herbage,
Grass of the roofs that is blasted
Before the *^g*standing grain.*^{-g}*
²⁷ I know your stayings
And your goings and comings,
And how you have raged against Me.
²⁸ Because you have raged against Me,
And your tumult has reached My ears,
I will place My hook in your nose
And My bit between your jaws;
And I will make you go back by the road
By which you came.

²⁹ "And this is the sign for you:*^h* This year you eat what grows of itself, and the next year what springs from that; and in the third year, sow and reap, and plant vineyards and eat their fruit. ³⁰ And the survivors of the House of Judah that have escaped shall regenerate its stock below and produce boughs above.

³¹ For a remnant shall come forth from Jerusalem,
Survivors from Mount Zion.
The zeal of the LORD of Hosts
Shall bring this to pass.

³² Assuredly, thus said the LORD concerning the king of Assyria:

He shall not enter this city:
He shall not shoot an arrow at it,
Or advance upon it with a shield,
Or pile up a siege mound against it.
³³ He shall go back
By the way he came;
He shall not enter this city

— declares the LORD.

---

^{g-g} Emendation yields "east wind"; see note at Isa. 37.27.
^h I.e. Hezekiah.

³⁴ I will protect and save this city for My sake,
And for the sake of My servant David."

³⁵ That night an angel of the Lord went out and struck down
one hundred and eighty-five thousand in the Assyrian camp, and
the following morning they were all dead corpses.
³⁶ So King Sennacherib of Assyria broke camp and retreated,
and stayed in Nineveh. ³⁷ While he was worshiping in the temple
of his god Nisroch, his sons Adrammelech and Sarezer struck him
down with the sword. They fled to the land of Ararat, and his son
Esarhaddon succeeded him as king.

20 In those days Hezekiah fell dangerously ill. The prophet
Isaiah son of Amoz came and said to him, "Thus said the Lord:
Set your affairs in order, for you are going to die; you will not get
well." ² Thereupon Hezekiah turned his face to the wall and
prayed to the Lord. He said, ³ "Please, O Lord, remember how
I have walked before You sincerely and wholeheartedly, and have
done what is pleasing to You." And Hezekiah wept profusely.

⁴ Before Isaiah had gone out of the middle court, the word of
the Lord came to him: ⁵ "Go back and say to Hezekiah, the ruler
of My people: Thus said the Lord, the God of your father David:
I have heard your prayer, I have seen your tears. I am going to
heal you; on the third day you shall go up to the House of the
Lord. ⁶ And I will add fifteen years to your life. I will also rescue
you and this city from the hands of the king of Assyria. I will
protect this city for My sake and for the sake of My servant
David."—⁷ Then Isaiah said, "Get a cake of figs." And they got
one, and they applied it to the rash, and he recovered.—⁸ Hezekiah asked Isaiah, "What is the sign that the Lord will heal me
and that I shall go up to the House of the Lord on the third day?"
⁹ Isaiah replied, "This is the sign for you from the Lord that the
Lord will do the thing which He has promised: Shall^a the shadow
advance ten steps or recede ten steps?" ¹⁰ Hezekiah said, "It is

---

^a *Cf. Targum.*

easy for the shadow to lengthen ten steps, but not for the shadow to recede ten steps." [11] So the prophet Isaiah called to the LORD, and He made the shadow which had descended on the dial[b] of Ahaz recede ten steps.

[12] At that time, King Berodach-[c]baladan son of Baladan of Babylon sent [envoys with] a letter and a gift to Hezekiah, for he had heard about Hezekiah's illness. [13] [d-]Hezekiah heard about them[-d] and he showed them all his treasure-house—the silver, the gold, the spices, and the fragrant oil—and his armory, and everything that was to be found in his storehouses. There was nothing in his palace or in all his realm that Hezekiah did not show them. [14] Then the prophet Isaiah came to King Hezekiah. "What," he demanded of him, "did those men say to you? Where have they come to you from?" "They have come," Hezekiah replied, "from a far country, from Babylon." [15] Next he asked, "What have they seen in your palace?" And Hezekiah replied, "They have seen everything that is in my palace. There was nothing in my storehouses that I did not show them."

[16] Then Isaiah said to Hezekiah, "Hear the word of the LORD: [17] A time is coming when everything in your palace which your ancestors have stored up to this day will be carried off to Babylon; nothing will remain behind, said the LORD. [18] And some of your sons, your own issue, whom you will have fathered, will be taken to serve as eunuchs in the palace of the king of Babylon." [19] Hezekiah declared to Isaiah, "The word of the LORD that you have spoken is good." For he thought, "It means that [e-]safety is assured for[-e] my time."

[20] The other events of Hezekiah's reign, and all his exploits, and how he made the pool and the conduit and brought the water into the city, are recorded in the Annals of the Kings of Judah. [21] Hezekiah slept with his fathers, and his son Manasseh succeeded him as king.

---

[b] *Heb. "steps." A model of a dial with steps has been discovered in Egypt.*
[c] *Several mss. and the parallel Isa. 39.1 read "Merodach."*
[d-d] *Isa. 39.2 reads "Hezekiah was pleased by their coming."*
[e-e] *Lit. "there shall be safety and faithfulness in."*

21 Manasseh was twelve years old when he became king, and he reigned fifty-five years in Jerusalem; his mother's name was Hephzibah. ² He did what was displeasing to the LORD, following the abhorrent practices of the nations which the LORD had dispossessed before the Israelites. ³ He rebuilt the shrines which his father Hezekiah had destroyed; he erected altars for Baal and made a sacred post, as King Ahab of Israel had done. He bowed down to all the host of heaven and worshiped them, ⁴ and he built altars for them in the House of the LORD, of which the LORD had said, "I will establish My name in Jerusalem." ⁵ He built altars for all the hosts of heaven in the two courts of the House of the LORD. ⁶ He consigned his son to the fire; he practiced soothsaying and divination, and consulted ghosts and familiar spirits; he did much that was displeasing to the LORD, to vex Him. ⁷ The sculptured image of Asherah which he made, he placed in the House concerning which the LORD had said to David and to his son Solomon, "In this House and in Jerusalem, which I chose out of all the tribes of Israel, I will establish My name forever. ⁸ And I will not again cause the feet of Israel to wander from the land which I gave to their fathers, if they will but faithfully observe all that I have commanded them—all the Teachings with which My servant Moses charged them." ⁹ But they did not obey, and Manasseh led them astray to do greater evil than the nations which the LORD had destroyed before the Israelites. ¹⁰ Therefore the LORD spoke through His servants the prophets: ¹¹ "Because King Manasseh of Judah has done these abhorrent things—he has outdone in wickedness all that the Amorites did before his time —and because he led Judah to sin with his fetishes, ¹² assuredly, thus said the LORD, the God of Israel: I am going to bring such a disaster on Jerusalem and Judah that both ears of everyone who hears about it will tingle. ¹³ I will *-apply to Jerusalem the measuring line of Samaria and the weights of the House of Ahab;⁻ᵃ I will wipe Jerusalem clean as one wipes a dish and turns it upside

---

ᵃ⁻ᵃ *I.e. I will bring the same fate upon it.*

down. [14] And I will cast off the remnant of My own people and deliver them into the hands of their enemies. They shall be plunder and prey to all their enemies [15] because they have done what is displeasing to Me and have been vexing Me from the day that their fathers came out of Egypt to this day."

[16] Moreover, Manasseh put so many innocent persons to death that he filled Jerusalem [with blood] from end to end—besides the sin he committed in causing Judah to do what was displeasing to the LORD.

[17] The other events of Manasseh's reign, and all his actions, and the sins he committed, are recorded in the Annals of the Kings of Judah. [18] Manasseh slept with his fathers and was buried in the garden of his palace, in the garden of Uzza; and his son Amon succeeded him as king.

[19] Amon was twenty-two years old when he became king, and he reigned two years in Jerusalem; his mother's name was Meshullemeth daughter of Haruz of Jotbah. [20] He did what was displeasing to the LORD, as his father Manasseh had done. [21] He walked in all the ways of his father, worshiping the fetishes which his father had worshiped and bowing down to them. [22] He forsook the LORD, the God of his fathers, and did not follow the way of the LORD.

[23] Amon's courtiers conspired against him; and they killed the king in his palace. [24] But the people of the land put to death all who had conspired against King Amon, and the people of the land made his son Josiah king in his stead. [25] The other events of Amon's reign [and] his actions are recorded in the Annals of the Kings of Judah. [26] He was buried in his tomb in the garden of Uzza; and his son Josiah succeeded him as king.

22

Josiah was eight years old when he became king, and he reigned thirty-one years in Jerusalem. His mother's name was Jedidah daughter of Adaiah of Bozkath. [2] He did what was pleasing to the LORD and he followed all the ways of his ancestor David; he did not deviate to the right or to the left.

3 In the eighteenth year of King Josiah, the king sent the scribe Shaphan son of Azaliah son of the scribe Meshullam to the House of the LORD, saying, 4 "Go to the high priest Hilkiah and let him weigh*a* the silver which has been deposited in the House of the LORD, which the guards of the threshold have collected from the people. 5 And let it be delivered to the overseers of the work who are in charge at the House of the LORD, that they in turn may pay it out to the workmen that are in the House of the LORD, for the repair of the House: 6 to the carpenters, the laborers, and the masons, and for the purchase of wood and quarried stones for repairing the House. 7 However, no check is to be kept on them for the silver which is delivered to them, for they deal honestly."

8 Then the high priest Hilkiah said to the scribe Shaphan, "I have found a scroll of the Teaching in the House of the LORD." And Hilkiah gave the scroll to Shaphan, who read it. 9 The scribe Shaphan then went to the king and reported to the king: "Your servants have melted down the silver that was deposited in the House, and they have delivered it to the overseers of the work who are in charge at the House of the LORD." 10 The scribe Shaphan also told the king, "The high priest Hilkiah has given me a scroll"; and Shaphan read it to the king.

11 When the king heard the contents of the scroll of the Teaching, he rent his clothes. 12 And the king gave orders to the priest Hilkiah, and to Ahikam son of Shaphan, Achbor son of Michaiah, the scribe Shaphan, and Asaiah the king's minister: 13 "Go, inquire of the LORD on my behalf, and on behalf of the people, and on behalf of all Judah, concerning the words of this scroll that has been found. For great indeed must be the wrath of the LORD that has been kindled against us, because our fathers did not obey the words of this scroll to do all that has been prescribed for us."

14 So the priest Hilkiah, and Ahikam, Achbor, Shaphan, and Asaiah went to the prophetess Huldah—the wife of Shallum son of Tikvah son of Harhas, the keeper of the wardrobe—who was

---

a *Meaning of Heb. uncertain. Emendation yields "pour out," cf. v. 9.*

living in Jerusalem in the Mishneh,^b and they spoke to her. ¹⁵ She responded: "Thus said the LORD, the God of Israel: Say to the man who sent you to me: ¹⁶ Thus said the LORD: I am going to bring disaster upon this place and its inhabitants, in accordance with all the words of the scroll which the king of Judah has read. ¹⁷ Because they have forsaken Me and have made offerings to other gods and vexed Me with all their deeds, My wrath is kindled against this place and it shall not be quenched. ¹⁸ But say this to the king, who sent you to inquire of the LORD: Thus said the LORD, the God of Israel: As for the words which you have heard—¹⁹ because your heart was softened and you humbled yourself before the LORD when you heard what I decreed against this place and its inhabitants—that it will become a desolation and a curse—and because you rent your clothes and wept before Me, I for My part have listened— declares the LORD. ²⁰ Assuredly, I will gather you to your fathers and you will be laid in your tomb in peace. Your eyes shall not see all the disaster which I will bring upon this place." So they brought back the reply to the king.

23 At the king's summons, all the elders of Judah and Jerusalem assembled before him. ² The king went up to the House of the LORD, together with all the men of Judah and all the inhabitants of Jerusalem, and the priests and prophets—all the people, young and old. And he read to them the entire text of the covenant scroll which had been found in the House of the LORD. ³ The king stood ^aby the pillar^{-a} and solemnized the covenant before the LORD: that they would follow the LORD and observe His commandments, His injunctions, and His laws with all their heart and soul; that they would fulfill all the terms of this covenant as inscribed upon the scroll. And all the people ^bentered into^{-b} the covenant.

⁴ Then the king ordered the high priest Hilkiah, the priests of the second rank, and the guards of the threshold to bring out of

^b *A quarter in Jerusalem; cf. Zeph. 1.10.*
^{a-a} *Or "on a platform," cf. Targum.*
^{b-b} *Cf. Targum.*

the Temple of the LORD all the objects made for Baal and Asherah[c] and all the host of heaven. He burned them outside Jerusalem in the fields[d] of Kidron, and he removed the ashes to Bethel. 5 He suppressed the idolatrous priests whom the kings of Judah had appointed [e]to make offerings[-e] at the shrines in the towns of Judah and in the environs of Jerusalem, and those who made offerings to Baal, to the sun and moon and constellations —all the host of heaven. 6 He brought out the [image of] Asherah from the House of the LORD to the Kidron Valley outside Jerusalem, and burned it in the Kidron Valley; he beat it to dust and scattered its dust over the burial ground of the common people. 7 He tore down the cubicles of the male prostitutes in the House of the LORD, at the place where the women wove coverings[d] for Asherah.

8 He brought all the priests from the towns of Judah [to Jerusalem] and defiled the shrines where the priests had been making offerings—from Geba to Beer-sheba. He also demolished the shrines of the gates, which were at the entrance of the gate of Joshua, the city prefect—[d]which were on a person's left [as he entered] the city gate.[-d] 9 [f]The priests of the shrines, however, did not ascend the altar of the LORD in Jerusalem, but they ate unleavened bread along with their kinsmen.[f] 10 He also defiled Topheth, which is in the Valley of Ben-hinnom, so that no one might consign his son or daughter to the fire of Molech. 11 He did away with the horses that the kings of Judah had dedicated to the sun, [g]at the entrance[-g] of the House of the LORD, near the chamber of the eunuch Nathan-melech, which was in the precincts.[d] He burned the chariots of the sun. 12 And the king tore down the altars made by the kings of Judah on the roof by the upper chamber of Ahaz, and the altars made by Manasseh in the two courts of the House of the LORD. He [h]removed them quickly from there[-h] and scattered their rubble in the Kidron Valley. 13 The king also defiled the shrines facing Jerusalem, to the south

c For this goddess, cf. I Kings 18.19; ordinarily asherah is rendered "sacred post" e.g. II Kings 17.16.
d Meaning of Heb. uncertain.
e-e Lit. "and he offered."
f-f This verse may be understood in connection with vv. 21-23.
g-g Heb. "from entering."
h-h Heb. "ran from there." Emendation yields "smashed them there."

of the [i-]Mount of the Destroyer,[-i] which King Solomon of Israel had built for Ashtoreth, the abomination of the Sidonians, for Chemosh, the abomination of Moab, and for Milcom, the detestable thing of the Ammonites.[j] 14 He shattered their pillars and cut down their sacred posts and covered their sites with human bones.

15 As for the altar in Bethel [and] the shrine made by Jeroboam son of Nebat who caused Israel to sin—that altar, too, and the shrine as well, he tore down. He burned down the shrine and beat it to dust, and he burned the sacred post.

16 Josiah turned and saw the graves that were there on the hill; and he had the bones taken out of the graves and burned on the altar. Thus he defiled it, in fulfillment of the word of the LORD foretold by the man of God who foretold these happenings. 17 He asked, "What is the marker I see there?" And the men of the town replied, "That is the grave of the man of God who came from Judah and foretold these things that you have done to the altar of Bethel."[k] 18 "Let him be," he said, "let no one disturb his bones." So they left his bones undisturbed together with the bones of the prophet[l] who came from Samaria.[m]

19 Josiah also abolished all the cult places in the towns of Samaria, which the kings of Israel had built, vexing [the LORD]. He dealt with them just as he had done to Bethel: 20 He slew on the altars all the priests of the shrines who were there, and he burned human bones on them. Then he returned to Jerusalem.

21 The king commanded all the people, "Offer the passover sacrifice to the LORD your God as prescribed in this scroll of the covenant." 22 Now the passover sacrifice had not been offered in that manner in the days of the chieftains who ruled Israel, or during the days of the kings of Israel and the kings of Judah. 23 Only in the eighteenth year of King Josiah was such a passover sacrifice offered in that manner to the LORD in Jerusalem.

---

i-i *Heb.* har ha-mashhith: *a derogatory play on* har ha-mishhah *("Mount of Ointment");* Mishnah Middoth 2.4.
j *Cf. I Kings 11.5, 7.*
k *Cf. I Kings 13.2-3.*
l *See I Kings 13.31-32 and note "m" below.*
m *The prophet lived in Bethel which, in Josiah's time, was part of the Assyrian province of Samaria.*

24 Josiah also did away with [n-]the necromancers and the mediums,[-n] the idols and the fetishes—all the detestable things that were to be seen in the land of Judah and Jerusalem. Thus he fulfilled the terms of the Teaching recorded in the scroll which the priest Hilkiah had found in the House of the LORD. 25 There was no king like him before who turned back to the LORD with all his heart and soul and might, in full accord with the Teaching of Moses; nor did any like him arise after him.

26 However, the LORD did not turn away from His awesome wrath which had blazed up against Judah because of all the things Manasseh did to vex Him. 27 The LORD said, "I will also banish Judah from My presence as I banished Israel; and I will reject the city of Jerusalem which I chose and the House where I said My name would abide."

28 The other events of Josiah's reign, and all his actions, are recorded in the Annals of the Kings of Judah. 29 In his days, Pharaoh Neco, king of Egypt, marched against the king of Assyria[o] to the River Euphrates; King Josiah marched toward him, but when he confronted him at Megiddo, [Pharaoh Neco] slew him. 30 His servants conveyed his body in a chariot from Megiddo to Jerusalem, and they buried him in his tomb. Then the people of the land took Jehoahaz; they anointed him and made him king in place of his father.

31 Jehoahaz was twenty-three years old when he became king, and he reigned three months in Jerusalem; his mother's name was Hamutal daughter of Jeremiah of Libnah. 32 He did what was displeasing to the LORD, just as his fathers had done. 33 Pharaoh Neco imprisoned him in Riblah in the region of Hamath, to keep him from reigning in Jerusalem. And he imposed on the land an indemnity of one hundred talents of silver and a talent of gold. 34 Then Pharaoh Neco appointed Eliakim son of Josiah king in place of his father Josiah, changing his name to Jehoiakim. He took Jehoahaz and [p-]brought him[-p] to Egypt, where he died. 35 Jehoiakim gave Pharaoh the silver and the gold, and he made

n-n *Lit. "the ghosts and the familiar spirits."*
o *I.e. the Chaldean Empire; cf. Isa. 52.4 and note.*
p-p *So II Chron. 36.4; Heb. here "he came."*

an assessment on the land to pay the money demanded by Pharaoh. He exacted from the people of the land the silver and gold to be paid Pharaoh Neco, according to each man's assessment. 36 Jehoiakim was twenty-five years old when he became king, and he reigned eleven years in Jerusalem; his mother's name was Zebudah daughter of Pedaiah of Rumah. 37 He did what was displeasing to the LORD, just as his ancestors had done.

24

In his days, King Nebuchadnezzar of Babylon came up, and Jehoiakim became his vassal for three years. Then he turned and rebelled against him. 2 The LORD let loose against him the raiding bands of the Chaldeans, Arameans, Moabites, and Ammonites; He let them loose against Judah to destroy it, in accordance with the word which the LORD had spoken through His servants the prophets. 3 All this befell Judah at the command of the LORD, who banished [them] from His presence because of all the sins that Manasseh had committed, 4 and also because of the blood of the innocent which he shed. For he filled Jerusalem with the blood of the innocent, and the LORD would not forgive.

5 The other events of Jehoiakim's reign, and all of his actions, are recorded in the Annals of the Kings of Judah. 6 Jehoiakim slept with his fathers, and his son Jehoiachin succeeded him as king. 7 The king of Egypt did not venture out of his country again, for the king of Babylon had seized all the land that had belonged to the king of Egypt, from the Wadi of Egypt to the River Euphrates.

8 Jehoiachin was eighteen years old when he became king, and he reigned three months in Jerusalem; his mother's name was Nehushta daughter of Elnathan of Jerusalem. 9 He did what was displeasing to the LORD, just as his father had done. 10 At that time, the troops^a of King Nebuchadnezzar of Babylon marched against Jerusalem, and the city came under siege. 11 King Nebuchadnezzar of Babylon advanced against the city while his troops

---

^{a} *Heb. "servants."*

were besieging it. [12] Thereupon King Jehoiachin of Judah, along with his mother, and his courtiers, commanders, and officers, surrendered to the king of Babylon. The king of Babylon took him captive in the eighth year of his reign. [13] He carried off [b-]from Jerusalem[-b] all the treasures of the House of the LORD and the treasures of the royal palace; he stripped off all the golden decorations in the Temple of the LORD—which King Solomon of Israel had made—as the LORD had warned. [14] He exiled all of Jerusalem: all the commanders and all the warriors—ten thousand exiles—as well as all the craftsmen and smiths; only the poorest people in the land were left. [15] He deported Jehoiachin to Babylon; and the king's wives and officers and the notables of the land were brought as exiles from Jerusalem to Babylon. [16] All the able men, to the number of seven thousand—all of them warriors, trained for battle—and a thousand craftsmen and smiths were brought to Babylon as exiles by the king of Babylon. [17] And the king of Babylon appointed Mattaniah, Jehoiachin's[c] uncle, king in his place, changing his name to Zedekiah.

[18] [d]Zedekiah was twenty-one years old when he became king, and he reigned eleven years in Jerusalem; his mother's name was Hamutal daughter of Jeremiah of Libnah. [19] He did what was displeasing to the LORD, just as Jehoiakim had done. [20] Indeed, Jerusalem and Judah [e-]were a cause of anger for the LORD, so that[-e] He cast them out of His presence.

25 Zedekiah rebelled against the king of Babylon. [1] And in the ninth year of his[a] reign, on the tenth day of the tenth month, Nebuchadnezzar moved against Jerusalem with his whole army. He besieged it; and they built towers against it all around. [2] The city continued in a state of siege until the eleventh year of King Zedekiah. [3] By the ninth day [of the fourth month][b] the famine had become acute in the city; there was no food left for the common people.

[b-b] Heb. "from there."
[c] Heb. "his."
[d] For the rest of this book cf. Jer. 39 and 52.
[e-e] Meaning of Heb. uncertain.

[a] I.e. Zedekiah's.
[b] Cf. Jer. 52.6.

⁴ Then [the wall of] the city was breached. All the soldiers [left the city] by night through the gate between the double walls, which is near the king's garden—the Chaldeans were all around the city; and [the king] set out for the Arabah.ᶜ ⁵ But the Chaldean troops pursued the king, and they overtook him in the steppes of Jericho as his entire force left him and scattered. ⁶ They captured the king and brought him before the king of Babylon at Riblah; and they put him on trial. ⁷ They slaughtered Zedekiah's sons before his eyes; then Zedekiah's eyes were put out. He was chained in bronze fetters and he was brought to Babylon.

⁸ On the seventh day of the fifth month—that was the nineteenth year of King Nebuchadnezzar of Babylon—Nebuzaradan, the chief of the guards, an officer of the king of Babylon, came to Jerusalem. ⁹ He burned the House of the LORD, the king's palace, and all the houses of Jerusalem; he burned down ᵈ⁻the house of every notable person.⁻ᵈ ¹⁰ The entire Chaldean force that was with the chief of the guard tore down the walls of Jerusalem on every side. ¹¹ The remnant of the people that was left in the city, the defectors who had gone over to the king of Babylon —and the remnant of the population—were taken into exile by Nebuzaradan, the chief of the guards. ¹² But some of the poorest in the land were left by the chief of the guards, to be vinedressers and field hands.

¹³ The Chaldeans broke up the bronze columns of the House of the LORD, the stands, and the bronze tank that was in the House of the LORD; and they carried the bronze away to Babylon. ¹⁴ They also took all the pails, scrapers, snuffers, ladles, and all the other bronze vessels used in the service. ¹⁵ The chief of the guards took whatever was of gold and whatever was of silver: fire pans and sprinkling bowls. ¹⁶ The two columns, the one tank, and the stands which Solomon provided for the House of the LORD —all these objects contained bronze beyond weighing. ¹⁷ The one column was eighteen cubits high. It had a bronze capital above it; the height of the capital was three cubits, and there was

ᶜ *Hoping to escape across the Jordan.*
ᵈ⁻ᵈ *Meaning of Heb. uncertain.*

a meshwork [decorated] with pomegranates about the capital, all made of bronze. And the like was true of the other column with its meshwork.

18 The chief of the guards also took Seraiah, the chief priest, Zephaniah, the deputy priest, and the three guardians of the threshold. 19 And from the city he took a eunuch who was in command of the soldiers; five royal privy councillors who were present in the city; the scribe of the army commander, who was in charge of mustering the people of the land; and sixty of the common people who were inside the city. 20 Nebuzaradan, the chief of the guards, took them and brought them to the king of Babylon at Riblah. 21 The king of Babylon had them struck down and put to death at Riblah, in the region of Hamath.

Thus Judah was exiled from its land. 22 King Nebuchadnezzar of Babylon put Gedaliah son of Ahikam son of Shaphan in charge of the people whom he left in the land of Judah. 23 When the officers of the troops and their men heard that the king of Babylon had put Gedaliah in charge, they came to Gedaliah at Mizpah with Ishmael son of Nethaniah, Johanan son of Kareah, Seraiah son of Tanhumeth the Netophathite, and Jaazaniah son of the Maachite, together with their men. 24 Gedaliah reassured[e] them and their men saying, "Do not be afraid [f-]of the servants of the Chaldeans.[-f] Stay in the land and serve the king of Babylon, and it will go well with you."

25 In the seventh month, Ishmael son of Nethaniah son of Elishama, who was of royal descent, came with ten men and they struck down Gedaliah and he died; [they also killed] the Judeans and the Chaldeans who were present with him at Mizpah. 26 And all the people, young and old, and the officers of the troops set out and went to Egypt because they were afraid of the Chaldeans.

27 In the thirty-seventh year of the exile of King Jehoiachin of Judah, on the twenty-seventh day of the twelfth month, King Evil-merodach of Babylon, in the year he became king, [g-]took

e Lit. "took an oath to them."
f-f Jer. 40.9 reads "to serve the Chaldeans."
g-g Lit. "raised the head of."

note of·ᵍ King Jehoiachin of Judah and released him from prison. ²⁸ He spoke kindly to him, and gave him a throne above those of other kings who were with him in Babylon. ²⁹ His prison garments were removed, and [Jehoiachin] received regular rations by his favor for the rest of his life. ³⁰ A regular allotment of food was given him at the instance of the king—an allotment for each day —all the days of his life.

ישעיה
ISAIAH

יִשַׁעְיָה
ISAIAH

1 ¹ The prophecies of Isaiah son of Amoz, who prophesied concerning Judah and Jerusalem in the reigns of Uzziah, Jotham, Ahaz, and Hezekiah, kings of Judah.

² Hear, O heavens, and give ear, O earth,
For the LORD has spoken:
"I reared children and brought them up—
And they have rebelled against Me!
³ An ox knows its owner,
An ass its master's crib:
Israel does not know,
My people takes no thought."

⁴ Ah, sinful nation!
People laden with iniquity!
Brood of evildoers!
Depraved children!
They have forsaken the LORD,
Spurned the Holy One of Israel,
Turned their backs [on Him].

⁵ Why do you seek further beatings,
That you continue to offend?
Every head is ailing,
And every heart is sick.
⁶ From head to foot
No spot is sound:

All bruises, and welts,
And festering sores—
Not pressed out, not bound up,
Not softened with oil.
7 Your land is a waste,
Your cities burnt down;
Before your eyes, the yield of your soil
Is consumed by strangers—
A wasteland *-as overthrown by strangers!-a
8 Fair*b* Zion is left
Like a booth in a vineyard,
Like a hut in a cucumber field,
Like a city beleaguered.
9 Had not the LORD of Hosts
Left us some survivors,
We should be like Sodom,
Another Gomorrah.

10 Hear the word of the LORD,
You chieftains of Sodom;
Give ear to our God's instruction,
You folk of Gomorrah!
11 "What need have I of all your sacrifices?"
Says the LORD.
"I am sated with burnt offerings of rams,
And suet of fatlings,
And blood of bulls;
And I have no delight
In lambs and he-goats.
12 That you come to appear before Me—
Who asked that *c*-of you?
Trample My courts
13   no more;
Bringing oblations is futile,-c
Incense is offensive to Me.

a-a *Emendation yields "like Sodom overthrown."*
b *Lit. "Daughter."*
c-c *Others "of you, to trample My courts?/ 13 Bring no more vain oblations."*

New moon and sabbath,
Proclaiming of solemnities,
d-Assemblies with iniquity,-d
I cannot abide.
14 Your new moons and fixed seasons
Fill Me with loathing;
They are become a burden to Me,
I cannot endure them.
15 And when you lift up your hands,
I will turn My eyes away from you;
Though you pray at length,
I will not listen.
Your hands are stained with crime—
16 Wash yourselves clean;
Put your evil doings
Away from My sight.
Cease to do evil;
17 Learn to do good.
Devote yourselves to justice;
e-Aid the wronged.-e
Uphold the rights of the orphan;
Defend the cause of the widow.

18 "Come, e-let us reach an understanding-e
                                    —says the LORD.
Be your sins like crimson,
They can turn snow-white;
Be they red as dyed wool,
They can become like fleece."
19 If, then, you agree and give heed,
You will eat the good things of the earth;
20 But if you refuse and disobey,
f-You will be devoured [by] the sword.-f—
For it was the LORD who spoke.

d-d Septuagint "Fast and assembly"; cf. Joel 1.14.
e-e Meaning of Heb. uncertain.
f-f Or "You will be fed the sword."

²¹ Alas, she has become a harlot,
The faithful city
That was filled with justice,
Where righteousness dwelt—
But now murderers.
²² Your^g silver has turned to dross;
^{e-}Your wine is cut with water.^{-e}
²³ Your rulers are rogues
And cronies of thieves,
Every one avid for presents
And greedy for gifts;
They do not judge the case of the orphan,
And the widow's cause never reaches them.

²⁴ Assuredly, this is the declaration
Of the Sovereign, the LORD of Hosts,
The Mighty One of Israel:
"Ah, I will get satisfaction from My foes;
I will wreak vengeance on My enemies!
²⁵ I will turn My hand against you,
And smelt out your dross ^{h-}as with lye,^{-h}
And remove all your slag:
²⁶ I will restore your magistrates as of old,
And your counselors as of yore.
After that you shall be called
City of Righteousness, Faithful City."

²⁷ ⁱZion shall be saved in the judgment;
Her repentant ones, in the retribution.^j
²⁸ But rebels and sinners shall all be crushed,
And those who forsake the LORD shall perish.

²⁹ Truly, you^k shall be shamed
Because of the terebinths you desired,

^g *I.e. Jerusalem's.*
^{h-h} *Emendation yields "in a crucible"; cf. 48.10.*
ⁱ *Others "Zion shall be saved by justice,/Her repentant ones by righteousness."*
^j *For this meaning cf. 5.16; 10.22.*
^k *Heb. "they."*

And you shall be confounded
Because of the gardens you coveted.
30 For you shall be like a terebinth
Wilted of leaf,
And like a garden
That has no water,
31 ᶦ‑Stored wealth⁻ᶦ shall become as tow,
And he who amassed it a spark;
And the two shall burn together,
With none to quench.

2 The word that Isaiah son of Amoz prophesied concerning
Judah and Jerusalem.

2 In the days to come,
The Mount of the LORD's House
Shall stand firm above the mountains
And tower above the hills;
And all the nations
Shall gaze on it with joy.
3 And the many peoples shall go and shall say:
"Come,
Let us go up to the Mount of the LORD,
To the House of the God of Jacob;
That He may instruct us in His ways,
And that we may walk in His paths."
For instruction shall come forthᵃ from Zion,
The word of the LORD from Jerusalem.
4 Thus He will judge among the nations
And arbitrate for the many peoples,
And they shall beat their swords into plowsharesᵇ
And their spears into pruning hooks:
Nation shall not take up

ᶦ⁻ᶦ Connecting hason with hasan "store" (23.18) and hosen "treasure" (33.6).
ᵃ I.e. oracles will be obtainable.
ᵇ More exactly, the iron points with which wooden plows were tipped.

Sword against nation;
They shall never again know[c] war.

⁵ O House of Jacob!
Come, let us walk
By the light of the LORD.
⁶ For you have forsaken [the ways of] your people,
O House of Jacob!
[d]For they are full [of practices] from the East,
And of soothsaying like the Philistines;
They abound in customs[e] of the aliens.[-d]
⁷ Their land is full of silver and gold,
There is no limit to their treasures;
Their land is full of horses,
There is no limit to their chariots.
⁸ And their land is full of idols;
They bow down to the work of their hands,
To what their own fingers have wrought.
⁹ But man shall be humbled,
And mortal brought low—
[f]Oh, do not forgive them![-f]

¹⁰ Go deep into the rock,
Bury yourselves in the ground,
Before the terror of the LORD
And His dread majesty!
¹¹ Man's haughty look shall be brought low,
And the pride of mortals shall be humbled.
None but the LORD shall be
Exalted in that day.

¹² For the LORD of Hosts has ready a day
Against all that is proud and arrogant,
Against all that is lofty—so that it is brought low:
¹³ Against all the cedars of Lebanon,

---

[c] *Cf. Judg. 3.2.*
[d-d] *Emendation yields "For they are full of divination/And have abundance of soothsaying,/ Like Philistines/And like alien folk."*
[e] *Cf. Targum; lit. "children."*
[f-f] *Meaning of Heb. uncertain. Emendation yields "And their idols with them"; cf. vv. 17-21.*

Tall and stately,
And all the oaks of Bashan;
¹⁴ Against all the high mountains
And all the lofty hills;
¹⁵ Against every soaring tower
And every mighty wall;
¹⁶ Against all the ᵍˉships of Tarshishˉᵍ
And all the gallant barks.
¹⁷ Then man's haughtiness shall be humbled
And the pride of man brought low.
None but the LORD shall be
Exalted in that day.

¹⁸ As for idols, they shall vanish completely.
¹⁹ And men shall enter caverns in the rock
And hollows in the ground—
Before the terror of the LORD
And His dread majesty,
When He comes forth to overawe the earth.

²⁰ On that day, men shall fling away,
To the ʰ-flying foxesˉʰ and the bats,
The idols of silver
And the idols of gold
Which they made for worshiping.
²¹ And they shall enter the clefts in the rocks
And the crevices in the cliffs,
Before the terror of the LORD
And His dread majesty,
When He comes forth to overawe the earth.

²² Oh, cease to glorify man,
Who has only a breath in his nostrils!
For by what does he merit esteem?

ᵍ⁻ᵍ *Probably a type of large ship.*
ʰ⁻ʰ *Exact meaning of Heb. uncertain.*

3 For lo!
The Sovereign LORD of Hosts
Will remove from Jerusalem and from Judah
Prop and stay,
Every prop of food
And every prop of water:ª
² Soldier and warrior,
Magistrate and prophet,
Augur and elder;
³ Captain of fifty,
Magnate and counselor,
Skilled artisan and expert enchanter;ᵇ
⁴ And Heᶜ will make boys their rulers,
And babes shall govern them.
⁵ So the people shall oppress one another—
Each oppressing his fellow:
The young shall bully the old,
And the despised [shall bully] the honored.

⁶ For should a man seize his brother,
ᵈ⁻In whose father's house there is clothing:⁻ᵈ
"Come, be a chief over us,
And let this ruinᵉ be under your care,"
⁷ The other will thereupon protest,
"I will not be a dresser of wounds,
With no food or clothing in my own house.
You shall not make me chief of a people!"

⁸ Ah, Jerusalem has stumbled,
And Judah has fallen,
Because by word and deed
They insult the LORD,
Defying His majestic glance.

ª *Emendation yields "clothing"; cf. v. 7; 4.1.*
ᵇ *Emendation yields "craftsman."*
ᶜ *Heb. "I."*
ᵈ⁻ᵈ *Emendation yields "His father's son, saying . . . ."*
ᵉ *Meaning of Heb. uncertain. Emendation yields "wound."*

⁹ Their partiality in judgment*ᶠ* accuses them;
They avow their sins like Sodom,
They do not conceal them.
Woe to them! For ill
Have they served themselves.
¹⁰ (Hail*ᵍ* the just man, for he shall fare well;
He shall eat the fruit of his works.
¹¹ Woe to the wicked man, for he shall fare ill;
As his hands have dealt, so shall it be done to him.)
¹² My people's rulers are babes,
It is governed by women.*ʰ*
O my people!
Your leaders are misleaders;
They have confused the course of your paths.

¹³ The LORD stands up to plead a cause,
He rises to champion peoples.*ⁱ*
¹⁴ The LORD will bring this charge
Against the elders and officers of His people:
"It is you who have ravaged the vineyard;
That which was robbed from the poor is in your houses.
¹⁵ How dare you crush My people
And grind the faces of the poor?"
                              —says my Lord GOD of Hosts.

¹⁶ The LORD said:
"Because the daughters of Zion
Are so vain
And walk with *ʲ*heads thrown back,*ʲ*
With roving eyes,
And with mincing gait,
Making a tinkling with their feet"—
¹⁷ My Lord will bare*ᵏ* the pates

ᶠ So Targum; cf. Deut. 1.17.
ᵍ Emendation yields "Happy is."
ʰ Emendation yields "boys"; cf. v. 4 (and v. 5).
ⁱ Septuagint "His people"; cf. vv. 14, 15.
ʲ⁻ʲ Lit. "throats bent back."
ᵏ So Saadia. To bare a woman's head in public was an intolerable humiliation: cf. Mishnah Baba Kamma 8.6.

Of the daughters of Zion,
The LORD will uncover their heads.

18 In that day, my LORD will strip off the finery[l] of the anklets, the fillets, and the crescents; 19 of the eardrops, the bracelets, and the veils; 20 the turbans, the armlets, and the sashes; of the talismans and the amulets; 21 the signet rings and the nose rings; 22 of the festive robes, the mantles, and the shawls; the purses, 23 the lace gowns, and the linen vests; and the kerchiefs and the capes.

24 And then—
Instead of perfume, there shall be rot;
And instead of an apron, a rope;
Instead of a diadem of beaten-work,
A shorn head;
Instead of a rich robe,
A girding of sackcloth;
[m-]A burn instead of beauty.[-m]

25 Her[n] men shall fall by the sword,
Her fighting manhood in battle;
26 And her gates shall lament and mourn,
And [o-]she shall be emptied,[-o]
Shall sit on the ground.

4 In that day, seven women shall take hold of one man, saying,
"We will eat our own food
And wear our own clothes;
Only let us be called by your name—
Take away our disgrace!"

---

[l] Many of the articles named in vv. 18-24 cannot be identified with certainty.
[m-m] The complete Isaiah scroll from Qumran, hereafter 1QIs[a], reads "For shame shall take the place of beauty"; cf. note k.
[n] I.e. Zion's; cf. vv. 16, 17; Heb. "your."
[o-o] Meaning of Heb. uncertain. Emendation yields "her wall"; cf. Lam. 2.8.

2 ^aIn that day,
The radiance of the LORD
Will lend beauty and glory,
And the splendor of ^{b-}the land^{-b}
[Will give] dignity and majesty,
To the survivors of Israel.
3 And those who remain in Zion
And are left in Jerusalem—
All who are inscribed for life in Jerusalem—
Shall be called holy.

4 When my Lord has washed away
The filth of ^{c-}the daughters of Zion,^{-c}
And from Jerusalem's midst
Has rinsed out her infamy—
In a spirit of judgment
And in a spirit of purging

5 the LORD will create^d over the whole shrine and meeting place
of Mount Zion cloud by day and smoke with a glow of flaming fire
by night. Indeed, over ^{e-}all the glory^{-e} shall hang a canopy, 6 which
shall serve as a pavilion for shade from heat by day and for shelter
and protection against drenching rain.

5

Let me sing for my beloved
A song of my lover about his vineyard.

My beloved had a vineyard
^{a-}On a fruitful hill.^{-a}
2 He broke the ground, cleared it of stones,
And planted it with choice vines.

---

^a *For the interpretation of this verse cf. 28.5. For "radiance," cf. Septuagint and the Syriac*
semha, *and for "splendor," cf. the meaning of* peri *in 10.12.*
^{b-b} *Emendation yields "my Lord"; cf. the parallelism (in reverse order) in 3.17.*
^{c-c} *Emendation yields "Daughter Zion," i.e. Zion personified; cf. 1.8 and note.*
^d *Emendation yields "spread"; cf. Ps. 105.39.*
^{e-e} *Emendation yields "His whole shrine."*

^{a-a} *Meaning of Heb. uncertain.*

He built a watchtower inside it,
He even hewed a wine press in it;
For he hoped it would yield grapes.
Instead, it yielded wild grapes.
³ "Now, then,
Dwellers of Jerusalem
And men of Judah,
You be the judges
Between Me and My vineyard:
⁴ What more could have been done for My vineyard
That I failed to do in it?
Why, when I hoped it would yield grapes,
Did it yield wild grapes?

⁵ "Now I am going to tell you
What I will do to My vineyard:
I will remove its hedge,
That it may be ravaged;
I will break down its wall,
That it may be trampled.
⁶ And I will *ᵃ⁻*make it a desolation;⁻ᵃ
It shall not be pruned or hoed,
And it shall be overgrown with briers and thistles.
And I will command the clouds
To drop no rain on it."

⁷ For the vineyard of the LORD of Hosts
Is the House of Israel,
And the seedlings he lovingly tended
Are the men of Judah.
ᵇAnd He hoped for justice,
But behold, injustice;
For equity,
But behold, iniquity!

ᵇ *This sentence contains two word-plays: "And He hoped for* mishpaṭ,/*And there is* mispaḥ
(exact meaning uncertain);/For ṣedaqah,/*But there is* ṣeʻaqah *(lit. "outcry").*

⁸ Ah,
Those who add house to house
And join field to field,
Till there is room for none but you
To dwell in the land!
⁹ In my hearing [said] the LORD of Hosts:
Surely, great houses
Shall lie forlorn,
Spacious and splendid ones
Without occupants.
¹⁰ For ten acres of vineyard
Shall yield just one *bath*,ᶜ
And a field sown with a *homer* of seed
Shall yield a mere *ephah.*

¹¹ Ah,
Those who chase liquor
From early in the morning,
And till late in the evening
Are inflamed by wine!
¹² ᵈ-Who, at their banquets,
Have-ᵈ lyre and lute,
Timbrel, flute, and wine;
But who never give a thought
To the plan of the LORD,
And take no note
Of what He is designing.
¹³ Assuredly,
My people will suffer exile
For not giving heed,
Its multitude victims of hunger
And its masses parched with thirst.
¹⁴ Assuredly,
Sheol has opened wide its gullet
And parted its jaws in a measureless gape;

ᶜ *I.e. of wine. The* bath *was the liquid equivalent of the* ephah; *and the* homer *was ten*
baths *or* ephahs *(Ezek. 45.11).*
ᵈ⁻ᵈ *Emendation yields "Whose interests are" (* mish'ehem, *from* sha'ah *"to turn to," 17.7,8;*
31.1).

And down into it shall go
That splendor and tumult,
That din and revelry.
¹⁵ Yea, man is bowed,
And mortal brought low;
Brought low is the pride of the haughty.
¹⁶ And the LORD of Hosts is exalted by judgment,
The Holy God proved holy by retribution.
¹⁷ ^eThen lambs shall graze
As in their meadows,
And strangers shall feed
On the ruins of the stout.

¹⁸ Ah,
Those who haul sin with cords of falsehood
And iniquity as with cart ropes!
¹⁹ Who say,^f
"Let Him speed, let Him hasten His purpose,
If we are to give thought;
Let the plans of the Holy One of Israel
Be quickly fulfilled,
If we are to give heed."

²⁰ Ah,
Those who call evil good
And good evil;
Who present darkness as light
And light as darkness;
Who present bitter as sweet
And sweet as bitter!
²¹ Ah,
Those who are so wise—
In their own opinion;
So clever—
In their own judgment!

^e *Meaning of verse uncertain. Emendation yields "Then lambs shall graze/In the pasture of*
the fat [rams],/And kids shall feed/On the ranges of the stout [bucks]." The lambs and the
kids are the poor, and the rams and bucks are the rich oppressors (cf. Ezek. 34.17-22).
^f *By way of retort to verse 12.*

22 Ah,
Those who are so doughty—
As drinkers of wine,
And so valiant—
As mixers of drink!
23 Who vindicate him who is in the wrong
In return for a bribe,
And withhold vindication
From him who is in the right.

24 Assuredly,
As straw is consumed by a tongue of fire
And hay *g*shrivels as it burns,*g*
Their stock shall become like rot,
And their buds shall blow away like dust.
For they have rejected the instruction of the LORD of Hosts,
Spurned the word of the Holy One of Israel.

25 That is why
The LORD's anger was roused
Against His people,
Why He stretched out His arm against it
And struck it,
So that the mountains quaked,*h*
And its corpses lay
Like refuse in the streets.
Yet his anger has not turned back,
And His arm is outstretched still.
26 He will raise an ensign to a nation*i* afar,
Whistle to one at the end of the earth.
There it comes with lightning speed!
27 In its ranks, none is weary or stumbles,
They never sleep or slumber;
The belts on their waists do not come loose,
Nor do the thongs of their sandals break.

g-g Emendation yields "is burned by flame"; cf. 33.11-12; 47.14.
h An allusion to the destructive earthquake in the reign of King Uzziah: Amos 1.1; Zech. 14.5;
cf. Isa. 9.18a.
i Heb. "nations."

²⁸ Their arrows are sharpened,
And all their bows are drawn.
Their horses' hoofs are like flint,
Their chariot wheels like the whirlwind.
²⁹ Their roaring is like a lion's,
They roar like the great beasts;
When they growl and seize a prey,
They carry it off and none can recover it.

³⁰ But in that day, a roaring shall resound over him like that of
the sea*ʲ*; and then he shall look below and, behold,
Distressing darkness, with light;
Darkness, *ᵃ⁻*in its lowering clouds.*⁻ᵃ*

6 In the year that King Uzziah died, I beheld my Lord seated
on a high and lofty throne; and the skirts of His robe filled the
Temple. ² Seraphs stood in attendance on Him. Each of them had
six wings: with two he covered his face, with two he covered his
legs, and with two he would fly.

³ And one would call to the other,
"Holy, holy, holy!
The LORD of Hosts!
His presence fills all the earth!"

⁴ The doorposts*ᵃ* would shake at the sound of the one who
called, and the House kept filling with smoke. ⁵ I cried,

"Woe is me; I am lost!
For I am a man *ᵇ⁻*of unclean lips*⁻ᵇ*
And I live among a people
Of unclean lips;
Yet my own eyes have beheld
The King LORD of Hosts."

ʲ *I.e. the* LORD *will intervene and come to his aid. Cf. 29.6-7; 30.27. This verse may constitute
a transition between chapters 8 and 9.*

ᵃ *Meaning of Heb. uncertain.*
ᵇ⁻ᵇ *I.e. speaking impiety; cf. 9.16, and contrast "pure of speech (lit. 'lip')" in Zeph. 3.9.*

⁶ Then one of the seraphs flew over to me with a live coal, which he had taken from the altar with a pair of tongs.⁷ He touched it to my lips and declared,

> "Now that this has touched your lips,
> Your guilt shall depart
> And your sin be purged away."

⁸ Then I heard the voice of my Lord saying, "Whom shall I send? Who will go for us?" And I said, "Here am I; send me."
⁹ And He said, "Go, say to that people:
'Hear, indeed, but do not understand;
See, indeed, but do not grasp.'
¹⁰ Dull that people's mind,
Stop its ears,
And seal its eyes—
Lest, seeing with its eyes
And hearing with its ears,
It also grasp with its mind,
And repent and save*c* itself."

¹¹ I asked, "How long, my Lord?" And He replied:
"Till towns lie waste without inhabitants
And houses without people,
And the ground lies waste and desolate—
¹² For the LORD will banish the population—
And deserted sites are many
In the midst of the land.
¹³ "But while a tenth part yet remains in it, it shall repent. It shall be ravaged like the terebinth and the oak, of which stumps are left even when they are felled: its stump shall be a holy seed."

c Lit. "heal."

7 In the reign of Ahaz son of Jotham son of Uzziah, king of Judah, King Rezin of Aram and King Pekah son of Remaliah of Israel marched upon Jerusalem to attack it; but they were not able to attack it.

2 Now, when it was reported to the House of David that Aram had allied itself with Ephraim, their hearts and the hearts of their people trembled as trees of the forest sway before a wind. 3 But the LORD said to Isaiah, "Go out with your son Shear-jashub[a] to meet Ahaz at the end of the conduit of the Upper Pool, by the road of the Fuller's Field. 4 And say to him: Be firm and be calm. Do not be afraid and do not lose heart on account of those two smoking stubs of firebrands, on account of the raging of Rezin and his Arameans and the son of Remaliah.[b] 5 Because the Arameans—with Ephraim and the son of Remaliah—have plotted against you, saying, 6 'We will march against Judah and invade and conquer it, and we will set up as king in it the son of Tabeel,'[b] 7 thus said my Lord GOD:

It shall not succeed,
It shall not come to pass.
8 For the chief city of Aram is Damascus,
And the chief of Damascus is Rezin;
9 The chief city of Ephraim is Samaria,
And the chief of Samaria is the son of Remaliah.[c]
[d-]And in another sixty-five years,
Ephraim shall be shattered as a people.[-d]
If you will not believe, [e-]for you cannot be trusted[-e] . . . ."

10 The LORD spoke further to Ahaz: 11 "Ask for a sign from the LORD your God, anywhere down to Sheol or up to the sky." 12 But Ahaz replied, "I will not ask, and I will not test the LORD." 13 "Listen, House of David," [Isaiah] retorted, "is it not enough for you to treat men as helpless that you also treat my God as

---

[a] Meaning "(only) a remnant will turn back," i.e. repent; cf. 6.13;10.21.
[b] To refer to a person only as "the son of—" is slighting; cf. note at I Sam. 10.11.
[c] The thought is continued by 8.8b-10; cf. II Chron. 13.8-12.
[d-d] Brought down from v. 8 for clarity.
[e-e] Others "surely, you shall not be established."

helpless?[f] [14] Assuredly, my Lord will give you a sign of His own accord! Look, the young woman is with child and about to give birth to a son. Let her name him Immanuel.[g] ([15] By the time he learns to reject the bad and choose the good, people will be feeding on curds and honey.) [16] For before the lad knows to reject the bad and choose the good, the ground whose two kings you dread shall be abandoned. [17] The LORD will cause to come upon you and your people and your ancestral house such days as never have come since Ephraim turned away from Judah—that selfsame king of Assyria![h]

[18] "In that day, the LORD will whistle to the flies at the ends of the water channels of Egypt and to the bees in the land of Assyria; [19] and they shall all come and alight in the rugged wadis, and in the clefts of the rocks, and in all the thornbrakes, and in all the watering places.

[20] "In that day, my Lord will cut away with the razor that is hired beyond the Euphrates—with the king of Assyria[i]—the hair of the head and[j]the hair of the feet,[j] and it shall clip off the beard as well. [21] And in that day, each man shall save alive a heifer of the herd and two animals of the flock. [22] (And he shall obtain so much milk that he shall eat curds.) Thus everyone who is left in the land shall feed on curds and honey.

[23] "For in that day, every spot where there could stand a thousand vines worth a thousand shekels of silver[k] shall become a wilderness of thornbush and thistle. [24] One will have to go there with bow and arrows,[l] for the country shall be all thornbushes and thistles. [25] But the perils of thornbush and thistle shall not spread to any of the hills that could only be tilled with a hoe;[m] and here cattle shall be let loose, and [n]sheep and goats[n] shall tramp about."

[f] *By insisting on soliciting the aid of Assyria (see II Kings 16.7 ff.; cf. below, v. 20). "Treat as helpless" follows the translation of Saadia; cf. Gen. 19.11.*
[g] *Meaning "with us is God."*
[h] *Cf. note on v. 13.*
[i] *Who was hired by Ahaz; cf. notes on vv. 13 and 17.*
[j-j] *I.e. the pubic hair.*
[k] *I.e. all the best farm land, corresponding to the hairiest parts of the body; v. 20.*
[l] *Because of dangerous beasts.*
[m] *Marginal farm land, too steep for the plow, corresponding to areas of the body with scant hair.*
[n-n] *See note at Exod. 12.3.*

8 The LORD said to me, "Get yourself a large sheet and write on it *ᵃ*in common script*⁻ᵃ* 'For Maher-shalal-hash-baz';*ᵇ* ² and call reliable witnesses, the priest Uriah and Zechariah son of Jeberechiah, to witness for Me." ³ I was intimate with the prophetess,*ᶜ* and she conceived and bore a son; and the LORD said to me, "Name him Maher-shalal-hash-baz.*ᵇ* ⁴ For before the boy learns to call 'Father' and 'Mother,' the wealth of Damascus and the spoils of Samaria, *ᵈ*and the delights of Rezin and of the son of Remaliah,*⁻ᵈ* shall be carried off before the king of Assyria."

⁵ Again the LORD spoke to me, thus:
 ⁶ "Because that people has spurned
 The gently flowing waters of Siloam"*ᵉ*—
⁷ Assuredly,
My Lord will bring up against them
The mighty, massive waters of the Euphrates,
The king of Assyria and all his multitude.
It shall rise above all its channels,
And flow over all its beds,
⁸ And swirl through Judah like a flash flood
Reaching up to the neck.*ᶠ*

*ᵍ*But with us is God,
Whose wings are spread
As wide as your land is broad!
⁹ Band together, O peoples—you shall be broken!
Listen to this, you remotest parts of the earth:
Gird yourselves—you shall be broken;
Gird yourselves—you shall be broken!

ᵃ⁻ᵃ *Meaning of Heb. uncertain.*
ᵇ *I.e. "Pillage hastens, looting speeds," indicating that two cities are to be pillaged at an early date; see v. 4.*
ᶜ *I.e. Isaiah's wife.*
ᵈ⁻ᵈ *Brought up from v. 6 for clarity.*
ᵉ *The conduit—and later the tunnel—of Siloam conveyed into Jerusalem the waters of Gihon, which symbolize "the LORD of Hosts who dwells on Mount Zion" (v. 18). For the nature of the rejection see note at 7.13.*
ᶠ *I.e. Judah shall be imperiled, but, in contrast to Aram and Ephraim (v. 4), not destroyed.*
ᵍ *See note c at 7.9.*

¹⁰ Hatch a plot—it shall be foiled;
Agree on action—it shall not succeed.
For with us is God!

¹¹ For this is what the LORD said to me, when He took me by
the hand*h* and charged me not to walk in the path of that people:
¹² "'You must not call conspiracy*j*
What that people calls conspiracy,*j*
Nor revere what it reveres,
Nor hold it in awe.
¹³ None but the LORD of Hosts
Shall you account holy;
Give reverence to Him alone,
Hold Him alone in awe.
¹⁴ He shall be *k-*for a sanctuary,
A stone*-k* men strike against:
A rock men stumble over
For the two Houses of Israel,
And a trap and a snare for those
Who dwell in Jerusalem.
¹⁵ The masses shall trip over these
And shall fall and be injured,
Shall be snared and be caught.
¹⁶ Bind up the message,
Seal the instruction with My disciples."

¹⁷ So I will wait for the LORD, who is hiding His face from the
House of Jacob, and I will trust in Him. ¹⁸ Here stand I and the
children the LORD has given me as signs and portents in Israel
from the LORD of Hosts, who dwells on Mount Zion.

¹⁹ Now, should people say to you, "Inquire of the ghosts and
familiar spirits that chirp and moan; for a people may inquire of
its divine beings*l*—of the dead on behalf of the living—²⁰ for
instruction and message," surely, for one who speaks thus there

---

h I.e. singled me out; cf. 41.9, 13; 42.6; 45.1; Jer. 31.32 [31].
i The Heb. forms here and in vv. 13 and 19 are plural, to include the disciples (v. 16) and the children (v. 18).
j Meaning of Heb. uncertain. Emendation yields "holy"; cf. v. 13.
k-k Emendation yields ". . . for His holy domain (cf. Ps. 114.2)/A stone. . . ."
l I.e. the shades of the dead; cf. I Sam. 28.13.

shall be no dawn. [21] *m*-And he shall go about in it wretched and hungry; and when he is hungry, he shall rage and revolt against his king and his divine beings.-*m* He may turn his face upward [22] or he may look below, but behold,

Distress and darkness, *n*-with no daybreak;-*n*
Straitness and gloom, *n*-with no dawn.-*n*

[23] For *o*-if there were to be-*o* any break of day for that [land] which is in straits, only the former [king] would have brought abasement to the land of Zebulun and the land of Naphtali— while the later one would have brought honor to the Way of the Sea, the other side of the Jordan, and Galilee of the Nations.*p*

9

*a*The people that walked in darkness
Have seen a brilliant light;
On those who dwelt in a land of gloom
Light has dawned.
[2] You have magnified that nation,
Have given it great joy;
They have rejoiced before You
As they rejoice at reaping time,
As they exult
When dividing spoil.

[3] For the yoke that they bore
And the stick for their back—
The rod of their taskmaster—
You have broken as on the day of Midian.*b*
[4] Truly, all the boots put on *c*-to stamp with-*c*
And all the garments donned in infamy
Have been fed to the flames,

m-m *This sentence would read well after v. 22.*
n-n *Meaning of Heb. uncertain.*
o-o *So lQIsᵃ; the others have "there is not."*
p *Meaning of verse uncertain. The rendering here assumes that "the former [king]" refers to Pekah (cf. II Kings 15.29) and "the later" to Hoshea (ibid. 30). For the construction lu . . . ka'eth, see Judg. 13.23.*

ᵃ *See note j at 5.30.*
ᵇ *See Judg. 7-8.*
c-c *Meaning of Heb. uncertain; emendation yields "in wickedness"; cf. Targum.*

Devoured by fire.
⁵ For a child has been born to us,
A son has been given us.
And authority has settled on his shoulders.
He has been named
"The Mighty God is planning grace;*d*
The Eternal Father, a peaceable ruler"—
⁶ In token of abundant authority
And of peace without limit
Upon David's throne and kingdom,
That it may be firmly established
In justice and in equity
Now and evermore.
The zeal of the LORD of Hosts
Shall bring this to pass.

⁷ My Lord
*e*Let loose a word*e* against Jacob
And it fell upon Israel.
⁸ But all the people noted*f*—
Ephraim and the inhabitants of Samaria—
In arrogance and haughtiness:
⁹ "Bricks have fallen—
We'll rebuild with dressed stone;
Sycamores have been felled—
We'll grow cedars instead!"
¹⁰ So the LORD let *g*the enemies of Rezin*g*
Triumph over it
And stirred up its foes—
¹¹ Aram from the east
And Philistia from the west—
Who devoured Israel
With greedy mouths.

---

d As in 25.1.
e-e Septuagint reads "Let loose pestilence"; cf. Amos 4.10. In vv. 7-20 Isaiah alludes to and
   builds upon Amos 4.10-12.
f 1QIsᵃ reads "shouted."
g-g Emendation yields "its enemies."

Yet His anger has not turned back,
And His arm is outstretched still.

12 For the people has not turned back
To Him who struck it
And has not sought
The LORD of Hosts.
13 So the LORD will cut off from Israel
Head and tail,
Palm branch and reed,
In a single day.
14 Elders *h-*and magnates*-h*—
Such are the heads;
Prophets who give false instruction,
Such are the tails;*i*
15 That people's leaders have been misleaders,
So they that are led have been confused.
16 That is why my Lord
Will not spare*j* their youths,
Nor show compassion
To their orphans and widows;
For all are ungodly and wicked,
And every mouth speaks impiety.

17 Already wickedness has blazed forth like a
    fire
Devouring thorn and thistle.
It has kindled the thickets of the wood,
*k-*Which have turned into billowing smoke.*-k*

*l-*Yet His anger has not turned back,
And His arm is outstretched still.*-l*

---

h-h *Emendation yields "who practice partiality."*
i *Emendation yields "palm branches"; the elders and the prophets are the leaders, the people
are the led; cf. 3.1-2, 12.*
j *Cf. Arabic* samuha.
k-k *Meaning of Heb. uncertain.*
l-l *Moved down from v. 16 for clarity.*

¹⁸ By the fury of the LORD of Hosts,
The earth was shaken.[m]
Next, the people became like devouring fire:
No man spared his countryman.
¹⁹ They snatched on the right, but remained hungry,
And consumed on the left without being sated.
Each devoured the flesh of his [n]own kindred[n]—
²⁰ Manasseh Ephraim's, and Ephraim Manasseh's,[o]
And both of them against Judah![p]

Yet His anger has not turned back,
And His arm is outstretched still.

10 Ha!

Those who write out evil writs
And compose iniquitous documents,
² To subvert the cause of the poor,
To rob of their rights the needy of My people;
That widows may be their spoil,
And fatherless children their booty!
³ What will you do on the day of punishment,
When the calamity comes from afar?
To whom will you flee for help,
And how will you save your carcasses[a]
⁴ From collapsing under [fellow] prisoners,
From falling beneath the slain?

Yet His anger has not turned back,
And his arm is outstretched still.

⁵ Ha!
Assyria, rod of My anger,

---

[m] Cf. note at 5.25.
[n-n] Meaning of Heb. uncertain. Emendation yields "fellow"; cf. Targum.
[o] Alludes to the civil wars of II Kings 15.10, 14-16, 25.
[p] Cf. 7.1-9.

[a] Meaning of Heb. uncertain; for "carcasses," compare the rendering of kabod in v. 16;
22.18.

b-In whose hand, as a staff, is My fury!*-b*
6 I send him against an ungodly nation,
I charge him against a people that provokes Me,
To take its spoil and to seize its booty
And to make it a thing trampled
Like the mire of the streets.
7 But he has evil plans,
His mind harbors evil designs;
For he means to destroy,
To wipe out nations, not a few.
8 For he thinks,
"After all, *c*-I have kings as my captains!*-c*
9 Was Calno any different from Carchemish?
Or Hamath from Arpad?
Or Samaria from Damascus?
10 *d*-Since I was able to seize
The insignificant kingdoms,
Whose images exceeded
Jerusalem's and Samaria's,*-d*
11 Shall I not do to Jerusalem and her images
What I did to Samaria and her idols?"

12 But when my Lord has carried out all his purpose on Mount
Zion and in Jerusalem, He*e* will punish the majestic pride and
overbearing arrogance of the king of Assyria. 13 For he thought,
"By the might of my hand have I wrought it,
By my skill, for I am clever:
I have erased the borders of peoples;
I have plundered their treasures,
Even exiled their vast populations.*f*
14 I was able to seize, like a nest,
The wealth of peoples;
As one gathers abandoned eggs,
So *I* gathered all the earth:

---

b-b *Emendation yields "Who is a staff in the hand of My fury."*
c-c *Emendation yields "all the kingdoms fared alike!"*
d-d *Emendation yields "Since I was able to seize/Those kingdoms and their images,/Why is Jerusalem better than Samaria?"*
e *Heb. "I."*
f *According to vv. 6-7, Assyria was to plunder, but not to exile.*

Nothing so much as flapped a wing
Or opened a mouth to peep."

¹⁵ Does an ax boast over him who hews with it,
Or a saw magnify itself above him who wields it?
As though the rod swung him who lifts it,
As though the staff lifted the man^g!

¹⁶ Assuredly,
The Sovereign LORD of Hosts will send
A wasting away in its^h fatness;
And under its bodyⁱ shall burn
A burning like that of fire,
^jDestroying frame and flesh.
It shall be like a sick man who pines away.^j
¹⁷ Yea, the Light of Israel will be fire
And its Holy One flame,
Which will burn and consume its thorns
And its thistles in a single day,
¹⁸ And the mass of its scrub and its farm land.
¹⁹ What trees remain of its scrub
Shall be so few that a boy may record them.

²⁰ And in that day,
The remnant of Israel
And the escaped of the House of Jacob
Shall lean no more upon him that beats it,^k
But shall lean sincerely
On the LORD, the Holy One of Israel.
²¹ Only a remnant shall return,
Only a remnant of Jacob,
To Mighty God.
²² Even if your people, O Israel,
Should be as the sands of the sea,

^g Lit. "not-wood."
^h Presumably Israel's. These verses would read well after 9.16.
ⁱ Cf. note at v. 3.
^{j-j} Brought up from v. 18 for clarity.
^k I.e. upon Assyria (see v. 24). Ahaz's reliance on Assyria was interpreted by Isaiah as lack
of faith in the Lord; see 7.13 with note.

Only a remnant of it shall return.
Destruction is decreed;
Retribution comes like a flood!
23 For my Lord GOD of Hosts is carrying out
A decree of destruction upon all the land.

24 Assuredly, thus said my Lord GOD of Hosts: "O My people that dwells in Zion, have no fear of Assyria, who beats you with a rod and wields his staff over you as did the Egyptians. 25 For very soon My wrath will have spent itself, and *l*My anger that was bent on wasting them."*-l* 26 The LORD of Hosts will brandish a scourge over him as when He beat Midian at the Rock of Oreb,*m* and will wield His staff as He did over the Egyptians by the sea.

27 And in that day,
His burden shall drop from your back,
*n-*And his yoke from your neck;
The yoke shall be destroyed because of fatness.

28 He advanced upon Aiath,
He proceeded to Migron,
At Michmas he deposited his baggage.
29 They made the crossing;
"Geba is to be our night quarters!"*-n*
Ramah was alarmed;
Gibeah of Saul took to flight.
30 "Give a shrill cry, O Bath-gallim!
Hearken, Laishah!
Take up the cry, Anathoth!"
31 Madmenah ran away;
The dwellers of Gebim sought refuge.

l-l Presumably Assyria; meaning of Heb. uncertain. Emendation yields "My anger against the world shall cease."
m See Judg. 7.25.
n-n Emendation yields "And his yoke shall leave your neck./He came up from Jeshimon/ 28 By the ascent of Aiath,/He proceeded to Migron;/At Michmas he commanded his forces:/29 'Make the crossing;/Geba is to be our night quarters!' " Jeshimon is the southeast corner of the Jordan Valley, Nu. 21.20: 23.28; Aiath is elsewhere called Ai.

³² This same day at Nob
He shall stand and wave his hand.°

O mount of Fair Zion!
O hill of Jerusalem!
³³ Lo! The Sovereign LORD of Hosts
Will hew off the tree-crowns with an ax:
The tall ones shall be felled,
The lofty ones cut down:
³⁴ The thickets of the forest shall be hacked away with iron,
And the Lebanon trees shall fall ᵖ⁻in their majesty.⁻ᵖ

11 But a shoot shall grow out of the stump of Jesse,
A twig shall sprout from his stock.
² The spirit of the LORD shall alight upon him:
A spirit of wisdom and insight,
A spirit of counsel and valor,
A spirit of devotion and reverence for the LORD.
³ ᵃ⁻He shall sense the truth⁻ᵃ by his reverence for the LORD:
He shall not judge by what his eyes behold,
Nor decide by what his ears perceive.
⁴ Thus he shall judge the poor with equity
And decide with justice for the lowly of the land.
He shall strike down a landᵇ with the rod of his mouth
And slay the wicked with the breath of his lips.
⁵ Justice shall be the girdle of his loins,
And faithfulness the girdle of his waist.
⁶ The wolf shall dwell with the lamb,
The leopard lie down with the kid;
ᶜ⁻The calf, the beast of prey, and the fatling⁻ᶜ together,
With a little boy to herd them.
⁷ The cow and the bear shall graze,

° *I.e. the Assyrian king, arriving at Nob (close to Jerusalem), shall beckon his army onward;
cf. 13.2.*
ᵖ⁻ᵖ *Or "by the bronze," connecting Heb. 'addir with Akkadian* urudū, *"bronze."*

ᵃ⁻ᵃ *Lit. "His sensing (shall be)"; meaning of Heb. uncertain.*
ᵇ *Emendation yields "the ruthless."*
ᶜ⁻ᶜ *1QIsᵃ reads: "The calf and the beast of prey shall feed"; so too the Septuagint.*

Their young shall lie down together;
And the lion, like the ox, shall eat straw.
8 A babe shall play
Over a viper's hole,
And an infant pass*^d* his hand
Over an adder's den.
9 In all of *^e*My sacred mount*^{-e}*
Nothing evil or vile shall be done;
For the land shall be filled with devotion to the LORD
As water covers the sea.

10 In that day,
The stock of Jesse that has remained standing
Shall become a standard to peoples—
Nations shall seek his counsel,
And his abode shall be honored.

11 In that day, My Lord will apply His hand again to redeeming the other part*^f* of His people from Assyria—as also from Egypt, Pathros, Nubia, Elam, Shinar, Hamath, and the coastlands.

12 He will hold up a signal to the nations
And assemble the banished of Israel,
And gather the dispersed of Judah
From the four corners of the earth.

13 Then Ephraim's envy shall cease
And Judah's harassment shall end;
Ephraim shall not envy Judah,
And Judah shall not harass Ephraim.
14 They shall pounce on the back of Philistia to the west,
And together plunder the peoples of the east;
Edom and Moab shall be subject to them
And the children of Ammon shall obey them.

---

^d *Meaning of Heb. uncertain.*
^{e-e} *I.e. the Holy Land; cf. Exod. 15.17; Ps. 78.54.*
^f *I.e. the part outside the Holy Land; lit. "the rest that will remain."*

¹⁵ The LORD will dry up the tongue of the Egyptian sea.—He will raise His hand over the Euphrates with the might*d* of His wind and break it into seven wadis, so that it can be trodden dry-shod. ¹⁶ Thus there shall be a highway for the other part*f* of His people out of Assyria, such as there was for Israel when it left the land of Egypt.

12 In that day, you shall say:
"I give thanks to You, O LORD!
Although You were wroth with me,
Your wrath has turned back and You comfort me,
² Behold the God who gives me triumph!
I am confident, unafraid;
For Yah the LORD is my strength and might,*a*
And He has been my deliverance."

³ Joyfully shall you draw water
From the fountains of triumph,
⁴ And you shall say on that day:
"Praise the LORD, proclaim His name.
Make His deeds known among the peoples;
Declare that His name is exalted.
⁵ Hymn the LORD,
For He has done gloriously;
Let this be made known
In all the world!
⁶ Oh, shout for joy,
You who dwell in Zion!
For great in your midst
Is the Holy One of Israel."

ª *Others "song."*

13 The "Babylon" Pronouncement, a prophecy of Isaiah son of Amoz.

2 "Raise a standard upon a bare hill,
Cry aloud to them;
Wave a hand, and let them enter
The gates of the nobles!
3 I have summoned My purified guests
To execute My wrath;
Behold, I have called My stalwarts,
My proudly exultant ones."[a]

4 Hark! a tumult on the mountains—
As of[b] a mighty force;
Hark! an uproar of kingdoms,
Nations assembling!
The Lord of Hosts is mustering
A host for war.
5 They come from a distant land,
From the end of the sky—
The Lord with the weapons of His wrath—
To ravage all the earth!

6 Howl!
For the day of the Lord is near;
It shall come like havoc from Shaddai.[c]
7 Therefore all hands shall grow limp,
And all men's hearts shall sink;
8 And, overcome by terror,
They shall be seized by pangs and throes,
Writhe like a woman in travail.
They shall gaze at each other in horror,
Their faces [d]livid with fright.[-d]

---

[a] *The impending slaughter is spoken of as a sacrificial meal, for which the guests were notified to purify themselves ritually; cf. Zeph. 1.7.*
[b] *Meaning of Heb. uncertain.*
[c] *Traditionally rendered "the Almighty."*
[d-d] *Taking the root lhb as a variant of bhl: others "shall be faces of flame."*

⁹ Lo! The day of the LORD is coming
With pitiless fury and wrath,
To make the earth a desolation,
To wipe out the sinners upon it.
¹⁰ The stars and constellations of heaven
Shall not give off their light;
The sun shall be dark when it rises,
And the moon shall diffuse no glow.

¹¹ "And I will requite to the world its evil,
And to the wicked their iniquity;
I will put an end to the pride of the arrogant
And humble the haughtiness of tyrants.
¹² I will make people scarcer than fine gold,
And men than gold of Ophir."

¹³ Therefore ᵉ⁻shall heaven be shaken,⁻ᵉ
And earth leap out of its place,
At the fury of the LORD of Hosts
On the day of His burning wrath.
¹⁴ Then like gazelles that are chased,
And like sheep that no man gathers,
Each man shall turn back to his people,
They shall flee everyone to his land.
¹⁵ All who remain shall be pierced through,
All who ᶠ⁻are caught⁻ᶠ
Shall fall by the sword.
¹⁶ And their babes shall be dashed to pieces in their sight,
Their homes shall be plundered,
And their wives shall be raped.

¹⁷ "Behold,
I stir up the Medes against them,
Who do not value silver
Or delight in gold.
¹⁸ Their bows shall shatter the young;

ᵉ⁻ᵉ Lit. "I will shake heaven."
ᶠ⁻ᶠ Meaning of Heb. uncertain; emendation yields "flee."

They shall show no pity to infants,
They shall not spare the children."

19 And Babylon, glory of kingdoms,
Proud splendor of the Chaldeans,
Shall become like Sodom and Gomorrah
Overturned by God.
20 Nevermore shall it be settled
Nor dwelt in through all the ages.
No Arab shall pitch his tent there,
No shepherds make flocks lie down there.
21 But beasts*b* shall lie down there,
And the houses be filled with owls;*b*
There shall ostriches make their home,
And there shall goat-demons dance.
22 And jackals*b* shall abide in its castles
And dragons*b* in the palaces of pleasure.
Her hour is close at hand;
Her days will not be long.

14 But the LORD will pardon Jacob, and will again choose Israel, and will settle them on their own soil. And strangers shall join them and shall cleave to the House of Jacob. 2 For peoples shall take them*a* and bring them to their homeland; and the House of Israel shall possess them*b* as slaves and handmaids on the soil of the LORD. They shall be captors of their captors and masters to their taskmasters.

3 And when the LORD has given you rest from your sorrow and trouble, and from the hard service that you were made to serve, 4 you shall recite this song of scorn over the king of Babylon:

How is the taskmaster vanished,
How is oppression*c* ended!

a *I.e. the House of Jacob.*
b *I.e. the peoples.*
c *Reading* marhebah *with 1QIs*a *(cf. Septuagint). The traditional reading* madhebah *is of unknown meaning.*

⁵ The LORD has broken the staff of the wicked,
The rod of tyrants
⁶ That smote peoples in wrath
With stroke unceasing,
That belabored nations in fury
In relentless pursuit.

⁷ All the earth is calm, untroubled;
Loudly it cheers.
⁸ Even pines rejoice at your fate,
And cedars of Lebanon:
"Now that you have lain down,
None shall come up to fell us."

⁹ Sheol below was astir
To greet your coming—
Rousing for you the shades
Of all earth's chieftains,
Raising from their thrones
All the kings of nations.
¹⁰ All speak up and say to you,
"So you have been stricken as we were,
You have become like us!
¹¹ Your pomp is brought down to Sheol,
And the strains of your lutes!
Worms are to be your bed,
Maggots your blanket!"

¹² How are you fallen from heaven,
O Shining One, son of Dawn!ᵈ
How are you felled to earth,
O vanquisher of nations!

¹³ Once you thought in your heart,
"I will climb to the sky;

ᵈ *A character in some lost myth.*

381

Higher than the stars of God
I will set my throne.
I will sit in the mount of assembly,*
On the summit of Zaphon:*
¹⁴ I will mount the back of a cloud—
I will match the Most High."
¹⁵ Instead, you are brought down to Sheol,
To *the bottom of the Pit.*
¹⁶ They who behold you stare;
They peer at you closely:
"Is this the man
Who shook the earth,
Who made realms tremble,
¹⁷ Who made the world like a waste
And wrecked its towns,
*Who never released his prisoners to their homes?"
¹⁸ All the kings of nations
Were laid, every one, in honor*
Each in his tomb;
¹⁹ While you were left lying unburied,
Like loathsome carrion,*
Like a trampled corpse
[In] the clothing of slain gashed by the sword
Who sink to the very stones of the Pit.
²⁰ You shall not have a burial like them;
Because you destroyed *your country,
Murdered your people.*

Let the breed of evildoers
Nevermore be named!
²¹ Prepare a slaughtering block for his sons

ᶜ *I.e. the assembly of the gods in council.*
ᶠ *The abode of the gods; cf. Ps. 48.3.*
ᵍ⁻ᵍ *A region of the netherworld reserved for those who have not received decent burial; cf. Ezek. 32.21 ff.*
ʰ⁻ʰ *Emendation yields "Who chained to his palace gate/All the kings of nations?/Yet they were all laid in honor. . . ." The practice of chaining captive chieftains to gates is attested in Mesopotamia.*
ⁱ *So several ancient versions; cf. postbiblical neṣel, "Putrefying flesh or blood."*
ʲ⁻ʲ *Emendation yields ". . . countries,/Murdered peoples."*

Because of the guilt of their father.[k]
Let them not arise to possess the earth!
Then the world's face shall be covered with
  towns.

[22] I will rise up against them—declares the LORD of Hosts—and will wipe out from Babylon name and remnant, kith and kin—declares the LORD—[23] and I will make it a home of bitterns,[l] pools of water. I will sweep it with a broom of extermination—declares the LORD of Hosts.

[24] The LORD of Hosts has sworn this oath:
"As I have designed, so shall it happen;
What I have planned, that shall come to pass:
[25] To break Assyria in My land,
To crush him on My mountain."[m]
And his yoke shall drop off them,
And his burden shall drop from their[n] backs.
[26] That is the plan that is planned
For all the earth;
That is why an arm is poised
Over all the nations.
[27] For the LORD of Hosts has planned,
Who then can foil it?
It is His arm that is poised,
And who can stay it?

[28] This pronouncement was made in the year that King Ahaz died:

[29] Rejoice not, all Philistia,
Because the staff of him that beat you is broken.
For from the stock of a snake there sprouts an asp,
A flying seraph[o] branches out from it.

[k] Heb. "fathers."
[l] Meaning of Heb. uncertain.
[m] Heb. "mountains"; for the designation of the entire land of Israel as the Lord's mountain,
  cf. 11.9.
[n] Heb. "his." The last two lines of this verse would read well after v. 26.
[o] Others "fiery serpent"; cf. Nu. 21.6, 8.

³⁰ ^{p-}The first-born of the poor shall graze^{-p}
And the destitute lie down secure.
^{q-}I will kill your stock by famine,^{-q}
And it shall slay the very last of you.
³¹ Howl, O gate; cry out, O city;
Quake, all Philistia!
^{r-}For a stout one is coming from the north
And there is no straggler in his ranks.^{-r}

³² And what will he answer the messengers of that nation?
That Zion has been established by the LORD:
In it, the needy of His people shall find shelter.

15 The "Moab" Pronouncement.

Ah, in the night Ar was sacked,
Moab was ruined;
Ah, in the night Kir was sacked,
Moab was ruined.

² He went up to the temple to weep,
Dibon^a [went] to the outdoor shrines.
Over Nebo and Medeba
Moab is wailing;
On every head is baldness,
Every beard is shorn.
³ In its streets, they are girt with sackcloth;
On its roofs, in its squares,
Everyone is wailing,
Streaming with tears.
⁴ Heshbon and Elealeh cry out,
Their voice carries to Jahaz.

---

^{p-p} *Emendation yields "The poor shall graze in His pasture." This line and the next would read well after v. 32.*
^{q-q} *Emendation yields "It shall kill your offspring with its venom (zar'ekh berosho)."*
^{r-r} *Meaning of Heb. uncertain; the rendering "stout one" is suggested by the Syriac 'ashshīn.*
^a *Regarded as the principal city of Moab.*

Therefore,
b-The shock troops of Moab shout,*-b*
His body is convulsed.
5 My heart cries out for Moab—
His fugitives flee down to Zoar,
To Eglath-shelishiyah.
For the ascent of Luhith
They ascend with weeping;
On the road to Horonaim
They raise a cry of anguish.

6 Ah, the waters of Nimrim
Are become a desolation;
The grass is sear,
The herbage is gone,
Vegetation is vanished.

7 Therefore,
The gains they have made, and their stores,
They carry to the Wadi of Willows.

8 Ah, the cry has compassed
The country of Moab:
All the way to Eglaim her wailing,
Even at Beer-elim her wailing!

9 Ah, the waters of Dimon are full of blood*c*
For I pour added [water] on Dimon;
I drench*d* it—for Moab's refugees—
With soil*e* for its remnant.

---

b-b *Change of vocalization yields "The loins of Moab are trembling."*
c *Emendation yields "tears."*
d *Cf. 16.9.*
e *Emendation yields "tears"; cf. Ugaritic 'dm't.*

16 [a]Dispatch as messenger
The ruler of the land,
From Sela in the wilderness
To the mount of Fair Zion:

2 "Like fugitive birds,
Like nestlings driven away,
Moab's villagers linger
By the fords of the Arnon.
3 Give advice,
[b]Offer counsel.[b]
At high noon make
Your shadow like night:
Conceal the outcasts,
Betray not the fugitives.
4 Let [c]Moab's outcasts[c]
Find asylum in you;
Be a shelter for them
Against the despoiler."

For violence has vanished,
Rapine is ended,
And marauders have perished from this land.
5 And a throne shall be established in goodness
In the tent of David,
And on it shall sit in faithfulness
A ruler devoted to justice
And zealous for equity.[d]

6 "We have heard of Moab's pride—
Most haughty is he—

[a] *Meaning of vv. 1 and 2 uncertain.*
[b-b] *Meaning of Heb. uncertain.*
[c-c] *Heb. "my outcasts, Moab."*
[d] *14.32, above, would read well here.*

Of his pride and haughtiness and arrogance,
And of the iniquity in him."[e]

7 Ah, let Moab howl;
Let all in Moab howl!
For the raisin-cakes[f] of Kir-hareseth
You shall moan most pitifully.
8 The vineyards of Heshbon are withered,
And the vines of Sibmah;
[b-]Their tendrils spread
To Baale-goiim,[-b]
And reached to Jazer,
And strayed to the desert;
Their shoots spread out
And crossed the sea.

9 Therefore,
As I weep for Jazer,
So I weep for Sibmah's vines;
O Heshbon and Elealeh,
I drench you with my tears.
[g-]Ended are the shouts
Over your fig and grain harvests.[-g]
10 Rejoicing and gladness
Are gone from the farm land;
In the vineyards no shouting
Or cheering is heard.
No more does the treader
Tread wine in the presses—
The shouts [h-]have been silenced.[-h]

11 Therefore,
Like a lyre my heart moans for Moab,
And my very soul for Kir-heres.

[e] Baddaw *is a suffixed form of the preposition* bede: *Nah. 2.13; Hab. 2.13; Job 39.25; with suffixes, Job 11.3, 41.4.*
[f] *Jer. 48.36 has "men."*
[g-g] *Jer. 48.32 reads "A ravager has come down/Upon your fig and grape harvests."*
[h-h] *Lit. "I have silenced."*

¹² And when it has become apparent that Moab has gained nothing in the outdoor shrine, he shall come to pray in his temple —but to no avail.

¹³ That is the word that the LORD spoke concerning Moab long ago. ¹⁴ And now the LORD has spoken: In three years, fixed like the years of a hired laborer, Moab's population, with all its huge multitude, shall shrink. Only a remnant shall be left, of no consequence.

17 The "Damascus" Pronouncement.

Behold,
Damascus shall cease to be a city;
It shall become a heap of ruins.
² ᵃ⁻The towns of Aroer shall be deserted;⁻ᵃ
They shall be a place for flocks
To lie down, with none disturbing.

³ Fortresses shall cease from Ephraim,ᵇ
And sovereignty from Damascus;
The remnant of Aram shall become
Like the mass of Israelites
　　　　　　—declares the LORD of Hosts.

⁴ In that day,
The mass of Jacob shall dwindle,
And the fatness of his body become lean:
⁵ After being like the standing grain
Harvested by the reaper—
Who reaps ears by the armful—
He shall be like the ears that are gleaned
In the Valley of Rephaim.
⁶ Only gleanings shall be left of him,
As when one beats an olive tree:

ᵃ⁻² *Emendation yields (cf. Septuagint) "Its towns shall be deserted forevermore."*
ᵇ *Emendation yields "Aram."*

Two berries or three on the topmost branch,
Four or five ^con the boughs of the crown^{-c}
　　　　—declares the LORD, the God of Israel.

⁷ In that day, men shall turn to their Maker, their eyes look to the Holy One of Israel; ⁸ they shall not turn to the altars that their own hands made, or look to the sacred posts and incense stands that their own fingers wrought.

⁹ In that day, their fortress cities shall be like the deserted sites which ^dthe Horesh and the Amir^{-d} abandoned because of the Israelites; and there shall be desolation.

¹⁰ Truly, you have forgotten the God who saves you
And have not remembered the Rock who shelters you;
That is why, though you plant a delightful^e sapling,
What you sow proves a disappointing slip.
¹¹ On the day that you plant, you see it grow,
On the morning you sow, you see it bud—
But the branches wither away
On a day of sickness and mortal agony.

¹² Ah, the roar of many peoples
That roar as roars the sea,
The rage of nations that rage
As rage the mighty waters—
¹³ Nations raging like massive waters!
But He shouts at them, and they flee far away,
Driven like chaff before winds in the hills,
And like tumbleweed before a gale.
¹⁴ At eventide, lo, terror!
By morning, it is no more.
Such is the lot of our despoilers,
The portion of them that plunder us.

^{c-c} Lit. "on her boughs, the many-branched one."
^{d-d} Septuagint reads "the Amorites and the Hivites."
^e Emendation yields "true." So Vulgate (cf. Septuagint); cf. Jer. 2.21.

18 Ah,

a-Land in the deep shadow of wings,*-a*
Beyond the rivers of Nubia!

² Go, swift messengers,
To a nation *b*-far and remote,
To a people thrust forth and away*-b*—
A nation of gibber and chatter*c*—
Whose land is cut off by streams;
d-Which sends out envoys by sea,
In papyrus vessels upon the water!*-d*

³ [Say this:]
"All you who live in the world
And inhabit the earth,
When a flag is raised in the hills, take note!
When a ram's horn is blown, give heed!"
⁴ For thus the Lord said to me:
"I rest calm and confident*e* in My habitation—
Like a scorching heat upon sprouts,
f-Like a rain-cloud in the heat of reaping time."*-f*
⁵ For before the harvest,*g* yet after the budding,
When the blossom has hardened into berries,
He will trim away the twigs with pruning hooks,
And lop off the trailing branches.*h*
⁶ They shall all be left
To the kites of the hills
And to the beasts of the earth;

---

a-a Or "Most sheltered land"; cf. e.g. 30.2,3; Ps. 36.8; 57.2; 61.5.
b-b Meaning of Heb. uncertain.
c Meaning of Heb. uncertain; cf. 28.10. Biblical writers often characterize distant nations by their unintelligible speech; cf. 33.19; Deut. 28.49; Jer. 5.15.
d-d Brought down from beginning of verse for clarity. The Hebrew verb for "sends" agrees in gender with "nation," not with "land."
e Cf. hibbit "to rely" (Job 6.19). The related noun mabbaṭ occurs with similar meaning in Isa. 20.5,6.
f-f I.e. like a threat of disaster; cf. Eccl. 11.4.
g Emendation yields "vintage."
h A figure of speech for the defeated enemy.

The kites shall summer on them
And all the beasts of the earth shall winter on them.

⁷ In that time,
Tribute shall be brought to the LORD of Hosts
[From] a people far and remote,
From a people thrust forth and away—
A nation of gibber and chatter,
Whose land is cut off by streams—
At the place where the name of the LORD of Hosts abides,
At Mount Zion.

19 The "Egypt" Pronouncement.

Mounted on a swift cloud,
The LORD will come to Egypt;
Egypt's idols shall tremble before Him,
And the heart of the Egyptians shall sink within them.

² "I will incite Egyptian against Egyptian:
They shall war with each other,
Every man with his fellow,
City with city
And kingdom with kingdom.ᵃ
³ Egypt shall be drained of spirit,
And I will confound its plans;
So they will consult the idols and the shades
And the ghosts and the familiar spirits.
⁴ And I will place the Egyptians
At the mercy of a harsh master,
And a ruthless king shall rule them"
          —declares the Sovereign, the LORD of Hosts.

ᵃ *I.e. the various districts of Egypt, which in Isaiah's time were governed by hereditary princes.*

5 Water shall fail from the seas,
Rivers dry up and be parched,
6 Channels turn foul as they ebb,
And Egypt's canals run dry.
Reed and rush shall decay,
7 *b-*And the Nile papyrus by the Nile-side*-b*
And everything sown by the Nile
Shall wither, blow away, and vanish.
8 The fishermen shall lament;
All who cast lines in the Nile shall mourn,
And those who spread nets on the water shall languish.
9 The flax workers, too, shall be dismayed,
Both carders and weavers chagrined.*b*
10 *c*Her foundations shall be crushed,
And all who make dams shall be despondent.

11 Utter fools are the nobles of Tanis;
The sagest of Pharaoh's advisers
[Have made] absurd predictions.
How can you say to Pharaoh,
"I am a scion of sages,
A scion of Kedemite kings"?*d*
12 Where, indeed, are your sages?
Let them tell you, let them discover
What the Lord of Hosts has planned against Egypt.
13 The nobles of Tanis have been fools,
The nobles of Memphis deluded;
Egypt has been led astray
By the chiefs of her tribes.
14 The Lord has mixed within her
A spirit of distortion,
Which shall lead Egypt astray in all her undertakings
As a vomiting drunkard goes astray;
15 Nothing shall be achieved in Egypt

b-b *Meaning of Heb. uncertain.*
c *Meaning of verse uncertain; emendation yields "Her drinkers shall be dejected, /And all her brewers despondent."*
d *Or "advisers." The wisdom of the Kedemites was proverbial; cf. I Kings 5.10.*

By either head or tail,
Palm branch or reed.[e]

[16] In that day, the Egyptians shall be like women, trembling and terrified because the LORD of Hosts will raise His hand against them. [17] And the land of Judah shall also be the dread of the Egyptians; they shall quake whenever anybody mentions it to them, because of what the LORD of Hosts is planning against them. [18] In that day, there shall be several[f] towns in the land of Egypt speaking the language of Canaan and swearing loyalty to the LORD of Hosts; one[g] shall be called Town of Heres.[h]

[19] In that day, there shall be an altar to the LORD inside the land of Egypt and a pillar to the LORD at its border.[i] [20] They shall serve as a symbol and reminder of the LORD of Hosts in the land of Egypt, so that when [the Egyptians] cry out to the LORD against oppressors, He will send them a savior and champion to deliver them. [21] For the LORD will make Himself known to the Egyptians, and the Egyptians shall acknowledge the LORD in that day, and they shall serve [Him] with sacrifice and oblation and shall make vows to the LORD and fulfill them. [22] The LORD will first afflict and then heal the Egyptians; when they turn back to the LORD, He will respond to their entreaties and heal them.

[23] In that day, there shall be a highway from Egypt to Assyria. The Assyrians shall join with the Egyptians and Egyptians with the Assyrians, and then the Egyptians together with the Assyrians shall serve [the LORD].

[24] In that day, Israel shall be a third partner with Egypt and Assyria as a blessing[j] on earth; [25] for the LORD of Hosts will bless them, saying, "Blessed be My people Egypt, My handiwork Assyria, and My very own Israel."

---

[e] *I.e. a man of either high or low station; cf. 9.13, 14.*
[f] *Lit. "five."*
[g] *Or "each one."*
[h] *Meaning uncertain. Many Heb. mss. read* heres, *"sun," which may refer to Heliopolis, i.e. Sun City, in Egypt. Targum's "Beth Shemesh" (cf. Jer. 43.13) has the same meaning.*
[i] *As a symbol of the Lord's sovereignty over Egypt.*
[j] *I.e. a standard by which blessing is invoked; cf. Gen. 12.2 with note.*

20 It was the year that the Tartan*a* came to Ashdod—being sent by King Sargon of Assyria—and attacked Ashdod and took it. ² Previously,*b* the LORD had spoken to Isaiah son of Amoz, saying, "Go, untie the sackcloth from your loins and take your sandals off your feet," which he had done, going naked and barefoot. ³ And now the LORD said, "It is a sign and a portent for Egypt and Nubia. Just as My servant Isaiah has gone naked and barefoot for three years, ⁴ so shall the king of Assyria drive off the captives of Egypt and the exiles of Nubia, young and old, naked and barefoot and with bared buttocks—to the shame of Egypt! ⁵ And they shall be dismayed and chagrined because of Nubia their hope and Egypt their boast. ⁶ In that day, the dwellers of this coastland shall say, 'If this could happen to those we looked to, to whom we fled for help and rescue from the king of Assyria, how can we ourselves escape?' "

21 *a-*The "Desert of the Sea" Pronouncement.*-a*

Like the gales
That race through the Negeb,
It comes from the desert,
The terrible land.
² A harsh prophecy
Has been announced to me:
"The betrayer is *b-*betraying,
The ravager ravaging.*-b*
Advance, Elam!
Lay siege, Media!
*c-*I have put an end
To all her sighing."*-c*

---

a An Assyrian title meaning "General"; cf. II Kings 18.17 and note.
b Lit. "At that time."

a-a Emendation yields "The 'From the Desert' Pronouncement," agreeing with the phrase farther on in the verse.
b-b Emendation yields "betrayed . . . ravaged"; cf. 33.1.
c-c Emendation yields "Put an end to all her merrymaking!"

³ Therefore my loins
Are seized with trembling;
I am gripped by pangs
Like a woman in travail,
Too anguished to hear,
Too frightened to see.
⁴ My mind is confused,
I shudder in panic.
My night of pleasure
He has turned to terror:
⁵ "Set the table!"
To "Let the watchman watch!"
"Eat and drink!"
To "Up, officers! grease*ᵈ* the shields!"

⁶ For thus my LORD said to me:
"Go, set up a sentry;
Let him announce what he sees.
⁷ He will see mounted men,
Horsemen in pairs—
Riders on asses,
Riders on camels—
And he will listen closely,
Most attentively."
⁸ And *ᵉ*[like] a lion he*ᵉ* called out:
ᶠ"On my Lord's lookout*ᶠ* I stand
Ever by day,
And at my post I watch
Every night.
⁹ And there they come, mounted men—
Horsemen in pairs!"
Then he spoke up and said,
"Fallen, fallen is Babylon,
And all the images of her gods
Have crashed to the ground!"

ᵈ *Emendation yields "grasp."*
ᵉ⁻ᵉ *1Qlsᵃ reads "The watcher."*
ᶠ⁻ᶠ *Or "On a lookout, my lord."*

10 *g*-My threshing, the product of my threshing floor:-*g*
What I have heard from the LORD of Hosts,
The God of Israel—
That I have told to you.

11 The "Dumah"*h* Pronouncement.

A call comes to me from Seir:
"Watchman, what of the night?
Watchman, what of the night?"
12 The watchman replied,
"Morning came, and so did night.
If you would inquire, inquire.
Come back again."

13 The "In the Steppe" Pronouncement.

In the scrub, in the steppe, you will lodge,
O caravans of the Dedanites!
14 Meet the thirsty with water,
You who dwell in the land of Tema;
Greet the fugitive with bread.
15 For they have fled before swords:
Before the whetted sword,
Before the bow that was drawn,
Before the stress of war.

16 For thus my Lord has said to me: "In another year, fixed like the years of a hired laborer, all the multitude of Kedar shall vanish; 17 the remaining bows of Kedar's warriors shall be few in number; for the LORD, the God of Israel, has spoken.

---

g-g Connection of Heb. uncertain.
h Name of a people; cf. Gen. 25.14.

22

The *a*-"Valley of Vision"-*a* Pronouncement.

*b*What can have happened to you
That you have gone, all of you, up on the roofs,
2 O you who were full of tumult,
You clamorous town,
You city so gay?
Your slain are not the slain of the sword
Nor the dead of battle.*c*
3 Your officers have all departed,
They fled far away;
Your survivors were all taken captive,
a-Taken captive without their bows.*a*
4 That is why I say, "Let me be,
I will weep bitterly.
Press not to comfort me
For the ruin of *d*-my poor people."-*d*

5 For my Lord GOD of Hosts had a day
Of tumult and din and confusion—
e-Kir raged in the Valley of Vision,
And Shoa on the hill;-*e*
6 While Elam bore the quiver
In troops of mounted men,
And Kir bared the shield—
7 And your choicest lowlands
Were filled with chariots and horsemen:
They stormed at Judah's*f* gateway
8 And pressed beyond its screen.*g*

a-a Meaning of Heb. uncertain.
b Vv. 1-3 describe a scene of mourning to take place in Jerusalem in the near future. In the ancient Near East, public weeping took place on the low flat roofs as well as in the streets and squares; cf. above, 15.3; Jer. 48.38.
c I.e. executed, instead of dying in battle.
d-d Lit. "the young woman, my people."
e-e Meaning of Heb. uncertain. On Kir see II Kings 16.9; Amos 1.5; 9.7; on Shoa see Ezek. 23.23.
f Brought up from 8a for clarity.
g Judah's gateway is the upper course of the Valley of Elah. The screen is the fortress Azekah, at the mouth of the gateway, which was captured by the Assyrians.

You gave thought on that day
To the arms in the Forest House,[h]
⁹ And you took note of the many breaches
In the City of David.

¹⁰ [i-]And you collected the water of the Lower Pool;[-i] and you counted the houses of Jerusalem and pulled houses down to fortify the wall; ¹¹ and you constructed a basin between the two walls for the water of the old pool.

But you gave no thought to Him who planned it,
You took no note of Him who designed it long before.
¹² My Lord GOD of Hosts summoned on that day
To weeping and lamenting,
To tonsuring and girding with sackcloth.
¹³ Instead, there was rejoicing and merriment,
Killing of cattle and slaughtering of sheep,
Eating of meat and drinking of wine:
"Eat and drink, for tomorrow we die!"
¹⁴ Then the LORD of Hosts revealed Himself to my
ears:
"This iniquity shall never be forgiven you
Until you die," said my Lord GOD of Hosts.

¹⁵ Thus said my Lord GOD of Hosts: Go in to see that steward, that Shebna, in charge of the palace:
¹⁶ What have you here, and whom have you here,
That you have hewn out a tomb for yourself here?—
O you who have hewn your[j] tomb on high;
O you who have hollowed out for yourself[j] an abode in the
cliff!
¹⁷ The LORD is about to shake you
[k-]Severely, fellow,[-k] and then wrap you around Himself.[l]
¹⁸ Indeed, He will wind you about Him [m-]as a headdress,
a turban.[-m]

---

[h] See I Kings 7.2-5; 10.16-17.
[i-i] This clause would read well after the prose part of v. 11a.
[j] Heb. "his," "himself."
[k-k] Emendation yields "as a garment is shaken out."
[l] I.e. and walk off with you; cf. Jer. 43.12.
[m-m] Emendation yields "as a turban is wound about."

Off to a broad land!
There shall you die, and there shall be the ⁿ⁻chariots bearing your body,⁻ⁿ
O shame of your master's house!
¹⁹ For I will hurl you from your station
And you shall be torn down from your stand.

²⁰ And in that day, I will summon My servant Eliakim son of Hilkiah, ²¹ and I will invest him with your tunic, gird him with your sash, and deliver your authority into his hand; and he shall be a father to the inhabitants of Jerusalem and the men of Judah. ²² I will place the keys of David's palace on his shoulders; and what he unlocks none may shut, and what he locks none may open. ²³ He shall be a seat of honor to his father's^o household. I will fix him as a peg in a firm place, ²⁴ on which all the substance of his father's^o household shall be hung: ^{a-}the sprouts and the leaves^{-a}—all the small vessels, from bowls to all sorts of jars.

²⁵ ^pIn that day—declares the LORD of Hosts—the peg fixed in a firm place shall give way: it shall be cut down and shall fall, and the weight it supports shall be destroyed. For it is the LORD who has spoken.

23 The "Tyre" Pronouncement.

Howl, you ^{a-}ships of Tarshish!^{-a}
For havoc has been wrought, not a house is left;
As they came from the land of Kittim,
This was revealed to them.

² Moan, you coastland dwellers,
You traders of Sidon!
You^b were filled with men who crossed the sea.

ⁿ⁻ⁿ *Emendation yields "abode (cf. v. 16) of your body" (cf. 10.3, 16).*
^o *Emendation yields "master's"; cf. v. 18 end.*
^p *Apparently continues v. 19.*

^{a-a} *See note at 2.16.*
^b *I.e. Sidon.*

3 Over many waters
Your^c revenue came:
From the trade of nations,
From the grain of Shihor,
The harvest of the Nile.
4 Be ashamed, O Sidon!
For the sea—this stronghold of the sea—declares,
^{d-}"I am as one who has^{-d} never labored,
Never given birth,
Never raised youths
Or reared maidens!"
5 When the Egyptians heard it, they quailed
As when they heard about Tyre.

6 Pass on to Tarshish—
Howl, you coastland dwellers!
7 Was such your merry city
In former times, of yore?
Did her feet carry her off
To sojourn far away?
8 Who was it that planned this
For crown-wearing Tyre,
Whose merchants were nobles,
Whose traders the world honored?
9 The LORD of Hosts planned it—
To defile all glorious beauty,
To shame all the honored of the world.

10 ^{e-}Traverse your land like the Nile,
Fair Tarshish;^{-e}
This is a harbor^f no more.

11 The LORD poised His arm o'er the sea
And made kingdoms quake;
It was He decreed destruction

^c Heb. "her."
^{d-d} Lit. "I have."
^{e-e} Meaning of Heb. uncertain. Emendation yields "Pass on to the land of Kittim, / You ships of Tarshish."
^f Meaning of Heb. uncertain; taking mezah as a by-form of mahoz: cf. Ps. 107.30.

For Phoenicia's^g strongholds,
[12] And said,
"You shall be gay no more,
O plundered one, Fair Maiden Sidon.
Up, cross over to Kittim—
Even there you shall have no rest."

[13] [h]Behold the land of Chaldea—
This is the people that has ceased to be.
Assyria, which founded it for ships,
Which raised its watchtowers,
Erected its ramparts,
Has turned it into a ruin.

[14] Howl, O ships of Tarshish,
For your stronghold is destroyed!

[15] In that day, Tyre shall remain forgotten for seventy years, equaling the lifetime of one king. After a lapse of seventy years, it shall go with Tyre as with the harlot in the ditty:

[16] Take a lyre, go about the town,
Harlot long forgotten;
Sweetly play, make much music,
To bring you back to mind.

[17] For after a lapse of seventy years, the LORD will take note of Tyre, and she shall resume her [i]"fee-taking" and "play the harlot"[i] with all the kingdoms of the world, on the face of the earth. [18] But her profits and "hire" shall be consecrated to the LORD. They shall not be treasured or stored; rather shall her profits go to those who abide before the LORD, that they may eat their fill and clothe themselves elegantly.

---

[g] Heb. "Canaan's."
[h] Meaning of verse uncertain. Emendation yields "The land of Kittim itself—/Which the Sidonian people founded,/Whose watchtowers they raised,/Whose citadels they erected—/Exists no more;/Assyria has turned it into a ruin."
[i-i] I.e. "trading . . . trade."

24 Behold,

The LORD will strip the earth bare,
'And lay it waste,
And twist its surface,
And scatter its inhabitants.
2 Layman and priest shall fare alike,
Slave and master,
Handmaid and mistress,
Buyer and seller,
Lender and borrower,
Creditor and debtor.
3 The earth shall be bare, bare;
It shall be plundered, plundered;
For it is the LORD who spoke this word.

4 The earth is withered, sear;
The world languishes, it is sear;
*a-*The most exalted people on earth*-a* languish.
5 For the earth was defiled
Under its inhabitants;
Because they transgressed teachings,
Violated laws,
Broke the ancient covenant.*b*
6 That is why a curse consumes the earth,
And its inhabitants pay the penalty;
That is why earth's dwellers have dwindled,
And but few men are left.
7 The new wine fails,
The vine languishes;
And all the merry-hearted sigh.
8 Stilled is the merriment of timbrels,
Ended the clamor of revelers,
Stilled the merriment of lyres.

---

a-a *Change of vocalization yields "both sky and earth."*
b *I.e. the moral law which is binding on all men (cf. Gen. 9.4-6).*

⁹ They drink their wine without song;
Liquor tastes bitter to the drinker.
¹⁰ Towns are broken,ᶜ empty;
Every house is shut, none enters;
¹¹ Even over wine, a cry goes up in the streets:
The sun has set on all joy,
The gladness of the earth is banished.
¹² Desolation is left in the town
And the gate is battered to ruins.
¹³ For thus shall it be among the peoples
In the midst of the earth:
As when the olive tree is beaten out,
Like gleanings when the vintage is over.

¹⁴ These shall lift up their voices,
Exult in the majesty of the LORD.
They shall shout from the sea:
¹⁵ Therefore, honor the LORD with lights
In the coastlands of the sea—
The name of the LORD, the God of Israel.
¹⁶ From the end of the earth
We hear singing:
Glory to the righteous!
ᵈ⁻And I said:⁻ᵈ
ᵉ⁻I waste away! I waste away! Woe is me!
The faithless have acted faithlessly;
The faithless have broken faith!⁻ᵉ

¹⁷ ᶠ⁻Terror, and pit, and trap⁻ᶠ
Upon you who dwell on earth!
¹⁸ He who flees at the report of the terror
Shall fall into the pit;
And he who climbs out of the pit
Shall be caught in the trap.

ᶜ Emendation yields "left."
ᵈ⁻ᵈ Change of vocalization yields "They shall say."
ᵉ⁻ᵉ Meaning of Heb. uncertain. Emendation yields "Villain [Arabic razīl], foolish villain!/
    The faithless who acted faithlessly/Have been betrayed in turn."
ᶠ⁻ᶠ Heb. paḥad wa-paḥath, wa-paḥ.

For sluices are opened on high,
And earth's foundations tremble.

19 The earth is breaking, breaking;
The earth is crumbling, crumbling.
The earth is tottering, tottering;
20 The earth is swaying like a drunkard;
It is rocking to and fro like a hut.
Its iniquity shall weigh it down,
And it shall fall, to rise no more.

21 In that day, the LORD will punish
The host of heaven in heaven
And the kings of the earth on earth.
22 They shall be gathered in a dungeon
As captives are gathered;
And shall be locked up in a prison.
But after many days they shall be remembered.

23 Then the moon shall be ashamed,
And the sun shall be abashed.
For the LORD of Hosts will reign
On Mount Zion and in Jerusalem,
And the Presence will be revealed to His elders.

25 O LORD, You are my God;
I will extol You, I will praise Your name.
For You planned graciousness[a] of old,
Counsels of steadfast faithfulness.

2 For You have turned a city into a stone heap,
A walled town into a ruin,
The citadel of strangers[b] into rubble,[c]

---

[a] See 9.5, with note.
[b] Emendation yields "arrogant men."
[c] Meaning of Heb. uncertain.

Never to be rebuilt.

³ Therefore a fierce people must honor You,
A city of cruel nations must fear You.
⁴ For You have been a refuge for the poor man,
A shelter for the needy man in his distress—
Shelter from rainstorm, shade from heat.
When the fury of tyrants was like a winter*ᶜ* rainstorm,
⁵ The rage of strangers*ᵇ* like heat in the desert,
You subdued the heat with the shade of clouds,
The singing*ᵈ* of the tyrants was vanquished.

⁶ The LORD of Hosts will make on this mount*ᵉ*
For all the peoples
A banquet of *ᶜ*rich viands,
A banquet of choice wines—
Of rich viands seasoned with marrow,
Of choice wines *ᶜ* well refined.
⁷ And He will destroy on this mount*ᵉ* the shroud
That is drawn over the faces of all the peoples
And the covering that is spread
Over all the nations:
⁸ He will destroy death*ᶠ* forever.
My Lord GOD will wipe the tears away
From all faces
And will put an end to the reproach of *ᵍ*His people*ᵍ*
Over all the earth—
For it is the LORD who has spoken.

⁹ In that day they shall say:
This is our God;
We trusted in Him, and He delivered us.
This is the LORD, in whom we trusted;
Let us rejoice and exult in His deliverance!

ᵈ *Meaning of Heb. uncertain. Emendation yields "rainstorm"; cf. v.4d.*
ᵉ *I.e. the Holy Land, as in 11.9; 14.25; 57.13.*
ᶠ *Perhaps an allusion to the mass killings committed by the Assyrians; cf. 10.7; 14.20.*
ᵍ⁻ᵍ *Emendation yields "peoples."*

¹⁰ For the hand of the LORD shall descend
Upon this mount,*ᵉ*
And Moab*ʰ* shall be trampled under Him
As straw is threshed to bits at Madmenah.*ⁱ*
¹¹ Then He will spread out His hands in their home-
land,*ʲ*
As a swimmer spreads his hands out to swim,
And He will humble their pride
Along with *ᵏ*the emblems of their power.*ᵏ*
¹² Yea, the secure fortification of their*ˡ* walls
He will lay low and humble,
Will raze to the ground, to the very dust.

26 In that day, this song shall be sung
In the land of Judah:
Ours is a mighty city;
He makes victory our inner and outer wall.
² Open the gates, and let
A righteous nation enter,
[A nation] that keeps faith.
³ The confident mind You guard in safety,
In safety because it trusts in You.

⁴ Trust in the LORD for ever and ever,
For in Yah the LORD you have an everlasting Rock.
⁵ For He has brought low those who dwelt high up,
Has humbled the secure city,
Humbled it to the ground,
Leveled it with the dust—
⁶ To be trampled underfoot,
By the feet of the needy,
By the soles of the poor.

ʰ Emendation yields "Assyria"; cf. 14.25.
ⁱ A village near Jerusalem; see 10.31. Emendation yields "As straw gets shredded in the threshing."
ʲ Lit. "midst."
ᵏ⁻ᵏ Meaning of Heb. uncertain. Emendation yields "their citadels"; cf. the next verse.
ˡ Heb. "your."

⁷ The path is level for the righteous man;
O Just One, You make smooth the course of the righteous.

⁸ For Your just ways, O LORD, we look to You;
We long for the name by which You are called.
⁹ At night I yearn for You with all my being,
I seek You with all *ᵃ*the spirit within me.*ᵃ*
For when Your judgments are wrought on earth,
The inhabitants of the world learn righteousness.
¹⁰ But when the scoundrel is spared, he learns not righteousness;
In a place of integrity, he does wrong—
He ignores the majesty of the LORD.

¹¹ O LORD!
They see not Your hand exalted.
Let them be shamed as they behold
Your zeal for Your people
And fire consuming Your adversaries.
¹² *ᵇ*O LORD!
May You appoint well-being for us,
Since You have also requited all our misdeeds.

¹³ O LORD our God!
Lords other than You possessed us,
But only Your name shall we utter.
¹⁴ They are dead, they can never live;
Shades, they can never rise;
Of a truth, You have dealt with them and wiped them out,
Have put an end to all mention of them.
¹⁵ *ᶜ*When You added to the nation, O LORD,
When You added to the nation,
Extending all the boundaries of the land,
You were honored.
¹⁶ O LORD! In their distress, they sought You;

ᵃ⁻ᵃ *Emendation yields "my spirit in the morning."*
ᵇ *Meaning of verse uncertain.*
ᶜ *Meaning of vv. 15-16 uncertain.*

Your chastisement reduced them
To anguished[d] whispered prayer.
17 Like a woman with child
Approaching childbirth,
Writhing and screaming in her pangs,
So are we become because of You, O LORD.
18 We were with child, we writhed—
It is as though we had given birth to wind;
We have won no victory on earth;
The inhabitants of the world have not [e-]come to life![-e]
19 Oh, let Your dead revive!
Let corpses[f] arise!
Awake and shout for joy,
You who dwell in the dust!—
For Your dew is like the dew on fresh growth;
You make the land of the shades [e-]come to life.[-e]

20 Go, my people, enter your chambers,
And lock your doors behind you.
Hide but a little moment,
Until the indignation passes.
21 For lo!
The LORD shall come forth from His place
To punish the dwellers of the earth
For their iniquity;
And the earth shall disclose its bloodshed
And shall no longer conceal its slain.

27 In that day the LORD will punish
With His great, cruel, mighty sword
Leviathan the Elusive[a] Serpent—
Leviathan the Twisting[a] Serpent;
He will slay the Dragon of the sea.[b]

d Lit. "anguish"; taking saqun as a noun formed like zadon and sason.
e-e Meaning of Heb. uncertain.
f Grammar of Heb. unclear.

a Meaning of Heb. uncertain.
b The monster which the Lord vanquished of old (cf. 51.9; Ps. 74.13-14) was the embodiment
of chaos; here it stands for the forces of evil in the present world.

² In that day,
They shall sing of it:[c]
"Vineyard of Delight."[d]
³ I the LORD keep watch over it,
I water it every moment;
[e]That no harm may befall it,[e]
I watch it night and day.
⁴ There is no anger in Me:
[a]If one offers Me thorns and thistles,
I will march to battle against him,
And set all of them on fire.[a]
⁵ But if he holds fast to My refuge,
[a]He makes Me his friend;
He makes Me his friend.[a]

⁶ [In days] to come Jacob shall strike root,
Israel shall sprout and blossom,
And the face of the world
Shall be covered with fruit.

⁷ Was he beaten as his beater has been?
Did he suffer such slaughter as his slayers?
⁸ [f]Assailing them[f] with fury unchained,
His pitiless blast bore them off
On a day of gale.

⁹ [g]Assuredly, by this alone
Shall Jacob's sin be purged away;
This is the only price
For removing his guilt:
That he make all the altar-stones
Like shattered blocks of chalk—
With no sacred post left standing,
Nor any incense altar.

[c] Apparently the earth; cf. 26.21.
[d] So some mss. (cf. Amos 5.11); other mss. and the editions have "Wine."
[e-e] Meaning of Heb. uncertain; emendation yields "My eye is open upon it."
[f-f] Lit. "Striving with her"; meaning of verse uncertain.
[g] This verse would read well before v. 6; the thought of vv. 7-8, dealing with the punishment of Israel's enemies, is continued in vv. 10-11.

¹⁰ Thus fortified cities lie desolate,
Homesteads deserted, forsaken like a wilderness;
There calves graze, there they lie down
ʰ⁻And consume its boughs.
¹¹ When its crown is withered, they break;⁻ʰ
Women come and make fires with them.
For they are a people without understanding;
That is why
Their Maker will show them no mercy,
Their Creator will deny them grace.

¹² And in that day, the LORD will beat out [the peoples like grain] from the channel of the Euphrates to the Wadi of Egypt; and you shall be picked up one by one, O children of Israel! ¹³ And in that day, a great ram's horn shall be sounded; and the strayed who are in the land of Assyria and the expelled who are in the land of Egypt shall come and worship the LORD on the holy mount, in Jerusalem.

28 Ah, the proud crowns of the drunkards of Ephraim,
Whose glorious beauty is but wilted flowers
On the heads of men bloatedᵃ with rich food,
Who are overcome by wine!

² Lo, my Lord has something strong and mighty,
Like a storm of hail,
A shower of pestilence.
Something like a storm of massive, torrential rainᵇ
Shall be hurled with force to the ground.
³ Trampled underfoot shall be
The proud crowns of the drunkards of Ephraim,
⁴ The wilted flowers—
On the heads of men bloatedᵃ with rich food—
That are his glorious beauty.

ʰ⁻ʰ *Meaning of Heb. uncertain. Emendation yields "Or like a terebinth whose boughs/Break when its crown is withered."*

ᵃ *Ge is contracted from ge'e; cf. Ibn Ezra.*
ᵇ *Lit. "water."*

They shall be like an early fig
Before the fruit harvest;
Whoever sees it devours it
While it is still ^cin his hand.^{-c}

⁵ In that day, the Lord of Hosts shall become a crown of beauty
and a diadem of glory for the remnant of His people, ⁶ and a spirit
of judgment for him who sits in judgment and of valor for those
who repel attacks at the gate.

⁷ But these are also muddled by wine
And dazed by liquor:
Priest and prophet
Are muddled by liquor;
They are confused by wine,
They are dazed by liquor;
They are muddled in their visions,
They stumble in judgment.
⁸ Yea, all tables are covered
With vomit and filth,
So that no space is left.

⁹ ^d"To whom would he give instruction?
To whom expound a message?
To those newly weaned from milk,
Just taken away from the breast?
¹⁰ That same mutter upon mutter,
Murmur upon murmur,
Now here, now there!"

¹¹ Truly, as one who speaks to that people in a stammer-
ing jargon and an alien tongue ¹² is he who declares to them,
"This is the resting place, let the weary rest;^e this is the place
of repose." They refuse to listen. ¹³ To them the word of the
Lord is:

"Mutter upon mutter,
Murmur upon murmur,
Now here, now there."
And so they will march,^{f}
But they shall fall backward,
And be injured and snared and captured.

^{14} Hear now the word of the LORD,
You men of mockery,
^{g}Who govern that people^{-g}
In Jerusalem!
^{15} For you have said,
"We have made a covenant with Death,
Concluded a pact with Sheol.
When the sweeping flood passes through,
It shall not reach us;
For we have made falsehood our refuge,
Taken shelter in treachery."
^{16} Assuredly,
Thus said the Lord GOD:
"Behold, I will found in Zion,
Stone by stone,
^{h}A tower of precious cornerstones,$^{-h}$
Exceedingly firm;
He who trusts need not fear.
^{17} But I will apply judgment as a measuring line
And retribution^i as weights;^{j}
And hail shall sweep away the refuge of falsehood,
And flood-waters carry off your shelter.
^{18} Your covenant with Death shall be annulled,
Your pact with Sheol shall not endure;
When the sweeping flood passes through,
You shall be its victims.
^{19} It shall catch you
Every time it passes through;

---

^{f} *I.e. embark on the political adventure.*
$^{g-g}$ *Or "Composers of taunt-verses for that people."*
$^{h-h}$ *Meaning of Heb. uncertain.*
^{i} *As in 1.27; 5.16; 10.22.*
^{j} *I.e. I will make judgment and retribution My plan of action; cf. 34.11; II Kings 21.13.*

It shall pass through every morning,
Every day and every night.
And it shall be sheer horror
To grasp the message."

20 The couch is too short for stretching out,
And the cover too narrow for curling up!

21 For the LORD will arise
As on the hill of Perazim,
He will rouse Himself
As in the vale of Gibeon,
To do His work—
Strange is His work!
And to perform His task—
Astounding is His task!*k*
22 Therefore, refrain from mockery,
Lest your bonds be tightened.
For I have heard a decree of destruction
From my Lord GOD of Hosts
Against all the land.

23 Give diligent ear to my words,
Attend carefully to what I say.
24 Does he who plows to sow
Plow all the time,
Breaking up and furrowing his land?
25 When he has smoothed its surface,
Does he not rather broadcast black cumin
And scatter cumin,
Or set wheat in a row,*l*
Barley in a strip,
And emmer in a patch?
26 For He teaches him the right manner,
His God instructs him.

k Instead of giving victory, as at Baal-perazim and Gibeon (cf. II Sam. 5.19-25; I Chron. 14.9-16), He will inflict punishment.
l In some Near Eastern countries, wheat is actually planted rather than scattered.

²⁷ So, too, black cumin is not threshed with a threshing-
board,
Nor is the wheel of a threshing sledge rolled over cumin;
But black cumin is beaten out with a stick
And cumin with a rod.
²⁸ It is cereal that is crushed.ᵐ
For ⁿ-even ifⁿ he threshes it thoroughly,
And the wheel of his sledge ʰ-and his horses overwhelm
it,⁻ʰ
He does not crush it.
²⁹ That, too, is ordered by the LORD of Hosts;
His counsel is unfathomable,
His wisdom marvelous.

29 "Ah, Ariel,ᵃ Ariel,
City where David camped!
Add year to year,
Let festivals come in their cycles!
² And I will harass Ariel,
And there shall be sorrow and sighing.
ᵇ-She shall be to Me like Ariel.⁻ᵇ
³ And I will camp against you ᶜ-round about;⁻ᶜ
I will lay siege to you ᵇ-with a mound,⁻ᵇ
And I will set up siegeworks against you.
⁴ And you shall speak from lower than the ground,
Your speech shall be humbler than the sod;
Your speech shall sound like a ghost's from the ground,
Your voice shall chirp from the sod.
⁵ And like fine dust shall be
The multitude of ᵈ-your strangers;⁻ᵈ
And like flying chaff,
The multitude of tyrants."

ᵐ *Emendation yields "threshed."*
ⁿ⁻ⁿ *Taking* lo *as equivalent to* lu.

ᵃ *A poetic name of Jerusalem; cf. 33.7.*
ᵇ⁻ᵇ *Meaning of Heb. uncertain.*
ᶜ⁻ᶜ *Meaning of Heb. uncertain; Septuagint reads "like David"; cf. v. 1.*
ᵈ⁻ᵈ *Manuscript 1QIsᵃ reads "haughty men."*

And suddenly, in an instant,
6 She shall be remembered of the LORD of Hosts
With roaring, and shaking, and deafening noise,
Storm, and tempest, and blaze of consuming fire.
7 Then, like a dream, a vision of the night,
Shall be the multitude of nations
That war upon Ariel,
And all her besiegers, and the siegeworks against her,
And those who harass her.
8 Like one who is hungry
And dreams he is eating,
But wakes to find himself empty;
And like one who is thirsty
And dreams he is drinking,
But wakes to find himself faint
And utterly parched—
So shall be all the multitude of nations
That war upon Mount Zion.

9 Act stupid and be stupefied!
Act blind and be blinded!
(They are drunk, but not from wine,
They stagger, but not from liquor.)
10 For the LORD has spread over you
A spirit of deep sleep,
And has shut your eyes, the prophets,
And covered your heads, the seers;
11 So that all prophecy has been to you
Like the words of a sealed document.

If it is handed to one who can read and he is asked to read it,
he will say, "I can't, because it is sealed"; 12 and if the document
is handed to one who cannot read and he is asked to read it, he
will say, "I can't read."

¹³ My Lord said:
Because that people has approached [Me] with its mouth
And honored Me with its lips,
But has kept its heart far from Me,
And its worship of Me has been
A commandment of men, learned by rote—
¹⁴ Truly, I shall further baffle that people
With bafflement upon bafflement;
And the wisdom of its wise shall fail,
And the prudence of its prudent shall vanish.

¹⁵ Ha! Those who would hide their plans
Deep from the LORD!
Who do their work in dark places
And say, "Who sees us, who takes note of us?"
¹⁶ ^{e-}How perverse of you!
Should the potter be accounted as the clay?^{-e}
Should what is made say of its Maker,
"He did not make me,"
And what is formed say of Him who formed it,
^{f-}"He did not understand?"^{-f}
¹⁷ Surely, in a little while,
Lebanon will be transformed into farm land,
And farm land accounted as mere brush.
¹⁸ In that day, the deaf shall hear even written words,
And the eyes of the blind shall see
Even in darkness and obscurity.
¹⁹ Then the humble shall have increasing joy through the
    LORD,
And the neediest of men shall exult
In the Holy One of Israel.
²⁰ For the tyrant shall be no more,
The scoffer shall cease to be;
And those diligent for evil shall be wiped out,
²¹ Who cause men to lose their lawsuits,

^{e-e} *Meaning of first line uncertain; emendation yields "Should the potter be accounted/Like the jugs or like the clay?"*
^{f-f} *Emendation yields "He did not fashion me."*

Laying a snare for the arbiter at the gate,
And wronging by falsehood
Him who was in the right.

²² Assuredly, thus said the LORD to the House of Jacob, ᵍ⁻who redeemed Abraham:⁻ᵍ

No more shall Jacob be shamed,
No longer his face grow pale.

²³ For when he—that is, his children—behold what My hands have wrought in his midst, they will hallow My name.

Men will hallow the Holy One of Jacob
And stand in awe of the God of Israel.
²⁴ And the confused shall acquire insight
And grumblers accept instruction.

30 Oh, disloyal sons!

—declares the LORD—

Making plans
Against My wishes,
Weaving schemes
Against My will,
Thereby piling
Guilt on guilt—
² Who set out to go down to Egypt
Without asking Me,
To seek refuge with Pharaoh,
To seek shelter under the protection of Egypt.

³ The refuge with Pharaoh shall result in your shame;
The shelter under Egypt's protection, in your chagrin.
⁴ Though his officers are present in Zoan,ᵃ

ᵍ⁻ᵍ *Emendation yields "whose fathers He redeemed."*
ᵃ *Or "Tanis."*

And his messengers[b] reach as far as Hanes,
5 They all shall come to shame
Because of a people that does not avail them,
That is of no help or avail,
But [brings] only chagrin and disgrace.

6 [c-]The "Beasts of the Negeb" Pronouncement.

Through a[-c] land of distress and hardship,
Of lion and roaring[d] king-beast,
Of viper and flying seraph,[e]
They convey their wealth on the backs of asses,
Their treasures on camels' humps,
To a people of no avail.
7 For the help of Egypt
Shall be vain and empty.
Truly, I say of this,
[f-]"They are a threat that has ceased."[-f]

8 Now,
Go, write it down on a tablet
And inscribe it in a record,
That it may be with them for future days,
A witness[g] forever.
9 For it is a rebellious people,
Faithless children,
Children who refused to heed
The instruction of the LORD;
10 Who said to the seers,
"Do not see,"
To the prophets, "Do not prophesy truth to us;
Speak to us falsehoods,
Prophesy delusions.

---

b Emendation yields "kings"; cf. 19.2 with note.
c-c Meaning of Heb. uncertain; emendation yields "Through the wasteland of the Negeb/ Through a. . . ."
d Meaning of Heb. uncertain.
e See note on 14.29.
f-f Meaning of Heb. uncertain. Emendation yields "Disgrace and chagrin"; cf. v. 5.
g Understanding 'ad, with Targum, as a variant of 'ed.

[11] Leave the way!
Get off the path!
Let us hear no more
About the Holy One of Israel!"

[12] Assuredly,
Thus said the Holy One of Israel:
Because you have rejected this word,
And have put your trust and reliance
In that which is fraudulent and tortuous—
[13] Of a surety,
This iniquity shall work on you
Like a spreading breach that occurs in a lofty wall,
Whose crash comes sudden and swift.
[14] It is smashed as one smashes an earthen jug,
Ruthlessly shattered
So that no shard is left in its breakage
To scoop coals from a brazier,
Or ladle water from a puddle.

[15] For thus said my Lord GOD,
The Holy One of Israel,
"You shall triumph by stillness and quiet;
Your victory shall come about
Through calm and confidence."
But you refused.
[16] "No," you declared.
"We shall flee on steeds"—
Therefore you shall flee!
"We shall ride on swift mounts"—
Therefore your pursuers shall prove swift!
[17] One thousand before the shout of one—
You shall flee at the shout of five;
Till what is left of you

Is like a mast on a hilltop,
Like a pole upon a mountain.

18 Truly, the LORD is waiting to show you grace,
Truly, He will arise to pardon you.
For the LORD is a God of justice;
Happy are all who wait for Him.

19 Indeed, O people in Zion, dwellers of Jerusalem, you shall not have cause to weep. He will grant you His favor at the sound of your cry; He will respond as soon as He hears it. 20 My Lord will provide for you meager bread and scant water. Then your Guide will no more *d*-be ignored,-*d* but your eyes will watch your Guide; 21 and, whenever you deviate to the right or to the left, your ears will heed the command from behind you: "This is the road; follow it!" 22 And you will treat as unclean the silver overlay of your images and the golden plating of your idols. You will cast*h* them away like a menstruous woman. "Out!" you will call to them.

23 So rain shall be provided for the seed with which you sow the ground, and the bread which the ground brings forth shall be rich and fat. Your livestock, in that day, shall graze in broad pastures; 24 as for the cattle and the asses which till the soil, they shall partake of salted fodder that has been winnowed with shovel and fan.

25 And on every high mountain and on every lofty hill, there shall appear brooks and watercourses—on a day of heavy slaughter, when towers topple. 26 And the light of the moon shall become like the light of the sun, and the light of the sun shall become sevenfold, like the light of the seven days, when the LORD binds up His people's wounds and heals the injuries it has suffered.

27 Behold the *i*-LORD Himself-*i*
Comes from afar

h *Change of vocalization yields "keep."*
i-i *Lit. "the name of the LORD."*

In blazing wrath,
j-With a heavy burden*-j*—
His lips full of fury,
His tongue like devouring fire,
[28] And his breath like a raging torrent
Reaching halfway up the neck—
To set a misguiding yoke*k* upon nations
And a misleading bridle upon the jaws of peoples.

[29] For you, there shall be singing
As on a night when a festival is hallowed;
There shall be rejoicing as when they march
With flute, *l*-with timbrels, and with lyres*-l*
To the Rock of Israel on the Mount of the LORD.

[30] For the LORD will make His majestic voice heard
And display the sweep of His arm
In raging wrath,
In a devouring blaze of fire,
In tempest, and rainstorm, and hailstones.
[31] Truly, Assyria, who beats with the rod,
Shall be cowed by the voice of the LORD;
[32] *d*-And each time the appointed staff passes by,
The LORD will bring down [His arm] upon him
And will do battle with him as he waves it.*-d*
[33] The Topheth*m* has long been ready for him;
He too is destined for Melech*n*—
His fire-pit has been made both wide and deep,
With plenty of fire and firewood,
And with the breath of the LORD
Burning in it like a stream of sulfur.

---

j-j Presumably with a heavy load of punishment. Meaning of Heb. uncertain.
k Interpreting naphath like Arabic nāf; meaning of line uncertain.
l-l Brought up from v. 32 for clarity.
m A site near Jerusalem at which human beings were sacrificed by fire in periods of paganizing;
   see II Kings 23.10.
n Cf. Molech, Lev. 18.21; 20.2-5.

31 Ha!

Those who go down to Egypt for help
And rely upon horses!
They have put their trust in abundance of chariots,
In vast numbers of riders,
And they have not turned to the Holy One of Israel,
They have not sought the LORD.

² But He too is wise!
He has brought on misfortune,
And has not canceled His word.
So He shall rise against the house of evildoers,
And the allies*a* of the workers of iniquity.
³ For the Egyptians are man, not God,
And their horses are flesh, not spirit;
And when the LORD stretches out His arm,
The helper shall trip
And the helped one shall fall,
And both shall perish together.

⁴ For thus the LORD has said to me:
As a lion—a great beast—
Growls over its prey
And, when the shepherds gather
In force against him,
Is not dismayed by their cries
Nor cowed by their noise—
So the LORD of Hosts will descend to make war
Against the mount and the hill of Zion.

⁵ Like the birds that fly, even so will the LORD of Hosts shield
Jerusalem, shielding and saving, protecting and rescuing.
⁶ *b-*Return, O children of Israel,*-b* to Him to whom they have

---

a *Lit. "help."*
b-b *Emendation yields "Then the children of Israel shall return."*

been so shamefully false; 7 for in that day everyone will reject his idols of silver and idols of gold, which your hands have made for your guilt.

8 Then Assyria shall fall,
Not by the sword of man;
A sword not of humans shall devour him.
He shall shrivel*c* before the sword,
And his young men *d*-pine away.*-d*
9 His rock shall melt with terror,
And his officers shall *e*-collapse from weakness*-e*—
Declares the LORD, who has a fire in Zion,
Who has an oven in Jerusalem.*f*

32 Behold, a king shall reign in righteousness,
And ministers shall govern with justice;
2 Every one of them shall be
Like a refuge from gales,
A shelter from rainstorms;
Like brooks of water in a desert,
Like the shade of a massive rock
In a languishing land.

3 Then the eyes of those who have sight shall not be sealed,
And the ears of those who have hearing shall listen;
4 And the minds of the thoughtless shall attend and note,
And the tongues of mumblers shall speak with fluent eloquence.
5 No more shall a villain be called noble,
Nor shall "gentleman" be said of a knave.
6 For the villain speaks villainy
And plots treachery;
To act impiously

---

c *From root* nss; *cf. 10.18; others "flee."*
d-d *From root* mss; *cf. 10.18; others "become tributary."*
e-e *Cf. note* c; *meaning of Heb. uncertain.*
f *Cf. 30.33.*

And to preach disloyalty against the LORD;
To leave the hungry unsatisfied
And deprive the thirsty of drink.
⁷ As for the knave, his tools are knavish.
He forges plots
To destroy the poor with falsehoods
And the needy when they plead their cause.
⁸ But the noble has noble intentions
And is constant in noble acts.

⁹ You carefree women,
Attend, hear my words!
You confident ladies,
Give ear to my speech!
¹⁰ *ᵃ⁻In little more than a year,⁻ᵃ*
You shall be troubled, O confident ones,
When the vintage is over
And no ingathering takes place.
¹¹ Tremble, you carefree ones!
Quake, O confident ones!
Strip yourselves naked,
Put the cloth about your loins!
¹² Lament *ᵇ⁻upon the breasts,⁻ᵇ*
For the pleasant fields,
For the spreading grapevines,
¹³ For my people's soil—
It shall be overgrown with briers and thistles—
Aye, and for all the houses of delight,
For the city of mirth.
¹⁴ For the castle shall be abandoned,
The noisy city forsaken;
Citadel and tower shall become
ᶜ⁻Bare places⁻ᶜ forever,
A stamping ground for wild asses,
A pasture for flocks*ᵈ*—

ᵃ⁻ᵃ *Meaning of Heb. uncertain.*
ᵇ⁻ᵇ *Emendation yields "for the fields."*
ᶜ⁻ᶜ *Meaning of Heb. uncertain; emendation yields "Brushland, desert."*
ᵈ *Emendation yields "onagers"; cf. Job 39.5.*

¹⁵ Till a spirit from on high is poured out on us,
And wilderness is transformed into farm land,
While farm land rates as mere brush.ᵉ
¹⁶ Then justice shall abide in the wilderness
And righteousness shall dwell on the farm land.
¹⁷ For the work of righteousness shall be peace,
And the effect of righteousness, calm and confidence
forever.
¹⁸ Then my people shall dwell in peaceful homes,
In secure dwellings,
In untroubled places of rest.
¹⁹ ᶠAnd the brush shall sink and vanish,
Even as the city is laid low.

²⁰ Happy shall you be who sow by all waters,
Who ᵍ⁻send out cattle and asses to pasture.⁻ᵍ

33 Ha, you ravager who are not ravaged,
You betrayer who have not been betrayed!
When you have done ravaging, you shall be ravaged;
When you have finished betraying, you shall be betrayed.

² O LORD, be gracious to us!
It is to You we have looked;
ᵃ⁻Be their arm⁻ᵃ every morning,
Also our deliverance in time of stress.
³ At [Your] roaring, peoples have fled;
Before Your majesty nations have scattered;
⁴ And spoilᵇ was gathered as locusts are gathered,
Itᶜ was amassedᵈ as grasshoppers are amassed.ᵉ

ᵉ *I.e. the transformed wilderness will surpass in fertility what is now used as farm land.*
ᶠ *Meaning of verse uncertain.*
ᵍ⁻ᵍ *Lit. "let loose the feet of cattle and asses"; cf. 7.25 end.*

ᵃ⁻ᵃ *Emendation yields "You have been our help."*
ᵇ *Heb. "your spoil."*
ᶜ *Meaning of Heb. uncertain. Emendation yields "booty"; cf. v. 23.*
ᵈ *Taking šqq as a cognate of qšš.*
ᵉ *Apparently for food; cf. Lev. 11.22.*

⁵ The LORD is exalted,
He dwells on high!
[Of old] He filled Zion
With justice and righteousness.
⁶ Faithfulness to *ᶠ-Your charge-ᶠ* was [her] wealth,
Wisdom and devotion [her] triumph,
Reverence for the LORD—that was her*ᵍ* treasure.

⁷ Hark! The Arielites*ʰ* cry aloud;
Shalom's*ⁱ* messengers weep bitterly.
⁸ Highways are desolate,
Wayfarers have ceased.
A covenant has been renounced,
Cities*ʲ* rejected
ᵏ-Mortal man⁻ᵏ* despised.
⁹ The land is wilted and withered;
Lebanon disgraced and moldering,
Sharon is become like a desert,
And Bashan and Carmel are stripped bare.

¹⁰ "Now I will arise," says the LORD,
"Now I will exalt Myself, now raise Myself high.
¹¹ You shall conceive hay,
Give birth to straw;
My*ˡ* breath will devour you like fire.
¹² Peoples shall be burnings of lime,*ᵐ*
Thorns cut down that are set on fire.
¹³ Hear, you who are far, what I have done;
You who are near, note My might."

¹⁴ Sinners in Zion are frightened,
The godless are seized with trembling:
"Who of us can dwell with the devouring fire:

ᶠ⁻ᶠ *Meaning of Heb. uncertain.*
ᵍ *Heb. "his."*
ʰ *So a few manuscripts; cf. 29.1.*
ⁱ *I.e. Jerusalem's; cf. Salem (Heb. Shalem), Ps. 76.3.*
ʲ *1QIsᵃ reads "A pact."*
ᵏ⁻ᵏ *Emendation yields "an obligation."*
ˡ *Heb. "your."*
ᵐ *Emendation yields "brambles"; cf. 32.13.*

Who of us can dwell with the never-dying blaze?"
15 He who walks in righteousness,
Speaks uprightly,
Spurns profit from fraudulent dealings,
Waves away a bribe instead of grasping it,
Stops his ears against listening to infamy,
Shuts his eyes against looking at evil—
16 Such a one shall dwell in lofty security,
With inaccessible cliffs for his stronghold,
With his food supplied
And his drink assured.

17 When your eyes behold *n*-a king in his beauty,-*n*
When they contemplate the land round about,
18 Your throat*o* shall murmur in awe,
"Where is one who could count? Where is one who could
weigh?
Where is one who could count [all these] towers?"
19 No more shall you see the barbarian folk,
The people of speech too obscure to comprehend,
So stammering of tongue that they are not understood.

20 When you gaze upon Zion, our city of assembly,
Your eyes shall behold Jerusalem
As a secure homestead,
A tent not to be transported,
Whose pegs shall never be pulled up,
And none of whose ropes shall break.
21 For there the LORD in His greatness shall be for us
Like a region of rivers, of broad streams,
Where no floating vessels can sail
And no mighty craft can travel—
p-Their*q* ropes are slack,
They cannot steady the sockets of their masts,
They cannot spread a sail.-*p*

n-n *Emendation yields "perfection of beauty"; cf. Ps. 50.2.*
o *As in 59.13 and elsewhere; others "heart."*
p-p *Brought up from v. 23 for clarity. The passage means that the Lord will render Jerusalem
as inaccessible to enemies as if it were surrounded by an impassable sea.*
q *Heb. "Your."*

²² For the LORD shall be our ruler,
The LORD shall be our prince,
The LORD shall be our king:
He shall deliver us.
²³ Then ^{r-}shall indeed much spoil be divided,^{-r}
Even the lame shall seize booty.
²⁴ And none who lives there shall say, "I am sick";
It shall be inhabited by folk whose sin has been forgiven.

34 Approach, O nations, and listen,
Give heed, O peoples!
Let the earth and those in it hear;
The world, and what it brings forth.
² For the LORD is angry at all the nations,
Furious at all their host;
He has doomed them, consigned them to slaughter.
³ Their slain shall be left lying,
And the stench of their corpses shall mount;
And the hills shall be drenched with their blood,
⁴ ^{a-}All the host of heaven shall molder.^{-a} ·
The heavens shall be rolled up like a scroll,
And all their host shall wither
Like a leaf withering on the vine,
Or shriveled fruit on a fig tree.

⁵ For My sword shall ^{b-}be drunk^{-b} in the sky;
Lo, it shall come down upon Edom,
Upon the people I have doomed,
To wreak judgment.
⁶ The LORD has a sword; it is sated with blood,
It is gorged with fat—
The blood of lambs and he-goats,
The kidney fat of rams.
For the LORD holds a sacrifice in Bozrah,

^{r-r} *Meaning of Heb. uncertain; emendation yields "even a blind man shall divide much spoil."*
^{a-a} *1QIs^a reads "And the valleys shall be cleft,/And all the host of heaven shall wither."*
^{b-b} *1QIs^a reads "be seen"; cf. Targum.*

A great slaughter in the land of Edom.
[7] Wild oxen shall fall *with them,*
Young bulls with mighty steers;
And their land shall be drunk with blood,
Their soil shall be saturated with fat.
[8] For it is the LORD's day of retribution,
The year of vindication for Zion's cause.
[9] Its*d* streams shall be turned to pitch
And its soil to sulfur.

Its land shall become burning pitch,
[10] Night and day it shall never go out;
Its smoke shall rise for all time.
Through the ages it shall lie in ruins;
Through the aeons none shall traverse it.
[11] *Jackdaws and owls* shall possess it;
Great owls and ravens shall dwell there.
He shall measure it with a line of chaos
And with weights of emptiness.*
[12] *It shall be called, "No kingdom is there,"*
Its nobles and all its lords shall be nothing.
[13] Thorns shall grow up in its palaces,
Nettles and briers in its strongholds.
It shall be a home of jackals,
An abode of ostriches.
[14] *Wildcats shall meet hyenas,
Goat-demons shall greet each other;
There too the lilith*h* shall repose
And find herself a resting place.
[15] There the arrow-snake shall nest and lay eggs,
And shall brood and hatch in its shade.
There too the buzzards shall gather
With one another.
[16] Search and read it in the scroll of the LORD:
Not one of these shall be absent,

---

c-c Emendation yields "with fatted calves."
d I.e. Edom's.
e-e Meaning of Heb. uncertain.
f I.e. He shall plan chaos and emptiness for it; cf. 28.17; Lam. 2.8.
g Most of the creatures in vv. 14-15 cannot be identified with certainty.
h A kind of demon.

Not one shall miss its fellow.
For His[i] mouth has spoken,
It is His spirit that has assembled them,
17 And it is He who apportioned it to them by lot,
Whose hand divided it for them with the line.
They shall possess it for all time,
They shall dwell there through the ages.

35 The arid desert shall be glad,
The wilderness shall rejoice
And shall blossom like a rose.[a]
2 It shall blossom abundantly,
It shall also exult and shout.
It shall receive the glory of Lebanon,
The splendor of Carmel and Sharon.
They shall behold the glory of the LORD,
The splendor of our God.

3 Strengthen the hands that are slack;
Make firm the tottering knees!
4 Say to the anxious of heart,
"Be strong, fear not;
Behold your God!
Requital is coming,
The recompense of God—
He Himself is coming to give you triumph."

5 Then the eyes of the blind shall be opened,
And the ears of the deaf shall be unstopped.
6 Then the lame shall leap like a deer,
And the tongue of the dumb shall shout aloud;
For waters shall burst forth in the desert,
Streams in the wilderness.
7 Torrid earth shall become a pool;
Parched land, fountains of water;

i *Heb. "My."*
a *Lit. "crocus."*

430

The home of jackals, a pasture[b];
The abode [of ostriches],[c] reeds and rushes.

[8] And a highway shall appear there,
Which shall be called the Sacred Way.
No one unclean shall pass along it,
But it shall be for them.[d]
[e-]No traveler, not even fools, shall go astray.[-e]
[9] No lion shall be there,
No ferocious beast shall set foot on it—
These shall not be found there.
But the redeemed shall walk it;
[10] And the ransomed of the LORD shall return,
And come with shouting to Zion,
Crowned with joy everlasting.
They shall attain joy and gladness,
While sorrow and sighing flee.

36 [a]In the fourteenth year of King Hezekiah, King Sennacherib of Assyria marched against all the fortified towns of Judah and seized them. [2] From Lachish, the king of Assyria sent the Rabshakeh,[b] with a large force, to King Hezekiah in Jerusalem. [The Rabshakeh] took up a position near the conduit of the Upper Pool, by the road of the Fuller's Field; [3] and Eliakim son of Hilkiah who was in charge of the palace, Shebna the scribe, and Joah son of Asaph the recorder went out to him.

[4] The Rabshakeh said to them, "You tell Hezekiah: Thus said the Great King, the king of Assyria: What makes you so confident? [5] I suppose[c] mere talk makes counsel and valor for war! Look, on whom are you relying, that you have rebelled against me? [6] You are relying on Egypt, that splintered reed of a staff, which enters and punctures the palm of anyone who leans on it.

[b] *Meaning of Heb. uncertain; emendation yields "a marsh."*
[c] *Cf. 34.13.*
[d] *Emendation yields "for His people."*
[e-e] *Meaning of Heb. uncertain.*

[a] *Chapters 36-39 occur also as II Kings 18.13-20.19, with a number of variants, some of which will be cited here in the footnotes.*
[b] *An Assyrian title; cf. "Tartan," 20.1.*
[c] *II Kings 18.20 "You must think."*

That's what Pharaoh king of Egypt is like to all who rely on him.
7 And if you tell me that you are relying on the LORD your God,
He is the very one whose shrines and altars Hezekiah did away
with, telling Judah and Jerusalem, 'You must worship only at this
altar!' 8 Come now, make this wager with my master, the king of
Assyria: I'll give you two thousand horses, if you can produce
riders to mount them. 9 So how could you refuse anything, even
to the deputy of one of my master's lesser servants, relying on
Egypt for chariots and horsemen? 10 And do you think I have
marched against this land to destroy it without the LORD? The
LORD Himself told me: Go up against that land and destroy it."

11 Eliakim, Shebna, and Joah replied to the Rabshakeh, "Please,
speak to your servants in Aramaic, since we understand it; do not
speak to us in Judean in the hearing of the people on the wall."
12 But the Rabshakeh replied, "Was it to your master and to you
that my master sent me to speak those words? It was precisely to
the men who are sitting on the wall—who will have to eat their
dung and drink their urine with you." 13 And the Rabshakeh
stood and called out in a loud voice in Judean: 14 "Hear the words
of the Great King, the king of Assyria! Thus said the king: Don't
let Hezekiah deceive you, for he will not be able to save you.
15 Don't let Hezekiah make you rely on the LORD, saying: 'The
LORD will surely save us; this city will not fall into the hands of
Assyria!' 16 Don't listen to Hezekiah. For thus said the king of
Assyria: Make your peace with me and come out to me,[d] so that
you may all eat from your vines and your fig trees and drink water
from your cisterns, 17 until I come and take you away to a land like
your own, a land of bread and wine, of grain [fields] and vineyards. 18 Beware of letting Hezekiah mislead you by saying, 'The
LORD will save us.' Did any of the gods of the other nations save
his land from the king of Assyria? 19 Where were the gods of
Hamath and Arpad? Where were the gods of Sepharvaim? And
did they[e] save Samaria from me? 20 Which among all the gods of
those countries saved their countries from me, that the LORD
should save Jerusalem from me?" 21 But they were silent and did

d *I.e. to my representative the Rabshakeh.*
e *I.e. the gods of Samaria.*

not answer him with a single word; for the king's order was: "Do not answer him."

²² And so Eliakim son of Hilkiah who was in charge of the palace, Shebna the scribe, and Joah son of Asaph the recorder came to Hezekiah with their clothes rent, and they reported to him what the Rabshakeh had said.

37 When King Hezekiah heard this, he rent his clothes and covered himself with sackcloth and went into the House of the LORD. ² He also sent Eliakim, who was in charge of the palace, Shebna the scribe, and the senior priests, covered with sackcloth, to the prophet Isaiah son of Amoz. ³ They said to him, "Thus said Hezekiah: This day is a day of distress, of chastisement, and of disgrace. ᵃ‑The babes have reached the birthstool, but the strength to give birth is lacking.‑ᵃ ⁴ Perhaps the LORD your God will take note of the words of the Rabshakeh, whom his master the king of Assyria has sent to blaspheme the living God, and will mete out judgment for the words that the LORD your God has heard—if you will offer up prayer for the surviving remnant."

⁵ When King Hezekiah's ministers came to Isaiah, ⁶ Isaiah said to them, "Tell your master as follows: Thus said the LORD: Do not be frightened by the words of blasphemy against Me that you have heard from the minions of the king of Assyria. ⁷ I will delude ᵇ him: he will hear a rumor and return to his land, and I will make him fall by the sword in his land."

⁸ The Rabshakeh, meanwhile, heard that [the king] had left Lachish; he turned back and found the king of Assyria attacking Libnah. ⁹ But [the king of Assyria] learned that King Tirhakah of Nubia had come out to fight him; and when he heard it, he sent messengers to Hezekiah, saying, ¹⁰ "Tell this to King Hezekiah of Judah: Do not let your God, on whom you are relying, mislead you into thinking that Jerusalem will not be delivered into the hands of the king of Assyria. ¹¹ You yourself have heard what the kings of Assyria have done to all the lands, how they have an-

---

ᵃ‑ᵃ *I.e. the situation is desperate, and we are at a loss.*
ᵇ *Lit. "put a spirit in."*

nihilated them; and can you escape? [12] Were the nations that my predecessors[c] destroyed—Gozan, Haran, Rezeph, and the Bethedenites in Telassar—saved by their gods? [13] Where is the king of Hamath? and the king of Arpad? and the kings of Lair, Sepharvaim, Hena, and Ivvah?"

[14] Hezekiah received the letter from the messengers and read it. Hezekiah then went up to the House of the LORD and spread it out before the LORD. [15] And Hezekiah prayed to the LORD: [16] "O LORD of Hosts, enthroned on the Cherubim! You alone are God of all the kingdoms of the earth. You made the heavens and the earth. [17] O LORD, incline Your ear and hear, open Your eye and see. Hear all the words that Sennacherib has sent to blaspheme the living God! [18] True, O LORD, the kings of Assyria have annihilated all the nations[d] and their lands [19] and have committed their gods to the flames and have destroyed them; for they are not gods, but man's handwork of wood and stone. [20] But now, O LORD our God, deliver us from his hands, and let all the kingdoms of the earth know that You, O LORD, alone [are God]."[e]

[21] Then Isaiah son of Amoz sent this message to Hezekiah: "Thus said the LORD, the God of Israel, to whom you have prayed, concerning King Sennacherib of Assyria—[22] this is the word that the LORD has spoken concerning him:

Fair Maiden Zion despises you,
She mocks at you;
Fair Jerusalem shakes
Her head at you.
[23] Whom have you blasphemed and reviled?
Against whom made loud your voice
And haughtily raised your eyes?
Against the Holy One of Israel!
[24] Through your servants you have blasphemed my Lord.
Because you thought,
'Thanks to my vast chariotry,

[c] Lit. "fathers."
[d] So II Kings 19.17, and 13 mss. here; most mss. and the editions read "lands."
[e] Supplied from II Kings 19.19.

434

It is I who have climbed the highest mountains,
To the remotest parts of the Lebanon,
And have cut down its loftiest cedars,
Its choicest cypresses,
And have reached its highest peak,
*f*Its densest forest.*f*
25 It is I who have drawn*g*
And drunk water.
I have dried up with the soles of my feet
All the streams of Egypt.'
26 Have you not heard? Of old
I planned that very thing,
I designed it long ago,
And now have fulfilled it.
And it has come to pass,
Laying fortified towns waste in desolate heaps.
27 Their inhabitants are helpless,
Dismayed and shamed.
They were but grass of the field
And green herbage,
Grass of the roofs *h*that is blasted
Before the east wind.*-h*
28 I know your stayings
And your goings and comings,
And how you have raged against Me.
29 Because you have raged against Me,
And your tumult has reached My ears,
I will place My hook in your nose
And My bit between your jaws;
And I will make you go back by the road
By which you came.

30 "And this is the sign for you:*i* This year you eat what grows
of itself, and the next year what springs from that, and in the third
year sow and reap and plant vineyards and eat their fruit. 31 And

---

f-f Lit. "Its farm land forest"; exact meaning of Heb. uncertain.
g Or "dug"; meaning of Heb. uncertain.
h-h So ms. 1QIs*a*; cf. II Kings 19.26. The usual reading in our passage means, literally, "and
a field (?) before standing grain."
i I.e. Hezekiah.

the survivors of the House of Judah that have escaped shall renew
its trunk below and produce boughs above.

32 For a remnant shall come forth from Jerusalem,
Survivors from Mount Zion.
The zeal of the LORD of Hosts
Shall bring this to pass.

33 "Assuredly, thus said the LORD concerning the king of Assyria:
He shall not enter this city;
He shall not shoot an arrow at it,
Or advance upon it with a shield,
Or pile up a siege mound against it.
34 He shall go back
By the way he came,
He shall not enter this city

—declares the LORD;
35 I will protect and save this city for My sake
And for the sake of My servant David."

36 [That night]^j an angel of the LORD went out and struck down
one hundred and eighty-five thousand in the Assyrian camp, and
the following morning they were all dead corpses.
37 So King Sennacherib of Assyria broke camp and retreated,
and stayed in Nineveh. 38 While he was worshiping in the temple
of his god Nisroch, he was struck down with the sword by his sons
Adrammelech and Sarezer. They fled to the land of Ararat, and
his son Esarhaddon succeeded him as king.

38 In those days Hezekiah fell dangerously ill. The prophet
Isaiah son of Amoz came and said to him, "Thus said the LORD:
Set your affairs in order, for you are going to die; you will not get
well." 2 Thereupon Hezekiah turned his face to the wall and

j Supplied from II Kings 19.35.

prayed to the LORD. ³ "Please, O LORD," he said, "remember how I have walked before You sincerely and wholeheartedly, and have done what is pleasing to You." And Hezekiah wept profusely.

⁴ Then the word of the LORD came to Isaiah: ⁵ "Go and tell Hezekiah: Thus said the LORD, the God of your father David: I have heard your prayer, I have seen your tears. I hereby add fifteen years to your life. ⁶ I will also rescue you and this city from the hands of the king of Assyria. I will protect this city. ⁷ And this is the sign for you from the LORD that the LORD will do the thing which He has promised: ⁸ I am going to make the shadow on the steps, which has descended on the dial*ᵃ* of Ahaz because of the sun, recede ten steps." And the sun['s shadow] receded ten steps, the same steps it had descended.

⁹ A poem by Hezekiah king of Judah when he recovered from the illness he had suffered:

ⁱ⁰ *ᵇ*I had thought:
I must depart in the middle of my days;
I have been consigned to the gates of Sheol
For the rest of my years.
¹¹ I thought, I shall never see Yah,*ᶜ*
Yah in the land of the living,
Or ever behold men again
Among those who inhabit the earth.
¹² My dwelling is pulled up and removed from me
Like a tent of shepherds;
My life is rolled up like a web
And cut from the thrum.

*ᵈ⁻*Only from daybreak to nightfall
Was I kept whole,
¹³ Then it was as though a lion
Were breaking all my bones;
I cried out until morning.

ᵃ *Heb. "steps." A model of a dial with steps has been discovered in Egypt.*
ᵇ *Meaning of verse uncertain in part.*
ᶜ *I.e. visit His Temple. For "Yah" see 12.2; 26.4.*
ᵈ⁻ᵈ *Meaning of Heb. uncertain.*

(Only from daybreak to nightfall
Was I kept whole.)^{-d}
14 I piped like a swift or a crane,
I moaned like a dove,
As my eyes, all worn, looked to heaven:
"My Lord, I am in straits;
Be my surety!"

15 What can I say? ^{d-}He promised me,^{-d}
And He it is who has wrought it.
^{d-}All my sleep had fled
Because of the bitterness of my soul.
16 My Lord, for all that and despite it
My life-breath is revived;^{-d}
You have restored me to health and revived me.
17 Truly, it was for my own good
That I had such great bitterness:
You saved my life
From the pit of destruction,
For You have cast behind Your back
All my offenses.
18 For it is not Sheol that praises You,
Not [the Land of] Death that extols You;
Nor do they who descend into the Pit
Hope for Your grace.
19 The living, only the living
Can give thanks to You
As I do this day;
Fathers^e relate to children
Your acts of grace:
20 "[It has pleased] the LORD to deliver us,
That is why we offer up music^f
All the days of our lives
At the House of the LORD."

^e *Heb. singular.*
^f*Neginothai is a poetic form of* neginoth.

²¹ When Isaiah said, "Let them take a cake of figs and apply it to the rash, and he will recover," ²² Hezekiah asked, "What will be the sign that I shall go up to the House of the LORD?"

39

At that time, Merodach-baladan son of Baladan, the king of Babylon, sent [envoys with] a letter and a gift to Hezekiah, for he had heard about his illness and recovery. ² Hezekiah was pleased by their coming, and he showed them his treasure house —the silver, the gold, the spices, and the fragrant oil—and all his armory, and everything that was to be found in his storehouses. There was nothing in his palace or in all his realm that Hezekiah did not show them. ³ Then the prophet Isaiah came to King Hezekiah. "What," he demanded of him, "did those men say to you? Where have they come to you from?" "They have come to me," replied Hezekiah, "from a far country, from Babylon." ⁴ Next he asked, "What have they seen in your palace?" And Hezekiah replied, "They have seen everything there is in my palace. There was nothing in my storehouses that I did not show them."

⁵ Then Isaiah said to Hezekiah, "Hear the word of the LORD of Hosts: ⁶ A time is coming when everything in your palace, which your ancestors have stored up to this day, will be carried off to Babylon; nothing will be left behind, said the LORD. ⁷ And some of your sons, your own issue, whom you will have fathered, will be taken to serve as eunuchs in the palace of the king of Babylon." ⁸ Hezekiah declared to Isaiah, "The word of the LORD that you have spoken is good." For he thought, "It means that ^a-safety is assured for^{-a} my time."

40

Comfort, oh comfort My people,
Says your God.
² Speak tenderly to Jerusalem,
And declare to her

---

^{a-a} Lit. "there shall be safety and faithfulness in."

That her term of service is over,
That her iniquity is expiated;
For she has received at the hand of the LORD
Double for all her sins.

³ A voice rings out:
"Clear in the desert
A road for the LORD!
Level in the wilderness
A highway for our God!
⁴ Let every valley be raised,
Every hill and mount made low.
Let the rugged ground become level
And the ridges become a plain.
⁵ The Presence of the LORD shall appear,
And all flesh, as one, shall behold—
For the LORD Himself has spoken."

⁶ A voice rings out: "Proclaim!"
ᵃ⁻Another asks,⁻ᵃ "What shall I proclaim?"
"All flesh is grass,
All its goodness like flowers of the field:
⁷ Grass withers, flowers fade
When the breath of the LORD blows on them.
Indeed, man is but grass:
⁸ Grass withers, flowers fade—
But the word of our God is always fulfilled!"

⁹ Ascend a lofty mountain,
O herald of joy to Zion;
Raise your voice with power,
O herald of joy to Jerusalem—
Raise it, have no fear;
Announce to the cities of Judah:
Behold your God!

ᵃ⁻ᵃ *1QIsᵃ and Septuagint read "And I asked."*

440

¹⁰ Behold, the Lord GOD comes in might,
And His arm wins triumph for Him;
See, His reward^b is with Him,
His recompense before Him.
¹¹ Like a shepherd He pastures His flock:
He gathers the lambs in His arms
And carries them in His bosom;
Gently He drives the mother sheep.

¹² Who measured the waters with the hollow of his hand,
And gauged the skies with a span,
And meted earth's dust with a measure,^c
And weighed the mountains with a scale
And the hills with a balance?
¹³ Who has plumbed the mind of the LORD,
What man could tell Him His plan?
¹⁴ Whom did He consult, and who taught Him,
Guided Him in the way of right?
Who guided Him in knowledge
And showed Him the path of wisdom?

¹⁵ The nations are but a drop in a bucket,
Reckoned as dust on a balance;
The very coastlands He lifts like motes.
¹⁶ Lebanon is not fuel enough,
Nor its beasts enough for sacrifice.
¹⁷ All nations are as naught in His sight;
He accounts them as less than nothing.

¹⁸ To whom, then, can you liken God,
What form compare to Him?
¹⁹ The idol? A woodworker shaped it,
And a smith overlaid it with gold,
^dForging links of silver.^{-d}
²⁰ As a gift, he chooses the mulberry^e—

^b *The reward and recompense to the cities of Judah; cf. Jer. 31.14, 16.*
^c *Heb. shalish "third," probably a third of an ephah.*
^{d-d} *Meaning of Heb. uncertain.*
^e *Heb. mesukkan; according to a Jewish tradition, preserved by Jerome, a kind of wood; a similar word denotes a kind of wood in Akkadian.*

A wood that does not rot—
Then seeks a skillful woodworker
To make a firm idol,
That will not topple.

21 Do you not know?
Have you not heard?
Have you not been told
From the very first?
Have you not discerned
d-How the earth was founded?*-d*
22 It is He who is enthroned above the vault of the earth,
So that its inhabitants seem as grasshoppers;
Who spread out the skies like gauze,
Stretched them out like a tent to dwell in.
23 He brings potentates to naught,
Makes rulers of the earth as nothing.
24 Hardly are they planted,
Hardly are they sown,
Hardly has their stem
Taken root in earth,
When He blows upon them and they dry up,
And the storm bears them off like straw.

25 To whom, then, can you liken Me,
To whom can I be compared?
                                        —says the Holy One.
26 Lift high your eyes and see:
Who created these?
He who sends out their host by count,
Who calls them each by name:
Because of His great might and vast power,
Not one fails to appear.

²⁷ Why do you say, O Jacob,
Why declare, O Israel,
"My way is hid from the LORD,
My cause is ignored by my God"?
²⁸ Do you not know?
Have you not heard?
The LORD is God from of old,
Creator of the earth from end to end,
He never grows faint or weary,
His wisdom cannot be fathomed.
²⁹ He gives strength to the weary,
Fresh vigor to the spent.
³⁰ Youths may grow faint and weary,
And young men stumble and fall;
³¹ But they who trust in the LORD shall renew their strength
As eagles grow new plumes:ᶠ
They shall run and not grow weary,
They shall march and not grow faint.

41

Stand silent before Me, coastlands,
And let nations ᵃ⁻renew their strength.⁻ᵃ
Let them approach to state their case;
Let us come forward together for argument.
² Who has roused a victorᵇ from the East,
Summoned him to His service?
Has delivered up nations to him,
And trodden sovereigns down?
Has rendered theirᶜ swords like dust,
Theirᶜ bows like wind-blown straw?
³ He pursues them, he goes on unscathed;
No shackleᵈ is placed on his feet.
⁴ Who has wrought and achieved this?
He who announced the generations from the start—

ᶠ *Alluding to a popular belief that eagles regain their youth when they molt; cf. Ps. 103.5.*

ᵃ⁻ᵃ *Connection of Heb. uncertain.*

ᵇ *Lit. "victory."*

ᶜ *Heb. "his."*

ᵈ *'rḥ has this meaning in Old Aramaic.*

I, the LORD, who was first
And will be with the last as well.

5 The coastlands look on in fear,
The ends of earth tremble.

They draw near and come;
6 Each one helps the other,
Saying to his fellow, "Take courage!"
7 The woodworker encourages the smith;
He who flattens with the hammer
[Encourages] him who pounds the anvil.
He says of the riveting, "It is good!"
And he fixes it with nails,
That it may not topple.

8 But you, Israel, My servant,
Jacob, whom I have chosen,
Seed of Abraham My friend—
9 You whom I drew from the ends of the earth
And called from its far corners,
To whom I said: You are My servant;
I chose you, I have not rejected you—
10 Fear not, for I am with you,
Be not frightened, for I am your God;
I strengthen you and I help you,
I uphold you with My victorious right hand.
11 Shamed and chagrined shall be
All who contend with you;
They who strive with you
Shall become as naught and shall perish.
12 You may seek, but shall not find
Those who struggle with you;
Less than nothing shall be
The men who battle against you.

¹³ For I the LORD am your God,
Who grasped your right hand,
Who say to you: Have no fear;
I will be your help.
¹⁴ Fear not, O worm Jacob,
O ^{e-}men of^{-e} Israel:
I will help you

—declares the LORD—

I, your Redeemer, the Holy One of Israel.
¹⁵ I will make of you a threshing-board,
A new thresher, with many spikes;
You shall thresh mountains to dust,
And make hills like chaff.
¹⁶ You shall winnow them
And the wind shall carry them off;
The whirlwind shall scatter them.
But you shall rejoice in the LORD,
And glory in the Holy One of Israel.

¹⁷ The poor and the needy
Seek water,^f and there is none;
Their tongue is parched with thirst.
I the LORD will respond to them.
I, the God of Israel, will not forsake them.
¹⁸ I will open up streams on the bare hills
And fountains amid the valleys;
I will turn the desert into ponds,
The arid land into springs of water.
¹⁹ I will plant cedars in the wilderness,
Acacias and myrtles and oleasters;
I will set cypresses in the desert,
Box trees and elms as well—
²⁰ That men may see and know,
Consider and comprehend

^{e-e} *Emendation yields "maggot."*
^f *I.e. on the homeward march through the desert.*

445

That the LORD's hand has done this,
That the Holy One of Israel has wrought it.

²¹ Submit your case, says the LORD;
Offer your pleas, says the King of Jacob.
²² Let them approach*g* and tell us what will happen.
Tell us what has occurred,*h*
And we will take note of it;
Or announce to us what will occur,
That we may know the outcome.
²³ Foretell what is yet to happen,
That we may know that you are gods!
Do anything, good or bad,
That we may be awed and see.*i*
²⁴ Why, you are less than nothing,
Your effect is less than nullity;
One who chooses you is an abomination.

²⁵ I have roused him from the north, and he has come,
From the sunrise, one who invokes My name;
And he has trampled rulers like mud,
Like a potter treading clay.
²⁶ Who foretold this from the start, that we may note it;
From aforetime, that we may say, "He is right"?
Not one foretold, not one announced;
No one has heard your utterance!
²⁷ *j-*The things once predicted to Zion—
Behold, here they are!*-j*
And again I send a herald to Jerusalem.
²⁸ But I look and there is not a man;
Not one of them can predict
Or respond when I question him.
²⁹ See, they are all nothingness,
Their works are nullity,
Their statues are naught and nil.

g Taking yaggishu *intransitively; cf.* hiqriv, *Exod. 14.10.*
h I.e. former prophecies by your gods which have been fulfilled.
i Change of vocalization yields "fear"; cf. v. 10.
j-j Meaning of Heb. uncertain.

42 This is My servant, whom I uphold,
My chosen one, in whom I delight.
I have put My spirit upon him,
He shall teach the true way to the nations.
² He shall not cry out or shout aloud,
Or make his voice heard in the streets.
³ *a*-He shall not break even a bruised reed,
Or snuff out even a dim wick.-*a*
He shall bring forth the true way.
⁴ He shall not grow dim or be bruised
Till he has established the true way on earth;
And the coastlands shall await his teaching.

⁵ Thus said God the LORD,
Who created the heavens and stretched them out,
Who spread out the earth and what it brings forth,
Who gave breath to the people upon it
And life to those who walk thereon:
⁶ I the LORD, in My grace, have summoned you,
And I have grasped you by the hand.
I created you, and appointed you
A *b*-covenant-people,-*b* *c*-a light of nations-*c*—
⁷ *d*-Opening eyes deprived of light,-*d*
Rescuing prisoners from confinement,
From the dungeon those who sit in darkness.
⁸ I am the LORD, that is My name;
I will not yield My glory to another,
Nor My renown to idols.
⁹ See, the things once predicted have come,
And now I foretell new things,
Announce to you ere they sprout up.
¹⁰ Sing to the LORD a new song,
His praise from the ends of the earth—

---

a-a *Or "A bruised reed, he shall not be broken;/A dim wick, he shall not be snuffed out."*
b-b *Lit. "covenant of a people"; meaning of Heb. uncertain.*
c-c *See 49.6 and note.*
d-d *An idiom meaning "freeing the imprisoned"; cf. 61.1.*

*-*You who sail the sea and you creatures in it,
You coastlands*-* and their inhabitants!
¹¹ Let the desert and its towns cry aloud,
The villages where Kedar dwells;
Let Sela's inhabitants shout,
Call out from the peaks of the mountains.
¹² Let them do honor to the LORD,
And tell His glory in the coastlands.

¹³ The LORD goes forth like a warrior,
Like a fighter He whips up His rage.
He yells, He roars aloud,
He charges upon His enemies.
¹⁴ "I have kept silent *far too long,*
Kept still and restrained Myself;
Now I will scream like a woman in labor,
I will pant and I will gasp.
¹⁵ Hills and heights will I scorch,
Cause all their green to wither;
I will turn rivers into isles,⁸
And dry the marshes up.
¹⁶ I will lead the blind
By a road they did not know,
And I will make them walk
By paths they never knew.
I will turn darkness before them to light,
Rough places into level ground.
These are the promises—
I will keep them without fail.
¹⁷ Driven back and utterly shamed
Shall be those who trust in an image,
Those who say to idols,
'You are our gods!' "

¹⁸ Listen, you who are deaf;
You blind ones, look up and see!

---

c-c *Emendation yields "Let the sea roar and its creatures, / The coastlands. . . ." Cf. Ps. 98.7.*
f-f *Lit. "from of old."*
g *Emendation yields "desert."*

¹⁹ Who is so blind as My servant,
So deaf as the messenger I send?
Who is so blind as the chosen^h one,
So blind as the servant of the LORD?
²⁰ Seeing many things, ⁱ⁻ he gives⁻ⁱ no heed;
With ears open, he hears nothing.
²¹ ^jThe LORD desires His [servant's] vindication,
That he may magnify and glorify [His] Teaching.

²² Yet it is a people plundered and despoiled:
All of them are trapped in holes,
Imprisoned in dungeons.
They are given over to plunder, with none to rescue them;
To despoilment, with none to say "Give back!"
²³ If only you would listen to this,
Attend and give heed from now on!
²⁴ Who was it gave Jacob over to despoilment
And Israel to plunderers?
Surely, the LORD against whom they^k sinned
In whose ways they would not walk
And whose Teaching they would not obey.
²⁵ So He poured out wrath upon them,
His anger and the fury of war.
It blazed upon them all about, but they heeded not;
It burned among them, but they gave it no thought.

43 But now thus said the LORD
Who created you, O Jacob,
Who formed you, O Israel:
Fear not, for I will redeem you;
I have singled you out by name,
You are Mine.
² When you pass through water,
I will be with you;
Through streams,

^h *Meaning of Heb. uncertain.*
ⁱ⁻ⁱ *Heb. "you give"*
^j *Meaning of verse uncertain; cf. 43.9-12.*
^k *Heb. "we."*

They shall not overwhelm you.
When you walk through fire,
You shall not be scorched;
Through flame,
It shall not burn you.
³ For I the LORD am your God,
The Holy One of Israel, your Savior.
I give Egypt as a ransom for you,
Ethiopia and Saba in exchange for you.
⁴ Because you are precious to Me,
And honored, and I love you,
I give men in exchange for you
And peoples in your stead.

⁵ Fear not, for I am with you:
I will bring your folk from the East,
Will gather you out of the West;
⁶ I will say to the North, "Give back!"
And to the South, "Do not withhold!
Bring My sons from afar,
And My daughters from the end of the earth—
⁷ All who are linked to My name,
Whom I have created,
Formed, and made for My glory—
⁸ Setting free that people,
Blind though it has eyes
And deaf though it has ears."

⁹ All the nations assemble as one,
The peoples gather.
Who among them declared this,
Foretold to us the things that have happened?
Let them produce their witnesses and be vindicated,
That men, hearing them, may say, "It is true!"ᵃ

ᵃ *I.e. that the other nations' gods are real.*

10 My witnesses are *you*

—declares the LORD—

My servant, whom I have chosen.
To the end that you*b* may take thought,
And believe in Me,
And understand that I am He:
Before Me no god was formed,
And after Me none shall exist—
11 None but Me, the LORD.
Beside Me, none can grant triumph.
12 I alone foretold the deliverance
And I brought it to pass;
I announced it,
And no strange god was among you.
So you are My witnesses

—declares the LORD—

And I am God.
13 Ever since day was, I am He;
None can deliver from My hand.
When I act, who can reverse it?

14 Thus said the LORD,
Your Redeemer, the Holy One of Israel:
For your sake *c*I send to Babylon;
I will bring down all [her] bars,
And the Chaldeans shall raise their voice in lamenta-
tion.*-c*
15 I am your Holy One, the LORD,
Your King, the Creator of Israel.

16 Thus said the LORD,
Who made a road through the sea
And a path through mighty waters,
17 Who destroyed*d* chariots and horses,

b *Emendation yields "they."*
c-c *Meaning of Heb. uncertain.*
d *Understanding* hoṣi, *here, as equivalent to Aramaic* sheṣi.

And all the mighty host—
They lay down to rise no more,
They were extinguished, quenched like a wick:
18 Do not recall what happened of old,
Or ponder what happened of yore!
19 I am about to do something new;
Even now it shall come to pass,
Suddenly you shall perceive it:
I will make a road through the wilderness
And rivers* in the desert.
20 The wild beasts shall honor Me,
Jackals and ostriches,
For I provide water in the wilderness,
Rivers in the desert,
To give drink to My chosen people,
21 The people I formed for Myself
That they might declare my praise.

22 But you have not worshiped Me, O Jacob,
That you should be weary of Me, O Israel.
23 You have not brought Me your sheep for burnt offer-
ings,
Nor honored Me with your sacrifices.
I have not burdened you with meal offerings,
Nor wearied you about frankincense.
24 You have not bought Me fragrant reed with money,
Nor sated Me with the fat of your sacrifices.
Instead, you have burdened Me with your sins,
You have wearied Me with your iniquities.
25 It is I, I who—for My own sake*—
Wipe your transgressions away
And remember your sins no more.
26 Help me remember!
Let us join in argument,
Tell your version,

* 1QIs* reads "paths"; cf. v. 16.
* I.e. in order to put an end to the profanation of My holy name; cf. 48.9-11.

That you may be vindicated.
²⁷ Your earliest ancestor sinned,
And your spokesmen transgressed against Me.
²⁸ So I profaned ^{g-}the holy princes;^{-g}
I abandoned Jacob to proscription^h
And Israel to mockery.

44

But hear, now, O Jacob My servant,
Israel whom I have chosen!
² Thus said the Lord, your Maker,
Your Creator who has helped you since birth:
Fear not, My servant Jacob,
Jeshurun^a whom I have chosen,
³ Even as I pour water on thirsty soil,
And rain upon dry ground,
So will I pour My spirit on your offspring,
My blessing upon your posterity.
⁴ And they shall sprout like^b grass,
Like willows by watercourses.
⁵ One shall say, "I am the Lord's,"
Another shall use the name "Jacob,"
Another shall mark his arm "the Lord's,"^c
And adopt the name "Israel."

⁶ Thus said the Lord, the King of Israel,
Their Redeemer, the Lord of Hosts:
I am the first and I am the last,
And there is no god but Me.
⁷ ^dWho like Me can announce,
Can foretell it—and match Me thereby?
Even as I told the future to an ancient people,
So let him foretell coming events to them.
⁸ Do not be frightened, do not be shaken!

---

^{g-g} *Emendation yields "My holy name"; see preceding note.*
^h *Emendation yields "insult."*

^a *A name for Israel; see note on Nu. 23.10; cf. Deut. 32.15; 33.5, 26.*
^b *Lit. "in among."*
^c *It was customary to mark a slave with the owner's name.*
^d *Meaning of verse uncertain.*

Have I not from of old predicted to you?
I foretold, and you are My witnesses.
Is there any god, then, but Me?
"There is no other rock; I know none!"

⁹ The makers of idols
All work to no purpose;
And the things they treasure
Can do no good,
As they themselves can testify.
They neither look nor think,
And so they shall be shamed.
¹⁰ Who would fashion a god
Or cast a statue
That can do no good?
¹¹ Lo, all its adherents shall be shamed;
They are craftsmen, are merely human.
Let them all assemble and stand up!
They shall be cowed, and they shall be shamed.

¹² ᵉThe craftsman in iron, with his tools,
Works itᶠ over charcoal
And fashions it by hammering,
Working with the strength of his arm.
Should he go hungry, his strength would ebb;
Should he drink no water, he would grow faint.

¹³ The craftman in wood measures with a line
And marks out a shape with a stylus;
He forms it with scraping tools,
Marking it out with a compass.
He gives it a human form,
The beauty of a man, to dwell in a shrine.
¹⁴ For his use he cuts down cedars;
He chooses plane trees and oaks.

ᵉ *The meaning of parts of vv. 12-13 is uncertain.*
ᶠ *I.e. the image he is making.*

He sets aside trees of the forest;
Or plants firs, and the rain makes them grow.
¹⁵ All this serves man for fuel:
He takes some to warm himself,
And he builds a fire and bakes bread.
He also makes a god of it and worships it,
Fashions an idol and bows down to it!
¹⁶ Part of it he burns in a fire:
On that part he roasts^g meat,
He eats^g the roast and is sated;
He also warms himself and cries, "Ah,
I am warm! I can feel^h the heat!"
¹⁷ Of the rest he makes a god—his own carving!
He bows down to it, worships it;
He prays to it and cries,
"Save me, for you are my god!"

¹⁸ They have no wit or judgment:
Their eyes are besmeared, and they see not;
Their minds, and they cannot think.
¹⁹ They do not give thought,
They lack the wit and judgment to say:
"Part of it I burned in a fire;
I also baked bread on the coals,
I roasted meat and ate it—
Should I make the rest an abhorrence?
Should I bow to a block of wood?"
²⁰ He pursues ashes!ⁱ
A deluded mind has led him astray,
And he cannot save himself;
He never says to himself,
"The thing in my hand is a fraud!"

²¹ Remember these things, O Jacob,
For you, O Israel, are My servant:

^g *Transposing the Heb. verbs for clarity.*
^h *Lit. "see."*
ⁱ *Lit. "He shepherds ashes."*

I fashioned you, you are My servant—
O Israel, never forget Me.[j]
22 I wipe away your sins like a cloud,
Your transgressions like mist—
Come back to Me, for I redeem you.

23 Shout, O heavens, for the LORD has acted;
Shout aloud, O depths of the earth!
Shout for joy, O mountains,
O forests with all your trees!
For the LORD has redeemed Jacob,
Has glorified Himself through Israel.

24 Thus said the LORD, your Redeemer,
Who formed you in the womb:
It is I, the LORD, who made everything,
Who alone stretched out thc heavens
And unaided[k] spread out the earth;
25 Who annul the omens of diviners,
And make fools of the augurs;
Who turn sages back
And make nonsense of their knowledge;
26 But confirm the word of My[l] servant
And fulfill the prediction of My[l] messengers.
It is I who say of Jerusalem, "It shall be inhabited,"
And of the towns of Judah, "They shall be rebuilt;
And I will restore their ruined places."
27 [I,] who said to the deep, "Be dry;
I will dry up your floods,"
28 Am the same who says of Cyrus, "He is My shepherd;[m]
He shall fulfill all My purposes!
He shall say of Jerusalem, 'She shall be rebuilt,'
And to the Temple: 'You shall be founded again.' "

j Emendation yields "them," these things.
k Lit. "with none beside me," or (following many Heb mss., kethib, and ancient versions)
"who was with me?"
l Heb. "His."
m I.e. the king whom I have designated.

45 Thus said the LORD to Cyrus, His anointed one—
Whose right hand ^aHe has^{-a} grasped,
Treading down nations before him,
^bUngirding the loins of kings,^{-b}
Opening doors before him
And letting no gate stay shut:
² I will march before you
And level ^cthe hills that loom up;^{-c}
I will shatter doors of bronze
And cut down iron bars.
³ I will give you treasures concealed in the dark
And secret hoards—
So that you may know that I am the LORD,
The God of Israel, who call you by name.
⁴ For the sake of My servant Jacob,
Israel My chosen one,
I call you by name,
I hail you by title, though you have not known Me.
⁵ I am the LORD and there is none else;
Beside Me, there is no god.
I engird you, though you have not known Me,
⁶ So that they may know, from east to west,
That there is none but Me.
I am the LORD and there is none else,
⁷ I form light and create darkness,
I make weal and create woe—
I the LORD do all these things.
⁸ Pour down, O skies, from above!
Let the heavens rain down victory!
Let the earth open up and triumph sprout,
Yes, let vindication spring up:
I the LORD have created it.

---

^{a-a} *Heb. "I have." Cf. note at 8.11.*
^{b-b} *I.e. I made them helpless; one who wished to move freely belted his garment around the
waist; cf. "engird" v. 5.*
^{c-c} *Meaning of Heb. uncertain.*

⁹ Shame on him who argues with his Maker,
Though naught but a potsherd of earth!
Shall the clay say to the potter, "What are you doing?
ᵈ⁻Your work has no handles"?⁻ᵈ
¹⁰ Shame on him who asks his father, "What are
you begetting?"
Or a woman, "What are you bearing?"

¹¹ Thus said the LORD,
Israel's Holy One and Maker:
ᵉ⁻Will you question Me⁻ᵉ on the destiny of My children,
Will you instruct Me about the work of My hands?
¹² It was I who made the earth
And created man upon it;
My own hands stretched out the heavens,
And I marshaled all their host.
¹³ It was I who roused himᶠ for victory
And who level all roads for him.
He shall rebuild My city
And let My exiled people go
Without price and without payment
　　　　　　　—said the LORD of Hosts.

¹⁴ Thus said the LORD:
Egypt's wealth and Nubia's gains
And men of Seba, ᵍ⁻long of limb,⁻ᵍ
Shall pass over to you and be yours,
Pass over and follow you in fetters,
Bow low to you
And reverently address you:
"Only among you is God,
There is no other god at all!
¹⁵ You are indeed a God who concealed Himself,
O God of Israel, who bring victory!
¹⁶ Those who fabricate idols,

ᵈ⁻ᵈ *Emendation yields "To its maker, 'You have no hands'?"*
ᵉ⁻ᵉ *Heb. imperative.*
ᶠ *I.e. Cyrus.*
ᵍ⁻ᵍ *Emendation yields "bearing tribute." For "tribute" cf. Ezra 4.20; 6.8; Neh. 5.4.*

Shamed are they and disgraced,
All of them, to a man.
17 But Israel has won through the LORD
Triumph everlasting.
You shall not be shamed or disgraced
In all the ages to come!"

18 For thus said the LORD,
The Creator of heaven who alone is God,
Who formed the earth and made it,
Who alone established it—
He did not create it a waste,
But formed it for habitation:
I am the LORD, and there is none else.
19 I did not speak in secret,
At a site in a land of darkness;
I did not say to the stock of Jacob,
"Seek Me out in a wasteland"—
I the LORD, who foretell reliably,
Who announce what is true.

20 Come, gather together,
Draw nigh, you remnants of the nations!
No foreknowledge had they who carry their wooden
   images
And pray to a god who cannot give success.
21 Speak up, compare testimony—
Let them even take counsel together!
Who announced this aforetime,
Foretold it of old?
Was it not I the LORD?
Then there is no god beside Me,
No God exists beside Me
Who foretells truly and grants success.
22 Turn to Me and gain success,

All the ends of earth!
For I am God, and there is none else.
23 By Myself have I sworn,
From My mouth has issued truth,
A word that shall not turn back:
To Me every knee shall bend,
Every tongue swear loyalty.
24 *h-*They shall say: "Only through the LORD
Can I find victory and might.*-h*
When people *i-*trust in*-i* Him,
All their adversaries are put to shame.
25 It is through the LORD that all the offspring of Israel
Have vindication and glory."

46 Bel*a* is bowed, Nebo*a* is cowering,
Their images are a burden for beasts and cattle;
The things you*b* would carry [in procession]
Are now piled as a burden
On tired [beasts].
2 They cowered, they bowed as well,
They could not rescue the burden,*c*
And they themselves went into captivity.

3 Listen to Me, O House of Jacob,
All that are left of the House of Israel,
Who have been carried since birth,
Supported since leaving the womb:
4 Till you grow old, I will still be the same;
When you turn gray, it is I who will carry;
I was the Maker, and I will be the Bearer;
And I will carry and rescue [you].

5 To whom can you compare Me
Or declare Me similar?

---

h-h Emendation yields "Only in the LORD/Are there victory and might for man."
i-i Lit. "come to"; for this idiom cf. Ps. 65.3; Job 6.20.

a Babylonian deities.
b Emendation yields "they."
c Emendation yields "him who carried [them]"; cf. Targum.

To whom can you liken Me,
So that we seem comparable?
⁶ Those who squander gold from the purse
And weigh out silver on the balance,ᵈ
They hire a metal worker to make it into a god,
To which they bow down and prostrate themselves.
⁷ They must carry it on their backs and transport it;
When they put it down, it stands,
It does not budge from its place.
If they cry out to it, it does not answer;
It cannot save them from their distress.
⁸ Keep this in mind, and ᵉstand firm!ᵉ
Take this to heart, you sinners!
⁹ Bear in mind what happened of old;
For I am God, and there is none else,
I am divine, and there is none like Me.
¹⁰ I foretell the end from the beginning,
And from the start, things that had not occurred.
I say: My plan shall be fulfilled;
I will do all I have purposed.
¹¹ I summoned that swooping bird from the East;ᶠ
From a distant land, the man for My purpose.
I have spoken, so I will bring it to pass;
I have designed it, so I will complete it.
¹² Listen to Me, you ᵍstubborn of heart,ᵍ
Who are far from victory:
¹³ I am bringing My victory close;
It shall not be far,
And My triumph shall not be delayed.
I will grant triumph in Zion
To Israel, in whom I glory.

ᵈ Lit. "beam (of the balance)."
ᵉ⁻ᵉ Meaning of Heb. uncertain.
ᶠ I.e. Cyrus; cf. 41.2-3; 44.28-45.1.
ᵍ⁻ᵍ Septuagint reads, "who have lost heart."

47 Get down, sit in the dust,
Fair Maiden Babylon;
Sit, dethroned, on the ground,
O Fair Chaldea;
Nevermore shall they call you
The tender and dainty one.
² Grasp the handmill and grind meal.
Remove your veil,
Strip off your train, bare your leg,
Wade through the rivers.
³ Your nakedness shall be uncovered,
And your shame shall be exposed.
I will take vengeance,
*ᵃ*And let no man intercede.
⁴ Our Redeemer—LORD of Hosts is His name—
Is the Holy One of Israel.*⁻ᵃ*
⁵ Sit silent; retire into darkness,
O Fair Chaldea;
Nevermore shall they call you
Mistress of Kingdoms.

⁶ I was angry at My people,
I defiled My heritage;
I put them into your hands,
But you showed them no mercy.
Even upon the aged you made
Your yoke exceedingly heavy.
⁷ You thought, "I shall always be
The mistress still."
You did not take these things to heart,
You gave no thought to the end of it.

ᵃ⁻ᵃ *Meaning of Heb. uncertain; emendation yields "And not be appeased,/Says our Redeemer, whose name is LORD of Hosts,/The Holy One of Israel."*

8 And now hear this, O pampered one—
Who dwell in security,
Who think to yourself,
"I am, and there is none but me;
I shall not become a widow
Or know loss of children"—
9 Both these things shall come upon you,
Suddenly, in one day:
Loss of children and widowhood
Shall come upon you in full measure,
Despite your many enchantments
And all your countless spells.
10 You were secure in your wickedness;
You thought, "No one can see me."
It was your skill and your science
That led you astray.
And you thought to yourself,
"I am, and there is none but me."
11 Evil is coming upon you
Which you will not know how to *b*-charm away;*-b*
Disaster is falling upon you
Which you will not be able to appease;
Coming upon you suddenly
Is ruin of which you know nothing.
12 Stand up, with your spells and your many enchantments
On which you labored since youth!
Perhaps you'll be able to profit,
Perhaps you *c*-will find strength.*-c*
13 You are helpless, despite all your art.
Let them stand up and help you now,
The scanners*d* of heaven, the star-gazers,
Who announce, month by month,
Whatever will come upon you.
14 See, they are become like straw,
Fire consumes them;

b-b *Meaning of Heb. uncertain; emendation yields "bribe."*
c-c *Taking 'aras as a variant of 'asar; cf. II Chron. 20.37.*
d *Meaning of Heb. uncertain.*

They cannot save themselves
From the power of the flame;
This is no coal for warming oneself,
No fire to sit by!
15 This is what they have profited you—
The traders you dealt with since youth—
Each has wandered off his own way,
There is none to save you.

48 Listen to this, O House of Jacob,
Who bear the name Israel
And have issued from the waters*a* of Judah,
Who swear by the name of the LORD
And invoke the God of Israel—
Though not in truth and sincerity—
2 For you*b* are called *c*after the Holy City*c*
And you*b* do lean on the God of Israel,
Whose name is LORD of Hosts:

3 Long ago, I foretold things that happened,
From My mouth they issued, and I announced them;
Suddenly I acted, and they came to pass.
4 Because I know how stubborn you are
(Your neck is like an iron sinew
And your forehead bronze),
5 Therefore I told you long beforehand,
Announced things to you ere they happened—
That you might not say, "My idol caused them,
My carved and molten images ordained them."
6 You have *d*heard all this; look, must you not acknowledge
it?*d*
As of now, I announce to you new things,
Well-guarded secrets you did not know.
7 Only now are they created, and not of old;

---

a Emendation yields "loins."
b Heb. "they."
c-c Emendation yields "the holy people."
d-d Meaning of Heb. uncertain.

*d-*Before today*-d* you had not heard them;
You cannot say, "I knew them already."
8 You had never heard, you had never known,
Your ears were not opened of old.

Though I know that you are treacherous,
That you were called a rebel from birth,
9 For the sake of My name I control My wrath;
To My own glory, *d-*I am patient*-d* with you,
And I will not destroy you.
10 See, I refine you, but not as silver;
I test you in the furnace of affliction.
11 For My sake, My own sake, do I act—
Lest [My name]*ᵉ* be dishonored!
I will not give My glory to another.

12 Listen to Me, O Jacob,
Israel, whom I have called:
I am He—I am the first,
And I am the last as well.
13 My own hand founded the earth,
My right hand spread out the skies.

I call unto them, let them stand up.
14 Assemble, all of you, and listen!
Who among you*ᶠ* foretold these things:
d-"He whom the LORD loves
Shall work His will against Babylon,
And, with His might, against Chaldea"?*-d*
15 I, I predicted, and I called him;
I have brought him and he shall succeed in his mission.
16 Draw near to Me and hear this:
From the beginning, I did not speak in secret;
From the time anything existed, I was there.*ᵍ*

ᵉ These words are supplied in some ancient versions; cf. v.9.
ᶠ Heb "them."
ᵍ I.e. I foretold it through prophets.

"And now the Lord GOD has sent me, ^{h-}endowed
with His spirit."^{-h}

¹⁷ Thus said the LORD your Redeemer,
The Holy One of Israel:
I the LORD am your God,
Instructing you for your own benefit.
Guiding you in the way you should go.
¹⁸ If only you would heed My commands!
Then your prosperity would be like a river,
Your triumph like the waves of the sea.
¹⁹ Your offspring would be as many as the sand,
Their issue as many as its grains.^d
Their name would never be cut off
Or obliterated from before Me.

²⁰ Go forth from Babylon,
Flee from Chaldea!
Declare this with loud shouting,
Announce this,
Bring out the word to the ends of the earth!
²¹ Say: "The LORD has redeemed
His servant Jacob!"
They have known no thirst,
Though He led them through parched places;
He made water flow for them from the rock;
He cleaved the rock and water gushed forth.

²² There is no safety—said the LORD—for the wicked.

49 Listen, O coastlands, to me,
And give heed, O nations afar:
The LORD appointed me before I was born,
He named me while I was in my mother's womb.

^{h-h} *Lit. "and His spirit."*

² He made my mouth like a sharpened blade,
He hid me in the shadow of His hand,
And He made me like a polished arrow;
He concealed me in His quiver.
³ And He said to me, "You are My servant,
Israel in whom I glory."
⁴ I thought, "I have labored in vain,
I have spent my strength for empty breath."
But my case rested with the LORD,
My recompense was in the hands of my God.
⁵ And now the LORD has resolved—
He who formed me in the womb to be His servant—
To bring back Jacob to Himself,
That Israel may be restored to Him.
And I have been honored in the sight of the LORD,
My God has been my strength.
⁶ For He has said:
"It is too little that you should be My servant
In that I raise up the tribes of Jacob
And restore the survivors of Israel:
I will also make you a light*a* of nations,
That My salvation may reach the ends of the earth."

⁷ Thus said the LORD,
The Redeemer of Israel, his Holy One,
*b-*To the despised being,
To the abhorred nation,*-b*
To the slave of rulers:
Kings shall see and stand up;
Nobles, and they shall prostrate themselves—
To the honor of the LORD, who is faithful,
To the Holy One of Israel who chose you.

⁸ Thus said the LORD:
In an hour of favor I answer you,

ª *I.e. the agent of good fortune; cf. 42.1-4; 51.4-5.*
b-b *Meaning of Heb. uncertain. Emendation yields "Whose being is despised,/Whose body is detested"; cf. 51.23.*

467

And on a day of salvation I help you—
I created you and appointed you *‑a covenant people‑*—
Restoring the land,
Allotting anew the desolate holdings,
⁹ Saying to the prisoners, "Go free,"
To those who are in darkness, "Show yourselves."
They shall pasture along the roads,
On every bare height shall be their pasture.
¹⁰ They shall not hunger or thirst,
Hot wind and sun shall not strike them;
For He who loves them will lead them,
He will guide them to springs of water.
¹¹ I will make all My mountains a road,
And My highways shall be built up.
¹² Look! These are coming from afar,
These from the north and the west,
And these from the land of Sinim.*ᵈ*
¹³ Shout, O heavens, and rejoice, O earth!
Break into shouting, O hills!
For the LORD has comforted His people,
And has taken back His afflicted ones in love.

¹⁴ Zion says,
"The LORD has forsaken me,
My Lord has forgotten me."
¹⁵ Can a woman forget her baby,
Or disown the child of her womb?
Though she might forget,
I never could forget you.
¹⁶ See, I have engraved you
On the palms of My hands,
Your walls are ever before Me.
¹⁷ Swiftly your children are coming;
Those who ravaged and ruined you shall leave you.
¹⁸ Look up all around you and see:

‑ See note b-b at 42.6.
ᵈ *1QIsᵃ reads "the Syenians"; cf. Ezek. 30.6.*

They are all assembled, are come to you!
As I live

—declares the LORD—
You shall don them all like jewels,
Deck yourself with them like a bride.
19 As for your ruins and desolate places
And your land laid waste—
You shall soon be crowded with settlers,
While destroyers stay far from you.
20 The children *ᵉyou thought you had lostᵉ
Shall yet say in your hearing,
"The place is too crowded for me;
Make room for me to settle."
21 And you will say to yourself,
"Who bore these for me
When I was bereaved and barren,
Exiled and disdained*ᶠ—
By whom, then, were these reared?
I was left all alone—
And where have these been?"

22 Thus said the Lord GOD:
I will raise My hand to nations
And lift up My ensign to peoples;
And they shall bring your sons in their bosoms,
And carry your daughters on their backs.
23 Kings shall tend your children,
Their queens shall serve you as nurses.
They shall bow to you, face to the ground,
And lick the dust of your feet.
And you shall know that I am the LORD—
Those who trust in Me shall not be shamed.

24 Can spoil be taken from a warrior,
Or captives retrieved from a victor?

ᵉ⁻ᵉ *Lit. "of your bereavement."*
ᶠ *Meaning of Heb. uncertain.*

²⁵ Yet thus said the LORD:
Captives shall be taken from a warrior
And spoil shall be retrieved from a tyrant;
For *I* will contend with your adversaries,
And *I* will deliver your children.
²⁶ I will make your oppressors eat their own flesh,
They shall be drunk with their own blood as with wine.
And all mankind shall know
That I the LORD am your Savior,
The Mighty One of Jacob, your Redeemer.

50

Thus said the LORD:
^aWhere is the bill of divorce
Of your mother whom I dismissed?
And which of My creditors was it
To whom I sold you off?
You were only sold off for your sins,
And your mother dismissed for your crimes.
² Why, when I came, was no one there,
Why, when I called, would none respond?
Is my arm, then, too short to rescue,
Have I not the power to save?
With a mere rebuke I dry up the sea,
And turn rivers into desert.
Their fish stink from lack of water;
They lie dead ^bof thirst.^{-b}
³ I clothe the skies in blackness
And make their raiment sackcloth.

⁴ ^cThe Lord GOD gave me a skilled tongue,
To know how to speak timely words to the weary.^{-c}
Morning by morning, He rouses,
He rouses my ear
To give heed like disciples.

---

^a *The mother (the country) has not been formally divorced, nor the children (the people) sold
because of poverty. Therefore there is no obstacle to their restoration.*
^{b-b} *Change of vocalization yields "on the parched ground"; cf. 44.3.*
^{c-c} *Meaning of Heb. uncertain.*

⁵ The Lord GOD opened my ears,
And I did not disobey,
I did not run away.
⁶ I offered my back to the floggers,
And my cheeks to those who tore out my hair.
I did not hide my face
From insult and spittle.
⁷ But the Lord GOD will help me—
Therefore I feel no disgrace;
Therefore I have set my face like flint,
And I know I shall not be shamed.
⁸ My Vindicator is at hand—
Who dare contend with me?
Let us stand up together!ᵈ
Who would be my opponent?
Let him approach me!
⁹ Lo, the Lord GOD will help me—
Who can get a verdict against me?
They shall all wear out like a garment,
The moth shall consume them.

¹⁰ Who among you reveres the LORD
And heeds the voice of His servant?—
Though he walk in darkness
And have no light,
Let him trust in the name of the LORD
And rely upon his God.
¹¹ But you are all kindlers of fire,
ᵉ⁻Girding on⁻ᵉ firebrands.
Walk by the blaze of your fire,
By the brands that you have lit!
This has come to you from My hand:
ᶜ⁻You shall lie down in pain.⁻ᶜ

ᵈ *I.e. as opponents in court; cf. Nu. 35.12.*
ᵉ⁻ᵉ *Emendation yields "Lighters of."*

51 Listen to Me, you who pursue justice,
You who seek the LORD:
Look to the rock you were hewn from,
To the quarry you were dug from.
² Look back to Abraham your father
And to Sarah who brought you forth.
For he was only one when I called him,
But I blessed him and made him many.

³ Truly the LORD has comforted Zion,
Comforted all her ruins;
He has made her wilderness like Eden,
Her desert like the Garden of the LORD.
Gladness and joy shall abide there,
Thanksgiving and the sound of music.

⁴ Hearken to Me, *ª*My people,*ª*
And give ear to Me, O *ª*My nation,*ª*
For teaching shall go forth*ᵇ* from Me,
My way for the light of peoples.
In a moment I will bring it:
⁵ The triumph I grant is near,
The success I give has gone forth.
My arms shall *ᶜ*provide for*ᶜ* the peoples;
The coastlands shall trust in Me,
They shall look to My arm.

⁶ Raise your eyes to the heavens,
And look upon the earth beneath:
Though the heavens should melt away like smoke,
And the earth wear out like a garment,
And its inhabitants die out *ᵈ*as well,*ᵈ*

ª⁻ª *Several mss. read "O peoples . . . O nations"; cf. end of this verse and verse 5.*
ᵇ *I.e. through My servant Israel; cf. 42.1-5: 49.6.*
ᶜ⁻ᶜ *Lit. "judge."*
ᵈ⁻ᵈ *Emendation yields "like gnats."*

My victory shall stand forever,
My triumph shall remain unbroken.

⁷ Listen to Me, you who care for the right,
O people who lay My instruction to heart!
Fear not the insults of men,
And be not dismayed at their jeers;
⁸ For the moth shall eat them up like a garment,
The worm*c* shall eat them up like wool.
But My triumph shall endure forever,
My salvation through all the ages.

⁹ Awake, awake, clothe yourself with splendor,
O arm of the LORD!
Awake as in days of old,
As in former ages!
It was you that hacked Rahab*f* in pieces,
That pierced the Dragon.*f*
¹⁰ It was you that dried up the Sea,
The waters of the great deep;
That made the abysses of the Sea
A road the redeemed might walk.
¹¹ So let the ransomed of the LORD return,
And come with shouting to Zion,
Crowned with joy everlasting.
Let them attain joy and gladness,
While sorrow and sighing flee.

¹² I, I am He who comforts you!
What ails you that you fear
Man who must die,
Mortals who fare like grass?
¹³ You have forgotten the LORD your Maker,
Who stretched out the skies and made firm the earth!

c Heb. sas, *another word for "moth."*
f Names of primeval monsters.

And you live all day in constant dread
Because of the rage of an oppressor
Who is aiming to cut [you] down.
Yet of what account is the rage of an oppressor?
14 ^gQuickly the crouching one is freed;
He is not cut down and slain,
And he shall not want for food.
15 For I the LORD your God—
Who stir up the sea into roaring waves,
Whose name is LORD of Hosts—
16 ^{h-}Have put My words in your mouth
And sheltered you with My hand;^{-h}
I, who plantedⁱ the skies and made firm the earth,
Have said to Zion: You are My people!
17 Rouse, rouse yourself!
Arise, O Jerusalem,
You who from the LORD's hand
Have drunk the cup of His wrath,
You who have drained to the dregs
The bowl, the cup of reeling!
18 She has none to guide her
Of all the sons she bore;
None takes her by the hand,
Of all the sons she reared.^j
19 These two things have befallen you:
Wrack and ruin—who can console you?
Famine and sword—^{k-}how shall I^{-k} comfort you?
20 Your sons lie in a swoon
At the corner of every street—
Like an antelope caught in a net—
Drunk with the wrath of the LORD,
With the rebuke of your God.
21 Therefore,
Listen to this, unhappy one,

^g *Meaning of verse uncertain. Emendation yields (cf. Jer. 11.19; Job 14.7-9) "Quickly the tree buds anew;/It does not die though cut down,/And its sap does not fail."*
^{h-h} *I.e. I have chosen you to be a prophet-nation; cf. 49.2; 59.21.*
ⁱ *Emendation yields "stretched out"; cf. Syriac version and v. 13.*
^j *To guide a drunken parent home was a recognized filial duty in ancient Canaan and Egypt.*
^{k-k} *Several ancient versions render "who can."*

Who are drunk, but not with wine!
²² Thus said the LORD, your Lord,
Your God who champions His people:
Herewith I take from your hand
The cup of reeling,[1]
The bowl, the cup of My wrath;
You shall never drink it again.
²³ I will put it in the hands of your tormentors,
Who have commanded you,
"Get down, that we may walk over you"—
So that you made your back like the ground,
Like a street for passers-by.

52 Awake, awake, O Zion!
Clothe yourself in splendor;
Put on your robes of majesty,
Jerusalem, holy city!
For the uncircumcised and the unclean
Shall never enter you again.
² Arise, shake off the dust,
Sit [on your throne], Jerusalem!
Loose the bonds from your neck,
O captive one, Fair Zion!

³ For thus said the LORD:
You were sold for no price,
And shall be redeemed without money.
⁴ For thus said the Lord GOD:
Of old, My people went down
To Egypt to sojourn there;
But Assyria has robbed them,
Giving nothing in return.[a]
⁵ What therefore do I gain here?

—declares the LORD—

[1] *A figure of speech for a dire fate; cf. Jer. 25.15 ff.*

[a] *Whereas the Israelites themselves sought hospitality in Egypt, Assyria (i.e. the Chaldean Empire) has exiled them by force.*

For My people has been carried off for nothing,
Their mockers howl

—declares the LORD—

And constantly, unceasingly,
My name is reviled.
⁶ Assuredly, My people shall learn My name,
Assuredly [they shall learn] on that day
That I, the one who promised,
Am now at hand.

⁷ How welcome on the mountain
Are the footsteps of the herald
Announcing happiness,
Heralding good fortune,
Announcing victory,
Telling Zion, "Your God is King!"
⁸ Hark!
Your watchmen raise their voices,
As one they shout for joy;
For every eye shall behold
The LORD's return to Zion.
⁹ Raise a shout together,
O ruins of Jerusalem!
For the LORD will comfort His people,
Will redeem Jerusalem.
¹⁰ The LORD will bare His holy arm
In the sight of all the nations,
And the very ends of earth shall see
The victory of our God.

¹¹ Turn, turn away, touch naught unclean
As you depart from there;
Keep pure, as you go forth from there,
You who bear the vessels of the LORD!ᵇ
¹² For you will not depart in haste,

ᵇ Cf. Ezra 1.7-8; 5.14-15.

Nor will you leave in flight;
For the LORD is marching before you,
The God of Israel is your rear guard.

¹³ Indeed, My servant shall prosper,
Be exalted and raised to great heights.
¹⁴ Just as the many were appalled at him*ᶜ*—
So marred was his appearance, unlike that of man,
His form, beyond human semblance—
¹⁵ Just so he shall startle*ᵈ* many nations.
Kings shall be silenced because of him,
For they shall see what has not been told them,
Shall behold what they never have heard.

53

"Who can believe what we have heard?
Upon whom has *ᵃ*the arm of the LORD*⁻ᵃ* been revealed?
² For he has grown, by His favor, like a tree-crown,
Like a tree-trunk out of arid ground.
He had no form or beauty, that we should look at him:
No charm, that we should find him pleasing.
³ He was despised, *ᵇ⁻*shunned by men,*⁻ᵇ*
A man of suffering, familiar with disease.
*ᶜ⁻*As one who hid his face from us,*⁻ᶜ*
He was despised, we held him of no account.
⁴ Yet it was our sickness that he was bearing,
Our suffering that he endured.
We accounted him plagued,
Smitten and afflicted by God;
⁵ But he was wounded because of our sins,
Crushed because of our iniquities.
He bore the chastisement that made us whole,
And by his bruises we were healed.
⁶ We all went astray like sheep,

ᶜ *Heb. "you."*
ᵈ *Meaning of Heb. uncertain.*

ᵃ⁻ᵃ *I.e. the vindication which the arm of the LORD effects.*
ᵇ⁻ᵇ *Meaning of Heb. uncertain.*
ᶜ⁻ᶜ *I.e. as a leper; cf. Lev. 13.45 ff.*

Each going his own way;
And the LORD visited upon him
The guilt of all of us."

7 He was maltreated, yet he was submissive,
He did not open his mouth;
Like a sheep being led to slaughter,
Like a ewe, dumb before those who shear her,
He did not open his mouth.
8 By oppressive judgment he was taken away,
b-Who could describe his abode?*-b*
For he was cut off from the land of the living
Through the sin of My people, who deserved the punishment.
9 And his grave was set among the wicked,
d-And with the rich, in his death*-d*—
Though he had done no injustice
And had spoken no falsehood.
10 But the LORD chose to crush him *b*-by disease,
That, if he made himself an offering for guilt,*-b*
He might see offspring*e* and have long life,
And that through him the LORD's purpose might prosper.
11 Out of his anguish he shall see it;*f*
He shall enjoy it to the full through his devotion.*g*

"My righteous servant makes the many righteous,
It is their punishment that he bears;
12 Assuredly, I will give him the many as his portion,
He shall receive the multitude as his spoil.
For he exposed himself to death
And was numbered among the sinners,
Whereas he bore the guilt of the many
And made intercession for sinners."

---

d-d *Emendation yields "And his tomb with evildoers."*
e *Emendation yields "His arm," i.e. His vindication; cf. v. 1 with note.*
f *I.e. The arm of the Lord; see preceding note.*
g *For this sense of* da'ath *see 11.2,9.*

54 Shout, O barren one,
You who bore no child!
Shout aloud for joy,
You who did not travail!
For the children of the wife forlorn
Shall outnumber those of the espoused

—said the LORD.

² Enlarge the site of your tent,
^{a-}Extend the size of your dwelling,^{-a}
Do not stint!
Lengthen the ropes, and drive the pegs firm.
³ For you shall spread out to the right and the left;
Your offspring shall dispossess nations^b
And shall people the desolate towns.

⁴ Fear not, you shall not be shamed;
Do not cringe, you shall not be disgraced.
For you shall forget
The reproach of your youth,
And remember no more
The shame of your widowhood.
⁵ For He who made you will espouse you—
His name is "LORD of Hosts";
The Holy One of Israel will redeem you,
Who is called "God of all the Earth."

⁶ The LORD has called you back
As a wife forlorn and forsaken.
Can one cast off the wife of his youth?

—said your God.

⁷ For a little while I forsook you,
But with vast love I will bring you back.
⁸ In slight anger, for a moment,

---

^{a-a} Lit. "Let the cloths of your dwelling extend."
^b I.e. the foreigners who had occupied regions from which Israelites had been exiled; cf.
II Kings 17.24.

I hid My face from you;
But with kindness everlasting
I will take you back in love
    —said the LORD your Redeemer.
9 For this to Me is like the waters[c] of Noah:
As I swore that the waters of Noah
Nevermore would flood the earth,
So I swear that I will not
Be angry with you or rebuke you.
10 For the mountains may move
And the hills be shaken,
But my loyalty shall never move from you,
Nor My covenant of friendship be shaken
    —said the LORD, who takes you back in love.

11 Unhappy, storm-tossed one, uncomforted!
I will lay carbuncles[d] as your building stones
And make your foundations of sapphires.
12 I will make your battlements of rubies,
Your gates of precious stones,
The whole encircling wall of gems.
13 And all your children shall be disciples of the LORD,
And great shall be the happiness of your children;
14 You shall be established through righteousness.
You shall be safe from oppression,
And shall have no fear;
From ruin, and it shall not come near you.
15 [e]Surely no harm can be done
Without My consent:
Whoever would harm you
Shall fall because of you.
16 It is I who created the smith
To fan the charcoal fire
And produce the tools for his work;

[c] Other Heb. mss. and the ancient versions read "days."
[d] Taking pukh as a by-form of nophekh; so already Rashi.
[e] Meaning of verse uncertain.

So it is I who create
The instruments of havoc.
[17] No weapon formed against you
Shall succeed,
And every tongue that contends with you at law
You shall defeat.
Such is the lot of the servants of the LORD,
Such their triumph through Me

—declares the LORD.

55 Ho, all who are thirsty,
Come for water,
Even if you have no money;
Come, buy food and eat:
Buy food without money,
Wine and milk without cost.
[2] Why do you spend money for what is not bread,
Your earnings for what does not satisfy?
Give heed to Me,
And you shall eat choice food
And enjoy the richest viands.
[3] Incline your ear and come to Me;
Hearken, and you shall be revived.
And I will make with you an everlasting covenant,
The enduring loyalty promised to David.
[4] [a-]As I made him a leader[b] of peoples,
A prince and commander of peoples,
[5] So you shall summon a nation you did not know,
And a nation that did not know you
Shall come running to you[-a]—
For the sake of the LORD your God,
The Holy One of Israel who has glorified you.

[a-a] *Cf. II Sam. 22.44-45 // Ps. 18.44-45.*
[b] *Cf. Targum; others "witness."*

6 Seek the LORD while He can be found,
Call to Him while He is near.
7 Let the wicked give up his ways,
The sinful man his plans;
Let him turn back to the LORD,
And He will pardon him;
To our God,
For He freely forgives.

8 For My plans are not your plans,
Nor are My ways[c] your ways[c]

—declares the LORD.
9 But as the heavens are high above the earth,
So are My ways[c] high above your ways[c]
And My plans above your plans.
10 For as the rain or snow drops from heaven
And returns not there,
But soaks the earth
And makes it bring forth vegetation,
Yielding [d-seed for sowing and bread for eating,-d]
11 So is the word that issues from My mouth:
It does not come back to Me unfulfilled,
But performs what I purpose,
Achieves what I sent it to do.
12 Yea, you shall leave[e] in joy and be led home secure.
Before you, mount and hill shall shout aloud,
And all the trees of the field shall clap their hands.
13 Instead of the brier, a cypress shall rise;
Instead of the nettle, a myrtle shall rise.
These shall stand as a testimony to the LORD,
As an everlasting sign that shall not perish.

---

[c] *Emendation yields "words"; cf. v. 11 and 40.8.*
[d-d] *Lit. "seed for the sower and bread for the eater."*
[e] *I.e. leave the Babylonian exile.*

56

Thus said the LORD:
Observe what is right and do what is just;
For soon My salvation shall come,
And my deliverance be revealed.

2 Happy is the man who does this,
The man who holds fast to it:
Who keeps the sabbath and does not profane it,
And stays his hand from doing any evil.

3 Let not the foreigner say,
Who has attached himself to the LORD,
"The LORD will keep me apart from His people";
And let not the eunuch say,
"I am a withered tree."
4 For thus said the LORD:
"As regards the eunuchs who keep My sabbaths,
Who have chosen what I desire
And hold fast to My covenant—
5 I will give them, in My House
And within My walls,
A monument and a name
Better than sons or daughters.
I will give them an everlasting name
Which shall not perish.
6 As for the foreigners
Who attach themselves to the LORD,
To minister to Him.
And to love the name of the LORD,
To be His servants—
All who keep the sabbath and do not profane it,
And who hold fast to My covenant—

⁷ I will bring them to My sacred mount
And let them rejoice in My house of prayer.
Their burnt offerings and sacrifices
Shall be welcome on My altar;
For My House shall be called
A house of prayer for all peoples."
⁸ Thus declares the Lord GOD,
Who gathers the dispersed of Israel:
"I will gather still more to those already gathered."

⁹ All you wild beasts, come and devour,
All you beasts of the forest!
¹⁰ The*a* watchmen are blind, all of them,
They perceive nothing.
They are all dumb dogs
That cannot bark;
They lie sprawling,*b*
They love to drowse.
¹¹ Moreover, the dogs are greedy;
They never know satiety.
*c*As for the shepherds, they know not
What it is to give heed.*c*
Everyone has turned his own way,
Every last one seeks his own advantage.
¹² "Come, I'll buy some wine;
Let us swill liquor.
And tomorrow will be just the same,
Or even much grander!"

57 The righteous man perishes,
And no one considers;
Pious men are taken away,
And no one gives thought
That because of evil

ᵃ Heb. "His."
ᵇ Meaning of Heb. uncertain.
ᶜ⁻ᶜ Meaning of Heb. uncertain. Emendation yields "Neither do the shepherds ever know
sufficiency (hon)." Cf. hon in Prov. 30.15,16.

The righteous was taken away.
2 Yet he shall come to peace,
a-He shall have rest on his couch*-a*
Who walked straightforward.

3 But as for you, come closer,
You sons of a sorceress,
You offspring of an adulterer and a harlot!*b*
4 With whom do you act so familiarly?
At whom do you open your mouth
And stick out your tongue?
Why, you are children of iniquity,
Offspring of treachery—
5 You who inflame*c* yourselves
Among the terebinths,
Under every verdant tree;
Who slaughter children in the wadis,
Among*d* the clefts of the rocks.
6 *e*-With such*f* are your share and portion,*-e*
They, they are your allotment;
To them you have poured out libations,
Presented offerings.
Should I relent in the face of this?

7 On a high and lofty hill
You have set your couch;
There, too, you have gone up
To perform sacrifices.
8 Behind the door and doorpost
You have directed your thoughts;
e-Abandoning Me, you have gone up
On the couch you made so wide.
You have made a covenant with them,*f*

---

a-a Heb. *"They shall have rest on their couches."*
b Lit. *"she acts the harlot."*
c I.e. *in some frenzied idolatrous rite.*
d Heb *"under."*
e-e Meaning of Heb. uncertain.
f The cult-trees referred to above in v. 5.

You have loved bedding with them;[g]
You have chosen lust.[h]
[9] You have approached[-e] the king[i] with oil,
You have provided many perfumes.
And you have sent your envoys afar,
Even down to the nether world.[j]
[10] Though wearied by much travel,
You never said, "I give up!"
You found gratification for your lust,[h]
And so you never cared.
[11] [k-]Whom do you dread and fear,
That you tell lies?[-k]
But you gave no thought to Me,
You paid no heed.
It is because I have stood idly by [l-]so long[-l]
That you have no fear of Me.
[12] I hereby pronounce [m-]judgment upon your deeds:[-m]
[n-]Your assorted [idols][-n] shall not avail you,
[13] Shall not save you when you cry out.
They shall all be borne off by the wind,
Snatched away by a breeze.
But those who trust in Me shall inherit the land
And possess My holy mountain.

[14] [The Lord] says:
Build up, build up a highway!
Clear a road!
Remove all obstacles
From the road of My people!
[15] For thus said He who high aloft
Forever dwells, whose name is holy:
I dwell on high, in holiness;
Yet with the contrite and the lowly in spirit—

---

[g] *I.e. with the objects behind door and doorpost.*
[h] *Like Ugaritic* yd, *from root* ydd, *"to love."*
[i] *Or "Molech."*
[j] *I.e. you have brought tribute to alien cults as to a king.*
[k-k] *Emendation yields "Them you dreaded and feared,/And so you gave them thought."*
[l-l] *Emendation yields "and shut My eyes."*
[m-m] *Lit. "your retribution and your deeds."*
[n-n] *Brought up from v. 13 for clarity.*

Reviving the spirits of the lowly,
Reviving the hearts of the contrite.
16 For I will not always contend,
I will not be angry forever:
Nay, I [e]who make spirits flag,[e]
Also create the breath of life.
17 For their[o] sinful greed I was angry;
I struck them and turned away in My wrath.
[p]Though stubborn, they follow the way of their hearts,[p]
18 I note how they fare and will heal them:
I will guide them and mete out solace to them,
And to the mourners among them
19 heartening,[q] comforting[r] words:
It shall be well,
Well with the far and the near
—said the LORD—
And I will heal them.
20 But the wicked are like the troubled sea
Which cannot rest,
Whose waters toss up mire and mud.
21 There is no safety
—said my God—
For the wicked.

58 Cry with full throat, without restraint;
Raise your voice like a ram's horn!
Declare to My people their transgression,
To the House of Jacob their sin.

2 To be sure, they seek Me daily,
Eager to learn My ways.
Like a nation that does what is right,
That has not abandoned the laws of its God,

o *I.e. Israel's. Cf. "My people," v. 14.*
p-p *Meaning of Heb. uncertain. Emendation yields "When they have walked broken in the contrition of their hearts."*
q *Lit. "the vigor of"; cf. Eccl. 12.1 and postbiblical* bori.
r *The Heb.* nib *is otherwise unknown; its meaning is inferred from that of* nid *(cf. the verb* nad *"to condole") in the parallel expression in Job 16.5.*

They ask Me for the right way,
They are eager for the nearness of God:
3 "Why, when we fasted, did You not see?
When we starved our bodies, did You pay no heed?"
Because on your fast day
You see to your business
And oppress all your laborers!
4 Because you fast in strife and contention,
And you strike with a wicked fist!
Your fasting today is not such
As to make your voice heard on high.
5 Is such the fast I desire,
A day for men to starve their bodies?
Is it bowing the head like a bulrush
And lying in sackcloth and ashes?
Do you call that a fast,
A day when the LORD is favorable?
6 No, this is the fast I desire:
To unlock the fetters of wickedness,
And untie the cords of *a-*the yoke*-a*
To let the oppressed go free;
To break off every yoke.
7 It is to share your bread with the hungry,
And to take the wretched poor into your home;
When you see the naked, to clothe him,
And not to ignore your own kin.

8 Then shall your light burst through like the dawn
And your healing spring up quickly;
Your Vindicator shall march before you,
The Presence of the LORD shall be your rear guard.
9 Then, when you call, the LORD will answer;
When you cry, He will say: Here I am.
If you banish *a-*the yoke*-a* from your midst,
*b-*The menacing hand,*-b* and evil speech,

---

a-a *Change of vocalization yields "lawlessness"; cf.* muṭṭeh, *Ezek. 9.9.*
b-b *Lit. "Extending the finger."*

¹⁰ And you offer your compassion^c to the hungry
And satisfy the famished creature—
Then shall your light shine in darkness,
And your gloom shall be like noonday.
¹¹ The LORD will guide you always;
He will slake your thirst in ^{d-}parched places^{-d}
And give strength to your bones.
You shall be like a watered garden,
Like a spring whose waters do not fail.
¹² Men from your midst shall rebuild ancient ruins,
You shall restore foundations laid long ago.
And you shall be called
"Repairer of fallen walls,
Restorer of lanes for habitation."
¹³ If you ^{e-}refrain from trampling^{-e} the sabbath,
From pursuing your affairs on My holy day;
If you call the sabbath "delight,"
The LORD's holy day "honored";
And if you honor it and go not your ways
Nor look to your affairs, nor strike bargains—
¹⁴ Then you ^{f-}can seek the favor of the LORD.^{-f}
I will set you astride the heights of the earth,
And let you enjoy the heritage of your father Jacob—
For the mouth of the LORD has spoken.

59

No, the LORD's arm is not too short to save,
Or His ear too dull to hear;
² But your iniquities have been a barrier
Between you and your God,
Your sins have made Him turn His face away
And refuse to hear you.
³ For your hands are defiled with crime^a
And your fingers with iniquity.
Your lips speak falsehood,

^c *Some Heb. mss. and ancient versions read "bread."*
^{d-d} *Meaning of Heb. uncertain.*
^{e-e} *Lit. "turn back your foot from."*
^{f-f} *Cf. Ps. 37.4; Job 22.26-27; 27.10.*
^a *Or "blood."*

Your tongue utters treachery.
4 No one sues justly
Or pleads honestly;
They rely on emptiness and speak falsehood,
Conceiving wrong and begetting evil.

5 They hatch adder's eggs
And weave spider webs;
He who eats of those eggs will die,
And if one is crushed, it hatches out a viper.
6 Their webs will not serve as a garment,
What they make cannot serve as clothing;
Their deeds are deeds of mischief,
Their hands commit lawless acts,
7 Their feet run after evil,
They hasten to shed the blood of the innocent.
Their plans are plans of mischief,
Destructiveness and injury are on their roads.
8 They do not care for the way of integrity,
There is no justice on their paths.
They make their courses crooked,
No one who walks in them cares for integrity.

9 "That is why redress is far from us,
And vindication does not reach us.
We hope for light, and lo! there is darkness;
For a gleam, and we must walk in gloom.
10 We grope, like blind men along a wall;
Like those without eyes we grope.
We stumble at noon, as if in darkness;
*b-*Among the sturdy, we are*-b* like the dead.
11 We all growl like bears
And moan like doves.
We hope for redress, and there is none;
For victory, and it is far from us.

b-b *Meaning of Heb. uncertain. Emendation yields "In the daytime. . . ."*

490

¹² For our many sins are before You,
Our guilt testifies against us.
We are aware of our sins,
And we know well our iniquities:
¹³ Rebellion, faithlessness to the LORD,
And turning away from our God,
Planning fraud and treachery,
Conceiving lies and uttering them with the throat.ᶜ
¹⁴ And so redress is turned back
And vindication stays afar,
Because honesty stumbles in the public square
And uprightness cannot enter.
¹⁵ Honesty has been lacking,
He who turns away from evil is despoiled."

The LORD saw and was displeased
That there was no redress.
¹⁶ He saw that there was no man,
He gazed long, but no one intervened.
Then His own arm won Him triumph,
His victorious right handᵈ supported Him.
¹⁷ He donned victory like a coat of mail,
With a helmet of triumph on His head;
He clothed Himself with garments of retribution,
Wrapped himself in zeal as in a robe.
¹⁸ ᵉ⁻According to their deserts,
So shall He repay⁻ᵉ fury to His foes;
He shall make requital to His enemies,
Requital to the distant lands.
¹⁹ From the west, they shall revereᶠ the name of the
    LORD,
And from the east, His Presence.
For He shall come like a hemmed-in stream
Which the wind of the LORD drives on;
²⁰ He shall come as redeemer to Zion,

ᶜ Lit. "heart"; see note at 33.18 and frequently elsewhere.
ᵈ Cf. Ps. 98.1-2.
ᵉ⁻ᵉ Meaning of Heb. uncertain.
ᶠ Or (with a number of mss. and editions) "see."

To those in Jacob who turn back from sin
—declares the LORD.

21 And this shall be My covenant with them, said the LORD:
My spirit*g* which is upon you, and the words which I have
placed in your mouth shall not be absent from your mouth,
nor from the mouth of your children, nor from the mouth of
your children's children—said the LORD—from now on, for all
time.*h*

60 Arise, shine, for your light has dawned;
The Presence of the LORD has shone upon you!
2 Behold! Darkness shall cover the earth,
And thick clouds the peoples;
But upon you the LORD will shine,
And His Presence be seen over you.
3 And nations shall walk by your light;
Kings, by your shining radiance.

4 Raise your eyes and look about:
They have all gathered and come to you.
Your sons shall be brought from afar,
Your daughters like babes on shoulders.
5 As you behold, you will glow;
Your heart will throb and thrill—
For the wealth of the sea*a* shall pass on to you,
The riches of nations shall flow to you.
6 Dust clouds of camels shall cover you,
Dromedaries of Midian and Ephah.
They all shall come from Sheba;
They shall bear gold and frankincense,
And shall herald the glories of the LORD.
7 All the flocks of Kedar shall be assembled for you,
The rams of Nebaioth shall serve your needs;

g *I.e. the gift of prophecy; cf., e.g., 61.1.*
h *Israel is to be a prophet-nation; cf. 51.16.*

a *Emendation yields "coastlands."*

They shall be welcome offerings on My altar,
And I will add glory to My glorious House.

8 Who are these that float like a cloud,
Like doves to their cotes?
9 *b*-Behold, the coastlands await me,*-b*
With *c*-ships of Tarshish*-c* in the lead,
To bring your sons from afar,
And their*d* silver and gold as well—
For the name of the LORD your God,
For the Holy One of Israel, who has glorified you.
10 Aliens shall rebuild your walls,
Their kings shall wait upon you—
For in anger I struck you down,
But in favor I take you back.
11 Your gates shall always stay open—
Day and night they shall never be shut—
To let in the wealth of the nations,
With their kings in procession.

12 For the nation or the kingdom
That does not serve you shall perish;
Such nations shall be destroyed.

13 The majesty of Lebanon shall come to you—
Cypress and pine and box—
To adorn the site of My Sanctuary,
To glorify the place where My feet rest.

14 Bowing before you, shall come
The children of those who tormented you;
Prostrate at the soles of your feet
Shall be all those who reviled you;
And you shall be called
"City of the LORD,

---

b-b *Emendation yields "The vessels of the coastlands are gathering."*
c-c *See note at 2.16.*
d *I.e. of the people of the coastlands.*

Zion of the Holy One of Israel."
15 Whereas you have been forsaken,
Rejected, with none passing through,
I will make you a pride everlasting,
A joy for age after age.
16 You shall suck the milk of the nations,
Suckle at royal breasts.[e]
And you shall know
That I the LORD am your Savior,
I, The Mighty One of Jacob, am your Redeemer.

17 Instead of copper I will bring gold,
Instead of iron I will bring silver;
Instead of wood, copper;
And instead of stone, iron.
And I will appoint Well-being as your government,
Prosperity as your officials.
18 The cry "Violence!"
Shall no more be heard in your land,
Nor "Wrack and ruin!"
Within your borders.
And you shall name your walls "Victory"
And your gates "Renown."

19 No longer shall you need the sun
For light by day,
Nor the shining of the moon
For radiance [by night[f]];
For the LORD shall be your light everlasting,
Your God shall be your glory.
20 Your sun shall set no more,
Your moon no more withdraw;
For the LORD shall be a light to you forever,
And your days of mourning shall be ended.
21 And your people, all of them righteous,

e Lit. "breasts of kings" or "breasts of kingdoms."
f So 1QIs[a], Septuagint, and Targum.

Shall possess the land for all time;
They are the shoot that I planted,
My handiwork in which I glory.
²² The smallest shall become a clan;
The least, a mighty nation.
I the LORD will speed it in due time.

61

The spirit of the Lord GOD is upon me,
Because the LORD has anointed me;
He has sent me as a herald of joy to the humble,
To bind up the wounded of heart,
To proclaim release to the captives,
Liberation to the imprisoned;
² To proclaim a year of the LORD's favor
And a day of vindication by our God;
To comfort all who mourn—
³ ^{a-}To provide for^{-a} the mourners in Zion—
To give them a turban instead of ashes,
Festive ointment instead of mourning,
A garment of splendor instead of a drooping spirit.
They shall be called terebinths of victory,
Planted by the LORD for His glory.
⁴ And they shall build the ancient ruins,
Raise up the desolations of old,
And renew the ruined cities,
The desolations of many ages.
⁵ Strangers shall stand and pasture your flocks,
Aliens shall be your plowmen and vine-trimmers;
⁶ While you shall be called "Priests of the LORD,"
And termed "Servants of our God."
You shall enjoy the wealth of nations
And ^{a-}revel^{-a} in their riches.
⁷ Because your shame was double—
^{b-}Men cried, "Disgrace is their portion"^{-b}—

^{a-a} *Meaning of Heb. uncertain.*
^{b-b} *Emendation yields "They inherited disgrace as their portion."*

Assuredly,
They shall have a double share in their land,
Joy shall be theirs for all time.
8 For I the LORD love justice,
I hate *robbery with a burnt offering.*
I will pay them their wages faithfully,
And make a covenant with them for all time.
9 Their offspring shall be known among the nations,
Their descendants in the midst of the peoples.
All who see them shall recognize
That they are a stock the LORD has blessed.

10 I greatly rejoice in the LORD,
My whole being exults in my God.
For He has clothed me with garments of triumph,
Wrapped me in a robe of victory,
Like a bridegroom adorned with a turban,
Like a bride bedecked with her finery.
11 For as the earth brings forth her growth
And a garden makes the seed shoot up,
So the Lord GOD will make
Victory and renown shoot up
In the presence of all the nations.

62 For the sake of Zion I will not be silent,
For the sake of Jerusalem I will not be still,
Till her victory emerge resplendent
And her triumph like a flaming torch.
2 Nations shall see your victory,
And every king your majesty;
And you shall be called by a new name
Which the LORD Himself shall bestow.
3 You shall be a glorious crown
In the hand of the LORD,

c-c *Emendation yields "the robbing of wages."*

And a royal diadem
In the palm of your God.

⁴ Nevermore shall you be called "Forsaken,"
Nor shall your land be called "Desolate";
But you shall be called "I delight in her,"
And your land "Espoused."
For the LORD takes delight in you,
And your land shall be espoused.
⁵ As a youth espouses a maiden,
*ᵃYour sons⁻ᵃ shall espouse you;
And as a bridegroom rejoices over his bride,
So will your God rejoice over you.

⁶ Upon your walls, O Jerusalem,
I have set watchmen,
Who shall never be silent
By day or by night.
O you, the LORD's remembrancers,ᵇ
Take no rest
⁷ And give no rest to Him,
Until He establish Jerusalem
And make her renowned on earth.

⁸ The LORD has sworn by His right hand,
By His mighty arm:
Nevermore will I give your new grain
To your enemies for food,
Nor shall foreigners drink the new wine
For which you have labored.
⁹ But those who harvest it shall eat it
And give praise to the LORD;
And those who gather it shall drink it
In My sacred courts.
¹⁰ Pass through, pass through the gates!

ᵃ⁻ᵃ *Change of vocalization yields "He who rebuilds you."*
ᵇ *I.e. the watchmen just mentioned.*

Clear the road for the people;
Build up, build up the highway,
Remove the rocks!
Raise an ensign over the peoples!
11 See, the LORD has proclaimed
To the end of the earth:
Announce to Fair Zion,
Your Deliverer is coming!
See, his reward is with Him,
His recompense before Him.*c*
12 And they shall be called, "The Holy People,
The Redeemed of the LORD,"
And you shall be called, "Sought Out,
A City Not Forsaken."

63 Who is this coming from Edom,
In crimsoned garments from Bozrah—
[Who is] this, majestic in attire,
a-Pressing forward-*a* in His great might?
"It is I, who contend victoriously,
b-Powerful to give triumph."-*b*

2 Why is your clothing so red,
Your garments like his who treads grapes?*c*
3 "I trod out a vintage alone;
d-Of the peoples-*d* no man was with Me.
I trod them down in My anger,
Trampled them in My rage;
Their life-blood*e* bespattered My garments,
And all My clothing was stained.
4 For I had planned a day of vengeance,
And My year of redemption arrived.
5 Then I looked, but there was none to help;

c See note at 40.10.

a-a *Meaning of Heb. uncertain; emendation yields "striding."*
b-b *Change of vocalization yields "Who contest triumphantly"; cf. 19.20.*
c *Lit. "in a press."*
d-d *Emendation yields "Peoples, and . . . ."*
e *Meaning of Heb. uncertain.*

I stared, but there was none to aid—
So My own arm wrought the triumph,
And *f*My own rage*f* was My aid.
⁶ I trampled peoples in My anger,
*g*I made them drunk with*g* My rage,
And I hurled their glory to the ground."

⁷ I will recount the kind acts of the LORD,
The praises of the LORD—
For all that the LORD has wrought for us,
The vast bounty to the House of Israel
That He bestowed upon them
According to His mercy and His great kindness.
⁸ He thought: Surely they are My people,
Children who will not play false.
*h*So He was their Deliverer.
⁹ In all their troubles He was troubled,
And the angel of His Presence delivered them.*h*
In His love and pity
He Himself redeemed them,
Raised them, and exalted them
All the days of old.
¹⁰ But they rebelled, and grieved
His holy spirit;
Then He became their enemy,
And Himself made war against them.
¹¹ Then they*i* remembered the ancient days,
*j*Him, who pulled His people*j* out [of the water]:
"Where is He who brought them up from the Sea
Along with the shepherd*k* of His flock?
Where is He who put
In their midst His holy spirit,
¹² Who made His glorious arm

---

f-f Many mss. read weṣidqathi "My victorious [right hand]"; cf. 59.16.
g-g Many mss. and Targum read "I shattered them in"; cf. 14.25.
h-h Ancient versions read "So He was their Deliverer./⁹In all their troubles./No [so kethib] angel or messenger,/His own Presence delivered them." Cf. Deut. 4.37 and note.
i Heb. "he."
j-j Heb. moshe 'ammo, a play on the name Moshe (Moses).
k So many mss. and ancient versions; other texts "shepherds."

March at the right hand of Moses,
Who divided the waters before them
To make Himself a name for all time,
13 Who led them through the deeps
So that they did not stumble—
As a horse in a desert,
14 Like a beast descending to the plain?"
'Twas the spirit of the LORD *-gave them rest;*
Thus did You shepherd Your people
To win for Yourself a glorious name.

15 Look down from heaven and see,
From Your holy and glorious height!
Where is Your zeal, Your power?
Your yearning and Your love
Are being withheld from us!*
16 Surely You are our Father:
Though Abraham regard us not,
And Israel recognize us not,
You, O LORD, are our Father;
From of old, Your name is "Our Redeemer."
17 Why, LORD, do You make us stray from Your ways,
And turn our hearts away from revering You?
Relent for the sake of Your servants,
The tribes that are Your very own!
18 Our foes have trampled Your Sanctuary,
Which Your holy people *-possessed but a little while.-*
19 We have become as a people You never ruled,
To which Your name was never attached.

If You would but tear open the heavens and come down,
So that mountains would quake before You—
64 1 *As when fire kindles brushwood,
And fire makes water boil—
To make Your name known to Your adversaries

-l Emendation yields "guided them."
*m Heb. "me." Emendation yields "[Where are] Your yearning and Your love?/Let them not
be restrained!"*
n-n Meaning of Heb. uncertain.

a Meaning of vv. 1-4 uncertain.

So that nations will tremble at Your Presence,
2 When You did wonders we dared not hope for,
You came down
And mountains quaked before You.
3 Such things had never been heard or noted.
No eye has seen [them], O God, but You,
Who act for those who trust in You.[b]
4 Yet you have struck him who would gladly do justice,
And remember You in Your ways.
It is because You are angry that we have sinned;
[c]We have been steeped in them from of old,
And can we be saved?[-c]
5 We have all become like an unclean thing,
And all our virtues like a filthy rag.
We are all withering like leaves,
And our iniquities, like a wind, carry us off.
6 Yet no one invokes Your name,
Rouses himself to cling to You.
For You have hidden Your face from us,
And [d]made us melt because of[-d] our iniquities.
7 But now, O LORD, You are our Father;
We are the clay, and You are the Potter,
We are all the work of Your hands.
8 Be not implacably angry, O LORD,
Do not remember iniquity forever.
Oh, look down to Your people, to us all!
9 Your holy cities have become a desert:
Zion has become a desert,
Jerusalem a desolation.
10 Our holy Temple, our pride,
Where our fathers praised You,
Has been consumed by fire:
And all that was dear to us is ruined.
11 At such things will You restrain Yourself, O LORD,
Will You stand idly by and let us suffer so heavily?

[b] Heb. "Him"
[c-c] Emendation yields "Because You have hidden Yourself we have offended." For the thought
  cf. 63.17.
[d-d] Emendation yields "delivered us into the hands of. . . ."

65

*ᵃ*I responded to*⁻ᵃ* those who did not ask,
I was at hand to those who did not seek Me;
I said, "Here I am, here I am,"
To a nation that did not invoke My name.
² I constantly held out My hands
To a disloyal people,
Who walk the way that is not good,
Following their own designs;
³ The people who provoke My anger,
Who continually, to My very face,
Sacrifice in gardens and burn incense on tiles;
⁴ Who sit inside tombs
And pass the night in secret places;
Who eat the flesh of swine,
With broth of unclean things in their bowls;
⁵ Who say, "Keep your distance! Don't come closer!
*ᵇ*For I would render you consecrated."*⁻ᵇ*
Such things make My anger rage,
Like fire blazing all day long.
⁶ See, this is recorded before Me;
I will not stand idly by, but will repay,
Deliver *ᶜ*their*ᵈ* sins*⁻ᶜ* into their bosom,
⁷ And the sins of their fathers as well
　　　　　　　　　　　　　　—said the LORD—
For they made offerings upon the mountains
And affronted Me upon the hills.
I will count out their recompense in full,*ᵉ*
Into their bosoms.

⁸ Thus said the LORD:
As, when new wine is present in the cluster,
One says, "Don't destroy it; there's good in it,"

ᵃ⁻ᵃ Lit. "I let Myself be inquired of. . . ."
ᵇ⁻ᵇ Taking qedashtikha as equivalent to qiddashtikhakh, cf. Ezek. 44.19; others "For I am holier than thou."
ᶜ⁻ᶜ Brought up from v. 7 for clarity.
ᵈ Heb. "your."
ᵉ Taking rishonah as equivalent to beroshah; cf. Lev. 5.24. Meaning of Heb. uncertain.

So will I do for the sake of My servants,
And not destroy everything.
⁹ I will bring forth offspring from Jacob,
From Judah heirs to My mountains;
My chosen ones shall take possession,
My servants shall dwell thereon.
¹⁰ Sharon*f* shall become a pasture for flocks,
And the Valley of Achor a place for cattle to lie down,
For My people who seek Me.

¹¹ But as for you who forsake the LORD,
Who ignore My holy mountain,
Who set a table for Luck*g*
And fill a mixing bowl for Destiny:*g*
¹² I will destine you for the sword,
You will all kneel down to be slaughtered—
Because, when I called, you did not answer,
When I spoke, you would not listen.
You did what I hold evil,
And chose what I do not want.

¹³ Assuredly, thus said the Lord GOD:
My servants shall eat, and you shall hunger;
My servants shall drink, and you shall thirst;
My servants shall rejoice, and you shall be shamed;
¹⁴ My servants shall shout in gladness,
And you shall cry out in anguish,
Howling in heartbreak.
¹⁵ You shall leave behind a name
By which My chosen ones shall curse:
"So may the Lord GOD slay you!"
But His servants shall be given a *h*-different name.-*h*
¹⁶ For whoever blesses himself in the land
Shall bless himself by the true God;
And whoever swears in the land

f Emendation yields "Jeshimon," the bleak southeast corner of the Jordan Valley; cf. Nu. 21.20; 23.8.
g Names of heathen deities.
h-h I.e. a name to be used in blessing.

Shall swear by the true God.
The former troubles shall be forgotten,
Shall be hidden from My eyes.

¹⁷ For behold! I am creating
A new heaven and a new earth;
The former things shall not be remembered,
They shall never come to mind.
¹⁸ Be glad, then, and rejoice forever
In what I am creating.
For I shall create Jerusalem as a joy,
And her people as a delight;
¹⁹ And I will rejoice in Jerusalem
And delight in her people.
Never again shall be heard there
The sounds of weeping and wailing.
²⁰ No more shall there be an infant or graybeard
Who does not live out his days.
He who dies at a hundred years
Shall be reckoned a youth,
And he who fails to reach a hundred
Shall be reckoned accursed.
²¹ They shall build houses and dwell in them,
They shall plant vineyards and enjoy their fruit.
²² They shall not build for others to dwell in,
Or plant for others to enjoy.
For the days of My people shall be
As long as the days of a tree,
My chosen ones shall outliveⁱ
The work of their hands.
²³ They shall not toil to no purpose;
They shall not bear children ^{j-}for terror,^{-j}
But they shall be a people blessed by the Lord,
And their offspring shall remain with them.
²⁴ Before they pray, I will answer;

ⁱ *Lit. "wear out."*
^{j-j} *Emendation yields "in vain."*

While they are still speaking, I will respond.
25 The wolf and the lamb shall graze together,
And the lion shall eat straw like the ox,
And the serpent's food shall be earth.
In all My sacred mount*k*
Nothing evil or vile shall be done

—said the LORD.

66 Thus said the LORD:
The heaven is My throne
And the earth is My footstool:
Where could you build a house for Me,
What place could serve as My abode?
2 All this was made by My hand,
And thus it all came into being

—declares the LORD.

Yet to such a one I look:
To the poor and broken-hearted,
Who is concerned about My word.

3 *a*As for those who slaughter oxen and slay humans,
Who sacrifice sheep and immolate*b* dogs,
Who present as oblation the blood of swine,
Who offer*c* incense and worship false gods—
Just as they have chosen their ways
And take pleasure in their abominations,
4 So will I choose to mock them,
To bring on them the very thing they dread.
For I called and none responded,
I spoke and none paid heed.
They did what I hold evil
And chose what I do not want.

k See note at 11.9.
a Vv. 3-4 refer to practioners of idolatrous rites; cf. v. 17 and 57.5-8; 65.1-12.
b Lit. "break the necks of."
c Heb. mazkir refers to giving the "token portion" ('azkarah); cf. Lev. 2.2, etc.

⁵ Hear the word of the LORD,
You who are concerned about His word!
Your kinsmen who hate you,
Who spurn you because of Me,ᵈ are saying,
"Let the LORD manifest His Presence,
So that we may look upon your joy."
But theirs shall be the shame.
⁶ Hark, tumult from the city,
Thunder from the Temple!
It is the thunder of the LORD
As He deals retribution to His foes.

⁷ Before she labored, she was delivered;
Before her pangs came, she bore a son.
⁸ Who ever heard the like?
Who ever witnessed such events?
Can a land pass through travail
In a single day?
Or is a nation born
All at once?
Yet Zion travailed
And at once bore her children!
⁹ Shall I who bring on labor not bring about birth?
              —says the LORD.
Shall I who cause birth shut the womb?
              —said your GOD.
¹⁰ Rejoice with Jerusalem and be glad for her,
All you who love her!
Join in her jubilation,
All you who mourned over her—
¹¹ That you may suck from her breast
Consolation to the full,
That you may draw from her bosomᵉ
Glory to your delight.

ᵈ Lit. "My name."
ᵉ Cf. Akkadian zīzu, Arabic zīzat "udder."

506

¹² For thus said the LORD:
I will extend to her
Prosperity like a stream,
The wealth of nations
Like a wadi in flood;
And you shall drink of it.
You shall be carried on shoulders
And dandled upon knees.
¹³ As a mother comforts her son
So I will comfort you;
You shall find comfort in Jerusalem.
¹⁴ You shall see and your heart shall rejoice,
Your limbs shall flourish like grass.
The power of the LORD shall be revealed
In behalf of His servants;
But He shall rage against His foes.

¹⁵ See, the LORD is coming with fire—
His chariots are like a whirlwind—
To vent His anger in fury,
His rebuke in flaming fire.
¹⁶ For with fire will the LORD contend,
With His sword, against all flesh;
And many shall be the slain of the LORD.

¹⁷ Those who sanctify and purify themselves to enter the groves, *f*imitating one in the center,*f* eating the flesh of the swine, the reptile, and the mouse, shall one and all come to an end—declares the LORD. ¹⁸ *g*For I [know] their deeds and purposes.

[The time] has come to gather all the nations and tongues; they shall come and behold My glory. ¹⁹ I will set a sign among them, and send from them survivors to the nations: to Tarshish, Pul, and Lud—that draw the bow—to Tubal, Javan, and the distant

f-f *Meaning of Heb uncertain.*
g *Exact construction of this verse uncertain; for the insertions in brackets, cf. Kimhi.*

coasts, that have never heard My fame nor beheld My glory. They shall declare My glory among these nations. ²⁰ And out of all the nations, said the LORD, they shall bring all your brothers on horses, in chariots and drays, on mules and dromedaries, to Jerusalem My holy mountain as an offering to the LORD—just as the Israelites bring an offering in a pure vessel to the House of the LORD. ²¹ And from them likewise I will take some to be ʰ˙levitical priests,˙ʰ said the LORD.

²² For as the new heaven and the new earth
Which I will make
Shall endure by My will
> —declares the LORD—
So shall your seed and your name endure.
²³ And new moon after new moon,
And sabbath after sabbath,
All flesh shall come to worship Me
> —said the LORD.

²⁴ They shall go out and gaze
On the corpses of the men who rebelled against Me:
Their worms shall not die,
Nor their fire be quenched;
They shall be a horror
To all flesh.

> And new moon after new moon,
> And sabbath after sabbath,
> All flesh shall come to worship Me
> > —said the LORD.

ʰ˙ʰ *Some Heb. mss. read "priests and Levites."*

ירמיה

JEREMIAH

יִרְמְיָה
JEREMIAH

1 The words of Jeremiah son of Hilkiah, one of the priests at Anathoth in the territory of Benjamin. ² The word of the LORD came to him in the days of King Josiah son of Amon of Judah, in the thirteenth year of his reign, ³ and throughout the days of King Jehoiakim son of Josiah of Judah, and until the end of the eleventh year of King Zedekiah son of Josiah of Judah, when Jerusalem went into exile in the fifth month.

⁴ The word of the LORD came to me:

⁵ Before I created you in the womb, I selected you;
Before you were born, I consecrated you;
I appointed you a prophet concerning the nations.

⁶ I replied:
Ah, Lord GOD!
I don't know how to speak,
For I am still a boy.
⁷ And the LORD said to me:
Do not say, "I am still a boy,"
But go wherever I send you
And speak whatever I command you.
⁸ Have no fear of them,
For I am with you to deliver you

—declares the LORD.

⁹ The LORD put out His hand and touched my mouth, and the LORD said to me: Herewith I put My words into your mouth.

10 See, I appoint you this day
Over nations and kingdoms:
To uproot and to pull down,
To destroy and to overthrow,
To build and to plant.

11 The word of the LORD came to me: What do you see, Jeremiah? I replied: I see a branch of an almond tree.[a]
12 The LORD said to me:
You have seen right,
For I am watchful[b] to bring My word to pass.

13 And the word of the LORD came to me a second time: What do you see? I replied:
I see a steaming pot,
[c-]Tipped away from the north.[-c]
14 And the LORD said to me:
From the north shall disaster break loose
Upon all the inhabitants of the land!
15 For I am summoning all the peoples
of the kingdoms of the north

—declares the LORD.

They shall come, and shall each set up a throne
Before the gates of Jerusalem,
Against its walls round about,
And against all the towns of Judah.
16 And I will argue My case against them[d]
For all their wickedness:
They have forsaken Me
And sacrificed to other gods
And worshiped the works of their hands.

17 So you, gird up your loins,
Arise and speak to them
All that I command you.

[a] *Heb.* shaqed.
[b] *Heb.* shoqed.
[c-c] *Meaning of Heb. uncertain.*
[d] *I.e. against Jerusalem and Judah.*

Do not break down before them,
Lest I break you before them.
¹⁸ I make you this day
A fortified city,
And an iron pillar,
And bronze walls
Against the whole land—
Against Judah's kings and officers,
And against its priests and citizens.ᵉ
¹⁹ They will attack you,
But they shall not overcome you;
For I am with you—declares the LORD—to save you.

2 The word of the LORD came to me, saying, ² Go proclaim to Jerusalem: Thus said the LORD:
I accounted to your favor
The devotion of your youth,
Your love as a bride—
How you followed Me in the wilderness,
In a land not sown.
³ Israel was holy to the LORD,
The first fruits of His harvest.
All who ate of it were held guilty;
Disaster befell them

> —declares the LORD.

⁴ Hear the word of the LORD, O House of Jacob,
Every clan of the House of Israel!
⁵ Thus said the LORD:
What wrong did your fathers find in Me
That they abandoned Me
And went after delusion and were deluded?
⁶ They never asked themselves, "Where is the LORD,
Who brought us up from the land of Egypt,

ᶜ *Lit. "the people of the land."*

Who led us through the wilderness,
A land of deserts and pits,
A land of drought and darkness,
A land no man had traversed,
Where no human being had dwelt?"
7 I brought you to this country of farm land
To enjoy its fruit and its bounty;
But you came and defiled My land,
You made My possession abhorrent.
8 The priests never asked themselves, "Where is the LORD?"
The guardians of the Teaching ignored Me;
The rulers*a* rebelled against Me,
And the prophets prophesied by Baal
And followed what can do no good.

9 Oh, I will go on accusing you
     —declares the LORD—
And I will accuse your children's children!
10 Just cross over to the isles of the Kittim and look,
Send to Kedar and observe carefully;
See if aught like this has ever happened:
11 Has any nation changed its gods
Even though they are no-gods?
But My people has exchanged its glory
For what can do no good.
12 Be appalled, O heavens, at this;
Be horrified, utterly dazed!
     —says the LORD.
13 For My people have done a twofold wrong:
They have forsaken Me, the Fount of living waters,
And hewed them out cisterns, broken cisterns,
Which cannot even hold water.

14 Is Israel a bondman,
Is he a home-born slave?

a Lit. "shepherds"; cf. 3.15; 23.1 ff.

Then why is he given over to plunder?
[15] Lions have roared over him,
Have raised their cries.
They have made his land a waste,
His cities desolate, without inhabitants.
[16] Those, too, in Noph and Tahpanhes[b]
[c]Will lay bare[-c] your head.
[17] See, [d]that is the price you have paid
For forsaking the LORD your God[-d]
[c]While He led you in the way.[-c]
[18] What, then, is the good of your going to Egypt
To drink the waters of the Nile?
And what is the good of your going to Assyria
To drink the waters of the Euphrates?
[19] Let your misfortune reprove you,
Let your afflictions rebuke you;
Mark well how bad and bitter it is
That you forsake the LORD your God,
That awe for Me is not in you
——declares the Lord GOD of Hosts.
[20] For long ago you[e] broke your yoke,
Tore off your yoke-bands,
And said, "I will not work!"[f]
On every high hill and under every verdant tree,
You recline as a whore.
[21] I planted you with noble vines,
All with choicest seed;
Alas, I find you changed
Into a base, an alien vine!
[22] Though you wash with natron
And use much lye,
Your guilt is ingrained before Me
——declares the Lord GOD.
[23] How can you say, "I am not defiled,
I have not gone after the Baalim"?

[b] Cities in Egypt. The Egyptians, like the Assyrians, will prove a disappointment; cf. v. 36.
[c-c] Meaning of Heb. uncertain.
[d-d] Lit. "that is what your forsaking the LORD your God is doing to you."
[e] For the form, cf. shaqqamti, Judg. 5.7; others "I."
[f] Following the kethib; qere "transgress."

Look at your deeds in the Valley,*g*
Consider what you have done!
Like a lustful she-camel,
*c*Restlessly running about,*c*
24 Or like a wild ass used to the desert,
Snuffing the wind in her eagerness,
Whose passion none can restrain,
None that seek her need grow weary—
In her season, they'll find her!

25 Save your foot from going bare,
And your throat from thirst.
But you say, "It is no use.
No, I love the strangers,*h*
And after them I must go."
26 Like a thief chagrined when he is caught,
So is the House of Israel chagrined—
They, their kings, their officers,
And their priests and prophets.
27 They said to wood, "You are my father,"
To stone, "You gave birth to me,"
While to Me they turned their backs
And not their faces.
But in their hour of calamity they cry,
"Arise and save us!"
28 And where are those gods
You made for yourself?
Let them arise and save you, if they can,
In your hour of calamity.
For your gods have become, O Judah,
As many as your towns!
29 Why do you call Me to account?
You have all rebelled against Me

—declares the LORD.

30 To no purpose did I smite your children;

g *I.e. of Hinnom; cf. 7.31-32; 32.35.*
h *I.e. other gods.*

They would not accept correction.
Your sword has devoured your prophets
Like a ravening lion.
31 ᶜO generation, behold ᶜ the word of the LORD!
Have I been like a desert to Israel,
Or like a land of deep gloom?
Then why do My people say, "We have broken loose,
We will not come to You any more?"
32 Can a maiden forget her jewels,
A bride her adornments?
Yet My people have forgotten Me—
Days without number.

33 How skillfully you plan your way
To seek out love!
Why, you have even taught
The worst of women your ways.
34 Moreover, on your garments is found
The lifeblood of the innocent poor—
You did not catch them breaking in.ⁱ
ᶜYet, despite all these things,ᶜ
35 You say, "I have been acquitted;
Surely, His anger has turned away from me."
Lo, I will bring you to judgment
For saying, "I have not sinned."

36 How you cheapen yourself,
By changing your course!
You shall be put to shame through Egypt,
Just as you were put to shame through Assyria.
37 From this way, too, you will come out
ʲWith your hands on your head;ʲ
For the LORD has rejected those you trust,
You will not prosper with them.

ⁱ *In which case there might have been an excuse for killing them; cf. Exod. 22.1.*
ʲ⁻ʲ *A gesture of wild grief; cf. II Sam. 13.19.*

517

3 [The word of the LORD came to me] as follows: If a man divorces his wife, and she leaves him and marries another man, can he ever go back to her? Would not such a land be defiled?*a* Now you have whored with many lovers: can you return to Me? —says the LORD.

> 2 Look up to the bare heights, and see:
> Where have they not lain with you?
> You waited for them on the roadside
> Like a bandit*b* in the wilderness.
> And you defiled the land
> With your whoring and your debauchery.
> 3 And when showers were withheld
> And the late rains did not come,
> You had the brazenness*c* of a street woman,
> You refused to be ashamed.
> 4 Just now you called to Me, "Father!
> You are the Guide of my youth.
> 5 Does one hate*d* for all time?
> Does one rage*d* forever?"
> That is how you spoke;
> You did wrong, and *e*had your way.*-e*

6 The LORD said to me in the days of King Josiah: Have you seen what Rebel Israel did, going to every high mountain and under every leafy tree, and whoring there? 7 I thought: After she has done all these things, she will come back to Me. But she did not come back; and her sister, Faithless Judah, saw it. 8 I noted: Because Rebel Israel had committed adultery, I cast her off and handed her a bill of divorce; yet her sister, Faithless Judah, was not afraid—she too went and whored. 9 Indeed, the land was defiled by her casual immorality, as she committed adultery with

---

a Cf. Deut. 24.1-4.
b Lit. "Arab."
c Lit. "forehead."
d Cf. Akkadian parallels nadāru and shamāru.
e-e Meaning of Heb. uncertain.

stone and with wood.*f* 10 And after all that, her sister, Faithless Judah, did not return to Me wholeheartedly, but insincerely—declares the LORD.

11 And the LORD said to me: Rebel Israel has shown herself more in the right than Faithless Judah. 12 Go, make this proclamation toward the north, and say: Turn back, O Rebel Israel—declares the LORD. I will not look on you in anger, for I am compassionate—declares the LORD; I do not bear a grudge for all time. 13 Only recognize your sin; for you have transgressed against the LORD, and scattered your favors*g* among strangers under every leafy tree, and you have not heeded Me—declares the LORD.

14 Turn back, rebellious children—declares the LORD. Though I have rejected*h* you, I will take you, one from a town and two from a clan, and bring you to Zion. 15 And I will give you shepherds after My own heart, who will pasture you with knowledge and skill.

16 And when you increase and are fertile in the land, in those days—declares the LORD—men shall no longer speak of the Ark of the Covenant of the LORD, nor shall it come to mind. They shall not mention it, or miss it, or make another. 17 At that time, they shall call Jerusalem "Throne of the LORD," and all nations shall assemble there, in the name of the LORD, at Jerusalem. They*i* shall no longer follow the willfulness of their evil hearts. 18 In those days, the House of Judah shall go with the House of Israel; they shall come together from the land of the north to the land I gave your fathers as a possession.

19 I had resolved to adopt you as My child, and I gave you a desirable land—the fairest heritage of all the nations; and I thought you would surely call Me "Father," and never cease to be loyal to Me. 20 Instead, you have broken faith with Me, as a woman breaks faith with a paramour, O House of Israel—declares the LORD.

f She deserted her God for idols of stone and wood.
g Lit. "ways."
h Taking baʿalti as equivalent to baḥalti; cf. note at 31.32.
i I.e. Israel and Judah.

21 Hark! On the bare heights is heard
The suppliant weeping of the people of Israel,
For they have gone a crooked way,
Ignoring the LORD their God.

22 Turn back, O rebellious children,
I will heal your afflictions!

"Here we are, we come to You,
For You, O LORD, are our God!
23 *j-*Surely, futility comes from the hills,
Confusion from the mountains.*-j*
Only through the LORD our God
Is there deliverance for Israel.
24 But the Shameful Thing*k* has consumed
The possessions of our fathers ever since our youth—
Their flocks and herds,
Their sons and daughters.
25 Let us lie down in our shame,
Let our disgrace cover us;
For we have sinned against the LORD our God,
We and our fathers from our youth to this day,
And we have not heeded the LORD our God."

4 If you return, O Israel

—declares the LORD—

If you return to Me,
If you remove your abominations from My presence
And do not waver,
2 And *a-*swear, "As the LORD lives,"*-a*
In sincerity, justice, and righteousness—
Nations shall bless themselves by you*b*
And praise themselves by you.*b*

---

j-j *I.e. the pagan rites celebrated on the hills are futile; exact force of Heb. uncertain.*
k *Heb.* Bosheth, *a contemptuous substitute for Baal.*

a-a *I.e. profess the worship of the LORD.*
b *Heb.* "him."

³ For thus said the LORD to the men of Judah and to Jerusalem:

Break up the untilled ground,
And do not sow among thorns.
⁴ Openᶜ your hearts to the LORD,
Remove the thickening about your hearts—
O men of Judah and inhabitants of Jerusalem—
Lest My wrath break forth like fire,
And burn, with none to quench it,
Because of your wicked acts.

⁵ Proclaim in Judah,
Announce in Jerusalem,
And say:
"Blow the horn in the land!"
Shout aloud and say:
"Assemble, and let us go
Into the fortified cities!"
⁶ Set up a signpost: To Zion.
Take refuge, do not delay!
For I bring evil from the north,
And great disaster.
⁷ The lion has come up from his thicket:
The destroyer of nations has set out,
Has departed from his place,
To make your land a desolation;
Your cities shall be ruined,
Without inhabitants.
⁸ For this, put on sackcloth,
Mourn and wail;
For the blazing anger of the LORD
Has not turned away from us.
⁹ And in that day

—declares the LORD—

The mind of the king

ᶜ Lit. "circumcise"; cf. Deut. 10.16 and 30.6.

And the mind of the nobles shall fail,
The priests shall be appalled,
And the prophets stand aghast.

10 *d-*And I said:*-d* Ah, Lord God! Surely You have deceived this
people and Jerusalem, saying:
It shall be well with you—
Yet the sword threatens the very life!

11 At that time, it shall be said concerning this people and
Jerusalem:
The conduct of *e-*My poor people*-e* is like searing wind
From the bare heights of the desert—
It will not serve to winnow or to fan.
12 A full blast from them comes against Me:
Now I in turn will bring charges against them.

13 Lo, he *f* ascends like clouds,
His chariots are like a whirlwind,
His horses are swifter than eagles.
Woe to us, we are ruined!
14 Wash your heart clean of wickedness,
O Jerusalem, that you may be rescued.
How long will you harbor within you
Your evil designs?

15 Hark, one proclaims from Dan
And announces calamity from Mount Ephraim!
16 Tell the nations: Here they are!
Announce concerning Jerusalem:
Watchers *f* are coming from a distant land,
They raise their voices against the towns of Judah.
17 Like guards of fields, they surround her on every side.
For she has rebelled against Me
—declares the Lord.

d-d *Septuagint reads "And they shall say."*
e-e *Lit. "the daughter that is My people"; so, frequently, in poetry.*
f *I.e. the invader of v. 7.*

522

¹⁸ Your conduct and your acts
Have brought this upon you;
This is your bitter punishment;
It pierces your very heart.

¹⁹ Oh, my suffering,^g my suffering!
How I writhe!
Oh, the walls of my heart!
My heart moans within me,
I cannot be silent;
For ^{h-}I hear^{-h} the blare of horns,
Alarms of war.
²⁰ Disaster overtakes disaster,
For all the land has been ravaged.
Suddenly my tents have been ravaged,
In a moment, my tent cloths.
²¹ How long must I see standards
And hear the blare of horns?

²² My people are stupid,
They give Me no heed;
They are foolish children,
They are not intelligent.
They are clever at doing wrong,
But unable to do right.

²³ I look at the earth,
It is unformed and void;
At the skies,
And their light is gone.
²⁴ I look at the mountains,
They are quaking;
And all the hills are rocking.
²⁵ I look: no man is left,
And all the birds of the sky have fled.

^g Lit. "entrails."
^{h-h} Lit. "you, O my being, hear." Change of vocalization yields "I hear the blare of horns, / My inner being, alarms of war."

26 I look: the farm land is desert,
And all its towns are in ruin—
Because of the LORD,
Because of His blazing anger.
(27 For thus said the LORD:
The whole land shall be desolate,
But I will not make an end of it.)
28 For this the earth mourns,
And skies are dark above—
Because I have spoken, I have planned,
And I will not relent or turn back from it.

29 At the shout of horseman and bowman
The whole city flees.
They enter the thickets,
They clamber up the rocks.
The whole city is deserted,
Not a man remains there.
30 And you, who are doomed to ruin,
What do you accomplish by wearing crimson,
By decking yourself in jewels of gold,
By enlarging your eyes with kohl?
You beautify yourself in vain:
Lovers despise you,
They seek your life!
31 I hear a voice as of one in travail,
Anguish as of a woman bearing her first child,
The voice of Fair Zion
Panting, stretching out her hands:
"Alas for me! I faint
Before the killers!"

5   Roam the streets of Jerusalem,
     Search its squares,
     Look about and take note:
     You will not find a man,
     There is none who acts justly,
     Who seeks integrity—
     That I should pardon her.
     ² Even when they say, "As the LORD lives,"
     They are sure to be swearing falsely.
     ³ O LORD, Your eyes look for integrity.
     You have struck them, but they sensed no pain;
     You have consumed them, but they would accept
       no discipline.
     They made their faces harder than rock,
     They refused to turn back.

     ⁴ I thought: These are just poor folk;
     They act foolishly;
     For they do not know the way of the LORD,
     The rules of their God.
     ⁵ So I will go to the wealthy
     And speak with them:
     Surely they know the way of the LORD,
     The rules of their God.
     But they as well had broken the yoke,
     Had snapped the bonds.
     ⁶ Therefore,
     The lion of the forest strikes them down,
     The wolf of the desert ravages them.
     A leopard lies in wait by their towns;
     Whoever leaves them will be torn in pieces.

For their transgressions are many,
Their rebellious acts unnumbered.

7 Why should I forgive you?
Your children have forsaken Me
And sworn by no-gods.
When I fed them their fill,
They committed adultery
And went trooping to the harlot's house.
8 They were *a*-well-fed, lusty*-a* stallions,
Each neighing at another's wife.
9 Shall I not punish such deeds?

—says the LORD—

Shall I not bring retribution
On a nation such as this?
10 Go up among her vines*b* and destroy;
Lop off her trailing branches,
For they are not of the LORD.
(But do not make an end.)
11 For the House of Israel and the House of Judah
Have betrayed Me

—declares the LORD.

12 They have been false to the LORD
And said: "*c*-It is not so!*-c*
No trouble shall come upon us,
We shall not see sword or famine.
13 The prophets shall prove mere wind
For the Word is not in them;
Thus-and-thus shall be done to them!"

14 Assuredly, thus said the LORD,
The God of Hosts:
Because they*d* said that,
I am putting My words into your mouth as fire,
And this people shall be firewood,

---

a-a *Meaning of Heb. uncertain.*
b *Lit. "rows."*
c-c *Or "Not He": cf. Deut. 32.39; Isa. 43.13.*
d *Heb. "you."*

Which it will consume.
¹⁵ Lo, I am bringing against you, O House of Israel,
A nation from afar

—declares the LORD;

It is an enduring nation,
It is an ancient nation;
A nation whose language you do not know—
You will not understand what they say.
¹⁶ ^{e-}Their quivers^{-e} are like a yawning grave—
They are all mighty men.
¹⁷ They will devour your harvest and food,
They will devour your sons and daughters,
They will devour your flocks and herds,
They will devour your vines and fig trees.
They will batter down with the sword
The fortified towns on which you rely.

¹⁸ But even in those days—declares the LORD—I will not make
an end of you. ¹⁹ And when they^d ask, "Because of what did the
LORD our God do all these things?" you shall answer them, "Be-
cause you forsook Me and served alien gods on your own land,
you will have to serve foreigners in a land not your own."

²⁰ Proclaim this to the House of Jacob
And announce it in Judah:
²¹ Hear this, O foolish people,
Devoid of intelligence,
That have eyes but can't see,
That have ears but can't hear!
²² Should you not revere Me

—says the LORD—

Should you not tremble before Me,
Who set the sand as a boundary to the sea,
As a limit for all time, not to be transgressed?
Though its waves toss, they cannot prevail;

^{e-e} *Emendation yields "Whose mouths."*

Though they roar, they cannot pass it.
23 Yet this people has a wayward and defiant heart;
They have turned aside and gone their way.
24 They have not said to themselves,
."Let us revere the LORD our God,
Who gives the rain,
The early and late rain in season,
Who keeps for our benefit
The weeks appointed for harvest."
25 It is your iniquities that have diverted these things,
Your sins that have withheld the bounty from you.
26 For among My people are found wicked men,
*a-*Who lurk, like fowlers lying in wait;*-a*
They set up a trap to catch men.
27 As a cage is full of birds,
So their houses are full of guile;
That is why they have grown so wealthy.
28 They have become fat and sleek;
They *f-*pass beyond the bounds of wickedness,*f*
And they prosper.
They will not judge the case of the orphan,
Nor give a hearing to the plea of the needy.
29 Shall I not punish such deeds

—says the LORD—

Shall I not bring retribution
On a nation such as this?
30 An appalling, horrible thing
Has happened in the land:
31 The prophets prophesy falsely,
And the priests *a-*rule accordingly;*-a*
And My people like it so.
But what will you do at the end of it?

---

f-f Some ancient versions read "have transgressed My words for evil."

6 Flee for refuge, O people of Benjamin,
Out of the midst of Jerusalem!
Blow the horn in Tekoa,
Set up a signal at Beth-haccherem!
For evil is appearing from the north,
And great disaster.
2 *a*-Fair Zion, the lovely and delicate,
I will destroy.-*a*
3 Against her come shepherds with their flocks,
They pitch tents all around her;
Each grazes *b*-the sheep under his care.-*b*
4 *c*-Prepare for-*c* battle against her:
"Up! we will attack at noon."
"Alas for us! for day is declining,
The shadows of evening grow long."
5 "Up! let us attack by night,
And wreck her fortresses."

6 For thus said the LORD of Hosts:
Hew down her trees,
And raise a siege-mound against Jerusalem.
d-She is the city destined for punishment;-*d*
Only fraud is found in her midst.
7 As a well flows with water,
So she flows with wickedness.
Lawlessness and rapine are heard in her;
Before Me constantly are sickness and wounds.
8 Accept rebuke, O Jerusalem,
Lest I come to loathe you,
Lest I make you a desolation,
An uninhabited land.

a-a *Meaning of Heb. uncertain.*
b-b *Understanding* yado *as in Ps. 95.7.*
c-c *Lit. "Consecrate."*
d-d *Emendation yields "She is the city of falseness."*

⁹ Thus said the LORD of Hosts:
ᵉ⁻Let them glean⁻ᵉ over and over, as a vine,
The remnant of Israel;
Pass your hand again,
Like a vintager,
Over its branches.

¹⁰ ᶠTo whom shall I speak,
Give warning that they may hear?
Their ears are blocked
And they cannot listen.
See, the word of the LORD has become for them
An object of scorn; they will have none of it.
¹¹ But I am filled with the wrath of the LORD,
I cannot hold it in.

Pour it on the infant in the street,
And on the company of youths gathered together!
Yes, men and women alike shall be captured,
Elders and those of advanced years.
¹² Their houses shall pass to others,
Fields and wives as well,
For I will stretch out My arm
Against the inhabitants of the country
                    —declares the LORD.
¹³ For from the smallest to the greatest,
They are all greedy for gain;
Priest and prophet alike,
They all act falsely.
¹⁴ They offer healing offhand
For the wounds of My people,
Saying, "All is well, all is well,"
When nothing is well.
¹⁵ They have acted shamefully;
They have done abhorrent things—

ᵉ⁻ᵉ *Emendation yields "Glean" (singular).*
ᶠ *The prophet speaks.*

Yet they do not feel shame,
And they cannot be made to blush.
Assuredly, they shall fall among the falling,
They shall stumble at the time when I punish them
—said the LORD.

¹⁶ Thus said the LORD:
Stand by the roads and consider,
Inquire about ancient paths:
Which is the road to happiness?
Travel it, and find tranquillity for yourselves.
But they said, "We will not."
¹⁷ And I raised up watchmen[g] for you:
"Hearken to the sound of the horn!"
But they said, "We will not."
¹⁸ Hear well, O nations,
And know, "ᵃ"O community, what is in store for them."ᵃ
¹⁹ Hear, O earth!
I am going to bring disaster upon this people,
The outcome of their own schemes;
For they would not hearken to My words,
And they rejected My Instruction.
²⁰ What need have I of frankincense
That comes from Sheba,
Or fragrant cane from a distant land?
Your burnt offerings are not acceptable
And your sacrifices are not pleasing to Me.
²¹ Assuredly, thus said the LORD:
I shall put before this people stumbling blocks
Over which they shall stumble—
Fathers and children alike,
Neighbor and friend shall perish.

²² Thus said the LORD:
See, a people comes from the northland,

g _I.e. prophets._

A great nation is roused
From the remotest parts of the earth.
23 They grasp the bow and javelin;
They are cruel, they show no mercy;
The sound of them is like the roaring sea.
They ride upon horses,
Accoutered like a man for battle,
Against you, O Fair Zion!

24 "We have heard the report of them,
Our hands fail;
Pain seizes us,
Agony like a woman in childbirth.
25 Do not go out into the country,
Do not walk the roads!
For the sword of the enemy is there,
Terror on every side."

26 *g*-My poor people,-*g*
Put on sackcloth
And strew dust on yourselves!
Mourn, as for an only child;
Wail bitterly,
For suddenly the destroyer
Is coming upon us.

27 I have made you an assayer of My people
—A refiner*a*—
You are to note and assay their ways.
28 They are copper and iron:
They are all stubbornly defiant;
They *h*-deal basely-*h*
All of them act corruptly.
29 *a*-The bellows puff;
The lead is consumed by fire.-*a*

g-g *Lit. "Daughter that is my people"; so, frequently, in poetry. See 4.11 and note.*
h-h *See note at Lev. 19.16.*

Yet the smelter smelts to no purpose—
The dross*a* is not separated out.
³⁰ They are called "rejected silver,"
For the LORD has rejected them.

7 The word which came to Jeremiah from the LORD: ² Stand at the gate of the House of the LORD, and there proclaim this word: Hear the word of the LORD, all you of Judah who enter these gates to worship the LORD!

³ Thus said the LORD of Hosts, the God of Israel: Mend your ways and your actions, and I will *a-*let you dwell*-a* in this place. ⁴ Don't put your trust in illusions and say, "The Temple of the LORD, the Temple of the LORD, the Temple of the LORD are these [buildings]." ⁵ No, if you really mend your ways and your actions; if you execute justice between one man and another; ⁶ if you do not oppress the stranger, the orphan, and the widow; if you do not shed the blood of the innocent in this place; if you do not follow other gods, to your own hurt—⁷ then only will I *a-*let you dwell*-a* in this place, in the land which I gave to your fathers for all time. ⁸ See, you are relying on illusions that are of no avail. ⁹ Will you steal and murder and commit adultery and swear falsely, and sacrifice to Baal, and follow other gods whom you have not experienced,*b* ¹⁰ and then come and stand before Me in this House which bears My name and say, "We are safe"?—[Safe] to do all these abhorrent things! ¹¹ Do you consider this House, which bears My name, to be a den of thieves? As for Me, I have been watching—declares the LORD.

¹² Just go to My place at Shiloh, where I had established My name formerly, and see what I did to it because of the wickedness of My people Israel. ¹³ And now, because you do all these things —declares the LORD—and though I spoke to you persistently, you would not listen; and though I called to you, you would not respond—¹⁴ therefore I will do to the House which bears My name, on which you rely, and to the place which I gave you and

---

a-a Meaning of Heb. uncertain. Change of vocalization yields "dwell with you"; so Aquila and Vulgate.
b See note at Deut. 11.28.

your fathers just what I did to Shiloh. ¹⁵ And I will cast you out of My presence as I cast out your brothers, the whole brood of Ephraim.

¹⁶ As for you, do not pray for this people, do not raise a cry of prayer on their behalf, do not plead with Me; for I will not listen to you. ¹⁷ Don't you see what they are doing in the towns of Judah and in the streets of Jerusalem? ¹⁸ The children gather sticks, the fathers build the fire, and the mothers knead dough, to make cakes for the Queen of Heaven,ᶜ and they pour libations to other gods, to vex Me. ¹⁹ Is it Me they are vexing?—says the LORD. It is rather themselves, to their own disgrace. ²⁰ Assuredly, thus said the Lord GOD: My wrath and My fury will be poured out upon this place, on man and on beast, on the trees of the field and the fruit of the soil. It shall burn, with none to quench it.

²¹ Thus said the LORD of Hosts, the God of Israel: Add your burnt offerings to your other sacrifices and eat the meat! ²² For when I freed your fathers from the land of Egypt, I did not speak with them or command them concerning burnt offerings or sacrifice. ²³ But this is what I commanded them: Do My bidding, that I may be your God and you may be My people; walk only in the way that I enjoin upon you, that it may go well with you. ²⁴ Yet they did not listen or give ear; they followed their own counsels, the willfulness of their evil hearts. They have gone backward, not forward, ²⁵ from the day your fathers left the land of Egypt until today. And though I kept sending all My servants, the prophets, to themᵈ daily and persistently, ²⁶ they would not listen to Me or give ear. They stiffened their necks, they acted worse than their fathers.

²⁷ You shall say all these things to them, but they will not listen to you; you shall call to them, but they will not respond to you. ²⁸ Then say to them: This is the nation that would not obey the LORD their God, that would not accept rebuke. Faithfulness has perished, vanished from their mouths.

ᶜ *I.e. the mother goddess (Ishtar, Astarte) in whose honor these cakes were baked.*
ᵈ *Heb. "you."*

²⁹ Shear your locks and cast them away,
Take up a lament on the heights,
For the LORD has spurned and cast off
The brood that provoked His wrath.

³⁰ For the people of Judah have done what displeases Me—
declares the LORD. They have set up their abominations in the
House which is called by My name, and they have defiled it.
³¹ And they have built the shrines of Topheth in the Valley of
Ben-hinnom to burn their sons and daughters in fire—which I
never commanded, which never came to My mind.
³² Assuredly, a time is coming—declares the LORD—when men
shall no longer speak of Topheth or the Valley of Ben-hinnom,
but of the Valley of Slaughter; and they shall bury in Topheth until no room is left. ³³ The carcasses of this people shall be food for
the birds of the sky and the beasts of the earth, with none to fright-
en them off, ³⁴ And I will silence in the towns of Judah and the
streets of Jerusalem the sound of mirth and gladness, the voice
of bridegroom and bride. For the whole land shall fall to ruin.

8 At that time—declares the LORD—the bones of the kings of
Judah, of its officers, of the priests, of the prophets, and of the
inhabitants of Jerusalem shall be taken out of their graves ² and
exposed to the sun, the moon, and all the host of heaven which
they loved and served and followed, to which they turned and
bowed down. They shall not be gathered for reburial; they shall
become dung upon the face of the earth. ³ And death shall be
preferable to life for all that are left of this wicked folk, in all the
other places to which I shall banish them—declares the LORD of
Hosts.

⁴ Say to them: Thus said the LORD:
When men fall, do they not get up again?
If they turn aside, do they not turn back?

5 Why is this people—Jerusalem—rebellious
With a persistent rebellion?
They cling to deceit,
They refuse to return.
6 I have listened and heard:
They do not speak honestly.
No one regrets his wickedness
And says, "What have I done!"
They all persist in their wayward course
Like a steed dashing forward in the fray.
7 Even the stork in the sky knows her seasons,
And the turtledove, swift, and crane
Keep the time of their coming;
But My people pay no heed
To the law of the LORD.
8 How can you say, "We are wise,
And we possess the Instruction of the LORD"?
Assuredly, for naught has the pen labored,
For naught the scribes!
9 The wise shall be put to shame,
Shall be dismayed and caught;
See, they reject the word of the LORD,
So their wisdom amounts to nothing.

10 Assuredly, I will give their wives to others,
And their fields to dispossessors;
For from the smallest to the greatest,
They are all greedy for gain;
Priest and prophet alike,
They all act falsely.
11 They offer healing offhand
For the wounds of My poor people,
Saying, "All is well, all is well,"
When nothing is well.

¹² They have acted shamefully;
They have done abhorrent things—
Yet they do not feel shame,
They cannot be made to blush.
Assuredly, they shall fall among the falling,
They shall stumble at the time of their doom

—said the LORD.

¹³ *^a*I will make an end of them*^{-a}*

—declares the LORD:
No grapes left on the vine,
No figs on the fig tree,
The leaves all withered;
*^b*Whatever I have given them is gone.*^{-h}*
¹⁴ Why are we sitting by?
Let us gather into the fortified cities
And meet our doom there.
For the LORD our God has doomed us,
He has made us drink a bitter draft,
Because we sinned against the LORD.
¹⁵ We hoped for good fortune, but no happiness
came;
For a time of relief—instead there is terror!
¹⁶ The snorting of their horses was heard from Dan;
At the loud neighing of their steeds
The whole land quaked.
They came and devoured the land and what was in it,
The towns and those who dwelt in them.

¹⁷ Lo, I will send serpents against you,
Adders that cannot be charmed,
And they shall bite you

—declares the LORD.

---

^{a-a} *Meaning of Heb. uncertain; change of vocalization yields "Their fruit harvest has been gathered in."*
^{b-b} *Meaning of Heb. uncertain.*

18 ᵇ⁻When in grief I would seek comfort,⁻ᵇ
My heart is sick within me.

19 ᶜ"Is not the LORD in Zion,
Is not her King within her?
Why then did they anger Me with their images,
With alien futilities?"

Hark! The outcry of my poor people
From the land far and wide:
20 "Harvest is past,
Summer is gone,
But we have not been saved."
21 Because my people is shattered I am shattered;
I am dejected, seized by desolation.
22 Is there no balm in Gilead,
Can no physician be found?
Why has healing not yet
Come to my poor people?
23 Oh, that my head were water,
My eyes a fount of tears!
Then would I weep day and night
For the slain of my poor people.

9 Oh, to be in the desert,
At an encampment for wayfarers!
Oh, to leave my people,
To go away from them—
For they are all adulterers,
A band of rogues.

2 They bend their tongues like bows;
They are valorous in the land
For treachery, not for honesty;

ᶜ *Here God is speaking.*

They advance from evil to evil.
And they do not heed Me
—declares the LORD.
³ Beware, every man of his friend!
Trust not even a brother!
For every brother takes advantage,
Every friend ᵃis base in his dealings.ˉᵃ
⁴ One man cheats the other,
They will not speak truth;
They have trained their tongues to speak falsely;
ᵇˉThey wear themselves out working iniquity.
⁵ You dwell in the midst of deceit.
In their deceit,ˉᵇ they refuse to heed Me
—declares the LORD.

⁶ Assuredly, thus said the LORD of Hosts:
Lo, I shall smelt and assay them—
ᵇˉFor what else can I do because of My poor people?ˉᵇ
⁷ Their tongue is a sharpened arrow,
They use their mouths to deceive.
One speaks to his fellow in friendship,
But lays an ambush for him in his heart.
⁸ Shall I not punish them for such deeds?
—says the LORD—
Shall I not bring retribution
On such a nation as this?

⁹ For the mountains I take up weeping and wailing,
For the pastures in the wilderness, a dirge.
They are laid waste; no man passes through,
And no sound of cattle is heard.
Birds of the sky and beasts as well
Have fled and are gone.

ᵃˉᵃ *See note at Lev. 19.16.*
ᵇˉᵇ *Meaning of Heb. uncertain.*

¹⁰ I will turn Jerusalem into rubble,
Into dens for jackals;
And I will make the towns of Judah
A desolation without inhabitants.

¹¹ What man is so wise
That he understands this?
To whom has the Lord's mouth spoken,
So that he can explain it:
Why is the land in ruins,
Laid waste like a wilderness,
With none passing through?

¹² The Lord replied: Because they forsook the Teaching I had set before them. They did not obey Me and they did not follow it, ¹³ but followed their own willful heart and followed the Baalim, as their fathers had taught them. ¹⁴ Assuredly, thus said the Lord of Hosts, the God of Israel: I am going to feed that people wormwood and make them drink a bitter draft. ¹⁵ I will scatter them among nations which they and their fathers never knew; and I will dispatch the sword after them until I have consumed them.

¹⁶ Thus said the Lord of Hosts:
Listen!
Summon the dirge-singers, let them come;
¹⁷ Send for the skilled women, let them come.
Let them quickly start a wailing for us,
That our eyes may run with tears,
Our pupils flow with water.

¹⁸ For the sound of wailing
Is heard from Zion:
How we are despoiled!
How greatly we are shamed!

Ah, we must leave our land,
Abandon^c our dwellings!

19 Hear, O women, the word of the LORD,
Let your ears receive the word of His mouth,
And teach your daughters wailing,
And one another lamentation.
20 For death has climbed through our windows,
Has entered our fortresses,
To cut off babes from the streets,
Young men from the squares.

21 Speak thus—says the LORD:
The carcasses of men shall lie
Like dung upon the fields,
Like sheaves behind the reaper,
With none to pick them up.

22 Thus said the LORD:
Let not the wise man glory in his wisdom;
Let not the strong man glory in his strength;
Let not the rich man glory in his riches.
23 But only in this should one glory:
In his earnest devotion to Me.
For I the LORD act with kindness,
Justice, and equity in the world;
For in these I delight

—declares the LORD.

24 Lo, days are coming—declares the LORD—when I will take
note of everyone ^{d-}circumcised in the foreskin:^{-d} 25 of Egypt,
Judah, Edom, the Ammonites, Moab, and all the desert dwellers
who have the hair of their temples clipped. For all these nations
are uncircumcised, but all the House of Israel are ^{e-}uncircumcised
of heart.^{-e}

^c *Lit. "They abandoned."*
^{d-d} *Force of Heb. uncertain.*
^{e-e} *I.e. their minds are blocked to God's commandments.*

541

10 Hear the word which the LORD has spoken to you, O House of Israel!

² Thus said the LORD:
Do not learn to go the way of the nations,
And do not be dismayed by portents in the sky;
Let the nations be dismayed by them!
³ For *ᵃ*the laws of the nations*⁻ᵃ* are delusions:
For it is the work of a craftsman's hands.
He cuts down a tree in the forest with an ax,
⁴ He adorns it with silver and gold,
He fastens it*ᵇ* with nails and hammer,
So that it does not totter.
⁵ They are like a scarecrow in a cucumber patch,
They cannot speak.
They have to be carried,
For they cannot walk.
Be not afraid of them, for they can do no harm;
Nor is it in them to do any good.

⁶ O LORD, there is none like You!
You are great and Your name is great in power.
⁷ Who would not revere You, O King of the nations?
For that is Your due,
Since among all the wise of the nations
And among all their royalty
There is none like You.
⁸ But they are both dull and foolish;
ᶜ[Their] doctrine is but delusion;*⁻ᶜ*
It is a piece of wood,
⁹ Silver beaten flat, that is brought from Tarshish,
And gold from Uphaz,
The work of a craftsman and the goldsmith's hands;

ᵃ⁻ᵃ *Emendation yields "the objects that the nations fear."*
ᵇ *Heb. "them."*
ᶜ⁻ᶜ *Meaning of Heb. uncertain.*

Their clothing is blue and purple,
All of them are the work of skilled men.
[10] But the LORD is truly God:
He is a living God,
The everlasting King.
At His wrath, the earth quakes,
And nations cannot endure His rage.

[11] [d]Thus shall you say to them: Let the gods who did not make heaven and earth perish from the earth and from under these heavens.

[12] He made the earth by His might,
Established the world by His wisdom,
And by His understanding stretched out the skies.
[13] [e-]When He makes His voice heard,[-e]
There is a rumbling of water in the skies;
He makes vapors rise from the end of the earth,
He makes lightning for the rain,
And brings forth wind from His treasuries.
[14] Every man is proved dull, without knowledge;
Every goldsmith is put to shame because of the idol,
For his molten image is a deceit—
There is no breath in them.
[15] They are delusion, a work of mockery;
In their hour of doom, they shall perish.
[16] Not like these is the Portion of Jacob;
For it is He who formed all things,
And Israel is His very own tribe:
LORD of Hosts is His name.

[17] Gather up your bundle[e] from the ground,
You who dwell under siege!
[18] For thus said the LORD: I will fling away the inhabitants of the land this time: I will harass them so that they shall [f-]feel it.[-f]

---

[d] *This verse is in Aramaic.*
[e-e] *Lit. "At the sound of His making."*
[f-f] *Emendation yields "have to leave."*

¹⁹ Woe unto me for my hurt,
My wound is severe!
I thought, "This is my sickness
And I must bear it."
²⁰ My tents are ravaged,
All my tent cords are broken.
My children have gone forth from me
And are no more;
No one is left to stretch out my tents
And hang my tent cloths.
²¹ For the shepherds ᵍ were dull
And did not seek the LORD;
Therefore they have not prospered,
And all their flock is scattered.
²² Hark, a noise! It is coming,
A great commotion out of the north,
That the towns of Judah may be made a desolation,
A haunt of jackals.

²³ I know, O LORD, that man's road is not his [to choose],
That man, as he walks, cannot direct his own steps.
²⁴ Chastise me, O LORD, but in measure;
Not in Your wrath, lest You reduce me to naught.
²⁵ Pour out Your wrath on the nations who have not
    heeded You,
Upon the clans that have not invoked Your name.
For they have devoured Jacob,
Have devoured and consumed him,
And have laid desolate his homesteads.

11 The word which came to Jeremiah from the LORD:

² "Hear the terms of this covenant, and recite them to the men of Judah and the inhabitants of Jerusalem! ³ And say to them,

ᵍ *I.e. rulers.; cf. note at 2.8.*

Thus said the Lord, the God of Israel: Cursed be the man who will not obey the terms of this covenant, ⁴ which I enjoined upon your fathers when I freed them from the land of Egypt, the iron crucible, saying, 'Obey Me and observe them,^a just as I command you, that you may be My people and I may be your God'—⁵ in order to fulfill the oath which I swore to your fathers, to give them a land flowing with milk and honey, as is now the case." And I responded, "Amen, Lord."

⁶ And the Lord said to me, "Proclaim all these things through the towns of Judah and the streets of Jerusalem: Hear the terms of this covenant, and perform them. ⁷ For I have repeatedly and persistently warned your fathers from^b the time I brought them out of Egypt to this day, saying: Obey My commands. ⁸ But they would not listen or give ear; they all followed the willfulness of their evil hearts. So I have applied to them all the terms^c of this covenant, because they did not do what I commanded them to do."

⁹ The Lord said to me, "A conspiracy exists among the men of Judah and the inhabitants of Jerusalem. ¹⁰ They have returned to the iniquities of their fathers of old, who refused to heed My words. They, too, have followed other gods and served them. The House of Israel and the House of Judah have broken the covenant which I made with their fathers."

¹¹ Assuredly, thus said the Lord: I am going to bring upon them disaster from which they will not be able to escape. Then they will cry out to me, but I will not listen to them. ¹² And the townsmen^d of Judah and the inhabitants of Jerusalem will go and cry out to the gods to which they sacrifice; but they will not be able to rescue them in their time of disaster. ¹³ For your gods have become as many as your towns, O Judah, and you have set up as many altars to Shame^e as there are streets in Jerusalem—altars for sacrifice to Baal.

¹⁴ As for you, do not pray for this people, do not raise a cry of

---

^a *I.e. the terms of the covenant.*
^b *Lit. "at."*
^c *I.e. the punishments prescribed for violation.*
^d *Lit. "towns."*
^e *See note at 3.24.*

545

prayer on their behalf; for I will not listen when they call to Me
on account of their disaster.

> ¹⁵ Why should My beloved be in My House,
> ^{f-}Who executes so many vile designs?
> The sacral flesh will pass away from you,
> For you exult while performing your evil deeds.^{-f}
> ¹⁶ The LORD named you
> "Verdant olive tree,
> Fair, with choice fruit."
> But with a great roaring sound
> He has set it on fire,
> And its boughs are broken.^g

¹⁷ The LORD of Hosts, who planted you, has decreed disaster
for you, because of the evil wrought by the House of Israel and
the House of Judah, who angered Me by sacrificing to Baal.

> ¹⁸ The LORD informed me, and I knew—
> Then You let me see their deeds.
> ¹⁹ For I was like a docile lamb
> Led to the slaughter;
> I did not realize
> That it was against me
> They fashioned their plots:
> "Let us destroy the tree with its fruit,^h
> Let us cut him off from the land of the living.
> That his name be remembered no more!"
> ²⁰ O LORD of Hosts, O just Judge,
> Who test the thoughts and the mind,
> Let me see Your retribution upon them,
> For I lay my case before You.

²¹ Assuredly, thus said the LORD of Hosts concerning the men
of Anathoth who seek your life and say, "You must not prophesy

---

^{f-f} *Meaning of Heb. uncertain. Emendation yields "Who does such vile deeds? /Can your
treacheries be canceled by sacral flesh /That you exult while performing your evil deeds?"*
^g *Emendation yields "burned."*
^h *Or "sap."*

any more in the name of the LORD, or you will die by our hand"—²² assuredly, thus said the LORD of Hosts: "I am going to deal with them: the young men shall die by the sword, their boys and girls shall die by famine. ²³ No remnant shall be left of them, for I will bring disaster on the men of Anathoth, the year of their doom."

12

You will win,ᵃ O LORD, if I make claim against You,
Yet I shall present charges against You:
Why does the way of the wicked prosper?
Why are the workers of treachery at ease?
² You have planted them, and they have taken root,
They spread, they even bear fruit.
You are present in their mouths,
But far from their thoughts.
³ Yet You, LORD, have noted and observed me;
You have tested my heart, and found it with You.
Drive them out like sheep to the slaughter,
Prepare them for the day of slaying!

⁴ How long must the land languish,
And the grass of all the countryside dry up?
Must beasts and birds perish,
Because of the evil of its inhabitants,
Who say, "He will not look upon our future"?ᵇ

⁵ ᶜIf you race with the foot-runners and they exhaust you,
How then can you compete with horses?
If you are ᵈ⁻secure onlyᵈ in a tranquil land,
How will you fare in the jungle of the Jordan?
⁶ For even your kinsmen and your father's house,
Even they are treacherous toward you,
They cry after you as a mob.

ᵃ Lit. "be in the right."
ᵇ Septuagint reads "ways."
ᶜ God here replies to Jeremiah's plea in vv. 1-3.
ᵈ⁻ᵈ Some Septuagint mss. read "not secure."

Do not believe them
When they speak cordially to you.

7 I have abandoned My House,
I have deserted My possession,
I have given over My dearly beloved
Into the hands of her enemies.
8 My own people*e* acted toward Me
Like a lion in the forest;
She raised her voice against Me—
Therefore I have rejected her.
9 *f-*My own people acts toward Me
Like a bird of prey [or] a hyena;
Let the birds of prey surround her!*-f*
Go, gather all the wild beasts,
Bring them to devour!

10 Many shepherds have destroyed My vineyard,
Have trampled My field,
Have made My delightful field
A desolate wilderness.
11 *g-*They have*-g* made her a desolation;
Desolate, she pours out grief to Me.
The whole land is laid desolate,
But no man gives it thought.
12 Spoilers have come
Upon all the bare heights of the wilderness.
For a sword of the LORD devours
From one end of the land to the other;
No flesh is safe.
13 They have sown wheat and reaped thorns,
They have endured pain to no avail.
Be shamed, then, by your harvest—
By the blazing wrath of the LORD!

---

e Lit. *"possession"*; the land as well as the people, as is clear in v. 14.
f-f Meaning of Heb. uncertain.
g-g Heb. *"He has."*

¹⁴ Thus said the LORD: As for My wicked neighbors who encroach on the heritage which I gave to My people Israel—I am going to uproot them from their soil, and I will uproot the House of Judah out of the midst of them. ¹⁵ Then, after I have uprooted them, I will take them back into favor, and restore them each to his own inheritance and his own land. ¹⁶ And if they learn the ways of My people, to swear by My name—"As the LORD lives" —just as they once taught My people to swear by Baal, then they shall be *ʰ*built up in the midst of*⁻ʰ* My people. ¹⁷ But if they do not give heed, I will tear out that nation, tear it out and destroy it—declares the LORD.

13 Thus the LORD said to me: "Go buy yourself a loincloth of linen, and put it around your loins, but do not dip it into water." ² So I bought the loincloth in accordance with the LORD's command, and put it about my loins. ³ And the word of the LORD came to me a second time: ⁴ "Take the loincloth which you bought, which is about your loins, and go at once to Perath*ᵃ* and cover it up there in a cleft of the rock." ⁵ I went and buried it at Perath, as the LORD had commanded me. ⁶ Then, after a long time, the LORD said to me, "Go at once to Perath and take from there the loincloth which I commanded you to bury there." ⁷ So I went to Perath and dug up the loincloth from the place where I had buried it; and found the loincloth ruined; it was not good for anything.

⁸ The word of the LORD came to me: ⁹ Thus said the LORD: Even so will I ruin the overweening pride of Judah and Jerusalem. ¹⁰ This wicked people who refuse to heed My bidding, who follow the willfulness of their own hearts, who follow other gods and serve them and worship them, shall become like that loincloth, which is not good for anything. ¹¹ For as the loincloth clings close to the loins of a man, so I brought close to Me the whole House of Israel and the whole House of Judah—declares the LORD—that

ʰ⁻ʰ Or "incorporated into."

ᵃ Or "the Euphrates"; cf. "Parah," Josh. 18.23.

they might be My people, for fame, and praise, and splendor. But they would not obey.

¹² And speak this word to them: Thus said the LORD, the God of Israel: "Every jar should be filled with wine." And when they say to you, "Don't we know that every jar should be filled with wine?" ¹³ say to them, "Thus said the LORD: I am going to fill with drunkenness all the inhabitants of this land, and the kings who sit on the throne of David, and the priests and the prophets, and all the inhabitants of Jerusalem. ¹⁴ And I will smash them one against the other, parents and children alike—declares the LORD; no pity, compassion, or mercy will stop Me from destroying them."

¹⁵ Attend and give ear; be not haughty,
For the LORD has spoken.
¹⁶ Give honor to the LORD your God
Before He brings darkness,
Before your feet stumble
On the mountains in shadow—
When you hope for light,
And it is turned to darkness
And becomes deep gloom.
¹⁷ For if you will not give heed,
My inmost self must weep,
Because of your arrogance;
My eye must stream and flow
With copious tears,
Because the flock of the LORD
Is taken captive.

¹⁸ Say to the king and the queen mother,
"Sit in a lowly spot;
For your diadems are abased,
Your glorious crowns."
¹⁹ The cities of the Negeb are shut,

There is no one to open them;
b-Judah is exiled completely,
All of it exiled.-*b*
20 Raise your eyes and behold
Those who come from the north:
Where are the sheep entrusted to you,
The flock you took pride in?
21 *c*-What will you say when they appoint as your heads
Those among you whom you trained to be tame?-*c*
Shall not pangs seize you
Like a woman in childbirth?
22 And when you ask yourself,
"Why have these things befallen me?"
It is because of your great iniquity
That your skirts are lifted up,
Your limbs exposed.

23 Can the Ethiopian change his skin,
Or the leopard his spots?
Just as much can you do good,
Who are practiced in doing evil!
24 So I will scatter you*d* like straw that flies
Before the desert wind.
25 This shall be your lot,
Your measured portion from Me

—declares the LORD.

Because you forgot Me
And trusted in falsehood,
26 I in turn will lift your skirts over your face
And your shame shall be seen.
27 I behold your adulteries,
Your lustful neighing,
Your unbridled depravity, your vile acts
On the hills of the countryside.
Woe to you, O Jerusalem,

b-b *I.e. most of Judah has been annexed by an alien people.*
c-c *Meaning of Heb. uncertain.*
d *Heb. "them."*

Who will not be clean!
How much longer shall it be?

14 The word of the LORD which came to Jeremiah concerning
the droughts.

² Judah is in mourning,
Her settlements languish.
Men are bowed to the ground,
And the outcry of Jerusalem rises.
³ Their nobles sent their servants for water;
They came to the cisterns, they found no water.
They returned, their vessels empty.
They are shamed and humiliated,
They cover their heads.
⁴ *ᵃ⁻Because of the ground there is dismay,⁻ᵃ*
For there has been no rain on the earth.
The plowmen are shamed,
They cover their heads.
⁵ Even the hind in the field
Forsakes her newborn fawn,
Because there is no grass.
⁶ And the wild asses stand on the bare heights,
Snuffing the air like jackals;
Their eyes pine,
Because there is no herbage.

⁷ Though our iniquities testify against us,
Act, O LORD, for the sake of Your name;
Though our rebellions are many
And we have sinned against You.
⁸ O Hope of Israel,
Its deliverer in time of trouble,
Why are You like a stranger in the land,

ᵃ⁻ᵃ *Meaning of Heb. uncertain.*

Like a traveler who stops only for the night?
⁹ Why are You like a man who is stunned,
Like a warrior who cannot give victory?
Yet You are in our midst, O LORD,
And Your name is attached to us—
Do not forsake us!

¹⁰ Thus said the LORD concerning this people: "Truly, they love to stray, they have not restrained their feet; so the LORD has no pleasure in them. Now He will recall their iniquity and punish their sin."

¹¹ And the LORD said to me, "Do not pray for the benefit of this people. ¹² When they fast, I will not listen to their outcry; and when they present burnt offering and meal offering, I will not accept them. I will exterminate them by war, famine, and disease."

¹³ I said, "Ah, Lord GOD! The prophets are saying to them, 'You shall not see the sword, famine shall not come upon you, but I will give you unfailing security in this place.' "

¹⁴ The LORD replied: It is a lie that the prophets utter in My name. I have not sent them nor commanded them. I have not spoken to them. A lying vision, an empty divination, the deceit of their own contriving—that is what they prophesy to you! ¹⁵ Assuredly, thus said the LORD concerning the prophets who prophesy in My name, though I have not sent them, and who say, "Sword and famine shall not befall this land": Those very prophets shall perish by sword and famine. ¹⁶ And the people to whom they prophesy shall be left lying in the streets of Jerusalem because of the famine and the sword, with none to bury them—they, their wives, their sons, and their daughters. I will pour out upon them [the requital of] their wickedness.

¹⁷ And do you speak to them thus:
Let my eyes run with tears,
Day and night let them not cease,
For ᵇ⁻my hapless people⁻ᵇ has suffered

ᵇ⁻ᵇ *Lit. "the maiden daughter, My people."*

A grievous injury, a very painful wound.
¹⁸ If I go out to the country—
Lo, the slain of the sword.
If I enter the city—
Lo, ᶜthose who are sick with⁻ᶜ famine.
Both priest and prophet roam*ª* the land,
They know not where.

¹⁹ Have You, then, rejected Judah?
Have You spurned Zion?
Why have You smitten us
So that there is no cure?
Why do we hope for happiness,
But find no good;
For a time of healing,
And meet terror instead?
²⁰ We acknowledge our wickedness, O LORD—
The iniquity of our fathers—
For we have sinned against You.
²¹ For Your name's sake, do not disown us;
Do not dishonor Your glorious throne.
Remember, do not annul Your covenant with us.
²² Can any of the false gods of the nations give rain?
Can the skies of themselves give showers?
Only You can, O LORD our God!
So we hope in You,
For only You made all these things.

15 The LORD said to me, "Even if Moses and Samuel were to
ᵃ⁻intercede with Me,⁻ᵃ I would not be won over to that people.
Dismiss them from My presence, and let them go forth! ² And if
they ask you, 'To what shall we go forth?' answer them, 'Thus
said the LORD:

ᶜ⁻ᶜ *Lit. "the sicknesses of."*
ᵃ⁻ᵃ *Lit. "stand before Me," as Jeremiah is doing now; cf. 18.20.*

Those destined for the plague, to the plague;
Those destined for the sword, to the sword;
Those destined for famine, to famine;
Those destined for captivity, to captivity.
³ And I will appoint over them four kinds[b] [of punishment]—
declares the LORD—the sword to slay, the dogs to drag, the birds
of the sky, and the beasts of the earth to devour and destroy.
⁴ I will make them a horror to all the kingdoms of the earth, on
account of King Manasseh son of Hezekiah of Judah, and of what
he did in Jerusalem.' "

⁵ But who will pity you, O Jerusalem,
Who will console you?
Who will turn aside to inquire
About your welfare?
⁶ You cast Me off

                   —declares the LORD—

You go ever backward.
So I have stretched out My hand to destroy you;
I cannot relent.
⁷ I will scatter them as with a winnowing fork
Through the settlements of the earth.
I will bereave, I will destroy My people,
For they would not turn back from their ways.
⁸ Their widows shall be more numerous
Than the sands of the seas.
I will bring against them—
[b]Young men and mothers together[-b]—
A destroyer at noonday.
I will bring down suddenly upon them
Alarm[b] and terror.
⁹ She who bore seven is forlorn,
Utterly disconsolate;
Her sun has set while it is still day,

---

b Meaning of Heb. uncertain.

She is shamed and humiliated.
The remnant of them I will deliver to the sword,
To the power of their enemies
> —declares the LORD.

10 Woe is me, my mother, that you ever bore me—
A man of conflict and strife with all the land!
I have not lent,
And I have not borrowed;
Yet everyone curses me.

11 The LORD said:
b-Surely, a mere remnant of you
Will I spare for a better fate!*-b*
By the enemy *c*-from the north*-c*
In a time of distress and a time of disaster,
Surely, I will have you struck down!
12 *d*-Can iron break iron and bronze?*-d*
13 *b*-I will hand over your wealth and your treasures
As a spoil, free of charge,
Because of all your sins throughout your territory.
14 And I will bring your enemies
By way of a land you have not known.*-b*
For a fire has flared in My wrath,
It blazes against you.

15 O Lord, You know—
Remember me and take thought of me,
Avenge me on those who persecute me;
Do not yield to Your patience,
e-Do not let me perish!*-e*
Consider how I have borne insult
On Your account.
16 When Your words were offered, I devoured them;
Your word brought me the delight and joy

c-c *Moved up from v. 12 for clarity.*
d-d *Emendation yields "He shall shatter iron—iron and bronze!"*
e-e *Lit. "Do not take me away."*

Of knowing that Your name is attached to me,
O Lord, God of Hosts.
¹⁷ I have not sat in the company of revelers
And made merry!
I have sat lonely because of Your hand upon me,
For You have filled me with gloom.
¹⁸ Why must my pain be endless,
My wound incurable,
Resistant to healing?
You have been to me like a spring that fails,
Like waters that cannot be relied on.

¹⁹ Assuredly, thus said the Lord:
If you turn back, I shall take you back
And you shall stand before Me;
If you produce what is noble
Out of the worthless,
You shall be My spokesman.
They shall come back to you,
Not you to them.
²⁰ Against this people I will make you
As a fortified wall of bronze:
They will attack you,
But they shall not overcome you,
For I am with you to deliver and save you
—declares the Lord.
²¹ I will save you from the hands of the wicked
And rescue you from the clutches of the violent.

16 The word of the Lord came to me:
² You are not to marry and not to have sons and daughters in this place. ³ For thus said the Lord concerning any sons and daughters that may be born in this place, and concerning the mothers who bear them, and concerning the fathers who beget

them in this land: 4 They shall die gruesome deaths. They shall not be lamented or buried; they shall be like dung on the surface of the ground. They shall be consumed by the sword and by famine, and their corpses shall be food for the birds of the sky and the beasts of the earth.

5 For thus said the LORD:
Do not enter a house of mourning,*
Do not go to lament and to condole with them;
For I have withdrawn My favor from that people
        —declares the LORD—
My kindness and compassion.
6 Great and small alike shall die in this land,
They shall not be buried; men shall not lament them,
Nor gash and tonsure themselves for them.
7 They shall not break bread*b* for a mourner*c*
To comfort him for a bereavement,
Nor offer one a cup of consolation
For the loss of his father or mother.
8 Nor shall you enter a house of feasting,
To sit down with them to eat and drink.

9 For thus said the LORD of Hosts, the God of Israel: I am going to banish from this place, in your days and before your eyes, the sound of mirth and gladness, the voice of bridegroom and bride. 10 And when you announce all these things to that people, and they ask you, "Why has the LORD decreed upon us all this fearful evil? What is the iniquity and what the sin that we have committed against the LORD our God?" 11 say to them, "Because your fathers deserted Me—declares the LORD—and followed other gods and served them and worshiped them; they deserted Me and did not keep My Instruction. 12 And you have acted worse than your fathers, every one of you following the willfulness of his evil heart and paying no heed to Me. 13 Therefore I will hurl you out of this land to a land which neither you nor your fathers have known,

a *Lit. "religious gathering."*
b *So a few mss. Most mss. and the editions read "to them."*
c *Lit. "mourning."*

and there you will serve other gods, day and night; for I will show you no mercy."

[14] Assuredly, a time is coming—declares the Lord—when it shall no more be said, "As the Lord lives who brought the Israelites out of the land of Egypt," [15] but rather, "As the Lord lives who brought the Israelites out of the northland, and out of all the lands to which He had banished them." For I will bring them back to their land, which I gave to their fathers.

[16] Lo, I am sending for many fishermen
                —declares the Lord—
And they shall haul them out;
And after that I will send for many hunters,
And they shall hunt them
Out of every mountain and out of every hill
And out of the clefts of the rocks.
[17] For My eyes are on all their ways,
They are not hidden from My presence,
Their iniquity is not concealed from My sight.
[18] I will pay them in full—
Nay, doubly for their iniquity and their sins—
Because they have defiled My land
With the corpses of their abominations,[d]
And have filled My own possession
With their abhorrent things.

[19] O Lord, my strength and my stronghold,
My refuge in a day of trouble,
To You nations shall come
From the ends of the earth and say:
Our fathers inherited utter delusions,
Things that are futile and worthless.
[20] Can a man make gods for himself?
No-gods are they!

[d] *I.e. their lifeless idols.*

²¹ Assuredly, I will teach them,
Once and for all I will teach them
My power and My might.
And they shall learn that My name is LORD:

17 The guilt of Judah is inscribed
With a stylus of iron,
Engraved with an adamant point
On the tablet of their hearts,
*ᵃ⁻*And on the horns of their altars,
² While their children remember⁻ᵃ
Their altars and sacred posts,
By verdant trees,
Upon lofty hills.
³ ᵇ⁻Because of the sin of your shrines
Throughout your borders,
I will make your rampart a heap in the field,
And all your treasures a spoil.⁻ᵇ
⁴ ᶜ⁻You will forfeit, by your own act,⁻ᶜ
The inheritance I have given you;
I will make you a slave to your enemies
In a land you have never known.
For you have kindled the flame of My wrath
Which shall burn for all time.

⁵ Thus said the LORD:
Cursed is he who trusts in man,
Who makes mere flesh his strength,
And turns his thoughts from the LORD.
⁶ He shall be like a bushᵈ in the desert,
Which does not sense the coming of good:
It is set in the scorched places of the wilderness,
In a barren land without inhabitant.
⁷ Blessed is he who trusts in the LORD,

ᵃ⁻ᵃ *Meaning of Heb. uncertain. Emendation yields "Surely the horns of their altars/Are as*
a memorial against them."
ᵇ⁻ᵇ *Meaning of Heb. uncertain.*
ᶜ⁻ᶜ *Meaning of Heb. uncertain. Emendation yields "Your hand must let go."*
ᵈ *Or "tamarisk"; exact meaning of Heb. uncertain.*

Whose trust is the LORD alone.
⁸ He shall be like a tree planted by waters,
Sending forth its roots by a stream:
It does not sense the coming of heat,
Its leaves are ever fresh;
It has no care in a year of drought,
It does not cease to yield fruit.

⁹ Most devious is the heart;
It is perverse—who can fathom it?
¹⁰ I the LORD probe the heart,
Search the mind—
To repay every man according to his ways,
With the proper fruit of his deeds.

¹¹ ᵇ⁻Like a partridge hatching what she did not lay,⁻ᵇ
So is one who amasses wealth by unjust means;
In the middle of his life it will leave him,
And in the end he will be proved a fool.

¹² O Throne of Glory exalted from of old,
Our Sacred Shrine!
¹³ O Hope of Israel! O LORD!
All who forsake You shall be put to shame,
Those in the land who turn from You⁶
Shall be doomedᶠ men,
For they have forsaken the LORD,
The Fount of living waters.

¹⁴ Heal me, O LORD, and let me be healed;
Save me, and let me be saved;
For You are my glory.

¹⁵ See, they say to me:
"Where is the prediction of the LORD?

ᵉ Lit. "Me."
ᶠ Lit. "inscribed"; meaning of line uncertain.

Let it come to pass!"
[16] But I have not [g]evaded
Being a shepherd in your service,[g]
Nor have I longed for the fatal day.
You know the utterances of my lips,
They were ever before You.
[17] Do not be a cause of dismay to me;
You are my refuge in a day of calamity.
[18] Let my persecutors be shamed,
And let not me be shamed;
Let them be dismayed,
And let not me be dismayed.
Bring on them the day of disaster,
And shatter them with double destruction.

[19] Thus said the LORD to me: Go and stand in the People's Gate, by which the kings of Judah enter and by which they go forth, and in all the gates of Jerusalem, [20] and say to them: Hear the word of the LORD, O kings of Judah, and all Judah, and all the inhabitants of Jerusalem who enter by these gates! [21] Thus said the LORD: Guard yourselves for your own sake against carrying burdens[h] on the sabbath day, and bringing them through the gates of Jerusalem. [22] Nor shall you carry out burdens from your houses on the sabbath day, or do any work, but you shall hallow the sabbath day, as I commanded your fathers. ([23] But they would not listen or turn their ear; they stiffened their necks and would not pay heed or accept discipline.) [24] If you obey Me—declares the LORD—and do not bring in burdens through the gates of this city on the sabbath day, but hallow the sabbath day and do no work on it, [25] then through the gates of this city shall enter kings who sit upon the throne of David, with their officers—riding on chariots and horses, they and their officers— and the men of Judah and the inhabitants of Jerusalem. And this city shall be inhabited for all time. [26] And people shall come from the towns of Judah and from the environs of Jerusalem, and from

[g-g] *Exact force of Heb. uncertain. Emendation yields "urged you to [bring] misfortune."*
[h] *Or "merchandise."*

the land of Benjamin, and from the Shephelah, and from the hill country, and from the Negeb, bringing burnt offerings and sacrifices, meal offerings and frankincense, and bringing offerings of thanksgiving to the House of the LORD. ²⁷ But if you do not obey My command to hallow the sabbath day and to carry in no burdens through the gates of Jerusalem on the sabbath day, then I will set fire to its gates; it shall consume the fortresses of Jerusalem and it shall not be extinguished.

18 The word which came to Jeremiah from the LORD: ² "Go down to the house of a potter, and there I will impart My words to you." ³ So I went down to the house of a potter, and found him working at the wheel. ⁴ ᵃ⁻And if the vessel he was making was spoiled, as happens to clay in the potter's hands,⁻ᵃ he would make it into another vessel, such as the potter saw fit to make.

⁵ Then the word of the LORD came to me. ⁶ O House of Israel, can I not deal with you like this potter?—says the LORD. Just like clay in the hands of the potter, so are you in My hands, O House of Israel! ⁷ At one moment I may decree that a nation or a kingdom shall be uprooted and pulled down and destroyed; ⁸ but if that nation against which I made the decree turns back from its wickedness, I change My mind concerning the punishment I planned to bring on it. ⁹ At another moment I may decree that a nation or a kingdom shall be built and planted; ¹⁰ but if it does what is displeasing to Me and does not obey Me, then I change My mind concerning the good I planned to bestow upon it.

¹¹ And now, say to the men of Judah and the inhabitants of Jerusalem: Thus said the LORD: I am devising*ᵇ* disaster for you and laying plans against you. Turn back, each of you, from your wicked ways, and mend your ways and your actions! ¹² But they will say, "It is no use. We will keep on following our own plans; each of us will act in the willfulness of his evil heart."

ᵃ⁻ᵃ *So some mss. and one early edition. Most mss. and editions read "And if the vessel that he was making with clay in the potter's hands was spoiled."*
ᵇ *The same Hebrew word as is used above for "potter."*

¹³ Assuredly, thus said the LORD:
Inquire among the nations:
Who has heard anything like this?
Maiden Israel has done
A most horrible thing.
¹⁴ ᶜDoes one forsake Lebanon snow
From the mountainous rocks?
Does one abandon cool water
Flowing from afar?
¹⁵ Yet My people have forgotten Me:
They sacrifice to a delusion:
They are made to stumble in their ways—
The ancient paths—
And to walk instead on byways,
On a road not built up.
¹⁶ So their land will become a desolation,
An object of hissing ᵈ for all time.
Every passerby will be appalled
And will shake his head.ᵈ
¹⁷ Like the east wind, I will scatter them
Before the enemy.
ᵉ⁻I will look upon their back, not their face,⁻ᵉ
In their day of disaster.

¹⁸ They said,ᶠ "Come let us devise a plot against Jeremiah—for instruction shall not fail from the priest, nor counsel from the wise, nor oracle from the prophet. Come, let us strike him with the tongue, and we shall no longer have to listen to all those words of his."

¹⁹ Listen to me, O LORD—
And take note of ᵍ⁻what my enemies say!⁻ᵍ
²⁰ Should good be repaid with evil?
Yet they have dug a pit for me.

ᶜ Meaning of verse uncertain; cf. 2.13, 17.13.
ᵈ These actions were performed at the sight of ruin to ward off a like fate from the observer; cf. Lam. 2.15.
ᵉ⁻ᵉ Change of vocalization yields "I will show them [My] back and not [My] face."
ᶠ Cf. 20.10.
ᵍ⁻ᵍ Emendation yields "my case."

Remember how I stood before You
To plead in their behalf,
To turn Your anger away from them!
²¹ Oh, give their children over to famine,
Mow them down by the sword.
Let their wives be bereaved
Of children and husbands,
Let their men be struck down by the plague,
And their young men be slain in battle by the sword.
²² Let an outcry be heard from their houses
When You bring sudden marauders against them;
For they have dug a pit to trap me,
And laid snares for my feet.
²³ O Lord, You know
All their plots to kill me.
Do not pardon their iniquity,
Do not blot out their guilt from Your presence.
Let them be made to stumble before You—
Act against them in Your hour of wrath!

19 Thus said the Lord: Go buy a jug of potter's ware. And [take] some of the elders of the people and the priests, ² and go out to the Valley of Ben-hinnom—ᵃ⁻at the entrance of the Harsith Gate⁻ᵃ—and proclaim there the words which I will speak to you.

³ Say: "Hear the word of the Lord, O kings of Judah and inhabitants of Jerusalem! Thus said the Lord of Hosts, the God of Israel: I am going to bring such disaster upon this place that the ears of all who hear about it will tingle. ⁴ For they and their fathers and the kings of Judah have forsaken Me, and have made this place alien [to Me]; they have sacrificed in it to other gods whom they have not experienced,ᵇ and they have filled this place with the blood of the innocent. ⁵ They have built shrines to Baal, to put their children to the fire as burnt offerings to Baal—which

ᵃ⁻ᵃ *Others "by way of the Potsherd Gate"; meaning of Heb. uncertain.*
ᵇ *See note at Deut. 11.28.*

I never commanded, never decreed, and which never came to My mind. ⁶ Assuredly, a time is coming—declares the LORD—when this place shall no longer be called Topheth or Valley of Ben-hinnom, but Valley of Slaughter.

⁷ And I will frustrate*ᶜ* the plans of Judah and Jerusalem in this place. I will cause them to fall by the sword before their enemies, by the hand of those who seek their lives; and I will give their carcasses as food to the birds of the sky and the beasts of the earth. ⁸ And I will make this city an object of horror and hissing;*ᵈ* everyone who passes by it will be appalled and will hiss over all its wounds. ⁹ And I will cause them to eat the flesh of their sons and the flesh of their daughters, and they shall devour one another's flesh—because of the desperate straits to which they will be reduced by their enemies, who seek their life."

¹⁰ Then you shall smash the jug in the sight of the men who go with you, ¹¹ and say to them: "Thus said the LORD of Hosts: So will I smash this people and this city, as one smashes a potter's vessel, which can never be mended. And they shall bury in Topheth until no room is left for burying. ¹² That is what I will do to this place and its inhabitants—declares the LORD. I will make this city like Topheth: ¹³ the houses of Jerusalem and the houses of the kings of Judah shall be unclean, like that place Topheth—all the houses on the roofs of which offerings were made to the whole host of heaven and libations were poured out to other gods."

¹⁴ When Jeremiah returned from Topheth, where the LORD had sent him to prophesy, he stood in the court of the House of the LORD and said to all the people: ¹⁵ "Thus said the LORD of Hosts, the God of Israel: I am going to bring upon this city and upon all its villages all the disaster which I have decreed against it, for they have stiffened their necks and refused to heed My words."

ᶜ *Lit. "empty," Heb.* u-baqqothi, *a play on* baqbuq, *"jug" in v. 1.*
ᵈ *See note at 18.16.*

20 Pashhur son of Immer, the priest who was chief officer of the House of the Lord, heard Jeremiah prophesy these things. ² Pashhur thereupon had Jeremiah flogged and put in the cell*ᵃ* at the Upper Benjamin Gate in the House of the Lord. ³ The next day, Pashhur released Jeremiah from the cell.

But Jeremiah said to him, "The Lord has named you not Pashhur, but Magor-missabib.*ᵇ* ⁴ For thus said the Lord: I am going to deliver you and all your friends over to terror: they will fall by the sword of their enemies while you look on. I will deliver all Judah into the hands of the king of Babylon; he will exile them to Babylon or put them to the sword. ⁵ And I will deliver all the wealth, all the riches, and all the prized possessions of this city, and I will also deliver all the treasures of the kings of Judah into the hands of their enemies: they shall seize them as plunder and carry them off to Babylon. ⁶ As for you, Pashhur, and all who live in your house, you shall go into captivity. You shall come to Babylon; there you shall die and there you shall be buried, and so shall all your friends to whom you prophesied falsely."

⁷ You enticed me, O Lord, and I was enticed;
You overpowered me and You prevailed.
I have become a constant laughingstock,
Everyone jeers at me.
⁸ For every time I speak, I must cry out,
Must shout, "Lawlessness and rapine!"
For the word of the Lord causes me
Constant disgrace and contempt.
⁹ I thought, "I will not mention Him,
No more will I speak in His name"—
But [His word] was like a raging fire in my heart,
Shut up in my bones;
I could not hold it in, I was helpless.

ᵃ *Meaning of Heb. uncertain.*
ᵇ *I.e. "Terror all around"; cf. v. 10.*

¹⁰ I heard the whispers of the crowd—
Terror all around:
"Inform! Let us inform against him!"
All my [supposed] friends
Are waiting for me to stumble:
"Perhaps he can be entrapped,
And we can prevail against him
And take our vengeance on him."
¹¹ But the LORD is with me like a mighty warrior;
Therefore my persecutors shall stumble;
They shall not prevail and shall not succeed.
They shall be utterly shamed
With a humiliation for all time,
Which shall not be forgotten.
¹² O LORD of Hosts, You who test the righteous,
Who examine the heart and the mind,
Let me see Your retribution upon them,
For I lay my case before You.
¹³ Sing unto the LORD,
Praise the LORD,
For He has rescued the needy
From the hands of evildoers!

¹⁴ Accursed be the day
That I was born!
Let not the day be blessed
When my mother bore me!
¹⁵ Accursed be the man
Who brought my father the news
And said, "A boy
Is born to you,"
And gave him such joy!
¹⁶ Let that manᶜ become like the cities
Which the LORD overthrew without relenting!
Let him hear shrieks in the morning

ᶜ *Emendation yields "day."*

And battle shouts at noontide—
[17] Because [that day] he did not kill me before birth
So that my mother might be my grave,
And her womb big [with me] for all time.
[18] Why did I ever issue from the womb,
To see misery and woe,
To spend all my days in shame!

21 The word which came to Jeremiah from the LORD, when King Zedekiah sent to him Pashhur son of Malchiah and the priest Zephaniah son of Maaseiah, to say, [2] "Please inquire of the LORD on our behalf, for King Nebuchadrezzar of Babylon is attacking us. Perhaps the LORD will act for our sake in accordance with all His wonders, so that [Nebuchadrezzar] will withdraw from us."

[3] Jeremiah answered them, "Thus shall you say to Zedekiah: [4] Thus said the LORD, the God of Israel: I am going to turn around the weapons in your hands with which you are battling outside the wall against those who are besieging you—the king of Babylon and the Chaldeans—and I will take them into the midst of this city; [5] and I Myself will battle against you with an outstretched mighty arm, with anger and rage and great wrath. [6] I will strike the inhabitants of this city, man and beast: they shall die by a terrible pestilence. [7] And then—declares the LORD—I will deliver King Zedekiah of Judah and his courtiers and the people—those in this city who survive the pestilence, the sword, and the famine—into the hands of King Nebuchadrezzar of Babylon, into the hands of their enemies, into the hands of those who seek their lives. He will put them to the sword without pity, without compassion, without mercy.

[8] "And to this people you shall say: Thus said the LORD: I set before you the way of life and the way of death. [9] Whoever remains in this city shall die by the sword, by famine, and by pestilence; but whoever leaves and goes over to the Chaldeans who

are besieging you shall live; *"he shall at least gain his life.*-*a* 10 For I have set My face against this city for evil and not for good— declares the LORD. It shall be delivered into the hands of the king of Babylon, who will destroy it by fire."

11 To the House of the king of Judah: Hear the word of the LORD!
12 O House of David, thus said the LORD:
> Render just verdicts
> Morning by morning;
> Rescue him who is robbed
> From him who defrauded him.
> Else My wrath will break forth like fire
> And burn, with none to quench it,
> Because of your wicked acts.
> 13 I will deal with you, *b*-O inhabitants of the valley,
> O rock of the plain-*b*—declares the LORD—
> You who say, "Who can come down against us?
> Who can get into our lairs?"
> 14 I will punish you according to your deeds
> —declares the LORD.
>
> I will set fire to its forest;*c*
> It shall consume all that is around it.

22 Thus said the LORD: Go down to the palace of the king of Judah, where you shall utter this word. 2 Say: Hear the word of the LORD: O king of Judah, you who sit on the throne of David, and your courtiers and your subjects who enter these gates! 3 Thus said the LORD: Do what is just and right; rescue from the defrauder him who is robbed; do not wrong the stranger, the fatherless, and the widow; commit no lawless act, and do not shed the blood of the innocent in this place. 4 For if you fulfill this command, then through the gates of this palace shall enter kings of David's line who sit upon his throne, riding horse-drawn chariots, with their courtiers and their subjects. 5 But if you do not

a-a *Lit. "he shall have his life as booty."*
b-b *Force of Heb. uncertain.*
c *Perhaps a reference to the royal palace; cf. I Kings 7.2.*

heed these commands, I swear by Myself—declares the LORD—
that this palace shall become a ruin.

⁶ For thus said the LORD concerning the royal palace of Judah:
You are as Gilead to Me,
As the summit of Lebanon;
But I will make you a desert,
Uninhabited towns.
⁷ I will appoint destroyers against you,
Each with his tools;
They shall cut down your choicest cedars
And make them fall into the fire.

⁸ And when many nations pass by this city and one man asks
another, "Why did the LORD do thus to that great city?" ⁹ the
reply will be, "Because they forsook the covenant with the LORD
their God and bowed down to other gods and served them."

¹⁰ Do not weep for the dead*a*
And do not lament for him;
Weep rather for *b*him who is leaving,*-b*
For he shall never come back
To see the land of his birth!

¹¹ For thus said the LORD concerning Shallum*b* son of King
Josiah of Judah, who succeeded his father Josiah as king, but who
has gone forth from this place: He shall never come back. ¹² He
shall die in the place to which he was exiled, and he shall not see
this land again.

¹³ Ha! he who builds his house with unfairness
And his upper chambers with injustice,
Who makes his fellowman work without pay
And does not give him his wages,
¹⁴ Who thinks: I will build me a vast palace
With spacious upper chambers,
Provided with windows,

---

a *I.e. Josiah; see II Kings 23.29-30.*
b-b *I.e. the king called by his throne name Jehoahaz in II Kings 23.31 ff., and by his private
name Shallum here in v. 11 and in I Chron. 3.15.*

Paneled in cedar,
Painted with vermilion!
¹⁵ Do you think you are more a king
Because you compete in cedar?
Your father ^{c-}ate and drank^{-c}
And dispensed justice and equity—
Then all went well with him.
¹⁶ He upheld the rights of the poor and needy—
Then all was well.
^{d-}That is truly heeding Me^{-d}

—declares the LORD.

¹⁷ But your eyes and your mind are only
On ill-gotten gains,
On shedding the blood of the innocent,
On committing fraud and violence.

¹⁸ Assuredly, thus said the LORD concerning Jehoiakim son of Josiah, king of Judah:

^{e-}They shall not mourn for him,
"Ah, brother! Ah, sister!"
They shall not mourn for him,
"Ah, lord! Ah, his majesty!"^{-e}
¹⁹ He shall have the burial of an ass,
Dragged out and left lying
Outside the gates of Jerusalem.

²⁰ ^fClimb Lebanon and cry out,
Raise your voice in Bashan,
Cry out from Abarim,
For all your lovers are crushed.
²¹ I spoke to you when you were prosperous;
You said, "I will not listen."
That was your way ever since your youth,
You would not heed Me.
²² All your shepherds^g shall be devoured by the wind,
And your lovers shall go into captivity.

---

^{c-c} *I.e. he was content with the simple necessities of life.*
^{d-d} *Or "That is the reward for heeding Me."*
^{e-e} *They shall express neither sorrow at the loss of a relative nor grief at the death of a ruler.*
^f *Israel is addressed.*
^g *Change of vocalization yields "paramours."*

Then you shall be shamed and humiliated
Because of all your depravity.
23 You who dwell in Lebanon,
Nestled among the cedars,
h-How much grace will you have*-h*
When pains come upon you,
Travail as in childbirth!

24 As I live—declares the LORD—*i*-if you, O Coniah, son of
Jehoiakim, king of Judah, were*-i* a signet on my right hand, I
would tear you off even from there. 25 I will deliver you into the
hands of those who seek your life, into the hands of those you
dread, into the hands of King Nebuchadrezzar of Babylon and
into the hands of the Chaldeans. 26 I will hurl you and the mother
who bore you into another land, where you were not born; there
you shall both die. 27 They shall not return to the land which they
yearn to come back to.
28 Is this man Coniah
A wretched broken pot,
A vessel no one wants?
Why are he and his offspring hurled out,
And cast away in a land they knew not?
29 O land, land, land,
Hear the word of the LORD!
30 Thus said the LORD:
Record this man as without succession,
One who shall never be found acceptable;
For no man of his offspring shall be accepted
To sit on the throne of David
And to rule again in Judah.

23 Ah, shepherds who let the flock of My pasture stray and
scatter!—declares the LORD. 2 Assuredly, thus said the LORD, the
God of Israel, concerning the shepherds who should tend My

---

h-h Septuagint reads "How you will groan."
i-i Heb "If Coniah . . . were . . ."; Coniah (Jeconiah in 24.1) is identical with Jehoiachin,
   II Kings 24.8 ff.

people: It is you who let My flock scatter and go astray. You gave no thought to them, but I am going to give thought to you, for your wicked acts—declares the LORD. ³ And I Myself will gather the remnant of My flock from all the lands to which I have banished them, and I will bring them back to their pasture, where they shall be fertile and increase. ⁴ And I will appoint over them shepherds who will tend them; they shall no longer fear or be dismayed, and none of them shall be missing—declares the LORD.

⁵ See, a time is coming—declares the LORD—when I will raise up a true branch of David's line. He shall reign as king and shall prosper, and he shall do what is just and right in the land. ⁶ In his days Judah shall be delivered and Israel shall dwell secure. And this is the name by which he shall be called: "The LORD is our Vindicator."

⁷ Assuredly, a time is coming—declares the LORD—when it shall no more be said, "As the LORD lives, who brought the Israelites out of the land of Egypt," ⁸ but rather, "As the LORD lives, who brought out and led the offspring of the House of Israel from the northland and from all the lands to which I have banished them." And they shall dwell upon their own soil.

⁹ Concerning the prophets.

My heart is crushed within me,
All my bones are trembling;*a*
I have become like a drunken man,
Like one overcome by wine—
Because of the LORD and His holy word.
¹⁰ For the land is full of adulterers,
The land mourns because of *b*a curse;*b*
The pastures of the wilderness are dried up.
*c*For they run to do evil,
They strain to do wrong.*c*
¹¹ For both prophet and priest are godless;

ᵃ *Meaning of Heb. uncertain.*
ᵇ⁻ᵇ *A few Heb mss. and Septuagint read "these."*
ᶜ⁻ᶜ *Lit. "Their running is wickedness,/Their straining is iniquity."*

Even in My House I find their wickedness
                  —declares the LORD.
¹² Assuredly,
Their path shall become
Like slippery ground;
They shall be thrust into darkness
And there they shall fall;
For I will bring disaster upon them,
The year of their doom
                      —declares the LORD.
¹³ In the prophets of Samaria
I saw a repulsive thing:
They prophesied by Baal
And led My people Israel astray.
¹⁴ But what I see in the prophets of Jerusalem
Is something horrifying:
Adultery and false dealing.
They encourage evildoers,
So that no one turns back from his wickedness.
To Me they are all like Sodom,
And [all] its inhabitants like Gomorrah.

¹⁵ Assuredly, thus said the LORD of Hosts concerning the prophets:

I am going to make them eat wormwood
And drink a bitter draft;
For from the prophets of Jerusalem
Godlessness has gone forth to the whole land.

¹⁶ Thus said the LORD of Hosts:
Do not listen to the words of the prophets
Who prophesy to you.
They are deluding you,
The prophecies they speak are from their own minds,

Not from the mouth of the Lord.
¹⁷ They declare to men who despise Me:
"The Lord has said:
"All shall be well with you";
And to all who follow their willful hearts they say:
"No evil shall befall you."
¹⁸ But he who has stood in the council of the Lord,
And seen, and heard His word—
He who has listened to His word must obey.^d
¹⁹ ^{e-}Lo, the storm of the Lord goes forth in fury,
A whirling storm,
It shall whirl down upon the heads of the wicked.
²⁰ The anger of the Lord shall not turn back
Till it has fulfilled and completed His purposes.^{-e}
In the days to come
You shall clearly perceive it.

²¹ I did not send those prophets,
But they rushed in;
I did not speak to them,
Yet they prophesied.
²² If they have stood in My council,
Let them announce My words to My people
And make them turn back
From their evil ways and wicked acts.

²³ Am I only a God near at hand

—says the Lord—

And not a God far away?
²⁴ If a man enters a hiding place,
Do I not see him?

—says the Lord.

For I fill both heaven and earth

—declares the Lord.

^d *Change of vocalization yields "announce it"; cf. vv. 22, 28.*
^{e-e} *This section constitutes the word of God to which Jeremiah refers.*

²⁵ I have heard what the prophets say, who prophesy falsely in My name: "I had a dream, I had a dream." ²⁶ ᵃ-How long will there be-ᵃ in the minds of the prophets who prophesy falsehood —the prophets of their own deceitful minds— ²⁷ the plan to make My people forget My name, by means of the dreams which they tell each other, just as their fathers forgot My name because of Baal? ²⁸ Let the prophet who has a dream tell the dream; and let him who has received My word report My word faithfully! How can straw be compared to grain?—says the LORD. ²⁹ Behold, My word is like fire—declares the LORD—and like a hammer that shatters rock!

³⁰ Assuredly, I am going to deal with the prophets—declares the LORD—who steal My words from one another. ³¹ I am going to deal with the prophets—declares the LORD—who wagᵃ their tongues and make oracular utterances. ³² I am going to deal with those who prophesy lying dreams—declares the LORD—who relate them to lead My people astray with their reckless lies, when I did not send them or command them. They do this people no good—declares the LORD.

³³ And when this people—or a prophet or a priest—asks you, "What is the burdenᶠ of the LORD?" you shall answer them, ᵍ-What is the burden?-ᵍ I will cast you off—declares the LORD.

³⁴ As for the prophet or priest or layman who shall say "the burden of the LORD," I will punish that person and his house. ³⁵ Thus you shall speak to each other, every one to his fellow, "What has the LORD answered?" or "What has the LORD spoken?" ³⁶ But do not mention "the burden of the LORD" any more. ᵃ-Does a man regard his own word as a "burden,"-ᵃ that you pervert the words of the living God, the LORD of Hosts, our God? ³⁷ Thus you shall speak to the prophet, "What did the LORD answer you?" or "What did the LORD speak?" ³⁸ But if you say "the burden of the LORD"—assuredly, thus said the LORD: Because you said this thing, "the burden of the LORD," whereas I sent word to you not to say "the burden of the LORD," ³⁹ I will utterly ʰ-forget you-ʰ and I will cast you away from My presence,

---

ᶠ *I.e. pronouncement; cf. Isa. 13.1, where the word rendered "pronouncement" can also mean "burden."*

ᵍ⁻ᵍ *Septuagint and other versions read "You are the burden!"*

ʰ⁻ʰ *Some Heb. mss., Septuagint, and other versions read "lift you up," a word from the same root as "burden."*

together with the city which I gave to you and your fathers. [40] And I will lay upon you a disgrace for all time, shame for all time, which shall never be forgotten.

24 The LORD showed me two baskets of figs, placed in front of the Temple of the LORD. This was after King Nebuchadrezzar of Babylon had exiled King Jeconiah son of Jehoiakim of Judah, and the officials of Judah, and the craftsmen and smiths, from Jerusalem, and had brought them to Babylon. [2] One basket contained very good figs, like first-ripened figs, and the other basket contained very bad figs, so bad that they could not be eaten.

[3] And the LORD said to me, "What do you see, Jeremiah?" I answered, "Figs—the good ones are very good, and the bad ones very bad, so bad that they cannot be eaten."

[4] Then the word of the LORD came to me:

[5] Thus said the LORD, the God of Israel: As with these good figs, so will I single out for good the Judean exiles whom I have driven out from this place to the land of the Chaldeans. [6] I will look upon them favorably, and I will bring them back to this land; I will build them and not overthrow them; I will plant them and not uproot them. [7] And I will give them the understanding to acknowledge Me, for I am the LORD. And they shall be My people and I will be their God, when they turn back to Me with all their heart.

[8] And like the bad figs, which are so bad that they cannot be eaten—thus said the LORD—so will I treat King Zedekiah of Judah and his officials and the remnant of Jerusalem that is left in this land, and those who are living in the land of Egypt: [9] I will make them a horror—an evil—to all the kingdoms of the earth, a disgrace and a proverb, a byword and a curse[a] in all the places to which I banish them. [10] I will send the sword, famine, and pestilence against them until they are exterminated from the land which I gave to them and their fathers.

---

[a] *I.e. a standard by which men curse; cf. Gen. 12.2 and note; Zech. 8.13.*

25 The word which came to Jeremiah concerning all the people of Judah, in the fourth year of King Jehoiakim son of Josiah of Judah, which was the first year of King Nebuchadrezzar of Babylon. ² This is what the prophet Jeremiah said to all the people of Judah and to all the inhabitants of Jerusalem:

³ From the thirteenth year of King Josiah son of Amon of Judah to this day—these twenty-three years—the word of the LORD has come to me. I have spoken to you persistently, but you would not listen. ⁴ Moreover, the LORD constantly sent all his servants the prophets to you, but you would not listen or incline your ears to hear ⁵ when they said, "Turn back, everyone, from your evil ways and your wicked acts, that you may remain throughout the ages on the soil which the LORD gave to you and your fathers. ⁶ Do not follow other gods, to serve them and worship them. Do not vex Me with what your own hands have made,ᵃ and I will not bring disaster upon you." ⁷ But you would not listen to Me—declares the LORD; you vexed Me with what your hands made, to your own hurt.

⁸ Assuredly, thus said the LORD of Hosts: Because you would not listen to My words, ⁹ I am going to send for all the peoples of the north—declares the LORD—and for My servant, King Nebuchadrezzar of Babylon, and bring them against this land and its inhabitants, and against all those nations round about. I will exterminate them and make them a desolation, an object of hissingᵇ—ruins for all time. ¹⁰ And I will banish from them the sound of mirth and gladness, the voice of bridegroom and bride, and the sound of the handmill and the light of the lamp. ¹¹ This whole land shall be a desolate ruin.

And those nations shall serve the king of Babylon seventy years. ¹² When the seventy years are over, I will punish the king of Babylon and that nation and the land of the Chaldeans for

---

ᵃ *I.e. idols.*
ᵇ *Cf. note at 18.16.*

their sins—declares the LORD—and I will make it a desolation for all time. [13] And I will bring upon that land all that I have decreed against it, all that is recorded in this book—that which Jeremiah prophesied against all the nations. [14] For they too shall be enslaved by many nations and great kings; and I will requite them according to their acts and according to their conduct.

[15] For thus said the LORD, the God of Israel, to me: "Take from My hand this cup of wine—of wrath—and make all the nations to whom I send you drink of it. [16] Let them drink and retch and act crazy, because of the sword which I am sending among them."

[17] So I took the cup from the hand of the LORD and gave drink to all the nations to whom the LORD had sent me: [18] Jerusalem and the towns of Judah, and its kings and officials, to make them a desolate ruin, an object of hissing and a curse[c]—as is now the case; [19] Pharaoh king of Egypt, his courtiers, his officials, and all his people; [20] all [d-]the mixed peoples;[-d] all the kings of the land of Uz; all the kings of the land of the Philistines—Ashkelon, Gaza, Ekron, and what is left of Ashdod; [21] Edom, Moab and Ammon; [22] all the kings of Tyre and all the kings of Sidon, and all the kings of the coastland across the sea; [23] Dedan, Tema, and Buz, and all those who have their hair clipped; [24] all the kings of Arabia, and all the kings of [d-]the mixed peoples[-d] who live in the desert; [25] all the kings of Zimri[d] and all the kings of Elam and all the kings of Media; [26] all the kings of the north, whether far from or close to each other—all the [d-]royal lands which are on the earth.[-d] And last of all, the king of Sheshach[e] shall drink.

[27] Say to them: "Thus said the LORD of Hosts, the God of Israel: Drink and get drunk and vomit; fall and never rise again, because of the sword that I send among you." [28] And if they refuse to take the cup from your hand and drink, say to them, "Thus said the LORD of Hosts: You must drink! [29] If I am bringing the punishment first on the city that bears My name, can you expect to go unpunished? You will not go unpunished, for I am summoning the sword against all the inhabitants of the earth—declares the LORD of Hosts."

---

[c] Cf. note at 24.9.
[d-d] Meaning of Heb. uncertain.
[e] A cipher for Babel, Babylon.

³⁰ You are to prophesy all those things to them, and then say to them:

> The LORD roars from on high,
> He makes His voice heard from His holy dwelling;
> He roars aloud over His [earthly] abode;
> He utters shouts like the grape-treaders,
> Against all the dwellers on earth.
> ³¹ Tumult has reached the ends of the earth,
> For the LORD has a case against the nations,
> He contends with all flesh.
> He delivers the wicked to the sword
>   —declares the LORD.
> ³² Thus said the LORD of Hosts:
> Disaster goes forth
> From nation to nation;
> A great storm is unleashed
> From the remotest parts of earth.

³³ In that day, the earth shall be strewn with the slain of the LORD from one end to the other. They shall not be mourned, or gathered and buried; they shall become dung upon the face of the earth.

> ³⁴ Howl, you shepherds, and yell,
> Strew [dust] on yourselves, you lords of the flock!
> For the day of your slaughter draws near.
> ᵈ-I will break you in pieces,-ᵈ
> And you shall fall like a precious vessel.
> ³⁵ Flight shall fail the shepherds,
> And escape, the lords of the flock.
> ³⁶ Hark, the outcry of the shepherds,
> And the howls of the lords of the flock!
> For the LORD is ravaging their pasture.
> ³⁷ The peaceful meadows shall be wiped out
> By the fierce wrath of the LORD.

³⁸ Like a lion, He has gone forth from His lair;
The land has become a desolation,
Because of the oppressive^d wrath,
Because of His fierce anger.

26

At the beginning of the reign of King Jehoiakim son of Josiah of Judah, this word came from the LORD: ² Thus said the LORD: Stand in the court of the House of the LORD, and speak to [the men of] all the towns of Judah, who are coming to worship in the House of the LORD, all the words which I command you to speak to them. Do not omit anything. ³ Perhaps they will listen and turn back, each from his evil way, that I may renounce the punishment I am planning to bring upon them for their wicked acts.

⁴ Say to them: Thus said the LORD: If you do not obey Me, abiding by the Teaching which I have set before you, ⁵ heeding the words of My servants the prophets whom I have been sending to you persistently—but you have not heeded— ⁶ then I will make this House like Shiloh, and I will make this city a curse^a for all the nations of earth.

⁷ The priests and prophets and all the people heard Jeremiah speaking these words in the House of the LORD. ⁸ And when Jeremiah finished speaking all that the LORD had commanded him to speak to all the people, the priests and the prophets and all the people seized him, shouting, "You shall die! ⁹ How dare you prophesy in the name of the LORD that this House shall become like Shiloh and this city be made desolate, without inhabitants?" And all the people crowded about Jeremiah in the House of the LORD.

¹⁰ When the officials of Judah heard about this, they went up from the king's palace to the House of the LORD and held a session at the entrance of the New Gate of ^{b-}the House of^{-b} the LORD. ¹¹ The priests and prophets said to the officials and to all the people, "This man deserves the death penalty, for he

---

^a *Cf. note at 24.9.*
^{b-b} *So many mss. and ancient versions; other mss. and the editions omit these words.*

has prophesied against this city, as you yourselves have heard."
[12] Jeremiah said to the officials and to all the people, "It was the LORD who sent me to prophesy against this House and this city all the words you heard. [13] Therefore mend your ways and your acts, and heed the LORD your God, that the LORD may renounce the punishment He has decreed for you. [14] As for me, I am in your hands: do to me what seems good and right to you. [15] But know that if you put me to death, you and this city and its inhabitants will be guilty of shedding the blood of an innocent man. For in truth the LORD has sent me to you, to speak all these words to you."

[16] Then the officials and all the people said to the priests and prophets, "This man does not deserve the death penalty, for he spoke to us in the name of the LORD our God."

[17] And some of the elders of the land arose and said to the entire assemblage of the people, [18] "Micah the Morashtite, who prophesied in the days of King Hezekiah of Judah, said to all the people of Judah: 'Thus said the LORD of Hosts:

ᶜZion shall be plowed as a field,
Jerusalem shall become heaps of ruins
And the Temple Mount a shrine in the woods.'

[19] Did King Hezekiah of Judah, and all Judah, put him to death? Did he not rather fear the LORD and implore the LORD, so that the LORD renounced the punishment He had decreed against them? We are about to do great injury to ourselves!"

[20] There was also a man prophesying in the name of the LORD, Uriah son of Shemaiah from Kiriath-jearim, who prophesied against this city and this land the same things as Jeremiah. [21] King Jehoiakim and all his warriors and all the officials heard about his address, and the king wanted to put him to death. Uriah heard of this and fled in fear, and came to Egypt. [22] But King Jehoiakim sent men to Egypt, Elnathan son of Achbor and men with him to Egypt. [23] They took Uriah out of Egypt and brought him to King Jehoiakim, who had him put to the sword and his body thrown

ᶜ *Mic. 3.12.*

into the burial place of the common people. [24] However, Ahikam son of Shaphan protected Jeremiah, so that he was not handed over to the people for execution.

27

At the beginning of the reign of King Jehoiakim[a] son of Josiah of Judah, this word came to Jeremiah from the LORD:

[2] Thus said the LORD to me: Make for yourself thongs and bars of a yoke, and put them on your neck. [3] [b]And send them[-b] to the king of Edom, the king of Moab, the king of the Ammonites, the king of Tyre, and the king of Sidon, by envoys who have come to King Zedekiah of Judah in Jerusalem; [4] and give them this charge to their masters: Thus said the LORD of Hosts, the God of Israel: Say this to your masters: [5] It is I who made the earth, and the men and beasts who are on the earth, by My great might and My outstretched arm; and I give it to whomever I deem proper. [6] I herewith deliver all these lands to My servant, King Nebuchadnezzar of Babylon; I even give him the wild beasts to serve him. [7] All nations shall serve him, his son and his grandson—until the turn of his own land comes, when many nations and great kings shall subjugate him. [8] The nation or kingdom that does not serve him—King Nebuchadnezzar of Babylon—and does not put its neck under the yoke of the king of Babylon, that nation I will visit—declares the LORD —with sword, famine, and pestilence, until I have destroyed it by his hands. [9] As for you, give no heed to your prophets, augurs, dreamers,[c] diviners, and sorcerers, who say to you, "Do not serve the king of Babylon." [10] For they prophesy falsely to you—with the result that you shall be banished from your land; I will drive you out and you shall perish. [11] But the nation which puts its neck under the yoke of the king of Babylon, and serves him, will be left by Me on its own soil—declares the LORD—to till it and dwell on it.

[a] *Emendation yields "Zedekiah"; so a few mss. and Syriac; cf. vv. 3 and 12.*
[b-b] *Emendation yields "And send," i.e. a message.*
[c] *Lit. "dreams."*

¹² I also spoke to King Zedekiah of Judah in just the same way: "Put your necks under the yoke of the king of Babylon; serve him and his people, and live! ¹³ Otherwise you will die together with your people, by sword, famine, and pestilence, as the LORD has decreed against any nation that does not serve the king of Babylon. ¹⁴ Give no heed to the words of the prophets who say to you, 'Do not serve the king of Babylon,' for they prophesy falsely to you. ¹⁵ I have not sent them—declares the LORD—and they prophesy falsely in My name, with the result that I will drive you out and you shall perish, together with the prophets who prophesy to you."

¹⁶ And to the priests and to all that people I said: "Thus said the LORD: Give no heed to the words of the prophets who prophesy to you, 'The vessels of the House of the LORD shall shortly be brought back from Babylon,' for they prophesy falsely to you. ¹⁷ Give them no heed. Serve the king of Babylon, and live! Otherwise this city shall become a ruin. ¹⁸ If they are really prophets and the word of the LORD is with them, let them intercede with the LORD of Hosts not to let the vessels remaining in the House of the LORD, in the royal palace of Judah, and in Jerusalem, go to Babylon!

¹⁹ "For thus said the LORD of Hosts concerning the columns, the tank,ᵈ the stands, and the rest of the vessels remaining in this city, ²⁰ which King Nebuchadnezzar of Babylon did not take when he exiled King Jeconiah son of Jehoiakim of Judah, from Jerusalem to Babylon, with all the nobles of Judah and Jerusalem— ²¹ thus said the LORD of Hosts, the God of Israel, concerning the vessels remaining in the House of the LORD, in the royal palace of Judah, and in Jerusalem: ²² They shall be brought to Babylon, and there they shall remain, until I take note of them—declares the LORD of Hosts—and bring them up and restore them to this place."

ᵈ *Lit. "sea"; cf. I Kings 7.23 ff.*

28 That year, early in the reign of King Zedekiah of Judah, in the fifth month of the fourth year, the prophet Hananiah son of Azzur, who was from Gibeon, spoke to me in the House of the LORD, in the presence of the priests and all the people. He said: 2 "Thus said the LORD of Hosts, the God of Israel: I hereby break the yoke of the king of Babylon. 3 In two years, I will restore to this place all the vessels of the House of the LORD which King Nebuchadnezzar of Babylon took from this place and brought to Babylon. 4 And I will bring back to this place King Jeconiah son of Jehoiakim of Judah, and all the Judean exiles who went to Babylon—declares the LORD. Yes, I will break the yoke of the king of Babylon."

5 Then the prophet Jeremiah answered the prophet Hananiah in the presence of the priests and of all the people who were standing in the House of the LORD. 6 The prophet Jeremiah said: "Amen! May the LORD do so! May the LORD fulfill what you have prophesied and bring back from Babylon to this place the vessels of the House of the LORD and all the exiles! 7 But just listen to this word which I address to you and to all the people: 8 The prophets who lived before you and me from ancient times prophesied war, disaster, and pestilence against many lands and great kingdoms. 9 So if a prophet prophesies good fortune, then only when the word of the prophet comes true can it be known that the LORD really sent him."

10 But the prophet Hananiah removed the bar from the neck of the prophet Jeremiah, and broke it; 11 and Hananiah said in the presence of all the people, "Thus said the LORD: So will I break the yoke of King Nebuchadnezzar of Babylon from off the necks of all the nations, in two years." And the prophet Jeremiah went on his way.

12 After the prophet Hananiah had broken the bar from off the neck of the prophet Jeremiah, the word of the LORD came to Jeremiah: 13 "Go say to Hananiah: Thus said the LORD: You broke

bars of wood, but *ᵃ·you shall·ᵃ* make bars of iron instead. ¹⁴ For thus said the LORD of Hosts, the God of Israel: I have put an iron yoke upon the necks of all those nations, that they may serve King Nebuchadnezzar of Babylon—and serve him they shall! I have even given the wild beasts to him."

¹⁵ And the prophet Jeremiah said to the prophet Hananiah, "Listen, Hananiah! The LORD did not send you, and you have given this people lying assurances. ¹⁶ Assuredly, thus said the LORD: I am going to banish you from off the earth. You shall die this year, for you have urged disloyalty to the LORD."

¹⁷ And the prophet Hananiah died that year, in the seventh month.

29 This is the text of the letter which the prophet Jeremiah sent from Jerusalem to the priests, the prophets, the rest of the elders of the exile community, and to all the people whom Nebuchadnezzar had exiled from Jerusalem to Babylon—² after King Jeconiah, the queen mother, the eunuchs, the officials of Judah and Jerusalem, and the craftsmen and smiths had left Jerusalem. ³ [The letter was sent] through Elasah son of Shaphan and Gemariah son of Hilkiah, whom King Zedekiah of Judah had dispatched to Babylon, to King Nebuchadnezzar of Babylon.

⁴ Thus said the LORD of Hosts, the God of Israel, to the whole community which I exiled from Jerusalem to Babylon: ⁵ Build houses and live in them, plant gardens and eat their fruit. ⁶ Take wives and beget sons and daughters; and take wives for your sons, and give your daughters to husbands, that they may bear sons and daughters. Multiply there, do not decrease. ⁷ And seek the welfare of the city to which I have exiled you and pray to the LORD in its behalf; for in its prosperity you shall prosper.

⁸ For thus said the LORD of Hosts, the God of Israel: Let not the prophets and diviners in your midst deceive you, and pay no heed to the dreams they*ᵃ* dream. ⁹ For they prophesy to you

---

ᵃ·ᵃ *Septuagint reads "I will."*

ᵃ *Heb. "you."*

in My name falsely; I did not send them—declares the LORD.

¹⁰ For thus said the LORD: When seventy years of Babylon are over, I will take note of you, and I will fulfill to you My promise of favor—to bring you back to this place. ¹¹ For I am mindful of the plans I have made concerning you—declares the LORD—plans for your welfare, not for disaster, to give you a hopeful future. ¹² When you call Me, and come and pray to Me, I will give heed to you. ¹³ You will search for Me and you will find Me, if only you seek Me wholeheartedly. ¹⁴ I will be at hand for you—declares the LORD—and I will restore your fortunes. And I will gather you from all the nations and from all the places to which I have banished you—declares the LORD—and I will bring you back to the place from which I have exiled you.

¹⁵ But you say, "The LORD has raised up prophets for us in Babylon."ᵇ

¹⁶ Thus said the LORD concerning the king who sits on the throne of David, and concerning all the people who dwell in this city, your brothers who did not go out with you into exile— ¹⁷ thus said the LORD of Hosts: I am going to let loose sword, famine, and pestilence against them and I will treat them as loathsome figs, so bad that they cannot be eaten.ᶜ ¹⁸ I will pursue them with the sword, with famine, and with pestilence; and I will make them a horror to all the kingdoms of the earth, a curse and an object of horror and hissingᵈ and scorn among all the nations to which I shall banish them, ¹⁹ because they did not heed My words—declares the LORD—when I persistently sent to them My servants, the prophets, and theyᵃ did not heed—declares the LORD.

²⁰ But you, the whole exile community which I banished from Jerusalem to Babylon, hear the word of the LORD! ²¹ Thus said the LORD of Hosts, the God of Israel, concerning Ahab son of Kolaiah and Zedekiah son of Maaseiah, who prophesy falsely to you in My name: I am going to deliver them into the hands of King Nebuchadrezzar of Babylon, and he shall put them to death before your eyes. ²² And the whole community of Judah in Baby-

---

ᵇ *This verse is continued in vv. 20 ff.*
ᶜ *Cf. 24.1 ff.*
ᵈ *Cf. note at 18.16.*

lonia shall use a curse derived from their fate: "May God make you like Zedekiah and Ahab, whom the king of Babylon consigned to the flames!"— [23] because they did vile things in Israel, committing adultery with the wives of their fellows and speaking in My name false words which I had not commanded them. I am He who knows and bears witness—declares the LORD.

[24] Concerning Shemaiah the Nehelamite you[e] shall say: [25] Thus said the LORD of Hosts, the God of Israel: Because you sent letters in your own name to all the people in Jerusalem, to the priest Zephaniah son of Maaseiah the priest and to the rest of the priests, as follows, [26] "The LORD appointed you priest in place of the priest Jehoiada, [f]to exercise authority[f] in the House of the LORD over every madman who wants to play the prophet, to put him into the cell [g]and into the stocks.[g] [27] Now why have you not rebuked Jeremiah the Anathothite, who plays the prophet among you? [28] For he has actually sent a message to us in Babylon to this effect: It will be a long time. Build houses and live in them, plant gardens and enjoy their fruit."—

[29] When the priest Zephaniah read this letter in the hearing of the prophet Jeremiah, [30] the word of the LORD came to Jeremiah: [31] Send a message to the entire exile community: Thus said the LORD concerning Shemaiah the Nehelamite: Because Shemaiah prophesied to you, though I did not send him, and made you false promises, [32] assuredly, thus said the LORD: I am going to punish Shemaiah the Nehelamite and his offspring. There shall be no man of his line dwelling among this people or seeing the good things I am going to do for My people—declares the LORD—for he has urged disloyalty toward the LORD.

30

The word which came to Jeremiah from the LORD: [2] Thus said the LORD, the God of Israel: Write down in a scroll all the words that I have spoken to you. [3] For days are coming—declares the LORD—when I will restore the fortunes of My people Israel

---

[e] *I.e. Jeremiah.*
[f-f] *Lit. "that there might be officials."*
[g-g] *Meaning of Heb. uncertain.*

and Judah, said the Lord; and I will bring them back to the land
which I gave their fathers, and they shall possess it. ⁴ And these
are the words which the Lord spoke concerning Israel and Judah:

⁵ Thus said the Lord:
We have heard cries of panic,
Terror without relief.
⁶ Ask and see:
Surely males do not bear young!
Why then do I see every man
With his hands on his loins
Like a woman in labor?
Why have all faces turned pale?
⁷ Ah, that day is awesome;
There is none like it!
It is a time of trouble for Jacob,
But he shall be delivered from it.

⁸ In that day—declares the Lord of Hosts—I will break the
yoke from off your neck and I will rip off your bonds. Strangers
shall no longer make slaves of them; ⁹ instead, they shall serve the
Lord their God and David, the king whom I will raise up for
them.

¹⁰ But you,
Have no fear, My servant Jacob
—declares the Lord—
Be not dismayed, O Israel!
I will deliver you from far away,
Your folk from their land of captivity.
And Jacob shall again have calm
And quiet with none to trouble him;
¹¹ For I am with you to deliver you
—declares the Lord.
I will make an end of all the nations
Among which I have dispersed you;

But I will not make an end of you!
I will not leave you unpunished,
But will chastise you in measure.

¹² For thus said the LORD:
Your injury is incurable,
Your wound severe;
¹³ ^{a-}No one pleads for the healing of your sickness,^{-a}
There is no remedy, no recovery for you.
¹⁴ All your lovers have forgotten you,
They do not seek you out;
For I have struck you as an enemy strikes,
With cruel chastisement,
Because your iniquity was so great
And your sins so many.
¹⁵ Why cry out over your injury,
That your wound is incurable?
I did these things to you
Because your iniquity was so great
And your sins so many.

¹⁶ Assuredly,
All who wanted to devour you shall be devoured,
And every one of your foes shall go into captivity;
Those who despoiled you shall be despoiled,
And all who pillaged you I will give up to pillage.
¹⁷ But I will bring healing to you
And cure you of your wounds

—declares the LORD.

Though they called you "Outcast,
That Zion whom no one seeks out,"
¹⁸ Thus said the LORD:
I will restore the fortunes of Jacob's tents
And have compassion upon his dwellings.

^{a-a} *Meaning of Heb. uncertain.*

The city shall be rebuilt on its mound,[b]
And the fortress in its proper place.
19 From them shall issue thanksgiving
And the sound of dancers.
I will multiply them,
And they shall not be few;
I will make them honored,
And they shall not be humbled.
20 His children shall be as of old,
And his community shall be established by My grace;
And I will punish all his oppressors.
21 His chieftain shall be one of his own,
His ruler shall come from his midst;
I will bring him near, that he may approach Me
—declares the LORD—
For who would otherwise dare approach Me?
22 You shall be My people,
And I will be your God.

23 Lo, the storm of the LORD goes forth in fury,
A raging tempest;
It shall whirl down upon the head of the wicked.
24 The anger of the LORD shall not turn back
Till it has fulfilled and completed His purposes.
In the days to come
You shall perceive it.
[31][1] [c]At that time—declares the LORD—I will be God to all the
clans of Israel, and they shall be My people.

31 2 Thus said the LORD:

The people escaped from the sword,
Found favor in the wilderness;
When Israel was marching homeward,
3 The LORD revealed Himself to me[a] of old.

b *I.e. on the mound of ruins left after its destruction.*
c *In some editions, this verse is 30.25.*

a *Emendation yields "him."*

Eternal love I conceived for you then;
Therefore I continue My grace to you.
⁴ I will build you firmly again,
O Maiden Israel!
Again you shall take up your timbrels
And go forth to the rhythm of the dancers.
⁵ Again you shall plant vineyards
On the hills of Samaria;
Men shall plant and live to enjoy them.
⁶ For the day is coming when watchmen
Shall proclaim on the heights of Ephraim:
Come, let us go up to Zion,
To the LORD our God!

⁷ For thus said the LORD:
Cry out in joy for Jacob,
Shout at the crossroads*ᵇ* of the nations!
Sing aloud in praise, and say:
ᶜ"Save, O LORD, Your people,*⁻ᶜ*
The remnant of Israel.
⁸ I will bring them in from the northland,
Gather them from the ends of the earth—
The blind and the lame among them,
Those with child and those in labor—
In a vast throng they shall return here.
⁹ They shall come with weeping,
And with compassion*ᵈ* will I guide them.
I will lead them to streams of water,
By a level road where they will not stumble.
For I am ever a Father to Israel,
Ephraim is My firstborn.

¹⁰ Hear the word of the LORD, O nations,
And tell it in the coastlands afar.
Say:

ᵇ Lit. "head."
ᶜ⁻ᶜ Emendation yields "The LORD has saved His people."
ᵈ For this meaning, cf. Zech. 12.10.

He who scattered Israel will gather them,
And will guard them as a shepherd his flock.
¹¹ For the LORD will ransom Jacob,
Redeem him from one too strong for him.
¹² They shall come and shout on the heights of Zion,
Radiant over the bounty of the LORD—
Over new grain and wine and oil,
And over sheep and cattle.
They shall fare like a watered garden,
They shall never languish again.
¹³ Then shall maidens dance gaily,
Young men and old alike.
I will turn their mourning to joy,
I will comfort them and cheer them in their grief.
¹⁴ I will give the priests their fill of fatness,
And My people shall enjoy My full bounty
                                    —declares the LORD.

¹⁵ Thus said the LORD:
A cry is heard ᵉ⁻in Ramah⁻ᵉ—
Wailing, bitter weeping—
Rachel weeping for her children.
She refuses to be comforted
For her children, who are gone.
¹⁶ Thus said the LORD:
Restrain your voice from weeping,
Your eyes from shedding tears;
For there is a reward for your labor
                                    —declares the LORD:
They shall return from the enemy's land.
¹⁷ And there is hope for your future
                                    —declares the LORD:
Your children shall return to their country.

¹⁸ I can hear Ephraim lamenting:
You have chastised me, and I am chastised

ᵉ⁻ᵉ *Or "on a height."*

Like a calf that has not been broken.
Receive me back, let me return,
For You, O LORD, are my God.
[19] Now that I have turned back, I am filled with remorse;
Now that I am made aware, I strike my thigh.*f*
I am ashamed and humiliated,
For I bear the disgrace of my youth.
[20] Truly, Ephraim is a dear son to Me,
A child that is dandled!
Whenever I have turned*g* against him,
My thoughts would dwell on him still.
That is why My heart yearns for him;
I will receive him back in love

—declares the LORD.

[21] Erect markers,
Set up signposts;*h*
Keep in mind the highway,
The road that you traveled.
Return, Maiden Israel!
Return to these towns of yours!
[22] How long will you waver,
O rebellious daughter?
(For the LORD has created something new on earth:
A woman courts*h* a man.)

[23] Thus said the LORD of Hosts, the God of Israel: They shall
again say this in the land of Judah and in its towns, when I restore
their fortunes:

"The LORD bless you,
Abode of righteousness,
O holy mountain!"

[24] Judah and all its towns alike shall be inhabited by the farmers
and *i*-such as move about-*i* with the flocks. [25] For I will give the
thirsty abundant drink, and satisfy all who languish.

---

f I.e. as a gesture of self-reproach.
g Lit. "spoken."
h Meaning of Heb. uncertain.
i-i Lit. "they shall travel."

26 At this I awoke and looked about, and my sleep^j had been pleasant to me.

27 See, a time is coming—declares the LORD—when I will sow the House of Israel and the House of Judah with seed of men and seed of cattle; 28 and just as I was watchful over them to uproot and to pull down, to overthrow and to destroy and to bring disaster, so I will be watchful over them to build and to plant—declares the LORD. 29 In those days, they shall no longer say, "Fathers have eaten sour grapes and children's teeth are blunted."^k 30 But everyone shall die for his own sins: whosoever eats sour grapes, his teeth shall be blunted.

31 See, a time is coming—declares the LORD—when I will make a new covenant with the House of Israel and the House of Judah. 32 It will not be like the covenant I made with their fathers, when I took them by the hand to lead them out of the land of Egypt, a covenant which they broke, so that I rejected^l them—declares the LORD. 33 But such is the covenant I will make with the House of Israel after these days—declares the LORD: I will put My Teaching into their inmost being and inscribe it upon their hearts. Then I will be their God, and they shall be My people. 34 No longer will they need to teach one another and say to one another, "Heed the LORD"; for all of them, from the least of them to the greatest, shall heed Me—declares the LORD.

> For I will forgive their iniquities,
> And remember their sins no more.

35 Thus said the LORD,
Who established the sun for light by day,
The laws of moon and stars for light by night,
Who stirs up the sea into roaring waves,
Whose name is LORD of Hosts:

^j *I.e. the vision in the preceding verses.*
^k *Others "set on edge."*
^l *Taking* ba'alti *as equivalent to* bahalti; *cf. 3.14.*

³⁶ If these laws should ever be annulled by Me
—declares the LORD—
Only then would the offspring of Israel cease
To be a nation before Me for all time.

³⁷ Thus said the LORD: If the heavens above could be measured, and the foundations of the earth below could be fathomed, only then would I reject all the offspring of Israel for all that they have done—declares the LORD.

³⁸ See, a time is coming—declares the LORD—when the city shall be rebuilt for the LORD from the Tower of Hananel to the Corner Gate; ³⁹ and the measuring line shall go straight out to the Gareb Hill, and then turn toward Goah. ⁴⁰ And the entire Valley of the Corpses and Ashes, and all the fields as far as the Wadi Kidron, and the corner of the Horse Gate on the east, shall be holy to the LORD. They shall never again be uprooted or overthrown.

32 The word which came to Jeremiah from the LORD in the tenth year of King Zedekiah of Judah, which was the eighteenth year of Nebuchadrezzar. ² At that time the army of the king of Babylon was besieging Jerusalem, and the prophet Jeremiah was confined in the prison compound attached to the palace of the king of Judah. ³ For King Zedekiah of Judah had confined him, saying, "How dare you prophesy: 'Thus said the LORD: I am delivering this city into the hands of the king of Babylon, and he shall capture it. ⁴ And King Zedekiah of Judah shall not escape from the Chaldeans; he shall be delivered into the hands of the king of Babylon, ᵃ⁻and he shall speak to him face to face and see him in person.⁻ᵃ ⁵ And Zedekiah shall be brought to Babylon, there to remain until I take note of him—declares the LORD. When you wage war against the Chaldeans, you shall not be successful.' "

ᵃ⁻ᵃ Lit. "and his mouth shall speak with his mouth, and his eyes shall see his eyes."

⁶ Jeremiah said: The word of the LORD came to me: ⁷ Hanamel, the son of your uncle Shallum, will come to you and say, "Buy my land in Anathoth, *ᵇ*for you are next in succession to redeem it by purchase."*⁻ᵇ* ⁸ And just as the LORD had said, my cousin Hanamel came to me in the prison compound and said to me, "Please buy my land in Anathoth, in the territory of Benjamin; for the right of succession is yours, and you have the duty of redemption. Buy it." Then I knew that it was indeed the word of the LORD.

⁹ So I bought the land in Anathoth from my cousin Hanamel. I weighed out the money to him, seventeen shekels of silver. ¹⁰ I wrote a deed, sealed it, and had it witnessed; and I weighed out the silver on a balance. ¹¹ I took the deed of purchase, the sealed text and the open one *ᶜ*according to rule and law,*⁻ᶜ* ¹² and gave the deed to Baruch son of Neriah son of Mahseiah in the presence of my kinsman Hanamel, of the witnesses *ᵈ*who were named*⁻ᵈ* in the deed, and all the Judeans who were sitting in the prison compound. ¹³ In their presence I charged Baruch as follows: ¹⁴ Thus said the LORD of Hosts, the God of Israel: "Take these documents, this deed of purchase, the sealed text and the open one, and put them into an earthen jar, so that they may last a long time." ¹⁵ For thus said the LORD of Hosts, the God of Israel: "Houses, fields, and vineyards shall again be purchased in this land."

¹⁶ But after I had given the deed to Baruch son of Neriah, I prayed to the LORD: ¹⁷ "Ah, Lord GOD! You made heaven and earth with Your great might and outstretched arm. Nothing is too wondrous for You! ¹⁸ You show kindness to the thousandth generation, but visit the guilt of the fathers upon their children after them. O great and mighty God whose name is LORD of Hosts, ¹⁹ wondrous in purpose and mighty in deed, whose eyes observe all the ways of men, so as to repay every man according to his ways, and with the proper fruit of his deeds! ²⁰ You displayed signs and marvels in the land of Egypt *ᵉ*with lasting effect,*⁻ᵉ* and

---

ᵇ⁻ᵇ *Lit. "for yours is the procedure of redemption by purchase."*
ᶜ⁻ᶜ *Force of Heb. uncertain.*
ᵈ⁻ᵈ *With many mss. and ancient versions; so ancient Near Eastern practice. Other mss. and the editions read "who wrote."*
ᵉ⁻ᵉ *Lit. "to this day."*

won renown in Israel and among mankind to this very day. ²¹ You freed Your people Israel from the land of Egypt with signs and marvels, with a strong hand and an outstretched arm, and with great terror. ²² You gave them this land which You had sworn to their fathers to give them, a land flowing with milk and honey, ²³ and they came and took possession of it. But they did not listen to You or follow Your Teaching; they did nothing of what You commanded them to do. Therefore You have caused all this misfortune to befall them. ²⁴ Here are the siege-mounds, raised against the city to storm it; and the city, because of sword and famine and pestilence, is at the mercy of the Chaldeans who are attacking it. What You threatened has come to pass—as You see. ²⁵ Yet You, Lord GOD, said to me: Buy the land for money and call in witnesses—when the city is at the mercy of the Chaldeans!"

²⁶ Then the word of the LORD came to Jeremiah:

²⁷ "Behold I am the LORD, the God of all flesh. Is anything too wondrous for Me? ²⁸ Assuredly, thus said the LORD: I am delivering this city into the hands of the Chaldeans and of King Nebuchadrezzar of Babylon, and he shall capture it. ²⁹ And the Chaldeans who have been attacking this city shall come and set this city on fire and burn it down—with the houses on whose roofs they made offerings to Baal and poured out libations to other gods, so as to vex Me. ³⁰ For the people of Israel and Judah have done nothing but evil in My sight since their youth; the people of Israel have done nothing but vex Me by their conduct—declares the LORD. ³¹ This city has aroused My anger and My wrath from the day it was built until this day; so that it must be removed from My sight ³² because of all the wickedness of the people of Israel and Judah who have so acted as to vex Me—they, their kings, their officials, their priests and prophets, and the men of Judah and the inhabitants of Jerusalem. ³³ They turned their backs to Me, not their faces; though I have taught them persistently, they do not give heed or accept rebuke. ³⁴ They placed

their abominations in the House which bears My name and defiled it; 35 and they built the shrines of Baal which are in the Valley of Ben-hinnom, where they offered up their sons and daughters to Molech—when I had never commanded, or even thought [of commanding], that they should do such an abominable thing, and so bring guilt on Judah.

36 But now, assuredly, thus said the LORD, the God of Israel, concerning this city of which you say, "It is being delivered into the hands of the king of Babylon through the sword, through famine, and through pestilence": 37 See, I will gather them from all the lands to which I have banished them in My anger and wrath, and in great rage; and I will bring them back to this place and let them dwell secure. 38 They shall be My people, and I will be their God. 39 I will give them a single heart and a single nature to revere Me for all time, and it shall be well with them and their children after them. 40 And I will make an everlasting covenant with them that I will not turn away from them and that I will treat them graciously; and I will put into their hearts reverence for Me, so that they do not turn away from Me. 41 I will delight in treating them graciously, and I will plant them in this land faithfully, with all My heart and soul.

42 For thus said the LORD: As I have brought this terrible disaster upon this people, so I am going to bring upon them the vast good fortune which I have promised for them. 43 And fields shall again be purchased in this land of which you say, "It is a desolation, without man or beast; it is delivered into the hands of the Chaldeans."

44 Fields shall be purchased, and deeds written and sealed, and witnesses called in the land of Benjamin and in the environs of Jerusalem, and in the towns of Judah; the towns of the hill country, the towns of the Shephelah, and the towns of the Negeb. For I will restore their fortunes—declares the LORD.

33 The word of the LORD came to Jeremiah a second time, while he was still confined in the prison compound, as follows:

²Thus said the LORD who is planning it,
The LORD who is shaping it to bring it about,
Whose name is LORD:
³Call to Me, and I will answer you,
And I will tell you wondrous things,
Secrets you have not known.

⁴For thus said the LORD, the God of Israel, concerning the houses of this city and the palaces of the kings of Judah that were torn down *ᵃ*for [defense] against the siege-mounds and against the sword, ⁵and were filled with those who went to fight the Chaldeans*⁻ᵃ*—with the corpses of the men whom I struck down in My anger and rage, hiding My face from this city because of all their wickedness: ⁶I am going to bring her relief and healing. I will heal them and reveal to them abundance*ᵃ* of true favor. ⁷And I will restore the fortunes of Judah and Israel, and I will rebuild them as of old. ⁸And I will purge them of all the sins which they committed against Me, and I will pardon all the sins which they committed against Me, by which they rebelled against Me. ⁹And she shall gain through Me renown, joy, fame, and glory above all the nations on earth, when they hear of all the good fortune I provide for them.*ᵇ* They will thrill and quiver because of all the good fortune and all the prosperity that I provide for her. ¹⁰Thus said the LORD: Again there shall be heard in this place, which you say is ruined, without man or beast—in the towns of Judah and the streets of Jerusalem that are desolate, without man, without inhabitants, without beast— ¹¹the sound of mirth and gladness, the voice of bridegroom and bride, the voice of those who cry, "Give thanks to the LORD of Hosts, for the LORD

ᵃ⁻ᵃ *Meaning of Heb. uncertain.*
ᵇ *I.e. for Judah and Israel.*

is good, for His kindness is everlasting!" as they bring thanksgiving offerings to the House of the LORD. For I will restore the fortunes of the land as of old—said the LORD.

¹² Thus said the LORD of Hosts: In this ruined place, without man and beast, and in all its towns, there shall again be a pasture for shepherds, where they can rest their flocks. ¹³ In the towns of the hill country, in the towns of the Shephelah, and in the towns of the Negeb, in the land of Benjamin and in the environs of Jerusalem and in the towns of Judah, sheep shall pass again under the hands of one who counts them—said the LORD. ¹⁴ See, days are coming—declares the LORD—when I will fulfill the promise which I made concerning the House of Israel and the House of Judah. ¹⁵ In those days and at that time, I will raise up a true branch of David's line, and he shall do what is just and right in the land. ¹⁶ In those days Judah shall be delivered and Israel shall dwell secure. And this is what she shall be called: "The LORD is our Vindicator." ¹⁷ For thus said the LORD: There shall never be an end to men of David's line who sit upon the throne of the House of Israel. ¹⁸ Nor shall there ever be an end to the line of the levitical priests before Me, of those who present burnt offerings and turn the meal offering to smoke and perform sacrifices.

¹⁹ The word of the LORD came to Jeremiah: ²⁰ Thus said the LORD: If you could break My covenant with the day and My covenant with the night, so that day and night should not come at their proper time, ²¹ only then could My covenant with My servant David be broken—so that he would not have a descendant reigning upon his throne—or with My ministrants, the levitical priests. ²² Like the host of heaven which cannot be counted, and the sand of the sea which cannot be measured, so will I multiply the offspring of My servant David, and of the Levites who minister to Me.

²³ The word of the LORD came to Jeremiah: ²⁴ You see what this people said: "The two families which the LORD chose have now

been rejected by Him." Thus they despise My people, ^aand regard them as no longer a nation.^{-a} ²⁵ Thus said the LORD: As surely as I have established My covenant with day and night—the laws of heaven and earth— ²⁶ so I will never reject the offspring of Jacob and My servant David; I will never fail to take from his offspring rulers for the descendants of Abraham, Isaac, and Jacob. Indeed, I will restore their fortunes and take them back in love.

34 The word which came to Jeremiah from the LORD, when King Nebuchadrezzar of Babylon and all his army, and all the kingdoms of the earth and all the peoples under his sway, were waging war against Jerusalem and all its towns:

² Thus said the LORD, the God of Israel: Go speak to King Zedekiah of Judah, and say to him: Thus said the LORD: I am going to deliver this city into the hands of the king of Babylon, and he will destroy it by fire ³ And you will not escape from him; you will be captured and handed over to him. ^aAnd you will see the king of Babylon face to face and speak to him in person;^{-a} and you will be brought to Babylon. ⁴ But hear the word of the LORD, O King Zedekiah of Judah! Thus said the LORD concerning you: You will not die by the sword. ⁵ You will die a peaceful death; and as incense^b was burned for your ancestors, the earlier kings who preceded you, so they will burn incense^b for you, and they will lament for you "Ah, lord!" For I Myself have made the promise —declares the LORD.

⁶ The prophet Jeremiah spoke all these words to King Zedekiah of Judah in Jerusalem, ⁷ when the army of the king of Babylon was waging war against Jerusalem and against the remaining towns of Judah—against Lachish and Azekah, for they were the only fortified towns of Judah that were left.

⁸ The word which came to Jeremiah from the LORD after King Zedekiah had made a covenant with all the people in Jerusalem to proclaim a release^c among them— ⁹ that everyone should set

^{a-a} *Meaning of Heb. uncertain.*
^{a-a} *For the idiom see note at 32.4.*
^b *Lit. "burnings."*
^c *Others "liberty."*

free his Hebrew slaves, both male and female, and that no one should keep his fellow Judean enslaved.

¹⁰ Everyone, officials and people, who had entered into the covenant agreed to set their male and female slaves free and not keep them enslaved any longer; they complied and let them go. ¹¹ But afterward they turned about and brought back the men and women they had set free, and forced them into slavery again. ¹² Then it was that the word of the LORD came to Jeremiah from the LORD:

¹³ Thus said the LORD, the God of Israel: I made a covenant with your fathers when I brought them out of the land of Egypt, the house of bondage, saying: ¹⁴ "In the seventh year *ᵈ* each of you must let go any fellow Hebrew *ᵉ*who may be sold*⁻ᵉ* to you; when he has served you six years, you must set him free." But your fathers would not obey Me or give ear. ¹⁵ Lately you turned about and did what is proper in My sight, and each of you proclaimed a release to his countrymen; and you made a covenant accordingly before Me in the House which bears My name. ¹⁶ But now you have turned back and have profaned My name; each of you has brought back the men and women whom you had given their freedom, and forced them to be your slaves again.

¹⁷ Assuredly, thus said the LORD: You would not obey Me and proclaim a release, each to his kinsman and countryman. Lo! I proclaim your release—declares the LORD—to the sword, to pestilence, and to famine; and I will make you a horror to all the kingdoms of the earth. ¹⁸ I will make the men who violated My covenant, who did not fulfill the terms of the covenant which they made before Me, [like] the calf which they cut in two so as to pass between the halves:*ᶠ* ¹⁹ the officers of Judah and Jerusalem, the officials, the priests, and all the people of the land who passed between the halves of the calf, ²⁰ shall be handed over to their enemies, to those who seek to kill them. Their carcasses shall become food for the birds of the sky and the beasts of the earth. ²¹ I will hand over King Zedekiah of Judah and his officers to their

ᵈ *I.e. of servitude. Lit. "After a period of seven years"; cf. Deut. 14.28 and 15.1.*
ᵉ⁻ᵉ *Or "who sells himself."*
ᶠ *Cf. Gen. 15.9-10, 17-21.*

enemies, who seek to kill them—to the army of the king of Babylon which has withdrawn from you. [22] I hereby give the command —declares the LORD—by which I will bring them back against this city. They shall attack it and capture it, and burn it down. I will make the towns of Judah a desolation, without inhabitant.

35 The word which came to Jeremiah from the LORD in the days of King Jehoiakim son of Josiah of Judah:

[2] Go to the house of the Rechabites and speak to them, and bring them to the House of the LORD, to one of the chambers, and give them wine to drink.

[3] So I took Jaazaniah son of Jeremiah son of Habazziniah, and his brothers, all his sons, and the whole household of the Rechabites; [4] and I brought them to the House of the LORD, to the chamber of the sons of Hanan son of Igdaliah, the man of God, which is next to the chamber of the officials and above the chamber of Maaseiah son of Shallum, the guardian of the threshold. [5] I set bowls full of wine and cups before the men of the house of the Rechabites, and said to them, "Have some wine."

[6] They replied. "We will not drink wine, for our ancestor, Jonadab son of Rechab, commanded us: 'You shall never drink wine, either you or your children. [7] Nor shall you build houses or sow fields[a] or plant vineyards, nor shall you own such things; but you shall live in tents all your days, so that you may live long upon the land where you sojourn.' [8] And we have obeyed our ancestor Jonadab son of Rechab in all that he commanded us: we never drink wine, neither we nor our wives nor our sons and daughters. [9] Nor do we build houses to live in, and we do not own vineyards or fields for sowing; [10] but we live in tents. We have obeyed and done all that our ancestor Jonadab commanded us. [11] But when King Nebuchadrezzar of Babylon invaded the country, we said, 'Come, let us go into Jerusalem because of the army of the Chaldeans and the army of Aram.' And so we are living in Jerusalem."

[a] *Lit. "seed."*

¹² Then the word of the Lord came to Jeremiah: ¹³ Thus said the LORD of Hosts, the God of Israel: Go say to the men of Judah and the inhabitants of Jerusalem: You can learn a lesson [here] about obeying My commands—declares the LORD. ¹⁴ The commands of Jonadab son of Rechab have been fulfilled: he charged his children not to drink wine, and to this day they have not drunk, in obedience to the charge of their ancestor. But I spoke to you persistently, and you did not listen to Me. ¹⁵ I persistently sent you all My servants, the prophets, to say: "Turn back, every one of you, from your wicked ways and mend your deeds; do not follow other gods or serve them. Then you may remain on the land which I gave to you and your fathers." But you did not give ear or listen to Me. ¹⁶ The family of Jonadab son of Rechab have indeed fulfilled the charge which their ancestor gave them; but this people has not listened to Me. ¹⁷ Assuredly, thus said the LORD, the God of Hosts, the God of Israel: I am going to bring upon Judah and upon all the inhabitants of Jerusalem all the disaster with which I have threatened them; for I spoke to them, but they would not listen; I called to them, but they would not respond.

¹⁸ And to the family of the Rechabites Jeremiah said: Thus said the LORD of Hosts, the God of Israel: Because you have obeyed the charge of your ancestor Jonadab and kept all his commandments, and done all that he enjoined upon you, ¹⁹ assuredly, thus said the LORD of Hosts, the God of Israel: There shall never cease to be a man of the line of Jonadab son of Rechab standing before Me.

36 In the fourth year of King Jehoiakim son of Josiah of Judah, this word came to Jeremiah from the LORD:

² "Get a scroll and write upon it all the words that I have spoken to you—concerning Israel and Judah and all the nations—from the time I first spoke to you in the days of Josiah to this day. ³ Perhaps when the House of Judah hear of all the disasters

I intend to bring upon them, they will turn back from their wicked ways, and I will pardon their iniquity and their sin." [4] So Jeremiah called Baruch son of Neriah; and Baruch wrote down in the scroll, at Jeremiah's dictation, all the words which the LORD had spoken to him.

[5] Jeremiah instructed Baruch, "I am in hiding; I cannot go to the House of the LORD. [6] But you go and read aloud the words of the LORD from the scroll which you wrote at my dictation, to the people in the House of the LORD on a fast day; thus you will also be reading them to all the Judeans who come in from the towns. [7] Perhaps their entreaty will be accepted by the LORD, if they turn back from their wicked ways. For great is the anger and wrath with which the LORD has threatened this people."

[8] Baruch son of Neriah did just as the prophet Jeremiah had instructed him—to read the words of the LORD from the scroll in the House of the LORD. [9] In the ninth month of the fifth year of King Jehoiakim son of Josiah of Judah, all the people in Jerusalem and all the people coming from Judah proclaimed a fast before the LORD in Jerusalem. [10] It was then that Baruch—in the chamber of Gemariah son of Shaphan the scribe, in the upper court, near the new gateway of the House of the LORD—read the words of Jeremiah from the scroll to all the people in the House of the LORD.

[11] Micaiah son of Gemariah son of Shaphan heard all the words of the LORD [read] from the scroll, [12] and he went down to the king's palace, to the chamber of the scribe. There he found all the officials in session: Elishama the scribe, Delaiah son of Shemaiah, Elnathan son of Achbor, Gemariah son of Shaphan, Zedekiah son of Hananiah, and all the other officials. [13] And Micaiah told them all that he had heard as Baruch read from the scroll in the hearing of the people.

[14] Then all the officials sent Jehudi son of Nethaniah son of Shelemiah son of Cushi to say to Baruch, "Take that scroll from

which you read to the people, and come along!" And Baruch took the scroll and came to them.

¹⁵ They said, ^{a-}"Sit down and read it^{-a} to us." And Baruch read it to them. ¹⁶ When they heard all these words, they turned to each other in fear; and they said to Baruch, "We must report all this to the king."

¹⁷ And they questioned Baruch further, "Tell us how you wrote down all these words ^{b-}that he spoke."^{-b} ¹⁸ He answered them, "He would dictate all those words to me, and I would write them down in the scroll in ink."

¹⁹ The officials said to Baruch, "Go into hiding, you and Jeremiah. Let no man know where you are!" ²⁰ And they went to the king in the court, after leaving the scroll in the chamber of the scribe Elishama. And they reported all these matters to the king.

²¹ The king sent Jehudi to get the scroll and he fetched it from the chamber of the scribe Elishama. Jehudi read it to the king and to all the officials who were in attendance on the king. ²² Since it was the ninth month, the king was sitting in the winter house, with a fire burning in the brazier before him. ²³ And every time Jehudi read three or four columns, [the king] would cut it up with a scribe's knife and throw it into the fire in the brazier, until the entire scroll was consumed by the fire in the brazier. ²⁴ Yet the king and all his courtiers who heard all these words showed no fear and did not tear their garments; ²⁵ moreover, Elnathan, Delaiah, and Gemariah begged the king not to burn the scroll, but he would not listen to them.

²⁶ The king ordered Jerahmeel, the king's son, and Seraiah son of Azriel, and Shelemiah son of Abdeel to arrest the scribe Baruch and the prophet Jeremiah. But the LORD hid them.

²⁷ The word of the LORD came to Jeremiah after the king had burned the scroll containing the words that Baruch had written at Jeremiah's dictation: ²⁸ Get yourself another scroll, and write upon it the same words that were in the first scroll which was

---

^{a-a} *Change of vocalization yields* "Read it again"; *cf. Targum and Septuagint.*
^{b-b} *Force of Heb. uncertain.*

burned by King Jehoiakim of Judah. [29] And concerning King Jehoiakim of Judah you shall say: Thus said the LORD: You burned that scroll, saying, "How dare you write in it that the king of Babylon will come and destroy this land and cause man and beast to cease from it?" [30] Assuredly, thus said the LORD concerning King Jehoiakim of Judah: He shall not have any of his line sitting on the throne of David; and his own corpse shall be left exposed to the heat by day and the cold by night. [31] And I will punish him and his offspring and his courtiers for their iniquity; I will bring on them and on the inhabitants of Jerusalem and on all the men of Judah all the disasters of which I have warned them —but they would not listen.

[32] So Jeremiah got another scroll and gave it to the scribe Baruch son of Neriah. And at Jeremiah's dictation, he wrote in it the whole text of the scroll which King Jehoiakim of Judah had burned; and more of the like was added.

37 Zedekiah son of Josiah became king instead of Coniah son of Jehoiakim, for King Nebuchadrezzar of Babylon set him up as king over the land of Judah. [2] Neither he nor his courtiers nor the people of the land gave heed to the words which the LORD spoke through the prophet Jeremiah.

[3] Yet King Zedekiah sent Jehucal son of Shelemiah and Zephaniah son of the priest Maaseiah to the prophet Jeremiah, to say, "Please pray on our behalf to the LORD our God." ([4] Jeremiah could still go in and out among the people, for they had not yet put him in prison. [5] The army of Pharaoh had set out from Egypt; and when the Chaldeans who were besieging Jerusalem heard the report, they raised the siege of Jerusalem.)

[6] Then the word of the LORD came to the prophet Jeremiah: [Answer them:] [7] Thus said the LORD, the God of Israel: Thus shall you say to the king of Judah who sent you to Me to inquire of Me: The army of Pharaoh, which set out to help you, will return

to its own land, to Egypt. [8] And the Chaldeans will come back and attack this city and they will capture it and destroy it by fire.

[9] Thus said the Lord: Do not delude yourselves into thinking, "The Chaldeans will go away from us." They will not. [10] Even if you defeated the whole army of the Chaldeans that are fighting against you, and only wounded men were left lying in their tents, they would get up and burn this city down!

[11] When the army of the Chaldeans raised the siege of Jerusalem on account of the army of Pharaoh, [12] Jeremiah was going to leave Jerusalem and go to the territory of Benjamin [a]to share in some property there[-a] among the people. [13] When he got to the Benjamin Gate, there was a guard officer there named Irijah son of Shelemiah son of Hananiah; and he arrested the prophet Jeremiah, saying, "You are defecting to the Chaldeans!" [14] Jeremiah answered, "That's a lie! I'm not defecting to the Chaldeans!" But Irijah would not listen to him; he arrested Jeremiah and brought him to the officials. [15] The officials were furious with Jeremiah; they beat him and put him into prison, in the house of the scribe Jonathan—for it had been made into a jail. [16] Thus Jeremiah came to the [a]pit and to the cells,[-a] and Jeremiah remained there a long time.

[17] Then King Zedekiah sent for him, and the king questioned him secretly in his palace. He asked, "Is there any word from the Lord?" "There is!" Jeremiah answered, and he continued, "You will be delivered into the hands of the king of Babylon." [18] And Jeremiah said to King Zedekiah, "What wrong have I done to you, to your courtiers, and to this people, that you have put me in jail? [19] And where are those prophets of yours who prophesied to you that the king of Babylon would never move against you and against this land? [20] Now, please hear me, O lord king, and grant my plea: Don't send me back to the house of the scribe Jonathan [b]to die there."[-b]

[21] So King Zedekiah gave instructions to lodge Jeremiah in the prison compound and to supply him daily with a loaf of bread

[a-a] *Meaning of Heb uncertain.*
[b-b] *Lit. "and let me not die there."*

from the Bakers' Street—until all the bread in the city was gone. Jeremiah remained in the prison compound.

38 Shephatiah son of Mattan, Gedaliah son of Pashhur, Jucal son of Shelemiah, and Pashhur son of Malchiah heard what Jeremiah was saying to all the people: ² "Thus said the LORD: Whoever remains in this city shall die by the sword, by famine, and by pestilence; but whoever surrenders to the Chaldeans shall live; *ᵃ*he shall at least gain his life*⁻ᵃ* and shall live. ³ Thus said the LORD: This city shall be delivered into the hands of the king of Babylon's army, and he shall capture it."

⁴ Then the officials said to the king, "Let that man be put to death, for he disheartens*ᵇ* the soldiers, and all the people who are left in this city, by speaking such things to them. That man is not seeking the welfare of this people, but their harm!" ⁵ King Zedekiah replied, "He is in your hands; the king cannot oppose you in anything!"

⁶ So they took Jeremiah and put him down in the pit of Malchiah, the king's son, which was in the prison compound; they let Jeremiah down by ropes. There was no water in the pit, only mud, and Jeremiah sank into the mud.

⁷ Ebed-melech the Ethiopian, a eunuch who was in the king's palace, heard that they had put Jeremiah in the pit. The king was then sitting at the Benjamin Gate; ⁸ so Ebed-melech left the king's palace, and spoke to the king: ⁹ "O lord king, those men have acted wickedly in all they did to the prophet Jeremiah; they have put him down in the pit, to die there of hunger." For there was no more bread in the city.

¹⁰ Then the king instructed Ebed-melech the Ethiopian, "Take with you thirty*ᶜ* men from here, and pull the prophet Jeremiah up from the pit before he dies." ¹¹ So Ebed-melech took the men with him, and went to the king's palace, to *ᵈ*a place below*⁻ᵈ* the treasury. There they got worn cloths and rags, which they let down to Jeremiah in the pit by ropes. ¹² And Ebed-melech the

---

ᵃ⁻ᵃ *Lit. "he shall have his life as booty"; cf. 21.9.*
ᵇ *Lit. "weakens the hands of."*
ᶜ *One ms. reads "three."*
ᵈ⁻ᵈ *Emendation yields "the wardrobe of."*

Ethiopian called to Jeremiah, "Put the worn cloths and rags under your armpits, inside the ropes." Jeremiah did so, ¹³ and they pulled Jeremiah up by the ropes and got him out of the pit. And Jeremiah remained in the prison compound.

¹⁴ King Zedekiah sent for the prophet Jeremiah, and had him brought to him at the third entrance of the House of the LORD. And the king said to Jeremiah, "I want to ask you something; don't conceal anything from me."

¹⁵ Jeremiah answered the king, "If I tell you, you'll surely kill me; and if I give you advice, you won't listen to me."

¹⁶ Thereupon King Zedekiah secretly promised Jeremiah on oath: "As the LORD lives who has ^{e-}given us this life,^{-e} I will not put you to death or leave you in the hands of those men who seek your life."

¹⁷ Then Jeremiah said to Zedekiah, "Thus said the LORD, the God of Hosts, the God of Israel: If you surrender to the officers of the king of Babylon, your life will be spared and this city will not be burned down. You and your household will live. ¹⁸ But if you do not surrender to the officers of the king of Babylon, this city will be delivered into the hands of the Chaldeans, who will burn it down; and you will not escape from them."

¹⁹ King Zedekiah said to Jeremiah, "I am worried about the Judeans who have defected to the Chaldeans; that they [the Chaldeans] might hand me over to them to abuse me."

²⁰ "They will not hand you over," Jeremiah replied. "Listen to the voice of the LORD, to what I tell you, that it may go well with you and your life be spared. ²¹ For this is what the LORD has shown me if you refuse to surrender: ²² All the women who are left in the palace of the king of Judah shall be brought out to the officers of the king of Babylon; and they shall say:

The men who were your friends
Have seduced you and vanquished you.
Now that your feet are sunk in the mire,
They have turned their backs [on you].

^{e-e} *Meaning of Heb. uncertain.*

²³ They will bring out all your wives and children to the Chaldeans, and you yourself will not escape from them. You will be captured by the king of Babylon, and *ᶠ*this city shall be burned down."*ᶠ*

²⁴ Zedekiah said to Jeremiah, "Don't let anyone know about this conversation, *ᵍ*or you will die.*ᵍ* ²⁵ If the officials should hear that I have spoken with you, and they should come and say to you, 'Tell us what you said to the king; hide nothing from us, *ʰ*or we'll kill you.*ʰ* And what did the king say to you?' ²⁶ say to them, 'I was presenting my petition to the king not to send me back to the house of Jonathan to die there.' "

²⁷ All the officials did come to Jeremiah to question him; and he replied to them just as the king had instructed him. So they stopped questioning him, for the conversation had not been overheard. ²⁸ Jeremiah remained in the prison compound until the day Jerusalem was captured.

When Jerusalem was captured. . . ,*ⁱ*

39 In the ninth year of King Zedekiah of Judah, in the tenth month, King Nebuchadrezzar of Babylon moved against Jerusalem with his whole army, and they laid siege to it. ² And in the eleventh year of Zedekiah, on the ninth day of the fourth month, the [walls of the] city were breached. ³ All the officers of the king of Babylon entered, and took up quarters at the middle gate— Nergal-sarezer, Samgar-nebo, Sarsechim the Rab-saris,*ᵃ* Nergal-sarezer the Rab-mag,*ᵃ* and all the rest of the officers of the king of Babylon.

⁴ When King Zedekiah of Judah saw them, he and all the soldiers fled. They left the city at night, by way of the king's garden, through the gate between the double walls; and he set out toward the Arabah.*ᵇ* ⁵ But the Chaldean troops pursued them, and they overtook Zedekiah in the steppes of Jericho. They captured him and brought him before King Nebuchadrezzar of Babylon at

---

ᶠ⁻ᶠ So Targum and Septuagint and some mss. Most mss. and the editions read "you will burn down this city by fire."

ᵍ⁻ᵍ Lit. "that you may not die."

ʰ⁻ʰ Lit. "that we may not kill you."

ⁱ This clause would read well before 39.3.

ᵃ Titles of officers.

ᵇ Hoping to escape across the Jordan.

Riblah in the region of Hamath; and he put him on trial. [6] The king of Babylon had Zedekiah's children slaughtered at Riblah before his eyes; the king of Babylon had all the nobles of Judah slaughtered. [7] Then the eyes of Zedekiah were put out and he was chained in bronze fetters, that he might be brought to Babylon.

[8] The Chaldeans burned down the king's palace and the houses[c] of the people by fire, and they tore down the walls of Jerusalem. [9] The remnant of the people that was left in the city, and the defectors who had gone over to him—the remnant of the people that was left—were exiled by Nebuzaradan, the chief of the guards, to Babylon. [10] But some of the poorest people who owned nothing were left in the land of Judah by Nebuzaradan, the chief of the guards, and he gave them vineyards and fields at that time.

[11] King Nebuchadrezzar of Babylon had given orders to Nebuzaradan, the chief of the guards, concerning Jeremiah: [12] "Take him and look after him; do him no harm, but grant whatever he asks of you." [13] So Nebuzaradan, the chief of the guards, and Nebushazban the Rab-saris, and Nergal-sarezer the Rab-mag, and all the commanders of the king of Babylon sent [14] and had Jeremiah brought from the prison compound. They committed him to the care of Gedaliah son of Ahikam son of Shaphan, [d-]that he might be left at liberty in a house.[-d] So he dwelt among the people.

[15] The word of the LORD had come to Jeremiah while he was still confined in the prison compound: [16] Go and say to Ebed-melech the Ethiopian: Thus said the LORD of Hosts, the God of Israel: I am going to fulfill My words concerning this city—for disaster, not for good—and they shall come true on that day in your presence. [17] But I will save you on that day—declares the LORD; you shall not be delivered into the hands of the men you dread. [18] I will rescue you, and you shall not fall by the sword. [e-]You shall escape with your life,[-e] because you trusted Me—declares the LORD.

[c] *Taking Heb. singular as collective, with Kimḥi.*
[d-d] *Meaning of Heb. uncertain.*
[e-e] *See note at 38.2.*

40 The word that came to Jeremiah from the LORD, after Nebuzaradan, the chief of the guards, set him free at Ramah, to which he had taken him, chained in fetters, among those from Jerusalem and Judah who were being exiled to Babylon.

² The chief of the guards took charge of Jeremiah, and he said to him, "The LORD your God threatened this place with this disaster; ³ and now the LORD has brought it about. He has acted as He threatened, because you sinned against the LORD and did not obey Him. That is why this has happened to you. ⁴ Now, I release you this day from the fetters which were on your hands. If you would like to go with me to Babylon, come, and I will look after you. And if you don't want to come with me to Babylon, you need not. See, the whole land is before you: go wherever seems good and right to you."—⁵ ªBut [Jeremiah] still did not turn back.ª—"Or go to Gedaliah son of Ahikam son of Shaphan, whom the king of Babylon has put in charge of the towns of Judah, and stay with him among the people, or go wherever you want to go."

The chief of the guards gave him an allowance of food, and dismissed him. ⁶ So Jeremiah came to Gedaliah son of Ahikam at Mizpah, and stayed with him among the people who were left in the land.

⁷ The officers of the troops in the open country, and their men with them, heard that the king of Babylon had put Gedaliah son of Ahikam in charge of the region, and that he had put in his charge the men, women, and children—of the poorest in the land —those who had not been exiled to Babylon.⁸ So they with their men came to Gedaliah at Mizpah—Ishmael son of Nethaniah; Johanan and Jonathan the sons of Kareah; Seraiah son of Tanhumeth; the sons of Ephai the Netophathite; and Jezaniah son of the Maacathite. ⁹ Gedaliah son of Ahikam son of Shaphan reas-

ª⁻ª *Meaning of Heb. uncertain.*

sured[b] them and their men, saying, "Do not be afraid to serve the Chaldeans. Stay in the land and serve the king of Babylon, and it will go well with you. [10] I am going to stay in Mizpah to attend upon the Chaldeans who will come to us. But you may gather wine and figs[c] and oil and put them in your own vessels, and settle in the towns you have occupied."

[11] Likewise, all the Judeans who were in Moab, Ammon, and Edom, or who were in other lands, heard that the king of Babylon had let a remnant stay in Judah, and that he had put Gedaliah son of Ahikam son of Shaphan in charge of them. [12] All these Judeans returned from all the places to which they had scattered. They came to the land of Judah, to Gedaliah at Mizpah, and they gathered large quantities of wine and figs.[c]

[13] Johanan son of Kareah, and all the officers of the troops in the open country, came to Gedaliah at Mizpah [14] and said to him, "Do you know that King Baalis of Ammon has sent Ishmael son of Nethaniah to kill you?" But Gedaliah son of Ahikam would not believe them. [15] Johanan son of Kareah also said secretly to Gedaliah at Mizpah, "Let me go and strike down Ishmael son of Nethaniah before anyone knows about it; otherwise he will kill you, and all the Judeans who have gathered about you will be dispersed, and the remnant of Judah will perish!"

[16] But Gedaliah son of Ahikam answered Johanan son of Kareah, "Do not do such a thing: what you are saying about Ishmael is not true!"

41 In the seventh month, Ishmael son of Nethaniah son of Elishama, who was of royal descent and one of the king's commanders, came with ten men to Gedaliah son of Ahikam at Mizpah; and they ate together there at Mizpah. [2] Then Ishmael son of Nethaniah and the ten men who were with him arose and struck down Gedaliah son of Ahikam son of Shaphan with the sword and killed him, because the king of Babylon had put him in charge of the land. [3] Ishmael also killed all the Judeans who

[b] *Lit. "swore to."*
[c] *Lit. "summer fruit."*

were with him—with Gedaliah in Mizpah—and the Chaldean soldiers who were stationed there.

⁴ The second day after Gedaliah was killed, when no one yet knew about it, ⁵ eighty men came from Shechem, Shiloh, and Samaria, their beards shaved, their garments torn, and their bodies gashed, carrying meal offerings and frankincense to present at the House of the LORD. ⁶ Ishmael son of Nethaniah went out from Mizpah to meet them, weeping as he walked. As he met them, he said to them, "Come to Gedaliah son of Ahikam." ⁷ When they came inside the town, Ishmael son of Nethaniah and the men who were with him slaughtered them [and threw their bodies] into a cistern.

⁸ But there were ten men among them who said to Ishmael, "Don't kill us! We have stores hidden in a field—wheat, barley, oil, and honey." So he stopped, and did not kill them along with their fellows.— ⁹ The cistern into which Ishmael threw all the corpses of the men he had killed ᵃ⁻in the affair of Gedaliah was the one that⁻ᵃ King Asa had constructed on account of King Baasha of Israel. That was the one which Ishmael son of Nethaniah filled with corpses.— ¹⁰ Ishmael carried off all the rest of the people who were in Mizpah, including the daughters of the king—all the people left in Mizpah, over whom Nebuzaradan, the chief of the guards, had appointed Gedaliah son of Ahikam. Ishmael son of Nethaniah carried them off, and set out to cross over to the Ammonites.

¹¹ Johanan son of Kareah, and all the army officers with him, heard of all the crimes committed by Ishmael son of Nethaniah. ¹² They took all their men and went to fight against Ishmael son of Nethaniah; and they encountered him by the great pool in Gibeon. ¹³ When all the people held by Ishmael saw Johanan son of Kareah and all the army officers with him, they were glad; ¹⁴ all the people whom Ishmael had carried off from Mizpah turned back and went over to Johanan son of Kareah. ¹⁵ But Ishmael son of Nethaniah escaped from Johanan with eight men, and went to the Ammonites.

ᵃ⁻ᵃ *Septuagint reads "was a large cistern, which. . . ."*

¹⁶ Johanan son of Kareah and all the army officers with him took all the rest of the people whom ^bhe had rescued from Ishmael son of Nethaniah^{-b} from Mizpah after he had murdered Gedaliah son of Ahikam—the men, soldiers, women, children, and eunuchs whom [Johanan] had brought back from Gibeon. ¹⁷ They set out, and they stopped at Geruth^c Chimham, near Bethlehem, on their way to go to Egypt ¹⁸ because of the Chaldeans. For they were afraid of them, because Ishmael son of Nethaniah had killed Gedaliah son of Ahikam, whom the king of Babylon had put in charge of the land.

42

Then all the army officers, with Johanan son of Kareah, Jezaniah son of Hoshaiah, and all the rest of the people, great and small, approached ² the prophet Jeremiah and said, "Grant our plea, and pray for us to the LORD your God, for all this remnant! For we remain but a few out of many, as you can see. ³ Let the LORD your God tell us where we should go and what we should do."

⁴ The prophet Jeremiah answered them, "Agreed: I will pray to the LORD your God as you request, and I will tell you whatever response the LORD gives for you. I will withhold nothing from you."

⁵ Thereupon they said to Jeremiah, "Let the LORD be a true and faithful witness against us! We swear that we will do exactly as the LORD your God instructs us through you! ⁶ Whether it is pleasant or unpleasant, we will obey the LORD our God to whom we send you, in order that it may go well with us when we obey the LORD our God."

⁷ After ten days, the word of the LORD came to Jeremiah. ⁸ He called Johanan son of Kareah and all the army officers, and the rest of the people, great and small, ⁹ and said to them, "Thus said the LORD, the God of Israel, to whom you sent me to present your

b-b *Emendation yields "Ishmael son of Nethaniah had carried off."*
c *Aquila reads "the sheepfolds of."*

supplication before Him: [10] If you remain in this land, I will build you and not overthrow, I will plant you and not uproot; for I regret the punishment I have brought upon you. [11] Do not be afraid of the king of Babylon, whom you fear; do not be afraid of him—declares the LORD—for I am with you to save you and to rescue you from his hands. [12] I will dispose him to be merciful to you: he shall show you mercy and *a*-bring you back to*-a* your own land.

[13] "But if you say, We will not stay in this land—thus disobeying the LORD your God— [14] if you say, No! We will go to the land of Egypt, so that we may not see war nor hear the sound of the horn, and so that we may not hunger for bread; there we will stay, [15] then hear the word of the LORD, O remnant of Judah! Thus said the LORD of Hosts, the God of Israel: If you turn your faces toward Egypt, and you go and sojourn there, [16] the sword that you fear shall overtake you there, in the land of Egypt, and the famine you worry over shall follow at your heels in Egypt too; and there you shall die. [17] All the men who turn their faces toward Egypt, in order to sojourn there, shall die by the sword, by famine, and by pestilence. They shall have no surviving remnant of the disaster which I will bring upon them. [18] For thus said the LORD of Hosts, the God of Israel: As My anger and wrath were poured out upon the inhabitants of Jerusalem, so will My wrath be poured out on you if you go to Egypt. You shall become *b*-an execration of woe, a curse*-b* and a mockery; and you shall never again see this place. [19] The LORD has spoken against you, O remnant of Judah! Do not go to Egypt! Know well, then—for I warn you this day [20] that you were deceitful at heart when you sent me to the LORD your God, saying, 'Pray for us to the LORD our God; and whatever the LORD our God may say, just tell us and we will do it.' [21] I told you today, and you have not obeyed the LORD your God in respect to all that He sent me to tell you— [22] know well, then, that you shall die by the sword, by famine, and by pestilence in the place where you want to go and sojourn."

a-a *Change of vocalization yields "let you dwell in."*
b-b *I.e. a standard by which men execrate and curse; cf. note at 24.9.*

43 When Jeremiah had finished speaking all these words to all the people—all the words of the LORD their God, with which the LORD their God had sent him to them— ² Azariah son of Hoshaiah and Johanan son of Kareah and all the arrogant men said to Jeremiah, "You are lying! The LORD our God did not send you to say, 'Don't go to Egypt and sojourn there'! ³ It is Baruch son of Neriah who is inciting you against us, so that we will be delivered into the hands of the Chaldeans to be killed or to be exiled to Babylon!"

⁴ So Johanan son of Kareah and all the army officers and the rest of the people did not obey the LORD's command to remain in the land of Judah. ⁵ Instead, Johanan son of Kareah and all the army officers took the entire remnant of Judah—those who had returned from all the countries to which they had been scattered and had sojourned in the land of Judah, ⁶ men, women, and children; and the daughters of the king and all the people whom Nebuzaradan the chief of the guards had left with Gedaliah son of Ahikam son of Shaphan, as well as the prophet Jeremiah and Baruch son of Neriah— ⁷ and they went to Egypt. They did not obey the LORD.

They arrived at Tahpanhes, ⁸ and the word of the LORD came to Jeremiah in Tahpanhes: ⁹ Get yourself large stones, and embed them in mortar in the brick structure at the entrance to Pharaoh's palace in Tahpanhes, with some Judeans looking on. ¹⁰ And say to them: Thus said the LORD of Hosts, the God of Israel: I am sending for My servant King Nebuchadrezzar of Babylon, and I^a will set his throne over these stones which I have embedded. He will spread out his pavilion^b over them. ¹¹ He will come and attack the land of Egypt, delivering

Those destined for the plague, to the plague,
Those destined for captivity, to captivity,
And those destined for the sword, to the sword.

ª *Septuagint reads "he."*
ᵇ *Meaning of Heb. uncertain.*

[12] And I[a] will set fire to the temples of the gods of Egypt; he will burn them down and carry them[c] off. He shall wrap himself up in the land of Egypt, as a shepherd wraps himself up in his garment. And he shall depart from there in safety. [13] He shall smash the obelisks of the Temple of the Sun which is in the land of Egypt, and he shall burn down the temples of the gods of Egypt.

44

The word which came to Jeremiah for all the Judeans living in the land of Egypt, living in Migdol, Tahpanhes, and Noph, and in the land of Pathros:

[2] Thus said the LORD of Hosts, the God of Israel: You have seen all the disaster that I brought on Jerusalem and on all the towns of Judah. They are a ruin today, and no one inhabits them, [3] on account of the wicked things they did to vex Me, going to make offerings in worship of other gods which they had not known— neither they nor you nor your fathers. [4] Yet I persistently sent to you all My servants the prophets, to say, "I beg you not to do this abominable thing which I hate." [5] But they would not listen or give ear, to turn back from their wickedness and not make offerings to other gods; [6] so My fierce anger was poured out, and it blazed against the towns of Judah and the streets of Jerusalem. And they became a desolate ruin, as they still are today

[7] And now, thus said the LORD, the God of Hosts, the God of Israel: Why are you doing such great harm to yourselves, so that every man and woman, child and infant of yours shall be cut off from the midst of Judah, and no remnant shall be left of you? [8] For you vex me by your deeds, making offering to other gods in the land of Egypt where you have come to sojourn, so that you shall be cut off and become a curse[a] and a mockery among all the nations of earth. [9] Have you forgotten the wicked acts of your forefathers, of the kings of Judah and their[b] wives, and your own wicked acts and those of your wives, which were committed in the land of Judah and in the streets of Jerusalem? [10] No one has

---

[c] I.e. the gods.

[a] See note at 24.9; 42.18.
[b] Heb. "his."

shown contrition to this day, and no one has shown reverence. You[c] have not followed the Teaching and the laws which I set before you and before your fathers.

11 Assuredly, thus said the LORD of Hosts, the God of Israel: I am going to set My face against you for punishment, to cut off all of Judah. 12 I will take the remnant of Judah who turned their faces toward the land of Egypt, to go and sojourn there, and they shall be utterly consumed in the land of Egypt. They shall fall by the sword, they shall be consumed by famine; great and small alike shall die by the sword and by famine, and they shall become an execration[a] and a desolation, a curse[a] and a mockery. 13 I will punish those who live in the land of Egypt as I punished Jerusalem, with the sword, with famine, and with pestilence. 14 Of the remnant of Judah who came to sojourn here in the land of Egypt, no survivor or fugitive shall be left to return to the land of Judah. Though they all long to return and dwell there, none shall return except [a few] survivors.

15 Thereupon they answered Jeremiah—all the men who knew that their wives made offerings to other gods; all the women present, a large gathering; and all the people who lived in Pathros in the land of Egypt: 16 "We will not listen to you in the matter about which you spoke to us in the name of the LORD. 17 On the contrary, we will do [d]everything which we have vowed[d] —to make offerings to the Queen of Heaven and to pour libations to her, as we used to do,[e] we and our fathers, our kings and our officials, in the towns of Judah and the streets of Jerusalem. For then we had plenty to eat, we were well-off, and suffered no misfortune. 18 But ever since we stopped making offerings to the Queen of Heaven and pouring libations to her, we have lacked everything, and we have been consumed by the sword and by famine. 19 And when we make offerings to the Queen of Heaven and pour libations to her, is it without our husbands' approval that we have made cakes [f]in her likeness[f] and poured libations to her?"

[c] Heb. "They."
[d-d] Lit. "everything that has gone forth from our mouth."
[e] Cf. 7.18.
[f-f] Meaning of Heb. uncertain.

²⁰ Jeremiah replied to all the people, men and women—all the people who argued with him. He said, ²¹ "Indeed, the offerings you presented in the towns of Judah and the streets of Jerusalem —you, your fathers, your kings, your officials, and the people of the land—were remembered by the LORD and brought to mind! ²² When the LORD could no longer bear your evil practices and the abominations you committed, your land became a desolate ruin and a curse,ᵃ without inhabitant, as is still the case. ²³ Because you burned incense and sinned against the LORD and did not obey the LORD, and because you did not follow His Teaching, His laws, and His exhortations, therefore this disaster has befallen you, as is still the case."

²⁴ Jeremiah further said to all the people and to all the women: "Hear the word of the LORD, all Judeans in the land of Egypt! ²⁵ Thus said the LORD of Hosts, the God of Israel: You and your wives have ᵍ⁻confirmed by deed what you spoke in words:⁻ᵍ 'We will fulfill the vows which we made, to burn incense to the Queen of Heaven and to pour libations to her.' So fulfill your vows; perform your vows!

²⁶ "Yet hear the word of the LORD, all Judeans who dwell in the land of Egypt! Lo, I swear by My great name—said the LORD— that none of the men of Judah in all the land of Egypt shall ever again invoke My name, saying, 'As the Lord GOD lives!' ²⁷ I will be watchful over them to their hurt, not to their benefit; all the men of Judah in the land of Egypt shall be consumed by sword and by famine, until they cease to be. ²⁸ Only the few who survive the sword shall return from the land of Egypt to the land of Judah. All the remnant of Judah who came to the land of Egypt to sojourn there shall learn whose word will be fulfilled—Mine or theirs!

²⁹ "And this shall be the sign to you—declares the LORD—that I am going to deal with you in this place, so that you may know that My threats of punishment against you will be fulfilled: ³⁰ Thus said the LORD: I will deliver Pharaoh Hophra, king of Egypt, into the hands of his enemies, those who seek his life, just

ᵍ⁻ᵍ *Lit. "spoken with your mouth and fulfilled by your hands."*

as I delivered King Zedekiah of Judah into the hands of King
Nebuchadrezzar of Babylon, his enemy who sought his life."

45 The word which the prophet Jeremiah spoke to Baruch
son of Neriah, when he was writing these words in a scroll at
Jeremiah's dictation, in the fourth year of King Jehoiakim son of
Josiah of Judah: ² Thus said the LORD, the God of Israel, concerning you,
Baruch: ³ You say, "Woe is me! The LORD has added grief to
my pain. I am worn out with groaning, and I have found no
rest." ⁴ Thus shall you speak to him: Thus said the LORD: I
am going to overthrow what I have built, and uproot what I
have planted—ᵃ-this applies to the whole land.⁻ᵃ ⁵ And do you
expect great things for yourself? Don't expect them. For I am
going to bring disaster upon all flesh—declares the LORD—but
I will ᵇ-at least grant you your life⁻ᵇ in all the places where you
may go.

46 The word of the LORD to the prophet Jeremiah concerning the nations.
² Concerning Egypt, about the army of Pharaoh Neco, king of
Egypt, which was at the river Euphrates near Carchemish, and
which was defeated by King Nebuchadrezzar of Babylon, in the
fourth year of King Jehoiakim son of Josiah of Judah.

³ Get ready buckler and shield,
And move forward to battle!
⁴ Harness the horses;
Mount, you horsemen!
Fall in line, helmets on!
Burnish the lances,
Don your armor!
⁵ Why do I see them dismayed,

ᵃ⁻ᵃ *Meaning of Heb. uncertain.*
ᵇ⁻ᵇ *Cf. note at 21.9.*

Yielding ground?
Their fighters are crushed,
They flee in haste
And do not turn back—
Terror all around!

—declares the LORD.

6 *a-*The swift cannot get away,
The warrior cannot escape.*-a*
In the north, by the river Euphrates,
They stagger and fall.

7 Who is this that rises like the Nile,
Like streams whose waters surge?
8 It is Egypt that rises like the Nile,
Like streams whose waters surge,
That said, "I will rise,
I will cover the earth,
I will wipe out towns
And those who dwell in them.
9 Advance, O horses,
Dash madly, O chariots!
Let the warriors go forth,
Cush and Put, that grasp the shield,
And the Ludim who grasp and draw the bow!"

10 But that day shall be for the Lord GOD of Hosts a day when He exacts retribution from His foes. The sword shall devour; it shall be sated and drunk with their blood. For the Lord GOD of Hosts is preparing a sacrifice in the northland, by the river Euphrates.

11 Go up to Gilead and get balm,
Fair Maiden Egypt.
In vain do you seek many remedies,
There is no healing for you.
12 Nations have heard your shame;

a-a *Lit. "Let not the swift get away,/Let not the warrior escape."*

The earth resounds with your screams.
For warrior stumbles against warrior;
The two fall down together.

13 The word which the LORD spoke to the prophet Jeremiah
about the coming of King Nebuchadrezzar of Babylon to attack
the land of Egypt:

14 Declare in Egypt, proclaim in Migdol,
Proclaim in Noph and Tahpanhes!
Say: Take your posts and stand ready,
For the sword has devoured all around you!
15 Why are your stalwarts swept away?
They did not stand firm,
For the LORD thrust them down;
16 He made many stumble,
They fell over one another.

They said:
"Up! let us return to our people,
To the land of our birth,
Because of the deadly*b* sword."
17 There they called Pharaoh king of Egypt:
b-"Braggart who let the hour go by."*-b*

18 As I live—declares the King,
Whose name is LORD of Hosts—
*b-*As surely as Tabor is among the mountains
And Carmel is by the sea,
So shall this come to pass.*-b*
19 Equip yourself for exile,
Fair Egypt, you who dwell secure!
For Noph shall become a waste,
Desolate, without inhabitants.

b-b *Meaning of Heb. uncertain.*

[20] Egypt is a handsome heifer—
A gadfly[c] from the north [d-]is coming, coming![-d]
[21] The mercenaries, too, in her midst
Are like stall-fed calves;
They too shall turn tail,
Flee as one, and make no stand.
Their day of disaster is upon them,
The hour of their doom.
[22] [b-]She shall rustle away like a snake[-b]
As they come marching in force;
They shall come against her with axes,
Like hewers of wood.
[23] They shall cut down her forest

—declares the LORD—

Though it cannot be measured;
For they are more numerous than locusts,
And cannot be counted.
[24] Fair Egypt shall be shamed,
Handed over to the people of the north.

[25] The LORD of Hosts, the God of Israel, has said: I will inflict punishment on Amon[e] of No and on Pharaoh—on Egypt, her gods, and her kings—on Pharaoh and all who rely on him. [26] I will deliver them into the hands of those who seek to kill them, into the hands of King Nebuchadrezzar of Babylon and into the hands of his subjects. But afterward she shall be inhabited again as in former days, declares the LORD.

[27] But you,
Have no fear, My servant Jacob,
Be not dismayed, O Israel!
I will deliver you from far away,
Your folk from their land of captivity;
And Jacob again shall have calm

[c] Or "butcher"; meaning of Heb. uncertain.
[d-d] Many mss. read "will come upon her."
[e] Tutelary deity of the city No (Thebes); cf. Nah. 3.8.

And quiet, with none to trouble him.
28 But you, have no fear,
My servant Jacob
—declares the LORD—
For I am with you.
I will make an end of all the nations
Among which I have banished you,
But I will not make an end of you!
I will not leave you unpunished,
But I will chastise you in measure.

47 The word of the LORD that came to the prophet Jeremiah concerning the Philistines, before Pharaoh conquered Gaza.

2 Thus said the LORD:
See, waters are rising from the north,
They shall become a raging torrent,
They shall flood the land and its creatures,
The towns and their inhabitants.
Men shall cry out,
All the inhabitants of the land shall howl,
3 At the clatter of the stamping hoofs of his stallions,
At the noise of his chariots,
The rumbling of their wheels,
Fathers shall not look to their children
Out of *-sheer helplessness*-*a*
4 Because of the day that is coming
For ravaging all the Philistines,
For cutting off every last ally
Of Tyre and Sidon.
For the LORD will ravage the Philistines,
The remnant from the island of Caphtor.
5 Baldness*b* has come upon Gaza,
Ashkelon is destroyed.

---

a-a Lit. "weakness of hands."
b Shaving the head and gashing the body were expressions of mourning; cf. Deut. 14.1.

O remnant of ^{c}their valley,$^{-c}$
How long will you ^{b}gash yourself?$^{-b}$

6 "O sword of the LORD,
When will you be quiet at last?
Withdraw into your sheath,
Rest and be still!"

7 How can it^d be quiet
When the LORD has given it orders
Against Ashkelon and the seacoast,
Given it assignment there?

48 Concerning Moab.^{a}

Thus said the LORD of Hosts, the God of Israel:
Alas, that Nebo should be ravaged,
Kiriathaim captured and shamed,
^{b}The stronghold^{-b} shamed and dismayed!
2 Moab's glory is no more;
In Heshbon they have planned^c evil against her:
"Come, let us make an end of her as a nation!"
You too, O Madmen, shall be silenced;^{d}
The sword is following you.
3 Hark! an outcry from Horonaim,
Destruction and utter ruin!

4 Moab is broken;
^{e}Her young ones cry aloud;$^{-e}$
5 They climb to Luhith
Weeping continually;
On the descent to Horonaim

$^{c-c}$ Septuagint reads "the Anakites"; cf. Josh. 11.22.
^{d} Heb. "you."

^{a} A number of parallels to this chapter occur in Isa. 15-16.
$^{b-b}$ Or "Misgab."
^{c} Heb. hashebu, play on Heshbon.
^{d} Heb. tiddommi, play on Madmen, the name of a town.
$^{e-e}$ Emendation yields "They cry aloud as far as Zoar"; cf. Isa. 15.5.

A distressing cry of anguish is heard:
⁶ Flee, save your lives!
*ᶠ*And be like Aroer in the desert.*ᶠ*

⁷ Surely, because of your trust
In your wealth and in your treasures,
You too shall be captured.
And Chemosh shall go forth to exile,
Together with his priests and attendants.
⁸ The ravager shall come to every town;
No town shall escape.
The valley shall be devastated
And the tableland laid waste
            —because the LORD has spoken.
⁹ Give *ᶠ*wings to Moab,
For she must go hence.*ᶠ*
Her towns shall become desolate,
With no one living in them.

¹⁰ Cursed be he who is slack in doing the LORD's work! Cursed
be he who withholds his sword from blood!

¹¹ Moab has been secure from his youth on—
He is settled on his lees
And has not been poured from vessel to vessel—
He has never gone into exile.
Therefore his fine flavor has remained
And his bouquet is unspoiled.

¹² But days are coming—declares the LORD—when I will send
men against him to tip him over; they shall empty his vessels and
smash his jars. ¹³ And Moab shall be shamed because of Chemosh, as the House of Israel were shamed because of Bethel, on
whom they relied.

ᶠ⁻ᶠ *Meaning of Heb. uncertain.*

¹⁴ How can you say: We are warriors,
Valiant men for war?
¹⁵ Moab is ravaged,
His towns have been entered,
His choice young men
Have gone down to the slaughter
    —declares the King whose name is LORD of Hosts.
¹⁶ The doom of Moab is coming close,
His downfall is approaching swiftly.
¹⁷ Condole with him, all who live near him,
All you who know him by name!
Say: "Alas, the strong rod is broken,
The lordly staff!"

¹⁸ Descend from glory
And sit in thirst,ᶠ
O inhabitant of Fair Dibon;
For the ravager of Moab has entered your town,
He has destroyed your fortresses.
¹⁹ Stand by the road and look out,
O inhabitant of Aroer.
Ask of him who is fleeing
And of her who is escaping:
Say, "What has happened?"
²⁰ Moab is shamed and dismayed;
Howl and cry aloud!
Tell at the Arnon
That Moab is ravaged!

²¹ Judgment has come upon the tableland—upon Holon, Jah-zah, and Mephaath; ²² upon Dibon, Nebo, and Beth-diblathaim; ²³ upon Kiriathaim, Beth-gamul, and Beth-meon; ²⁴ upon Kerioth and Bozrah—upon all the towns of the land of Moab, far and near.

25 The might of Moab has been cut down,
His strength is broken

—declares the LORD.

26 Get him drunk
For he vaunted himself against the LORD.
Moab shall vomit till he is drained,
And he too shall be a laughingstock.
27 Wasn't Israel a laughingstock to you?
Was he ever caught among thieves,
That you should *g-*shake your head*-g*
Whenever you speak of him?
28 Desert the cities
And dwell in the crags,
O inhabitants of Moab!
Be like a dove that nests
In the sides of a pit.

29 We have heard of Moab's pride—
Most haughty is he—
Of his arrogance and pride,
His haughtiness and self-exaltation.
30 I know his insolence—declares the LORD—the wickedness
that is in him,*h* the wickedness *i-*he has*-i* committed.
31 Therefore I will howl for Moab,
I will cry out for all Moab,
I*j* will moan for the men of Kir-heres.
32 With greater weeping than for Jazer
I weep for you, O vine of Sibmah,
Whose tendrils crossed the sea,
Reached to the sea,*f* to Jazer.
A ravager has come down
Upon your fig and grape harvests.
33 Rejoicing and gladness
Are gone from the farm land,
From the country of Moab;

g-g *I.e. in mockery.*
h *Cf. note at Isa. 16.6.*
i-i *Heb. "they have."*
j *Heb. "He."*

I have put an end to wine in the presses,
No one treads [the grapes] with shouting—
ᶠ The shout is a shout no more.ᶠ
³⁴ There is an outcry from Heshbon to Elealeh,
They raise their voices as far as Jahaz,
From Zoar to Horonaim and Eglath-shelishiah.
The waters of Nimrim
Shall also become desolation.
³⁵ And I will make an end in Moab

—declares the LORD—

Of those who offer at a shrine
And burn incense to their god.
³⁶ Therefore,
My heart moans for Moab like a flute;
Like a flute my heart moans
For the men of Kir-heres—
ᶠ Therefore,
The gains they have made shall vanishᶠ—
³⁷ For every head is bald
And every beard is shorn;
On all hands there are gashes,
And on the loins sackcloth.
³⁸ On all the roofs of Moab,
And in its squares
There is naught but lamentation;
For I have broken Moab
Like a vessel no one wants

—declares the LORD.

³⁹ How he is dismayed! Wail!
How Moab has turned his back in shame!
Moab shall be a laughingstock
And a shock to all those near him.

⁴⁰ For thus said the LORD:
See, he soars like an eagle

And spreads out his wings against Moab!
⁴¹ Kerioth shall be captured
And the strongholds shall be seized.
In that day, the heart of Moab's warriors
Shall be like the heart of a woman in travail.
⁴² And Moab shall be destroyed as a people,
For he vaunted himself against the LORD.
⁴³ ᵏ⁻Terror, and pit, and trap⁻ᵏ
Upon you who dwell in Moab!

—declares the LORD.

⁴⁴ He who flees from the terror
Shall fall into the pit;
And he who climbs out of the pit
Shall be caught in the trap.
For I will bring upon Moab
The year of their doom

—declares the LORD.

⁴⁵ In the shelter of Heshbon
Fugitives halt exhausted;
For fire went forth from Heshbon,
Flame from the midstˡ of Sihon,
Consuming the brow of Moab,
The pate of the people of Shaon.ᵐ
⁴⁶ Woe to you, O Moab!
The people of Chemosh are undone,
For your sons are carried off into captivity,
Your daughters into exile.
⁴⁷ But I will restore the fortunes of Moab in the days to come
—declares the LORD.

Thus far is the judgment on Moab.

ᵏ⁻ᵏ *See note at Isa. 24.17.*
ˡ *Emendation yields "house."*
ᵐ *Or "tumult."*

49 Concerning the Ammonites.

Thus said the LORD:
Has Israel no sons,
Has he no heir?
Then why has Milcom*a* dispossessed Gad,
And why have his people settled in Gad's*b* towns?
² Assuredly, days are coming

—declares the LORD—

When I will sound the alarm of war
Against Rabbah of the Ammonites;
It shall become a desolate mound,
And its villages shall be set on fire.
And Israel shall dispossess
Those who dispossessed him

—said the LORD.

³ Howl, O Heshbon, for Ai is ravaged!
Cry out, O daughters of Rabbah!
Gird on sackcloth, lament,
*c-*And run to and fro in the sheepfolds.*-c*
For Milcom shall go into exile,
Together with his priests and attendants.

⁴ *d-*Why do you glory in strength?
Your strength is drained,*-d*
O rebellious daughter,
You who relied on your treasures,
[Who said:] Who dare attack me?
⁵ I am bringing terror upon you

—declares the Lord GOD of Hosts—

From all those around you.
Every one of you shall be driven *e-*in every direction,*-e*
And none shall gather in the fugitives.

a The name of the Ammonite deity; vocalized Malcam here and in v. 3.
b Heb. "his."
c-c Meaning of Heb. uncertain.
d-d Meaning of Heb. uncertain; for "strength" cf. Akkadian emuqu.
e-e Lit. "each man straight ahead."

[6] But afterwards I will restore the fortunes of the Ammonites
—declares the LORD.

[7] Concerning Edom.

Thus said the LORD of Hosts:
Is there no more wisdom in Teman?
Has counsel vanished from the prudent?
Has their wisdom gone stale?
[8] Flee, turn away, sit down low,
O inhabitants of Dedan,
For I am bringing Esau's doom upon him,
The time when I deal with him.
[9] [f-]If vintagers were to come upon you,
Would they leave no gleanings?
Even thieves in the night
Would destroy only for their needs![-f]
[10] But it is I have bared Esau,
Have exposed his place of concealment;
He cannot hide.
His offspring is ravaged,
His kin and his neighbors—
[g-]He is no more.[-g]
[11] "Leave your orphans with me,
I will rear them;
Let your widows rely on me!"

[12] For thus said the LORD: If they who rightly should not drink
of the cup must drink it, are you the one to go unpunished? You
shall not go unpunished: you will have to drink! [13] For by Myself
I swear—declares the LORD—Bozrah shall become a desolation,
a mockery, a ruin, and a curse;[h] and all its towns shall be ruins
for all time.

[14] I have received tidings from the LORD,
And an envoy is sent out among the nations:

[f-f] *Obad. 1.5 reads: "If thieves were to come to you, / Marauders by night, / They would steal no more than they needed. / If vintagers came to you, / They would surely leave some gleanings."*

[g-g] *Some Septuagint mss. read "And there is none to say."*

[h] *Cf. note at 24.9 and 42.18.*

Assemble, and move against her,
And rise up for war!
[15] For I will make you least among nations,
Most despised among men.
[16] *ᶜYour horrible nature,ᶜ*
Your arrogant heart has seduced you,
You who dwell in clefts of the rock,
Who occupy the height of the hill!
Should you nest as high as the eagle,
From there I will pull you down

—declares the LORD.

[17] And Edom shall be a cause of appallment; whoever passes by will be appalled and will hissⁱ at all its wounds. [18] It shall be like the overthrow of Sodom and Gomorrah and their neighbors—said the LORD: no man shall live there, no human shall sojourn there. [19] It shall be as when a lion comes up out of the jungle of the Jordan against a secure pasture: in a moment ʲ⁻I can harry him out of it and appoint over it anyone I choose.⁻ʲ Then who is like Me? Who can summon Me? Who is the shepherd that can stand up against Me? [20] Hear, then, the plan which the LORD has devised against Edom, and what He has purposed against the inhabitants of Teman:

Surely the shepherd boys
Shall drag them away;
Surely the pasture shall be
Aghast because of them.
[21] At the sound of their downfall
The earth shall shake;
The sound of screaming
Shall be heard at the Sea of Reeds.
[22] See, like an eagle he flies up,
He soars and spreads his wings against Bozrah;

ⁱ *Cf. note at 18.16.*
ʲ⁻ʲ *Emendation yields "he can harry them [i.e. the sheep] out of it; and what champion could one place in charge of them?"*

And the heart of Edom's warriors in that day
Shall be like the heart of a woman in travail.

23 Concerning Damascus.

Hamath and Arpad are shamed,
For they have heard bad news.
They shake with anxiety,
Like[k] the sea which cannot rest.
24 Damascus has grown weak,
She has turned around to flee;
Trembling has seized her,
Pain and anguish have taken hold of her,
Like a woman in childbirth.
25 [l]How has the glorious city not been deserted,[l]
The citadel of my joy!
26 Assuredly, her young men shall lie fallen in
    her squares.
And all her warriors shall be stilled in that day
                    —declares the LORD of Hosts.
27 I will set fire to the wall of Damascus,
And it shall consume the fortresses of Ben-hadad.

28 Concerning Kedar and the kingdoms of Hazor, which
    King Nebuchadrezzar of Babylon conquered.

Thus said the LORD:
Arise, march against Kedar,
And ravage the Kedemites!
29 They will take away their tents and their flocks,
Their tent cloths and all their gear;
They shall carry off their camels,
And shall proclaim against them:
Terror all around!

---

[k] *So a few mss. Most mss. and editions read "In."*
[l-l] *Emendation yields "How has the glorious city been deserted"; so Vulgate.*

³⁰ Flee, wander far,
Sit down low, O inhabitants of Hazor

      —says the LORD.

For King Nebuchadrezzar of Babylon
Has devised a plan against you
And formed a purpose against you:
³¹ Rise up, attack a tranquil nation
That dwells secure

      —says the LORD—

That has no barred gates,
That dwells alone.
³² Their camels shall become booty,
And their abundant flocks a spoil;
And I will scatter to every quarter
Those who have their hair clipped;
And from every direction I will bring
Disaster upon them

      —says the LORD.

³³ Hazor shall become a lair of jackals,
A desolation for all time.
No man shall live there,
No human shall sojourn there.

³⁴ The word of the LORD that came to the prophet Jeremiah concerning Elam, at the beginning of the reign of King Zedekiah of Judah:

³⁵ Thus said the LORD of Hosts: I am going to break the bow of Elam, the mainstay of their strength. ³⁶ And I shall bring four winds against Elam from the four quarters of heaven, and scatter them to all those winds. There shall not be a nation to which the fugitives from Elam do not come. ³⁷ And I will break Elam before their enemies, before those who seek their lives; and I will bring disaster upon them, My flaming wrath—declares the LORD. And I will dispatch the sword after them until I have consumed them.

³⁸ And I will set My throne in Elam,
And wipe out from there king and officials
—says the LORD.
³⁹ But in the days to come I will restore the fortunes of Elam
—declares the LORD.

50 The word which the LORD spoke concerning Babylon, concerning the land of the Chaldeans, through the prophet Jeremiah:

² Declare among the nations, and proclaim;
Raise a standard, proclaim;
Hide nothing! Say:
Babylon is captured,
Bel^a is shamed,
Merodach^a is dismayed.
Her idols are shamed,
Her fetishes dismayed.
³ For a nation from the north has attacked her,
It will make her land a desolation.
No one shall dwell in it,
Both man and beast shall wander away.

⁴ In those days and at that time—declares the LORD—the people of Israel together with the people of Judah shall come, and they shall weep as they go to seek the LORD their God. ⁵ They shall inquire for Zion; in that direction their faces shall turn; ^{b-}they shall come^{-b} and attach themselves to the LORD by a covenant for all time, which shall never be forgotten. ⁶ My people were lost sheep: their shepherds led them astray, they drove them out to the mountains, they roamed from mount to hill, they forgot their own resting place. ⁷ All who encountered them devoured them; and their foes said, "We shall not be held guilty,

^a *Names of the city god of Babylon.*
^{b-b} *Heb. "come ye."*

because they have sinned against the LORD, the true Pasture, the Hope of their fathers—the LORD."

⁸ Flee from Babylon,
Leave the land of the Chaldeans,
And be like he-goats that lead the flock!
⁹ For see, I am rousing and leading
An assemblage of great nations against Babylon
From the lands of the north.
They shall draw up their lines against her,
There she shall be captured.
Their arrows are like those of ⸢a skilled warrior⸢
Who does not turn back without hitting the mark.
¹⁰ Chaldea shall be despoiled,
All her spoilers shall be sated

—declares the LORD.

¹¹ For you rejoiced, you exulted,
You who plundered My possession;
You stamped like a heifer treading grain,
You neighed like steeds.
¹² So your mother will be utterly shamed,
She who bore you will be disgraced.
Behold the end of the nations—
Wilderness, desert, and steppe!
¹³ Because of the LORD's wrath she shall not
be inhabited;
She shall be utterly desolate.
Whoever passes by Babylon will be appalled
And will hiss at all her wounds.

¹⁴ Range yourselves round about Babylon,
All you who draw the bow;
Shoot at her, don't spare arrows,
For she has sinned against the LORD.

⸢⸢ *So many mss., editions, and versions; other mss. and editions read "a warrior who bereaves."*

¹⁵ Raise a shout against her all about!
^{d-}She has surrendered;^{-d}
Her bastions have fallen,
Her walls are thrown down—
This is the LORD's vengeance.
Take vengeance on her,
Do to her as she has done!
¹⁶ Make an end in Babylon of sowers,
And of wielders of the sickle at harvest time.
Because of the deadly^e sword,
Each man shall turn back to his people,
They shall flee every one to his land.

¹⁷ Israel are scattered sheep, harried by lions. First the king of Assyria devoured them, and in the end King Nebuchadrezzar of Babylon crunched their bones. ¹⁸ Assuredly, thus said the LORD of Hosts, the God of Israel: I will deal with the king of Babylon and his land as I dealt with the king of Assyria. ¹⁹ And I will lead Israel back to his pasture, and he shall graze in Carmel and Bashan, and eat his fill in the hill country of Ephraim and in Gilead.

²⁰ In those days and at that time

—declares the LORD—
The iniquity of Israel shall be sought,
And there shall be none;
The sins of Judah,
And none shall be found;
For I will pardon those I allow to survive.

²¹ Advance against her—^{e-}the land of Merathaim^{-e}—
And against the inhabitants of Pekod;
Ruin and destroy after them to the last

—says the LORD—
Do just as I have commanded you.

---

^{d-d} *Lit. "She has given her hand"; meaning of Heb. uncertain.*
^e *Meaning of Heb. uncertain.*

²² Hark! War in the land
And vast destruction!
²³ How the hammer of the whole earth
Has been hacked and shattered!
How Babylon has become
An appallment among the nations!
²⁴ I set a snare for you, O Babylon,
And you were trapped unawares;
You were found and caught,
Because you challenged the LORD.
²⁵ The LORD has opened His armory
And brought out the weapons of His wrath;
For that is the task
Of my Lord GOD of Hosts
In the land of the Chaldeans.
²⁶ Come against her ᵉ'from every quarter;⁻ᵉ
Break open her granaries,
ᵉ'Pile her up like heaps of grain,⁻ᵉ
And destroy her, let her have no remnant!
²⁷ ᶠ'Destroy all⁻ᶠ her bulls,
Let them go down to slaughter.
Alas for them, their day is come,
The hour of their doom!
²⁸ Hark! fugitives are escaping
From the land of Babylon,
To tell in Zion of the vengeance of the LORD our God,
Vengeance for His Temple.

²⁹ Summon archers against Babylon,
All who draw the bow!
Encamp against her round about,
Let none of her people escape.
Pay her back for her actions,
Do to her just what she has done;
For she has acted insolently against the LORD,

ᶠ⁻ᶠ *Emendation yields "A sword against"; cf. vv. 35 ff.*

643

The Holy One of Israel.
³⁰ Assuredly, her young men shall fall in her squares,
And all her warriors shall perish in that day
—declares the LORD.
³¹ I am going to deal with you, O Insolence
—declares the Lord GOD of Hosts—
For your day is come, the time when I doom you:
³² Insolence shall stumble and fall,
With none to raise her up.
I will set her cities on fire,
And it shall consume everything around her.

³³ Thus said the LORD of Hosts:
The people of Israel are oppressed,
And so too the people of Judah;
All their captors held them,
They refused to let them go.
³⁴ Their Redeemer is mighty,
His name is LORD of Hosts.
He will champion their cause—
So as to give rest to the earth,
And unrest to the inhabitants of Babylon.

³⁵ A sword against the Chaldeans
—declares the LORD—
And against the inhabitants of Babylon,
Against its officials and its wise men!
³⁶ A sword against the diviners, that they be made fools of!
A sword against the warriors, that they be dismayed!
³⁷ A sword against its horses and chariots,
And against all the motley crowd in its midst,
That they become like women!
A sword against its treasuries, that they be pillaged!
³⁸ A drought^g against its waters, that they be dried up!
For it is a land of idols;

^g Horeb, *play on* hereb, *"sword" in preceding verses.*

They are besotted by their *-dread images.-*
³⁹ Assuredly,
-Wildcats and hyenas- shall dwell [there],
And ostriches shall dwell there;
It shall never be settled again,
Nor inhabited throughout the ages.

⁴⁰ It shall be as when God overthrew Sodom and Gomorrah and their neighbors—declares the LORD; no man shall live there, no human shall sojourn there.

⁴¹ Lo, a people comes from the northland;
A great nation and many kings are roused
From the remotest parts of the earth.
⁴² They grasp the bow and javelin,
They are cruel, they show no mercy;
The sound of them is like the roaring sea.
They ride upon horses,
Accoutered like a man for battle,
Against you, O Fair Babylon!
⁴³ The king of Babylon has heard the report of them,
And his hands are weakened;
Anguish seizes him,
Pangs like a woman in childbirth.
⁴⁴ It shall be as when a lion comes out of the jungle of the Jordan against a secure pasture: in a moment *ʰ-I can harry them out of it and appoint over it anyone I choose.-ʰ* Then who is like Me? Who can summon Me? Who is the shepherd that can stand up against Me? ⁴⁵ Hear, then, the plan which the LORD has devised against Babylon, and has purposed against the land of Chaldea:
Surely the shepherd boys
Shall drag them away;
Surely the pasture shall be
Aghast because of them.

ʰ-ʰ *See note at 49.19.*

⁴⁶ At the sound of Babylon's capture
The earth quakes,
And an outcry is heard among the nations.

51

Thus said the LORD:
See, I am rousing a destructive wind
Against Babylon and the inhabitants of Leb-kamai.ᵃ
² I will send strangersᵇ against Babylon, and they
    shall winnow her.
And they shall strip her land bare;
They shall beset her on all sides
On the day of disaster.
³ Letᶜ the archer draw his bow,
And let him stand ready in his coat of mail!
Show no pity to her young men,
Wipe out all her host!
⁴ Let them fall slain in the land of Chaldea,
Pierced through in her streets.

⁵ For Israel and Judah were not bereftᵈ
Of their God the LORD of Hosts,
But their land was filled with guilt
Before the Holy One of Israel.

⁶ Flee from the midst of Babylon
And save your lives, every one of you!
Do not perish for her iniquity;
For this is a time of vengeance for the LORD,
He will deal retribution to her.

⁷ Babylon was a golden cup in the LORD's hand,
It made the whole earth drunk;
The nations drank of her wine—
That is why the nations are mad.

ᵃ *A cipher for* Kasdim, *"Chaldea".*
ᵇ *Change of vocalization yields "winnowers."*
ᶜ *Some Heb mss. and ancient versions read "Let not" here and in next line.*
ᵈ *Lit. "widowed."*

⁸ Suddenly Babylon has fallen and is shattered;
Howl over her!
Get balm for her wounds:
Perhaps she can be healed.
⁹ We tried to cure Babylon
But she was incurable.
Let us leave her and go,
Each to his own land;
For her punishment reaches to heaven,
It is as high as the sky.
¹⁰ The Lord has proclaimed our vindication;
Come, let us recount in Zion
The deeds of the Lord our God.

¹¹ Polish the arrows,
Fill the quivers!
The Lord has roused the spirit of the kings of Media,
For His plan against Babylon is to destroy her.
This is the vengeance of the Lord,
Vengeance for His Temple.

¹² Raise a standard against the walls of Babylon!
Set up a blockade; station watchmen;
Prepare those in ambush.
For the Lord has both planned and performed
What He decreed against the inhabitants of Babylon.

¹³ O you who dwell by great waters,
With vast storehouses,
Your time is come, ᵉ⁻the hour of your end.⁻ᵉ
¹⁴ The Lord of Hosts has sworn by Himself:
I will fill you with men like a locust swarm,
They will raise a shout against you.

ᵉ⁻ᵉ *Meaning of Heb. uncertain.*

15 He made the earth by His might,
Established the world by His wisdom,
And by His understanding stretched out the skies.
16 /-When He makes His voice heard,-/
There is a rumbling of waters in the skies;
He makes vapors rise from the end of the earth,
He makes lightning for the rain,
And brings forth wind from His treasuries.
17 Every man is proved dull, without knowledge;
Every goldsmith is put to shame because of the idol,
For his molten image is a deceit—
There is no breath in them.
18 They are delusion, a work of mockery;
In their hour of doom, they shall perish.
19 Not like these is the Portion of Jacob,
For it is He who formed all things;
And [Israel is] His very own tribe.
LORD of Hosts is His name.

20 You are My war club, [My] weapons of battle;
With you I clubbed nations,
With you I destroyed kingdoms;
21 With you I clubbed horse and rider,
With you I clubbed chariot and driver,
22 With you I clubbed man and woman,
With you I clubbed graybeard and boy,
With you I clubbed youth and maiden;
23 With you I clubbed shepherd and flock,
With you I clubbed plowman and team,
With you I clubbed governors and prefects.
24 But I will requite Babylon and all the inhabitants
    of Chaldea
For all the wicked things they did to Zion before
    your eyes
                                        —declares the LORD.

f-f Lit. "At the sound of His making."

25 See, I will deal with you, O mountain of the destroyer
$\qquad$ —declares the LORD—
Destroyer of the whole earth!
I will stretch out My hand against you
And roll you down from the crags,
And make you a burnt-out mountain.
26 They shall never take from you
A cornerstone or foundation stone;
You shall be a desolation for all time
$\qquad$ —declares the LORD.
27 Raise a standard on earth,
Sound a horn among the nations,
Appoint nations against her,
Assemble kingdoms against her—
Ararat, Minni, and Ashkenaz—
Designate a marshal against her,
Bring up horses like swarming[e] locusts!
28 Appoint nations for war against her—
The kings of Media,
Her governors and all her prefects,
And all the lands they rule!

29 Then the earth quakes and writhes,
For the LORD's purpose is fulfilled against Babylon,
To make the land of Babylon
A waste without inhabitant.
30 The warriors of Babylon stop fighting,
They sit in the strongholds,
Their might is dried up,
They become women.
Her dwellings are set afire,
Her bars are broken.
31 Runner dashes to meet runner,
Messenger to meet messenger,
To report to the king of Babylon

That his city is captured, from end to end.
³² The fords are captured,
And the swamp thickets*ᵉ* are consumed in fire;
And the fighting men are in panic.

³³ For thus said the LORD of Hosts, the God of Israel:
Fair Babylon is like a threshing floor
Ready to be trodden;
In a little while her harvest time will come.

³⁴ "Nebuchadrezzar king of Babylon
Devoured me and discomfited me;
He swallowed me like a dragon,
He filled his belly with my dainties,
And set me down like an empty dish;
Then he *ᵉ*ʳinsed me out.ᵗᵉ
³⁵ Let the violence done me and my kindred
Be upon Babylon,"
Says the inhabitant of Zion;
"And let my blood be upon the inhabitants
of Chaldea,"
Says Jerusalem.

³⁶ Assuredly, thus said the LORD:
I am going to uphold your cause
And take vengeance for you;
I will dry up her sea
And make her fountain run dry.
³⁷ Babylon shall become rubble,
A den for jackals,
An object of horror and hissing,ᵍ
Without inhabitant.
³⁸ Like lions, they roar together,
They growl like lion cubs.
³⁹ ʰ⁻When they are heated, I will set out their drink

ᵍ *See note at 18.16.*

And get them drunk, that they may become hilarious[-h]
And then sleep an endless sleep,
Never to awake

—declares the LORD.

[40] I will lead them like lambs to slaughter,
Like rams and he-goats.
[41] How has Sheshach[i] been captured,
The praise of the whole earth been taken!
How has Babylon become
A horror to the nations!
[42] The sea has risen over Babylon,
She is covered by its roaring waves.
[43] Her towns are a desolation,
A land of desert and steppe,
A land that no man lives in
And no human passes through.
[44] And I will deal with Bel in Babylon,
And make him disgorge what he has swallowed,
And nations shall no more gaze on him with joy.
Even the wall of Babylon shall fall.

[45] Depart from there, O My people,
Save your lives, each of you,
From the furious anger of the LORD.
[46] Do not be downhearted or afraid
At the rumors heard in the land:
A rumor will come one year,
And another rumor the next year
Of violence in the land,
And of ruler against ruler.
[47] Assuredly, days are coming,
When I will deal with Babylon's images;
Her whole land shall be shamed,
And all her slain shall fall in her midst.
[48] Heavens and earth and all that is in them

[h-h] *Emendation yields "With poison (so Syriac) will I set out their drink / And get them drunk till they fall unconscious" (so ancient versions).*
[i] *See note at 25.26.*

Shall shout over Babylon;
For the ravagers shall come upon her from the north
—declares the LORD.
⁴⁹ Yes, Babylon is to fall
[For] the slain of Israel,
As the slain of all the earth
Have fallen through Babylon.

⁵⁰ You fugitives from the sword,
Go, don't delay!
Remember the LORD from afar,
And call Jerusalem to mind.
⁵¹ "We were shamed, we heard taunts;
Humiliation covered our faces,
When aliens entered
The sacred areas of the LORD's House."
⁵² Assuredly, days are coming
—declares the LORD—
When I will deal with her images,
And throughout her land the dying shall groan.
⁵³ Though Babylon should climb to the skies,
Though she fortify her strongholds up to heaven,
The ravagers would come against her from Me
—declares the LORD.

⁵⁴ Hark! an outcry from Babylon,
Great destruction from the land of the Chaldeans.
⁵⁵ For the LORD is ravaging Babylon;
He will put an end to her great din,
Whose roar is like waves of mighty waters,
Whose tumultuous noise resounds.
⁵⁶ For a ravager is coming upon Babylon,
Her warriors shall be captured, their bows shall
be snapped.
For the LORD is a God of requital,

He deals retribution.
⁵⁷ I will make her officials and wise men drunk,
Her governors and prefects and warriors;
And they shall sleep an endless sleep,
Never to awaken
            —declares the King whose name is LORD of Hosts.
⁵⁸ Thus said the LORD of Hosts:
Babylon's broad wall shall be knocked down,
And her high gates set afire.
Peoples shall labor for naught,
And nations have wearied themselves for fire.

⁵⁹ The instructions which the prophet Jeremiah gave to Seraiah son of Neriah son of Mahseiah, when the latter went with*ʲ* King Zedekiah of Judah to Babylonia, in the fourth year of [Zedekiah's] reign. Seraiah was quartermaster.*ᵉ* ⁶⁰ Jeremiah wrote down in one scroll all the disaster that would come upon Babylon, all these things which are written concerning Babylon. ⁶¹ And Jeremiah said to Seraiah, "When you get to Babylon, see that you read out all these words. ⁶² And say, 'O LORD, You Yourself have declared concerning this place that it shall be cut off, without inhabitant, man or beast; that it shall be a desolation for all time.' ⁶³ And when you finish reading this scroll, tie a stone to it and hurl it into the Euphrates. ⁶⁴ And say, 'Thus shall Babylon sink and never rise again, because of the disaster which I will bring upon it. And [nations] shall have wearied themselves [for fire].' "*ᵏ*

Thus far the words of Jeremiah.

52 *ᵃ*Zedekiah was twenty-one years old when he became king, and he reigned in Jerusalem for eleven years. His mother's name was Hamutal, daughter of Jeremiah of Libnah. ² He did what was displeasing to the LORD, just as Jehoiakim had done. ³ In-

ʲ *Emendation yields "at the instance of."*
ᵏ *Cf. v. 58, last line.*

ᵃ *For this chapter cf. chapter 39 above and II Kings 24-25.*

deed, Jerusalem and Judah *b*-were a cause of anger for the LORD, so that*-b* He cast them out of His presence.

Zedekiah rebelled against the king of Babylon. 4 And in the ninth year of his*c* reign, on the tenth day of the tenth month, King Nebuchadrezzar moved against Jerusalem with his whole army. They besieged it and built towers against it all around. 5 The city continued in a state of siege until the eleventh year of King Zedekiah. 6 By the ninth day of the fourth month, the famine had become acute in the city; there was no food left for the common people.

7 Then [the wall of] the city was breached. All the soldiers fled; they left the city by night through the gate between the double walls, which is near the king's garden—the Chaldeans were all around the city—and they set out for the Arabah.*d* 8 But the Chaldean troops pursued the king, and they overtook Zedekiah in the steppes of Jericho, as his entire force left him and scattered. 9 They captured the king and brought him before the king of Babylon at Riblah, in the region of Hamath; and he put him on trial. 10 The king of Babylon had Zedekiah's sons slaughtered before his eyes; he also had all the officials of Judah slaughtered at Riblah. 11 Then the eyes of Zedekiah were put out, and he was chained in bronze fetters. The king of Babylon brought him to Babylon and put him in prison, [where he remained] to the day of his death.

12 On the tenth day of the fifth month—that was the nineteenth year of King Nebuchadrezzar, the king of Babylon—Nebuzaradan, the chief of the guards, came *e*-to represent*-e* the king of Babylon in Jerusalem. 13 He burned the House of the LORD, the king's palace, and all the houses of Jerusalem; he burned down the house of *b*-every notable person.*-b* 14 The entire Chaldean force that was with the chief of the guards tore down all the walls of Jerusalem on every side. 15 The remnant of the people left in the city, the defectors who had gone over to the king of Babylon, and what remained of the craftsmen*f* were taken into exile by

b-b *Meaning of Heb. uncertain.*
c *I.e. Zedekiah's.*
d *See note at 39.4.*
e-e *Lit. "he stood before."*
f *Apparently after the deportation of II Kings 24.14; meaning of Heb. uncertain.*

Nebuzaradan, the chief of the guards. But some of the poorest elements of the population—[16] some of the poorest in the land —were left by Nebuzaradan, the chief of the guards, to be vine-dressers and field hands.

[17] The Chaldeans broke up the bronze columns of the House of the LORD, the stands, and the bronze tank that was in the House of the LORD; and they carried all the bronze away to Babylon. [18] They also took the pails, scrapers, snuffers, sprinkling bowls, ladles, and all the other bronze vessels used in the service. [19] The chief of the guards took whatever was of gold and whatever was of silver: basins, fire pans, sprinkling bowls, pails, lamp-stands, ladles, and jars. [20] The two columns, the one tank and the twelve bronze oxen which supported it, and the stands, which King Solomon had provided for the House of the LORD—all these objects contained bronze beyond weighing. [21] As for the columns, each was eighteen cubits high and twelve cubits in circumference; it was hollow, and [the metal] was four fingers thick. [22] It had a bronze capital above it; the height of each capital was five cubits, and there was a meshwork [decorated] with pomegranates about the capital, all made of bronze; and so for the second column, also with pomegranates. [23] There were ninety-six pomegranates *b*-facing outward;-*b* all the pomegranates around the meshwork amounted to one hundred.

[24] The chief of the guards also took Seraiah the chief priest and Zephaniah the deputy priest, and the three guardians of the threshold. [25] And from the city he took a eunuch who was in command of the soldiers; seven royal privy councilors, who were present in the city; the scribe of the army commander, who was in charge of mustering the people of the land; and sixty of the common people who were inside the city. [26] Nebuzaradan, the chief of the guards, took them and brought them to the king of Babylon at Riblah. [27] The king of Babylon had them struck down and put to death at Riblah, in the region of Hamath.

Thus Judah was exiled from its land. [28] This is the number of those whom Nebuchadrezzar exiled in the seventh year: 3,023 Judeans. [29] In the eighteenth year of Nebuchadrezzar, 832 persons [were exiled] from Jerusalem. [30] And in the twenty-third year of Nebuchadrezzar, Nebuzaradan, the chief of the guards, exiled 745 Judeans. The total came to 4,600 persons.

[31] In the thirty-seventh year of the exile of King Jehoiachin of Judah, on the twenty-fifth day of the twelfth month, King Evil-merodach of Babylon, in the year he became king, [g-]took note of[-g] King Jehoiachin of Judah and released him from prison. [32] He spoke kindly to him, and gave him a throne above those of other kings who were with him in Babylon. [33] He removed his prison garments and [Jehoiachim] ate regularly in his presence the rest of his life. [34] A regular allotment of food was given him by order of the king of Babylon, an allotment for each day, to the day of his death—all the days of his life.

g-g *Lit. "raised the head of."*

יחזקאל

EZEKIEL

יחזקאל

EZEKIEL

1

In the thirtieth year,*a* on the fifth day of the fourth month, when I was in the community of exiles by the Chebar Canal, the heavens opened and I saw visions of God. ² On the fifth day of the month—it was the fifth year of the exile of King Jehoiachin—³ the word of the LORD came to the priest Ezekiel son of Buzi, by the Chebar Canal, in the land of the Chaldeans. And the hand of the LORD came upon him there.

⁴ I looked, and lo, a stormy wind came sweeping out of the north—a huge cloud and flashing fire, surrounded by a radiance; and in the center of it, in the center of the fire, a gleam as of amber. ⁵ In the center of it were also the figures of four creatures. And this was their appearance:

They had the figures of human beings. ⁶ However, each had four faces, and each of them had four wings; ⁷ the legs of each were [fused into] a single rigid leg, and the feet of each were like a single calf's hoof;*b* and their sparkle*c* was like the luster of burnished bronze. ⁸ They had human hands below their wings. The four of them had their faces and their wings on their four sides. ⁹ Each one's wings touched those of the other. They did not turn when they moved; each could move in the direction of any of its faces.

¹⁰ Each of them had a human face [at the front]; each of the four had the face of a lion on the right; each of the four had the face of an ox on the left; and each of the four had the face of an eagle [at the back]. ¹¹ Such were their faces. As for their wings, they were separated: above, each had two touching those of the others, while the other two covered its body. ¹² And each could move

---

a We do not know the 30th of what.
b I.e. cleft in front.
c Or "plumage."

in the direction of any of its faces; they went wherever the spirit impelled them to go, without turning when they moved.

¹³ Such then was the appearance of the creatures. With them was something that looked like burning coals of fire. This fire, suggestive of torches, kept moving about among the creatures; the fire had a radiance, and lightning issued from the fire. ¹⁴ ^dDashing to and fro [among] the creatures was something that looked like flares.^{-d}

¹⁵ As I gazed on the creatures, I saw one wheel on the ground next to each of the four-faced creatures. ¹⁶ As for the appearance and structure of the wheels, they gleamed like beryl. All four had the same form; the appearance and structure of each was as of two wheels cutting through each other. ¹⁷ And when they moved, each could move in the direction of any of its four quarters; they did not veer when they moved. ¹⁸ Their rims were tall and frightening, for the rims of all four were covered all over with eyes. ¹⁹ And when the creatures moved forward, the wheels moved at their sides; and when the creatures were borne above the earth, the wheels were borne too. ²⁰ Wherever the spirit impelled them to go, they went—wherever the spirit impelled them—and the wheels were borne alongside them; for the spirit of the creatures was in the wheels. ²¹ When those moved, these moved; and when those stood still, these stood still; and when those were borne above the earth, the wheels were borne alongside them—for the spirit of the creatures was in the wheels.

²² Above the heads of the creatures was a form: an expanse, with an awe-inspiring gleam as of crystal, was spread out above their heads. ²³ Under the expanse, each had one pair of wings extended toward those of the others; and each had another pair covering its body. ²⁴ When they moved, I could hear the sound of their wings like the sound of mighty waters, like the sound of Shaddai,^e a tumult like the din of an army. When they stood still, they would let their wings droop. ²⁵ ^dFrom above the expanse over their heads came a sound.^{-d} When they stood still, they would let their wings droop.

d-d *Meaning of Heb. uncertain.*
e *Traditionally "the Almighty"; see Gen. 17.1.*

²⁶ Above the expanse over their heads was the semblance of a throne, in appearance like sapphire; and on top, upon this semblance of a throne, there was the semblance of a human form. ²⁷ From what appeared as his loins up, I saw a gleam as of amber —*ᵈ*what looked like a fire encased in a frame;*⁻ᵈ* and from what appeared as his loins down, I saw what looked like fire. There was a radiance all about him. ²⁸ Like the appearance of the bow which shines in the clouds on a day of rain, such was the appearance of the surrounding radiance. That was the appearance of the semblance of the Presence of the LORD. When I beheld it, I flung myself down on my face. And I heard the voice of someone speaking.

2 And He said to me, "O mortal, stand up on your feet that I may speak to you." ² As He spoke to me, a spirit entered into me and set me upon my feet; and I heard what was being spoken to me. ³ He said to me, "O mortal, I am sending you to the people of Israel, that nation of rebels, who have rebelled against Me.— They as well as their fathers have defied Me to this very day; ⁴ for the sons are brazen of face and stubborn of heart. I send you to them, and you shall say to them: 'Thus said the Lord GOD'— ⁵ whether they listen or not, for they are a rebellious breed—that they may know that there was a prophet among them.

⁶ "And you, mortal, do not fear them and do not fear their words, though thistles and thorns *ᵃ*press against*⁻ᵃ* you, and you sit upon scorpions. Do not be afraid of their words and do not be dismayed by them, though they are a rebellious breed; ⁷ but speak My words to them, whether they listen or not, for they are rebellious.

⁸ "And you, mortal, heed what I say to you: Do not be rebellious like that rebellious breed. Open your mouth and eat what I am giving you." ⁹ As I looked, there was a hand stretched out to me, holding a written scroll. ¹⁰ He unrolled it before me, and it was inscribed on both the front and the back; on it were written lamentations, dirges, and woes.

ᵃ⁻ᵃ *Lit. "are with."*

3 He said to me, "Mortal, eat what is offered you; eat this scroll, and go speak to the House of Israel." ² So I opened my mouth, and He gave me this scroll to eat, ³ as He said to me, "Mortal, feed your stomach and fill your belly with this scroll that I give you." I ate it, and it tasted as sweet as honey to me.

⁴ Then He said to me, "Mortal, go to the House of Israel and repeat My very words to them. ⁵ For you are sent, not to a people of unintelligible speech and difficult language, but to the House of Israel—⁶ not to the many peoples of unintelligible speech and difficult language, whose talk you cannot understand. If I sent you to them, they would listen to you. ⁷ But the House of Israel will refuse to listen to you, for they refuse to listen to Me; for the whole House of Israel are brazen of forehead and stubborn of heart. ⁸ But I will make your face as hard as theirs, and your forehead as brazen as theirs. ⁹ I will make your forehead like adamant, harder than flint. Do not fear them, and do not be dismayed by them, though they are a rebellious breed."

¹⁰ Then He said to me: "Mortal, listen with your ears and receive into your mind all the words that I speak to you. ¹¹ Go to your people, the exile community, and speak to them. Say to them: Thus says the Lord GOD—whether they listen or not." ¹² Then a spirit carried me away, and behind me I heard a great roaring sound: *ᵃ*-"Blessed is the Presence of the LORD, in His place,"*⁻ᵃ* ¹³ with the sound of the wings of the creatures beating against one another, and the sound of the wheels beside them —a great roaring sound. ¹⁴ A spirit seized me and carried me away. I went in bitterness, in the fury of my spirit, while the hand of the LORD was strong upon me. ¹⁵ And I came to the exile community that dwelt in Tel Abib by the Chebar Canal, and I remained where they dwelt. And for seven days I sat there stunned among them.

¹⁶ After those seven days, the word of the LORD came to me: ¹⁷ "O mortal, I appoint you watchman for the House of Israel;

ᵃ⁻ᵃ *Emendation yields "as the Presence of the LORD rose from where it stood."*

and when you hear a word from My mouth, you must warn them for Me. [18] If I say to a wicked man, 'You shall die,' and you do not warn him—you do not speak to warn the wicked man of his wicked course in order to save his life—he, the wicked man, shall die for his iniquity, but I will require a reckoning for his blood from you. [19] But if you do warn the wicked man, and he does not turn back from his wickedness and his wicked course, he shall die for his iniquity, but you will have saved your own life. [20] Again, if a righteous man abandons his righteousness and does wrong, when I put a stumbling block before him, he shall die. He shall die for his sins; the righteous deeds that he did shall not be remembered; but because you did not warn him, I will require a reckoning for his blood from you. [21] If, however, you warn the righteous man not to sin, and he, the righteous, does not sin, he shall live because he took warning, and you will have saved your own life."

[22] Then the hand of the LORD came upon me there, and He said to me, "Arise, go out to the valley, and there I will speak with you." [23] I arose and went out to the valley, and there stood the Presence of the LORD, like the Presence that I had seen at the Chebar Canal; and I flung myself down on my face. [24] And a spirit entered into me and set me upon my feet. And He spoke to me, and said to me: "Go, shut yourself up in your house. [25] As for you, O mortal, cords have been placed upon you, and you have been bound with them, and you shall not go out among them.[b] [26] And I will make your tongue cleave to your palate, and you shall be dumb; you shall not be a reprover to them, for they are a rebellious breed. [27] But when I speak with you, I will open your mouth, and you shall say to them, 'Thus says the Lord GOD!' He who listens will listen, and he who does not will not—for they are a rebellious breed."

[b] *I.e. the people.*

4 "And you, O mortal, take a brick and put it in front of you, and incise on it a city, Jerusalem. ² Set up a siege against it, and build towers against it, and cast a mound against it; pitch camps against it, and bring up battering rams round about it. ³ Then take an iron plate and place it as an iron wall between yourself and the city, and set your face against it.ᵃ Thus it shall be under siege, you shall besiege it. This shall be an omen for the House of Israel.

⁴ "Then lie on your left side, and let it bear the punishment of the House of Israel;ᵇ for as many days as you lie on it you shall bear their punishment. ⁵ For I impose upon you three hundred and ninety days, corresponding to the number of the years of their punishment; and so you shall bear the punishment for the House of Israel. ⁶ When you have completed these, you shall lie another forty days on your right side, and bear the punishment of the House of Judah.ᵇ I impose on you one day for each year.

⁷ "Then, with bared arm, set your face toward besieged Jerusalem and prophesy against it. ⁸ Now I put cords upon you, so that you cannot turn from side to side until you complete your days of siege.

⁹ "Further, take wheat, barley, beans, lentils, millet, and emmer. Put them into one vessel and bake them into bread. Eat it as many days as you lie on your side: three hundred and ninety. ¹⁰ The food that you eat shall be by weight, twenty shekels a day; this you shall eat in the space of a day. ¹¹ And you shall drink water by measure; drink a sixth of a hin in the space of a day.

¹² "Eat it as a barleyᶜ cake; you shall bake it on human excrement before their eyes. ¹³ So," said the LORD, "shall the people of Israel eat their bread, unclean, among the nations to which I will banish them." ¹⁴ Then I said, "Ah, Lord GOD, my person was never defiled; nor have I eaten anything that died of itself or was torn by beasts from my youth until now, nor has foul flesh entered my mouth." ¹⁵ He answered me, "See, I allow you cow's

ᵃ *I.e. in hostility.*
ᵇ *Since left and right also denote north and south (e.g. 16.46), the left side represents Israel, the northern kingdom, and the right side Judah, the southern kingdom.*
ᶜ *Meaning of Heb. uncertain.*

dung instead of human excrement; prepare your bread on that."
¹⁶ ^dAnd He said to me, "O mortal, I am going to break the staff
of bread in Jerusalem, and they shall eat bread by weight, in
anxiety, and drink water by measure, in horror, ¹⁷ so that, lacking
bread and water, they shall stare at each other, heartsick over
their iniquity. ¹ "And you, O mortal, take a sharp knife; use
it as a barber's razor and pass it over your head and beard.
Then take scales and divide the hair.^a ² When the days of siege
are completed, destroy a third part in fire in the city, take a third
and strike it with the sword all around ^{b-}the city,^{-b} and scatter a
third to the wind and unsheathe^c a sword after them.

³ "Take also a few [hairs] from there and tie them up in your
skirts. ⁴ And take some more of them and cast them into the fire,
and burn them in the fire. From this a fire shall go out upon the
whole House of Israel."

⁵ Thus said the Lord God: I set this Jerusalem in the midst of
nations, with countries round about her. ⁶ But she rebelled
against My rules and My laws, acting more wickedly than the
nations and the countries round about her; she^d rejected My rules
and disobeyed My laws. ⁷ Assuredly, thus said the Lord God:
Because you have outdone the nations that are round about you
—you have not obeyed My laws or followed My rules, nor have
you observed the rules of the nations round about you—⁸ assuredly, thus said the Lord God: I, in turn, am going to deal with
you, and I will execute judgments in your midst in the sight of
the nations. ⁹ On account of all your abominations, I will do
among you what I have never done, and the like of which I will
never do again.

¹⁰ Assuredly, parents shall eat their children in your midst,
and children shall eat their parents. I will execute judgments
against you, and I will scatter all your survivors in every direction.

¹¹ Assuredly, as I live—said the Lord God—because you defiled
My Sanctuary with all your detestable things and all your abomi-

^d *Resuming the thought of v.11.*

^a *Lit. "them."*
^{b-b} *Heb. "it."*
^c *Cf. v. 12; lit. "I will unsheathe."*
^d *Heb. "they."*

nations, I in turn will shear [you] away[e] and show no pity. I in turn will show no compassion: [12] One third of you shall die of pestilence or perish in your midst by famine, one third shall fall by the sword around you, and I will scatter one third in every direction and will unsheathe the sword after them. [13] I will vent all My anger and satisfy My fury upon them; and when I vent all My fury upon them, they shall know that I the LORD have spoken in My passion. [14] I will make you a ruin and a mockery among the nations round about you, in the sight of every passerby. [15] And when I execute judgment upon you in anger and rage and furious chastisement, you[f] shall be a mockery and a derision, a warning and a horror, to the nations round about you: I the LORD have spoken. [16] When I loose the deadly arrows of famine against those doomed to destruction, when I loose them against you to destroy you, I will heap more famine upon you and break your staff of bread. [17] I will let loose against you famine and wild beasts and they shall bereave you; pestilence and bloodshed shall sweep through you, and I will bring the sword upon you. I the LORD have spoken.

6 The word of the LORD came to me: [2] O mortal, turn your face toward the mountains of Israel and prophesy to them [3] and say: O mountains of Israel, hear the word of the Lord GOD. Thus said the Lord GOD to the mountains and the hills, to the streams and the valleys: See, I will bring a sword against you and destroy your shrines. [4] Your altars shall be wrecked and your incense stands smashed, and I will hurl down your slain in front of your fetishes. [5] I will cast the corpses of the people of Israel in front of their fetishes, and scatter your bones around your altars [6] in all your settlements. The towns shall be laid waste and the shrines shall be devastated. Thus your altars shall be laid waste and [a-]bear their punishment;[-a] your fetishes shall be smashed and annihilated, your incense stands cut down, and your handiwork wiped out; [7] and the slain shall fall in your midst. Then you shall know that

---

[e] Cf. Isa. 15.2 and Jer. 48.37; here an allusion to the symbolism in v.1.
[f] Heb. "she."

[a-a] Targum and other ancient versions read "shall be devastated."

I am the LORD. [8] Yet I will leave a remnant, in that some of you shall escape the sword among the nations and be scattered through the lands. [9] And those of you that escape will remember Me among the nations where they have been taken captive, [b]how I was brokenhearted through[b] their faithless hearts which turned away from Me, and through their eyes which lusted after their fetishes. And they shall loathe themselves for all the evil they committed and for all their abominable deeds. [10] Then they shall realize it was not without cause that I the LORD resolved to bring this evil upon them.

[11] Thus said the Lord GOD: Strike your hands together and stamp your feet and cry: Aha! over all the vile abominations of the House of Israel who shall fall by the sword, by famine, and by pestilence. [12] He who is far away shall die of pestilence, and he who is near shall fall by the sword, and he who survives and is protected shall die of famine. Thus I will spend My fury upon them. [13] And you shall know that I am the LORD, when your slain lie among the fetishes round about their altars, on every high hill, on all the mountaintops, under every green tree, and under every leafy oak—wherever they presented pleasing odors to all their fetishes.

[14] I will stretch out My hand against them, and lay the land waste and desolate in all their settlements, from the wilderness as far as Diblah;[c] then they shall know that I am the LORD.

7 The word of the LORD came to me: [2] You, O mortal, [say:] Thus said the Lord GOD to the land of Israel: Doom! Doom is coming upon the four corners of the land. [3] Now doom is upon you! I will let loose My anger against you and judge you according to your ways; I will requite you for all your abominations. [4] I will show you no pity and no compassion; but I will requite you for your ways and for the abominations in your midst. And you shall know that I am the LORD.

[5] Thus said the Lord GOD: [a]A singular disaster; a disaster[a] is

b-b *Emendation yields "how I broke."*
c *A few Heb. mss. read "Riblah"; cf. II Kings 23.33; 25.6 ff.*
a-a *A number of mss. and editions, as well as Targum, read "disaster after disaster."*

coming. [6] Doom is coming! The hour of doom is coming! It stirs against you; there it comes! [7] [b-]The cycle has come around for you, O inhabitants of the land; the time has come; the day is near. There is panic on the mountains, not joy.[-b] [8] Very soon I will pour out My wrath upon you and spend My anger on you; I will judge you according to your ways, and I will requite you for all your abominations. [9] I will show you no pity and no compassion; but I will requite you for your ways, and for the abominations in your midst. And you shall know it was I the LORD who punished.

[10] Here is the day! See, the [b-]cycle has come round; it has appeared. The rod has blossomed; arrogance has budded, [11] lawlessness has grown into a rod of wickedness. Nothing comes of them, nor of their abundance, nor of their wealth; nor is there preeminence among them.[-b] [12] The time has come, the day has arrived. Let not the buyer rejoice nor the seller mourn—for divine wrath shall overtake all her multitude. [13] For the seller shall not return to what he sold so long as they remain among the living. For the vision concerns all her multitude, it shall not be revoked. And because of his guilt, no man shall hold fast to his life.

[14] They have sounded the horn, and all is prepared; but no one goes to battle, for My wrath is directed against all her multitude. [15] The sword is outside and pestilence and famine are inside; he who is in the open shall die by the sword, he who is in the town shall be devoured by famine and pestilence. [16] And if any survive, they shall take to the mountains; they shall be [c-]like doves of the valley, moaning together[-c]—everyone for his iniquity. [17] All hands shall grow weak, and all knees shall turn to water. [18] They shall gird on sackcloth, and horror shall cover them; every face shall betray shame, and every head shall be made bald.

[19] They shall throw their silver into the streets, and their gold shall be treated as something unclean. Their silver and gold shall not avail to save them in the day of the LORD's wrath—to satisfy their hunger or to fill their stomachs. Because they made them stumble into guilt—[20] for out of their beautiful adornments, in

---

[b-b] *Meaning of Heb. uncertain.*
[c-c] *Emendation yields "like moaning doves. All of them shall perish."*

which they took pride, they made their images and their detestable abominations—therefore I will make them*d* an unclean thing to them. 21 I will give them as spoil to strangers, and as plunder to the wicked of the earth; and they shall defile them. 22 I will turn My face from them, and My treasures shall be defiled; ruffians shall invade it and defile it.

23 *b-*Forge the chain,*-b* for the land is full of bloody crimes, and the city is full of lawlessness. 24 I will bring in the worst of the nations to take possession of their houses; so shall I turn to naught the pride of the powerful, and their sanctuaries shall be defiled.

25 Horror*b* comes, and they shall seek safety, but there shall be none. 26 Calamity shall follow calamity, and rumor follow rumor. Then they shall seek vision from the prophet in vain; instruction shall perish from the priest, and counsel from the elders. 27 The king shall mourn, the prince shall clothe himself with desolation, and the hands of the people of the land shall tremble. I will treat them in accordance with their own ways and judge them according to their deserts. And they shall know that I am the LORD.

8 In the sixth year, on the fifth day of the sixth month, I was sitting at home, and the elders of Judah were sitting before me, and there the hand of the Lord GOD fell upon me. 2 As I looked, there was a figure which had the appearance of fire:*a* from what appeared as his loins down, [he was] fire; and from his loins up, his appearance was resplendent and had the color of amber. 3 He stretched out the form of a hand, and took me by the hair of my head. A spirit lifted me up between heaven and earth and brought me in visions of God to Jerusalem, to the entrance of the Penimith*b* Gate which faces north; that was the site of the infuriating image that provokes fury. 4 And the Presence of the God of Israel appeared there, like the vision that I had seen in the valley.*c*

5 And He said to me, "O mortal, turn your eyes northward." I turned my eyes northward, and there, *d-*north of the gate of the altar, was*-d* that infuriating image on the approach.*b* 6 And He said

---

d *I.e. their adornments.*

a *Septuagint "a man."*
b *Meaning of Heb. uncertain.*
c *See chapter 1 and 3.22-23.*
d-d *Meaning of Heb. uncertain; emendation yields "north of the gate was the altar of."*

to me, "Mortal, do you see what they are doing, the terrible abominations that the House of Israel is practicing here, *e*to drive Me far*-e* from My Sanctuary? You shall yet see even greater abominations!"

⁷ Then He brought me to the entrance of the court;*f* and I looked, and there was a hole in the wall. ⁸ He said to me, "Mortal, break through the wall"; so I broke through the wall and found an entrance. ⁹ And He said to me, "Enter and see the vile abominations that they are practicing here." ¹⁰ I entered and looked, and there all detestable forms of creeping things and beasts and all the fetishes of the House of Israel were depicted over the entire wall. ¹¹ Before them stood seventy men, elders of the House of Israel, with Jaazaniah son of Shaphan standing in their midst. Everyone had a censer in his hand, and a thick cloud of incense smoke ascended. ¹² Again He spoke to me, "O mortal, have you seen what the elders of the House of Israel are doing in the darkness, everyone in his image-covered chamber? For they say, 'The LORD does not see us; the LORD has abandoned the country.' " ¹³ And He said to me, "You shall see even more terrible abominations which they practice."

¹⁴ Next He brought me to the entrance of the north *g*gate of the House of the LORD;*-g* and there sat the women bewailing Tammuz.*h* ¹⁵ He said to me, "Have you seen, O mortal? You shall see even more terrible abominations than these."

¹⁶ Then He brought me into the inner court of the House of the LORD, and there, at the entrance to the Temple of the LORD, between the portico and the altar, were about twenty-five men, their backs to the Temple of the LORD and their faces to the east; they were bowing low to the sun in the east. ¹⁷ And He said to me, "Do you see, O mortal? Is it not enough for the House of Judah to practice the abominations that they have committed here, that they must fill the country with lawlessness and provoke Me still further and *i*thrust the branch to their nostrils?*-i* ¹⁸ I in turn will act with fury, I will show no pity or compassion; though they cry aloud to Me, I will not listen to them."

ᵉ⁻ᵉ *Or "at a distance."*
ᶠ *I.e. the outer court of the Temple.*
ᵍ⁻ᵍ *I.e. the gate of the inner court.*
ʰ *A Babylonian god.*
ⁱ⁻ⁱ *Apparently meaning "goad Me to fury"; "their" is a euphemism for "My."*

9 Then He called loudly in my hearing, saying, "Approach, you men in charge of the city, each bearing his weapons of destruction!" 2 And six men entered by way of the upper gate that faces north, each with his club in his hand; and among them was another, clothed in linen, with a writing case at his waist. They came forward and stopped at the bronze altar. 3 Now the Presence of the God of Israel had moved from the cherub on which it had rested to the platform*a* of the House. He called to the man clothed in linen with the writing case at his waist; 4 and the LORD said to him, "Pass through the city, through Jerusalem, and put a mark on the foreheads of the men who moan and groan because of all the abominations that are committed in it." 5 To the others He said in my hearing, "Follow him through the city and strike; show no pity or compassion. 6 Kill off graybeard, youth and maiden, women and children; but do not touch any person who bears the mark. Begin here at My Sanctuary." So they began with the elders who were in front of the House. 7 And He said to them, "Defile the House and fill the courts with the slain. Then go forth." So they went forth and began to kill in the city. 8 When they were out killing, and I remained alone, I flung myself on my face and cried out, "Ah, Lord GOD! Are you going to annihilate all that is left of Israel, pouring out Your fury upon Jerusalem?" 9 He answered me, "The iniquity of the Houses of Judah and Israel is very very great, the land is full of crime and the city is full of corruption. For they say, 'The LORD has forsaken the land, and the LORD does not see.' 10 I, in turn, will show no pity or compassion; I will give them their deserts." 11 And then the man clothed in linen with the writing case at his waist brought back word, saying, "I have done as You commanded me."

---

a The raised platform on which the Temple stood; cf. 47.1.

10 I looked, and on the expanse over the heads of the cherubs, there was something like a sapphire stone; an appearance resembling a throne could be seen over them. ² He spoke to the man clothed in linen and said, "Step inside the wheelwork, under the cherubs, and fill your hands with glowing coals from among the cherubs, and scatter them over the city." And he went in as I looked on. ³ Now the cherubs were standing on the south side of the House when the man entered, and the cloud filled the inner court. ⁴ But when the Presence of the LORD moved from the cherubs to the platform*a* of the House, the House was filled with the cloud, and the court was filled with the radiance of the Presence of the LORD. ⁵ The sound of the cherubs' wings could be heard as far as the outer court, like the voice of El Shaddai*b* when He speaks.

⁶ When He commanded the man dressed in linen: "Take fire from among the cherubs within the wheelwork," he went in and stood beside a wheel. ⁷ And a cherub stretched out his hand among the cherubs to the fire that was among the cherubs; he took some and put it into the hands of him who was clothed in linen, who took it and went out. ⁸ The cherubs appeared to have the form of a man's hand under their wings.

⁹ I could see that there were four wheels beside the cherubs, one wheel beside each of the cherubs; as for the appearance of the wheels, they gleamed like the beryl stone. ¹⁰ In appearance, the four had the same form, as if there were two wheels cutting through each other. ¹¹ And when they moved, each could move in the direction of any of its four quarters; they did not veer as they moved. The [cherubs] moved in the direction in which one of the heads faced, without turning as they moved. ¹² Their entire bodies—backs, hands, and wings—and the wheels, the wheels of the four of them, were covered all over with eyes. ¹³ It was these wheels that I had heard called "the wheelwork."*c* ¹⁴ Each one had four faces: One was a cherub's face, the second a

---

a See note at 47.1.
b See note at Gen. 17.1.
c See v. 2.

human face, the third a lion's face, and the fourth an eagle's face. ¹⁵ The cherubs ascended; those were the creatures that I had seen by the Chebar Canal. ¹⁶ Whenever the cherubs went, the wheels went beside them; and when the cherubs lifted their wings to ascend from the earth, the wheels did not roll away from their side. ¹⁷ When those stood still, these stood still; and when those ascended, these ascended with them, for the spirit of the creature was in them.

¹⁸ Then the Presence of the Lord left the platform^a of the House and stopped above the cherubs. ¹⁹ And I saw the cherubs lift their wings and rise from the earth, with the wheels beside them as they departed; and they^d stopped at the entrance of the eastern gate of the House of the Lord, with the Presence of the God of Israel above them. ²⁰ They were the same creatures that I had seen below the God of Israel at the Chebar Canal; so now I knew that they were cherubs.^e ²¹ Each one had four faces and each had four wings, with the form of human hands under the wings. ²² As for the form of their faces, they were the very faces that I had seen by the Chebar Canal—their appearance and ^ftheir features^f—and each could move in the direction of any of its faces.

11 Then a spirit lifted me up and brought me to the east gate of the House of the Lord, which faces eastward; and there, at the entrance of the gate, were twenty-five men, among whom I saw Jaazaniah son of Azzur and Pelatiah son of Benaiah, leaders of the people. ² [The Lord] said to me, "O mortal, these are the men who plan iniquity and plot wickedness in this city, ³ who say: 'There is no need now to build houses; this [city] is the pot, and we are the meat.'^a ⁴ I adjure you, prophesy against them; prophesy, O mortal!"

⁵ Thereupon the spirit of the Lord fell upon me, and He said to me, "Speak: Thus said the Lord: Such are your thoughts, O House of Israel; I know what comes into your mind. ⁶ Many have

^d *Lit. "it."*
^e *Because they had been called "cherubs" (cf. v.2).*
^{f-f} *Lit. "themselves."*

^a *I.e. the exiles will not return.*

you slain in this city; you have filled its streets with corpses. [7] Assuredly, thus says the Lord GOD: The corpses that you have piled up in it are the meat for which it is the pot; but you shall be taken out of it. [8] You feared the sword, and the sword I will bring upon you—declares the Lord GOD. [9] I will take you out of it and deliver you into the hands of strangers, and I will execute judgments upon you. [10] You shall fall by the sword; I will punish you at the border of Israel. And you shall know that I am the LORD. [11] This [city] shall not be a pot for you, nor you the meat in it; I will punish you at the border of Israel. [12] Then you shall know that I am the LORD, whose laws you did not follow and whose rules you did not obey, acting instead according to the rules of the nations around you."

[13] Now, as I prophesied, Pelatiah son of Benaiah dropped dead. I threw myself upon my face and cried out aloud, "Ah, Lord GOD! You are wiping out the remnant of Israel!"

[14] Then the word of the LORD came to me: [15] "O mortal, [I will save] your brothers, your brothers, the men of your kindred,[b] all of that very House of Israel to whom the inhabitants of Jerusalem say, 'Keep far from the LORD; the land has been given as a heritage to us.' [16] Say then: Thus said the Lord GOD: I have indeed removed them far among the nations and have scattered them among the countries, and I have become to them a diminished sanctity in the countries whither they have gone. [17] Yet say: Thus said the Lord GOD: I will gather you[b] from the peoples and assemble you out of the countries where you have been scattered, and I will give you the Land of Israel. [18] And they shall return there, and do away with all its detestable things and all its abominations. [19] I will give them one heart and put a new spirit in them;[c] I will remove the heart of stone from their bodies and give them a heart of flesh, [20] that they may follow My laws and faithfully observe My rules. Then they shall be My people and I will be their God. [21] But as for them whose heart is set upon their detestable things and their abominations, I will repay them for their conduct—declares the Lord GOD."

[b] *I.e. the exiles.*
[c] *Heb. "you."*

²² Then the cherubs, with the wheels beside them, lifted their wings, while the Presence of the God of Israel rested above them. ²³ The Presence of the LORD ascended from the midst of the city. ²⁴ A spirit carried me away and brought me in a vision by the spirit of God to the exile community in Chaldea. Then the vision that I had seen left me, ²⁵ and I told the exiles all the things that the LORD had shown me.

12 The word of the LORD came to me: ² O mortal, you dwell among the rebellious breed. They have eyes to see but see not, ears to hear but hear not; for they are a rebellious breed. ³ Therefore, mortal, get yourself gear for exile, and go into exile by day before their eyes. Go into exile from your home to another. place before their very eyes; perhaps they will take note, even though they are a rebellious breed. ⁴ Carry out your gear as gear for exile by day before their very eyes; and go out again in the evening before their eyes, as one who goes out into exile. ⁵ Before their eyes, break through the wall and carry [the gear] out through it; ⁶ before their eyes, carry it on your shoulder. Take it out in the dark, and cover your face that you may not see the land; for I make you a portent to the House of Israel.

⁷ I did just as I was ordered: I took out my gear by day as gear for exile, and in the evening I broke through the wall ᵃ⁻with my own hands.⁻ᵃ In the darkness I carried [the gear] out on my shoulder, carrying it before their eyes.

⁸ In the morning, the word of the LORD came to me: ⁹ O mortal, did not the House of Israel, that rebellious breed, ask you, "What are you doing?" ¹⁰ Say to them: Thus said the Lord GOD: This pronouncement concerns the prince in Jerusalem and all the House of Israel who are in it. ¹¹ Say: "I am a portent for you: As I have done, so shall it be done to them; they shall go into exile, into captivity. ¹² And the prince among them shall carry his gear on his shoulder as he goes out in the dark. Heᵇ shall break

ᵃ⁻ᵃ *Lit. "by hand."*
ᵇ *Heb. "They."*

through the wall in order to carry [his gear] out through it; he shall cover his face, because he himself shall not see the land with his eyes." [13] I will spread My net over him, and he shall be caught in My snare. I will bring him to Babylon, the land of the Chaldeans, but he shall not see it;[c] and there he shall die. [14] And all those around him, his helpers and all his troops, I will scatter in every direction; and I will unsheathe the sword after them. [15] Then, when I have scattered them among the nations and dispersed them through the countries, they shall know that I am the LORD. [16] But I will spare a few of them from the sword, from famine, and from pestilence, that they may recount all their abominable deeds among the nations to which they come; and they shall know that I am the LORD!

[17] The word of the LORD came to me: [18] O mortal, eat your bread in trembling and drink your water in fear and anxiety. [19] And say to the people of the land: Thus said the Lord GOD concerning the inhabitants of Jerusalem in the land of Israel: They shall eat their bread in anxiety and drink their water in desolation, because their land will be desolate of its multitudes on account of the lawlessness of all its inhabitants. [20] The inhabited towns shall be laid waste and the land shall become a desolation; then you shall know that I am the LORD.

[21] The word of the LORD came to me: [22] O mortal, what is this proverb that you have in the land of Israel, that you say, "The days grow many and every vision comes to naught?" [23] Assuredly, say to them, Thus said the Lord GOD: I will put an end to this proverb; it shall not be used in Israel any more. Speak rather to them: The days draw near, and the fulfillment of every vision. [24] For there shall no longer be any false vision or soothing divination in the House of Israel. [25] But whenever I the LORD speak what I speak, that word shall be fulfilled without any delay; in your days, O rebellious breed, I will fulfill every word I speak— declares the Lord GOD.

[c] Cf. II Kings 25.7.

²⁶ The word of the LORD came to me: ²⁷ See, O mortal, the House of Israel says, "The vision that he sees is far ahead, and he prophesies for the distant future." ²⁸ Assuredly, say to them: Thus said the Lord GOD: There shall be no more delay; whenever I speak a word, that word shall be fulfilled—declares the Lord GOD.

13 The word of the LORD came to me: ² O mortal, prophesy against the prophets of Israel who prophesy; say to those who prophesy out of their own imagination: Hear the word of the LORD! ³ Thus said the Lord GOD: Woe to the degenerate prophets, who follow their own fancy, without having had a vision! ⁴ Your prophets, O Israel, have been like jackals among ruins. ⁵ You did not enter the breaches and repair the walls for the House of Israel, that they might stand up in battle in the day of the LORD. ⁶ They prophesied falsehood and lying divination; they said, "Declares the LORD," when the LORD did not send them, and then they waited for their word to be fulfilled. ⁷ It was false visions you prophesied and lying divination you uttered, saying, "Declares the LORD," when I had not spoken.

⁸ Assuredly, thus said the Lord GOD: Because you speak falsehood and prophesy lies, assuredly, I will deal with you—declares the Lord GOD. ⁹ My hand will be against the prophets who prophesy falsehood and utter lying divination. They shall not remain in the assembly of My people, they shall not be inscribed in the lists of the House of Israel, and they shall not come back to the land of Israel. Thus shall you know that I am the Lord GOD.

¹⁰ Inasmuch as they have misled My people, saying, "It is well," when nothing is well, daubing with plaster the flimsy wall which ᵃ⁻the people⁻ᵃ was building, ¹¹ say to those daubers of plaster: It shall collapse; a driving rain shall descend—and you, O great hailstones, shall fall—and a hurricane wind shall rend it. ¹² Then, when the wall collapses, you will be asked, "What became of the plaster you daubed on?"

ᵃ⁻ᵃ *Heb. "it."*

¹³ Assuredly, thus said the Lord GOD: In My fury I will let loose hurricane winds; in My anger a driving rain shall descend, and great hailstones in destructive fury. ¹⁴ I will throw down the wall that you daubed with plaster, and I will raze it to the ground so that its foundation is exposed; and when it falls, you shall perish in its midst; then you shall know that I am the LORD. ¹⁵ And when I have spent My fury upon the wall and upon those who daubed it with plaster, I will say to you: Gone is the wall and gone are its daubers, ¹⁶ the prophets of Israel who prophesy about Jerusalem and see a vision of well-being for her when there is no well-being —declares the Lord GOD.

¹⁷ And you, O mortal, set your face against the women of your people, who prophecy out of their own imagination. Prophesy against them ¹⁸ and say: Thus said the Lord GOD: Woe to those who sew pads^b on all arm-joints and make bonnets^b for the head of every person, in order to entrap! Can you hunt down lives among My people, while you preserve your own lives? ¹⁹ You have profaned ^{c-}My name^{-c} among My people in return for handfuls of barley and morsels of bread; you have announced the death of persons who will not die and the survival of persons who will not live—lying to My people, who listen to your lies.

²⁰ Assuredly, thus said the Lord GOD: I am going to deal with your pads,^b ^{d-}by which^{-d} you hunt down lives like birds, and I will tear them from your arms and free the persons whose lives you hunt down like birds. ²¹ I will tear off your bonnets^b and rescue My people from your hands, and they shall no longer be prey in your hands; then you shall know that I am the LORD. ²² Because you saddened the heart of the innocent with lies, when I would not inflict suffering on him, and encouraged the wicked not to repent of his evil ways and so gain life—²³ assuredly, you shall no longer prophesy lies or practice divination! I will save My people from your hands, and you shall know that I am the LORD.

---

^b *Meaning of Heb. uncertain.*
^{c-c} *Heb. "Me."*
^{d-d} *Heb. "where."*

14 Certain elders of Israel came to me and sat down before me. ² And the word of the LORD came to me: ³ O mortal, these men have turned their thoughts upon their fetishes and set their minds upon the sin through which they stumbled: Shall I respond to their inquiry? ⁴ Now speak to them and tell them: Thus said the Lord GOD: If anyone of the House of Israel turns his thoughts upon his fetishes and sets his mind upon the sin through which he stumbled, and yet comes to the prophet, I the LORD will respond to him *ᵃ-as he comes with-ᵃ* his multitude of fetishes. ⁵ Thus I will hold the House of Israel to account for their thoughts, because they have all been estranged from Me through their fetishes.

⁶ Now say to the House of Israel: Thus said the Lord GOD: Repent, and turn back from your fetishes and turn your minds away from all your abominations. ⁷ For if any man of the House of Israel, or of the strangers who dwell in Israel, breaks away from Me and turns his thoughts upon his fetishes and sets his mind upon the sins through which he stumbled, and then goes to the prophet to inquire of Me through him, I the LORD will respond to him directly. ⁸ I will set My face against that man and make him a sign and a byword, and I will cut him off from the midst of My people. Then you shall know that I am the LORD.

⁹ And if a prophet is seduced and does speak a word [to such a man], it was I the LORD who seduced that prophet; I will stretch out My hand against him and destroy him from among My people Israel. ¹⁰ Thus they shall bear their punishment: The punishment of the inquirer and the punishment of the prophet shall be the same, ¹¹ so that the House of Israel may never again stray from Me and defile itself with all its transgressions. Then they shall be My people and I will be their God—declares the Lord GOD.

¹² The word of the LORD came to me: ¹³ O mortal, if a land were to sin against Me and commit a trespass, and I stretched out My

---

ᵃ⁻ᵃ *Emendation yields "directly, because of"; cf. v.7.*

hand against it and broke its staff of bread, and sent famine against it and cut off man and beast from it, [14] even if these three men—Noah, Daniel, and Job—should be in it, they would by their righteousness save only themselves—declares the Lord GOD. [15] Or, if I were to send wild beasts to roam the land and they depopulated it, and it became a desolation with none passing through it because of the beasts, [16] as I live—declares the Lord GOD—those three men in it would save neither sons nor daughters; they alone would be saved, but the land would become a desolation. [17] Or, if I were to bring the sword upon that land and say, "Let a sword sweep through the land so that I may cut off from it man and beast," [18] if those three men should be in it, as I live—declares the Lord GOD—they would save neither sons nor daughters, but they alone would be saved. [19] Or, if I let loose a pestilence against that land, and poured out My fury upon it in blood, cutting off from it man and beast, [20] should Noah, Daniel, and Job be in it, as I live—declares the Lord GOD—they would save neither son nor daughter; they would save themselves alone by their righteousness.

[21] Assuredly, thus said the Lord GOD: How much less [should any escape] now that I have let loose against Jerusalem all four of My terrible punishments—the sword, famine, wild beasts, and pestilence—to cut off man and beast from it! [22] Yet there are survivors left of it, [b-]sons and daughters who are being brought out.[-b] They are coming out to you; and when you see their ways and their deeds, you will be consoled for the disaster that I brought on Jerusalem, for all that I brought on it. [23] You will be consoled through them, when you see their ways and their deeds and realize that not without cause did I do all that I did in it—declares the Lord GOD.

15 The word of the LORD came to me: [2] O mortal, how is the wood of the grapevine better than the wood of any branch to be found among the trees of the forest? [3] Can wood be taken from

b-b *Several ancient versions read "who are bringing out sons and daughters."*

it for use in any work? Can one take a peg from it to hang any vessel on? 4 Now suppose it was thrown into the fire as fuel and the fire consumed its two ends and its middle was charred—is it good for any use? 5 Even when it was whole it could not be used for anything; how much less when fire has consumed it and it is charred! Can it still be used for anything?

6 Assuredly, thus said the Lord GOD: Like the wood of the grapevine among the trees of the forest, which I have designated to be fuel for fire, so will I treat the inhabitants of Jerusalem. 7 I will set My face against them; they escaped from fire, but fire shall consume them. When I set my face against them, you shall know that I am the LORD. 8 I will make the land a desolation, because they committed trespass—declares the Lord GOD.

16 The word of the LORD came to me: 2 O mortal, proclaim Jerusalem's abominations to her, 3 and say: Thus said the Lord GOD to Jerusalem: By origin and birth you are from the land of the Canaanites—your father was an Amorite and your mother a Hittite. 4 As for your birth, when you were born your navel cord was not cut, and you were not bathed in water to *a*-smoothe you;*-a* you were not rubbed with salt, nor were you swaddled. 5 No one pitied you enough to do any one of these things for you out of compassion for you; on the day you were born, you were left lying, rejected, in the open field. 6 When I passed by you and saw you wallowing in your blood, I said to you; "Live in spite of your blood." *b*-Yea, I said to you, "Live in spite of your blood."*-b* 7 I let you grow like the plants of the field; and you continued to grow up until you attained *a*-to womanhood,*-a* until your breasts became firm and your hair sprouted.

You were still naked and bare 8 when I passed by you [again] and saw that your time for love had arrived. *c*-So I spread My robe over you*-c* and covered your nakedness, and I entered into a covenant with you by oath—declares the Lord GOD; thus you became Mine. 9 I bathed you in water, and washed the blood off

a-a *Meaning of Heb. uncertain.*
b-b *This sentence is missing from some ancient versions and a few Heb. mss.*
c-c *An act symbolizing espousal; cf. Ruth 3.9.*

you, and anointed you with oil. [10] I clothed you with embroidered garments, and gave you sandals of *[a-]tahash*-leather*[-a]* to wear, and wound fine linen about your head, and dressed you in silks. [11] I decked you out in finery and put bracelets on your arms and a chain around your neck. [12] I put a ring in your nose, and earrings in your ears, and a splendid crown on your head. [13] You adorned yourself with gold and silver, and your apparel was of fine linen, silk, and embroidery. Your food was choice flour, honey, and oil. You grew more and more beautiful, and became fit for royalty. [14] Your beauty won you fame among the nations, for it was perfected through the splendor which I set upon you—declares the Lord GOD.

[15] But confident in your beauty and fame, you played the harlot: you lavished your favors on every passerby; *[a-]they were his.*[-a]* [16] You even took some of your cloths and made yourself *[a-]tapestried platforms[-a]* and fornicated on them—*[d-]not in the future; not in time to come.*[-d]* [17] You took your beautiful things, made of the gold and silver that I had given you, and you made yourself phallic images and fornicated with them. [18] You took your embroidered cloths to cover them; and you set My oil and My incense before them. [19] The food that I had given you—the choice flour, the oil, and the honey, which I had provided for you to eat —you set it before them for a pleasing odor.*[e]* And so it went— declares the Lord GOD. [20] You even took the sons and daughters that you bore to Me and sacrificed them to those [images] as food —as if your harlotries were not enough, [21] you slaughtered My children and presented them as offerings to them! [22] In all your abominations and harlotries, you did not remember the days of your youth, when you were naked and bare, and lay wallowing in your blood.

[23] After all your wickedness (woe, woe to you!)—declares the Lord GOD—[24] you built yourself an eminence and made yourself a mound in every square. [25] You built your mound at every crossroad; and you sullied your beauty and spread your legs to every passerby, and you multiplied your harlotries. [26] You played the

---

[d-d] *I.e. this actually happened; but meaning of Heb. uncertain.*
[e] *I.e. as a sacrifice; cf. Lev.2.2.*

whore with your neighbors, the lustful[f] Egyptians—you multiplied your harlotries to anger Me. ²⁷ Now, I will stretch out My arm against you and withhold your maintenance; and I will surrender you to the will of your enemies, the Philistine women, who are shocked by your lewd behavior.

²⁸ In your insatiable lust you also played the whore with the Assyrians; you played the whore with them, but were still unsated. ²⁹ You multiplied your harlotries with Chaldea, that land of traders; yet even with this you were not satisfied.

³⁰ ᵍ⁻How sick was your heart⁻ᵍ—declares the Lord GOD—when you did all those things, the acts of a self-willed whore, ³¹ building your eminence at every crossroad and setting your mound in every square! Yet you were not like a prostitute, for you spurned fees; ³² [you were like] the adulterous wife who welcomes strangers instead of her husband. ³³ Gifts are made to all prostitutes, but you made gifts to all your lovers, and bribed them to come to you from every quarter for your harlotries. ³⁴ You were the opposite of other women: you solicited instead of being solicited; you paid fees instead of being paid fees. Thus you were just the opposite!

³⁵ Now, O harlot, hear the word of the LORD. ³⁶ Thus said the Lord GOD: Because of your brazen effrontery, offering your nakedness to your lovers for harlotry—ʰ⁻just like the blood of your children, which you gave to all your abominable fetishes: ʰ—³⁷ I will assuredly assemble all the lovers to whom you gave your favors, along with everybody you accepted and everybody you rejected. I will assemble them against you from every quarter, and I will expose your nakedness to them, and they shall see all your nakedness. ³⁸ I will inflict upon you the punishment of women who commit adultery and murder, and I will direct bloody and impassioned fury against you. ³⁹ I will deliver you into their hands, and they shall tear down your eminence and level your mounds; and they shall strip you of your clothing and take away your dazzling jewels, leaving you naked and bare. ⁴⁰ Then they shall assemble a mob against you to pelt you with stones and

---

ᶠ *Lit. "big of phallus"; cf. 23.20.*
ᵍ⁻ᵍ *Change of vocalization yields "How furious I was with you"; lit. "How I was filled with your fury" (libbat, as in Akkadian and Old Aramaic).*
ʰ⁻ʰ *Construction of Heb. uncertain.*

pierce you with their swords. [41] They shall put your houses to the flames and execute punishment upon you in the sight of many women; thus I will put a stop to your harlotry, and you shall pay no more fees. [42] When I have satisfied My fury upon you and My rage has departed from you, then I will be tranquil; I will be angry no more.

[43] Because you did not remember the days of your youth, but infuriated Me with all those things, I [h-]will pay you back for your conduct[-h]—declares the Lord GOD.

Have you not committed depravity on top of all your other abominations? [44] Why, everyone who uses proverbs applies to you the proverb "Like mother, like daughter." [45] You are the daughter of your mother, who rejected her husband and children. And you are the sister of your sisters, who rejected their husbands and children; for you are daughters of a Hittite mother and an Amorite father. [46] Your elder sister was Samaria, who lived with her daughters to the north of you; your younger sister was Sodom, who lived with her daughters to the south of you. [47] Did you not walk in their ways and practice their abominations? Why, you were almost[a] more corrupt than they in all your ways. [48] As I live—declares the Lord GOD—your sister Sodom and her daughters did not do what you and your daughters did. [49] Only this was the sin of your sister Sodom: arrogance! She and her daughters had plenty of bread and untroubled tranquillity; yet she did not support the poor and the needy. [50] In their haughtiness, they committed abomination before Me; and so I removed them, as you saw.[i] [51] Nor did Samaria commit even half your sins. You committed more abominations than they, and by all the abominations that you committed you made your sisters look righteous. [52] Truly, you must bear the disgrace of serving as your sisters' advocate: Since you have sinned more abominably than they, they appear righteous in comparison. So be ashamed and bear your disgrace, because you have made your sisters look righteous.

[53] I will restore their fortunes—the fortunes of Sodom and her

---

[i] *Construed as second person feminine; cf.* qere, *vv. 47 and 51; and see above vv. 13, 18, 22, 31, 43.*

daughters and the fortunes of Samaria and her daughters—and your fortunes along with theirs. [54] Thus you shall bear your disgrace and feel your disgrace for behaving in such a way that they could take comfort. [55] Then your sister Sodom and her daughters shall return to their former state, and Samaria and her daughters shall return to their former state, and you and your daughters shall return to your former state. [56] Was not your sister Sodom a byword in your mouth in the days of your pride, [57] before your own wickedness was exposed? So must you now bear the mockery of the daughters of Aram[j] and all her neighbors, the daughters of Philistia who jeer at you on every side. [58] You yourself must bear your depravity and your abominations—declares the Lord.

[59] Truly, thus said the Lord God: I will deal with you as you have dealt, for you have spurned the pact and violated the covenant. [60] Nevertheless, I will remember the covenant I made with you in the days of your youth, and I will establish it with you as an everlasting covenant. [61] You shall remember your ways and feel ashamed, when you receive your older sisters and your younger sisters, and I give them to you as daughters, though they are not of your covenant. [62] I will establish My covenant with you, and you shall know that I am the Lord. [63] Thus you shall remember and feel shame, and you shall be too abashed to open your mouth again, when I have forgiven you for all that you did—declares the Lord God.

17 The word of the Lord came to me: [2] O mortal, propound a riddle and relate an allegory to the House of Israel. [3] Say: Thus said the Lord God: The great eagle with the great wings and the long pinions, [a]with the full plumage and the brilliant colors,[-a] came to the Lebanon range and seized the top of the cedar. [4] He plucked off its topmost bough and carried it off to the land of traders[b] and set it in a city of merchants. [5] He then took some of the seed of the land[c] and planted it in a fertile field; [d]he planted

---

[j] *Many Heb. mss. and editions read "Edom."*

[a-a] *This description suggests the golden eagle; the vulture, called by the same word in Heb. (nesher) has a bald head (Mic. 1.16) and dark feathers.*

[b] *Cf. 16.29.*

[c] *Emendation yields "cedar."*

[d-d] *Meaning of Heb. uncertain.*

and set it like a willow^{-d} beside abundant waters. ⁶ It grew and became a spreading vine of low stature; it became a vine, produced branches, and sent out boughs. [He had intended] that its twigs should turn to him, and that its roots should stay under him.

⁷ But there was another great eagle with great wings and full plumage; and this vine now bent its roots in his direction and sent out its twigs toward him, that he might water it more than the bed where it was planted—⁸ though it was planted in rich soil beside abundant water—so that it might grow branches and produce boughs and be a noble vine.

⁹ Say: Thus said the Lord GOD: Will it thrive? Will he^e not tear out its roots and rip off its crown, so that its entire foliage withers? It shall wither, despite any strong arm or mighty army [that may come] to remove it from its roots. ¹⁰ And suppose it is transplanted, will it thrive? When the east wind strikes it, it shall wither—wither upon the bed where it is growing.

¹¹ Then the word of the LORD came to me: ¹² Say to the rebellious breed: Do you not know what these things mean? Say: The king of Babylon came to Jerusalem, and carried away its king and its officers and brought them back with him to Babylon. ¹³ He took one of the seed royal and made a covenant with him and imposed an oath on him, and he carried away the nobles of the land—¹⁴ so that it might be a humble kingdom and not exalt itself, but keep his covenant and so endure.

¹⁵ But [that prince] rebelled against him and sent his envoys to Egypt to get horses and a large army. Will he succeed? Will he who does such things escape? Shall he break a covenant and escape? ¹⁶ As I live—declares the Lord GOD—in the very homeland of the king who made him king, whose oath he flouted and whose covenant he broke—right there, in Babylon, he shall die. ¹⁷ Pharaoh will not fight at his side with a great army and with numerous troops in the war, when mounds are thrown up and siege towers erected to destroy many lives. ¹⁸ He flouted a pact and broke a covenant; he gave his promise and did all these

^{e} *I.e. the first eagle.*

things—he shall not escape. ¹⁹ Assuredly, thus said the Lord GOD: As I live, I will pay him back for flouting My pact and breaking My covenant. ²⁰ I will spread My net over him and he shall be caught in My snare; I will carry him to Babylon and enter with him into judgment there for the trespass which he committed against Me. ²¹ And all the fugitives*f* of all his battalions shall fall by the sword, and those who remain shall scatter in every direction; then you will know that I the LORD have spoken.

²² Thus said the Lord GOD: Then I in turn will take and set [in the ground a slip] from the lofty top of the cedar; I will pluck a tender twig from the tip of its crown, and I will plant it on a tall, towering mountain. ²³ I will plant it in Israel's lofty highlands, and it shall bring forth boughs and produce branches*g* and grow into a noble cedar. Every bird of every feather shall take shelter under it, shelter in the shade of its boughs. ²⁴ Then shall all the trees of the field know that it is I the LORD who have abased the lofty tree and exalted the lowly tree, who have dried up the green tree and made the withered tree bud. I the LORD have spoken, and I will act.

18

The word of the LORD came to me: ² What do you mean by quoting this proverb upon the soil of Israel, "Fathers eat sour grapes and their children's teeth are blunted"?*a* ³ As I live— declares the Lord GOD—this proverb shall no longer be current among you in Israel. ⁴ Consider, all lives are Mine; the life of the father and the life of the son are both Mine. The person who sins, only he shall die.

⁵ Thus, if a man is righteous and does what is just and right: ⁶ If he has not eaten on the mountains*b* or raised his eyes to the fetishes of the House of Israel; if he has not defiled his neighbor's wife or approached a menstruous woman; ⁷ if he has not wronged anyone; if he has returned the debtor's pledge to him and has taken nothing by robbery; if he has given bread to the hungry and clothed the naked; ⁸ if he has not lent at advance interest or

---

f Many mss. read "picked men."
g Others "fruit."

a Others "set on edge."
b I.e. in idolatry. Emendation yields "with the blood"; cf. 33.25; Lev. 17.26.

exacted accrued interest;[c] if he has abstained from wrongdoing and executed true justice between man and man; 9 if he has followed My laws and kept My rules and acted honestly—he is righteous. Such a man shall live—declares the Lord GOD.

10 Suppose, now, that he has begotten a son who is a ruffian, a shedder of blood, who [d-]does any of these things,[-d] 11 whereas he himself did none of these things. That is, [the son] has eaten on the mountains,[b] has defiled his neighbor's wife, 12 has wronged the poor and the needy, has taken by robbery, has not returned a pledge, has raised his eyes to the fetishes, has committed abomination, 13 has lent at advance interest, or exacted accrued interest—shall he live? He shall not live! If he has committed any of these abominations, he shall die; he has forfeited his life.

14 Now suppose that he, in turn, has begotten a son who has seen all the sins that his father committed, but has taken heed and has not imitated them: 15 He has not eaten on the mountains[b] or raised his eyes to the fetishes of the House of Israel; he has not defiled his neighbor's wife; 16 he has not wronged anyone; he has not seized a pledge or taken anything by robbery; he has given his bread to the hungry and clothed the naked; 17 he has [e-]refrained from oppressing the poor;[-e] he has not exacted advance or accrued interest; he has obeyed My rules and followed My laws —he shall not die for the iniquity of his father, but shall live. 18 To be sure, his father, because he practiced fraud, robbed his brother, and acted wickedly among his kin, did die for his iniquity; 19 and now you ask, "Why has not the son shared the burden of his father's guilt?" But the son has done what is right and just, and has carefully kept all My laws: he shall live!

20 The person who sins, he alone shall die. A son shall not share the burden of a father's guilt, nor shall a father share the burden of a son's guilt; the righteousness of the righteous shall be accounted to him alone, and the wickedness of the wicked shall be accounted to him alone.

---

[c] *I.e. interest deducted in advance or interest added at the time of repayment; cf. Lev. 25.36.*
[d-d] *Meaning of Heb. uncertain.*
[e-e] *Lit. "turned his hand back from the poor." Emendation yields "abstained from wrongdoing"; cf. v.8.*

²¹ Moreover, if the wicked man repents of all the sins that he committed and keeps all My laws and does what is just and right, he shall live; he shall not die. ²² None of the transgressions he committed shall be remembered against him; because of the righteousness he has practiced, he shall live. ²³ Is it my desire that a wicked man shall die?—says the Lord GOD. It is rather that he shall turn back from his ways and live.

²⁴ So, too, if a righteous man turns away from his righteousness and does wrong, practicing the very abominations that the wicked man practiced, shall he live? None of the righteous deeds that he did shall be remembered; because of the treachery he has practiced and the sins he has committed—because of these, he shall die.

²⁵ Yet you say, "The way of the Lord is unfair." Listen, O House of Israel: Is My way unfair? It is your ways that are unfair! ²⁶ When a righteous man turns away from his righteousness and does wrong, he shall die for it; he shall die for the wrong he has done. ²⁷ And if a wicked man turns back from the wickedness that he practiced and does what is just and right, such a man shall save his life. ²⁸ Because he took heed and turned back from all the transgressions that he committed, he shall live; he shall not die.

²⁹ Yet the House of Israel say, "The way of the LORD is unfair." Are My ways unfair, O House of Israel? It is your ways that are unfair! ³⁰ Be assured, O House of Israel, I will judge each one of you according to his ways—declares the Lord GOD. Repent and turn back from your transgressions; let them not be a stumbling block of guilt for you. ³¹ Cast away all the transgressions by which you have offended, and get yourselves a new heart and a new spirit, that you may not die, O House of Israel. ³² For it is not My desire that anyone shall die—declares the Lord GOD. Repent, therefore, and live!

19 And you are to intone a dirge over the princes of Israel,
² and say:

> What a lioness was your mother
> Among the lions!
> Crouching among the great beasts,
> She reared her cubs.
> ³ She raised up one of her cubs,
> He became a great beast;
> He learned to hunt prey—
> He devoured men.
> ⁴ Nations heeded [the call] against him;
> He was caught in their snare.
> They dragged him off with hooks
> To the land of Egypt.
> ⁵ When she saw herself frustrated,
> Her hope defeated,
> She took another of her cubs
> And set him up as a great beast.
> ⁶ He stalked among the lions,
> He was a great beast;
> He learned to hunt prey—
> He devoured men.
> ⁷ He *ᵃ*ravished their widows,*ᵃ*
> Laid waste their cities;
> The land and all in it were appalled
> At the sound of his roaring.
> ⁸ Nations from the countries round about
> Arrayed themselves against him.
> They spread their net over him,
> He was caught in their snare.
> ⁹ With hooks he was put in a cage,
> They carried him off to the king of Babylon

ᵃ⁻ᵃ *Emendation yields "ravaged their castles."*

And confined him in a fortress,
So that never again should his roar be heard
On the hills of Israel.

10 Your mother was like a vine *b*-in your blood,-*b*
Planted beside streams,
With luxuriant boughs and branches
Thanks to abundant waters.
11 And she had a mighty rod*c*
Fit for a ruler's scepter.*c*
It towered highest *d*-among the leafy trees,-*d*
It was conspicuous by its height,
By the abundance of its boughs.
12 But plucked up in a fury,
She was hurled to the ground.
The east wind withered her branches,
They broke apart and dried up;
And her mighty rod was consumed by fire.
13 Now she is planted in the desert,
In ground that is arid and parched.
14 Fire has issued from her twig-laden branch
And has consumed her boughs,
She is left without a mighty rod,
A scepter to rule with.

This is a dirge, and it has become a [familiar] dirge.

20 In the seventh year, on the tenth day of the fifth month, certain elders of Israel came to inquire of the LORD, and sat down before me. 2 And the word of the LORD came to me:

3 O mortal, speak to the elders of Israel and say to them: Thus said the Lord GOD: Have you come to inquire of Me? As I live, I will not respond to your inquiry—declares the Lord GOD.

b-b *Meaning of Heb. uncertain; emendation yields "in a vineyard."*
c *Heb. plural.*
d-d *Meaning of Heb. uncertain.*

4 ^{a}-Arraign, arraign them, O mortal!$^{-a}$ Declare to them the abhorrent deeds of their fathers. 5 Say to them: Thus said the Lord GOD:

On the day that I chose Israel, I ^{b}-gave My oath^{-b} to the stock of the House of Jacob; when I made Myself known to them in the land of Egypt, I gave my oath to them. When I said, "I the LORD am your God," 6 that same day I swore to them to take them out of the land of Egypt into a land flowing with milk and honey, a land which I had sought out for them, the fairest of all lands.

7 I also said to them: Cast away, every one of you, the detestable things ^{c}-that you are drawn to,$^{-c}$ and do not defile yourselves with the fetishes of Egypt—I the LORD am your God. 8 But they defied Me and refused to listen to Me. They did not cast away the detestable things they were drawn to, nor did they give up the fetishes of Egypt. Then I resolved to pour out My fury upon them, to vent all My anger upon them there, in the land of Egypt. 9 But I acted for the sake of My name, that it might not be profaned in the sight of the nations among whom they were. For it was before their eyes that I had made Myself known to Israel^{d} to bring them out of the land of Egypt.

10 I brought them out of the land of Egypt and I led them into the wilderness. 11 I gave them My laws and taught them My rules, by the pursuit of which a man shall live. 12 Moreover, I gave them My sabbaths to serve as a sign between Me and them, that they might know that it is I the LORD who sanctify them. 13 But the House of Israel rebelled against Me in the wilderness; they did not follow My laws and they rejected My rules—by the pursuit of which a man shall live—and they grossly desecrated My sabbaths. Then I thought to pour out My fury upon them in the wilderness and to make an end of them; 14 but I acted for the sake of My name, that it might not be profaned in the sight of the nations before whose eyes I had led them out. 15 However, I swore^{b} to them in the wilderness that I would not bring them into the land flowing with milk and honey, the fairest of all lands, which I had assigned [to them], 16 for they had rejected My rules, disobeyed

---

$^{a\text{-}a}$ Lit. "Will you arraign them, will you arraign, O mortal?"
$^{b\text{-}b}$ Lit. "raised My hand."
$^{c\text{-}c}$ Lit. "of his eyes."
^{d} Lit. "them."

My laws, and desecrated My sabbaths; their hearts followed after their fetishes. [17] But I had pity on them and did not destroy them; I did not make an end of them in the wilderness.

[18] I warned their children in the wilderness: Do not follow the practices of your fathers, do not keep their ways, and do not defile yourselves with their fetishes. [19] I the LORD am your God: Follow My laws and be careful to observe My rules. [20] And hallow My sabbaths, that they may be a sign between Me and you, that you may know that I the LORD am your God.

[21] But the children rebelled against Me: they did not follow My laws and did not faithfully observe My rules, by the pursuit of which man shall live; they profaned My sabbaths. Then I resolved to pour out My fury upon them, to vent all My anger upon them, in the wilderness. [22] But I held back My hand and acted for the sake of My name, that it might not be profaned in the sight of the nations before whose eyes I had led them out. [23] However, I swore[b] to them in the wilderness that I would scatter them among the nations and disperse them through the lands, [24] because they did not obey My rules, but rejected My laws, profaned My sabbaths, and looked with longing to the fetishes of their fathers. [25] Moreover, I gave them laws that were not good and rules by which they could not live: [26] When they set aside every first issue of the womb, I defiled them by their very gifts[e]—that I might render them desolate,[f] that they might know that I am the LORD.

[27] Now, O mortal, speak to the House of Israel and say to them: Thus said the Lord GOD: By this too your fathers affronted Me and committed trespass against Me: [28] When I brought them to the land that I had sworn[b] to give them, and they saw any high hill or any leafy tree, they slaughtered their sacrifices there and presented their offensive offerings there; there they produced their pleasing odors and poured out their libations. [29] Then I said to them, "What is this shrine which you visit?" (Therefore such [a shrine] is called bamah[g] to this day.)

[30] Now say to the House of Israel: Thus said the Lord GOD: If you defile yourselves as your fathers did and go astray after their

---

[c] See v. 31.
[f] Emendation yields "guilty."
[g] As if from ba "visit" and mah "what."

detestable things, [31] and if to this very day you defile yourselves in the presentation of your gifts by making your children pass through the fire to all your fetishes, shall I respond to your inquiry, O House of Israel? As I live—declares the Lord GOD— I will not respond to you. [32] And what you have in mind shall never come to pass—when you say, "We will be like the nations, like the families of the lands, worshiping wood and stone." [33] As I live—declares the Lord GOD—I will reign over you with a strong hand, and with an outstretched arm, and with overflowing fury. [34] With a strong hand and an outstretched arm and overflowing fury I will bring you out from the peoples and gather you from the lands where you are scattered, [35] and I will bring you into the wilderness of the peoples; and there I will enter into judgment with you face to face. [36] As I entered into judgment with your fathers in the wilderness of the land of Egypt, so will I enter into judgment with you—declares the Lord GOD. [37] I will make you pass under the shepherd's staff,[h] and I will bring you into the bond[i] of the covenant. [38] I will remove from you those who rebel and transgress against Me; I will take them out of the countries where they sojourn, but they shall not enter the land of Israel. Then you shall know that I am the LORD.

[39] As for you, O House of Israel, thus said the Lord GOD: Go, every one of you, and worship his fetishes and continue,[i] if you will not obey Me; but do not profane My holy name any more with your idolatrous gifts. [40] For only on My holy mountain, on the lofty mount of Israel—declares the Lord GOD—there, in the land, the entire House of Israel, all of it, must worship Me. There I will accept them, and there I will take note of your contributions and the choicest offerings of all your sacred things. [41] When I bring you out from the peoples and gather you from the lands in which you are scattered, I will accept you as a pleasing odor; and I will be sanctified through you in the sight of the nations. [42] Then, when I have brought you to the land of Israel, to the country that I swore[b] to give to your fathers, you shall know that I am the LORD. [43] There you will recall your ways and all the acts by which

---

[h] *I.e. to be counted; see Lev. 27.32.*
[i] *Meaning of Heb. uncertain.*

you defiled yourselves; and you will loathe yourselves for all the evils that you committed. ⁴⁴ Then, O House of Israel, you shall know that I am the LORD, when I deal with you for My name's sake —not in accordance with your evil ways and corrupt acts—declares the Lord GOD.

21 The word of the LORD came to me: ² O mortal, set your face toward Teman,ᵃ and proclaim to Darom,ᵃ and prophesy against the brushland of the Negeb.ᵃ ³ Say to the brushland of the Negeb: Hear the word of the LORD. Thus said the Lord GOD: I am going to kindle a fire in you, which shall devour every tree of yours, both green and withered. Its leaping flame shall not go out, and every face from south to north shall be scorched by it. ⁴ Then all flesh shall recognize that I the LORD have kindled it; it shall not go out. ⁵ And I said, "Ah, Lord GOD! They say of me: He is just a riddlemonger."

⁶ Then the word of the LORD came to me: ⁷ O mortal, set your face toward Jerusalem and proclaim against her sanctuaries and prophesy against the land of Israel. ⁸ Say to the land of Israel: Thus said the LORD: I am going to deal with you! I will draw My sword from its sheath, and I will wipe out from you both the righteous and the wicked. ⁹ In order to wipe out from you both the righteous and the wicked, My sword shall assuredly be unsheathed against all flesh from south to north; ¹⁰ and all flesh shall know that I the LORD have drawn My sword from its sheath, not to be sheathed again.

¹¹ And you, O mortal, sigh; with tottering limbs and bitter grief, sigh before their eyes. ¹² And when they ask you, "Why do you sigh?" answer, "Because of the tidings that have come." Every heart shall sink and all hands hang nerveless; every spirit shall grow faint and all knees turn to water because of the tidings that have come. It is approaching, it shall come to pass—declares the Lord GOD.

¹³ The word of the LORD came to me: ¹⁴ O mortal, prophesy

ᵃ *Teman, Darom, and Negeb are three terms for "the south." The allusion is to Jerusalem (v.7), which was always approached from Babylon by way of the north.*

and say: Thus said the Lord GOD: A sword! A sword has been whetted and polished. ¹⁵ It has been whetted to wreak slaughter; *ᵇ*[therefore] it has been ground to a brilliant polish.*⁻ᵇ* *ᶜ*How can we rejoice? My son, it scorns*⁻ᶜ* the rod and every stick. ¹⁶ It has been given to be polished and then grasped in the hand; for this has the sword been whetted, for this polished— to be put into the hand of a slayer. ¹⁷ Cry and wail, O mortal, for this shall befall My people, this shall befall all the chieftains of Israel: they shall be cast before the sword together with My people; oh, strike the thigh [in grief]. ¹⁸ *ᶜ*Consider: How shall it fail to happen, seeing that it even scorns the rod?*⁻ᶜ* —says the Lord GOD.

¹⁹ Further, O mortal, prophesy, striking hand against hand. Let the sword strike a second time and yet a third time; it is a sword for massacre, a sword for great carnage, that presses*ᶜ* upon them. ²⁰ Thus hearts shall lose courage and many shall fall. At all their gates I have appointed slaughter*ᶜ* by the sword. Ah! it is made to flash brilliantly, it is honed*ᶜ* for slaughter. ²¹ Be united,*ᵈ* go to the right, turn left; whither are you bound? ²² I, too, will strike hand against hand and will satisfy My fury upon you; I the LORD have spoken.

²³ The word of the LORD came to me: ²⁴ And you, O mortal, choose two roads on which the sword of the king of Babylon may advance, both issuing from the same country; and select a spot, select it where roads branch off to [two] cities. ²⁵ Choose a way for the sword to advance on Rabbah of the Ammonites or on fortified Jerusalem in Judah. ²⁶ For the king of Babylon has stood at the fork of the road, where two roads branch off, to perform divination: he has shaken arrows, consulted teraphim, and inspected the liver.*ᵉ* ²⁷ In his right hand came up the omen against Jerusalem—to set battering rams, to proclaim murder, to raise battle shouts, to set battering rams against the gates, to cast up mounds, to erect towers.

²⁸ *ᶠ*In their eyes, the oaths they had sworn to them were like empty divination; but this shall serve to recall their guilt, for

---

ᵇ⁻ᵇ *Lit. "it has been polished in order that it may have lightning."*
ᶜ⁻ᶜ *Meaning of Heb. uncertain.*
ᵈ *Meaning of Heb. uncertain; Targum reads "Be whetted." Cf. vv. 14-16.*
ᵉ *I.e., of a sacrificed animal.*
ᶠ *The inhabitants of Jerusalem disregarded their oaths to the Babylonians; cf. 17.13 ff.*

which they shall be taken to task. ²⁹ Assuredly, thus said the Lord GOD: For causing your guilt to be recalled, your transgressions to be uncovered, and your sins to be revealed—all your misdeeds —because you have brought yourselves to [My] mind, you shall be taken to task.

³⁰ And to you, O dishonored wicked prince of Israel, whose day has come—the time set for your punishment—³¹ thus said the Lord GOD: Remove the turban and lift off the crown! This shall not remain as it is; exalt the low and abase the high. ³² Ruin, an utter ruin I will make it. ᶜIt shall be no moreᶜ until he comes to whom it rightfully belongs; and I will give it to him.

³³ Further, O mortal, prophesy and say: Thus said the Lord GOD concerning the Ammonites and their blasphemies: Proclaim: O sword! O sword unsheathed for slaughter, polished to the utmost, to a flashing brilliance! ³⁴ Because they have prophesied falsely about you and have divined deceitfully concerning you, you shall be wielded over the necks of the dishonored wicked ones, for their day has come, the time ᶜset for their punishment.ᶜ

³⁵ ᵍReturn it to its sheath!ᵍ In the place where you were created, in the land of your origin, I will judge you. ³⁶ I will pour out My indignation upon you, I will blow upon you with the fire of My wrath; and I will deliver you into the hands of barbarians, craftsmen of destruction. ³⁷ You shall be fuel for the fire, your blood shall sink into the earth, you shall not be remembered, for I the LORD have spoken.

22 The word of the LORD came to me: ² Further, O mortal, ᵃarraign, arraignᵃ the city of bloodshed; declare to her all her abhorrent deeds! ³ Say: Thus said the Lord GOD: O city in whose midst blood is shed, so that your hour is approaching; within which fetishes are made, so that you have become un-

---

ᵍ⁻ᵍ *Emendation yields "Return to your scabbard!" In this and the following verses, the prophet describes the future punishment of Babylon, still symbolized by the sword.*

ᵃ⁻ᵃ *Lit. "will you arraign, arraign."*

clean! [4] You stand guilty of the blood you have shed, defiled by the fetishes you have made. You have brought on your day; [b-]you have reached your year.[-b] Therefore I will make you the mockery of the nations and the scorn of all the lands. [5] Both the near and the far shall scorn you, O besmirched of name, O laden with iniquity!

[6] Every one of the princes of Israel in your midst used his strength for the shedding of blood. [7] Fathers and mothers have been humiliated within you; strangers have been cheated in your midst; orphans and widows have been wronged within you. [8] You have despised My holy things and profaned My sabbaths.

[9] Base[c] men in your midst were intent on shedding blood; in you they have eaten [d-]upon the mountains;[-d] and they have practiced depravity in your midst. [10] In you they have uncovered their fathers' nakedness;[e] in you they have ravished women during their impurity. [11] They have committed abhorrent acts with other men's wives; in their depravity they have defiled their own daughters-in-law; in you they have ravished their own sisters, daughters of their fathers. [12] They have taken bribes within you to shed blood. You have taken advance and accrued interest;[f] you have defrauded your countrymen to your profit. You have forgotten Me—declares the Lord GOD.

[13] Lo, I will strike My hands over the ill-gotten gains that you have amassed, and over the bloodshed that has been committed in your midst. [14] Will your courage endure, will your hands remain firm in the days when I deal with you? I the LORD have spoken and I will act. [15] I will scatter you among the nations and disperse you through the lands; I will consume the uncleanness out of you. [16] You shall be dishonored in the sight of nations, and you shall know that I am the LORD.

[17] The word of the LORD came to me: [18] O mortal, the House of Israel has become dross to Me; they are all copper, tin, iron, and lead. [But in a crucible, the dross shall turn into silver.] [19] Assuredly, thus said the Lord GOD: Because you have all be-

---

b-b *Some Babylonian mss. and ancient versions read "the time of your years has come."*
c *Meaning of Heb. uncertain.*
d-d *I.e. in idolatry. Emendation yields "with the blood," cf. Lev. 19.26.*
e *I.e. have cohabited with a former wife of the father; cf. Lev. 18.7-8.*
f *Cf. note at 18.8.*

come dross, I will gather you into Jerusalem. [20] As silver, copper, iron, lead, and tin are gathered into a crucible to blow the fire upon them, so as to melt them, so will I gather you in My fierce anger and cast you [into the fire] and melt you. [21] I will gather you and I will blow upon you the fire of My fury, and you shall be melted in it. [22] As silver is melted in a crucible, so shall you be melted in it. And you shall know that I the LORD have poured out My fury upon you.

[23] The word of the LORD came to me: [24] O mortal, say to her: You are an uncleansed land, ᶜnot to be washed with rainᶜ on the day of indignation. [25] ᵍHer gang of prophetsᵍ are like roaring lions in her midst, rending prey. They devour human beings; they seize treasure and wealth; they have widowed many women in her midst. [26] Her priests have violated My Teaching: they have profaned what is sacred to Me, they have not distinguished between the sacred and the profane, they have not taught the difference between the unclean and the clean, and they have closed their eyes to My sabbaths. I am profaned in their midst. [27] Her officials are like wolves rending prey in her midst; they shed blood and destroy lives to win ill-gotten gain. [28] Her prophets, too, daub the wall for them with plaster:ʰ They prophesy falsely and divine deceitfully for them; they say, "Thus said the Lord GOD," when the LORD has not spoken. [29] And the people of the land have practiced fraud and committed robbery; they have wronged the poor and needy, have defrauded the stranger without redress. [30] And I sought a man among them to repair the wall or to stand in the breach before Me in behalf of this land, that I might not destroy it; but I found none. [31] I have therefore poured out My indignation upon them; I will consume them with the fire of My fury. I will repay them for their conduct—declares the Lord GOD.

ᵍ⁻ᵍ *Septuagint reads "Whose chieftains."*
ʰ *Cf. 13.10 ff.*

23 The word of the LORD came to me: ² O mortal, once there were two women, daughters of one mother. ³ They played the whore in Egypt; they played the whore while still young. There their breasts were squeezed, and there their virgin nipples were handled. ⁴ Their names were: the elder one, Oholah;*ᵃ* and her sister, Oholibah.*ᵇ* They became Mine, and they bore sons and daughters. As for their names, Oholah is Samaria, and Oholibah is Jerusalem.

⁵ Oholah whored while she was Mine, and she lusted after her lovers, after the Assyrians, warriors*ᶜ* ⁶ clothed in bluc, governors and prefects, horsemen mounted on steeds—all of them handsome young fellows. ⁷ She bestowed her favors upon them— upon all the pick of the Assyrians—and defiled herself with all their fetishes after which she lusted. ⁸ She did not give up the whoring she had begun with the Egyptians; for they had lain with her in her youth, and they had handled her virgin nipples and had poured out their lust upon her. ⁹ Therefore I delivered her into the hands of her lovers, into the hands of the Assyrians after whom she lusted. ¹⁰ They exposed her nakedness; they seized her sons and daughters, and she herself was put to the sword. And because of the punishment inflicted upon her, she became a byword among women.

¹¹ Her sister Oholibah saw this; yet her lusting was more depraved than her sister's, and her whoring more debased. ¹² She lusted after the Assyrians, governors and prefects, warriors*ᶜ* gorgeously clad, horsemen mounted on steeds—all of them handsome young fellows. ¹³ And I saw how she had defiled herself. Both of them followed the same course, ¹⁴ but she carried her harlotries further. For she saw men sculptured upon the walls, figures of Chaldeans drawn in vermilion, ¹⁵ girded with belts round their waists, and with flowing turbans on their heads, all of them looking like officers—a picture of Babylonians whose native land was Chaldea. ¹⁶ At the very sight of them she lusted

ᵃ *I.e. "Tent."*
ᵇ *I.e. "My Tent Is in Her."*
ᶜ *Meaning of Heb. uncertain.*

after them, and she sent messengers for them to Chaldea. [17] So the Babylonians came to her for lovemaking and defiled her with their whoring; and she defiled herself with them until she turned from them in disgust. [18] She flaunted her harlotries and exposed her nakedness, and I turned from her in disgust, as I had turned disgusted from her sister. [19] But she whored still more, remembering how in her youth she had played the whore in the land of Egypt; [20] she lusted for concubinage with them, whose members were like those of asses and whose organs[c] were like those of stallions. [21] Thus you reverted to the wantonness of your youth, remembering[d] your youthful breasts, when the men of Egypt handled your nipples.

[22] Assuredly, Oholibah, thus said the Lord God: I am going to rouse against you the lovers from whom you turned in disgust, and I will bring them upon you from all around—[23] the Babylonians and all the Chaldeans, [the people of] Pekod, Shoa, and Koa, and all the Assyrians with them, all of them handsome young fellows, governors and prefects, officers and warriors,[c] all of them riding on horseback. [24] They shall attack you with fleets[c] of wheeled chariots and a host of troops; they shall set themselves against you on all sides with bucklers, shields, and helmets. And I will entrust your punishment to them, and they shall inflict their punishments on you. [25] I will direct My passion against you, and they shall deal with you in fury: they shall cut off your nose and ears. The last of you shall fall by the sword; they[e] shall take away your sons and daughters, and your remnant shall be devoured by fire. [26] They shall strip you of your clothing and take away your dazzling jewels. [27] I will put an end to your wantonness and to your whoring in the land of Egypt, and you shall not long for them nor remember Egypt any more.

[28] For thus said the Lord God: I am going to deliver you into the hands of those you hate, into the hands of those from whom you turned in disgust. [29] They shall treat you with hate, and they shall take away all you have toiled for, and leave you naked and bare; your naked whoredom, wantonness, and harlotry will be

[d] *Lit. "for the sake of."*
[e] *I.e. the former lovers, vv. 22 ff.*

exposed. [30] These things shall be done to you for your harlotries with the nations, for defiling yourself with their fetishes. [31] You walked in your sister's path; therefore I will put her cup into your hand.

[32] Thus said the Lord GOD:

You shall drink of your sister's cup,
So deep and wide;
It shall cause derision and scorn,
It holds so much.
[33] You shall be filled with drunkenness and woe.
The cup of desolation and horror,
The cup of your sister Samaria—
[34] You shall drink it and drain it,
And gnaw its shards;
And you shall tear your breasts.

For I have spoken—declares the Lord GOD.

[35] Assuredly, thus said the Lord GOD: Because you have forgotten Me and cast Me behind your back, you in turn must suffer for your wanton whoring.

[36] Then the LORD said to me: O mortal, arraign*f* Oholah and Oholibah, and charge them with their abominations. [37] For they have committed adultery, and blood is on their hands; truly they have committed adultery with their fetishes, and have even offered to them as food the children they bore to Me. [38] At the same time they also did this to Me: they defiled My sanctuary and profaned My sabbaths. [39] On the very day that they slaughtered their children to their fetishes, they entered My sanctuary to desecrate it. That is what they did in My House.

[40] Moreover, they sent for men to come from afar, [men] to whom a messenger was sent; and they came. For them, [Oholibah,] you bathed, painted your eyes, and donned your finery; [41] and you sat on a grand couch with a set table in front of it— and it was My incense and My oil you laid upon it. [42] And the noise of a carefree multitude was there, *of numerous men brought drunk from the desert;* and they put bracelets on their

f Lit. "will you arraign"; cf. 22.2.

arms and splendid crowns upon their heads. [43] Then I said, [c]"To destruction with adultery! Look, they are still going on with those same fornications of hers."[-c] [44] And they would go to her as one goes to a prostitute; that is how they went to Oholah and Oholibah, wanton women. [45] But righteous men shall punish them with the punishments for adultery and for bloodshed, for they are adulteresses and have blood on their hands.

[46] For thus said the Lord GOD: Summon an assembly against them, and make them an object of horror and plunder. [47] Let the assembly pelt them with stones and cut them down with their swords; let them kill their sons and daughters, and burn down their homes. [48] I will put an end to wantonness in the land; and all the women shall take warning not to imitate your wantonness. [49] They shall punish you for your wantonness, and you shall suffer the penalty for your sinful idolatry. And you shall know that I am the Lord GOD.

24

In the ninth year, on the tenth day of the tenth month, the word of the LORD came to me: [2] O mortal, record this date, this exact day; for this very day the king of Babylon has laid siege to Jerusalem. [3] Further, speak in an allegory to the rebellious breed and say to them: Thus said the Lord GOD:

> Put the caldron [on the fire], put it on,
> And then pour water into it.
> [4] Collect in it the pieces [of meat].
> Every choice piece, thigh and shoulder;
> Fill it with the best cuts[a]—
> [5] Take the best of the flock.
> Also pile the cuts[b] under it;
> Get it boiling briskly,
> And cook the cuts in it.
> [6] Assuredly, thus said the Lord GOD:
> Woe to the city of blood—
> A caldron whose scum[c] is in it,

[a] Lit. "limbs."
[b] Emendation yields "wood"; cf. v. 10.
[c] Or "rust."

Whose scum has not been cleaned out!
Empty it piece by piece;
^{d-}No lot has fallen upon it.^{-d}
⁷ For the blood she shed is still in her;
She set it upon a bare rock;
She did not pour it out on the ground
To cover it with earth.
⁸ She^e set her blood upon the bare rock,
So that it was not covered,
So that it may stir up [My] fury
To take vengeance.
⁹ Assuredly, thus said the Lord GOD:
Woe to the city of blood!
I in turn will make a great blaze.
¹⁰ Pile on the logs,
Kindle the fire,
Cook the meat through
And ^{f-}stew it completely,^{-f}
And let the bones be charred.
¹¹ Let it stand empty on the coals,
Until it becomes so hot
That the copper glows.
Then its uncleanness shall melt away in it,
And its rust be consumed.
¹² ^{d-}It has frustrated all effort,
Its thick scum will not leave it—
Into the fire with its scum!^{-d}

¹³ For your vile impurity—because I sought to cleanse you of your impurity, but you would not be cleansed—you shall never be clean again until I have satisfied My fury upon you. ¹⁴ I the LORD have spoken: It shall come to pass and I will do it. I will not refrain or spare or relent. You shall be punished according to your ways and your deeds—declares the Lord GOD.

---

^{d-d} *Meaning of Heb. uncertain.*
^e *Heb. "I."*
^{f-f} *Emendation yields "Pour out the broth."*

¹⁵ The word of the LORD came to me: ¹⁶ O mortal, I am about to take away the delight of your eyes from you through pestilence; but you shall not lament or weep or let your tears flow. ¹⁷ Moan softly; observe no mourning for the dead: Put on your turban and put your sandals on your feet; do not cover over your upper lip, and do not eat the bread of comforters."^g

¹⁸ In the evening my wife died, and in the morning I did as I had been commanded. And when I spoke to the people that morning, ¹⁹ the people asked me, "Will you not tell us what these things portend for us, that you are acting so?" ²⁰ I answered them, "The word of the LORD has come to me: ²¹ Tell the House of Israel: Thus said the Lord GOD: 'I am going to desecrate My Sanctuary, your pride and glory, the delight of your eyes and the desire of your heart; and the sons and daughters you have left behind shall fall by the sword. ²⁴ ^hAnd Ezekiel shall become a portent for you: you shall do just as he has done, when it happens; and you shall know that I am the Lord GOD.' ²² Accordingly, you shall do as I have done: you shall not cover over your upper lips nor eat the bread of comforters;^g ²³ and your turbans shall remain on your heads, and your sandals upon your feet. You shall not lament or weep, but you shall be heartsick because of your iniquities and shall moan to one another."^h

²⁵ You, O mortal, take note: On the day that I take their stronghold from them, their pride and joy, the delight of their eyes and the longing of their hearts—their sons and daughters—²⁶ on that day a fugitive will come to you, to let you hear it with your own ears. ²⁷ On that day your mouth shall be opened to the fugitive, and you shall speak and no longer be dumb. So you shall be a portent for them, and they shall know that I am the LORD.

---

^g *Lit. "men."*
^h *Verse 24 moved up for clarity.*

25 The word of the LORD came to me: [2] O mortal, set your face toward the Ammonites and prophesy against them. [3] Say to the Ammonites: Hear the word of the Lord GOD! Thus said the Lord GOD: Because you cried "Aha!" over My sanctuary when it was desecrated, and over the land of Israel when it was laid waste, and over the House of Judah when it went into exile—[4] assuredly, I will deliver you to the Kedemites as a possession. They shall set up their encampments among you and pitch their dwellings in your midst; they shall eat your produce and they shall drink your milk. [5] I will make Rabbah a pasture for camels and Ammon a place for sheep to lie down. And you shall know that I am the LORD.

[6] For thus said the Lord GOD: Because you clapped your hands and stamped your feet and rejoiced over the land of Israel with such utter scorn—[7] assuredly, I will stretch out My hand against you and give you as booty to the nations; I will cut you off from among the peoples and wipe you out from among the countries and destroy you. And you shall know that I am the LORD.

[8] Thus said the Lord GOD: Because Moab *-and Seir-*^a said, "See the House of Judah is like all other nations"—[9] assuredly, I will lay bare the flank of Moab, all its towns to the last one—Beth-jeshimoth, Baal-meon, and Kiriathaim, the glory of the country. [10] I will deliver it, together with Ammon, to the Kedemites as their possession. Thus Ammon shall not be remembered among the nations, [11] and I will mete out punishments to Moab. And they shall know that I am the LORD.

[12] Thus said the Lord GOD: Because Edom acted vengefully against the House of Judah and incurred guilt by wreaking revenge upon it—[13] assuredly, thus said the Lord GOD: I will stretch out My hand against Edom and cut off from it man and beast, and I will lay it in ruins; from Tema to Dedan they shall fall by the

^a-a Lacking in some Septuagint mss.

sword. [14] I will wreak My vengeance on Edom through My people Israel, and they shall take action against Edom in accordance with My blazing anger; and they shall know My vengeance—declares the Lord GOD.

[15] Thus said the Lord GOD: Because the Philistines, in their ancient hatred, acted vengefully, and with utter scorn sought revenge and destruction—[16] assuredly, thus said the Lord GOD: I will stretch out My hand against the Philistines and cut off the Cherethites and wipe out the last survivors of the seacoast. [17] I will wreak frightful vengeance upon them by furious punishment; and when I inflict My vengeance upon them, they shall know that I am the LORD.

26 In the eleventh year, on the first of the month,[a] the word of the LORD came to me: [2] O mortal, because Tyre gloated over Jerusalem, "Aha! The gateway[b] of the peoples is broken, it has become mine; I shall be filled, now that it is laid in ruins"— [3] assuredly, thus said the Lord GOD:
> I am going to deal with you, O Tyre!
> I will hurl many nations against you,
> As the sea hurls its waves.
> [4] They shall destroy the walls of Tyre
> And demolish her towers;
> And I will scrape her soil off her
> And leave her a naked rock.
> [5] She shall be in the heart of the sea
> A place for drying[c] nets;
> For I have spoken it
> > —declares the Lord GOD.
> She shall become spoil for the nations,
> [6] And her daughter-towns in the country
> Shall be put to the sword.
> And they shall know that I am the LORD.

[a] *The month is not indicated.*
[b] *Targum reads "trafficker"; cf. 27.3.*
[c] *Lit. "spreading out."*

⁷ For thus said the Lord GOD: I will bring from the north, against Tyre, King Nebuchadrezzar of Babylon, a king of kings, with horses, chariots, and horsemen—a great mass of troops.

⁸ Your daughter-towns in the country
He shall put to the sword;
He shall erect towers against you,
And cast up mounds against you,
And raise [a wall of] bucklers against you.
⁹ He shall turn the force of his battering rams
Against your walls
And smash your towers with his axes.*d*
¹⁰ From the cloud raised by his horses
Dust shall cover you;
From the clatter of horsemen
And wheels and chariots,
Your walls shall shake—
When he enters your gates
As men enter a breached city.
¹¹ With the hoofs of his steeds
He shall trample all your streets.
He shall put your people to the sword,
And your mighty pillars shall crash to the ground.
¹² They shall plunder your wealth
And loot your merchandise.
They shall raze your walls
And tear down your splendid houses,
And they shall cast into the water
Your stones and timber and soil.
¹³ I will put an end to the murmur of your songs,
And the sound of your lyres shall be heard no more.
¹⁴ I will make you a naked rock,
You shall be a place for drying*c* nets;
You shall never be rebuilt.
For I have spoken

—declares the Lord GOD.

d Lit. "swords."

¹⁵ Thus said the Lord GOD to Tyre: The coastlands shall quake at the sound of your downfall, when the wounded groan, when slaughter is rife within you. ¹⁶ All the rulers of the sea shall descend from their thrones; they shall remove their robes and strip off their embroidered garments. They shall clothe themselves with trembling, and shall sit on the ground; they shall tremble every moment, and they shall be aghast at you. ¹⁷ And they shall intone a dirge over you, and they shall say to you:

> How you have perished, ᵉ‑you who were peopled‑ᵉ from the
>   seas,
> O renowned city!
> Mighty on the sea were she and her inhabitants,
> Who cast their terror on all ᶠ‑its inhabitants.‑ᶠ
> ¹⁸ Now shall the coastlands tremble
> On the day of your downfall,
> And the coastlands by the sea
> Be terrified at your end.

¹⁹ For thus said the Lord GOD: When I make you a ruined city, like cities empty of inhabitants; when I bring the deep over you, and its mighty waters cover you, ²⁰ then I will bring you down, with those who go down to the Pit, to the people of old. I will install you in the nether world, with those that go down to the Pit, like the ruins of old, so that you shall not be inhabited and shall not radiate⁸ splendor in the land of the living. ²¹ I will make you a horror, and you shall cease to be; you shall be sought, but shall never be found again—declares the Lord GOD.

27

The word of the LORD came to me: ² Now you, O mortal, intone a dirge over Tyre. ³ Say to Tyre:

> O you who dwell at the gateway of the sea,
> Who trade with the peoples on many coastlands:
> Thus said the Lord GOD:
> ᵃ‑O Tyre, you boasted,

ᵉ‑ᵉ *Septuagint reads "vanished."*
ᶠ‑ᶠ *I.e., of the sea. Emendation yields "the dry land."*
⁸ *Understanding* nathatti *as second person singular feminine; cf. 16.50 and note. But meaning of Heb. uncertain.*
ᵃ‑ᵃ *Emendation yields: "O Tyre, you are a ship/Perfect in beauty."*

I am perfect in beauty.⁻ᵃ
⁴ Your frontiers were on the high seas,
Your builders perfected your beauty.
⁵ From cypress trees of Senir
They fashioned your planks;
They took a cedar from Lebanon
To make a mast for you.
⁶ From oak trees of Bashan
They made your oars;
Of boxwood from the isles of Kittim,
Inlaid with ivory,
They made your decks.
⁷ Embroidered linen from Egypt
Was the cloth
That served you for sails;
Of blue and purple from the coasts of Elishah
Were your awnings.
⁸ The inhabitants of Sidon and Arvad
Were your rowers;
ᵇ⁻Your skilled men, O Tyre,⁻ᵇ were within you,
They were your pilots.
⁹ Gebal's elders and craftsmen were within you,
Making your repairs.

All the ships of the sea, with their crews,
Were ᶜ⁻in your harborᶜ
To traffic in your wares.
¹⁰ Men of Paras, Lud, and Put
Were in your army,
Your fighting men;
They hung shields and helmets in your midst,
They lent splendor to you.
¹¹ Men of Arvad and Helech
Manned your walls all around,
And men of Gammad were stationed in your towers;

ᵇ⁻ᵇ *Emendation yields "The skilled men of Zemar"; cf. Gen. 10.18.*
ᶜ⁻ᶜ *Lit. "in you".*

They hung their quivers all about your walls;
They perfected your beauty.
¹² Tarshish traded with you because of your wealth of all kinds of goods; they bartered silver, iron, tin, and lead for your wares. ¹³ Javan, Tubal, and Meshech—they were your merchants; they trafficked with you in human beings and copper utensils. ¹⁴ From Beth-togarmah they bartered horses, horsemen, and mules for your wares. ¹⁵ The people of Dedan were your merchants; many coastlands traded under your rule and rendered you tribute in ivory tusks and ebony. ¹⁶ Aram traded with you because of your wealth of merchandise, dealing with you in turquoise, purple stuff, embroidery, fine linen, coral, and agate.^d ¹⁷ Judah and the land of Israel were your merchants; they trafficked with you in wheat of ^e⁻Minnith and Pannag,⁻^e honey, oil, and balm. ¹⁸ Because of your wealth of merchandise, because of your great wealth, Damascus traded with you in Helbon wine and white wool. ¹⁹ ^f⁻Vedan and Javan from Uzal traded for your wares; they trafficked with you in polished iron, cassia, and calamus. ²⁰ Dedan was your merchant in saddlecloths for riding.^f ²¹ Arabia and all Kedar's chiefs were traders under your rule; they traded with you in lambs, rams, and goats. ²² The merchants of Sheba and Raamah were your merchants; they bartered for your wares all the finest spices, all kinds of precious stones, and gold. ²³ Haran, Canneh, and Eden, the merchants of Sheba, Assyria, and Chilmad traded with you. ²⁴ ^f⁻These were your merchants in choice fabrics, embroidered cloaks of blue, and many-colored carpets tied up with cords and preserved with cedar—among your wares.^f ²⁵ The ships of Tarshish were in the service of your trade.

^gSo you were full and richly laden
On the high seas.
²⁶ Your oarsmen brought you out
Into the mighty waters;
The tempest wrecked you
On the high seas.
²⁷ Your wealth, your wares, your merchandise,

---

^d The exact identity of these stones is uncertain.
^e⁻e Meaning of Heb. uncertain; cf. "Minnith," Judg. 11.33.
^f⁻f Meaning of Heb. uncertain.
^g Resuming the description of Tyre as a ship, as in vv. 3b-9a.

Your sailors and your pilots,
The men who made your repairs,
Those who carried on your traffic,
And all the fighting men within you—
All the multitude within you—
Shall go down into the depths of the sea
On the day of your downfall.
28 At the outcry of your pilots
The billows shall heave;
29 And all the oarsmen and mariners,
All the pilots of the sea,
Shall come down from their ships
And stand on the ground.
30 They shall raise their voices over you
And cry out bitterly;
They shall cast dust on their heads
And strew ashes on themselves.
31 On your account, they shall make
Bald patches on their heads,
And shall gird themselves with sackcloth.
They shall weep over you, broken-hearted,
With bitter lamenting;
32 They shall intone a dirge over you as they wail,
And lament for you thus:

Who was like Tyre when she was silenced
In the midst of the sea?
33 When your wares were unloaded from the seas,
You satisfied many peoples;
With your great wealth and merchandise
You enriched the kings of the earth.
34 But when you were wrecked on the seas,
In the deep waters sank your merchandise
And all the crew aboard you.
35 All the inhabitants of the coastlands

Are appalled over you;
Their kings are aghast,
Their faces contorted.*f*
[36] The merchants among the peoples hissed*h* at you;
You have become a horror,
And have ceased to be forever.

28 The word of the LORD came to me: [2] O mortal, say to the prince of Tyre: Thus said the Lord GOD:

Because you have been so haughty and have said, "I am a god; I sit enthroned like a god in the heart of the seas," whereas you are not a god but a man, though you deemed your mind equal to a god's*a*—

[3] Yes, you are wiser than Daniel;
In no hidden matter can anyone
Compare to you.
[4] By your shrewd understanding
You have gained riches,
And have amassed gold and silver
In your treasuries.
[5] By your great shrewdness in trade
You have increased your wealth,
And you have grown haughty
Because of your wealth.

[6] Assuredly, thus said the Lord GOD: Because you have deemed your mind equal to a god's,

[7] I swear I will bring against you
Strangers, the most ruthless of nations.
They shall unsheathe their swords
Against your prized shrewdness,
And they shall strike down*b* your splendor.
[8] They shall bring you down to the Pit;
In the heart of the sea you shall die
The death of the slain.

h I.e. to ward off the calamity from the viewer; cf. Jer. 18.16; 49.17; Job 27.23; Lam. 2.15.
a This sentence is continued in v. 6; vv. 3-5 are parenthetical.
b Meaning of Heb. uncertain.

⁹ Will you still say, "I am a god"
Before your slayers,
When you are proved a man, not a god,
At the hands of those who strike you down?
¹⁰ By the hands of strangers you shall die
The death of the uncircumcised;ᶜ
For I have spoken
                    —declares the Lord GOD.

¹¹ The word of the LORD came to me: ¹² O mortal, intone a
dirge over the king of Tyre and say to him: Thus said the Lord
GOD:
You were the seal of perfection,
Full of wisdom and flawless in beauty.
¹³ You were in Eden, the garden of God;
Every precious stone was your adornment:
Carnelian, chrysolite, and amethyst;
Beryl, lapis lazuli, and jasper;
Sapphire, turquoise, and emerald;
And gold ᵈ⁻beautifully wrought for you,
Mined for you, prepared the day you were created.⁻ᵈ
¹⁴ ᵇ⁻I created you as a cherub
With outstretched shielding wings;⁻ᵇ
And you resided on God's holy mountain;
You walked among stones of fire.
¹⁵ You were blameless in your ways,
From the day you were created
Until wrongdoing was`found in you.
¹⁶ By your far-flung commerce
You were filled with lawlessness
And you sinned.
So I have struck you down
From the mountain of God,
And I have destroyed you, O shielding cherub,
From among the stones of fire.

ᶜ *According to popular belief, those who die uncircumcised and those left unburied are relegated
to the lower level of the nether world; cf. 31.18; 32.19 ff.*
ᵈ⁻ᵈ *Meaning of Heb. uncertain. On the stones, see note at Exod. 28.17.*

[17] You grew haughty because of your beauty,
You debased your wisdom for the sake of your splendor;
I have cast you to the ground,
I have made you an object for kings to stare at.
[18] By the greatness of your guilt,
Through the dishonesty of your trading,
You desecrated your sanctuaries.
So I made a fire issue from you,
And it has devoured you;
I have reduced you to ashes on the ground,
In the sight of all who behold you.
[19] All who knew you among the peoples
Are appalled at your doom.
You have become a horror
And have ceased to be forever.

[20] The word of the LORD came to me: [21] O mortal, set your face toward Sidon and prophesy against her. [22] Say: Thus said the Lord GOD:

I am going to deal with you, O Sidon.
I will gain glory in your midst;
And they shall know that I am the LORD,
When I wreak punishment upon her
And show Myself holy through her.
[23] I will let pestilence loose against her
And bloodshed into her streets.
And the slain shall fall in her midst
When the sword comes upon her from all sides.
And they shall know that I am the LORD.

[24] Then shall the House of Israel no longer be afflicted with prickling briers and lacerating thorns from all the neighbors who despise them; and they shall know that I am the Lord GOD.

[25] Thus said the Lord GOD: When I have gathered the House of Israel from the peoples among which they have been dis-

persed, and have shown Myself holy through them in the sight of the nations, they shall settle on their own soil, which I gave to My servant Jacob, ²⁶ and they shall dwell on it in security. They shall build houses and plant vineyards, and shall dwell on it in security, when I have meted out punishment to all those about them who despise them. And they shall know that I the LORD am their God.

29 In the tenth year, on the twelfth day of the tenth month, the word of the LORD came to me: ² O mortal, turn your face against Pharaoh king of Egypt, and prophesy against him and against all Egypt. ³ Speak these words:

Thus said the Lord GOD:
I am going to deal with you, O Pharaoh king of Egypt,
Mighty monster, sprawling in your*a* channels,
Who said,
My Nile is my own;
I made it for myself.
⁴ I will put hooks in your jaws,
And make the fish of your channels
Cling to your scales;
I will haul you up from your channels,
With all the fish of your channels.
Clinging to your scales.
⁵ And I will fling you into the desert,
With all the fish of your channels.
You shall be left lying in the open,
Ungathered and unburied:
I have given you as food
To the beasts of the earth
And the birds of the sky.
⁶ Then all the inhabitants of Egypt shall know
That I am the LORD.

a Lit. "its."

Because you[b] were a staff of reed
To the House of Israel:
7 When they grasped you with the hand, you would
    splinter,
And wound all their shoulders,[c]
And when they leaned on you, you would break,
And make all their loins unsteady.[d]

8 Assuredly, thus said the Lord GOD: Lo, I will bring a sword against you, and will cut off man and beast from you, 9 so that the land of Egypt shall fall into desolation and ruin. And they shall know that I am the LORD—because he boasted, "The Nile is mine, and I made it." 10 Assuredly, I am going to deal with you and your channels, and I will reduce the land of Egypt to utter ruin and desolation, [e]from Migdol to Syene, all the way to the border of Nubia.[-e] 11 No foot of man shall traverse it, and no foot of beast shall traverse it; and it shall remain uninhabited for forty years. 12 For forty years I will make the land of Egypt the most desolate of desolate lands, and its cities shall be the most desolate of ruined cities. And I will scatter the Egyptians among the nations and disperse them throughout the countries.

13 Further, thus said the Lord GOD: After a period of forty years I will gather the Egyptians from the peoples among whom they were dispersed. 14 I will restore the fortunes of the Egyptians and bring them back to the land of their origin, the land of Pathros,[f] and there they shall be a lowly kingdom. 15 It shall be the lowliest of all the kingdoms, and shall not lord it over the nations again. I will reduce the Egyptians,[g] so that they shall have no dominion over the nations. 16 Never again shall they be the trust of the House of Israel, recalling its guilt in having turned to them. And they shall know that I am the Lord GOD.

17 In the twenty-seventh year, on the first day of the first month, the word of the LORD came to me: 18 O mortal, King Nebuchadrezzar of Babylon has made his army expend vast labor on

---

b Lit. "they."
c Septuagint and Syriac read, "palms"; cf. II Kings 18.21; Isa. 36.6.
d Taking 'amad as a by-form of ma'ad; cf. Syriac translation.
e-e I.e. the length of Egypt, from north to south. Syene is modern Aswan.
f I.e. southern Egypt.
g Heb. "them."

Tyre; every head is rubbed bald and every shoulder scraped. But he and his army have had no return for the labor he expended on Tyre. [19] Assuredly, thus said the Lord GOD: I will give the land of Egypt to Nebuchadrezzar, king of Babylon. He shall carry off her wealth and take her spoil and seize her booty; and she shall be the recompense of his army. [20] As the wage for which he labored, for what they did for Me, I give him the land of Egypt —declares the Lord GOD.

[21] On that day I will [h-]endow the House of Israel with strength, and you shall be vindicated[-h] among them. And they shall know that I am the LORD.

30 The word of the LORD came to me: [2] O mortal, prophesy and say: Thus said the Lord GOD:

Wail, alas for the day!
[3] For a day is near;
A day of the LORD is near.
It will be a day of cloud,
An hour of [invading] nations.
[4] A sword shall pierce Egypt,
And Nubia shall be seized with trembling,
When men fall slain in Egypt
And her wealth is seized
And her foundations are overthrown.
[5] Nubia, Put, and Lud, and all [a-]the mixed populations,[-a] and Cub, and the inhabitants of the allied countries shall fall by the sword with them.
[6] Thus said the LORD:
Those who support Egypt shall fall,
And her proud strength shall sink;
There they shall fall by the sword,
From Migdol to Syene
—declares the Lord GOD.

[h-h] Lit. *"cause a horn to sprout for the House of Israel, and I will grant you opening of the mouth."*

[a-a] *Meaning of Heb. uncertain.*

⁷ They shall be the most desolate of desolate lands, and her cities shall be the most ruined of cities, ⁸ when I set fire to Egypt and all who help her are broken. Thus they shall know that I am the LORD.

⁹ On that day, messengers shall set out at My bidding to strike terror into confident Nubia. And they shall be seized with trembling on Egypt's day [of doom]—for it is at hand.

¹⁰ Thus said the Lord GOD: I will put an end to the wealth of Egypt through King Nebuchadrezzar of Babylon. ¹¹ He, together with his troops, the most ruthless of the nations, shall be brought to ravage the land. And they shall unsheathe the sword against Egypt and fill the land with the slain.

¹² I will turn the channels into dry ground, and I will deliver the land into the hands of evil men. I will lay waste the land and everything in it by the hands of strangers. I the LORD have spoken.

¹³ Thus said the Lord GOD: I will destroy the fetishes and make an end of the idols in Noph; and no longer shall there be a prince in the land of Egypt; and I will strike the land of Egypt with fear. ¹⁴ I will lay Pathros waste, I will set fire to Zoan, and I will execute judgment on No. ¹⁵ I will pour out my anger upon Sin, the stronghold of Egypt, and I will destroy the wealth of No. ¹⁶ I will set fire to Egypt; Sin shall writhe in anguish and No shall be torn apart; ᵃ⁻and Noph [shall face] adversaries in broad daylight.⁻ᵃ ¹⁷ The young men of Avenᵇ and Pi-beseth shall fall by the sword, and those [towns] shall go into captivity. ¹⁸ In Tehaphnehesᶜ daylight shall be withheld,ᵈ when I break there the power of Egypt, and there her proud strength comes to an end. [The city] itself shall be covered with cloud, and its daughter towns shall go into captivity.

¹⁹ Thus I will execute judgment on Egypt;
And they shall know that I am the LORD.

²⁰ In the eleventh year, on the seventh day of the first month, the word of the LORD came to me: ²¹ O mortal, I have broken the

ᵇ Elsewhere called "On"; cf. Gen. 41.45,50; 46.20.
ᶜ Elsewhere vocalized "Tahpanhes"; e.g. Jer. 2.16; 44.1.
ᵈ Some Heb. mss. and editions read "darkened".

arm of Pharaoh king of Egypt; it has not been bound up to be healed nor firmly bandaged to make it strong enough to grasp the sword. ²² Assuredly, thus said the Lord GOD: I am going to deal with Pharaoh king of Egypt. I will break his arms, both the sound one and the injured, and make the sword drop from his hand. ²³ I will scatter the Egyptians among the nations and disperse them throughout the countries. ²⁴ I will strengthen the arms of the king of Babylon and put My sword in his hand; and I will break the arms of Pharaoh, and he shall groan before him with the groans of one struck down. ²⁵ I will make firm the arms of the king of Babylon, but the arms of Pharaoh shall fail. And they shall know that I am the LORD, when I put My sword into the hand of the king of Babylon, and he lifts it against the land of Egypt. ²⁶ I will scatter the Egyptians among the nations and disperse them throughout the countries. Thus they shall know that I am the LORD.

31 In the eleventh year, on the first day of the third month, the word of the LORD came to me: ² O mortal, say to Pharaoh king of Egypt and his hordes:

> Who was comparable to you in greatness?
> ³ Assyria was a cedar in Lebanon
> With beautiful branches and ᵃ⁻shady thickets,⁻ᵃ
> Of lofty stature,
> With its top among ᵇ⁻leafy trees.⁻ᵇ
> ⁴ Waters nourished it,
> The deep made it grow tall,
> Washing with its streams
> The place where it was planted,
> Making its channels well up
> ᶜ⁻To all⁻ᶜ the trees of the field.
> ⁵ Therefore it exceeded in stature
> All the trees of the field;

ᵃ⁻ᵃ *Meaning of Heb. uncertain.*
ᵇ⁻ᵇ *Septuagint reads "clouds."*
ᶜ⁻ᶜ *Meaning of Heb. uncertain; emendation yields "more than for all."*

Its branches multiplied and its boughs grew long
Because of the abundant water
That welled up for it.
⁶ In its branches nested
All the birds of the sky;
All the beasts of the field
Bore their young under its boughs,
And in its shadow lived
All the great nations.
⁷ It was beautiful in its height,
In the length of its branches,
Because its stock stood
By abundant waters.
⁸ Cedars in the garden of God
Could not compare with it;
Cypresses could not match its boughs,
And plane trees could not vie with its branches;
No tree in the garden of God
Was its peer in beauty.
⁹ I made it beautiful
In the profusion of its branches;
And all the trees of Eden envied it
In the garden of God.

¹⁰ Assuredly, thus said the Lord GOD: Because it*d* towered high
in stature, and thrust its top up among the *b-*leafy trees,*-b* and it
was arrogant in its height, ¹¹ I delivered it into the hands of the
mightiest of nations. They treated it as befitted its wickedness. I
banished it. ¹² Strangers, the most ruthless of nations, cut it down
and abandoned it; its branches fell on the mountains and in every
valley; its boughs were splintered in every watercourse of the
earth; and all the peoples of the earth departed from its shade
and abandoned it. ¹³ Upon its fallen trunk all the birds of the sky
nest, and all the beasts of the field lodge among its boughs—
¹⁴ so that no trees by water should exalt themselves in stature or

---

d Heb. "you."

set their tops among the *b*-leafy trees,-*b* and that no well watered tree may reach up to them in height. For they are all consigned to death, to the lowest part of the nether world,*e* together with human beings who descend into the Pit.

15 Thus said the Lord GOD: On the day it went down to Sheol, I closed*f* the deep over it and covered it; I held back its streams, and the great waters were checked. I made Lebanon mourn deeply for it, and all the trees of the field languished on its account. 16 I made nations quake at the crash of its fall, when I cast it down to Sheol with those who descend into the Pit; and all the trees of Eden, the choicest and best of Lebanon, all that were well watered, were consoled in the lowest part of the nether-world. 17 They also descended with it into Sheol, to those slain by the sword, together with its supporters,*g* they who had lived under its shadow among the nations.

18 [Now you know] who is comparable to you in glory and greatness among the trees of Eden. And you too shall be brought down with the trees of Eden to the lowest part of the nether-world; you shall lie among the uncircumcised and those slain by the sword. Such shall be [the fate of] Pharaoh and all his hordes —declares the Lord GOD.

32 In the twelfth year, on the first day of the twelfth month, the word of the LORD came to me: 2 O mortal, intone a dirge over Pharaoh king of Egypt. Say to him:

a-O great beast among the nations,-*a* you are doomed!
You are like the dragon in the seas,
Thrusting through their*b* streams,
Stirring up the water with your feet
And muddying their streams!
3 Thus said the Lord GOD:
I will cast My net over you
In an assembly of many peoples,
And you shall be hauled up in My toils.

e *To which popular belief relegated those who died uncircumcised or by the sword; cf. v.18.*
f *Cf. Aramaic 'abulla, "gate."*
g *Heb. "arm."*

a-a *Meaning of Heb. uncertain.*
b *Heb. "your."*

⁴ And I will fling you to the ground,
Hurl you upon the open field,
I will cause all the birds of the sky
To settle upon you,
I will cause the beasts of all the earth
To batten on you.
⁵ I will cast your carcass upon the hills
And fill the valleys with your ᵃ⁻rotting flesh.⁻ᵃ
⁶ I will drench the earth
With your oozing blood upon the hills,
And the water courses shall be filled with your [gore].
⁷ When you are snuffed out,
I will cover the sky
And darken its stars;
I will cover the sun with clouds
And the moon shall not give its light.
⁸ All the lights that shine in the sky
I will darken above you;
And I will bring darkness upon your land
                              —declares the Lord GOD.
⁹ I will vex the hearts of many peoples
When I bring your ᶜ⁻shattered remnants⁻ᶜ among the
     nations,
To countries which you never knew.
¹⁰ I will strike many peoples with horror over your fate;
And their kings shall be aghast over you,
When I brandish My sword before them.
They shall tremble continually,
Each man for his own life,
On the day of your downfall.
¹¹ For thus said the Lord GOD:
The sword of the king of Babylon shall come upon you.
¹² I will cause your multitude to fall
By the swords of warriors,
All the most ruthless among the nations.

ᶜ⁻ᶜ *Septuagint reads "captives."*

They shall ravage the splendor of Egypt,
And all her masses shall be wiped out.
13 I will make all her cattle vanish from beside abundant
waters;
The feet of man shall not muddy them any more,
Nor shall the hoofs of cattle muddy them.
14 Then I will let their waters settle,
And make their rivers flow like oil
—declares the Lord GOD:
15 When I lay the land of Egypt waste,
When the land is emptied of [the life] that filled it,
When I strike down all its inhabitants.
And they shall know that I am the LORD.
16 This is a dirge, and it shall be intoned;
The women of the nations shall intone it,
They shall intone it over Egypt and all her multitude
—declares the Lord GOD.

17 In the twelfth year, on the fifteenth day of the month,*d* the word of the LORD came to me: 18 *e*O mortal, wail [the dirge]— along with the women of the mighty nations—over the masses of Egypt, accompanying their descent to the lowest part of the nether world, among those who have gone down into the Pit. 19 *f-*Whom do you surpass in beauty? Down with you, and be laid to rest with the uncircumcised! 20 They shall lie amid those slain by the sword,*f* *e*[amid those slain by] the sword [Egypt] has been dragged and left with all her masses.

21 From the depths of Sheol the mightiest of warriors speak to him and his allies; the uncircumcised, the slain by the sword, have gone down and lie [there]. 22 Assyria is there with all her company, their graves round about, all of them slain, fallen by the sword. 23 Their graves set in the farthest recesses of the Pit, all her company are round about her tomb, all of them slain, fallen by the sword—they who struck terror in the land of the living. 24 There too is Elam and all her masses round about her tomb,

d Presumably the twelfth month; cf. v. 1.
e Construction of these verses uncertain.
f-f Cf. 31.18 ff. and note e on 31.14.

all of them slain, fallen by the sword—they who descended uncircumcised to the lowest part of the nether world, who struck terror in the land of the living—now they bear their shame with those who have gone down to the Pit. ²⁵ They made a bed for her among the slain, with all her masses; their graves are round about her. They are all uncircumcised, slain by the sword. Though their terror was once spread over the land of the living, they bear their shame with those who have gone into the Pit; they are placed among the slain. ²⁶ Meshech and Tubal and all their masses are there; their graves are round about. They are all uncircumcised, pierced through by the sword—they who once struck terror in the land of the living. ²⁷ And they do not lie with the fallen uncircumcised warriors, who went down to Sheol with their battle gear, who put their swords beneath their heads and their iniquities*g* upon their bones—for the terror of the warriors was upon the land of the living. ²⁸ And you too shall be shattered amid the uncircumcised, and lie among those slain by the sword. ²⁹ Edom is there, her kings and all her chieftains, who, for all their might, are laid among those who are slain by the sword; they too lie with the uncircumcised and with those who have gone down to the Pit. ³⁰ All the princes of the north and all the Sidonians are there, who went down in disgrace with the slain, in spite of the terror that their might inspired; and they lie, uncircumcised, with those who are slain by the sword, and bear their shame with those who have gone down to the Pit.

³¹ These Pharaoh shall see, and he shall be consoled for all his masses, those of Pharaoh's men slain by the sword and all his army—declares the Lord GOD. ³² *h-*I strike terror into the land of the living; Pharaoh*-h* and all his masses are laid among the uncircumcised, along with those who were slain by the sword—said the Lord GOD.

---

g *Emendation yields "shields."*
h-h *Emendation yields "because he struck terror in the land of the living, Pharaoh."*

33 The word of the LORD came to me: ² O mortal, speak to
your fellow countrymen and say to them: When I bring the sword
against a country, the citizens of that country take one of their
number and appoint him their watchman. ³ Suppose he sees the
sword advancing against the country, and he blows the horn and
warns the people. ⁴ If anybody hears the sound of the horn but
ignores the warning, and the sword comes and dispatches him,
his blood shall be on his own head. ⁵ Since he heard the sound
of the horn but ignored the warning, his bloodguilt shall be upon
himself; had he taken the warning, he would have saved his life.
⁶ But if the watchman sees the sword advancing and does not
blow the horn, so that the people are not warned, and the sword
comes and destroys one of them, that person was destroyed for
his own sins; however, I will demand a reckoning for his blood
from the watchman.

⁷ Now, O mortal, I have appointed you a watchman for the
House of Israel; and whenever you hear a message from My
mouth, you must transmit My warning to them. ⁸ When I say to
the wicked, "Wicked man, you shall die," but you have not
spoken to warn the wicked man against his way, he, that wicked
man, shall die for his sins, but I will demand a reckoning for his
blood from you. ⁹ But if you have warned the wicked man to turn
back from his way, and he has not turned from his way, he shall
die for his own sins, but you will have saved your life.

¹⁰ Now, O mortal, say to the House of Israel: This is what you
have been saying, "Our transgressions and our sins weigh heavily
upon us; we are sick at heart about them. How can we survive?"
¹¹ Say to them: As I live—declares the Lord GOD—it is not My
desire that the wicked shall die, but that the wicked turn from his
[evil] ways and live. Turn back, turn back from your evil ways,
that you may not die, O House of Israel!

¹² Now, O mortal, say to your fellow countrymen: The righ-
teousness of the righteous shall not save him when he transgres-

ses, nor shall the wickedness of the wicked cause him to stumble when he turns back from his wickedness. The righteous shall not survive through *ᵃhis righteousnessᵃ* when he sins. ¹³ When I say of the righteous "He shall surely live," and, relying on his righteousness, he commits iniquity, none of his righteous deeds shall be remembered; but for the iniquity that he has committed he shall die. ¹⁴ So, too, when I say to the wicked, "You shall die," and he turns back from his sinfulness and does what is just and right—¹⁵ if the wicked man restores a pledge, makes good what he has taken by robbery, follows the laws of life,*ᵇ* and does not commit iniquity—he shall live, he shall not die. ¹⁶ None of the sins that he committed shall be remembered against him; since he does what is just and right, he shall live.

¹⁷ Your fellow countrymen say, "The way of the Lord is unfair." But it is their way that is unfair! ¹⁸ When a righteous man turns away from his righteous deeds and commits iniquity, he shall die *ᶜfor it.ᶜ* ¹⁹ And when a wicked man turns back from his wickedness and does what is just and right, it is he who shall live by virtue of these things. ²⁰ And will you say, "The way of the Lord is unfair?" I will judge each one of you according to his ways, O House of Israel!

²¹ In the twelfth year of our exile, on the fifth day of the tenth month, a fugitive came to me from Jerusalem and reported, "The city has fallen." ²² Now the hand of the LORD had come upon me the evening before the fugitive arrived, and He opened my mouth before he came to me in the morning; thus my mouth was opened and I was no longer speechless.

²³ The word of the LORD came to me: ²⁴ O mortal, those who live in these ruins in the land of Israel argue, "Abraham was but one man, yet he was granted possession of the land. We are many; surely, the land has been given as a possession to us." ²⁵ Therefore say to them: Thus said the Lord GOD: You eat with the blood, you raise your eyes to your fetishes, and you shed blood—yet you expect to possess the land! ²⁶ You have relied on

ᵃ⁻ᵃ *Heb. "it."*
ᵇ *Cf. Lev. 18.5.*
ᶜ⁻ᶜ *Or "in spite of them," i.e. his righteous deeds.*

your sword, you have committed abominations, you have all defiled other men's wives—yet you expect to possess the land!

²⁷ Thus shall you speak to them: Thus said the Lord GOD: As I live, those who are in the ruins shall fall by the sword, and those who are in the open I have allotted as food to the beasts, and those who are in the strongholds and caves shall die by pestilence. ²⁸ I will make the land a desolate waste, and her proud glory shall cease; and the mountains of Israel shall be desolate, with none passing through. ²⁹ And they shall know that I am the LORD, when I make the land a desolate waste on account of all the abominations which they have committed.

³⁰ Note well, O mortal: your fellow countrymen who converse about you by the walls and in the doorways of their houses and say to each other and propose to one another, "Come and hear what word has issued from the LORD." ³¹ They will come to you ᵈ⁻in crowds and sit before you in throngs⁻ᵈ and will hear your words, but they will not obey them. For ᵉ⁻they produce nothing but lust with their mouths;⁻ᵉ and their hearts pursue nothing but gain. ³² To them you are just a singer of bawdy songs, who has a sweet voice and plays skillfully; they hear your words, but will not obey them. ³³ But when itᶠ comes—and come it will—they shall know that a prophet has been among them.

34

The word of the LORD came to me: ² O mortal, prophesy against the shepherdsᵃ of Israel. Prophesy, and say to them:

To the shepherds: Thus said the Lord GOD: Ah, you shepherds of Israel, who have been tending yourselves! Is it not the flock that the shepherds ought to tend? ³ You partake of the fat,ᵇ you clothe yourselves with the wool, and you slaughter the fatlings; but you do not tend the flock. ⁴ You have not sustained the weak, healed the sick, or bandaged the injured; you have not brought back the strayed, or looked for the lost; but you have driven them with harsh rigor, ⁵ and they have been scattered for want of any-

---

ᵈ⁻ᵈ *Meaning of Heb. uncertain. Lit. "as a people come, and sit before you as My people."*
ᵉ⁻ᵉ *Meaning of Heb. uncertain.*
ᶠ *I.e. the punishment predicted.*

ᵃ *I.e. rulers.*
ᵇ *Septuagint and Vulgate, reading the Hebrew consonants with different vowels, translate "milk."*

one to tend them; scattered, they have become prey for every wild beast. ⁶ My sheep stray through all the mountains and over every lofty hill; My flock is scattered all over the face of the earth, with none to take thought of them and none to seek them. ⁷ Hear then, O shepherds, the word of the LORD! ⁸ As I live—declares the Lord GOD: Because My flock has been a spoil—My flock has been a prey for all the wild beasts, for want of anyone to tend them since My shepherds have not taken thought of My flock, for the shepherds tended themselves instead of tending the flock— ⁹ hear indeed, O shepherds, the word of the LORD: ¹⁰ Thus said the Lord GOD: I am going to deal with the shepherds! I will demand a reckoning of them for My flock, and I will dismiss them from tending the flock. The shepherds shall not tend themselves any more; for I will rescue My flock from their mouths, and it shall not be their prey. ¹¹ For thus said the Lord GOD: Here am I! I am going to take thought for My flock and I will seek them out. ¹² As a shepherd seeks out his flock when some [animals] in his flock have gotten separated, so I will seek out My flock, I will rescue them from all the places to which they were scattered on a day of cloud and gloom. ¹³ I will take them out from the peoples and gather them from the countries, and I will bring them to their own land, and will pasture them on the mountains of Israel, by the watercourses and in all the settled portions of the land. ¹⁴ I will feed them in good grazing land, and the lofty hills of Israel shall be their pasture. There, in the hills of Israel, they shall lie down in a good pasture and shall feed on rich grazing land. ¹⁵ I Myself will graze My flock, and I Myself will let them lie down —declares the Lord GOD. ¹⁶ I will look for the lost, and I will bring back the strayed; I will bandage the injured, and I will sustain the weak; and the fat and healthy ones I will destroy.ᶜ I will tend them rightly.

¹⁷ And as for you, My flock, thus said the Lord GOD: I am going to judge between one animal and another.

To the rams and the bucks: ¹⁸ Is it not enough for you to graze

ᶜ *Several ancient versions read "guard."*

on choice grazing ground, but you must also trample with your feet what is left from your grazing? And is it not enough for you to drink *d-*clear water,*-d* but you must also muddy with your feet what is left? ¹⁹ And must My flock graze on what your feet have trampled and drink what your feet have muddied? ²⁰ Assuredly, thus said the Lord GOD to them: Here am I, I am going to decide between the stout animals and the lean. ²¹ Because you pushed with flank and shoulder against the feeble ones and butted them with your horns until you scattered them abroad, ²² I will rescue My flock and they shall no longer be a spoil. I will decide between one animal and another.

²³ Then I will appoint a single shepherd over them to tend them—My servant David. He shall tend them, he shall be a shepherd to them. ²⁴ I the LORD will be their God, and My servant David shall be a ruler among them—I the LORD have spoken. ²⁵ And I will grant them a covenant of friendship. I will banish vicious beasts from their land, and they shall live secure in the wasteland, they shall even sleep in the woodland. ²⁶ I will make *e-*these and the environs of My hill*-e* a blessing: I will send down the rain in its season, rains that bring blessing. ²⁷ The trees of the field shall yield their fruit and the land shall yield its produce. [My people] shall continue secure on its own soil. They shall know that I am the LORD when I break the bars of their yoke and rescue them from those who enslave them. ²⁸ They shall no longer be a spoil for the nations, and the beasts of the earth shall not devour them; they shall dwell secure and untroubled. ²⁹ I shall establish for them *e-*a planting of renown;*-e* they shall no more be carried off by famine, and they shall not have to bear again the taunts of the nations.*ᶠ* ³⁰ They shall know that I the LORD their God am with them and they, the House of Israel, are My people—declares the Lord GOD.

³¹ For you, My flock, flock that I tend, are men; and I, your Shepherd, am your God—declares the Lord GOD.

ᵈ⁻ᵈ *Lit. "water that has settled."*
ᵉ⁻ᵉ *Meaning of Heb. uncertain.*
ᶠ *Cf. 36.30.*

35

The word of the LORD came to me: ² O mortal, set your face against Mount Seir and prophesy against it. ³ Say to it: Thus said the Lord GOD: I am going to deal with you, Mount Seir: I will stretch out My hand against you and make you an utter waste. ⁴ I will turn your towns into ruins, and you shall be a desolation; then you shall know that I am the LORD. ⁵ Because you harbored an ancient hatred and handed the people of Israel over to the sword in their time of calamity, the time set for their punishment—⁶ assuredly, as I live, declares the Lord GOD, ᵃ⁻I will doom you with blood; blood shall pursue you; I swear that, for your bloodthirsty hatred, blood shall pursue you.⁻ᵃ ⁷ I will make Mount Seir an utter waste, and I will keep all passersby away from it. ⁸ I will cover its mountains with the slain; men slain by the sword shall lie on your hills, in your valleys, and in all your watercourses. ⁹ I will make you a desolation for all time; your towns shall never be inhabited. And you shall know that I am the LORD.

¹⁰ Because you thought "The two nations and the two lands shall be mine and we shall possess them"—ᵇ⁻although the LORD was there⁻ᵇ—¹¹ assuredly, as I live, declares the Lord GOD, I will act with the same anger and passion that you acted with in your hatred of them. And I will make Myself known through them when I judge you. ¹² You shall know that I the LORD have heard all the taunts you uttered against the hills of Israel: "They have been laid waste; they have been given to us as prey." ¹³ And you spoke arrogantly against Me and ᶜ⁻multiplied your words⁻ᶜ against Me: I have heard it.

¹⁴ Thus said the LORD God: When the whole earth rejoices, I will make you a desolation. ¹⁵ As you rejoiced when the heritage of the House of Israel was laid waste, so will I treat you: the hill country of Seir and the whole of Edom, all of it, shall be laid waste. And they shall know that I am the LORD.

ᵃ⁻ᵃ *Meaning of Heb. uncertain.*
ᵇ⁻ᵇ *Meaning of Heb. uncertain; emendation yields "and the LORD heard it."*
ᶜ⁻ᶜ *Emendation yields "and spoke arrogantly."*

36 And you, O mortal, prophesy to the mountains of Israel and say: O mountains of Israel, hear the word of the LORD: ² Thus said the Lord GOD: Because the enemy gloated over you, "Aha! Those ancient heights have become our possession!" ³ therefore prophesy, and say: Thus said the Lord GOD: Just because ^{a-}they eagerly lusted to see you become a possession of the other nations round about, so that you have become the butt of gossip in every language and of the jibes from every people^{-a}—⁴ truly, you mountains of Israel, hear the word of the Lord GOD: Thus said the Lord GOD to the mountains and the hills, to the watercourses and the valleys, and to the desolate wastes and deserted cities which have become a prey and a laughingstock to the other nations round about:

⁵ Assuredly, thus said the Lord GOD: I have indeed spoken in My blazing wrath against the other nations and against all of Edom which, ^{a-}with wholehearted glee and with contempt, have made My land a possession for themselves for pasture and for prey.^{-a} ⁶ Yes, prophesy about the land of Israel, and say to the mountains and the hills, to the watercourses and to the valleys, Thus said the Lord GOD: Behold, I declare in My blazing wrath: Because you have suffered the taunting of the nations, ⁷ thus said the Lord GOD: I hereby swear that the nations which surround you shall, in their turn, suffer disgrace. ⁸ But you, O mountains of Israel, shall yield your produce and bear your fruit for My people Israel, for their return is near. ⁹ For I will care for you: I will turn to you, and you shall be tilled and sown. ¹⁰ I will settle a large population on you, the whole House of Israel; the towns shall be resettled, and the ruined sites rebuilt. ¹¹ I will multiply men and beasts upon you, and they shall increase and be fertile, and I will resettle you as you were formerly, and will make you more prosperous than you were at first. And you shall know that I am the LORD. ¹² I will lead men—My people Israel—to you, and

---

^{a-a} *Exact meaning of Heb. uncertain.*

they shall possess you. You shall be their heritage, and you shall not again cause them to be bereaved.

13 Thus said the Lord GOD: Because they say to you, "You are [a land] that devours men, you have been a bereaver of your nations,"*b* 14 assuredly, you shall devour men no more, you shall never again bereave your nations—declares the Lord GOD. 15 No more will I allow the jibes of the nations to be heard against you, no longer shall you suffer the taunting of the peoples; and never again shall you cause your nations to stumble*c*—declares the Lord GOD.

16 The word of the LORD came to me: 17 O mortal, when the House of Israel dwelt on their own soil, they defiled it with their ways and their deeds; their ways were in My sight like the uncleanness of a menstruous woman. 18 So I poured out My wrath on them for the blood which they shed upon their land, and for the fetishes with which they defiled it. 19 I scattered them among the nations, and they were dispersed through the countries: I punished them in accordance with their ways and their deeds. 20 But when they came *d*-to those nations,-*d* they caused My holy name to be profaned,*e* in that it was said of them, "These are the people of the LORD, yet they had to leave His land." 21 Therefore I am concerned for My holy name, which the House of Israel have caused to be profaned among the nations to which they have come.

22 Say to the House of Israel: Thus said the Lord GOD: Not for your sake will I act, O House of Israel, but for My holy name, which you have caused to be profaned among the nations to which you have come. 23 I will sanctify My great name which has been profaned among the nations—among whom you have caused it to be profaned. And the nations shall know that I am the LORD—declares the Lord GOD—when I manifest My holiness before their eyes through you. 24 I will take you from among the nations and gather you from all the countries, and I will bring you

---

b I.e. Israel and Judah; cf. 37.15-22.
c Many mss. read "be bereaved"; cf. vv. 13-14.
d-d Lit. "the nations they came to."
e I.e. the exile of Israel was taken by the nations to be evidence of the LORD's weakness.

back to your own land. ²⁵ I will sprinkle clean water upon you, and you shall be clean: I will cleanse you from all your uncleanness and from all your fetishes. ²⁶ And I will give you a new heart and put a new spirit into you: I will remove the heart of stone from your body and give you a heart of flesh; ²⁷ and I will put My spirit into you. Thus I will cause you to follow My laws and faithfully to observe My rules. ²⁸ Then you shall dwell in the land which I gave to your fathers, and you shall be My people and I will be your God.

²⁹ And when I have delivered you from all your uncleanness, I will summon the grain and make it abundant, and I will not bring famine upon you. ³⁰ I will make the fruit of your trees and the crops of your fields abundant, so that you shall never again be humiliated before the nations because of famine. ³¹ Then you shall recall your evil ways and your base conduct, and you shall loathe yourselves for your iniquities and your abhorrent practices. ³² Not for your sake will I act—declares the Lord GOD—take good note! Be ashamed and humiliated because of your ways, O House of Israel!

³³ Thus said the Lord GOD: When I have cleansed you of all your iniquities, I will people your settlements, and the ruined places shall be rebuilt; ³⁴ and the desolate land, after lying waste in the sight of every passerby, shall again be tilled. ³⁵ And men shall say, "That land, once desolate, has become like the garden of Eden; and the cities, once ruined, desolate, and ravaged, are now populated and fortified." ³⁶ And the nations that are left around you shall know that I the LORD have rebuilt the ravaged places and replanted the desolate land. I the LORD have spoken and will act.

³⁷ Thus said the Lord GOD: Moreover, in this I will respond to the House of Israel and act for their sake: I will multiply their people like sheep. ³⁸ As Jerusalem is filled with sacrificial sheep during her festivals, so shall the ruined cities be filled with flocks of people. And they shall know that I am the LORD.

37 The hand of the LORD came upon me. He took me out by the spirit of the LORD and set me down in the valley. It was full of bones. ² He led me all around them; there were very many of them spread over the valley, and they were very dry. ³ He said to me, "O mortal, can these bones live again?" I replied, "O Lord GOD, only You know." ⁴ And He said to me, "Prophesy over these bones and say to them: O dry bones, hear the word of the LORD! ⁵ Thus said the Lord GOD to these bones: I will cause breath to enter you and you shall live again. ⁶ I will lay sinews upon you, and cover you with flesh, and form skin over you. And I will put breath into you, and you shall live again. And you shall know that I am the LORD!"

⁷ I prophesied as I had been commanded. And while I was prophesying, suddenly there was a sound of rattling, and the bones came together, bone to matching bone. ⁸ I looked, and there were sinews on them, and flesh had grown, and skin had formed over them; but there was no breath in them. ⁹ Then He said to me, "Prophesy to the breath, prophesy, O mortal! Say to the breath: Thus said the Lord GOD: Come, O breath, from the four winds, and breathe into these slain, that they may live again." ¹⁰ I prophesied as He commanded me. The breath entered them, and they came to life and stood up on their feet, a vast multitude.

¹¹ And He said to me: O mortal, these bones are the whole House of Israel. They say, "Our bones are dried up, our hope is gone; we are doomed." ¹² Prophesy, therefore, and say to them: Thus said the Lord GOD: I am going to open your graves and lift you out of the graves, O My people, and bring you to the land of Israel. ¹³ You shall know, O My people, that I am the LORD when I have opened your graves and lifted you out of your graves. ¹⁴ I will put My breath into you and you shall live again, and I will set you upon your own soil. Then you shall

know that I the LORD have spoken and have acted—declares
the LORD.

15 The word of the LORD came to me: 16 And you, O mortal, take
a stick and write on it, "Of Judah and the Israelites associated
with him"; and take another stick and write on it, "Of Joseph—
the stick of Ephraim—and all the House of Israel associated with
him." 17 Bring them close to each other, so that they become one
stick, joined together in your hand. 18 And when any of your
people ask you, "Won't you tell us what these actions of yours
mean?" 19 answer them, "Thus said the Lord GOD: I am going to
take the stick of Joseph—which is in the hand of Ephraim—and
of the tribes of Israel associated with him, and I will place the stick
of Judah *-upon it-* and make them into one stick; they shall be
joined in My hand." 20 You shall hold up before their eyes the
sticks which you have inscribed, 21 and you shall declare to them:
Thus said the Lord GOD: I am going to take the Israelite people
from among the nations they have gone to, and gather them from
every quarter, and bring them to their own land. 22 I will make
them a single nation in the land, on the hills of Israel, and one
king shall be king of them all. Never again shall they be two
nations, and never again shall they be divided into two kingdoms.
23 Nor shall they ever again defile themselves by their fetishes and
their abhorrent things, and by their other transgressions. I will
save them in all their settlements where they sinned, and I will
cleanse them. Then they shall be My people, and I will be their
God.

24 My servant David shall be king over them; there shall be one
shepherd for all of them. They shall follow My rules and faithfully
obey My laws. 25 Thus they shall remain in the land which I gave
to My servant Jacob and in which your fathers dwelt; they and
their children and their children's children shall dwell there
forever, with My servant David as their prince for all time. 26 I will
make a covenant of friendship with them—it shall be an everlasting covenant with them—I will establish* them and multiply

a-a *Meaning of Heb. uncertain.*

them, and I will place My sanctuary among them forever. ²⁷ My Presence*ᵇ* shall rest over them; I will be their God and they shall be My people. ²⁸ And when My sanctuary abides among them forever, the nations shall know that I the LORD do sanctify Israel.

38 The word of the LORD came to me; ² O mortal, turn your face toward Gog of the land of Magog, the chief prince of Meshech and Tubal. Prophesy against him ³ and say: Thus said the Lord GOD: Lo, I am coming to deal with you, O Gog, chief prince of Meshech and Tubal! ⁴ I will turn you around and put hooks in your jaws, and lead you out with all your army, horses, and horsemen, all of them clothed in splendor, a vast assembly, all of them with bucklers and shields, wielding swords. ⁵ Among them shall be Persia, Cush, and Put, everyone with shield and helmet; ⁶ Gomer and all its cohorts, Beth-togarmah [in] the remotest parts of the north and all its cohorts—the many peoples with you.*ᵃ* ⁷ Be ready, prepare yourselves, you and all the battalions mustered about you, and hold yourself in reserve for them.*ᵇ* ⁸ After a long time you shall be summoned; in the distant future you shall march against the land [of a people] restored from the sword, gathered from the midst of many peoples—against the mountains of Israel, which have long lain desolate—[a people] liberated from the nations, and now all dwelling secure. ⁹ You shall advance, coming like a storm; you shall be like a cloud covering the earth, you and all your cohorts, and the many peoples with you.

¹⁰ Thus said the Lord GOD: On that day, a thought will occur to you, and you will conceive a wicked design. ¹¹ You will say, "I will invade a land of open towns, I will fall upon a tranquil people living secure, all of them living in unwalled towns and lacking bars and gates, ¹² in order to take spoil and seize plunder"—to turn your hand against repopulated wastes, and against a people gathered from among nations, acquiring livestock and possessions, living at the center of the earth. ¹³ Sheba and Dedan, and

ᵇ *Lit. "dwelling place."*

ᵃ *I.e. with Gog.*
ᵇ *Septuagint reads "Me."*

the merchants and all the magnates of Tarshish will say to you, "Have you come to take spoil? Is it to seize plunder that you assembled your hordes—to carry off silver and gold, to make off with livestock and goods, to gather an immense booty?"

14 Therefore prophesy, O mortal, and say to Gog: Thus said the Lord GOD: Surely, on that day, when My people Israel are living secure, you will ᶜ‑take note,‑ᶜ 15 and you will come from your home in the farthest north, you and many peoples with you—all of them mounted on horses, a vast horde, a mighty army—16 and you will advance upon My people Israel, like a cloud covering the earth. This shall happen on that distant day: I will bring you to My land, that the nations may know Me when, before their eyes, I manifest My holiness through you, O Gog!

17 Thus said the Lord GOD: Why, you are the one I spoke of in ancient days through My servants, the prophets of Israel, who prophesied for years in those days that I would bring you against them!

18 On that day, when Gog sets foot on the soil of Israel—declares the Lord GOD—My raging anger shall flare up. 19 For I have decreed in My indignation and in My blazing wrath: On that day, a terrible earthquake shall befall the land of Israel. 20 The fish of the sea, the birds of the sky, the beasts of the field, all creeping things that move on the ground, and every human being on earth shall quake before Me. Mountains shall be overthrown, cliffs shall topple, and every wall shall crumble to the ground. 21 ᵈ‑I will then summon the sword against him throughout My mountains‑ᵈ—declares the Lord GOD—and every man's sword shall be turned against his brother. 22 I will punish him with pestilence and with bloodshed; and I will pour torrential rain, hailstones, and sulfurous fire upon him and his hordes and the many peoples with him. 23 Thus will I manifest My greatness and My holiness, and make Myself known in the sight of many nations. And they shall know that I am the LORD.

ᶜ‑ᶜ *Septuagint reads "rouse yourself."*
ᵈ‑ᵈ *Meaning of Heb. uncertain.*

39 And you, O mortal, prophesy against Gog and say: Thus said the Lord GOD: I am going to deal with you, O Gog, chief prince of Meshech and Tubal! ² I will turn you around and ᵃ‑drive you on,‑ᵃ and I will take you from the far north and lead you toward the mountains of Israel. ³ I will strike your bow from your left hand and I will loosen the arrows from your right hand. ⁴ You shall fall on the mountains of Israel, you and all your battalions and the peoples who are with you; and I will give you as food to carrion birds of every sort and to the beasts of the field, ⁵ as you lie in the open field. For I have spoken—declares the Lord GOD. ⁶ And I will send a fire against Magog and against those who dwell secure in the coastlands. And they shall know that I am the LORD. ⁷ I will make My holy name known among My people Israel, and never again will I let My holy name be profaned. And the nations shall know that I the LORD am holy in Israel. ⁸ Ah! it has come, it has happened—declares the Lord GOD: this is that day that I decreed.

⁹ Then the inhabitants of the cities of Israel will go out and make fires and feed them with the weapons—shields and bucklers, bows and arrows, clubs and spears; they shall use them as fuel for seven years. ¹⁰ They will not gather firewood in the fields or cut any in the forests, but will use the weapons as fuel for their fires. They will despoil those who despoiled them and plunder those who plundered them—declares the Lord GOD.

¹¹ On that day I will assign to Gog a burial site there in Israel —the Valley of the Travelers, east of the Sea. It shall block the path of travelers, for there Gog and all his multitude will be buried. It shall be called the Valley of Gog's Multitude. ¹² The House of Israel shall spend seven months burying them, in order to cleanse the land; ¹³ all the people of the land shall bury them. ᵃ‑The day I manifest My glory shall bring renown to them‑ᵃ— declares the Lord GOD. ¹⁴ And they shall appoint men to serve permanently, to traverse the land and bury any invaders who

---

ᵃ‑ᵃ *Meaning of Heb. uncertain.*

remain above ground, in order to cleanse it. The search shall go on for a period of seven months. [15] As those who traverse the country make their rounds, any one of them who sees a human bone shall erect a marker beside it, until the buriers have interred them in the Valley of Gog's Multitude. [16] *-There shall also be a city named Multitude.-*[a] And thus the land shall be cleansed.

[17] And you, O mortal, say to every winged bird and to all the wild beasts: Thus said the Lord GOD: Assemble, come and gather from all around for the sacrificial feast which I am preparing for you—a great sacrificial feast—upon the mountains of Israel, and eat flesh and drink blood. [18] You shall eat the flesh of warriors and drink the blood of the princes of the earth: rams, lambs, he-goats, and bulls—fatlings of Bashan all of them. [19] You shall eat fat to satiety and drink your fill of blood from the sacrificial feast that I have prepared for you. [20] And you shall sate yourselves at My table with horses, charioteers,[b] warriors, and all fighting men— declares the Lord GOD. [21] Thus will I manifest My glory among the nations, and all the nations shall see the judgment that I executed and the power that I wielded against them.

[22] From that time on, the House of Israel shall know that I the LORD am their God. [23] And the nations shall know that the House of Israel were exiled only for their iniquity, because they trespassed against Me, so that I hid My face from them and delivered them into the hands of their adversaries, and they all fell by the sword. [24] When I hid My face from them, I dealt with them according to their uncleanness and their transgressions.

[25] Assuredly, thus said the Lord GOD: I will now restore the fortunes of Jacob and take the whole House of Israel back in love; and I will be zealous for My holy name. [26] They will bear[c] their shame and all their trespasses that they committed against Me, when they dwell in their land secure and untroubled, [27] when I have brought them back from among the peoples and gathered them out of the lands of their enemies and have manifested My holiness through them in the sight of many nations. [28] They shall

[b] *Lit. "chariots"; Septuagint reads "riders."*
[c] *Change of diacritical point yields "forget."*

know that I the Lord am their GOD when, having exiled them among the nations, I gather them back into their land and leave none of them behind. ²⁹ I will never again hide My face from them, for I will pour out My spirit upon the House of Israel—declares the Lord GOD.

40 In the twenty-fifth year of our exile,ᵃ the fourteenth year after the city had fallen, at the beginning of the year, the tenth day of the month—on that very day—the hand of the LORD came upon me, and He brought me there. ² He brought me, in visions of God, to the Land of Israel, and He set me down on a very high mountainᵇ on which there seemed to be the outline of a city ᶜ˙on the south.˙ᶜ ³ He brought me over to it, and there, standing at the gate, was a man who shone like copper. In his hand were a cord of linen and a measuring rod. ⁴ The man spoke to me: "Mortal, look closely and listen attentively and note well everything I am going to show you—for you have been brought here in order to be shown—and report everything you see to the House of Israel."

⁵ Along the outside of the Temple [area] ran a wall on every side. The rod that the man held was six cubits long, plus one handbreadth for each cubit; and when he applied it to that structure, it measured one rod deepᵈ and one rod high.

⁶ He went up to the gate that faced eastward and mounted its steps. He measured the threshold of the gate; it was one rod deepᵈ—ᵉ˙the one threshold was one rod deep.˙ᵉ ⁷ Each recess was one rod wide and one rod deep, with [a partition of] 5 cubits between recesses; and the threshold of the gate, at the inner vestibule of the gate, was one rod deep. ⁸ ᵉ˙For when he measured it at the inner vestibule of the gate, it was one rod [deep].˙ᵉ ⁹ Next he measured the vestibule of the gate, and it measured 8 cubits

---

ᵃ *I.e. the exile of King Jehoiachin; see 1.2.*
ᵇ *Cf. Isa.2.1, Mic. 4.1.*
ᶜ⁻ᶜ *Septuagint reads facing [me]."*
ᵈ *In this description, the Hebrew word which ordinarily corresponds to the English "width" sometimes designates a measurement from an opening or outer surface inward, and so corresponds to the English "depth"; and the word which ordinarily corresponds to English "length" designates the distance from side to side of a vestibule or a passage, and so corresponds to the English "width."*
ᵉ⁻ᵉ *Meaning of Heb. uncertain.*

and its supports 2 cubits; the vestibule of the gate was at its inner end. [10] *f* On either side of this eastern gate there were three recesses, all three of the same size; of identical sizes were also the supports*g* on either side. [11] He measured the opening of the gate and found it 10 cubits wide, while the gate itself measured 13 cubits across.*h* [12] At the fronts of the recesses on either side were *e*-barriers of one cubit;*-e* the recesses on either side were 6 cubits [deep]. [13] Their openings faced each other directly across the gate passage, so that when he measured from rear*e* of recess to rear*e* of recess he obtained a width of 25 cubits.*i* [14] *e*-He made the vestibule*j*—60 cubits—and the gate next to the support on every side of the court.*-e* [15] And [the distance] from the front of the outer*e* gate to the front of the inner vestibule of the gate was 50 cubits. [16] The recesses—and their supports—had windows *e*-with frames*-e* on the interior of the gate complex on both sides, and the interiors of the vestibules also had windows on both sides; and the supports were adorned with palms.

[17] He took me into the outer court. There were chambers there, and there was a pavement laid out all around the court. There were 30 chambers on the pavement. [18] The pavements flanked the gates; the depth of the lower*k* pavements paralleled that of the gates. [19] Then he measured the width of *l*-the lower*k* court, from in front of the inner gate to in front of the outer gate*-l*—100 cubits.

e-After the east [gate], the north [gate].*-e* [20] Next he measured the gate of the outer court that faced north: its length and its width, [21] its three recesses on either side and its supports, as also its vestibule. It measured, like the first gate, 50 cubits in length and 25 cubits in width. [22] Its windows and [those of] its vestibule, as also its palm trees, corresponded to those of the gate that faced east. [From the outside] one had to climb 7 steps to reach it, and

f This verse would read well before v. 7.

g In connection with recesses, the "supports" are partitions.

h The opening was perhaps narrowed by a stone on each side for receiving the hinge of a door-leaf.

i Since each of the recesses was 6 cubits deep (v. 7a) and the passage in the middle was 13 cubits wide (v. 11).

j Elim here is the same as elam in vv. 16, 21, 22, etc.

k The outer court and its gates were 8 steps lower than the inner ones: v. 34.

l-l In this rendering, the adjectives "lower" and "inner" are construed, not with the nouns they stand next to in the Hebrew, but with those which they agree with in gender.

its vestibule was *m-*ahead of them.*-m* [23] Like the east gate, the north gate faced a gate leading into the inner forecourt; and when he measured the distance from gate to gate, it was 100 cubits.

[24] Then he took me to the south side. There was also a gate on the south side, and he got the same measurements as before for its supports and its vestibule. [25] Both it and its vestibule had windows like the aforementioned ones. It was 50 cubits long and 25 cubits wide. [26] Its staircase consisted of 7 steps; its vestibule was *m-*ahead of them,*-m* and its supports were decorated on both sides with palm trees. [27] The inner court likewise had a gate facing south; and on the south side, too, he measured a distance of 100 cubits from the [outer] gate to the [inner] gate.

[28] He now took me into the inner forecourt through its south gate. When he measured this south gate, it had the same measurements as the foregoing. [29] Its recesses, its supports, and its vestibule had the same measurements. Both it and its vestibule had windows on both sides; it was 50 cubits long and 25 cubits wide—[30] *n-*vestibules on both sides, 25 cubits long, 5 cubits wide. *n* [31] Its vestibule, however, gave on the outer court.*o* Its supports were adorned on either side with palms, and its staircase consisted of 8 steps.

[32] Then he took me to the eastern side of the inner forecourt; and when he measured the gate there, he got the same measurements: [33] its recesses, supports, and vestibule had the above measurements. Both it and its vestibule had windows on both sides; it was 50 cubits long and 25 cubits wide, [34] and its vestibule gave on the outer court. Its supports were decorated on both sides with palm trees, and its staircase consisted of 8 steps.

[35] Then he took me to the north gate, and found its measurements to be identical, [36] with the same recesses, supports, vestibule, windows on both sides, and a length of 50 cubits and a width of 25 cubits. [37] Its supports*p* gave on the outer court; its supports were decorated on both sides with palm trees; and its staircase consisted of 8 steps.

---

m-m *Septuagint reads "at its inner end."*

n-n *Connection unclear; wanting in some Heb. mss. and versions.*

o *I.e. in the inner gates the vestibules were situated at their entrances, and so they were true vestibules, in contrast to the "inner vestibules" of the outer gate.*

p *Septuagint reads "vestibules"; cf. vv. 31,34.*

³⁸ A chamber opened into the gate;^q there the burnt offering would be washed. ³⁹ And inside the vestibule of the gate, there were two tables on each side, at which the burnt offering, the sin offering, and the guilt offering were to be slaughtered; ⁴⁰ while outside—^{r-}as one goes up toward^{-r} the opening of the north gate —there were two tables on one side, and there were two tables on the other side of the gate's vestibule. ⁴¹ Thus there were four tables on either flank of the gate—eight tables in all—at which [the sacrifices] were to be slaughtered. ⁴² As for the four tables for the burnt offering^s—they were of hewn stone, one and a half cubits long, one and half cubits wide, and one cubit high—^{t-}on them were laid out the instruments with which burnt offerings and sacrifices were slaughtered.^{-t} ⁴³ Shelves,^e one handbreadth wide, were attached all around the inside; and the sacrificial flesh was [laid] on the tables.

⁴⁴ There were ^{u-}chambers for singers^{-u} in the inner forecourt: [one] beside the north gate facing south, and one beside the east^v gate facing north. ⁴⁵ [The man] explained to me: "The chamber that faces south is for the priests who perform the duties of the Temple; ⁴⁶ and the chamber that faces north is for the priests who perform the duties of the altar—they are the descendants of Zadok, who alone of the descendants of Levi may approach the LORD to minister to Him."

⁴⁷ He then measured the forecourt: 100 cubits long and 100 cubits broad—foursquare. In front of the Temple stood the altar. ⁴⁸ He took me into the portico of the Temple and measured it. The jambs^w of the portico were 5 cubits deep on either side. The width of the gate-opening was ^{x-}[14 cubits, and the flanking wall of the gate was]^{-x} 3 cubits on either side. ⁴⁹ The portico was 20 cubits wide^y and 11^z cubits deep, and ^{aa-}it was

^q Heb. "gates"; the reference is apparently to the north gate; cf. v. 40 and Lev. 1.11; 4.24; 7.2.
^{r-r} Emendation yields "the vestibule at."
^s See v. 39.
^{t-t} This clause would read well after v. 43.
^{u-u} Septuagint reads "two chambers."
^v Septuagint reads "south."
^w I.e. the edges of the flanking walls.
^{x-x} Preserved in the Septuagint.
^y See note on v.5.
^z Septuagint reads "12"; see note j on 41.13.
^{aa-aa} Septuagint reads "it was reached by 10 steps."

by steps that it was reached.⁻ᵃᵃ There were columns by the jambs on either side.

41 He then led me into the great hall. He measured the jambs, 6 cubits on either side; such was the depthᵃ of each jamb.ᵇ ² The entrance was 10 cubits wide, and the flanking walls of the entrance were each 5 cubits wide. Next he measured the depth [of the hall], 40 cubits, and the width, 20 cubits. ³ And then he entered the inner room. He measured each jamb of the entrance, 2 cubits [deep]; the entrance itself, 6 cubits across; and the width of ᶜ[the flanking wall on either side of]⁻ᶜ the entrance, 7 cubits. ⁴ Then he measured the depth, 20 cubits; and the width at the inner end of the great hall was also 20 cubits. And he said to me, "This is the Holy of Holies."

⁵ Then he measured the wall of the Temple. [It was] 6 cubits [thick] on every side of the Temple, and the side-chamber measured 4 cubits [across].ᵈ ⁶ The side-chambers were arranged one above the other, in 33 sections.ᵉ All around, there were projections in the Temple wall to serve the side-chambers as supports, so that [their] supports should not be the Temple wall itself. ⁷ The ᶠ⁻winding passage⁻ᶠ of the side-chambers widened from story to story; ᵍ⁻and since the structure was furnished all over with winding passages from story to story, the structure itself became wider from story to story.⁻ᵍ It was by this means that one ascended from the bottom story to the top one by way of the middle one.

⁸ I observed that the Temple was surrounded by a raised pavement—the foundations of the side chambers; its elevation was a rod's length, or 6 cubits. ⁹ The outer wall of the side chamber was 5 cubits thick, and that which served as a walk between the Temple's side chambers ¹⁰ and the chamber complexesʰ was 20 cubits

ᵃ *See note on 40.5.*
ᵇ *This sense is demanded by the context; usually,* ohel *means "tent."*
ᶜ⁻ᶜ *Preserved in the Septuagint.*
ᵈ *I.e. on the ground level; cf. v. 7.*
ᵉ *Lit. "times." Emendation yields "in three sections of three tiers each," i.e. one section next to each of the two side walls of the Temple and one next to its rear wall; cf. v. 7.*
ᶠ⁻ᶠ *So Targum; cf. Mishnah Tamid 1.1.*
ᵍ⁻ᵍ *Exact meaning of Heb. uncertain, but for the general sense cf. I Kings 6.6a, 8b.*
ʰ *See 42.1 ff.*

wide all around the Temple. [11] Of entrances to the side chambers giving on the walk, there was one entrance on the north side and one entrance on the south side; and the space[i] of the walk was 5 cubits thick all around. [12] And the structure that fronted on the vacant space at the [Temple's] western end was 70 cubits deep;[a] the walls of the structure were 5 cubits thick on every side; and it was 90 cubits wide.[a]

[13] He measured the [total] depth of the Temple, 100 cubits;[j] and the depth of the vacant space and of the structure, with its walls, also came to 100 cubits.[k] [14] The front side of the Temple, like the vacant space on the east, was 100 cubits wide.[l] [15] He also measured the width[a] of the structure facing the vacant space in the rear, inclusive of its ledges,[m] 100 cubits.

Both the great hall inside and the portico next to the court [16] —[n-]the thresholds[-n]—and the windows [o-]with frames[-o] and the ledges[p] at the threshold, all over the three parts of each, were completely overlaid[o] with wood. There was wainscoting from the floor to the windows, including the window [frame]s [17] and extending above the openings, [q-]both in the inner Temple and outside.[-q] And all over the wall, [q-]both in the inner one and in the outer,[-q] ran a pattern.[o] [18] It consisted of cherubs and palm trees, with a palm tree between every two cherubs. Each cherub had two faces: [19] a human face turned toward the palm tree on one side and a lion's face turned toward the palm tree on the other side. This was repeated all over the Temple; [20] the cherubs and the palm trees were carved on[r] the wall from the floor to above the openings.

[i] *Emendation yields "parapet."*
[j] *Comprising the 5 cubits of 40.48, the 12 of 40.49 (see note there), the 6 of 41.1, the 40 of 41.2, the 2 of 41.3, the 20 of 41.4, the 6 of 41.5a, the 4 of 41.5b, and the 5 of 41.9.*
[k] *The structure was 70 cubits deep and its front and rear walls each 5 cubits thick (v.12). The remaining 20 cubits are accounted for by the vacant space; cf. 42.1-3.*
[l] *To the inside width of 20 cubits (40.49; 41.2-4) must be added on each side: one Temple wall of 6 cubits equals 12; one side chamber wall of 5 cubits equals 10; one side chamber's inner depth of 4 cubits equals 8; a walk's width of 20 cubits (40.9-10) equals 40; and a parapet's thickness of 5 cubits (v.11) equals 10; totaling 100 cubits.*
[m] *Emendation yields "walls" cf. v.12.*
[n-n] *Septuagint reads "were paneled."*
[o-o] *Meaning of Heb. uncertain.*
[p] *Here perhaps designating the door frames, since it is these that (as required by the continuation of the verse) are situated at the threshold and consist of three parts (a lintel and two doorposts).*
[q-q] *Meaning perhaps the great hall and the vestibule; cf. v.5.*
[r] *Heb. "and."*

As regards the great hall, [21] the great hall had four doorposts; and before the Shrine was something resembling [22] a wooden altar 3 cubits high and 2 cubits long and having inner corners;[s] and its length[t] and its walls were of wood. And he said to me, "This is the table[u] that stands before the LORD." [23] The great hall had a double door, and the Shrine likewise had [24] a double door, and each door had two [o-]swinging leaves:[-o] two for the one door and two [o-]such leaves[-o] for the other. [25] Cherubs and palm trees were carved on these—on the doors of the hall—just as they were carved on the walls; and there was a lattice[o] of wood outside in front of the portico. [26] And there were windows [o-]with frames[-o] and palm trees on the flanking walls of the portico on either side [of the entrance] [o-]and [on] the Temple's side-chambers and [on] the lattices.[o]

42

He took me out, by way of the northern gate, into the outer court, and he led me [westward] up to a [u-]complex of chambers[-a] that ran parallel to the northern ends of the vacant space and the structure. [2] The width[b] of its facade—[c-]its north side, the one from which it was entered[-c]—was 100 cubits, and its depth[b] was 50 cubits. [3] At right angles to the 20 cubits[d] of the inner court and to the pavement of the outer court,[e] the complex rose ledge by ledge[f] in three tiers. [4] There was an areaway, 10 cubits wide and [g-]a road of one cubit,[-g] running along the inner-court side of the chamber complex, but its entrances were on its north side. [5] Here its upper chambers were cut back, because ledges took away from them as construction proceeded backward from the bottom ones and then from the middle ones. [6] For they were arranged in three tiers, and they had no columns like those of the chambers in the

---

[s] *Apparently meaning that it had a rim around the top, like the table of Exod. 25.25; see the final note on the present verse.*

[t] *Septuagint reads "base."*

[u] *Serving to hold the bread of display; cf. Exod. 25.30; 40.22-23; I Kings 7.48.*

[a-a] *Heb. simply "chambers," and so elsewhere.*

[b] *See note d at 40.6.*

[c-c] *Lit. "the north entrance"; but cf. v.4.*

[d] *I.e. the vacant space; cf. 41.13 with note k.*

[e] *Cf. 40.17.*

[f] *Because this part of the inner court was considerably higher than the outer; 40.28-31 and 41.8, 9b-10.*

[g-g] *Septuagint and Syriac read "and 100 cubits long"; cf. vv. 2-3.*

courts.[h] That is why the rise proceeded by stages: from the ground, from the bottom ones, and from the middle ones. [7] In the outer court, a wall 50 cubits long ran parallel to the chamber complex up to the chambers in the outer court;[h] [8] for the chambers in the outer court were themselves 50 cubits deep, thus completing 100 cubits alongside the edifice.[i] [9] Thus, at the foot of that complex of chambers ran a passage[j]—[k]of a width set by the wall in the outer court[-k]—which one entered from the east in order to gain access to them from the outer court.

[10] There was another chamber complex to the east[l] of the vacant space and the structure, [11] likewise with a passage in front— just like the complex on the north side, with which this one agreed in width[b] and depth[b] and in the exact layout of its exits and entrances. [12] Accordingly, the entrances to the chamber complex on the south side were approached from the east by the entrance at the head of [m]the corresponding passage along the matching wall.[-m]

[13] And he said to me, "The northern chambers and the southern chambers by the vacant space are the consecrated chambers in which the priests who have access to the LORD shall eat the most holy offerings. There they shall deposit the most holy offerings—the meal offerings, the sin offerings, and the guilt offerings, for the place is consecrated. [14] When the priests enter, they shall not proceed from the consecrated place to the outer court without first leaving here the vestments in which they minister, for the [vestments] are consecrated. Before proceeding to the area open to the people,[n] they shall put on other garments."

[15] When he had finished the measurements of the inner Temple [area], he led me out by way of the gate which faces east, and he measured off the entire area. [16] He measured the east side with the measuring rod, 500 [cubits]—in rods, by the measuring rod. He turned [17] [and] measured the north side: 500 [cubits]—in rods, by the measuring rod. He turned [18] [and] measured the

[h] *See vv. 8-9 referring to chambers along the west wall.*
[i] *Apparently meaning the chamber complex of v.1.*
[j] *So* kethib; qere *"thing giving access."*
[k-k] *Brought up from v. 10 for clarity.*
[l] *Septuagint reads "south"; cf. v.13.*
[m-m] *Exact meaning of Heb. uncertain; the phrase apparently refers back to vv. 7-8.*
[n] *Cf. 44.19 and note d.*

south side: 500 [cubits]—in rods, by the measuring rod. [19] Then he turned to the west side [and] measured it: 500 cubits—in rods, by the measuring rod. [20] Thus he measured it on the four sides; it had a wall completely surrounding it, 500 [cubits] long [o-]on each side,[-o] to separate the consecrated from the unconsecrated.

43 Then he led me to a gate, the gate that faced east. [2] And there, coming from the east with a roar like the roar of mighty waters, was the Presence of the God of Israel, and the earth was lit up by His Presence. [3] The vision was like the vision I had seen when I[a] came to destroy the city, the very same vision that I had seen by the Chebar Canal. Forthwith, I fell on my face.

[4] The Presence of the LORD entered the Temple by the gate that faced eastward. [5] A spirit carried me into the inner court, and lo, the Presence of the LORD filled the Temple; [6] and I heard speech addressed to me from the Temple, though [the] man[b] was standing beside me. [7] It said to me:

O mortal, this is the place of My throne and the place for the soles of My feet, where I will dwell in the midst of the people Israel forever. The House of Israel and their kings must not again defile My holy name by their apostasy and by the corpses of their kings [c-]at their death.[-c] [8] When they placed their threshold next to My threshold and their doorposts next to My doorposts with only a wall between Me and them,[d] they would defile My holy name by the abominations that they committed, and I consumed them in My anger. [9] Therefore, let them put their apostasy and the corpses of their kings far from Me, and I will dwell among them forever.

[10] [Now] you, O mortal, describe the Temple to the House of Israel,[e] and let them measure its design. But let them be ashamed of their iniquities: [11] When they are ashamed of all they have

o-o Lit. "and 500 wide."

a Six mss. and two ancient versions read "He."

b I.e. the guide of 40.3 ff.

c-c So with a number of Heb. mss. The usual vocalization yields "their shrines."

d The south wall of the First Temple enclosure was also the north wall of the royal enclosure; the two communicated by the Gate of the Guard (II Kings 11.19). Thus Temple and palace could be regarded as a single dwelling ("tent") in the sense of Num. 19.14, and the death of a king in the palace would defile the Temple. Hence the zoning provisions of 45.2 ff.

e In accordance with the three preceding chapters; cf. 40.4.

done, make known to them the plan of the Temple and its layout, its exits and entrances—its entire plan, and all the laws and instructions pertaining to its entire plan. Write it down before their eyes, that they may faithfully follow its entire plan and all its laws. [12] Such are the instructions for the Temple on top of the mountain: the entire area of its enclosure shall be most holy. Thus far the instructions for the Temple.

[13] [f]And these are the dimensions of the altar, in cubits where each is a cubit and a handbreadth. The trench[g] shall be a cubit deep and a cubit wide, with a rim one span high around its edge. And the height[h] shall be as follows: [14] From the trench in the ground to the lower ledge, which shall be a cubit wide: 2 cubits; from the [i]lower ledge to the upper[i] ledge, which shall likewise be a cubit wide: 4 cubits; [15] and the height of the altar hearth shall be 4 cubits, with 4 horns projecting upward from the hearth: 4 cubits. [16] Now the hearth shall be 12 cubits long and 12 broad, square, with 4 equal sides. [17] Hence, the [upper] base [j] shall be 14 cubits broad, with 4 equal sides. The surrounding rim shall be half a cubit [high],[k] and the surrounding trench shall measure one cubit. And the ramp[l] shall face east.

[18] Then he[b] said to me: O mortal, thus said the Lord GOD: These are the directions for the altar on the day it is erected, so that burnt offerings may be offered up on it and blood dashed against it. [19] You shall give to the levitical priests who are of the stock of Zadok, and so eligible to minister to Me—declares the Lord GOD—a young bull of the herd for a sin offering. [20] You shall take some of its blood and apply it to [m]the four horns [of the altar],[m] to the four corners of the base, and to the surrounding rim; thus you shall purge it and perform purification upon it. [21] Then you shall take the bull of sin offering and burn it in the [n]designated area[n] of the Temple, outside the Sanctuary.

[f] *Some of the terms and details in vv. 13-17 are obscure.*
[g] *Lit. "bosom."*
[h] *Lit. "bulge."*
[i-i] *Lit. "lesser ledge to the greater."*
[j] *Heb. 'azarah, which in v. 14 means "ledge." The altar consists of 3 blocks; each smaller than the one below it.*
[k] *Half a cubit is identical with the one span of v. 13.*
[l] *Leading up to the altar; cf. Exod. 20.23.*
[m-m] *Heb. "its four horns."*
[n-n] *Meaning of Heb. uncertain. Emendation yields "burning place"; cf. Lev. 6.2; Isa. 33.14; Ps. 102.4 (for the word), and Lev. 4.12; 6.4 (for the place).*

²² On the following day, you shall offer a goat without blemish as a sin offering; and the altar shall be purged [with it] just as it was purged with the bull. ²³ When you have completed the ritual of purging, you shall offer a bull of the herd without blemish and a ram of the flock without blemish. ²⁴ Offer them to the LORD; let the priests throw salt on them and offer them up as a burnt offering to the LORD. ²⁵ Every day, for seven days, you shall present a goat of sin offering, as well as a bull of the herd and a ram of the flock; you*ᵒ* shall present unblemished ones. ²⁶ Seven days they shall purge the altar and cleanse it; *ᵖ*thus shall it be consecrated.*ᵖ*

²⁷ And when these days are over, then from the eighth day onward the priests shall offer your burnt offerings and your offerings of well-being on the altar; and I will extend My favor to you —declares the Lord GOD.

44 Then he led me back to the outer gate of the Sanctuary that faced eastward; it was shut. ² And the LORD said to me: This gate is to be kept shut and is not to be opened! No one shall enter by it because the LORD, the God of Israel, has entered by it; therefore it shall remain shut. ³ Only the prince may sit in it and eat bread before the LORD, since he is a prince; he shall enter by way of *ᵃ*the vestibule of the gate,*ᵃ* and shall depart by the same way.

⁴ Then he led me, by way of the north gate, to the front of the Temple. I looked, and lo! the Presence of the LORD filled the Temple of the LORD; and I fell upon my face. ⁵ Then the LORD said to me: O mortal, mark well, look closely and listen carefully to everything that I tell you regarding all the laws of the Temple of the LORD and all the instructions regarding it. Note well who may enter the Temple and all who must be excluded from the Sanctuary. ⁶ And say to the rebellious House of Israel: Thus said the Lord GOD: Too long, O House of Israel, have you committed all your abominations, ⁷ admitting aliens, uncircumcised of spirit and uncircumcised of flesh, to be in My Sanctuary and profane

---

ᵒ *Heb. "they."*
ᵖ⁻ᵖ *Lit. "they shall fill its hands"; cf. note at Exod. 28.41.*
ᵃ⁻ᵃ *This does not contradict v.2 because the vestibule is at the inner end of the gate; cf. 40.9.*

My very Temple, when you offer up My food—the fat and the blood. You[b] have broken My covenant with all your abominations. [8] You have not discharged the duties concerning My sacred offerings, but have appointed them to discharge the duties of My Sanctuary for you.

[9] Thus said the Lord GOD: Let no alien, uncircumcised in spirit and flesh, enter My Sanctuary—no alien whatsoever among the people of Israel. [10] But the Levites who forsook Me when Israel went astray—straying from Me to follow their fetishes—shall suffer their punishment: [11] They shall be servitors in My Sanctuary, appointed over the Temple gates, and performing the chores of My Temple; they shall slaughter the burnt offerings and the sacrifices for the people. They shall attend on them and serve them. [12] Because they served the House of Israel in the presence of their fetishes and made them stumble into guilt, therefore—declares the Lord GOD—I have sworn concerning them that they shall suffer their punishment: [13] They shall not approach Me to serve Me as priests, to come near any of My sacred offerings, the most holy things. They shall bear their shame for the abominations which they committed. [14] I will make them watchmen of the Temple, to perform all its chores, everything that needs to be done in it.

[15] [c-]But the levitical priests descended from Zadok,[-c] who maintained the service of My sanctuary when the people of Israel went astray from Me—they shall approach Me to minister to Me; they shall stand before Me to offer Me fat and blood—declares the Lord GOD. [16] They alone may enter My sanctuary and they alone shall approach My table to minister to Me; and they shall keep My charge. [17] And when they enter the gates of the inner court, they shall wear linen vestments: they shall have nothing woolen upon them when they minister inside the gates of the inner court. [18] They shall have linen turbans on their heads and linen breeches on their loins; they shall not gird themselves with anything that causes sweat. [19] When they go out to the outer court—the outer court where the people are—they shall remove the

b Heb. "They."
c-c By contrast with the Levite-priests whose demotion has just been announced.

vestments in which they minister and shall deposit them in the sacred chambers;[d] they shall put on other garments, lest they make the people consecrated[e] by [contact with] their vestments. [20] They shall neither shave their heads nor let their hair go untrimmed; they shall keep their hair trimmed. [21] No priest shall drink wine when he enters into the inner court. [22] They shall not marry widows[f] or divorced women; they may marry only virgins of the stock of the House of Israel, or widows who are widows of priests.

[23] They shall declare to My people what is sacred and what is profane, and inform them what is clean and what is unclean. [24] In lawsuits, too, it is they who shall act as judges; they shall decide them in accordance with My rules. They shall preserve My teachings and My laws regarding all My fixed occasions; and they shall maintain the sanctity of My sabbaths.

[25] [A priest] shall not defile himself by entering [a house] where there is a dead person. He shall defile himself only for father or mother, son or daughter, brother or unmarried sister. [26] After he has become clean, seven days shall be counted off for him; [27] and on the day that he reenters the inner court of the Sanctuary to minister in the Sanctuary, he shall present his sin offering—declares the Lord GOD.

[28] This shall be their portion, for I am their portion; and no holding shall be given them in Israel, for I am their holding. [29] The meal offerings, sin offerings, and guilt offerings shall be consumed by them. Everything proscribed[g] in Israel shall be theirs. [30] All the choice first fruits of every kind, and all the gifts of every kind—of all your contributions—shall go to the priests. You shall further give the first of the yield of your baking[h] to the priest, that a blessing may rest upon your home.

[31] Priests shall not eat anything, whether bird or animal, that died or was torn by beasts.

---

[d] *Cf. 42. 13-14.*
[e] *Thereby rendering the people unfit for ordinary activity.*
[f] *I.e. of laymen.*
[g] *See Lev. 27.28.*
[h] *See Nu. 15.20-21.*

45 When you allot the land as an inheritance, you shall set aside from the land, as a gift sacred to the LORD, an area*ᵃ* 25,000 [cubits] long and 10,000*ᵇ* wide: this shall be holy through its entire extent. ² Of this, a square measuring a full 500 by 500 shall be reserved for the Sanctuary,*ᶜ* and 50 cubits for an open space all around it. ³ Of the aforesaid area, you shall measure off, as most holy and destined to include the Sanctuary, [a space] 25,000 long by 10,000 wide; ⁴ it is a sacred portion of the land; it shall provide space for houses for the priests, the ministrants of the Sanctuary who are qualified to minister to the LORD, as well as holy ground for the Sanctuary. ⁵ Another [space], 25,000 long by 10,000 wide, shall be the property of the Levites, the servants of the Temple—*ᵈ*twenty chambers.*⁻ᵈ* ⁶ Alongside the sacred reserve, you shall set aside [a space] 25,000 long by 5,000 wide, as the property of the city; it shall belong to the whole House of Israel. ⁷ And to the prince shall belong, on both sides of the sacred reserve and the property of the city and alongside the sacred reserve and the property of the city, on the west extending westward and on the east extending eastward, a portion*ᵃ* corresponding to one of the [tribal] portions that extend from the western border to the eastern border ⁸ of the land.*ᵉ* That shall be his property in Israel; and My princes shall no more defraud My people, but shall leave the rest of the land to the several tribes of the House of Israel.

⁹ Thus said the Lord GOD: Enough, princes of Israel! Make an end of lawlessness and rapine, and do what is right and just! Put a stop to your evictions of My people—declares the Lord GOD. ¹⁰ Have honest balances, an honest *ephah*, and an honest *bath.*ᶠ ¹¹ The *ephah* and the *bath* shall comprise the same volume, the *bath* a tenth of a *homer* and the *ephah* a tenth of a *homer;* their capacity shall be gauged by the *homer.* ¹² And the shekel shall

---

ᵃ *Lit. "length."*
ᵇ *Septuagint reads 20,000; cf. vv.3-5.*
ᶜ *Cf. 42.15 ff.*
ᵈ⁻ᵈ *Septuagint reads "for towns to dwell in."*
ᵉ *Cf. for all the foregoing 48.1 ff.*
ᶠ *The* ephah *is used for dry measure and the* bath *for liquid measure.*

weigh 20 *gerahs.* *ᵍ⁻*20 shekels, 25 shekels [and] 10 plus 5 shekels shall count with you as a *mina.* *⁻ᵍ*

¹³ This is the contribution you shall make: One-sixth of an *ephah* from every *homer* of wheat and one-sixth of an *ephah* from every *homer* of barley, ¹⁴ while the due from the oil—*ʰ⁻*the oil being measured by the *bath ⁻ʰ*—shall be one-tenth of a *bath* from every *kor.*—As 10 *baths* make a *homer,* so 10 *baths* make a *homer.* *ⁱ*—¹⁵ And [the due] from the flock shall be one animal from every 200. [All these shall be contributed] from Israel's products*ʰ* for meal offerings, burnt offerings, and offerings of well-being, to make expiation for them—declares the Lord Goᴅ. ¹⁶ In this contribution, the entire population must join with the prince in Israel.

¹⁷ But the burnt offerings, the meal offerings, and the libations on festivals, new moons, sabbaths—all fixed occasions—of the House of Israel shall be the obligation of the prince; he shall provide the sin offerings, the meal offerings, the burnt offerings, and the offerings of well-being, to make expiation for the House of Israel.

¹⁸ Thus said the Lord Goᴅ: On the first day of the first month, you shall take a bull of the herd without blemish, and you shall cleanse the Sanctuary. ¹⁹ The priest shall take some of the blood of the sin offering and apply it to the doorposts of the Temple, to the four corners of the ledge*ʰ* of the altar, and to the doorposts of the gate of the inner court. ²⁰ You shall do the same *ʲ⁻*on the seventh day of the month*ʲ* to purge the Temple from uncleannes caused by unwitting or ignorant persons.

²¹ On the fourteenth day of the first month you shall have the passover sacrifice; and during a festival of seven days unleavened bread shall be eaten. ²² On that day, the prince shall provide a bull of sin offering on behalf of himself and of the entire population; ²³ and during the seven days of the festival, he shall provide daily—for seven days—seven bulls and seven rams, without blemish, for a burnt offering to the Lᴏʀᴅ, and one goat daily for a sin offering. ²⁴ He shall provide a meal offering of an *ephah*ᵏ for each bull and an *ephah* for each ram, with a *hin* of oil to every

ᵍ⁻ᵍ *The Mesopatamian* mina *of 60 shekels; but the meaning of Heb. uncertain.*
ʰ⁻ʰ *Meaning of Heb. uncertain.*
ⁱ *The Vulgate reads* "kor"; homer *and* kor *are synonyms.*
ʲ⁻ʲ *Septuagint reads* "in the seventh month."
ᵏ *Of choice flour.*

ephah. ²⁵ So, too, during the festival of the seventh month, for seven days from the fifteenth day on, he shall provide the same sin offerings, burnt offerings, meal offerings, and oil.

46 Thus said the Lord GOD: The gate of the inner court which faces east shall be closed on the six working days; it shall be opened on the sabbath day and it shall be opened on the day of the new moon. ² The prince shall enter by way of the vestibule outside the gate, and shall attend at the gatepost while the priests sacrifice his burnt offering and his offering of well-being; he shall then bow low at the threshold of the gate and depart. The gate, however, shall not be closed until evening. ³ The common people*ᵃ* shall worship before the LORD on sabbaths and new moons at the entrance of the same gate.

⁴ The burnt offering which the prince presents to the LORD on the sabbath day shall consist of six lambs without blemish and one ram without blemish—⁵ with a meal offering of an *ephah* for the ram, a meal offering of as much as he wishes for the lambs, and a *hin* of oil with every *ephah.* ⁶ And on the day of the new moon, it shall consist of a bull of the herd without blemish, and six lambs and a ram—they shall be without blemish. ⁷ And he shall provide a meal offering of an *ephah* for the bull, an *ephah* for the ram, and as much as he can afford for the lambs, with a *hin* of oil to every *ephah.*

⁸ When the prince enters, he shall come in by way of the vestibule of the gate, and he shall go out the same way.

⁹ But on the fixed occasions, when the common people come before the LORD, whoever enters by the north gate to bow low shall leave by the south gate; and whoever enters by the south gate shall leave by the north gate. They shall not go back through the gate by which they came in, but shall go out *ᵇ*by the opposite one.*⁻ᵇ* ¹⁰ And as for the prince, he shall enter with them when they enter and leave when they leave.

¹¹ On festivals and fixed occasions, the meal offering shall be

---

ᵃ *I.e. those other than the priests, the Levites, and the prince; lit. "the people of the land."*
ᵇ⁻ᵇ *Lit. "straight before him."*

an *ephah* for each bull, an *ephah* for each ram, and as much as he wishes for the lambs, with a *hin* of oil for every *ephah*.

¹² The gate that faces east shall also be opened for the prince whenever he offers a freewill offering—be it burnt offering or offering of well-being—freely offered to the LORD, so that he may offer his burnt offering or his offering of well-being just as he does on the sabbath day. Then he shall leave, and the gate shall be closed after he leaves.

¹³ Each day you shall offer a lamb of the first year without blemish, as a daily burnt offering to the LORD; you shall offer one every morning. ¹⁴ And every morning regularly you shall offer a meal offering with it: a sixth of an *ephah*, with a third of a *hin* of oil to moisten the choice flour, as a meal offering to the LORD— a law for all time. ¹⁵ The lamb, the meal offering, and oil shall be presented every morning as a regular burnt offering.

¹⁶ Thus said the Lord GOD: If the prince makes a gift to any of his sons, it shall become the latter's inheritance; it shall pass on to his sons; it is their holding by inheritance. ¹⁷ But if he makes a gift from his inheritance to any of his subjects, it shall only belong to the latter until the year of release.ᶜ Then it shall revert to the prince; his inheritance must by all means pass on to his sons.

¹⁸ But the prince shall not take property away from any of the people and rob them of their holdings. Only out of his own holdings shall he endow his sons, in order that My people may not be dispossessed of their holdings.

¹⁹ Then he led me into the passage at the side of the gate to the sacred chambers of the priests, which face north, and there, at the rear of it, in the west, I saw a space. ²⁰ He said to me, "This is the place where the priests shall boil the guilt offerings and the sin offerings, and where they shall bake the meal offerings, so as not to take them into the outer court and ᵈ-make the people conse- crated."⁻ᵈ ²¹ Then he led me into the outer court and led me past the four corners of the court; and in each corner of the court

---

ᶜ *Cf. Lev. 25.10.*
ᵈ⁻ᵈ *See note e at 44.19.*

there was an enclosure. ²² These unroofed*ᵉ* enclosures, [each] 40 [cubits] long and 30 wide, were in the four corners of the court; the four corner enclosures had the same measurements. ²³ [On the inside,] running round the four of them, there was a row of masonry, equipped with hearths under the rows all around. ²⁴ He said to me, "These are the kitchens where the Temple servitors shall boil the sacrifices of the people."

47 He led me back to the entrance of the Temple, and I found that water was issuing from below the platform*ᵃ* of the Temple —eastward, since the Temple faced east—but the water was running out at the *ᵇ⁻*south of the altar,*⁻ᵇ* under the south wall of the Temple. ² Then he led me out by way of the northern gate and led me around to the outside of the outer gate that faces in the direction of the east;*ᶜ* and I found that water was gushing from [under] the south wall. ³ As the man went on eastward with a measuring line in his hand, he measured off a thousand cubits and led me across the water; the water was ankle deep. ⁴ Then he measured off another thousand and led me across the water, the water was knee deep. He measured off a further thousand and led me across the water; the water was up to the waist. ⁵ When he measured yet another thousand, it was a stream I could not cross; for the water had swollen into a stream that could not be crossed except by swimming. ⁶ "Do you see, O mortal?" he said to me; and he led me back to the bank of the stream.

⁷ As I came back, I saw trees in great profusion on both banks of the stream. ⁸ "This water," he told me, "runs out to the eastern region, and flows into the Arabah; and when it comes into the sea, into *ᵈ⁻*the sea of foul waters,*⁻ᵈ* the water will become wholesome. ⁹ Every living creature that swarms will be able to live wherever this stream goes; the fish will be very abundant once these waters have reached there. It will be wholesome, and everything will live

ᶜ So Mishnah Middoth 2.5; emendation yields "small."

ᵃ See note at 9.3.
ᵇ⁻ᵇ Connection unclear. Emendation yields "southeast."
ᶜ The end of the verse explains why he could not have made the detour by way of the south gate. For the reasons why he could not have proceeded to his present position directly by way of the east gate, see 43.1-2; 44.1-2.
ᵈ⁻ᵈ I.e. the Dead Sea.

wherever this stream goes. [10] Fishermen shall stand beside it all the way from En-gedi to En-eglaim; it shall be a place for drying nets; and the fish will be of various kinds [and] most plentiful, like the fish of the Great Sea. [11] But its swamps and marshes shall not become wholesome; they will serve to [supply] salt. [12] All kinds of trees for food will grow up on both banks of the stream. Their leaves will not wither nor their fruit fail; they will yield new fruit every month, because the water for them flows from the Temple. Their fruit will serve for food and their leaves for healing."

[13] Thus said the Lord GOD: These shall be the boundaries of the land that you shall allot to the twelve tribes of Israel. Joseph shall receive two portions, [14] and you shall share the rest equally. As I swore to give it to your fathers, so shall this land fall to you as your heritage. [15] These are the boundaries of the land:

As the northern limit: From the Great Sea by way of Hethlon, Lebo-[e]-hamath,[e] Zedad, [16] Beratah, Sibraim—which lies between the border of Damascus and the border of Hamath—[down to] Hazer-hatticon, which is on the border of Hauran. [17] Thus the boundary shall run from the Sea to [f]Hazer-enon,[f] to the north of the territory of Damascus, with the territory of Hamath to the north of it. That shall be the northern limit.

[18] As the eastern limit: A line between Hauran and Damascus, and between Gilead and the land of Israel: with the Jordan as a boundary, you shall measure down to the [d]Eastern Sea.[d] That shall be the eastern limit.

[19] The southern limit shall run: A line from Tamar to the waters of Meriboth-kadesh, along the Wadi [of Egypt and] the Great Sea. That is the southern limit.

[20] And as the western limit: The Great Sea shall be the boundary up to a point opposite Lebo-hamath. That shall be the western limit.

[21] This land you shall divide for yourselves among the tribes of Israel. [22] You shall allot it as a heritage for yourselves and for the strangers who reside among you, who have begotten children

e-e *Brought up from v. 16 for clarity.*
f-f *Apparently identical with Hazer-hatticon in v. 16.*

among you. You shall treat them as Israelite citizens; they shall receive allotments along with you among the tribes of Israel. ²³ You shall give the stranger an allotment within the tribe where he resides—declares the Lord GOD.

48 These are the names of the tribes:

At the northern end, along the Hethlon road, [from] Lebo-hamath to Hazar-enan—which is the border of Damascus, with Hamath to the north—from the eastern border to the Sea: Dan —one [tribe].

² Adjoining the territory of Dan, from the eastern border to the western border: Asher—one.

³ Adjoining the territory of Asher, from the eastern border to the western border: Naphtali—one.

⁴ Adjoining the territory of Naphtali, from the eastern border to the western border: Manasseh—one.

⁵ Adjoining the territory of Manasseh, from the eastern border to the western border: Ephraim—one.

⁶ Adjoining the territory of Ephraim, from the eastern border to the western border: Reuben—one.

⁷ Adjoining the territory of Reuben, from the eastern border to the western border: Judah—one.

⁸ Adjoining the territory of Judah, from the eastern border to the western border, shall be the reserve that you set aside: 25,000 [cubits] in breadth and in length equal to one of the portions from the eastern border to the western border; the Sanctuary shall be in the middle of it. ⁹ The reserve that you set aside for the LORD shall be 25,000 long and 10,000^a wide. ¹⁰ It shall be apportioned to the following: The sacred reserve for the priests shall measure 25,000 [cubits] on the north, ^{b-}10,000 on the west, 10,000 on the east, and 25,000 on the south,^{-b} with the LORD's Sanctuary in the middle of it. ¹¹ This consecrated area shall be for the priests of the line of Zadok, who kept My charge and did not

---

^a *Emendation yields "25,000"; cf. 45.3-6.*
^{b-b} *Lit. "10,000 in breadth on the west; 10,000 in breadth on the east; and 25,000 in length on the south."*

go astray, as the Levites did when the people of Israel went astray. [12] It shall be a special reserve for them out of the [total] reserve from the land, most holy, adjoining the territory of the Levites. [13] Alongside the territory of the priests, the Levites shall have [an area] 25,000 long by 10,000 wide; the total length shall be 25,000 and the breadth 10,000.[c] [14] None of it—the choicest of the land—may be sold, exchanged, or transferred; it is sacred to the LORD.

[15] The remaining 5,000 in breadth by 25,000 shall be for common use—serving the city for dwellings and pasture. The city itself shall be in the middle of it; [16] and these shall be its measurements: On the north side 4,500 cubits, on the south side 4,500, on the east side 4,500, and on the west side 4,500. [17] The pasture shall extend 250 cubits to the north of the city, 250 to the south, 250 to the east, and 250 to the west. [18] As for the remaining 10,000 to the east and 10,000 to the west, adjoining the long side[d] of the sacred reserve, the produce of these areas adjoining the sacred reserve shall serve as food for the workers in the city, [19] the workers in the city from all the tribes of Israel shall cultivate it. [20] The entire reserve, 25,000 square, you shall set aside as the sacred reserve plus the city property. [21] What remains on either side of the sacred reserve and the city property shall belong to the prince. The prince shall own [the land] from the border of the 25,000 [e]of the reserve[e] up to the eastern boundary, and from the border of the 25,000 on the west up to the western boundary, corresponding to the [tribal] portions. The sacred reserve, with the Temple Sanctuary in the middle of it [22] and the property of the Levites and the city property as well, shall be in the middle of the [area belonging] to the prince; [the rest of the land] between the territory of Judah and the territory of Benjamin shall belong to the prince.

[23] As for the remaining tribes:[f] From the eastern border to the western border: Benjamin—one.

[24] Adjoining the territory of Benjamin, from the eastern border to the western border: Simeon—one.

[c] *Septuagint reads 20,000; cf. note a.*
[d] *I.e. the south side.*
[e-e] *Emendation yields "on the east."*
[f] *The tribes not provided for in vv. 1-7, and lying south of the sacred gift.*

²⁵ Adjoining the territory of Simeon, from the eastern border to the western border: Issachar—one.
²⁶ Adjoining the territory of Issachar, from the eastern border to the western border: Zebulun—one.
²⁷ Adjoining the territory of Zebulun, from the eastern border to the western border: Gad—one.
²⁸ The other border of Gad shall be the southern boundary. This boundary shall run from Tamar to the waters of Meribath-kadesh, to the Wadi [of Egypt], and to the Great Sea.
²⁹ That is the land which you shall allot as a heritage to the tribes of Israel, and those are their portions—declares the Lord GOD.

³⁰ And these are the exits from the city: On its northern side, measuring 4,500 cubits, ³¹ the gates of the city shall be—three gates on the north—named for the tribes of Israel: the Reuben Gate: one; the Judah Gate: one; the Levi Gate: one. ³² On the eastern side, [measuring] 4,500 cubits—there shall be three gates: the Joseph Gate: one; the Benjamin Gate: one; and the Dan Gate: one. ³³ On the southern side, measuring 4,500 cubits, there shall be three gates: the Simeon Gate: one; the Issachar Gate: one; and the Zebulun Gate: one. ³⁴ And on the western side, [measuring] 4,500 cubits—there shall be three gates: the Gad Gate: one; the Asher Gate: one; the Naphtali Gate: one.
³⁵ Its circumference [shall be] 18,000 [cubits]; and the name of the city from that day on shall be "The LORD Is There."

THE TWELVE

HOSEA	הושע
JOEL	יואל
AMOS	עמוס
OBADIAH	עבדיה
JONAH	יונה
MICAH	מיכה
NAHUM	נחום
HABAKKUK	חבקוק
ZEPHANIAH	צפניה
HAGGAI	חגי
ZECHARIAH	זכריה
MALACHI	מלאכי

הושע

HOSEA

1 The word of the Lord that came to Hosea son of Beeri, in the reigns of Kings Uzziah, Jotham, Ahaz, and Hezekiah of Judah, and in the reign of King Jeroboam son of Joash of Israel.

2 When the Lord first spoke to Hosea, the Lord said to Hosea, "Go, get yourself *a-*a wife of whoredom and children of whoredom; the land will stray*b* from following the Lord."*-a* 3 So he went and married Gomer daughter of Diblaim. She conceived and bore him a son, 4 and the Lord instructed him, "Name him Jezreel; for, I will soon punish the House of Jehu*c* for the *d-*bloody deeds at Jezreel*-d* and put an end to the monarchy of the House of Israel. 5 In that day, I will break the bow of Israel in the Valley of Jezreel."

6 She conceived again and bore a daughter; and He said to him, "Name her Lo-ruhamah;*e* for I will no longer accept the House of Israel *f-*or pardon them.*f* (7 But I will accept the House of Judah. And I will give them victory through the Lord their God; I will not give them victory with bow and sword and battle, by horses and riders.)"

8 After weaning Lo-ruhamah, she conceived and bore a son. 9 Then He said, "Name him Lo-ammi;*g* for you*h* are not My people, and *i-*I will not be your [God]."*-i*

---

a-a *Force of Heb. uncertain.*
b *Lit. "whore away."*
c *Emendation yields "Israel"; cf. next note.*
d-d *See I Kings 21.1-24; II Kings 9.21-35. Emendation yields "the Baal days"; cf. 2.15.*
e *I.e. "Not-accepted"; cf. 2.3, 6, and 25.*
f-f *Meaning of Heb. uncertain; emendation yields "but will disown them"; cf. 9.15 and elsewhere.*
g *I.e. "Not-My-People."*
h *I.e. you and your fellow countrymen.*
i-i *Cf. 2.25.*

2 *a*The number of the people of Israel shall be like that of the sands of the sea, which cannot be measured or counted; and instead of being told, "You are Not-My-People,"*b* they shall be called Children-of-the-Living-God. ² The people of Judah and the people of Israel shall assemble together and appoint one head over them; and they shall rise from the ground*c*—for marvelous shall be *d*the day of Jezreel!*-d*

³ Oh, call*e* your brothers "My People,"
And your sisters "Lovingly Accepted"!

⁴ Rebuke*e* your mother, rebuke her—
For she is not My wife
And I am not her husband—
And let her put away her harlotry from her face
And her adultery from between her breasts.
⁵ Else will I strip her naked
And leave her as on the day she was born:
And I will make her like a wilderness,
Render her like desert land,
And let her die of thirst.
⁶ I will also disown her children;
For they are now a harlot's brood,
⁷ In that their mother has played the harlot,
She that conceived them has acted shamelessly—
Because she thought,
"I will go after my lovers,
Who supply my bread and my water,
My wool and my linen,
My oil and my drink."

---

a *Vv. 1-3 anticipate the conclusion of the chapter.*
b *See 1.9.*
c *Meaning, perhaps, "from their wretched condition," or "to ascendancy over the land."*
d-d *I.e. the day when the name Jezreel will convey a promise (2.23-25) instead of a threat (1.4-5).*
e *The Lord addresses Hosea and his fellow North Israelites; see 1.9. The mother is the nation; her children the individual North Israelites.*

8 Assuredly,
I will hedge up her* roads with thorns
And raise walls against her,
And she shall not find her paths.
9 Pursue her lovers as she will,
She shall not overtake them;
And seek them as she may,
She shall never find them.
Then she will say,
"I will go and return
To my first husband,
For then I fared better than now."

10 And she did not consider this:
It was I who bestowed on her
The new grain and wine and oil;
I who lavished silver on her
And gold—which they used for Baal.
11 Assuredly,
I will take back My new grain in its time
And My new wine in its season,
And I will snatch away My wool and My linen
That serve to cover her nakedness.
12 Now will I uncover her shame
In the very sight of her lovers,
And none shall save her from Me.
13 And I will end all her rejoicing:
Her festivals, new moons, and sabbaths—
All her festive seasons.
14 I will lay waste her vines and her fig trees,
Which she thinks are a fee
She received from her lovers;
I will turn them into brushwood,
And beasts of the field shall devour them.
15 Thus will I punish her

Heb. "your." Vv. 8-9 would read well after v. 15.

For the days of the Baalim,
On which she brought them offerings;
When, decked with earrings and jewels,
She would go after her lovers,
Forgetting Me

—declares the LORD.

16 Assuredly,
I will speak coaxingly to her
And lead her through the wilderness^g
And speak to her tenderly.
17 I will give her her vineyards from there,
And the Valley of Achor^h as a ^i-plowland of hope.^-i
There she shall respond as in the days of her youth,
When she came up from the land of Egypt.

18 And in that day

—declares the LORD—

You will call [Me] Ishi,^j
And no more will you call Me Baali.^j
19 For I will remove the names of the Baalim from her
  mouth,
And they shall nevermore be mentioned by name.

20 In that day, I will make a covenant for them with the beasts
of the field, the birds of the air, and the creeping things of the
ground; I will also banish^k bow, sword, and war from the land.
Thus I will let them lie down in safety.

21 And I will espouse you forever:
I will espouse you ^l-with righteousness and justice,
And with goodness and mercy,
22 And I will espouse you with faithfulness;^-l

---

^g *I.e. her ravaged land (see vv. 5, 10-11, 14); so Ibn Ezra.*
^h *A desolate region; cf. Isa. 65.10; see further Josh. 7.25-26.*
^i-i *Connecting pethah with pittah "to plow" (see Isa. 28.24). Meaning of Heb. uncertain;*
  others "door of hope."
^j *Both Ishi and Baali mean "my husband," but the latter also means "my Baal."*
^k *Lit. "break."*
^l-l *As the bride price which the Bridegroom will pay, He will confer these qualities on her, so*
  that she will never offend again.

Then you shall be devoted to the LORD.
²³ In that day,
I will respond

—declares the LORD—

I will respond to the sky,
And it shall respond to the earth;
²⁴ And the earth shall respond
With new grain and wine and oil,
And they shall respond to Jezreel.*m*
²⁵ I will sow her in the land as My own;
And take Lo-ruhamah back in favor;
And I will say to Lo-ammi, "You are My people,"
And he will respond, "[You are] my God."

3 The LORD said to me further, "Go, *a*-befriend a woman who, while befriended by a companion, consorts with others, just as the LORD befriends the Israelites,-*a* but they turn *b*-to other gods and love the cups of the grape."-*b*

² Then I hired her for fifteen [shekels of] silver, a *homer* of barley, and *c*-a *lethech* of barley;-*c* ³ and I stipulated with her, *d*-"In return,-*d* you are to go a long time without either fornicating or marrying; even I [shall not cohabit] with you."

⁴ For the Israelites shall go a long time without king and without officials, without sacrifice*e* and without cult pillars, and without ephod and teraphim. ⁵ Afterward, the Israelites will turn back and will seek the LORD their God and David their king—and they will thrill over the LORD and over His bounty in the days to come.

4 Hear the word of the LORD,
O people of Israel!
For the LORD has a case

m I.e. "God sows." The names of Hosea's children (1.3-8) are applied here to Israel.

a-a For "befriend," see Deut. 10.19. For God's befriending Israel, see Hos. 2.10.

b-b Meaning of Heb. uncertain; emendation yields " 'to other gods.' And so I befriended a woman of lust."

c-c Septuagint reads "a jar of wine."

d-d Lit. "for me."

e Emendation yields "altar."

Against the inhabitants of this land,
Because there is no honesty and no goodness
And no obedience to God in the land.
² [False] swearing, dishonesty, and murder,
And theft and adultery are rife;
Crime follows upon crime!
³ For that, the earth is withered:
Everything that dwells on it languishes—
Beasts of the field and birds of the sky—
Even the fish of the sea perish.

⁴ "Let no man rebuke, let no man protest!"
ᵃ⁻For this your people has a grievance against [you],
   O priest!⁻ᵃ
⁵ So you shall stumble by day,
And by night ᵇ⁻a prophet⁻ᵇ shall stumble as well,
And I will destroy your kindred.ᶜ
⁶ My people is destroyed because of [your] disobedience!
Because you have rejected obedience,
I reject you as My priest;
Because you have spurned the teaching of your God,
I, in turn, will spurn your children.
⁷ The more they increased, the more they sinned against
   Me:
I will change their dignity to dishonor.
⁸ They feed on My people's sin offerings,
And so they desire its iniquity.
⁹ Therefore, the people shall fare like the priests:
I will punish it for its conduct,
I will requite it for its deeds.
¹⁰ Truly, they shall eat, but not be sated;
They shall swill,ᵈ but not be satisfied,
Because they have forsaken the LORD
To practiceᵉ
¹¹   lechery.

ᵃ⁻ᵃ *For failing to reprove; but meaning of Heb. uncertain.*
ᵇ⁻ᵇ *Emendation yields "your children"; cf. v. 6 end.*
ᶜ *Lit. "mother."*
ᵈ *For this meaning of* hiznah *cf. v. 18.*
ᵉ *Cf. 12.7.*

Wine*f* and new wine destroy
The mind of
12   My people:
It consults its stick,*g*
Its rod*g* directs it!
A lecherous impulse has made them go wrong,
And they have strayed*h* from submission to their God.
13 They sacrifice on the mountaintops
And offer on the hills,
Under oaks, poplars, and terebinths
Whose shade is so pleasant.
That is why their*i* daughters fornicate
And their daughters-in-law commit adultery!
14 I will not punish their daughters for fornicating
Nor their daughters-in-law for committing adultery;
For they themselves *j*turn aside*j* with whores
And sacrifice with prostitutes,
And a people that is without sense*k* must stumble.
15 If you are a lecher, Israel—
Let not Judah incur guilt—
Do not come to Gilgal,*l*
Do not make pilgrimages to Beth-aven,*m*
And do not swear by the LORD!*n*

16 Ah, Israel has balked
Like a stubborn cow;
Therefore,
The LORD will graze him
On the range, like a sheep.*o*
17 *p*Ephraim is addicted to images—

f Emendation yields "New grain"; cf. 7.14; 9.1-2.
g I.e. its phallus, meaning "its lust."
h See note b at 1.2.
i Heb. "your," here and through v. 14.
j-j Meaning of Heb. uncertain.
k Cf. vv. 11-12.
l One who participates in the debaucheries of the open-air shrines is not fit to visit a temple building.
m Lit. "House of Delusion," substituted for Bethel (cf. Amos 4.4).
n I.e. you are not fit to profess His religion; see Jer. 12.16.
o Instead of giving them fodder in return for their work; cf. Isa. 30.23-24.
p Meaning of vv. 17-19 uncertain in part.

Let him be.
¹⁸ They drink to excess—
Their liquor turns against them.
They "love" beyond measure—
Disgrace is the "gift"
¹⁹ Which the wind ^{q-}is bringing;^{-q}
They shall garner shame from their sacrifices.

5

Hear this, O priests,
Attend, O House^a of Israel,
And give ear, O royal house;
For right conduct is your responsibility!
But you have been a snare to Mizpah
And a net spread out over Tabor;
^{2 b-}For when trappers dug deep pitfalls,
I was the only reprover of them all.^{-b}
³ Yes, I have watched Ephraim,
Israel has not escaped my notice:
Behold, you have fornicated, O Ephraim;
Israel has defiled himself!
⁴ Their habits do not let them
Turn back to their God;
Because of the lecherous impulse within them,
They pay no heed to the LORD.

^{5 c-}Israel's pride shall be humbled before his very eyes,
As Israel and Ephraim fall because of their sin
(And Judah falls with them).
⁶ Then they will go with their sheep and cattle
To seek the LORD, but they will not find Him.^{-c}

^{b-}He has cast them off:^{-b}
⁷ [Because] they have broken faith with the LORD,
Because ^{d-}they have^{-d} begotten

---

^{q-q} *Lit. "has bound up in the corners of its garment"; see note at Mal. 3.20.*

^a *Emendation yields "prophets."*
^{b-b} *Meaning of Heb. uncertain.*
^{c-c} *This passage would read well after 5.15; cf. 5.6 with 6.6.*
^{d-d} *Emendation yields "He has."*

Alien children.
Therefore, *b-*the new moon
Shall devour their portions.*-b*

8 Sound a ram's horn in Gibeah,
A trumpet in Ramah;
Give the alarm in Beth-aven;*e*
*f-*After you,*f* Benjamin!
9 Ephraim is stricken with horror
On a day of chastisement.

Against the tribes*g* of Israel
I proclaim certainties:
10 The officers of Judah have acted
Like shifters of field boundaries;
On them I will pour out
My wrath like water.
11 Ephraim is defrauded,
Robbed of redress,
Because he has witlessly
Gone after futility.*h*
12 For it is I who am like rot to Ephraim,
Like decay to the House of Judah;*i*
13 Yet when Ephraim became aware of his sickness,
Judah*i* of his sores,
Ephraim repaired to Assyria—
He sent envoys to a patron*j* king!
He will never be able to cure you,
Will not heal you of your sores.
14 No, I will be like a lion to Ephraim,
Like a great beast to the House of Judah;*i*
I, I will attack and stride away,
Carrying the prey that no one can rescue;

---

*e The three towns named, in the territory of Benjamin, are now being wrested from Israel by
Judah; see v. 10.*
f-f Emendation yields "Stir up."
g I.e. the kingdoms of Judah and Israel (Ephraim).
h Cf. Targum and Septuagint; but meaning of Heb. uncertain.
i Emendation yields "Israel."
*j Compare the verb ryb in the sense of "to champion, uphold the cause of," in Isa. 1.17; 3.13;
19.20 end; 51.22.*

773

¹⁵ And I will return to My abode—
Till they realize their guilt.
In their distress, they will seek Me
And beg for My favor.

6 ^a"Come, let us turn back to the LORD:
He attacked, and He can heal us;
He wounded, and He can bind us up.
² In two days He will make us whole again;
On the third day He will raise us up,
And we shall be whole by His favor.
³ Let us pursue obedience to the LORD,
And we shall become obedient.
His appearance is as sure as daybreak,
And He will come to us like rain,
Like latter rain that refreshes^b the earth."

⁴ What can I do for you, Ephraim,
What can I do for you, Judah,^c
When your goodness is like morning clouds,
Like dew so early gone?
⁵ That is why I have hewn down ^{d-}the prophets,^{-d}
Have slain them with the words of My mouth:
^{e-}And the day that dawned [brought on] your punish-
ment.^{-e}
⁶ For I desire goodness, not sacrifice;
Obedience to God, rather than burnt offerings.
^{7 f}But they, to a man, have transgressed the Covenant.
This is where they have been false to Me:
⁸ Gilead is a city of evildoers,
Tracked up with blood.
⁹ The gang of priests is

---

^a *As anticipated at the end of chapter 5, Israel seeks the Lord's favor; His answer begins with v. 4.*
^b *Taking* yoreh *as equivalent of* yarweh.
^c *Emendation yields "Israel"; cf. "Ephraim . . . Israel" in v. 10.*
^{d-d} *Emendation yields "your children"; cf. 9.13.*
^{e-e} *Cf. v. 3; but meaning of Heb. uncertain.*
^f *Meaning of vv. 7-11 unclear in part.*

Like the ambuscade of bandits
Who murder on the road to Shechem,
For they have encouraged[g] depravity.
¹⁰ In [h]the House of Israel[-h] I have seen
A horrible thing;
Ephraim has fornicated there,
Israel has defiled himself.
¹¹ [i](Even Judah has reaped a harvest of you!)[-i]

7

When I would restore My people's fortunes,
¹ When I would heal Israel,
The guilt of Ephraim reveals itself
And the wickedness of Samaria.
For they have acted treacherously,
With thieves breaking in
And bands raiding outside.
² And they do not consider
That I remembered all their wickedness.
Why, their misdeeds have been all around them,[a]
They have been ever before Me.

³ [b]In malice they make a king merry,
And officials in treachery.
⁴ They [c]commit adultery,[-c] all of them,
Like an oven fired by a baker,
Who desists from stoking only
From the kneading of the dough to its leavening.
⁵ The day they made our king sick
[And] officials with the poison of wine,
[d]He gave his hand to traitors.[-d]
⁶ [e]For they approach their ambush
With their hearts like an oven:[-e]
Through the night

---

[g] Heb. "done"; cf. 5.1-3.
[h-h] Emendation yields "Beth-shean."
[i-i] Cf. 5.9-10; but meaning of clause uncertain.

[a] Emendation yields "Me."
[b] Vv. 3-6 would read well in the order 4, 6, 3, 5.
[c-c] Emendation yields "rage."
[d-d] I.e. he trusted traitors; but meaning of verse uncertain.
[e-e] Meaning of Heb. uncertain.

Their baker[c] has slept;
In the morning, it flares up
Like a blazing fire.
[7] They all get heated like an oven
And devour their rulers—
None of them calls to Me.
All their kings have fallen [by their hand].

[8] [e-]Ephraim is among the peoples;
He is rotting away.
Ephraim is like a cake—
Incapable of turning.[-e]
[9] Strangers have consumed his strength,
But he has taken no notice;
Also, mold[f] is scattered over him,
But he has taken no notice.
[10] Though Israel's pride has been humbled
Before his very eyes,
They have not turned back
To their God the LORD;
They have not sought Him
In spite of everything.
[11] Instead, Ephraim has acted
Like a silly dove with no mind:
They have appealed to Egypt!
They have gone to Assyria!
[12] When they go, I will spread
My net over them,
I will bring them down
Like birds of the sky;
[e-]I will chastise them
When I hear their bargaining.[-e]
[13] Woe to them
For straying from Me;
Destruction to them

[f] *Like Akkadian* shību; *others "gray hairs."*

For rebelling against Me!
For I was their Redeemer;
Yet they have plotted treason against Me.

14 *g*But they did not cry out to Me sincerely
As they *h*-lay wailing.*-h*
They debauch*i* over new grain and new wine,
They are faithless*j* to Me.

15 *I* braced, *I* strengthened their arms,
And they plot evil against *Me!*
16 They come back;
They have been of no use,*e*
Like a slack bow.
Their officers shall fall by the sword,
Because of the stammering*k* of their tongues.
Such shall be [the results of] their jabbering*l*
In the land of Egypt.

8   [Put] a ram's horn to your mouth—
a-Like an eagle*-a* over the House of *b*-the LORD;*-b*
Because they have transgressed My covenant
And been faithless to My teaching.
2 Israel cries out to Me,
"O my God, we are devoted to You."*c*

3 Israel rejects what is good;
d-An enemy shall pursue him.*-d*
4 They have made kings,
But not with My sanction;
They have made officers,

---

g This verse would read well after 8.2.
h-h I.e. in penitence; cf. Isa. 58.5.
i Cf. Aramaic gar/yegur "to commit adultery"; for the thought, cf. 4.11.
j Taking yasuru as equivalent to yasoru, from sarar; cf. 9.15 end.
k Cf. Arabic zaghūm and zughmūm "a stammerer."
l I.e. the negotiations conducted in the Egyptian language.

a-a Meaning of Heb. uncertain.
b-b Emendation yields "Israel."
c See note g at 7.14.
d-d Emendation yields "They pursue delusion."

But not of My choice.
Of their silver and gold
They have made themselves images,
To their own undoing.
5 *e-*He rejects*-e* your calf, Samaria!
I am furious with them!
Will they never be capable of *f-*purity?
6 For it was Israel's doing;*-f*
It was only made by a joiner,
It is not a god.
No, the calf of Samaria shall be
Reduced to splinters!

7 They sow wind,
And they shall reap whirlwind—
Standing stalks devoid of ears
And yielding no flour.
If they do yield any,
Strangers shall devour it.
8 Israel is bewildered;*g*
They have now become among the nations
Like an unwanted vessel,
9 [Like] a lonely wild ass.
For they have gone up to Assyria,
*h-*Ephraim has*-h* courted friendship.
10 And while they are courting among the nations,
*i-*There I will hold them fast;*-i*
*a-*And they shall begin to diminish in number
From the burden of king [and] officers.*-a*

11 For Ephraim has multiplied altars—for guilt;
His altars have redounded to his guilt:
12 The many teachings I wrote for him
Have been treated as something alien.

---

e-e Emendation yields "I reject."
f-f Emendation yields "understanding,/That House of Israel?"
g A play on words: The Heb. root bala', which means "bewilder" here (cf. Isa. 28.7), means "devour" in the preceding verse.
h-h Emendation yields "In Egypt they have."
i-i Cf. 9.6; but meaning of Heb. uncertain.

¹³ ᵃ⁻When they present sacrifices to Me,⁻ᵃ
It is but flesh for them to eat:
The Lᴏʀᴅ has not accepted them.
Behold, He remembers their iniquity,
He will punish their sins:
Back to Egypt with them!
¹⁴ Israel has ignored his Maker
And built temples
(And Judah has fortified many cities).
So I will set fire to his cities,
And it shall consume their fortresses.

9

Rejoice not, O Israel,
As other peoples exult;
For you have strayed
Away from your God:
ᵃ⁻You have loved a harlot's fee
By every threshing floor of new grain.
² Threshing floor and winepress
Shall not join them,
And the new wine shall fail her.⁻ᵃ
³ They shall not be able to remain
In the land of the Lᴏʀᴅ.
But Ephraim shall return to Egypt
And shall eat unclean food in Assyria.ᵇ
⁴ It shall be for them like the food of mourners,
All who partake of which are defiled.
They will offer no libations of wine to the Lᴏʀᴅ,
And no sacrifices of theirs will be pleasing to Him;
But their food will be only for their hunger,
It shall not come into the House of the Lᴏʀᴅ.
⁵ What will you do about feast days,
About the festivals of the Lᴏʀᴅ?

ᵃ⁻ᵃ *Emendation and rearrangement yield: "You have loved fornication/By every threshing floor and press;/The new grain shall not join them,/And the new wine shall fail them."*
ᵇ *The lands of the heathen and the food there are unclean; cf. Ezek. 4.13; Amos 7.17.*

⁶ Behold, they have gone ᶜ⁻from destruction⁻ᶜ
[With] the silver they treasure.
Egypt shall ᵈ⁻hold them fast,⁻ᵈ
Mophᵉ shall receive them in burial.
Weeds are their heirs;
Prickly shrubs occupy their [old] homes.

⁷ The days of punishment have come
For your heavy guilt;
The days of requital have come—
Let Israel know it!

The prophet was distraught,
The inspired man driven mad
By constant harassment.
⁸ Ephraim watches for ᶠ⁻my God.
As for the prophet,⁻ᶠ
Fowlers' snares are on all his paths,
Harassment in the House of his God.
⁹ They have been as grievously corrupt
As in the days of Gibeah;ᵍ
He will remember their iniquity,
He will punish their sins.

¹⁰ I found Israel [as pleasing]
As grapes in the wilderness;
Your fathers seemed to Me
ʰ⁻Like the first fig to ripen on a fig tree.⁻ʰ
But when they came to Baal-peor,
They turned aside to shamefulness;ⁱ
ʲ⁻Then they became as detested
As they had been loved.⁻ʲ

ᶜ⁻ᶜ *Emendation yields "to Assyria."*
ᵈ⁻ᵈ *Cf. 8.10.*
ᵉ *Believed to be Memphis, elsewhere called Noph.*
ᶠ⁻ᶠ *Emendation yields "the prophet of my God."*
ᵍ *See Judg. 19-20.*
ʰ⁻ʰ *Emendation yields "like a ripe fig in a waterless waste"; cf. 13.5.*
ⁱ *Cf. Num. 25.1-3.*
ʲ⁻ʲ *Meaning of Heb. uncertain.*

¹¹ From birth, from the womb, from conception
Ephraim's glory shall be
Like birds that fly away.*k*
¹² Even if they rear their infants,
I will bereave them of men.
l-Woe to them indeed
When I turn away from them!*-l*
¹³ *j*-It shall go with Ephraim
As I have seen it go with Tyre,
Which was planted in a meadow;*-j*
Ephraim too must bring out
His children to slayers.
¹⁴ Give them, O LORD—give them what?
Give them a womb that miscarries,
And shriveled breasts!
¹⁵ All their misfortune [began] at Gilgal,
For there I disowned them.*m*
For their evil deeds
I will drive them out of My House.
I will accept them no more;
n-All their officials are-*n* disloyal.

¹⁶ *k*Ephraim*o* is stricken,
Their stock is withered;
They can produce no fruit.
Even if they do bear children,
I will slay their cherished offspring.

¹⁷ My God rejects them
Because they have not obeyed Him,
And they shall go wandering
Among the nations.

---

k *V. 16 would read well after v. 11.*
l-l *Emendation yields: "Even if they wean their babes,/They shall be dismayed because of them."*
m *The specific allusion is uncertain.*
n-n *Emendation yields "They are all."*
o *Targum reads "Their crown," i.e. of a tree.*

10 Israel is a ravaged vine
And its fruit is like it.
When his fruit was plentiful,
He made altars aplenty;
When his land was bountiful,
Cult pillars abounded.
² Now that his boughs[a] are broken up,
He feels his guilt;
He himself pulls apart his altars,
Smashes his pillars.

³ Truly, now they say,
"We have no king;
For, since we do not fear the LORD,
What can a king do to us?"
⁴ So they conclude agreements and make covenants
With false oaths,
And justice [b-]degenerates into poison weeds,
Breaking out[-b] on the furrows of the fields.

⁵ The inhabitants of Samaria fear
For the calf of Beth-aven;[c]
Indeed, its people and priestlings,
[d-]Whose joy it once was,[-d]
Mourn over it for the glory
That is departed from it.
⁶ It too shall be brought to Assyria
As tribute to a patron[e] king;
Ephraim shall be chagrined,
Israel shall be dismayed
Because of his plans.[f]

---

[a] Cf. II Sam. 18.14, where the word is rendered "thick growth."
[b-b] Cf. Amos 6.12; lit. "breaks out like poison weeds."
[c] See note m at 4.15.
[d-d] Meaning of Heb. uncertain.
[e] See note j at 5.13.
[f] Emendation yields "image," referring to the calf.

⁷ Samaria's monarchy[g] is vanishing
Like foam upon water,
⁸ Ruined shall be the shrines of [Beth-]aven,[c]
That sin of Israel.
Thorns and thistles
Shall grow on their altars.
They shall call to the mountains, "Bury us!"
To the hills, "Fall on us!"

⁹ You have sinned more, O Israel,
Than in the days of Gibeah.[h]
[d-]There they stand [as] at Gibeah!
Shall they not be overtaken
By a war upon scoundrels
¹⁰ As peoples gather against them?[-d]

When I chose [them], I broke them in,
Harnessing them for two furrows.
¹¹ Ephraim became a trained heifer,
But preferred to thresh;
I [i-]placed a yoke
Upon her sleek neck.[-i]
I will make Ephraim [j-]do advance plowing;[-j]
Judah[k] shall do [main] plowing!
Jacob shall do final plowing!
¹² "Sow righteousness for yourselves;
Reap [l]the fruits of[-l] goodness;
Break for yourselves betimes fresh ground
Of seeking the LORD,
So that you may obtain [m-]a teacher[-m] of righteousness."
¹³ You have plowed wickedness,
You have reaped iniquity—

[g] *The Heb. verb agrees with this word, not with "Samaria."*
[h] *See note at 9.9.*
[i-i] *Lit. "passed over the comeliness of its neck."*
[j-j] *Taking* rkb *in the sense of the Arabic* krb.
[k] *Emendation yields "Israel."*
[l-l] *Lit. "according to."*
[m-m] *Meaning of Heb. uncertain; Septuagint reads "the fruits."*

[And] you shall eat the fruits of treachery—
Because you relied on your way,[n]
On your host of warriors.
[14] But the din of war shall arise in your own people,
And all your fortresses shall be ravaged
As Beth-arbel was ravaged by Shalman[o]
On a day of battle,
When mothers and babes were dashed to death together.
[15] This [p]is what Bethel has done to you[p]
For your horrible wickedness:
[q]At dawn[q] shall Israel's monarchy
Utterly perish.

11

I fell in love with Israel
When he was still a child;
And I have called [him] My son
Ever since Egypt.
[2] [a]Thus were they called,
But they went their own way;
They sacrifice to Baalim[b]
And offer to carved images.
[3] I have pampered Ephraim,
Taking them in My[c] arms;
But they have ignored
My healing care.
[4] I drew them with human ties,
With cords of love;
But I seemed to them as one
Who imposed a yoke on their jaws,
Though I was offering them food.
[5] No!

---

[n] *Septuagint reads "chariots."*
[o] *Perhaps identical with the Shallum of II Kings 15.10ff.; cf. the atrocities of Shallum's rival, ibid. v. 16.*
[p-p] *Emendation yields "will I do to you, O House of Israel."*
[q-q] *Meaning, perhaps, "swiftly as the dawn"; cf. v. 7 above, "like foam upon water."*

[a] *Meaning of parts of vv. 2-7 uncertain.*
[b] *Emendation yields "calves"; cf. 8.4-6; 13.2.*
[c] *Heb. "his."*

They return to the land of Egypt,
And Assyria is their king.
Because they refuse to repent,
⁶ A sword shall descend upon their towns*d*
And consume their limbs
And devour *e*[them] because of their designs.*e*
⁷ *f*For My people persists
In its defection from Me;
When it is summoned upward,
It does not rise at all.*f*

⁸ How can I give you up, O Ephraim?
How surrender you, O Israel?
How can I make you like Admah,
Render you like Zeboiim?*g*
I have had a change of heart,
All My tenderness is stirred.
⁹ I will not act on My wrath,
Will not turn to destroy Ephraim.
For I am God, not man,
*f*The Holy One in your midst:
I will not come in fury.*f*

¹⁰ The LORD will roar like a lion,
And they shall march behind Him;
When He roars, His children shall come
Fluttering out of the west.
¹¹ They shall flutter from Egypt like sparrows,
From the land of Assyria like doves;
And I will settle them in their homes

      —declares the LORD.

---

d *Emendation yields "bodies," lit. "skins"; cf. Job 18.13.*
e-e *Emendation yields "their bones."*
f-f *Meaning of Heb. uncertain.*
g *Admah and Zeboiim were destroyed with neighboring Sodom and Gomorrah; cf. Gen. 10.19;*
14.2,8; Deut. 29.22.

12 Ephraim surrounds Me with deceit,
The House of Israel with guile.*ª*
ᵇ⁻(But Judah stands firm with God
And is faithful to the Holy One.)*⁻ᵇ*
² Ephraim tends the wind
And pursues the gale;
He is forever adding
Illusion to calamity.*ᶜ*
Now they make a covenant with Assyria,
Now oil is carried to Egypt.*ᵈ*

³ The Lord once indicted Judah,*ᵉ*
And punished Jacob for his conduct,
Requited him for his deeds.
⁴ In the womb he tried to supplant his brother;
Grown to manhood, he strove with a divine being,*ᶠ*
⁵ He strove with an angel and prevailed—
The other had to weep and implore him.
At Bethel [Jacob] would meet him,
There to commune with him.*ᵍ*
⁶ Yet the Lord, the God of Hosts,
Must be invoked as "Lord."*ʰ*
⁷ You must return to your God!
Practice goodness and justice,
And constantly trust in your God.

⁸ A trader who uses false balances,
Who loves to overreach,
⁹ Ephraim thinks,
"Ah, I have become rich;

ª *I.e. the deceit and guile they practice on each other (below vv. 8-9) is constantly noted by the Lord.*
ᵇ⁻ᵇ *Meaning of Heb. uncertain.*
ᶜ *Septuagint reads "futility."*
ᵈ *I.e. they foolishly depend on alliances instead of on the Lord; cf. 5.13; 7.10-11.*
ᵉ *Presumably the patriarch Judah. Emendation would yield "Israel"; cf. next note.*
ᶠ *Cf. Gen. 25.26 and 32.29.*
ᵍ *Heb. "us."*
ʰ *I.e. one should not invoke any of the angelic hosts.*

I have gotten power!
*b-*All my gains do not amount
To an offense which is real guilt."*-b*

¹⁰ I the LORD have been your God
Ever since the land of Egypt.
I will let you dwell in your tents*ⁱ* again
As in the days of old,*ʲ*
¹¹ When I spoke to the prophets;
For I granted many visions,
*b-*And spoke parables through the prophets.
¹² As for Gilead, it is worthless;
And to no purpose*-b* have they
Been sacrificing oxen in Gilgal:
The altars of these are also
Like stone heaps upon a plowed field.*ᵏ*

¹³ Then Jacob had to flee*ˡ* to the land of Aram;
There Israel served for a wife,
For a wife he had to guard [sheep].
¹⁴ But when the LORD
Brought Israel up from Egypt,
It was through a prophet;*ᵐ*
Through a prophet*ᵐ* they were guarded.
¹⁵ *ⁿ*Ephraim gave bitter offense,
And his Lord cast his crimes upon him
And requited him for his mockery.

13

When Ephraim spoke piety,
He was exalted in Israel;
But he incurred guilt through Baal,*ᵃ*
And so he died.

ⁱ I.e. securely; see II Kings 13.5.
ʲ Lit. "fixed season."
ᵏ I.e. the cults of Gilead and Gilgal are as worthless as that of Bethel.
ˡ This is the punishment mentioned in 12.3.
ᵐ I.e. not through an angel.
ⁿ Meaning of 12.15–13.1 uncertain.

ᵃ I.e. Baal-peor; cf. 9.10.

² And now they go on sinning;
They have made them molten images,
Idols, by their skill, from their silver,
Wholly the work of craftsmen.
b-Yet for these they appoint men to sacrifice;-*b*
They are wont to kiss calves!
³ Assuredly,
They shall be like morning clouds,
Like dew so early gone;
Like chaff whirled away from the threshing floor.
And like smoke from a lattice.
⁴ Only I the LORD have been your God
Ever since the land of Egypt;
You have never known a [true] God but Me,
You have never had a helper other than Me.
⁵ I looked after you in the desert,
In a thirsty land.
⁶ When they grazed, they were sated;
When they were sated, they grew haughty;
And so they forgot Me.
⁷ So I am become like a lion to them,
Like a leopard I lurk on the way;
⁸ Like a bear robbed of her young I attack them
And rip open the casing of their hearts;
c-I will devour them there like a lion,-*c*
The beasts of the field shall mangle them.

⁹ *b*-You are undone, O Israel!
You had no help but Me.-*b*
¹⁰ Where now is your king?
Let him save you!
Where are the chieftains in all your towns
Whom you demanded:
"Give me a king and officers"?

---

b-b *Meaning of Heb. uncertain.*
c-c *Emendation yields "There dogs shall devour them"; cf. Septuagint.*

¹¹ I give you kings in my ire,
And take them away in My wrath.

¹² Ephraim's guilt is bound up,
His sin is stored away.ᵈ
¹³ Pangs of childbirth assail him,
ᵇ⁻And the babe is not wise—
For this is no time to survive
At the birthstool of babes.⁻ᵇ

¹⁴ ᵉFrom Sheol itself I will save them,
Redeem them from very Death.
Where, O Death, are your plagues?
Your pestilence where, O Sheol?
ᶠRevenge shall be far from My thoughts.ᶠ

¹⁵ For though he flourish among reeds,
A blast, a wind of the LORD,
Shall come blowing up from the wilderness;
His fountain shall be parched,
His spring dried up.
That [wind] shall plunder treasures,
Every lovely object.

14 ¹ Samaria must bear her guilt,
For she has defied her God.
They shall fall by the sword,
Their infants shall be dashed to death,
And their women with child ripped open.

² Return, O Israel, to the LORD your God,
For you have fallen because of your sin.
³ Take words with you
And return to the LORD.
Say to Him:
ᵃ⁻"Forgive all guilt

ᵈ *I.e. for future retribution.*
ᵉ *This verse would read well before 14.5.*
ᶠ⁻ᶠ *Lit. "Satisfaction (for this meaning of* nḥm *see Deut. 32.36; Isa. 1.24) shall be hidden from My eyes."*
ᵃ⁻ᵃ *Meaning of Heb. uncertain.*

And accept what is good;
Instead of bulls we will pay
[The offering of] our lips.⁻ᵃ
⁴ Assyria shall not save us,
No more will we ride on steeds;ᵇ
Nor ever again will we call
Our handiwork our god,
Since in You alone orphans find pity!"

⁵ I will heal their affliction,ᶜ
Generously will I take them back in love;
For My anger has turned away from them.ᵈ
⁶ I will be to Israel like dew;
He shall blossom like the lily,
He shall strike root like a ᵉLebanon tree.⁻ᵉ
⁷ His boughs shall spread out far,
His beauty shall be like the olive tree's,
His fragrance like that of Lebanon.
⁸ They who sit in his shade shall be revived:
They shall bring to life new grain,
They shall blossom like the vine;
His scent shall be like the wine of Lebanon.ᶠ
⁹ Ephraim [shall say]:
"What more have I to do with idols?
When I respond and look to Him,
I become like a verdant cypress."
ᵃ⁻Your fruit is provided by Me.⁻ᵃ

¹⁰ He who is wise will consider these words,
He who is prudent will take note of them.
For the paths of the LORD are smooth;
The righteous can walk on them,
While sinners stumble on them.

ᵇ *I.e. we will no longer depend on an alliance with Egypt; cf. II Kings 18.24 // Isa. 36.9;
Isa. 30.16.*
ᶜ *For this meaning of* meshubah *see Jer. 2.19; 3.22.*
ᵈ *Heb. "him."*
ᵉ *Emendation yields "poplar."*
ᶠ *Emendation yields "Helbon"; cf. Ezek. 27.18.*

יוֹאֵל

JOEL

1 The word of the LORD that came to Joel son of Pethuel.

² Listen to this, O elders;
Give ear, all inhabitants of the land.
Has the like of this happened in your days
Or in the days of your fathers?
³ Tell your children about it,
And let your children tell theirs,
And their children the next generation!
⁴ What the cutter*a* has left, the locust has devoured;
What the locust has left, the grub has devoured;
And what the grub has left, the hopper has devoured.
⁵ Wake up, you drunkards, and weep,
Wail, all you swillers of wine—
For the new wine that is *b*-denied you!-*b*
⁶ For a nation has invaded my land,
Vast beyond counting,
With teeth like the teeth of a lion,
With the fangs of a lion's breed.
⁷ They have laid my vines waste
And splintered my fig trees:
They have stripped off their bark and thrown [it] away;
Their runners have turned white.

⁸ Lament—like a maiden girt with sackcloth
For the husband of her youth!
⁹ Offering and libation have ceased

---

^a *The Heb. terms translated "cutter, locust, grub, and hopper" are of uncertain meaning; they probably designate stages in the development of the locust.*
^{b-b} *Lit. "cut off from your mouth."*

From the House of the LORD;
The priests must mourn
Who minister to the LORD.
¹⁰ The country is ravaged,
The ground must mourn;
For the new grain is ravaged,
The new wine is dried up,
The new oil has failed.
¹¹ Farmers are dismayed
And vinedressers wail
Over wheat and barley;
For the crops of the field are lost.
¹² The vine has dried up,
The fig tree withers,
Pomegranate, palm, and apple—
All the trees of the field are sere.
And joy has dried up
Among men.

¹³ Gird yourselves and lament, O priests,
Wail, O ministers of the altar;
Come, spend the night in sackcloth,
O ministers of my God.
For offering and libation are withheld
From the House of your God.
¹⁴ Solemnize a fast,
Proclaim an assembly;
Gather the elders—all the inhabitants of the land—
In the House of the LORD your God,
And cry out to the LORD.

¹⁵ Alas for the day!
For the day of the LORD is near;
It shall come like havoc from Shaddai.^c

^c *Traditionally "the Almighty"; see Gen. 17.1.*

¹⁶ For food is cut off
Before our very eyes,
And joy and gladness
From the House of our God.
¹⁷ ᵈ⁻The seeds have shriveled
Under their clods.⁻ᵈ
The granaries are desolate,
Barns are in ruins,
For the new grain has failed.
¹⁸ How the beasts groan!
The herds of cattle are bewildered
Because they have no pasture,
And the flocks of sheep are dazed.ᵈ

¹⁹ To You, O LORD, I call.
For fireᵉ has consumed
The pastures in the wilderness,
And flameᵉ has devoured
All the trees of the countryside.
²⁰ The very beasts of the field
Cry out to You;
For the watercourses are dried up,
And fire has consumed
The pastures in the wilderness.

2

Blow a horn in Zion,
Sound an alarm on My holy mount!
Let all dwellers on earth tremble,
For the day of the LORD has come!
It is close—
² A day of darkness and gloom,
A day of densest cloud
Spread like soot over the hills.
A vast, enormous horde—

ᵈ⁻ᵈ *Meaning of Heb. uncertain.*
ᵉ *I.e. scorching heat.*

Nothing like it has ever happened,
And it shall never happen again
Through the years and ages.

³ Their vanguard is a consuming fire,
Their rear guard a devouring flame.
Before them the land was like the Garden of Eden,
Behind them, a desolate waste:
Nothing has escaped them.
⁴ They have the appearance of horses,
They gallop just like steeds.
⁵ With a clatter as of chariots
They bound on the hilltops,
With a noise like a blazing fire
Consuming straw;
Like an enormous horde
Arrayed for battle.
⁶ Peoples tremble before them,
All faces ^{a-}turn ashen.^{-a}
⁷ They rush like warriors,
They scale a wall like fighters.
And each keeps to his own track.
Their paths never cross;^b
⁸ No one jostles another,
Each keeps to his own course.
^{b-}And should they fall through a loophole,
They do not get hurt.^{-b}
⁹ They rush up the wall,
They dash about in the city;
They climb into the houses,
They enter like thieves
By way of the windows.
¹⁰ Before them earth trembles,
Heaven shakes,
Sun and moon are darkened,

^{a-a} *Meaning of Heb. uncertain; cf. Nah. 2.11.*
^b *Meaning of Heb. uncertain.*

794

And stars withdraw their brightness.
¹¹ And the LORD roars aloud
At the head of His army;
For vast indeed is His host,
Numberless are those that do His bidding.
For great is the day of the LORD,
Most terrible—who can endure it?
¹² "Yet even now"—says the LORD—
"Turn back to Me with all your hearts,
And with fasting, weeping, and lamenting."
¹³ Rend your hearts
Rather than your garments,
And turn back to the LORD your God.
For He is gracious and compassionate,
Slow to anger, abounding in kindness,
And renouncing punishment.
¹⁴ Who knows but He may turn and relent,
And leave a blessing behind
For meal offering and drink offering
To the LORD your God?^c

¹⁵ Blow a horn in Zion,
Solemnize a fast,
Proclaim an assembly!
¹⁶ Gather the people,
Bid the congregation purify themselves.^d
Bring together the old,
Gather the babes
And the sucklings at the breast;
Let the bridegroom come out of his chamber,
The bride from her canopied couch.
¹⁷ Between the portico and the altar,
Let the priests, the LORD's ministers, weep
And say:
"Oh, spare Your people, LORD!

^c *When the locusts depart, there will again be yield enough for offerings; see 1.9.*
^d *Cf. Exod. 19.10; Zeph. 1.7.*

Let not Your possession become a mockery,
To be taunted by nations!
Let not the peoples say,
'Where is their God?' "

¹⁸ Then the LORD was roused
On behalf of His land
And had compassion
Upon His people.
¹⁹ In response to His people
The LORD declared:
"I will grant you the new grain,
The new wine, and the new oil,
And you shall have them in abundance.
Nevermore will I let you be
A mockery among the nations.
²⁰ I will drive the northerner^e far from you,
I will thrust it into a parched and desolate land—
Its van to the Eastern Sea^f
And its rear to the Western Sea;^g
And the stench of it shall go up,
And the foul smell rise."
For [the LORD] shall work great deeds.

²¹ Fear not, O soil, rejoice and be glad;
For the LORD has wrought great deeds.
²² Fear not, O beasts of the field,
For the pastures in the wilderness
Are clothed with grass.
The trees have borne their fruit;
Fig tree and vine
Have yielded their strength.
²³ O children of Zion, be glad,
Rejoice in the LORD your God.
For He has given you the early rain in [His] kindness,

---

^e *I.e. the locusts. Emendation yields* "My multitude"; *cf.* "nation" (1.6), "horde," "army,"
and "host" (2.2, 5, 11, *and* 25).
^f *The Dead Sea.*
^g *The Mediterranean Sea.*

Now He makes the rain fall [as] formerly—
The early rain and the late—
24 And threshing floors shall be piled with grain,
And vats shall overflow with new wine and oil.

25 "I will repay you ^{h-}for the years^{-h}
Consumed by swarms and hoppers,
By grubs and locusts,
The great army I let loose against you.
26 And you shall eat your fill
And praise the name of the LORD your God
Who dealt so wondrously with you—
My people shall be shamed no more.
27 And you shall know
That I am in the midst of Israel:
That I the LORD am your God
And there is no other.
And My people shall be shamed no more."

3 After that,
I will pour out My spirit on all flesh;
Your sons and daughters shall prophesy;
Your old men shall dream dreams,
And your young men shall see visions.
2 I will even pour out My spirit
Upon male and female slaves in those days.

3 ^{a-}Before the great and terrible day of the LORD comes,^{-a}
I will set portents in the sky and on earth:
Blood and fire and pillars of smoke;
4 The sun shall turn into darkness
And the moon into blood.
5 But everyone who invokes the name of the LORD shall escape;
for there shall be a remnant on Mount Zion and in Jerusalem, as

the LORD promised. *b-Anyone who invokes the LORD will be among the survivors.-b*

4   For lo! in those days
And in that time,
When I restore the fortunes
Of Judah and Jerusalem,
² I will gather all the nations
And bring them down to the Valley of Jehoshaphat.*a*
There I will contend with them
Over My very own people, Israel,
Which they scattered among the nations.
For they divided My land among themselves
³ And cast lots over My people;
And they bartered a boy for a whore,
And sold a girl for wine, which they drank.

⁴ What is this you are doing to Me, O Tyre, Sidon, and all the districts of Philistia? Are you requiting Me for something I have done, or are you doing something for My benefit? Quick as a flash, I will pay you back; ⁵ for you have taken My gold and My silver, and have carried off My precious treasures to your palaces; ⁶ and you have sold the people of Judah and the people of Jerusalem to the Ionians, so that you have removed them far away from their homeland. ⁷ Behold, I will rouse them to leave the place you have sold them to, and I will pay you back: ⁸ I will deliver your sons and daughters into the hands of the people of Judah, and they will sell them into captivity to a distant nation—for the LORD has spoken.

⁹ Proclaim this among the nations:
Prepare for battle!
Arouse the warriors,
Let all the fighters come and draw near!

---

^{b-b} *Meaning of Heb. uncertain.*

^a *Here understood as "The LORD contends"; contrast v. 12.*

798

¹⁰ Beat your plowshares^{*b*} into swords,
And your pruning hooks into spears.
Let even the weakling say, "I am strong."
¹¹ *^c*Rouse yourselves*^c* and come,
All you nations;
Come together
From round about.
There *^c*bring down*^c*
Your warriors, O Lord!
¹² Let the nations rouse themselves and march up
To the Valley of Jehoshaphat;*^d*
For there I will sit in judgment
Over all the nations round about.
¹³ Swing the sickle,
For the crop is ripe;
Come and tread,
For the winepress is full,
The vats are overflowing!
For great is their wickedness.

¹⁴ Multitudes upon multitudes
In the Valley of Decision!
For the day of the Lord is at hand
In the Valley of Decision.
¹⁵ Sun and moon are darkened,
And stars withdraw their brightness.
¹⁶ And the Lord will roar from Zion,
And shout aloud from Jerusalem,
So that heaven and earth tremble.
But the Lord will be a shelter to His people,
A refuge to the children of Israel.
¹⁷ And you shall know that I the Lord your God
Dwell in Zion, My holy mount.
And Jerusalem shall be holy;
Nevermore shall strangers pass through it.

---

^b *See note at Isa. 2.4.*
^{c-c} *Meaning of Heb. uncertain.*
^d *Here understood as "The Lord judges"; contrast v. 2.*

¹⁸ And in that day,
The mountains shall drip with wine,
The hills shall flow with milk,
And all the watercourses of Judah shall flow with water;
A spring shall issue from the House of the LORD
And shall water the Wadi of the Acacias.
¹⁹ Egypt shall be a desolation,
And Edom a desolate waste,
Because of the outrage to the people of Judah,
In whose land they shed the blood of the innocent.
²⁰ But Judah shall be inhabited forever,
And Jerusalem throughout the ages.
²¹ Thus ^{e-}I will treat as innocent their blood
Which I have not treated as innocent;^{-e}
And the LORD shall dwell in Zion.

---

^{e-e} *Emendation yields "their unavenged blood shall be avenged."*

עמוס

AMOS

1 The words of Amos, a sheep breeder from Tekoa, who prophesied concerning Israel in the reigns of Kings Uzziah of Judah and Jeroboam son of Joash of Israel, two years before the earthquake.[a]

2 He proclaimed:
The LORD roars from Zion,
Shouts aloud from Jerusalem;
And the pastures of the shepherds shall languish,
And the summit of Carmel shall wither.

3 Thus said the LORD:
For three transgressions of Damascus,
For four, I will not revoke it:[b]
Because they threshed Gilead
With threshing boards of iron.
4 I will send down[c] fire upon the palace of Hazael,
And it shall devour the fortresses of Ben-hadad.[d]
5 I will break the gate bars of Damascus,
And wipe out the inhabitants from the Vale of Aven
And the sceptered ruler of Beth-eden;
And the people of Aram shall be exiled to Kir
　　　　　　　　　　　　　—said the LORD.

6 Thus said the LORD:
For three transgressions of Gaza,
For four, I will not revoke it:

---

[a] See Zech. 14.5.
[b] I.e. the decree of punishment.
[c] Cf. Lam. 1.13.
[d] Cf. II Kings 13.22-25.

Because they exiled[e] an entire population,
Which they delivered to Edom.[f]
[7] I will send down fire upon the wall of Gaza,
And it shall devour its fortresses;
[8] And I will wipe out the inhabitants of Ashdod
And the sceptered ruler of Ashkelon;
And I will turn My hand against Ekron,
And the Philistines shall perish to the last man
　　　　　　　　　　　　—said the Lord God.

[9] Thus said the Lord:
For three transgressions of Tyre,
For four, I will not revoke it:
Because they handed over
An entire population to Edom,[g]
Ignoring the covenant of brotherhood.[h]
[10] I will send down fire upon the wall of Tyre,
And it shall devour its fortresses.

[11] Thus said the Lord:
For three transgressions of Edom,
For four, I will not revoke it:
Because he pursued his brother with the sword
And repressed all pity,
Because his anger raged unceasing
And his fury stormed[i] unchecked.
[12] I will send down fire upon Teman,
And it shall devour the fortresses of Bozrah.

[13] Thus said the Lord:
For three transgressions of the Ammonites,
For four, I will not revoke it:
Because they ripped open the pregnant women of Gilead
In order to enlarge their own territory.
[14] I will set fire to the wall of Rabbah,

---

[e] *I.e. they cooperated in the annexation of Israelite territory; cf. Jer. 13.19 with note.*
[f] *Emendation yields "Aram"; cf. Isa. 9.11.*
[g] *Emendation yields "Aram."*
[h] *Cf. I Kings 5.26; 9.12-13.*
[i] *Cf. Akkadian* shamaru *and Jer. 3.5.*

And it shall devour its fortresses,
Amid shouting on a day of battle,
On a day of violent tempest.
¹⁵ Their king and his officers shall go
Into exile together

—said the LORD.

2 Thus said the LORD:
For three transgressions of Moab,
For four, I will not revoke it:
Because he burned the bones
Of the king of Edom to lime.
² I will send down fire upon Moab,
And it shall devour the fortresses of Kerioth.
And Moab shall die in tumult,
Amid shouting and the blare of horns;
³ I will wipe out the ruler from within her
And slay all her officials along with him

—said the LORD.

⁴ Thus said the LORD:
For three transgressions of Judah,
For four, I will not revoke it:
Because they have spurned the Teaching of the LORD
And have not observed His laws;
They are beguiled by the delusions
After which their fathers walked.
⁵ I will send down fire upon Judah,
And it shall devour the fortresses of Jerusalem.

⁶ Thus said the LORD:
For three transgressions of Israel,
For four, I will not revoke it:
Because they have sold for silver

Those whose cause was just,
And the needy for a pair of sandals.
⁷ [Ah,] you ᵃ⁻who trample the heads of the poor
Into the dust of the ground,
And make the humble walk a twisted course!⁻ᵃ
Father and son go to the same girl,
And thereby profane My holy name.
⁸ They recline by every altar
On garments taken in pledge,
And drink in the House of their God
Wine bought with fines they imposed.

⁹ Yet I
Destroyed the Amorite before them,
Whose stature was like the cedar's
And who was stout as the oak,
Destroying his boughs above
And his trunk below!
¹⁰ And I
Brought you up from the land of Egypt
And led you through the wilderness forty years,
To possess the land of the Amorite!
¹¹ And I raised up prophets from among your sons
And nazirites from among your young men.
Is that not so, O people of Israel?

—says the LORD.

¹² But you made the nazirites drink wine
And ordered the prophets not to prophesy.
¹³ ᵇ⁻Ah, I will slow your movements
As a wagon is slowed
When it is full of cut grain.⁻ᵇ
¹⁴ Flight shall fail the swift,
The strong shall find no strength,
And the warrior shall not save his life.
¹⁵ The bowman shall not hold his ground,
And the fleet-footed shall not escape,

ᵃ⁻ᵃ *Understanding* sho'afim *as equivalent to* shafim. *Emendation yields:* "Who crush on the
ground/The heads of the poor,/And push off the road/The humble of the land"; cf. Job
24.4.
ᵇ⁻ᵇ *Meaning of verse uncertain; alternatively:* "I will slow your movements/As a threshing
sledge (cf. Isa. 28.27-28) is slowed/When clogged by cut grain."

Nor the horseman save his life.
[16] Even the most stouthearted warrior
Shall run away unarmed[c] that day
—declares the LORD.

3 Hear this word, O people of Israel,
That the LORD has spoken concerning you,
Concerning the whole family that I brought up from Egypt:
[2] You alone have I singled out
Of all the families of the earth—
That is why I will call you to account
For all your iniquities.

[3] Can two walk together
Without having met?
[4] Does a lion roar in the forest
When he has no prey?
Does a great beast let out a cry from its den
Without having made a capture?
[5] Does a bird drop on the ground—in a trap—
With no snare there?
Does a trap spring up from the ground
Unless it has caught something?
[6] When a ram's horn is sounded in a town,
Do the people not take alarm?
Can misfortune come to a town
If the LORD has not caused it?
[7] Indeed, my Lord GOD does nothing
Without having revealed His purpose
To His servants the prophets.
[8] A lion has roared,
Who can but fear?
My Lord GOD has spoken,
Who can but prophesy?

---

[c] *Lit. "naked."*

⁹ Proclaim in the fortresses of Ashdod*a*
And in the fortresses of the land of Egypt!
Say:
Gather on the hill*b* of Samaria
And witness the great outrages within her
And the oppression in her midst.
¹⁰ They are incapable of doing right

—declares the LORD;

They store up lawlessness and rapine
In their fortresses.
¹¹ Assuredly,
Thus said my Lord GOD:
An enemy, all about the land!
He shall strip you of your splendor,
And your fortresses shall be plundered.
¹² Thus said the LORD:
As a shepherd rescues from the lion's jaws
Two shank bones or the tip of an ear,
So shall the Israelites escape
Who dwell in Samaria—
With the leg*c* of a bed or the head*c* of a couch.

¹³ Hear [this], and warn the House of Jacob

—says my Lord GOD, the God of Hosts—

¹⁴ That when I punish Israel for its transgressions,
I will wreak judgment on the altar*d* of Bethel,
And the horns of the altar shall be cut off
And shall fall to the ground.
¹⁵ I will wreck the winter palace
Together with the summer palace;
The ivory palaces shall be demolished,
And the great houses shall be destroyed

—declares the LORD.

a Septuagint reads "Assyria."
b Heb. plural; but cf. 4.1; 6.1.
c Meaning of Heb. uncertain.
d Heb. plural, but cf. "altar" in next line.

806

4 Hear this word, you cows of Bashan
On the hill of Samaria—
Who defraud the poor,
Who rob the needy;
Who say to your husbands,
"Bring, and let's carouse!"
² My Lord GOD swears by His holiness:
Behold, days are coming upon you
ᵃ⁻When you will be carried off in baskets,
And, to the last one, in fish baskets,
³ And taken out ⌊of the city⌋—
Each one through a breach straight ahead—
And flung on the refuse heap⁻ᵃ

—declares the LORD.

⁴ Come to Bethel and transgress;
To Gilgal, and transgress even more:
Present your sacrifices the next morning
And your tithes on the third day;
⁵ And burn a thank offering of leavened bread;ᵇ
And proclaim freewill offerings loudly.
For you love that sort of thing, O Israelites

—declares my Lord GOD.

⁶ I, on My part, have given you
Cleanness of teeth in all your towns,
And lack of food in all your settlements.
Yet you did not turn back to Me

—declares the LORD.

⁷ I therefore withheld the rain from you
Three months before harvest time:
I would make it rain on one town
And not on another;

ᵃ⁻ᵃ *Meaning of Heb. uncertain.*
ᵇ *Cf. Lev. 7.12-14; where, however, the bread is not to be burned.*

One field would be rained upon
While another on which it did not rain
Would wither.
⁸ So two or three towns would wander
To a single town to drink water,
But their thirst would not be slaked.
Yet you did not turn back to Me

      —declares the LORD.

⁹ I scourged you with blight and mildew;
Repeatedly*a* your gardens and vineyards,
Your fig trees and olive trees
Were devoured by locusts.
Yet you did not turn back to Me

      —declares the LORD.

¹⁰ I sent against you pestilence
In the manner of Egypt;*c*
I slew your young men with the sword,
Together with your captured horses,
And I made the stench of your armies
Rise in your very nostrils.
Yet you did not turn back to Me

      —declares the LORD.

¹¹ I have wrought destruction among you
As when God destroyed Sodom and Gomorrah;
You have become like a brand plucked from burning.
Yet you have not turned back to Me

      —declares the LORD.

¹² Assuredly,
*d-*Because I am doing that to you,*-d*
Even so will I act toward you, O Israel—
Prepare to meet your God, O Israel!

¹³ Behold,
He who formed the mountains,

---

c Alluding to the plagues at the time of the Exodus.
d-d Emendation yields "Because you are acting thus toward Me."

And created the wind,
And has told man what His wish*a* is,
Who turns blackness*e* into daybreak,
And treads upon the high places of the earth—
His name is the LORD, the God of Hosts.

5 Hear this word which I intone
As a dirge over you, O House of Israel:
2 Fallen, not to rise again,
Is Maiden Israel;
Abandoned on her soil
With none to lift her up.
3 For thus said my Lord GOD
About the House of Israel:
The town that marches out a thousand strong
Shall have a hundred left,
And the one that marches out a hundred strong
Shall have but ten left.

4 Thus said the LORD
To the House of Israel:
Seek Me, and you will live.
5 Do not seek Bethel,
Nor go to Gilgal,
Nor cross over*a* to Beer-sheba;
For Gilgal shall go into exile,
And Bethel shall become a delusion.
6 Seek the LORD, and you will live,
*b-*Else He will rush like fire upon*-b* the House of Joseph
And consume Bethel*c* with none to quench it.

7 [Ah,] you who turn justice into wormwood
And hurl righteousness to the ground!
[Seek the LORD,]

---

e Cf. Joel 2.2. Emendation yields "darkness"; cf. 5.8.

a I.e. into Judah; cf. I Kings 19.3.
b-b Meaning of Heb. uncertain.
c Septuagint reads "the House of Israel."

⁸ Who made the Pleiades and Orion,
Who turns deep darkness into dawn
And darkens day into night,
Who summons the waters of the sea
And pours them out upon the earth—
His name is the LORD!
⁹ ᵇ⁻It is He who hurls destruction upon strongholds,
So that ruin comes upon fortresses!⁻ᵇ

¹⁰ They hate the arbiter in the gate,
And detest him whose plea is just.
¹¹ Assuredly,
Because you ᵇ⁻impose a tax⁻ᵇ on the poor
And exact from him a levy of grain,
You have built houses of hewn stone,
But you shall not live in them;
You have planted delightful vineyards,
But shall not drink their wine.
¹² For I have noted how many are your crimes,
And how countless your sins—
You enemies of the righteous,
You takers of bribes,
You who subvert in the gate
The cause of the needy!

¹³ Assuredly,
At such a time the prudent man keeps silent,
For it is an evil time.

¹⁴ Seek good and not evil,
That you may live,
And that the LORD, the God of Hosts,
May truly be with you,
As you think.
¹⁵ Hate evil and love good,

And establish justice in the gate;
Perhaps the LORD, the God of Hosts,
Will be gracious to the remnant of Joseph.

¹⁶ Assuredly,
Thus said the LORD,
My Lord, the God of Hosts:
In every square there shall be lamenting,
In every street cries of "Ah, woe!"
And the farmhand shall be
Called to mourn,
And those skilled in wailing
To lament;
¹⁷ For there shall be lamenting
In every vineyard, too,
When I pass through your midst

—said the LORD.

¹⁸ Ah, you who wish
For the day of the LORD!
Why should you want
The day of the LORD?
It shall be darkness, not light!
¹⁹ —As if a man should run from a lion
And be attacked by a bear;
Or if he got indoors,
Should lean his hand on the wall
And be bitten by a snake!
²⁰ Surely the day of the LORD shall be
Not light, but darkness,
Blackest night without a glimmer.

²¹ I loathe, I spurn your festivals,
I am not appeased by your solemn assemblies.
²² If you offer Me burnt offerings—or your meal offerings—

I will not accept them;
I will pay no heed
To your gifts of fatlings.
²³ Spare Me the sound of your hymns,
And let Me not hear the music of your lutes.
²⁴ But let justice well up like water,
Righteousness like an unfailing stream.
²⁵ Did you offer sacrifice and oblation to Me
Those forty years in the wilderness,
O House of Israel?

²⁶ ᵈAnd you shall carry off your "king"—
Sikkuthᵉ and Kiyyun,ᵉ
The images you have made for yourselves
Of your astral deity—
²⁷ As I drive you into exile beyond Damascus
—Said the Lord, whose name is God of Hosts.ᶠ

6

Ah, you who are at ease in Zionᵃ
And confident on the hill of Samaria,
You notables of the leading nation
On whom the House of Israel ᵇ⁻pin their hopes:⁻ᵇ
² Cross over to Calneh and see,
Go from there to Great Hamath,
And go down to Gath of the Philistines:
Are [you] better than those kingdoms,
ᶜ⁻Or is their territory larger than yours?⁻ᶜ
³ ᵈ⁻Yet you ward off [the thought of] a day of woe
And convene a session of lawlessness.⁻ᵈ
⁴ They lie on ivory beds,
Lolling on their couches,

ᵈ *Vv. 26-27 would read well after 6.14.*
ᵉ *Two Akkadian names applied to Saturn, here deliberately pointed with the vowels of Heb.*
  shiqquṣ, *"detestable thing."*
ᶠ *I.e. who is Lord of all the astral bodies.*

ᵃ *Emendation yields "Joseph," cf. v. 6, and 5.6, 15, where "Joseph" denotes the northern*
  kingdom.
ᵇ⁻ᵇ *Taking ba l- as synonymous with ba 'ad; see Isa. 45.24 and note i-i.*
ᶜ⁻ᶜ *Emendation yields "Or is your territory larger than theirs?"*
ᵈ⁻ᵈ *Meaning of Heb. uncertain.*

Feasting on lambs from the flock
And on calves from the stalls.
5 *d-*They hum snatches of song
To the tune of the lute—
They account themselves musicians*-d* like David.
6 They drink [straight] from the wine bowls
And anoint themselves with the choicest oils—
But they are not concerned about the ruin of Joseph.
7 Assuredly, right soon
They shall head the column of exiles;
They shall loll no more at festive meals.

8 My Lord GOD swears by Himself:
I loathe *e-*the Pride of Jacob,*-e*
And I detest his fortresses.
I will declare forfeit city and inhabitants alike
　　　　　　　　　　—declares the LORD, the God of Hosts.
9 If ten people are left in one house, they shall die. *d-*10 And if someone's kinsman—who is to burn incense for him—comes to carry the remains out of a house,*-d* and he calls to the one at the rear of the house, "Are there any alive besides you?" he will answer, "No, none." And he will say, "Hush!"—so that no one may utter the name of the LORD.
11 For the LORD will command,
And the great house shall be smashed to bits,
And the little house to splinters.

12 Can horses gallop on a rock?
*f-*Can it be plowed with oxen?*-f*
Yet you have turned justice into poison weed
And the fruit of righteousness to wormwwod.
13 [Ah,] those who are so happy about Lo-dabar,*g*
Who exult, "By our might
We have captured Karnaim"!*g*
14 But I, O House of Israel,

---

e-e A poetic designation of the northern kingdom.
f-f Meaning of Heb. uncertain; emendation yields "Can one plow the sea with oxen?"
g Two towns east of the Jordan recovered for Israel by Jeroboam II (see II Kings 14.25). For Lo-dabar, cf. II Sam. 9.4, 5; 17.27; for Karnaim, cf. Gen. 14.5.

Will raise up a nation against you
    —declares the LORD, the God of Hosts—
Who will harass you from Lebo-hamath
To the Wadi Arabah.

7 This is what my Lord GOD showed me: He was creating [a plague of] locusts at the time when the late-sown crops were beginning to sprout—*ᵃ⁻* the late-sown crops after the king's reaping.*⁻ᵃ* ² When it had finished devouring the herbage in the land, I said, "O Lord GOD, pray forgive. How will Jacob survive? He is so small." ³ The LORD relented concerning this. "It shall not come to pass," said the LORD.

⁴ This is what the Lord GOD showed me: Lo, my Lord GOD was summoning *ᵇ⁻*to contend by*⁻ᵇ* fire, which consumed the Great Deep and was consuming the fields. ⁵ I said, "Oh, Lord GOD, refrain! How will Jacob survive? He is so small." ⁶ The LORD relented concerning this. "That shall not come to pass, either," said my Lord GOD.

⁷ This is what He showed me: He was standing on a wall *ᶜ⁻*checked with a plumb line*⁻ᶜ* and He was holding a plumb line.*ᵈ* ⁸ And the LORD asked me, "What do you see, Amos?" "A plumb line,"*ᵈ* I replied. And my Lord declared, "I am going to apply a plumb line*ᵈ* to My people Israel; I will pardon them no more. ⁹ The shrines of Isaac shall be laid waste, and the sanctuaries of Israel reduced to ruins; and I will turn upon the House of Jeroboam with the sword."

¹⁰ Amaziah, the priest of Bethel, sent this message to King Jeroboam of Israel: "Amos is conspiring against you within the House of Israel. The country cannot endure the things he is saying. ¹¹ For Amos has said, 'Jeroboam shall die by the sword, and Israel shall be exiled from its soil.'"

ᵃ⁻ᵃ *Meaning of Heb. uncertain. The king's reaping of fodder apparently occurred near the end of the rainy season, and whatever the locust destroyed after that could not be replaced for another year.*
ᵇ⁻ᵇ *Emendation yields "flaming."*
ᶜ⁻ᶜ *Or "destined for the pickax"; meaning of Heb. uncertain.*
ᵈ *Or "pickax"; meaning of Heb. uncertain.*

¹² Amaziah also said to Amos, "Seer, off with you to the land of Judah! ᵉ⁻Earn your living⁻ᵉ there, and do your prophesying there. ¹³ But don't ever prophesy again at Bethel; for it is a king's sanctuary and a royal palace." ¹⁴ Amos answered Amaziah: "I am not a prophet,ᶠ and I am not a prophet's disciple. I am a cattle breederᵍ and a tender of sycamore figs. ¹⁵ But the LORD took me away from following the flock, and the LORD said to me, 'Go, prophesy to My people Israel.' ¹⁶ And so, hear the word of the LORD. You say I must not prophesy about the House of Israel or preach about the House of Isaac; ¹⁷ but this, I swear, is what the LORD said: Your wife shall ʰ⁻play the harlot⁻ʰ in the town, your sons and daughters shall fall by the sword, and your land shall be divided up with a measuring line. And you yourself shall die on unclean soil;ⁱ for Israel shall be exiled from its soil."

8 This is what my Lord GOD showed me: There was a basket of figs.ᵃ ² He said, "What do you see, Amos?" "A basket of figs," I replied. And the LORD said to me: "The ᵇ⁻hour of doom⁻ᵇ has come for My people Israel; I will not pardon them again. ³ And the singing women of the palace shall howl on that day—declares my Lord GOD:

> So many corpses
> Left lying everywhere!
> Hush!"

⁴ Listen to this, you ᶜ⁻who devour the needy, annihilating the poor of the land,⁻ᶜ ⁵ saying, "If only the new moon were over, so that we could sell grain; the sabbath, so that we could offer wheat for sale, ᵈ⁻using an ephah that is too small, and a shekel that is

---

ᵉ⁻ᵉ *Lit. "eat bread."*
ᶠ *I.e. by profession.*
ᵍ *Meaning of Heb. uncertain; emendation yields "sheep breeder"; cf. the next verse and 1.1.*
ʰ⁻ʰ *Emendation yields "be ravished"; cf. Lam. 5.11.*
ⁱ *Cf. Hos. 9.3 and note.*

ᵃ *Heb. qayiṣ, lit. "summer fruit."*
ᵇ *Heb. qeṣ.*
ᶜ⁻ᶜ *Emendation yields "who on every new moon devour the needy, and on every sabbath the humble of the land"; cf. v. 5.*
ᵈ⁻ᵈ *Giving short measures of grain, but using oversize weights for the silver received in payment.*

too big,*d* tilting a dishonest scale, 6 and selling grain refuse as grain! We will buy the poor for silver, the needy for a pair of sandals." 7 The LORD swears by*e* the Pride of Jacob: "I will never forget any of their doings."

8 Shall not the earth shake for this
And all that dwell on it mourn?
Shall it not all rise like the Nile
And surge and subside like the Nile of Egypt?
9 And in that day

—declares my Lord GOD—

I will make the sun set at noon,
I will darken the earth on a sunny day.
10 I will turn your festivals into mourning
And all your songs into dirges;
I will put sackcloth on all loins
And tonsures on every head.
I will make it*f* mourn as for an only child,
All*g* of it as on a bitter day.

11 A time is coming—declares my Lord GOD—when I will send a famine upon the land: not a hunger for bread or a thirst for water, but for hearing the words of the LORD. 12 Men shall wander from *h-*sea to sea*-h* and from north to east to seek the word of the LORD, but they shall not find it.

13 In that day, the beautiful maidens and the young men shall faint with thirst—
14 Those who swear by the guilt of Samaria,
Saying, "As your god lives, Dan,"*i*
And "As the way to Beer-sheba lives"*j*—
They shall fall to rise no more.

e *Or "concerning"; cf. 6.8 with note.*
f *I.e. the earth; cf. vv. 8 and 9d.*
g *Lit. "the end."*
h-h *Emendation yields "south to west."*
i *See I Kings 12.28-29.*
j *See 5.5 with note.*

9 I saw my LORD standing by the altar, and He said: *a*-Strike the capitals so that the thresholds quake, and make an end of the first of them all.-*a* And I will slay the last of them with the sword; not one of them shall escape, and not one of them shall survive.

2 If they burrow down to Sheol,
From there My hand shall take them;
And if they ascend to heaven,
From there I will bring them down.
3 If they hide on the top of Carmel,
There I will search them out and seize them;
And if they conceal themselves from My sight
At the bottom of the sea,
There I will command
The serpent to bite them.
4 And if they go into captivity
Before their enemies,
There I will command
The sword to slay them.
I will fix My eye on them for evil
And not for good.

5 It is my Lord the GOD of Hosts
At whose touch the earth trembles
And all who dwell on it mourn,
And all of it swells like the Nile
And subsides like the Nile of Egypt;
6 Who built His chambers in heaven
And founded His vault on the earth,
Who summons the waters of the sea
And pours them over the land—
His name is the LORD.

a-a Meaning of Heb. uncertain.

⁷ To Me, O Israelites, you are
Just like the Ethiopians

—declares the LORD.

True, I brought Israel up
From the land of Egypt,
But also the Philistines from Caphtor
And the Arameans from Kir.
⁸ Behold, the Lord GOD has His eye
Upon the sinful kingdom:
I will wipe it off
The face of the earth!

But, I will not wholly wipe out
The House of Jacob

—declares the LORD.

⁹ For I will give the order
And shake the House of Israel—
Through all the nations—
As one shakes [sand] in a sieve,*b*
And not a pebble falls to the ground.
¹⁰ All the sinners of My people
Shall perish by the sword,
Who boast,
"Never shall the evil
Overtake us or come near us."

¹¹ In that day,
I will set up again the fallen booth of David:
I will mend its breaches and set up its ruins anew.
I will build it firm as in the days of old,
¹² *c-*So that they shall possess the rest of Edom
And all the nations once attached to My name*-c*
—Declares the LORD who will bring this to pass.

---

b *A coarse sieve used for cleansing grain of straw and stones, or sand of pebbles and shells.*
c-c *I.e. the House of David shall reestablish its authority over the nations that were ruled by David.*

¹³ A time is coming

—declares the LORD—

When the plowman shall meet the reaper,^{d}
And the treader of grapes
Him who holds the [bag of] seed;
When the mountains shall drip wine
And all the hills shall wave [with grain].

¹⁴ I will restore My people Israel.
They shall rebuild ruined cities and inhabit them;
They shall plant vineyards and drink their wine;
They shall till gardens and eat their fruits.
¹⁵ And I will plant them upon their soil,
Nevermore to be uprooted
From the soil I have given them

—said the LORD your God.

^{d} *Cf. Lev.* 26.5.

עבדיה
OBADIAH

1 The prophecy of Obadiah.

> We have received tidings from the LORD,
> And an envoy has been sent out among the nations:
> "Up! Let us rise up against her for battle."

> Thus said my Lord GOD concerning Edom:
> ² I will make you least among nations,
> You shall be most despised.
> ³ Your arrogant heart has seduced you,
> You who dwell in clefts of the rock,
> In your lofty abode.
> You think in your heart,
> "Who can pull me down to earth?"
> ⁴ Should you nest as high as the eagle,
> Should your eyrie be lodged 'mong the stars,
> Even from there I will pull you down
> —declares the LORD.

> ⁵ If thieves were to come to you,
> Marauders by night,
> They would steal no more than they needed.
> If vintagers came to you,
> They would surely leave some gleanings.
> How utterly you are destroyed!
> ⁶ How thoroughly rifled is Esau,
> How ransacked his hoards!

⁷ All your allies turned you back
At the frontier;
Your own confederates
Have duped and overcome you;
[Those who ate] your bread
Have planted snares under you.

He is bereft of understanding.
⁸ In that day

—declares the LORD—

I will make the wise vanish from Edom,
Understanding from Esau's mount.
⁹ Your warriors shall lose heart, O Teman,
And not a man on Esau's mount
Shall survive the slaughter.

¹⁰ For the outrage to your brother Jacob,
Disgrace shall engulf you,
And you shall perish forever.
¹¹ On that day when you stood aloof,
When aliens carried off his goods,
When foreigners entered his gates
And cast lots for Jerusalem,
You were as one of them.

¹² *ᵃ⁻How could you⁻ᵃ* gaze with glee
On your brother that day,
On his day of calamity!
How could you gloat
Over the people of Judah
On that day of ruin!
How could you loudly jeer
On a day of anguish!
¹³ How could you enter the gate of My people
On its day of disaster,

ᵃ⁻ᵃ *Lit. "Do not," and so through v. 14.*

Gaze in glee with the others
On its misfortune
On its day of disaster,
And lay hands on its wealth
On its day of disaster!
[14] How could you stand at the passes[b]
To cut down its fugitives!
How could you betray those who fled
On that day of anguish!
[15] As you did, so shall it be done to you;
Your conduct shall be requited.

Yea, against all nations
The day of the LORD is at hand.
[16] That same cup that you[c] drank on My Holy Mount
Shall all nations drink evermore,[d]
Drink till their speech grows thick,
And they become as though they had never been.
[17] But on Zion's mount a remnant shall survive,
And it shall be holy.[e]
The House of Jacob shall dispossess
Those who dispossessed them.
[18] The House of Jacob shall be fire,
And the House of Joseph flame,
And the House of Esau shall be straw;
They shall burn it and devour it,
And no survivor shall be left of the House of Esau
　　　　　　—for the LORD has spoken.

[19] [f]Thus they shall possess the Negeb and Mount Esau as well, the Shephelah and Philistia. They shall possess the Ephraimite country and the district of Samaria,[g] and Benjamin[h] along with Gilead. [20] And that exiled force of Israelites [shall possess] what

[b] *Meaning of Heb. uncertain.*
[c] *I.e. the Israelites.*
[d] *Emendation yields "at My hand," cf. Isa. 51.17; Jer. 25.15; Ps. 75.9.*
[e] *I.e. inviolate; cf. Jer. 2.3.*
[f] *Meaning of parts of vv. 19-21 uncertain.*
[g] *After the exile of the northern tribes, the city and district of Samaria were occupied mainly by non-Israelites.*
[h] *Emendation yields "the land of the Ammonites."*

belongs to the Phoenicians as far as Zarephath,[i] while the Jeru-salemite exile community of Sepharad[j] shall possess the towns of the Negeb. 21 For [k]liberators shall march up[-k] on Mount Zion to wreak judgment on Mount Esau; and dominion shall be the LORD's.

---

[i] *A town in southern Phoenicia; see I Kings 17.9.*
[j] *Probably Asia Minor, called Saparda in Persian cuneiform inscriptions.*
[k-k] *Several ancient versions read, "they (the exiles from Jerusalem named in the preceding verse) shall march up victorious."*

יונה
JONAH

1 The word of the Lord came to Jonah[a] son of Amittai: ² Go at once to Nineveh, that great city, and proclaim judgment upon it; for their wickedness has come before Me.

³ Jonah, however, started out to flee to Tarshish from the Lord's service. He went down to Joppa and found a ship going to Tarshish. He paid the fare and went aboard to sail with the others to Tarshish, away from the service of the Lord.

⁴ But the Lord cast a mighty wind upon the sea, and such a great tempest came upon the sea that the ship was in danger of breaking up. ⁵ In their fright, the sailors cried out, each to his own god; and they flung the ship's cargo overboard to make it lighter for them. Jonah, meanwhile, had gone down into the hold of the vessel, where he lay down and fell asleep. ⁶ The captain went over to him and cried out, "How can you be sleeping so soundly! Up, call upon your god! Perhaps the god will be kind to us and we will not perish."

⁷ The men said to one another, "Let us cast lots and find out on whose account this misfortune has come upon us." They cast lots and the lot fell on Jonah. ⁸ They said to him, "Tell us, you who have brought this misfortune upon us, what is your business? Where have you come from? What is your country, and of what people are you?" ⁹ "I am a Hebrew," he replied. "I worship the Lord, the God of Heaven, who made both sea and land." ¹⁰ The men were greatly terrified, and they asked him, "What have you done?" And when the men learned that he was fleeing from the service of the Lord—for so he told them—¹¹ they said to him, "What must we do to you to make the sea calm around

---

[a] *Mentioned in II Kings 14.25.*

us?" For the sea was growing more and more stormy. ¹² He answered, "Heave me overboard, and the sea will calm down for you; for I know that this terrible storm came upon you on my account." ¹³ Nevertheless, the men rowed hard to regain the shore, but they could not, for the sea was growing more and more stormy about them. ¹⁴ Then they cried out to the LORD: "Oh, please, LORD, do not let us perish on account of this man's life. Do not hold us guilty of killing an innocent person! For You, O LORD, by Your will, have brought this about." ¹⁵ And they heaved Jonah overboard, and the sea stopped raging.

¹⁶ The men feared the LORD greatly; they offered a sacrifice to the LORD and they made vows.

2 The LORD provided a huge fish to swallow Jonah; and Jonah remained in the fish's belly three days and three nights. ² Jonah prayed to the LORD his God from the belly of the fish. ³ He said:

> In my trouble I called to the LORD,
> And He answered me;
> From the belly of Sheol I cried out,
> And You heard my voice.
> ⁴ You cast me into the depths,
> Into the heart of the sea,
> The floods engulfed me;
> All Your breakers and billows
> Swept over me.
> ⁵ I thought I was driven away
> Out of Your sight:
> Would I ever gaze again
> Upon Your holy Temple?
> ⁶ The waters closed in over me,
> The deep engulfed me.
> Weeds twined around my head.
> ⁷ I sank to the base of the mountains;

The bars of the earth closed upon me forever.
Yet You brought my life up from the pit,
O LORD my God!
8 When my life was ebbing away,
I called the LORD to mind;
And my prayer came before You,
Into Your holy Temple.
9 They who cling to empty folly
Forsake their own welfare,*a*
10 But I, with loud thanksgiving,
Will sacrifice to You;
What I have vowed I will perform.
Deliverance is the LORD's!

11 The LORD commanded the fish, and it spewed Jonah out upon dry land

3 The word of the LORD came to Jonah a second time: 2 "Go at once to Nineveh, that great city, and proclaim to it what I tell you." 3 Jonah went at once to Nineveh in accordance with the LORD's command.

Nineveh was *a*an enormously large city*-a* a three days' walk across. 4 Jonah started out and made his way into the city the distance of one day's walk, and proclaimed: "Forty days more, and Nineveh shall be overthrown!"

5 The people of Nineveh believed God. They proclaimed a fast, and great and small alike put on sackcloth. 6 When the news reached the king of Nineveh, he rose from his throne, took off his robe, put on sackcloth, and sat in ashes. 7 And he had the word cried through Nineveh: "By decree of the king and his nobles: No man or beast—of flock or herd—shall taste anything! They shall not graze, and they shall not drink water! 8 They shall be covered with sackcloth—man and beast—and shall cry mightily to God. Let everyone turn back from his evil ways and from the injustice

a Meaning of Heb. uncertain.

a-a Lit. "a large city of God."

827

of which he is guilty. ⁹ Who knows but that God may turn and relent? He may turn back from His wrath, so that we do not perish."

¹⁰ God saw what they did, how they were turning back from their evil ways. And God renounced the punishment He had planned to bring upon them, and did not carry it out.

4 This displeased Jonah greatly, and he was grieved. ² He prayed to the Lord, saying, "O Lord! Isn't this just what I said when I was still in my own country? That is why I fled beforehand to Tarshish. For I know that You are a compassionate and gracious God, slow to anger, abounding in kindness, renouncing punishment. ³ Please, Lord, take my life, for I would rather die than live." ⁴ The Lord replied, "Are you that deeply grieved?"

⁵ Now Jonah had left the city and found a place east of the city. He made a booth there and sat under it in the shade, until he should see what happened to the city. ⁶ The Lord God provided a ricinus plant,ᵃ which grew up over Jonah, to provide shade for his head and save him from discomfort. Jonah was very happy about the plant. ⁷ But the next day at dawn God provided a worm, which attacked the plant so that it withered. ⁸ And when the sun rose, God provided a sultryᵇ east wind; the sun beat down on Jonah's head, and he became faint. He begged for death, saying, "I would rather die than live." ⁹ Then God said to Jonah, "Are you so deeply grieved about the plant?" "Yes," he replied, "so deeply that I want to die."

¹⁰ Then the Lord said: "You cared about the plant, which you did not work for and which you did not grow, which appeared overnight and perished overnight. ¹¹ And should not I care about Nineveh, that great city, in which there are more than a hundred and twenty thousand persons who do not yet know their right hand from their left, and many beasts as well!"ᶜ

ᵃ *Meaning of Heb. uncertain; others "gourd."*
ᵇ *Meaning of Heb. uncertain.*
ᶜ *Infants and beasts are not held responsible for their actions.*

מיכה
MICAH

1 The word of the LORD that came to Micah the Morashtite, who prophesied concerning Samaria and Jerusalem in the reigns of Kings Jotham, Ahaz, and Hezekiah of Judah.

[2] Listen, all you peoples,
Give heed, O earth, and all it holds;
And let my Lord GOD be your accuser—
My Lord from His holy abode.
[3] For lo! the LORD
Is coming forth from His dwelling place,
He will come down and stride
Upon the heights of the earth.
[4] The mountains shall melt under Him
And the valleys burst open—
Like wax before fire,
Like water cascading down a slope.

[5] All this is for the transgression of Jacob,
And for the sins of the House of Israel.
What is the transgression of Jacob
But Samaria,
And what the shrines[a] of Judah
But Jerusalem?
[6] So I will turn Samaria
Into a ruin in open country,
Into ground for planting vineyards;
For I will tumble her stones into the valley

---

[a] *Emendation yields "sins."*

And lay her foundations bare.
7 All her sculptured images shall be smashed,
And all her harlot's wealth be burned,
And I will make a waste heap of all her idols,
For they were amassed from fees for harlotry,
And they shall become harlots' fees again.

8 Because of this I will lament and wail;
I will go stripped and naked!
I will lament as sadly as the jackals,
As mournfully as the ostriches.
9 For her*b* wound is incurable,
It has reached Judah,
It has spread to the gate of my people,
To Jerusalem.

10 *c*Tell it not in Gath,
Refrain from weeping;*d*
In Beth-leaphrah,
Strew dust*e* over your [head].
11 Pass on, inhabitants of Shaphir!
Did not the inhabitants of Zaanan
Have to go forth naked in shame?
There is lamentation in Beth-ezel—
It will withdraw its support from you.
12 Though the inhabitants of Maroth
Hoped for good,
Yet disaster from the LORD descended
Upon the gate of Jerusalem.
13 Hitch the steeds to the chariot,
Inhabitant of Lachish!
It is the beginning
Of Fair Zion's guilt;
Israel's transgressions
Can be traced to you!

---

b *I.e. the nation's.*
c *Meaning of much of vv. 10-13 uncertain. They may refer to the transfer of part of western Judah to Philistine rule by Sennacherib of Assyria in the year 701 B.C.E.*
d *So that enemies may not gloat; cf. II Sam. 1.20.*
e *Heb. 'aphar, a play on Beth-leaphrah; vv. 10-15 contain several similar puns.*

¹⁴ Truly, you must give a farewell gift
To Moresheth-gath.
^{f-}The houses of Achzib are^{-f}
To the kings of Israel
Like a spring that fails.
¹⁵ A dispossessor will I bring to you
Who dwell in Mareshah;
At Adullam the glory
Of Israel shall set.
¹⁶ ^gShear off your hair and make yourself bald
For the children you once delighted in;
Make yourself as bald as a vulture,
For they have been banished from you.

2   Ah, those who plan iniquity
And design evil on their beds;
When morning dawns, they do it,
For they have the power.
² They covet fields, and seize them;
Houses, and take them away.
They defraud men of their homes,
And people of their land.

³ Assuredly, thus said the LORD: I am planning such a misfortune against this clan that you will not be able to free your necks from it. You will not be able to walk erect; it will be such a time of disaster.

⁴ In that day,
One shall recite a poem about you,
And utter a bitter lament,
And shall say:
^{a-}"My people's portion changes hands;
How it slips away from me!
Our field is allotted to a rebel.^b
We are utterly ravaged."^{-a}

^{f-f} *Emendation yields "Fair Achzib is."*
^g *A common rite of mourning; cf. Jer. 7.29.*

^{a-a} *Meaning of Heb. uncertain.*
^b *Emendation yields "ravager."*

⁵ Truly, none of you
Shall cast a lot cord^c
In the assembly of the LORD!

⁶ "Stop preaching!" they preach.
"That's no way to preach;
^{a-}Shame shall not overtake [us].
⁷ Is the House of Jacob condemned?^{-a}
Is the LORD's patience short?
Is such His practice?"

To be sure, My words are friendly
To those who walk in rectitude;
⁸ But ^{d-}an enemy arises against^{-d} My people.
You strip the mantle ^{e-}with the cloak^{-e}
Off such as pass unsuspecting,
^{a-}Who are turned away from war.^{-a}
⁹ You drive the women of My people away
From their pleasant homes;
You deprive their infants
Of My glory forever.
¹⁰ Up and depart!
This is no resting place;
^{a-}Because of [your] defilement
Terrible destruction shall befall.^{-a}

¹¹ If a man were to go about uttering
Windy, baseless falsehoods:
"I'll preach to you in favor of wine and liquor"—
He would be a preacher [acceptable] to that people.

¹² ^fI will assemble Jacob, all of you;
I will bring together the remnant of Israel;
I will make them all like sheep ^{g-}of Bozrah,^{-g}
Like a flock inside its pen^a—

^c On a piece of land, thus acquiring title to it; cf. Josh. 18.6 and Ps. 16.6.
^{d-d} Meaning of Heb. uncertain; emendation yields "you arise as enemies against."
^{e-e} Meaning of Heb. uncertain; emendation yields "off peaceful folk."
^f Vv. 12-13 may be an example of such "acceptable" preaching.
^{g-g} Emendation yields "in a fold (Arabic sīrah)."

832

They will be noisy with people.
¹³ One who makes a breach
Goes before them;
They enlarge it to a gate
And leave by it.
Their king marches before them,
The LORD at their head.

3 I said:
Listen, you rulers of Jacob,
You chiefs of the House of Israel!
For you ought to know what is right,
² ᵃBut you hate good and love evil.
³ You have devoured My people's flesh;
You have flayed the skin off them,
And their flesh off their bones.
ᵇ⁻And after tearing their skins off them,
And their flesh off their bones,⁻ᵇ
And breaking their bones to bits,
You have cut it up ᶜ⁻as into⁻ᶜ a pot,
Like meat in a caldron.
⁴ Someday they shall cry out to the LORD,
But He will not answer them;
At that time He will hide His face from them,
In accordance with the wrongs they have done.

⁵ Thus said the LORD to the prophets
Who lead My people astray,
Who cry "Peace!"
When they have something to chew,
But launch a war on him
Who fails to fill their mouths:
⁶ Assuredly,
It shall be night for you

ᵃ⁻ᵃ *Syntax of vv. 2-3 uncertain.*
ᵇ⁻ᵇ *Brought down from v. 2 for clarity.*
ᶜ⁻ᶜ *Meaning of Heb. uncertain; Septuagint and Syriac read "like flesh in."*

So that you cannot prophesy,
And it shall be dark for you
So that you cannot divine;
The sun shall set on the prophets,
And the day shall be darkened for them.
⁷ The seers shall be shamed
And the diviners confounded;
They shall cover their upper lips,*d*
Because no response comes from God.
⁸ But I,
I am filled with strength by the spirit of the LORD,
And with judgment and courage,
To declare to Jacob his transgressions
And to Israel his sin.

⁹ Hear this, you rulers of the House of Jacob,
You chiefs of the House of Israel,
Who detest justice
And make crooked all that is straight,
¹⁰ Who build Zion with crime,
Jerusalem with iniquity!
¹¹ Her rulers judge for gifts,
Her priests give rulings for a fee,
And her prophets divine for pay;
Yet they rely upon the LORD, saying,
"The LORD is in our midst;
No calamity shall overtake us."
¹² Assuredly, because of you
Zion shall be plowed as a field,
And Jerusalem shall become heaps of ruins,
And the Temple Mount
A shrine in the woods.

d *As a sign of mourning; cf. Ezek. 24.17, 22; Lev. 13.45.*

4   ^aIn the days to come,
The Mount of the LORD's House shall stand
Firm above the mountains;
And it shall tower above the hills.
The peoples shall gaze on it with joy,
² And the many nations shall go and shall say:
"Come,
Let us go up to the Mount of the LORD,
To the House of the God of Jacob;
That He may instruct us in His ways,
And that we may walk in His paths."
For instruction shall come forth^b from Zion,
The word of the LORD from Jerusalem.
³ Thus He will judge among the many peoples,
And arbitrate for the multitude of nations,
However distant;
And they shall beat their swords into plowshares^c
And their spears into pruning hooks.
Nation shall not take up
Sword against nation;
They shall never again know^d war;
⁴ But every man shall sit
Under his grapevine or fig tree
With no one to disturb him.
For it was the LORD of Hosts who spoke.
⁵ Though all the peoples walk
Each in the names of its gods,
We will walk
In the name of the LORD our God
Forever and ever.

⁶ In that day

—declares the LORD—

---

^a *For vv. 1-3 cf. Isa. 2.2-4.*
^b *I.e. oracles will be obtainable.*
^c *More exactly, the iron points with which wooden plows were tipped.*
^d *Cf. Judg. 3.2.*

I will assemble the lame [sheep]
And will gather the outcast
And those I have treated harshly;
7 And I will turn the lame into a remnant
And the expelled[e] into a populous nation.
And the LORD will reign over them on Mount Zion
Now and for evermore.

8 And you, O Migdal-eder,[f]
[g-]Outpost of Fair Zion,
It shall come to you:[-g]
The former monarchy shall return—
The kingship of [h-]Fair Jerusalem.[-h]

9 Now why do you utter such cries?
Is there no king in you,
Have your advisors perished,
That you have been seized by writhing
Like a woman in travail?
10 Writhe and scream,[g] Fair Zion,
Like a woman in travail!
For now you must leave the city
And dwell in the country—
And you will reach Babylon.
There you shall be saved,
There the LORD will redeem you
From the hands of your foes.
11 Indeed, many nations
Have assembled against you
Who think, "Let our eye
[g-]Obscenely gaze[-g] on Zion."
12 But they do not know
The design of the LORD,
They do not divine His intent:

---

[e] *Meaning of Heb. uncertain; emendation yields "weaklings"; cf. Ezek. 34.4.*
[f] *Apparently near Bethlehem; see Gen. 35.19-21.*
[g-g] *Meaning of Heb. uncertain.*
[h-h] *Emendation yields "the House of Israel"; cf. 5.1-2.*

He has gathered them
Like cut grain to the threshing floor.
¹³ Up and thresh, Fair Zion!
For I will give you horns of iron
And provide you with hoofs of bronze,
And you will crush the many peoples.
You[i] will devote their riches to the LORD,
Their wealth to the Lord of all the earth.

¹⁴ Now you gash yourself [g-]in grief.[-g]
They have laid siege to us;
They strike the ruler of Israel
On the cheek with a staff.

5 And you, O Bethlehem of Ephrath,[a]
Least among the clans of Judah,
From you one shall come forth
To rule Israel for Me—
One whose origin is from of old,
From ancient times.
² [b-]Truly, He will leave them [helpless]
Until she who is to bear has borne;[c]
Then the rest of his countrymen
Shall return to the children of Israel.[-b]
³ He shall stand and shepherd
By the might of the LORD,
By the power of the name
Of the LORD his God,
And they shall dwell [secure].
For lo, he shall wax great
To the ends of the earth;
⁴ And that shall afford safety.
Should Assyria invade our land

---

[i] *Heb.* -ti *serves here as the ending of the second person singular feminine; cf. Judg. 5.7 and note; Jer. 2.20; etc.*

[a] *The clan to which the Bethlehemites belonged; see I Sam. 17.12; Ruth 1.2; 4.11.*
[b-b] *Meaning of Heb. uncertain.*
[c] *I.e. a ruler, shepherd (v.3), to deliver Israel from the Assyrians (vv. 4-5).*

And tread upon our fortresses,^d
We will set up over it^e seven shepherds,
Eight princes of men,
⁵ Who will shepherd Assyria's land with swords,
The land of Nimrod ^fin its gates.^f
Thus he will deliver [us]
From Assyria, should it invade our land,
And should it trample our country.

⁶ The remnant of Jacob shall be,
In the midst of the many peoples,
Like dew from the LORD,
Like droplets on grass—
Which do not look to any man
Nor place their hope in mortals.

⁷ The remnant of Jacob
Shall be among the nations,
In the midst of the many peoples,
Like a lion among beasts of the wild,
Like a fierce lion among flocks of sheep,
Which tramples wherever it goes
And rends, with none to deliver.
⁸ Your hand shall prevail over your foes,
And all your enemies shall be cut down!

⁹ In that day

—declares the LORD—

I will destroy the horses in your midst
And wreck your chariots.
¹⁰ I will destroy the cities of your land
And demolish all your fortresses.
¹¹ I will destroy the sorcery you practice,
And you shall have no more soothsayers.
¹² I will destroy your idols

---

^d *Septuagint and Syriac read "soil"; cf. v. 5.*
^e *I.e. Assyria.*
^{f-f} *Emendation yields "with drawn blades"; cf. Ps. 37.14; 55.22.*

And the sacred pillars in your midst;
And no more shall you bow down
To the work of your hands.
¹³ I will tear down the sacred posts in your midst
And destroy your cities.*g*
¹⁴ In anger and wrath
Will I wreak retribution
On the nations*h* that have not obeyed.

6

Hear what the LORD is saying:
Come, present [My] case before the mountains,
And let the hills hear you pleading.

² Hear, you mountains, the case of the LORD—
*a*You firm*-a* foundations of the earth!
For the LORD has a case against His people,
He has a suit against Israel.

³ "My people!
What wrong have I done you?
What hardship have I caused you?
Testify against Me.
⁴ In fact,
I brought you up from the land of Egypt,
I redeemed you from the house of bondage,
And I sent before you
Moses, Aaron, and Miriam.

⁵ "My people,
Remember what Balak king of Moab
Plotted against you,
And how Balaam son of Beor
Responded to him.
[Recall your passage]

g *Emendation yields "idols."*
h *Emendation yields "arrogant."*

a-a *Emendation yields "Give ear, you."*

From Shittim to Gilgal*ᵇ*—
And you will recognize
The gracious acts of the LORD."

⁶ With what shall I approach the LORD,
Do homage to God on high?
Shall I approach Him with burnt offerings,
With calves a year old?
⁷ Would the LORD be pleased with thousands of rams,
With myriads of streams of oil?
Shall I give my firstborn for my transgression,
The fruit of my body for my sins?

⁸ "He has told you, O man, what is good,
And what the LORD requires of you:
Only to do justice
And to love goodness,
And *ᶜ*to walk modestly with your God;*⁻ᶜ*
⁹ *ᵈ⁻*Then will your name achieve wisdom."*⁻ᵈ*

Hark! The LORD
Summons the city:
*ᵉ⁻*Hear, O scepter;
For who can direct her
10   but you?*⁻ᵉ*
Will I overlook,*ᶠ* in the wicked man's house,
The granaries of wickedness
And the accursed short ephah?*ᵍ*
¹¹ Shall he*ʰ* be acquitted despite wicked balances
And a bag of fraudulent weights?—
¹² *ⁱ*Whose rich men are full of lawlessness,
And whose inhabitants speak treachery,
With tongues of deceit in their mouths.

ᵇ *I.e. the crossing of the Jordan; see Josh. 3.1, 14-4.19.*
ᶜ⁻ᶜ *Or "It is prudent to serve your God."*
ᵈ⁻ᵈ *Emendation yields "And it is worthwhile to revere His name."*
ᵉ⁻ᵉ *Meaning of Heb. uncertain.*
ᶠ *Taking ish as from* nashah *"to forget"; cf. Deut. 32.18.*
ᵍ *Cf. Amos 8.4-5.*
ʰ *Heb. "I"; change of vocalization yields "Will I acquit him."*
ⁱ *This verse would read well after "city" in v.9.*

¹³ I, in turn, have beaten you sore,
Have stunned [you] for your sins:
¹⁴ You have been eating without getting your fill,
^{e-}And there is a gnawing at your vitals;
You have been conceiving without bearing young,^{-e}
And what you bore I would deliver to the sword.
¹⁵ You have been sowing, but have nothing to reap;
You have trod olives, but have no oil for rubbing,
And grapes^j but have no wine to drink.
¹⁶ Yet ^{k-}you have kept^{-k} the laws of Omri,
And all the practices of the House of Ahab,
And have followed what they devised.
Therefore I will make you an object of horror
And ^{l-}her inhabitants^{-l} an object of hissing;^m
And you shall bear the mockery of peoples.ⁿ

7 Woe is me!^a
I am become like leavings of a fig harvest,
Like gleanings when the vintage is over,
There is not a cluster to eat,
Not a ripe fig I could desire.
² The pious are vanished from the land,
None upright are left among men;
All lie in wait to commit crimes,
One traps the other in his net.
^{3 b-}They are eager to do evil:
The magistrate makes demands,
And the judge [judges] for a fee;
The rich man makes his crooked plea,
And they grant it.^{-b}
⁴ The best of them is like a prickly shrub;
The [most] upright, worse than a barrier of thorns.

---

^j *Lit. "new wine."*
^{k-k} *Heb. "is kept."*
^{l-l} *I.e. those of the city of v. 9, apparently Samaria.*
^m *See note at Jer. 18.16.*
ⁿ *Heb. "My people."*

^a *The speaker is feminine (cf. 'elohayikh, v. 10), probably Samaria personified; cf. note l-l at 6.16.*
^{b-b} *Meaning of Heb. uncertain.*

*ᵇ⁻*On the day you waited for,*⁻ᵇ* your doom has come—
Now their confusion shall come to pass.
⁵ Trust no friend,
Rely on no intimate;
Be guarded in speech
With her who lies in your bosom.
⁶ For son spurns father,
Daughter rises up against mother,
Daughter-in-law against mother-in-law—
A man's own household
Are his enemies.
⁷ Yet I will look to the LORD,
I will wait for the God who saves me,
My God will hear me.

⁸ Do not rejoice over me,
O my enemy!*ᶜ*
Though I have fallen, I rise again;
Though I sit in darkness, the LORD is my light.
⁹ I must bear the anger of the LORD,
Since I have sinned against Him,
Until He champions my cause
And upholds my claim.
He will let me out into the light;
I will enjoy vindication by Him.
¹⁰ When my enemy*ᶜ* sees it,
She shall be covered with shame,
She who taunts me with "Where is He,
The LORD your God?"
My eyes shall behold her [downfall];
Lo, she shall be for trampling
Like mud in the streets.
¹¹ A day for mending your walls*ᵈ*—
That is a far-off day.
¹² This is rather a day when to you

ᶜ Heb. feminine, apparently referring to Damascus.
ᵈ To keep out tramplers (end of preceding verse); cf. Isa. 5.5; Ps. 80.13-14.

[Tramplers] will come streaming
From Assyria and the towns of Egypt—
From [every land from] Egypt to the Euphrates,
From sea to sea and from mountain to mountain—
¹³ And your*ᵉ* land shall become a desolation—
Because of those who dwell in it—
As the fruit of their misdeeds.

¹⁴ Oh, shepherd Your people with Your staff,
Your very own flock.
May they who dwell isolated
*ᶠ*In a woodland surrounded by farmland*ᶠ*
Graze*ᵍ* Bashan and Gilead
As in olden days.
¹⁵ *ʰ*I will show him*ʰ* wondrous deeds
As in the days when You sallied forth from the land of
  Egypt.
¹⁶ Let nations behold and be ashamed
Despite all their might;
Let them put hand to mouth;
Let their ears be deafened!
¹⁷ Let them lick dust like snakes,
Like crawling things on the ground!
*ᵇ*Let them come trembling out of their strongholds*ᵇ*
To the LORD our God;
Let them fear and dread You!

¹⁸ Who is a God like You,
Forgiving iniquity
And remitting transgression;
Who has not maintained His wrath forever
Against the remnant of His own people,
Because He loves graciousness!
¹⁹ He will take us back in love;
He will cover up our iniquities,

ᵉ *Heb. "the."*
ᶠ⁻ᶠ *I.e. the land west of the Jordan, which is represented as far less fertile than adjacent regions.*
ᵍ *Emendation yields "possess."*
ʰ⁻ʰ *Emendation yields "Show us."*

You will hurl all our[i] sins
Into the depths of the sea.
20 You will keep faith with Jacob,
Loyalty to Abraham,
As You promised on oath to our fathers
In days gone by.

[i] *Heb. "their."*

נחום
NAHUM

1 A pronouncement on Nineveh: The Book of the Prophecy of Nahum the Elkoshite.

² The Lord is a passionate, avenging God;
The Lord is vengeful and fierce in wrath.
The Lord takes vengeance on His enemies,
He rages against His foes.
³ The Lord is slow to anger and of great forbearance,
But the Lord does not remit all punishment.
He travels in whirlwind and storm,
And clouds are the dust on His feet.
⁴ He rebukes the sea and dries it up,
And He makes all rivers fail;
Bashan and Carmel languish,
And the blossoms*a* of Lebanon wither.
⁵ The mountains quake because of Him,
And the hills melt.
The earth heaves*b* before Him,
The world and all that dwell therein.
⁶ Who can stand before His wrath?
Who can resist His fury?
His anger pours out like fire,
And rocks are shattered because of Him.
⁷ The Lord is good to [those who hope in Him],
A haven on a day of distress;
He is mindful of those who seek refuge in Him.
⁸ And with a sweeping flood

a Lit. "bud."
b Meaning of Heb. uncertain.

He makes an end of ^cher place,^{-c}
And chases His enemies into darkness.
⁹ Why will you plot against the LORD?
He wreaks utter destruction:
No adversary^d opposes Him twice!
¹⁰ ^{b-}For like men besotted with drink,
They are burned up like tangled thorns,
Like straw that is thoroughly dried.^{-b}

¹¹ ^eThe base plotter
Who designed evil against the LORD
Has left you.
¹² Thus said the LORD:
^{b-}"Even as they^f were full and many,
Even so are they over and gone;
As surely as I afflicted you,
I will afflict you no more."^{-b}
¹³ And now
I will break off his yoke bar from you
And burst your cords apart.
¹⁴ The LORD has commanded concerning him:^g
^{b-}No posterity shall continue your name.^{-b}
I will do away with
The carved and graven images
In the temples of your gods;
I will make your grave
^{b-}Accord with your worthlessness.^{-b}

2   Behold on the hills
The footsteps of a herald
Announcing good fortune!
"Celebrate your festivals, O Judah,

---

^{c-c} *Meaning of Heb. uncertain; emendation yields "those who oppose Him."*
^d *Cf. Ugaritic* ṣrt.
^e *Vv. 11-14 would read well after 2.1.*
^f *I.e. the days of your affliction.*
^g *Heb. "you."*

Fulfill your vows.
Never again shall scoundrels invade you,
They have totally vanished."

2 ^aA shatterer has come up against you.
Man the guard posts,
Watch the road;
Steady your loins,
Brace all your strength!

3 For the LORD has restored ^{b-}the pride^c of Jacob
As well as the pride^c of Israel,^{-b}
Though marauders have laid them waste
And ravaged their branches.

4 His warriors' shields are painted red,
And the soldiers are clothed in crimson;
The chariots are like flaming torches,^d
On the day they are made ready.
^{e-}The [arrows of] cypress wood are poisoned,^{-e}
5 The chariots dash about frenzied in the fields,
They rush through the meadows.
They appear like torches,
They race like streaks of lightning.
6 ^{f-}He commands his burly men;
They stumble as they advance,
They hasten up to her wall,
Where ^{g-}wheeled shelters^{-g} are set up.^{-f}
7 ^{h-}The floodgates are opened,
And the palace is deluged.^{-h}

---

^a *This verse would read well after v.3.*
^{b-b} *"Jacob" refers to the northern kingdom (cf. Amos 6.8; 8.7); Israel refers to the southern
kingdom, regarded as the remnant of Israel after the fall of the northern kingdom (cf. Mic.
1.13-15).*
^c *Emendation yields "vine."*
^d *Understanding peladoth as equivalent to lappidoth.*
^{e-e} *Meaning of Heb. uncertain. Emendation yields "The horsemen charge"; cf. 3.3.*
^{f-f} *Meaning of Heb. uncertain.*
^{g-g} *To protect the crews that swung the battering rams.*
^{h-h} *I.e. the walls are breached and the palace is overrun.*

8 *i*-And Huzzab is exiled and carried away,*-i*
While her handmaidens *j*-escort [her]*-j*
As with the voices of doves,
Beating their breasts.
9 Nineveh has been like a [placid] pool of water
f-From earliest times;*-f*
Now they flee.
"Stop! Stop!"—
But none can turn them back.
10 "Plunder silver! Plunder gold!"
There is no limit to the treasure;
It is a hoard of all precious objects.

11 Desolation, devastation, and destruction!
Spirits sink,
Knees buckle,
All loins tremble,
All faces *k*-turn ashen.*-k*
12 What has become of that lions' den,
That pasture*l* of great beasts,
Where lion and lion's breed walked,
And lion's cub—with none to disturb them?
13 [Where is] the lion that tore victims for his cubs
And strangled for his lionesses,
And filled his lairs with prey
And his dens with mangled flesh?
14 I am going to deal with you
                    —declares the LORD of Hosts:
I will burn down *m*-her chariots in smoke,*-m*
And the sword shall devour your great beasts;
I will stamp out your killings from the earth,
And the sound of your messengers*n*
Shall be heard no more.

---

i-i *Meaning of Heb. uncertain. Emendation yields "And its mistress is led out and exiled."*
j-j *Emendation yields "moan."*
k-k *Meaning of Heb. uncertain; cf. note at Joel 2.6.*
l *Emendation yields "cave."*
m-m *Emendation yields "your thicket in fire."*
n *Emendation yields "devouring."*

848

3 Ah, city of crime,
Utterly treacherous,
Full of violence,
Where killing never stops!

² Crack of whip
And rattle of wheel,
Galloping steed
And bounding chariot!
³ Charging horsemen,
Flashing swords,
And glittering spears!
Hosts of slain
And heaps of corpses,
Dead bodies without number—
They stumble over bodies.
⁴ Because of the countless harlotries of the harlot,
The winsome mistress of sorcery,
Who ensnared*a* nations with her harlotries
And peoples with her sorcery,
⁵ I am going to deal with you
                              —declares the LORD of Hosts.
I will lift up your skirts over your face
And display your nakedness to the nations
And your shame to kingdoms.
⁶ I will throw loathsome things over you
And disfigure you
And make a spectacle of you.
⁷ All who see you will recoil from you
And will say,
"Nineveh has been ravaged!"
Who will console her?
Where shall I look for

---

a Meaning of Heb. uncertain.

Anyone to comfort you?
8 Were you any better than No-amon,*b*
Which sat by the Nile,
Surrounded by water—
Its rampart a river,*c*
Its wall *d-*consisting of sea?*-d*
9 Populous Nubia
And teeming Egypt,
Put and the Libyans—
They were her*e* helpers.
10 Yet even she was exiled,
She went into captivity.
Her babes, too, were dashed in pieces
At every street corner.
Lots were cast for her honored men,
And all her nobles were bound in chains.
11 You too shall be drunk
And utterly overcome;*a*
You too shall seek
A refuge from the enemy.
12 All your forts are fig trees
With*f* ripe fruit;
If shaken they will fall
Into the mouths of devourers.
13 Truly, the troops within you are women;
The gates of your land have opened themselves
To your enemies;
Fire has consumed your gate bars.

14 Draw water for the siege,
Strengthen your forts;
Tread the clay,
Trample the mud,
Grasp the brick mold!

*b Amon was the tutelary deity of No (Thebes; cf. Jer. 46.25), which the Assyrians had sacked
in 663 B.C.E.*
c Heb. "sea."
d-d Change of vocalization yields "water."
e Heb. "your."
f Emendation yields "Your troops are"; cf. next verse.

¹⁵ There fire will devour you,
The sword will put an end to you;
It will devour you like the grub.
^{a-}Multiply like grubs,
Multiply like locusts!^{-a}

¹⁶ You had more traders
Than the sky has stars—
The grubs cast their skins and fly away.
¹⁷ Your guards were like locusts,
Your marshals like piles of hoppers
Which settle on the stone fences
On a chilly day;
When the sun comes out, they fly away,
And where they are nobody knows.

¹⁸ Your shepherds are slumbering,
O king of Assyria;
Your sheep masters are ^{g-}lying inert;^{-g}
Your people are scattered^a over the hills,
And there is none to gather them.
¹⁹ There is no healing^h for your injury;
Your wound is grievous.
All who hear the news about you
Clap their hands over you.
For who has not suffered
From your constant malice?

---

^{g-g} *Lit. "dwelling"; emendation yields "asleep."*
^h *Heb.* kehah, *a variant of* gehah; *see Prov. 17.22.*

חבקוק

HABAKKUK

1 The pronouncement made by the prophet Habakkuk.

² How long, O LORD, shall I cry out
And You not listen,
Shall I shout to You, "Violence!"
And You not save?
³ Why do You make me see iniquity
ᵃ[Why] do You look⁻ᵃ upon wrong?—
Raiding and violence are before me,
Strife continues and contention ᵇ⁻goes on.⁻ᵇ
⁴ That is why decision fails
And justice never emerges;
For the villain hedges in the just man—
Therefore judgment emerges deformed.

⁵ "Look among the nations,
Observe well and be utterly astounded;
For a work is being wrought in your days
Which you would not believe if it were told.
⁶ For lo, I am raising up the Chaldeans,
That fierce, impetuous nation,
Who cross the earth's wide spaces
To seize homes not their own.
⁷ They are terrible, dreadful;
ᶜ⁻They make their own laws and rules.⁻ᶜ
⁸ Their horses are swifter than leopards,
Fleeter than wolves of the steppe.ᵈ
Their steeds gallop—ᵉ⁻their steeds⁻ᵉ

ᵃ⁻ᵃ *Targum and Syriac "So that I look."*
ᵇ⁻ᵇ *Meaning of Heb. uncertain.*
ᶜ⁻ᶜ *Lit. "Their law and majesty proceed from themselves."*
ᵈ *Understanding* 'ereb *as synonymous with* 'arabah; cf. Jer. 5.6.
ᵉ⁻ᵉ *The Qumran Habakkuk commentary (hereafter* 1QpHab) *reads "and spread [wings]."*

Come flying from afar.
Like vultures rushing toward food,
⁹ They all come, bent on rapine.
The thrust*ᵇ* of their van is forward,
And they amass captives like sand.
¹⁰ Kings they hold in derision,
And princes are a joke to them;
They laugh at every fortress,
They pile up earth and capture it.
¹¹ *ᵇ⁻*Then they pass on like the wind,
They transgress and incur guilt,
For they ascribe their might to their god."*⁻ᵇ*

¹² You, O LORD, are from everlasting;
My holy God, You*ᶠ* never die.
O LORD, You have made them a subject of contention;
O Rock, You have made them a cause for complaint.
¹³ You whose eyes are too pure to look upon evil,
Who cannot countenance wrongdoing,
Why do You countenance treachery,
And stand by idle
While the one in the wrong devours
The one in the right?
¹⁴ You have made mankind like the fish of the sea,
Like creeping things *ᵍ⁻*that have no ruler.*⁻ᵍ*
¹⁵ He has fished them all up with a line,
Pulled them up in his trawl,
And gathered them in his net.
That is why he rejoices and is glad.
¹⁶ That is why he sacrifices to his trawl
And makes offerings to his net;
For through them his portion*ʰ* is rich
And his nourishment fat.
¹⁷ Shall he then keep *ⁱ⁻*emptying his trawl,*⁻ⁱ*
And slaying nations without pity?

ᶠ Heb "we," a change made by a pious scribe.
ᵍ⁻ᵍ 1QpHab "[for him] to rule over"; cf. Gen. 1.28; Ps. 8.7-9.
ʰ Emendation yields "bread"; cf. Gen. 49.20.
ⁱ⁻ⁱ 1QpHab "drawing his sword."

2   I will stand on my watch,
Take up my station at the[a] post,
And wait to see what He will say to me,
What He[b] will reply to my complaint.

2 The LORD answered me and said:
Write the prophecy down,
Inscribe it clearly on tablets,
So that it can be read easily.
3 For [c]there is yet a prophecy[c] for a set term,
A truthful witness for a time that will come.
Even if it tarries, wait for it still;
For it will surely come, without delay:
4 [d]Lo, his spirit within him is puffed up, not upright,
But[d] the righteous man is rewarded with life
For his fidelity.
5 How much less then shall the defiant[e] go unpunished,
The treacherous, arrogant man
Who has made his maw as wide as Sheol,
Who is as insatiable as Death,
Who has harvested all the nations
And gathered in all the peoples!
6 Surely all these shall pronounce a satire against
    him,
A pointed epigram concerning him.
They shall say:
Ah, you who pile up what is not yours—
How much longer?—
And make ever heavier your load of indebtedness!
7 Right suddenly will your creditors[f] arise,

---

[a] *1QpHab reads "my."*
[b] *Taking 'ashib as equivalent to yashib.*
[c-c] *Emendation yields "the prophecy is a witness."*
[d-d] *Meaning of Heb. uncertain. Emendation yields "Lo there is a reward for the upright—/*
    the life breath within him—/And. . . ."
[e] *Connecting hyyn (1QpHab hwn) with the root hwn, Deut. 1.41; for the thought cf. Prov.*
    11.31. Meaning of rest of line uncertain.
[f] *Lit. "usurers".*

And those who remind^g you will awake,
And you will be despoiled by them.
^{8} Because you plundered many nations,
All surviving peoples shall plunder you—
For crimes against men and wrongs against lands,
Against cities and all their inhabitants.

^{9} Ah, you who have acquired gains
To the detriment of your own house,
$^{h\text{-}}$Who have destroyed many peoples$^{\text{-}h}$
In order to set your nest on high
To escape disaster!
^{10} You have plotted shame for your own house,
And guilt for yourself;
^{11} For a stone shall cry out from the wall,
And a rafter shall answer it from the woodwork.

^{12} Ah, you who have built a town with crime,
And established a city with infamy,
^{13} So that peoples have had to toil for the fire,^{i}
And nations to weary themselves for naught!
^{j}Behold, it is from the Lord of Hosts:
^{14} $^{k\text{-}}$For the earth shall be filled
With awe for the glory of the Lord
As water covers the sea.$^{\text{-}k}$

^{15} Ah, you who make others drink to intoxication
$^{l\text{-}}$As you pour out$^{\text{-}l}$ your wrath,
In order to gaze upon their nakedness!^{m}
^{16} You shall be sated with shame
Rather than glory:
Drink in your turn and stagger!^{n}
The cup in the right hand of the Lord

---

^{g} *Lit. "shake"; the same verb means "to call to mind" in Samaritan Aramaic.*
$^{h\text{-}h}$ *Brought up from v. 10 for clarity.*
^{i} *I.e. without profit.*
^{j} *Connection with the next four lines uncertain; they might read better after v. 20.*
$^{k\text{-}k}$ *Cf. Isa. 11.9.*
$^{l\text{-}l}$ *Meaning of Heb. uncertain. Emendation yields "from the bowl of."*
^{m} *Cf. Gen. 9.21-22.*
^{n} *Emendation yields "uncover yourself"; cf. Lam. 4.21.*

Shall come around to you,
And [o]disgrace to[o] your glory.
17 [p]For the lawlessness against Lebanon shall cover you,
The destruction of beasts shall overwhelm you[p]—
For crimes against men and wrongs against lands,
Against cities and all their inhabitants.

18 [q]What has the carved image availed,
That he who fashioned it has carved it
For an image and a false oracle—
That he who fashioned his product has trusted in it,
Making dumb idols?
19 Ah, you who say, "Wake up" to wood,
"Awaken" to inert stone!
Can that give an oracle?
Why, it is encased in gold and silver,
But there is no breath inside it.
20 But the LORD in His holy Abode—
Be silent before Him all the earth!

3

A prayer of the prophet Habakkuk. In the mode of *Shigionoth.*[a]

2 O LORD! I have learned of Your renown;
I am awed, O LORD, by Your deeds.
Renew them in these years,
Oh, make them known in these years!
Though angry, may You remember compassion.

3 God is coming from Teman,
The Holy One from Mount Paran. *Selah.*[b]
His majesty covers the skies,

o-o *Or "vomit of disgrace upon."*
p-p *Meaning of Heb. uncertain.*
q *This verse would read well after v. 19.*

a *Meaning uncertain; perhaps "psalms of supplication"; cf. Ps. 7.1.*
b *A musical direction of uncertain meaning.*

His splendor fills the earth:
⁴ ᶜIt is a brilliant light
Which gives off rays on every side—
And therein His glory is enveloped.ᶜ
⁵ Pestilence marches before Him,
And plague comes forth at His heels.
⁶ When He stands, He makes the earth shake;ᵈ
When He glances, He makes nations tremble.
The age-old mountains are shattered,
The primeval hills sink low.
ᶜHis are the ancient routes:
⁷ As a scene of havoc I beholdᶜ
The tents of Cushan;
Shaken are the pavilions
Of the land of Midian!

⁸ Are You wroth, O Lᴏʀᴅ, with Neharim?
Is Your anger against Neharim,
Your rage against Yamᵉ—
That You are driving Your steeds,
Your victorious chariot?
⁹ All bared and ready is Your bow.
ᶜSworn are the rods of the word.ᶜ   *Selah.*
You make the earth burst into streams,
¹⁰ The mountains rock at the sight of You,
A torrent of rain comes down;
Loud roars the deep,
ᶜThe sky returns the echo.ᶜ
¹¹ Sun [and] moon stand still on high
As Your arrows fly in brightness,
Your flashing spear in brilliance.
¹² You tread the earth in rage,
You trample nations in fury.

ᶜ⁻ᶜ *Meaning of Heb. uncertain.*
ᵈ *Cf. Targum and Septuagint.*
ᵉ *Neharim (lit. "Floods") and Yam (lit. "Sea") were marine monsters vanquished by the*
 Lᴏʀᴅ *in hoary antiquity. On Yam see Ps. 74.13; Job 7.12. A being called both Yam and*
 Nahar figures in early Canaanite literature.

¹³ You have come forth to deliver Your people,
To deliver Your anointed.^f
^{g-}You will smash the roof of the villain's house,
Raze it from foundation to top.   Selah.
¹⁴ You will crack [his] skull with Your^h bludgeon;
Blown away shall be his warriors,
Whose delight is to crush me suddenly,
To devour a poor man in an ambush.^{-g}
¹⁵ ⁱ⁻You will make Your steeds tread the sea,
Stirring the mighty waters.

¹⁶ I heard and my bowels quaked,
My lips quivered at the sound;
Rot entered into my bone,
I trembled where I stood.
Yet I wait calmly for the day of distress,
For a people to come to attack us.
¹⁷ Though the fig tree does not bud
And no yield is on the vine,
Though the olive crop has failed
And the fields produce no grain,
Though sheep have vanished from the fold
And no cattle are in the pen,⁻ⁱ
¹⁸ Yet will I rejoice in the LORD,
Exult in the God who delivers me.
¹⁹ My Lord GOD is my strength:
He makes my feet like the deer's
And lets me stride upon the heights.

^{c-}For the leader; with instrumental music.^{-c}

^f *I.e. the king of Judah.*
^{g-g} *Emendation yields: You will strike the heads of men of evil,/Smash the pates of Your adversaries. Selah./You will crack their skulls with Your bludgeon;/Dispersed, blown like chaff shall be they/Who lie in wait to swallow the innocent,/To devour the poor in an ambush.*
^h *Heb. "His."*
ⁱ⁻ⁱ *Or:* ¹⁵ *You will make Your steeds tread the sea,/Stirring the mighty waters,/*¹⁶ *That I may have rest on a day of distress,/When a people come up to attack us./But this report made my bowels quake,/These tidings made my lips quiver;/Rot entered into my bone,/I trembled where I stood:/*¹⁷ *That the fig tree does not bud,/And no yield is on the vine,/The olive crop has failed,/And the fields produce no grain;/The sheep have vanished from the fold,/And no cattle are in the pen.*

859

צפניה

ZEPHANIAH

1 The word of the LORD that came to Zephaniah son of Cushi son of Gedaliah son of Amariah son of Hezekiah, during the reign of King Josiah son of Amon of Judah.

> ² I will sweep everything away
> From the face of the earth
> > —declares the LORD.
> ³ I will sweep away man and beast;
> I will sweep away the birds of the sky
> And the fish of the sea.
> ^{a-}I will make the wicked stumble,^{-a}
> And I will destroy mankind
> From the face of the earth
> > —declares the LORD.

> ⁴ I will stretch out My arm against Judah
> And against all who dwell in Jerusalem;
> And I will wipe out from this place
> Every vestige of Baal,
> And the name of the priestlings^b along with the priests;
> ⁵ And those who bow down on the roofs
> To the host of heaven;
> And those who bow down and swear to the LORD
> But also swear by Malcam;^c
> ⁶ And those who have forsaken the LORD,
> And those who have not sought the LORD
> And have not turned to Him.

---

^{a-a} *Meaning of Heb. uncertain.*
^b *Heb.* kemarim, *a term used only of priests of heathen gods.*
^c *Apparently identical with "Milcom the abomination of the Ammonites"; cf. I Kings 11.5.*

⁷ Be silent before my Lord GOD,
For the day of the LORD is approaching;
For the LORD has prepared a ^{d-}sacrificial feast,^{-d}
Has bidden His guests purify themselves.
⁸ And on the day of the LORD's sacrifice
I will punish the officials
And the king's sons,^e
^{f-}And all who don a foreign vestment.
⁹ I will also punish on that day
Everyone who steps over the threshold,^{-f}
Who fill their master's^g palace
With lawlessness and fraud.
¹⁰ In that day there shall be

—declares the LORD—

A loud outcry from the Fish Gate,
And howling from the Mishneh,^h
And a sound of great anguish from the hills.
¹¹ The dwellers of the Machteshⁱ howl;
For all the tradesmen have perished,
All who weigh silver are wiped out.

¹² At that time,
I will search Jerusalem with lamps;
And I will punish the men
Who rest untroubled on their lees,
Who say to themselves,
"The LORD will do nothing, good or bad."
¹³ Their wealth shall be plundered
And their homes laid waste.
They shall build houses and not dwell in them,
Plant vineyards and not drink their wine.
¹⁴ The great day of the LORD is approaching,
Approaching most swiftly.

---

^{d-d} *I.e. a slaughter of sinners.*
^e *Apparently brothers of King Amon, who exercised influence during the minority of King Josiah (II Kings 22.1).*
^{f-f} *Apparently references to two customs of heathen worship; cf. II Kings 10.22 and I Sam. 5.5.*
^g *I.e. King Josiah's.*
^h *A quarter of Jerusalem; cf. II Kings 22.14.*
ⁱ *Another quarter of Jerusalem.*

*j*Hark, the day of the LORD!
It is bitter:
There a warrior shrieks!*j*
15 That day shall be a day of wrath,
A day of trouble and distress,
A day of calamity and desolation,
A day of darkness and deep gloom,
A day of densest clouds,
16 A day of horn blasts and alarms—
Against the fortified towns
And the lofty corner towers.
17 I will bring distress on the people,
And they shall walk like blind men,
Because they sinned against the LORD;
Their blood shall be spilled like dust,
And their fat*k* like dung.
18 Moreover, their silver and gold
Shall not avail to save them.
On the day of the LORD's wrath,
In the fire of His passion,
The whole land shall be consumed;
For He will make a terrible end
Of all who dwell in the land.

2   Gather together, gather,
a-O nation without shame,
2 Before the decree is born—
The day flies by like chaff-*a*—
Before the fierce anger
Of the LORD overtakes you,
Before the day of anger
Of the LORD overtakes you.
3 Seek the LORD,
All you humble of the land

j-j *Emendation yields: "The day of the* LORD *is faster than a runner, /Fleeter than a warrior";
cf. Ps. 19.6.*
k *Or "marrow"; meaning of Heb. uncertain.*

a-a *Meaning of Heb. uncertain. Emendation yields: "O straw (Aramaic* gel*) not gathered
in, /Before you are driven like flying chaff"; cf. Ps. 35.5.*

Who have fulfilled His law;
Seek righteousness,
Seek humility.
Perhaps you will find shelter
On the day of the LORD's anger.

⁴ Indeed, Gaza shall be deserted
And Ashkelon desolate;
Ashdod's people shall be expelled in broad daylight,
And Ekron shall be uprooted.
⁵ Ah, nation of Cherethites
Who inhabit the seacoast!
There is a word of the LORD against you,
O Canaan,ᵇ land of the Philistines:
I will lay you waste
Without inhabitants.

⁶ The seacoast Cherothᶜ shall become
An abode for shepherds and folds for flocks,
⁷ And shall be a portion for the remnant of the House of
    Judah;
On these [pastures] they shall graze [their flocks],
They shall ᵈ⁻lie downᵈ at eventide
In the houses of Ashkelon.
For the LORD their God will take note of them
And restore their fortunes.

⁸ I have heard the insults of Moab
And the jeers of the Ammonites,
Who have insulted My people
And gloated over their country.
⁹ Assuredly, as I live
        —declares the LORD of Hosts, the God of Israel—
Moab shall become like Sodom
And the Ammonites like Gomorrah:

ᵇ Or "Phoenicia," of which Philistia is regarded as an extension southward.
ᶜ Meaning of Heb. uncertain.
ᵈ⁻ᵈ Change of vocalization yields "rest [them]"; cf. Song of Songs 1.7.

Clumps^c of weeds and patches^c of salt,
And desolation evermore.
The remnant of My people shall plunder them,
The remainder of My nation shall possess them.
¹⁰ That is what they'll get for their haughtiness,
For insulting and jeering
At the people of the LORD of Hosts.
¹¹ The LORD will show Himself terrible against them,
Causing all the gods on earth to shrivel;^c
And all the coastlands of the nations
Shall bow down to Him—
Every man in his own home.

¹² You Cushites too—
^{e-}They shall be slain by My sword.^{-e}
¹³ And He will stretch out His arm against the north
And destroy Assyria;
He will make Nineveh a desolation,
Arid as the desert.
¹⁴ In it flocks shall lie down,
Every ^{c-}species of beast,
While jackdaws and owls roost on its capitals,
The great owl hoots in the window,
And the raven [croaks] on the threshold.
For he has stripped its cedarwork bare.^{-c}

¹⁵ Is this the gay city
That dwelt secure,
That thought in her heart,
"I am, and there is none but me"?
Alas, she is become a waste,
A lair of wild beasts!
Everyone who passes by her
Hisses and gestures with his hand.^f

---

^{e-e} *Emendation yields "shall be slain by the sword of the* LORD."
^f *To ward off a like fate from himself; cf. Jer. 18.16 and note.*

3 Ah, sullied, polluted,
Overbearing*a* city!
² She has been disobedient,
Has learned no lesson;
She has not trusted in the LORD,
Has not drawn near to her God.
³ The officials within her
Are roaring lions;
Her judges are wolves *b-*of the steppe,
They leave no bone until morning.*-b*
⁴ Her prophets are reckless,
Faithless fellows;
Her priests profane what is holy,
They give perverse rulings.
⁵ But the LORD in her midst is﹐righteous,
He does no wrong;
He issues judgment every morning,
As unfailing as the light.

The wrongdoer knows no shame!
⁶ I wiped out nations:
Their corner towers are desolate;
I turned their thoroughfares into ruins,
With none passing by;
Their towns lie waste without people,
Without inhabitants.
⁷ And I thought that she*c* would fear Me,
Would learn a lesson,
And that the punishment I brought on them*d*
Would not be *e-*lost on her.*-e*
Instead, all the more eagerly
They have practiced corruption in all their deeds.

---

a Meaning of Heb. uncertain. Emendation yields "harlot"; cf. Isa. 1.21.
b-b Meaning of Heb. uncertain.
c Heb. "you."
d Heb. "her."
e-e Lit. "cut off [from] her vision."

866

⁸ But wait for Me—says the LORD—
For the day when I arise as an accuser;ᶠ
When I decide to gather nations,
To bring kingdoms together,
To pour out My indignation on them,
All My blazing anger.
Indeed, by the fire of My passion
All the earth shall be consumed.
⁹ For then I will make the peoples pure of speech,
So that they all invoke the LORD by name
And serve Him with one accord.ᵍ
¹⁰ From beyond the rivers of Cush, My suppliantsᵇ
Shall bring offerings to Me in Fair Puzai.ʰ
¹¹ In that day,
You will no longer be shamed for all the deeds
By which you have defied Me.
For then I will remove
The proud and exultant within you,
And you will be haughty no more
On My sacred mount.ⁱ
¹² But I will leave within you
A poor, humble folk,
And they shall find refuge
In the name of the LORD.
¹³ The remnant of Israel
Shall do no wrong
And speak no falsehood;
A deceitful tongue
Shall not be in their mouths.
Only such as these shall graze and lie down,
With none to trouble them.

¹⁴ Shout for joy, Fair Zion,
Cry aloud, O Israel!
Rejoice and be glad with all your heart,

ᶠ *Understanding* 'ad *as equivalent to* 'ed, *with Septuagint and Syriac.*
ᵍ *Lit.* "back," *i.e. like beasts of burden.*
ʰ *Emendation yields "Zion." For the thought, cf. Isa. 18.1, 7.*
ⁱ *I.e. in My holy land; cf. Isa. 11.9; 57.13; 65.25.*

Fair Jerusalem!
¹⁵ The LORD has annulled the judgment against you,
He has swept away your foes.
Israel's Sovereign the LORD is within you;
You need fear misfortune no more.

¹⁶ In that day,
This shall be said to Jerusalem:
Have no fear, O Zion;
Let not your hands droop!
¹⁷ Your God the LORD is in your midst,
A warrior who brings triumph.
He will rejoice over you and be glad,
He will shout over you with jubilation.
He will ^{j-}soothe with His love
¹⁸ Those long disconsolate.^{-j}
I will take away from you ^{b-}the woe
Over which you endured mockery.^{-b}
¹⁹ At that time I will make [an end]
Of all who afflicted you.
And I will rescue the lame [sheep]
And gather the strayed;
And I will exchange their disgrace
For fame and renown in all the earth.
²⁰ At that time I will gather you,
And at [that] time I will bring you [home];
For I will make you renowned and famous
Among all the peoples on earth,
When I restore your fortunes
Before their^k very eyes

—said the LORD.

---

^{j-j} *Meaning of Heb. uncertain. Emendation yields "renew His love/As in the days of old."*
^k *Heb. "your."*

חגי

HAGGAI

1 In the second year of King Darius, on the first day of the sixth month, this word of the LORD came through the prophet Haggai to Zerubbabel son of Shealtiel, the governor of Judah, and to Joshua son of Jehozadak, the high priest:

² Thus said the LORD of Hosts: These people say, *ᵃ*-"The time has not yet come, *ᵃ* for rebuilding the House of the LORD."

³ And the word of the LORD through the prophet Haggai continued:

⁴ Is it a time for you to dwell in your paneled houses, while this House is lying in ruins? ⁵ Now thus said the LORD of Hosts: Consider how you have been faring! ⁶ You have sowed much and brought in little; you eat without being satisfied; you drink without getting your fill; you clothe yourselves, but no one gets warm; and he who earns anything earns it for a leaky purse.

⁷ *ᵇ*Thus said the LORD of Hosts: Consider how you have fared: ⁸ Go up to the hills and get timber, and rebuild the House; then I will look on it with favor and I will *ᶜ*-be glorified*ᶜ*—said the LORD.

⁹ You have been expecting much and getting little; and when you brought it home, I would blow on it!*ᵈ* Because of what?—says the LORD of Hosts. Because of My House which lies in ruins, while you all hurry to your own houses! ¹⁰ That is why the skies above you have withheld [their] moisture and the earth has withheld its yield, ¹¹ and I have summoned fierce heat upon the land —upon the hills, upon the new grain and wine and oil, upon all

---

ᵃ⁻ᵃ Lit. "It is not time for the coming of the time."
ᵇ Vv. 7-8 would read well after v. 11.
ᶜ⁻ᶜ Emendation yields "glorify it"; see 2.7-9.
ᵈ Meaning, perhaps, cast a curse on.

that the ground produces, upon man and beast, and upon all the fruits of labor.

¹² Zerubbabel son of Shealtiel and the high priest Joshua son of Jehozadak and all the rest of the people gave heed to the summons of the LORD their God and to the words of the prophet Haggai, when the LORD their God sent him; the people feared the LORD. ¹³ And Haggai, the LORD's messenger, fulfilling the LORD's mission, spoke to the people, "I am with you—declares the LORD."

¹⁴ Then the LORD roused the spirit of Zerubbabel son of Shealtiel, the governor of Judah, and the spirit of the high priest Joshua son of Jehozadak, and the spirit of all the rest of the people: They came and set to work on the House of the LORD of Hosts, their God, ¹⁵ on the twenty-fourth day of the sixth month.

2 In the second year of King Darius, ¹ on the twenty-first day of the seventh month, the word of the LORD came through the prophet Haggai:

² Speak to Zerubbabel son of Shealtiel, the governor of Judah, and to the high priest Joshua son of Jehozadak, and to the rest of the people: ³ Who is there left among you who saw this House in its former splendor? How does it look to you now? It must seem like nothing to you. ⁴ But be strong, O Zerubbabel—says the LORD—be strong, O high priest Joshua son of Jehozadak; be strong, all you people of the land—says the LORD—and act! For I am with you—says the LORD of Hosts. ⁵ So I promised you when you came out of Egypt, and My spirit is still in your midst. Fear not!

⁶ For thus said the LORD of Hosts: In just a little while longer I will shake the heavens and the earth, the sea and the dry land; ⁷ I will shake all the nations. And the precious things of all the nations shall come [here], and I will fill this House with glory, said the LORD of Hosts. ⁸ Silver is Mine and gold is Mine—says

the Lord of Hosts. [9] The glory of this latter House shall be greater than that of the former one, said the Lord of Hosts; and in this place I will grant prosperity—declares the Lord of Hosts.

[10] On the twenty-fourth day of the ninth [month], in the second year of Darius, the word of the Lord came to the prophet Haggai: [11] Thus said the Lord of Hosts: Seek a ruling from the priests, as follows: [12] If a man is carrying sacrificial flesh in a fold of his garment, and with that fold touches bread, stew, wine, oil, or any other food, will the latter become holy? In reply, the priests said, "No." [13] Haggai went on, "If someone defiled by a corpse touches any of these, will it be defiled?" And the priests responded, "Yes."

[14] Thereupon Haggai said: That is how this people and that is how this nation looks to Me—declares the Lord—and so, too, the work of their hands: whatever they offer there is defiled. [15] And now take thought, from this day backward:[a] As long as no stone had been laid on another in the House of the Lord, [16] if one came to a heap of twenty measures,[b] it would yield only ten; and if one came to a wine vat to skim off fifty measures, the press would yield only twenty. [17] I struck you—all the works of your hands—with blight and mildew and hail, but [c]you did not return[c] to Me—declares the Lord. [18] Take note, from this day forward—from the twenty-fourth day of the ninth month, from the day when the foundation was laid for the Lord's Temple—take note [19] while the seed is still in the granary, and the vine, fig tree, pomegranate, and olive tree have not yet borne fruit. For from this day on I will send blessings.

[20] And the word of the Lord came to Haggai a second time on the twenty-fourth day of the month: [21] Speak to Zerubbabel the governor of Judah: I am going to shake heaven and earth. [22] And I will overturn the thrones of kingdoms and destroy the might of the kingdoms of the nations. I will overturn chariots and their

---

[a] Or "forward."
[b] I.e. of grain.
[c-c] Lit. "there was not with you to Me"; cf. Amos. 4.9.

drivers; horses and their riders shall fall, each by the sword of his fellow. 23 On that day—declares the LORD of Hosts—I will take you, O My servant Zerubbabel son of Shealtiel—declares the LORD—and make you as a signet;[d] for I have chosen you—declares the LORD of Hosts.

[d] *I.e. bring you close to Me; contrast Jer. 22.24-30.*

זכריה

ZECHARIAH

1 In the eighth month of the second year of Darius, this word of the LORD came to the prophet Zechariah son of Berechiah son of Iddo:[a] 2 The LORD was very angry with your fathers. 3 Say to them further:

Thus said the LORD of Hosts: Turn back to me—says the LORD of Hosts—and I will turn back to you—said the LORD of Hosts. 4 Do not be like your fathers! For when the earlier prophets called to them, "Thus said the LORD of Hosts: Come, turn back from your evil ways and your evil deeds, they did not obey or give heed to Me—declares the LORD. 5 Where are your fathers now? And did the prophets live forever? 6 But the warnings and the decrees with which I charged My servants the prophets overtook your fathers—did they not?—and in the end they had to admit, 'The LORD has dealt with us according to our ways and our deeds, just as He purposed.' "

7 On the twenty-fourth day of the eleventh month of the second year of Darius—the month of Shebat—this word of the LORD came to the prophet Zechariah son of Berechiah son of Iddo:

8 In the night, I had a vision. I saw a man, mounted on a bay horse, standing *b*-among the myrtles-*b* in the Deep, and behind him were bay,*c* sorrel,*d* and white horses. 9 I asked, "What are those, my lord?" And the angel who talked with me answered, "I will let you know what they are." 10 Then the man who was standing *b*-among the myrtles-*b* spoke up and said, "These were sent out by the LORD to roam the earth."

---

a A clause like "Say to the people" is here understood; cf. 7.5.
b-b Septuagint reads "between the mountains"; cf. 6.1. In 6.1 ff. four teams of horses leave the LORD's abode to roam the four quarters of the earth; in 1.8 ff. they are about to reenter His abode after such a reconnaissance.
c Septuagint adds "dappled"; cf. 6.3.
d Meaning of Heb. uncertain. Emendation yields "black"; cf. 6.2.

[11] And in fact, they reported to the angel of the LORD who was standing [b-]among the myrtles,[-b] "We have roamed the earth, and have found all the earth dwelling in tranquility."[e] [12] Thereupon the angel of the LORD exclaimed, "O LORD of Hosts! How long will You withhold pardon from Jerusalem and the towns of Judah, which You placed under a curse seventy years ago?"

[13] The LORD replied with kind, comforting words to the angel who talked with me.

[14] Then the angel who talked with me said to me: "Proclaim! Thus said the LORD of Hosts: I am very jealous for Jerusalem— for Zion—[15] and I am very angry with those nations that are at ease; for I was only angry a little, but they overdid the punishment. [16] Assuredly, thus said the LORD: I graciously return to Jerusalem. My House shall be built in her—declares the LORD of Hosts—the measuring line is being applied to Jerusalem. [17] Proclaim further: Thus said the LORD of Hosts: My towns shall yet overflow with bounty. For the LORD will again comfort Zion; He will choose Jerusalem again."

2 I looked up, and I saw four horns.[a] [2] I asked the angel who talked with me, "What are those?" "Those," he replied, "are the horns that tossed Judah, Israel, and Jerusalem."[a] [3] Then the LORD showed me four smiths. [4] "What are they coming to do?" I asked. He replied: "Those are the horns that tossed Judah, so that no man could raise his head; and these men have come [b-]to throw them into a panic,[-b] to [c-]hew down[-c] the horns of the nations that raise a horn against the land of Judah, to toss it."

[5] I looked up, and I saw a man holding a measuring line. [6] "Where are you going?" I asked. "To measure Jerusalem," he replied, "to see how long and wide it is to be." [7] But the angel who talked with me came forward, and another angel came forward to meet him. [8] The former said to him, "Run to that young man and tell him:

[e] *Upheavals at the start of Darius' reign had encouraged hopes of an early restoration of the Davidic dynasty (cf. Hag. 2.21 ff.). Now these hopes were dashed.*

[a] *The four horns correspond to the four winds of v. 10.*

[b-b] *Meaning of Heb. uncertain; emendation yields "to sharpen ax heads."*

[c-c] *Meaning of Heb. uncertain.*

"Jerusalem shall be peopled as a city without walls, so many shall be the men and cattle it contains. ⁹ And I Myself—declares the LORD—will be a wall of fire all around it, and I will be a glory inside it.

¹⁰ "Away, away! Flee from the land of the north—says the LORD —though I swept you [there] like the four winds of heaven— declares the LORD."

¹¹ Away, escape, O Zion, you who dwell in Fair Babylon! ¹² For thus said the LORD of Hosts—He *ᵈ*who sent me after glory*ᵈ*— concerning the nations that have taken you as spoil: "Whoever touches you touches the pupil of *ᵉ*his own*ᵉ* eye. ¹³ For I will lift My hand against them, and they shall be spoil for those they enslaved." —Then you shall know that I was sent by the LORD of Hosts.

¹⁴ Shout for joy, Fair Zion! For lo, I come; and I will dwell in your midst—declares the LORD. ¹⁵ In that day many nations will attach themselves to the LORD and become His*ᶠ* people, and He*ᵍ* will dwell in your midst. Then you will know that I was sent to you by the LORD of Hosts.

¹⁶ The LORD will *ʰ*take Judah to Himself as His portion*ʰ* in the Holy Land, and He will choose Jerusalem once more.

¹⁷ Be silent, all flesh, before the LORD!

For He is roused from His holy habitation.

3 He further showed me Joshua, the high priest, standing before the angel of the LORD, and the Accuser*ᵃ* standing at his right to accuse him. ² But [the angel of] the LORD said to the Accuser, "The LORD rebuke you, O Accuser; may the LORD who has chosen Jerusalem rebuke you! For this is a brand plucked from the fire."*ᵇ* ³ Now Joshua was clothed in filthy garments when he stood before the angel. ⁴ The latter spoke up and said to his attendants,

---

ᵈ⁻ᵈ Emendation yields "whose Presence sent me."
ᵉ⁻ᵉ According to ancient Jewish tradition, a scribal change for "My."
ᶠ Heb. "My."
ᵍ Heb. "I."
ʰ⁻ʰ Emendation yields "allot to Judah its portion"; cf. Num. 34.17.
ᵃ Others "Satan."
ᵇ Joshua's father (Hag. 1.1; I Chron. 5.40-41) was exiled and his grandfather executed (II Kings 25.18-21) by the Babylonians, but Joshua returned.

"Take the filthy garments off him!" And he said to him, "See, I have removed your guilt from you, and you shall be clothed in [priestly] robes." [5] Then he[c] gave the order, "Let a pure[d] diadem be placed on his head." And they placed the pure diadem on his head and clothed him in [priestly] garments,[e] as the angel of the LORD stood by.

[6] And the angel of the LORD charged Joshua as follows: [7] "Thus said the LORD of Hosts: If you walk in My paths and keep My charge, you in turn will rule My House and guard My courts, and I will permit you to move about among these attendants. [8] Hearken well, O High Priest Joshua, you and your fellow priests sitting before you! For those men are a sign that I am going to bring My servant the Branch.[f] [9] For mark well this stone which I place before Joshua, a single stone with seven eyes.[g] I will execute its engraving—declares the LORD—and I will remove that country's guilt in a single day. [10] In that day—declares the LORD of Hosts—you will be inviting each other to the shade of vines and fig trees."

4 The angel who talked with me came back and woke me as a man is wakened from sleep. [2] He said to me, "What do you see?" And I answered, "I see a lampstand all of gold, with a bowl above it. The lamps on it are seven in number, and the [a]lamps above it have[-a] seven pipes; [3] and by it are two olive trees, one on the right of the bowl and one on its left." [4] I, in turn, asked the angel who talked with me, "What do those things mean, my lord?" [5] "Do you not know what those things mean?" asked the angel who talked with me; and I said, "No, my lord." [6] Then he explained to me as follows:[b]

"This is the word of the LORD to Zerubbabel:[c] Not by might,

---

[c] *Heb. "I."*
[d] *I.e. ritually pure.*
[e] *Joshua has now been rendered fit to associate with the heavenly beings (v. 7); cf. Isa. 6.6-8.*
[f] *I.e. the future king of David's line. See 6.12; Jer. 23.5-6; 33.15-16; cf. Isa. 11.1.*
[g] *Meaning of Heb. uncertain. The stone apparently symbolizes the God-given power of the future Davidic ruler; see below 4.6-7.*

[a-a] *Emendation yields "bowl above it has."*
[b] *The explanation is given in the last sentence of v. 10.*
[c] *A grandson of King Jehoiachin (I Chron. 3.17-19) and the secular head of the repatriated community (Hag. 1.1; etc.).*

nor by power, but by My spirit[d]—said the LORD of Hosts. [7] Whoever you are, O great mountain in the path of Zerubbabel, turn into level ground! For he shall produce that excellent stone; it shall be greeted with shouts of 'Beautiful! Beautiful!' "

[8] And the word of the LORD came to me: [9] "Zerubbabel's hands have founded this House and Zerubbabel's hands shall complete it. Then you shall know that it was the LORD of Hosts who sent me to you. [10] Does anyone scorn a day of small beginnings? When they see [e-]the stone of distinction[-e] in the hand of Zerubbabel, they shall rejoice.

"Those seven are the eyes of the LORD, ranging over the whole earth."

[11] "And what," I asked him, "are those two olive trees, one on the right and one on the left of the lampstand?" [12] And I further asked him, "What are the two tops[f] of the olive trees that feed their gold[g] through those two golden tubes?"[h] [13] He asked me, "Don't you know what they are?" And I replied, "No, my lord." [14] Then he explained, "They are the two [i-]anointed dignitaries[-i] who attend the Lord of all the earth."

5 I looked up again, and I saw a flying scroll. [2] "What do you see?" he asked. And I replied, "A flying scroll, twenty cubits long and ten cubits wide." [3] "That," he explained to me, "is the curse which goes out over the whole land. [a-]For everyone who has stolen, as is forbidden on one side [of the scroll], has gone unpunished; and everyone who has sworn [falsely], as is forbidden on the other side of it, has gone unpunished.[-a] [4] [But] I have sent it forth—declares the LORD of Hosts—and [the curse] shall enter the house of the thief and the house of the one who swears falsely by My name, and it shall lodge inside their houses and shall consume them to the last timber and stone."

[5] Then the angel who talked with me came forward and said,

---

[d] *I.e. Zerubbabel will succeed by means of spiritual gifts conferred upon him by the* LORD; *cf. Isa. 11.2 ff.*

[e-e] *Meaning of Heb. uncertain; others "plummet."*

[f] *Meaning of Heb. uncertain; literally "ears" (as of grain).*

[g] *Emendation yields "oil"; cf. v. 14.*

[h] *Or "funnels"; through them the oil runs from the olive trees into the bowl of vv. 2 and 3.*

[i-i] *I.e. the high priest and the king (cf. 3.8 with note); lit. "sons of oil."*

[a-a] *Meaning of Heb. uncertain.*

"Now look up and note this other object that is approaching."
⁶ I asked, "What is it?" And he said, "This tub*b* that is approaching—this," said he, "is their eye*c* in all the land." ⁷ And behold, a disk of lead was lifted, revealing a woman seated inside the tub.
⁸ "That," he said, "is Wickedness"; and, thrusting her down into the tub, he pressed the leaden weight into its mouth.

⁹ I looked up again and saw two women come soaring with the wind in their wings—they had wings like those of a stork—and carry off the tub between earth and sky. ¹⁰ "Where are they taking the tub?" I asked the angel who talked with me. ¹¹ And he answered, "To build a shrine for it in the land of Shinar,*d* [a stand] shall be erected for it, and it shall be set down there upon the stand."

6 I looked up again, and I saw: Four chariots were coming out from between the two mountains; the mountains were of copper. ² The horses of the first chariot were bay, the horses of the second chariot were black; ³ the horses of the third chariot were white, and the horses of the fourth chariot were spotted—dappled. ⁴ And I spoke up and asked the angel who talked with me: "What are those, my lord?" ⁵ In reply, the angel said to me, "Those are the four winds of heaven coming out after presenting themselves to the Lord of all the earth. ⁶ The one with the black horses is going out to the region of the north; the white ones *a*-have gone out*-a* to *b*-what is to the west of them;*-b* the spotted ones *a*-have gone out*-a* to the region of the south; ⁷ and *c*-the dappled ones have gone out. . . ."*-c* They were ready to start out and range the earth, and he gave them the order, "Start out and range the earth!" And they ranged the earth. ⁸ Then he alerted me, and said to me, "Take good note! Those that went out to the region of the north have *d*-done my pleasure*-d* in the region of the north."*e*

---

b *Heb.* ephah, *a measure of capacity.*
c *Septuagint and Syriac read* "guilt."
d *I.e. Babylonia; cf. Gen. 10.10; 11.2, 9.*

a-a *Change of vocalization yields* "will go out."
b-b *Cf.* 'ahor, "west," *Isa. 9.11. Emendation yields* "the region of the west."
c-c *Emendation yields* "the bay ones will go out to the region of the east."
d-d *Cf. postbiblical* naḥath ruaḥ, "gratification." *Emendation yields,* "done the LORD's pleasure."
e *I.e. Babylonia, whose communication with Judah was via North Mesopotamia and Syria; cf. 2.10-11.*

⁹ The word of the LORD came to me: ¹⁰ Receive from *f* the exiled community—from Heldai, Tobijah, and Jedaiah, who have come from Babylon—and you, in turn, proceed the same day to the house of Josiah son of Zephaniah. ¹¹ Take silver and gold and make crowns. Place [one] on the head of High Priest Joshua son of Jehozadak, ¹² and say to him, "Thus said the LORD of Hosts: Behold, a man called the Branch*g* shall branch out from the place where he is, and he shall build the Temple of the LORD. ¹³ He shall build the Temple of the LORD and shall assume majesty, and he shall sit on his throne and rule. And there shall also be a priest *h*-seated on his throne,-*h* and harmonious understanding shall prevail between them."

¹⁴ The crowns shall remain in the Temple of the LORD as a memorial to Helem,*i* Tobijah, Jedaiah, and Hen*j* son of Zephaniah. ¹⁵ Men from far away shall come and take part in the building of the Temple of the LORD, and you shall know that I have been sent to you by the LORD of Hosts—if only you will obey the LORD your God!

7 In the fourth year of King Darius, on the fourth day of the ninth month, Kislev, the word of the LORD came to Zechariah— ² when Bethel-sharezer *a*-and Regem-melech and his men sent-*a* to entreat the favor of the LORD, ³ [and] to address this inquiry to the priests of the House of the LORD and to the prophets: "Shall I weep and practice abstinence in the fifth month,*b* as I have been doing all these years?"

⁴ Thereupon the word of the LORD of Hosts came to me: ⁵ Say to all the people of the land and to the priests: When you fasted and lamented in the fifth and seventh months all these seventy years, did you fast for My benefit? ⁶ And when you eat and drink, who but you does the eating, and who but you does the drinking? ⁷ Look, this is the message that the LORD proclaimed through the

f Emendation yields "the gift of."
g See note at 3.8.
h-h Septuagint reads "on his right side."
i The Syriac version reads "Heldai"; cf. v. 10.
j In v. 10, "Josiah."
a-a Emendation yields "sent Regem-melech and his men."
b Because of the destruction of the Temple and Jerusalem; cf. II Kings 25.8 ff.

earlier prophets, when Jerusalem and the towns about her were peopled and tranquil, when the Negeb and the Shephelah were peopled.

⁸ And the word of the LORD to Zechariah continued: ⁹ Thus said the LORD of Hosts: Execute true justice; deal loyally and compassionately with one another. ¹⁰ Do not defraud the widow, the orphan, the stranger, and the poor; and do not plot evil against one another.—¹¹ But they refused to pay heed. They presented a balky back and turned a deaf ear. ¹² They hardened their hearts like adamant against heeding the instruction and admonition that the LORD of Hosts sent to them by His spirit through the earlier prophets; and a terrible wrath issued from the LORD of Hosts. ¹³ Even as He called and they would not listen, "So," said the LORD of Hosts, "let them call and I will not listen. ¹⁴ I dispersed them among all those nations which they had not known, and the land was left behind them desolate, without any who came and went. They caused a delightful land to be turned into a desolation."

8 The word of the LORD of Hosts came [to me]:

² Thus said the LORD of Hosts: I am very jealous for Zion, I am fiercely jealous for her. ³ Thus said the LORD: I have returned to Zion, and I will dwell in Jerusalem. Jerusalem will be called the City of Faithfulness, and the mount of the LORD of Hosts the Holy Mount.

⁴ Thus said the LORD of Hosts: There shall yet be old men and women in the squares of Jerusalem, each with staff in hand because of their great age. ⁵ And the squares of the city shall be crowded with boys and girls playing in the squares. ⁶ Thus said the LORD of Hosts: Though it will seem impossible to the remnant of this people in those days, shall it also be impossible to Me?—declares the LORD of Hosts. ⁷ Thus said the LORD of Hosts: I will rescue My people from the lands of the east and from the lands of the west, ⁸ and I will bring them home to dwell in Jerusa-

lem. They shall be My people, and I will be their God—in truth and sincerity.

⁹ Thus said the LORD of Hosts: Take courage, you who now hear these words which the prophets spoke when the foundations were laid for the rebuilding of the Temple, the House of the LORD of Hosts.

¹⁰ ªFor before that time, the earnings of men were nil, and profits from beasts were nothing. It was not safe to go about one's business on account of enemies; and I set all men against one another. ¹¹ But now I will not treat the remnant of this people as before—declares the LORD of Hosts—¹² but what it sows shall prosper: The vine shall produce its fruit, the ground shall produce its yield, and the skies shall provide their moisture. I will bestow all these things upon the remnant of this people. ¹³ And just as you were a curseᵇ among the nations, O House of Judah and House of Israel, so, when I vindicate you, you shall become a blessing.ᵇ Have no fear; take courage!

¹⁴ For thus said the LORD of Hosts: Just as I planned to afflict you and did not relent when your fathers provoked Me to anger —said the LORD of Hosts—¹⁵ so, at this time, I have turned and planned to do good to Jerusalem and to the House of Judah. Have no fear! ¹⁶ These are the things you are to do: Speak the truth to one another, render true and perfect justice in your gates. ¹⁷ And do not contrive evil against one another, and do not love perjury, because all those are things that I hate—declares the LORD.

¹⁸ And the word of the LORD of Hosts came to me, saying, ¹⁹ Thus said the LORD of Hosts: The fast of the fourth month, the fast of the fifth month, the fast of the seventh month, and the fast of the tenth monthᶜ shall become occasions for joy and gladness, happy festivals for the House of Judah; but you must love honesty and integrity.

²⁰ Thus said the LORD of Hosts: Peoples and the inhabitants of many cities shall yet come—²¹ the inhabitants of one shall go to the other and say, "Let us go and entreat the favor of the LORD,

ª Cf. Hag. 1.6.
ᵇ I.e. a standard by which men curse or bless; cf. Gen. 12.2 and note.
ᶜ Commemorating respectively the events of II Kings 25.3 ff. (Jer. 52.6 ff.); II Kings 25.8 ff. (Jer. 52.12 ff.); II Kings 25.25 ff. (Jer. 41); II Kings 25.1 ff. (Jer. 52.4).

let us seek the LORD of Hosts; I will go, too." [22] The many peoples and the multitude of nations shall come to seek the LORD of Hosts in Jerusalem and to entreat the favor of the LORD. [23] Thus said the LORD of Hosts: In those days, ten men from nations of every tongue will take hold—they will take hold of every Jew by a corner of his cloak and say, "Let us go with you, for we have heard that God is with you."

9 A pronouncement: The word of the LORD.

He will reside in the land of Hadrach and Damascus;
For all men's eyes will turn to the LORD—
Like all the tribes of Israel—
[2] Including Hamath, which borders on it,[a]
And Tyre and Sidon, though they are very wise.
[3] Tyre has built herself a fortress;
She has amassed silver like dust,
And gold like the mud in the streets.
[4] But my Lord will impoverish her;
He will hurl her wealth into the sea,
And she herself shall be consumed by fire.

[5] Ashkelon shall see it and be frightened,
Gaza shall tremble violently,
And Ekron, at the collapse of her hopes.
Kingship shall vanish from Gaza,
Ashkelon shall be without inhabitants,
[6] And [b-]a mongrel people[-b] shall settle in Ashdod.
I will uproot the grandeur of Philistia.

[7] But I will clean out the blood from its mouth,
And the detestable things from between its teeth.

---

[a] *I.e. on the land of Hadrach and Damascus.*
[b-b] *Heb.* mamzer; *cf. note at Deut. 23.3.*

Its survivors, too, shall belong to our God:
They shall become like a clan in Judah,
And Ekron shall be like the Jebusites.

8 And I will encamp in My House *ᶜ-against armies,-ᶜ*
Against any that come and go,
And no oppressor shall ever overrun them again;
For I have now taken note *ᵈ-with My own eyes.-ᵈ*

9 Rejoice greatly, Fair Zion;
Raise a shout, Fair Jerusalem!
Lo, your king is coming to you.
He is victorious, triumphant,
Yet humble, riding on an ass,
On a donkey foaled by a she-ass.
10 He*ᵉ* shall banish chariots from Ephraim
And horses from Jerusalem;
The warrior's bow shall be banished.
He shall call on the nations to surrender,*ᶠ*
And his rule shall extend from sea to sea
And from ocean to land's end.

11 *ᵍ*You, for your part, have released*ʰ*
Your prisoners from the dry pit,*ⁱ*
For the sake of the blood of your covenant,
12 [Saying], "Return to Bizzaron,*ʲ*
You prisoners of hope."
In return [I] announce this day:
I will repay you double.
13 For I have drawn Judah taut,
And applied [My hand] to Ephraim as to a bow,

ᶜ-ᶜ *Change of vocalization yields "as a garrison."*
ᵈ-ᵈ *Emendation yields "of their suffering"; cf. I Sam. 1.11.*
ᵉ *Heb. "I."*
ᶠ *Cf. Deut. 20.10-12 and note.*
ᵍ *Exact meaning and connection of vv. 11-12 uncertain.*
ʰ *Taking* shillaḥti *as a second person singular feminine form, with Septuagint; cf. Judg. 5.7
with note.*
ⁱ *I.e. a pit that serves as a dungeon rather than a cistern (both are called* bor *in Heb.).*
ʲ *Perhaps a nickname ("fortress") for Samaria (Heb.* Shomeron*).*

And I will arouse your sons, O Zion,
Against your sons, O Javan,
And make you like a warrior's sword.

¹⁴ And the LORD will manifest Himself to them,^k
And His arrows shall flash like lightning;
My Lord GOD shall sound the ram's horn
And advance in a stormy tempest.^l
¹⁵ The LORD of Hosts will protect them:
^m[His] slingstones shall devour and conquer;
They shall ⁿ⁻drink, shall rage as with⁻ⁿ wine,
And be filled [with it] like a dashing bowl,
Like the corners of an altar.
¹⁶ The LORD their God shall prosper them
On that day;
[He shall pasture] His people like sheep.
[They shall be] like crown jewels glittering on His soil.
¹⁷ How lovely, how beautiful they shall be,
Producing young men like new grain,
Young women like new wine!

10

Ask the LORD for rain
In the ^{a-}season of late rain.^{-a}
It is the LORD who causes storms;^b
And He will provide rainstorms ^{c-}for them,
Grass in the fields for everyone.^{-c}

² For the teraphim^d spoke delusion,
The augurs predicted falsely;
And dreamers speak lies
And console with illusions.

^k *I.e. Judah.*
^l *Lit. "tempests of wind"; for* teman *in the sense of wind, cf. Job 9.9; 39.26.*
^m *The meaning of much of the rest of the chapter is uncertain.*
ⁿ⁻ⁿ *Some Septuagint mss. read "drink blood like."*

^{a-a} *Septuagint reads "in its season/The early rain and the late." Cf. Deut. 11.14.*
^b *Meaning of Heb. uncertain.*
^{c-c} *Emendation yields "[producing] food for men,/Grass in the fields for cattle." Cf. Deut.*
11.14-15.
^d *Idols consulted for oracles; cf. I Sam. 15.23; Ezek. 21.26.*

That is why [My people] have strayed^b like a flock,
They suffer^b for lack of a shepherd.
³ My anger is roused against the shepherds,
And I will punish the he-goats.^{c}

For the LORD of Hosts has taken thought
In behalf of His flock, the House of Judah;
He will make them like majestic chargers in battle.
⁴ From them shall come ^{f}cornerstones,
From them tent pegs,^{f}
From them bows of combat,
And every captain shall also arise from them.
⁵ And together they shall be like warriors in battle,
Tramping in the dirt of the streets;
They shall fight, for the LORD shall be with them,
And they shall put horsemen to shame.
⁶ I will give victory to the House of Judah,
And triumph to the House of Joseph.
I will restore them, for I have pardoned them,
And they shall be as though I had never disowned them;
For I the LORD am their God,
And I will answer their prayers.
⁷ ^{g}Ephraim shall be like a warrior,
And they^g shall exult as with wine;
Their children shall see it and rejoice,
They shall exult in the LORD.
⁸ I will whistle to them and gather them,
For I will redeem them;
They shall increase ^{b}and continue increasing.$^{-b}$
⁹ For though I sowed them among the nations,
In the distant places they shall remember Me;
They shall escape with their children and shall return.
¹⁰ I will bring them back from the land of Egypt
And gather them from Assyria;
And I will bring them to the lands of Gilead and Lebanon,

^{c} *I.e. oppressive leaders; cf. Ezek. 34.17 ff.*
$^{f-f}$ *Emendation yields "shields and bucklers."*
$^{g-g}$ *Emendation yields "And when Ephraim is victorious,/They. . . ."*

And even they shall not suffice for them.
11 *b-*A hemmed-in force shall pass over the sea
And shall stir up waves in the sea;*-b*
And all the deeps of the Nile shall dry up.
Down shall come the pride of Assyria,
And the scepter of Egypt shall pass away.
12 But I will make them*h* mighty through the LORD,
And they shall *i-*march proudly*-i* in His name
                                   —declares the LORD.

11
Throw open your gates, O Lebanon,
And let fire consume your cedars!
2 Howl, cypresses, for cedars have fallen!
How the mighty are ravaged!
Howl, you oaks of Bashan,
For the stately forest is laid low!
3 Hark, the wailing of the shepherds,
For their *a-*rich pastures*-a* are ravaged;
Hark, the roaring of the great beasts,
For the jungle of the Jordan is ravaged.

4 Thus said my God the LORD: Tend the sheep meant for slaughter, 5 whose buyers will slaughter them with impunity, whose seller will say, "Praised be the LORD! I'll get rich," and whose shepherd will not pity them. 6 For I will pity the inhabitants of the land no more—declares the LORD—but I will place every man at the mercy of every other man and at the mercy of his king; they shall break the country to bits, and I will not rescue it from their hands.

7 So I tended the sheep meant for slaughter, *b-*for those poor men of the sheep.*-b* I got two staffs, one of which I named Favor and the other Unity, and I proceeded to tend the sheep. 8 But I lost *c-*the three shepherds*-c* in one month; then my patience with them was at an end, and they in turn were disgusted with me.

---

h *I.e. Judah and Ephraim.*
i-i *Meaning of Heb. uncertain. Emendation yields "have glory"; cf. Isa. 45.25.*

a-a *Meaning of Heb. uncertain.*
b-b *Emendation yields "for the sheep dealers"; cf. the word rendered "trader" in 14.21.*
c-c *Emendation yields "a third of the flock."*

⁹ So I declared, "I am not going to tend you; let the one that is to die die and the one that is to get lost get lost; and let the rest devour each other's flesh!"

¹⁰ Taking my staff Favor, I cleft it in two, so as to annul the covenant I had made with all the peoples;^d ¹¹ and when it was annulled that day, ^ethe same poor men of the sheep^e who watched^f me realized that it was a message from the Lord. ¹² Then I said to them, "If you are satisfied, pay me my wages; if not, don't." So they weighed out my wages, thirty shekels of silver—¹³ ^athe noble sum that I was worth in their estimation.^a The Lord said to me, "Deposit it in the treasury."^a And I took the thirty shekels and deposited it in the treasury in the House of the Lord. ¹⁴ Then I cleft in two my second staff, Unity, in order to annul the brotherhood between Judah and Israel.^g

¹⁵ The Lord said to me further: Get yourself the gear of a foolish shepherd. ¹⁶ For I am going to raise up in the land a shepherd who will neither miss the lost [sheep], nor seek the strayed,^a nor heal the injured, nor sustain the frail,^a but will feast on the flesh of the fat ones and ^atear off their hoofs.^a

¹⁷ Oh, the worthless shepherd
Who abandons the flock!
Let a sword descend upon his arm
And upon his right eye!
His arm shall shrivel up;
His right eye shall go blind.

12

A pronouncement: The word of the Lord concerning Israel.

The utterance of the Lord,
Who stretched out the skies
And made firm the earth,
And created man's breath within him:

---

^d *Perhaps alluding to the prediction of 14.1-3.*
^{e-e} *Emendation yields "the sheep dealers."*
^f *Emendation yields "hired."*
^g *Two mss. of the Septuagint have "Jerusalem"; cf. 12.2-3; 14.14.*

² Behold, I will make Jerusalem a bowl of reeling for the peoples all around. Judah shall be caught up in the siege upon Jerusalem, ³ when all the nations of the earth gather against her. In that day, I will make Jerusalem a stone for all the peoples to lift; all who lift it shall injure themselves. ⁴ In that day—declares the LORD—I will strike every horse with panic and its rider with madness. But I will ᵃ⁻watch over the House of Judah while I strike every horse of⁻ᵃ the peoples with blindness. ⁵ And the clans of Judah will say to themselves, ᵇ⁻"The dwellers of Jerusalem are a task set for us by⁻ᵇ their God, the LORD of Hosts." ⁶ In that day, I will make the clans of Judah like a flaming brazier among sticks and like a flaming torch among sheaves. They shall devour all the besieging peoples right and left; and Jerusalem shall continue on its site, in Jerusalem.ᶜ

⁷ The LORD will give victory to the tents of Judah first, so that the glory of the House of David and the glory of the inhabitants of Jerusalem may not be too great for Judah. ⁸ In that day, the LORD will shield the inhabitants of Jerusalem; and the feeblest of them shall be in that day like David, and the House of David like a divine being—like an angel of the LORD—at their head.

⁹ In that day I will ᵈ⁻all but annihilate⁻ᵈ all the nations that came up against Jerusalem. ¹⁰ But I will fill the House of David and the inhabitants of Jerusalem with a spirit of pity and compassion; and they shall lamentᵉ to Me about those who are slain, wailing over them as over a favorite son and showing bitter grief as over a firstborn. ¹¹ In that day, the wailing in Jerusalem shall be as great as the wailing at Hadad-rimmon in the plain of Megiddon.ᶠ ¹² The land shall wail, each family by itself: the family of the House of David by themselves, and their womenfolk by themselves; the family of the House of Nathan by themselves, and their womenfolk by themselves; ¹³ the family of the House of Levi by themselves, and their womenfolk by themselves; the family of the Shimeites by themselves, and their womenfolk by themselves;

ᵃ⁻ᵃ *Emendation yields "open the eyes of Judah while I strike all."*
ᵇ⁻ᵇ *Emendation yields "We will save the dwellers of Jerusalem with the help of."*
ᶜ *Emendation yields "safety."*
ᵈ⁻ᵈ *For the idiom cf. Gen. 43.30; it is also attested in postbiblical Hebrew.*
ᵉ *Meaning of Heb. uncertain.*
ᶠ *Usually "Megiddo."*

¹⁴ and all the other families, every family by itself, with their womenfolk by themselves.ᵍ

13 In that day a fountain shall be open to the House of David and the inhabitants of Jerusalem for purging and cleansing.

² In that day, too—declares the LORD of Hosts—I will erase the very names of the idols from the land; they shall not be uttered anymore. And I will also make the "prophets" and the ᵃ⁻unclean spirit⁻ᵃ vanish from the land. ³ If anyone "prophesies" thereafter, his own father and mother, who brought him into the world, will say to him, "You shall die, for you have lied in the name of the LORD"; and his own father and mother, who brought him into the world, will put him to death when he "prophesies." ⁴ In that day, every "prophet" will be ashamed of the "visions" [he had] when he "prophesied." In order to deceive, heʰ will not wear a hairy mantle,ᶜ ⁵ and he will declare, "I am not a 'prophet'; ᵈ⁻I am a tiller of the soil;⁻ᵈ you see, ᵉ⁻I was plied with the red stuff⁻ᵉ from my youth on." ⁶ And if he is asked, "What are those ᶠ⁻sores on your back?"⁻ᶠ he will reply, "From being beaten in the homes of my friends."ᵍ

⁷ ʰO sword!
Rouse yourself against My shepherd,
The man ⁱ⁻in charge of My flock⁻ⁱ
                    —says the LORD of Hosts.
Strike down the shepherd
And let the flock scatter;
And I will also turn My hand

ᵍ *In this way, apparently, they will prevail upon the Lord to spare the remnant of the besieging nations; cf. v. 10.*

ᵃ⁻ᵃ *To which abnormal human behavior was attributed.*

ᵇ *Heb. "They."*

ᶜ *In imitation of Elijah; cf. II Kings 1.8.*

ᵈ⁻ᵈ *I.e. I was addicted to wine like Noah, the tiller of the soil, (cf. Gen. 9.20-21), hence my hallucinations and ravings; cf. Prov. 23.33.*

ᵉ⁻ᵉ *Connecting 'adam with 'adom "red" (cf. Prov. 23.31); but meaning of Heb. uncertain.*

ᶠ⁻ᶠ *Lit. "sores between your arms"; cf. II Kings 9.24. Sores are sometimes symptoms of hysteria.*

ᵍ *Presumably for making drunken scenes; cf. Prov. 23.35.*

ʰ *Vv. 7-9 would read well after 11.17.*

ⁱ⁻ⁱ *Meaning of Heb. uncertain.*

Against all the shepherd boys.
8 Throughout the land

—declares the LORD—

Two thirds shall perish, shall die,
And one third of it shall survive.
9 That third I will put into the fire,
And I will smelt them as one smelts silver
And test them as one tests gold.
They will invoke Me by name,
And I will respond to them.
I will declare, "You are My people,"
And they will declare,
"The LORD is our God!"

14 Lo, a day of the LORD is coming when your*a* spoil shall be divided in your very midst! 2 For I will gather all the nations to Jerusalem for war: the city shall be captured, the houses plundered, and the women violated; and a part of the city shall go into exile. But the rest of the population shall not be uprooted from the city.

3 Then the LORD will come forth and make war on those nations as He is wont to make war on a day of battle. 4 On that day, He will set His feet on the Mount of Olives, near Jerusalem on the east; and the Mount of Olives shall split across from east to west, and one part of the Mount shall shift to the north and the other to the south, [forming] a huge gorge. 5 *b*And the Valley in the Hills shall be stopped up, for the Valley of the Hills shall reach only to Azal; it shall be stopped up as it was stopped up as a result of the earthquake in the days of King Uzziah of Judah. —And the LORD my God, with all the holy beings, will come to you.

6 *c*In that day, there shall be neither sunlight nor cold moonlight, 7 but there shall be a continuous day—only the LORD knows

---

a *Jerusalem is addressed.*
b *Vocalizing [we] nistam with Targum, Septuagint, and an old Heb. ms. Other mss. and printed editions read, "You (pl.) shall flee [to] the Valley in the Hills, for the Valley of the Hills shall reach up to Azal. You shall flee as you fled because of the earthquake. . . ."*
c *Meaning of verse uncertain; cf. Job 21.26.*

when—of neither day nor night, and there shall be light at eventide.

8 In that day, fresh water shall flow from Jerusalem, part of it to the Eastern Sea[d] and part to the Western Sea,[e] throughout the summer and winter.

9 And the LORD shall be king over all the earth; in that day there shall be one LORD with one name.[f]

10 Then the whole country shall become like the Arabah,[g] [h-]from Geba to Rimmon south of Jerusalem.[-h] The latter, however, shall perch high up where it is, and [i-]shall be inhabited[-i] from the Gate of Benjamin to the site of the Old Gate, down to the Corner Gate, and from the Tower of Hananel to the king's winepresses. 11 Never again shall destruction be decreed, and Jerusalem shall dwell secure.

12 As for those peoples that warred against Jerusalem, the LORD will smite them with this plague: their flesh shall rot away while they stand on their feet; their eyes shall rot away in their sockets; and their tongues shall rot away in their mouths.

13 In that day, a great panic from the LORD shall fall upon them, and everyone shall snatch at the hand of another, and everyone shall raise his hand against everyone else's hand. 14 Judah shall join the fighting in Jerusalem, and the wealth of all the nations round about—vast quantities of gold, silver, and clothing—shall be gathered in.

15 The same plague shall strike the horses, the mules, the camels, and the asses; the plague shall affect all the animals in those camps.

16 All who survive of all those nations that came up against Jerusalem shall make a pilgrimage year by year to bow low to the King LORD of Hosts and to observe the Feast of Booths. 17 Any of the earth's communities that does not make the pilgrimage to Jerusalem to bow low to the King LORD of Hosts shall receive no rain. 18 However, if the community of Egypt does not make this

[d] I.e. the Dead Sea; cf. Joel 2.20.
[e] I.e. the Mediterranean Sea; cf. Joel 2.20.
[f] I.e. the LORD alone shall be worshiped and shall be invoked by His true name.
[g] I.e. shall be depressed like the Jordan Valley.
[h-] I.e. from the northern border of the Kingdom of Judah (I Kings 15.22; II Kings 23.8) to the southern border (Josh. 15.32; 19.7).
[i-] Brought up from v. 11 for clarity.

pilgrimage, it shall not be visited by the same affliction with which the LORD will strike the other nations that do not come up to observe the Feast of Booths.[j] [19] Such shall be the punishment of Egypt and of all other nations that do not come up to observe the Feast of Booths.

[20] In that day, even the bells on the horses shall be inscribed "Holy to the LORD." The metal pots in the House of the LORD shall be like the basins before the altar; [21] indeed, every metal pot in Jerusalem and in Judah shall be holy to the LORD of Hosts. And all those who sacrifice shall come and take of these to boil [their sacrificial meat] in; in that day there shall be no more traders[k] in the House of the LORD of Hosts.

[j] *Because Egypt is not dependent on rain, it will suffer some other punishment, presumably that described in v. 12.*
[k] *To sell ritually pure vessels.*

מלאכי
MALACHI

1 A pronouncement: The word of the Lord to Israel through Malachi.

² I have shown you love, said the Lord. But you ask, "How have You shown us love?" After all—declares the Lord—Esau is Jacob's brother; yet I have accepted Jacob ³ and have rejected Esau. I have made his hills a desolation, his territory *a*a home for beasts*a* of the desert. ⁴ If Edom thinks, "Though crushed, we can build the ruins again," thus said the Lord of Hosts: They may build, but I will tear down. And so they shall be known as the region of wickedness, the people damned forever of the Lord. ⁵ Your eyes shall behold it, and you shall declare, "Great is the Lord beyond the borders of Israel!"

⁶ A son should honor his father, and a slave*b* his master. Now if I am a father, where is the honor due Me? And if I am a master, where is the reverence due Me?—said the Lord of Hosts to you, O priests who scorn My name. But you ask, "How have we scorned Your name?" ⁷ You offer defiled food on My altar. But you ask, "How have we defiled You*c*?" By saying, "The table of the Lord can be treated with scorn." ⁸ When you present a blind animal for sacrifice—it doesn't matter! When you present a lame or sick one—it doesn't matter! Just offer it to your governor: Will he accept you? Will he show you favor?—said the Lord of Hosts. ⁹ And now implore the favor of God! Will He be gracious to us? This is what you have done—will He accept any of you?

ᵃ⁻ᵃ *Meaning of Heb. uncertain.*
ᵇ *Septuagint and Targum add "should reverence"; cf. next part of verse.*
ᶜ *Septuagint "it."*

The Lord of Hosts has said: [10] If only you would lock My doors, and not kindle fire on My altar to no purpose! I take no pleasure in you—said the Lord of Hosts—and I will accept no offering from you. [11] For from where the sun rises to where it sets, My name is honored among the nations, and everywhere incense and pure oblation are offered to My name; for My name is honored among the nations—said the Lord of Hosts. [12] But you profane it when you say, "The table of the Lord is defiled and the meat,[a] the food, can be treated with scorn." [13] You say, "Oh, what a bother!" And so you degrade[a] it—said the Lord of Hosts—and you bring the stolen, the lame, and the sick; and you offer such as an oblation. Will I accept it from you?—said the Lord.

[14] A curse on the cheat who has an [unblemished] male in his flock, but for his vow sacrifices a blemished animal to the Lord! For I am a great King—said the Lord of Hosts—and My name is revered among the nations.

2 And now, O priests, this charge is for you: [2] Unless you obey and unless you lay it to heart, and do honor to My name—said the Lord of Hosts—I will send a curse and turn your blessings into curses. (Indeed, I have turned them into curses, because you do not lay it to heart.) [3] I will [a-]put your seed under a ban,[-a] and I will strew dung upon your faces, the dung of your festal sacrifices, and you shall be carried out to its [heap].

[4] Know, then, that I have sent this charge to you so that My covenant with Levi may endure—said the Lord of Hosts. [5] I had with him a covenant of life and well-being, which I gave to him, and of reverence, which he showed Me. For he stood in awe of My name.

[6] [b]Proper rulings were in his mouth,
And nothing perverse was on his lips;
He served Me with complete loyalty
And held the many back from iniquity.
[7] [c-]For the lips of a priest guard knowledge,

[a-a] *Meaning of Heb. uncertain.*
[b] *See Hag. 2.10-13; cf. Lev. 10.8-11; Deut. 33.8, 10.*
[c-c] *Or: For the lips of a priest are observed;/Knowledge and ruling are sought from his mouth.*

And men seek rulings from his mouth;⁻ᶜ
For he is a messenger of the LORD of Hosts.
⁸ But you have turned away from that course: You have made the many stumble through your rulings;ᵈ you have corrupted the covenant of the Levites—said the LORD of Hosts. ⁹ And I, in turn, have made you despicable and vile in the eyes of all the people, because you disregard My ways and show partiality in your rulings.

¹⁰ Have we not all one father? Did not one God create us? Why do we break faith with one another, profaning the covenant of our fathers? ¹¹ Judah has broken faith; abhorrent things have been done in Israel and in Jerusalem. For Judah has profaned what is holy to the LORD—what He desires—and espoused daughters of alien gods. ¹² May the LORD leave to him who does this ᵃ⁻no descendants⁻ᵃ dwelling in the tents of Jacob and presenting offerings to the LORD of Hosts. ¹³ And this you do ᵉ⁻as well:⁻ᵉ you cover the altar of the LORD with tears, weeping, and moaning, so that He refuses to regard the oblation any more and to accept ᶠ⁻what you offer.ᶠ ¹⁴ But you ask, "Because of what?" Because the LORD is a witness between you and the wife of your youth with whom you have broken faith, though she is your partner and covenanted spouse. ¹⁵ Did not the One make [all,] ᵃ⁻so that all remaining life-breath is His? And what does that One seek but godly folk? So be careful of your life-breath,⁻ᵃ and let no one break faith with the wife of his youth. ¹⁶ For I detest divorce—said the LORD, the God of Israel—ᵃ⁻and covering oneself with lawlessness as with a garment⁻ᵃ—said the LORD of Hosts. So be careful of your life-breath and do not act treacherously.

¹⁷ You have wearied the LORD with your talk. But you ask, "By what have we wearied [Him]?" By saying, "All who do evil are good in the sight of the LORD, and in them He delights," or else, "Where is the God of justice?"

ᵈ By ruling falsely that an act was licit or an object ritually pure.
ᵉ⁻ᵉ Lit. "a second time"; Septuagint reads "which I detest"; cf. v. 16.
ᶠ⁻ᶠ Lit. "from your hand."

3 Behold, I am sending My messenger to clear the way before Me, and the Lord whom you seek shall come to His Temple suddenly. As for the angel of the covenant[a] that you desire, he is already coming. [2] But who can endure the day of his coming, and who can hold out when he appears? For he is like a smelter's fire and like fuller's lye. [3] He shall act[b] like a smelter and purger of silver; and he shall purify the descendants of Levi and refine them like gold and silver, so that they shall present offerings in righteousness. [4] Then the offerings of Judah and Jerusalem shall be pleasing to the LORD as in the days of yore and in the years of old. [5] But [first] I will step forward to contend against you, and I will act as a relentless accuser against those who have no fear of Me: who practice sorcery, who commit adultery, who swear falsely, who cheat laborers of their hire, and who subvert [the cause of] the widow, orphan, and stranger—said the LORD of Hosts.

[6] [c]For I am the LORD—I have not changed; and you are the children of Jacob—you have not ceased to be. [7] From the very days of your fathers you have turned away from My laws and have not observed them. Turn back to Me, and I will turn back to you —said the LORD of Hosts. But you ask, "How shall we turn back?" [8] Ought man to defraud[d] God? Yet you are defrauding Me. And you ask, "How have we been defrauding You?" In tithe and contribution.[e] [9] You are suffering from a curse, yet you go on defrauding Me—the whole nation of you. [10] Bring the full tithe into the storehouse,[f] and let there be food in My House, and thus put Me to the test—said the LORD of Hosts. I will surely open the floodgates of the sky for you and pour down boundless blessing; [11] and I will banish the locusts[g] from you, so that they will not

---

[a] *Apparently the messenger of the previous sentence is regarded as Israel's tutelary angel.*
[b] *Lit. "sit."*
[c] *Vv. 6-12 resume the thought of 1.2-5.*
[d] *Heb. qaba', a play on the name of Jacob (v. 6); cf. Gen. 27.36.*
[e] *I.e. the contributions to the priests from the new grain, oil, and wine; see Num. 18.12.*
[f] *I.e. the public storehouse; see Neh. 13.10-13.*
[g] *Lit. "devourer."*

destroy the yield of your soil; and your vines in the field shall no longer miscarry—said the LORD of Hosts. [12] And all the nations shall account you happy, for you shall be the most desired of lands—said the LORD of Hosts.

[13] You have spoken hard words against Me—said the LORD. But you ask, "What have we been saying among ourselves against You?" [14] You have said, "It is useless to serve God. What have we gained by keeping His charge and walking in abject awe of the LORD of Hosts? [15] And so, we account the arrogant happy: they have indeed done evil and endured; they have indeed dared God and escaped." [16] In this vein have those who revere the LORD been talking to one another. The LORD has heard and noted it, and a scroll of remembrance has been written at His behest concerning those who revere the LORD and esteem His name. [17] And on the day that I am preparing, said the LORD of Hosts, they shall be My treasured possession; I will be tender toward them as a man is tender toward a son who ministers to him. [18] And you shall come to see the difference between the righteous and the wicked, between him who has served the LORD and him who has not served Him.

[19] For lo! That day is at hand, burning like an oven. All the arrogant and all the doers of evil shall be straw, and the day that is coming—said the LORD of Hosts—shall burn them to ashes and leave of them neither stock nor boughs. [20] But for you who revere My name a sun of victory shall rise *h-*to bring healing.*-h* You shall go forth and stamp like stall-fed calves, [21] and you shall trample the wicked to a pulp, for they shall be dust beneath your feet on the day that I am preparing—said the LORD of Hosts.

[22] Be mindful of the Teaching of My servant Moses, whom I charged at Horeb with laws and rules for all Israel.

---

h-h Lit. "with healing in the corners of its garments"; others "with healing in its wings."

²³ Lo, I will send the prophet Elijah to you before the coming of the awesome, fearful day of the LORD. ²⁴ He shall reconcile fathers with sons and sons with their fathers, so that, when I come, I do not strike the whole land with utter destruction.

> Lo, I will send the prophet Elijah to you before
> the coming of the awesome, fearful day of the LORD.